Richard Harland

**A lineal index to the Wesleyan hymn book and supplement**

Richard Harland

**A lineal index to the Wesleyan hymn book and supplement**

ISBN/EAN: 9783742835901

Manufactured in Europe, USA, Canada, Australia, Japa

Cover: Foto ©Angelika Wolter / pixelio.de

Manufactured and distributed by brebook publishing software (www.brebook.com)

Richard Harland

**A lineal index to the Wesleyan hymn book and supplement**

# A LINEAL INDEX

### TO THE

# WESLEYAN HYMN BOOK

### AND

## SUPPLEMENT:

#### BEING AN

ALPHABETICAL ARRANGEMENT OF EVERY LINE IN THE COLLECTION OF HYMNS FOR THE USE OF THE PEOPLE CALLED METHODISTS.

### BY

## RICHARD HARLAND.

SECOND THOUSAND.

LONDON:
SOLD FOR THE AUTHOR AT THE
WESLEYAN CONFERENCE OFFICE,
2, CASTLE STREET, CITY ROAD, AND AT 66, PATERNOSTER ROW.

BRADFORD: THOMAS BREAR.

1878.

# PREFACE.

A NEW book is generally considered imperfect without a preface; but in the present instance, where scissors and paste have been the chief editorial implements—not a line of the volume having been composed by himself—the author of this compilation lays no claim to literary merit, and feels that beyond a brief statement of his reasons for publishing his work, nothing is here necessary.

Some years ago he happened to meet with a copy of "A Complete Index to Dr. Watts' Psalms and Hymns; wherein Reference is had to each Line of the Works, and the Whole digested into an Easy and Natural Alphabetical order, agreeable to the Index to the First Lines of each Psalm and Hymn. By David Guy, of Rye, in Sussex, 1773 & 4," the sight of which gave definite form to a thought long present with the compiler of this manual—viz., that besides what is afforded by the indices usually appended to the

Wesleyan Hymn Book, some help in finding particular passages in that collection would be very acceptable to a large number of his brethren throughout the Methodist Connexion, who love their hymn book, and use it so extensively in their public and private devotional exercises. It has frequently happened to himself that some portion of a verse, suitable for a purpose then in view, presented itself to his mind, when, being unable to recall the preceding lines, such a volume as the present appeared to him to be a necessity. Sometimes, also, he saw or heard a line quoted which he would gladly have associated with its context, but was prevented by its not being the beginning of a hymn or verse; and on one occasion in particular, this want was so *painfully* felt by himself and others, that it still lingers in his remembrance. A young relative, evidently drawing near to death, asked him to read a hymn, of which he quoted a couplet. There were several other relatives present, but not one of them could find the hymn desired. The dying youth then took the book, to search for the hymn, but before he had found the place the summons came—he expired in the attempt.

The compiler naturally supposed that many others shared his own desire for such assistance as is here rendered, and this idea has been confirmed by finding that the late Rev. John Kirk had considered the desirability of publishing a Concordance to the Methodist Hymn Book, and even commenced the task of preparing one, which, however, other claims upon his time compelled him to relinquish. The Rev. J. Julian also prepared a Concordance to Wesley's Hymns, and advertised its publication; but, apparently, owing to his leaving the Wesleyan Ministry for that of the Church of England, the work was never issued. Some years ago, Mr. James Stelfox, the well-known hymnologist, in a letter to the *Methodist Recorder*, urged the compilation of such a work; yet, strange to say, no Lineal Index or Concordance to Wesley's Hymns has yet appeared, whilst Dr. Watts' Psalms and Hymns, although used by a very much smaller number of persons, have twice been thought worthy of alphabetical arrangement; there being in addition to the above-named work by Guy, another Lineal Index to Watts, issued some time ago by Dr. Rippon.

## PREFACE.

This work would have been set about long ago, but knowing that a new edition of the Hymn Book was intended, the author thought it best to wait its appearance. Since that event, he has given most of his leisure time to the task now completed. No pains have been spared to make the book as complete and as perfect as possible; every line in the printer's proof has been verified from the Hymn Book, and every line in the book discovered in the proof. The only object of the work is usefulness, and therefore the compiler ventures to present the result of his labours to the societies and congregations throughout the Methodist Connexion; trusting that to preachers, leaders, and others, it will prove a useful and valuable companion, and become their indispensable assistant in the use of that valuable *body of divinity* and *thesaurus of quotation*—THE WESLEYAN HYMN BOOK.

KETTLEWELL, SKIPTON,
   May, 1878.

# INDEX.

*Note.—The first line of each hymn is indicated by an asterisk (\*). The obelisk (†) denotes first lines of other verses.*

| A BAND | | A DROP |
|---|---|---|
| | Hymn | Verse |
| A band of love, a threefold cord | 504 | 2 |
| A blessing to mankind | 952 | 2 |
| A blessing to receive | 80 | 2 |
| A blest eternity shall be | 284 | 3 |
| A blood-besprinkled race | 387 | 2 |
| A boundless ocean of bright beams | 974 | 8 |
| A brand plucked from eternal fire | 30 | 1 |
| A bright harmonious throng | 222 | 4 |
| A broken heart for sacrifice | 574 | 6 |
| †A broken heart, my God, my King | 574 | 6 |
| A brother dead to God | 482 | 5 |
| A calm and heavenly frame | 787 | 1 |
| A Canaanite by birth | 164 | 1 |
| A candidate for glorious bliss | 467 | 1 |
| \*A charge to keep I have | 318 | 1 |
| A cheerful sojourner | 840 | 2 |
| A cheering fire by night | 704 | 3 |
| A child of wrath am I | 943 | 11 |
| A church must stand or fall | 822 | 4 |
| A citizen of heaven below | 72 | 4 |
| †A clod of living earth | 229 | 2 |
| A conscious unbeliever sigh | 861 | 2 |
| A constant paradise | 405 | 6 |
| A copy, Lord, of thine | 343 | 4 |
| A cordial for our fears | 742 | 1 |
| A cordial to the faint | 109 | 6 |
| A country far from mortal sight | 947 | 1 |
| A country in the skies | 68 | 6 |
| †A country of joy | 498 | 3 |
| A covert from the tempest be | 292 | 1 |
| A curse or blessing meet | 43 | 3 |
| A day of holy love | 958 | 3 |
| A day of resurrection | 958 | 3 |
| A day of sweet refection | 958 | 3 |
| A day without night | 499 | 8 |
| A day's march nearer home | 944 | 2 |
| A deeper displacence at sin | 100 | 3 |
| A deep where all our thoughts are drowned | 225 | 2 |
| A diligent and pious mind | 858 | 1 |
| A drop of that unbounded sea | 247 | 1 |
| †A drop of that unbounded sea | 513 | 2 |

| | Hymn | Verse |
|---|---|---|
| A dying wretch I flee | 799 | 7 |
| A fair terrestrial paradise | 111 | 4 |
| †A faithful witness of thy grace | 440 | 2 |
| A faithless and backsliding race | 298 | 3 |
| †A faith that doth the mountains move | 774 | 4 |
| A faith that purifies the heart | 774 | 3 |
| A faith that shows our sins forgiven | 774 | 4 |
| A faith that sweetly works by love | 774 | 4 |
| A faith that *would* by works be shown | 774 | 3 |
| A faith thou must thyself impart | 774 | 3 |
| A family of faith and love | 489 | 1 |
| A farewell voice may be | 799 | 4 |
| A far serener clime | 984 | 3 |
| A favour unto me | 551 | 5 |
| A fearful or a joyful doom | 43 | 3 |
| A fear lest I should ever grieve | 307 | 1 |
| A feeble thing of nought | 270 | 3 |
| A few from every land | 460 | 1 |
| A few more partings o'er | 984 | 5 |
| †A few more Sabbaths here | 984 | 6 |
| A few more seasons come | 984 | 1 |
| †A few more storms shall beat | 984 | 4 |
| †A few more struggles here | 984 | 5 |
| †A few more suns shall set | 984 | 3 |
| A few more toils, a few more tears | 984 | 5 |
| A few more years in pain | 356 | 4 |
| *A few more years shall roll | 984 | 1 |
| A flame of reciprocal love | 911 | 3 |
| A follower of my God | 472 | 3 |
| A form of godliness was mine | 91 | 2 |
| *A fountain of life and of grace | 79 | 1 |
| A fountain of water and blood | 371 | 2 |
| A friend before the throne of love | 186 | 1 |
| A full acquittance we receive | 11 | 4 |
| A fulness of pleasure that never can cloy | 808 | 8 |
| A general blessing make | 424 | 1 |
| †A glance of thine runs through the globe | 651 | 4 |
| A glimpse of love cannot suffice | 284 | 1 |
| A godly fear of sin impart | 186 | 6 |
| A God that on Calvary died | 371 | 2 |
| A God to glorify | 318 | 1 |
| A golden harp for me | 798 | 6 |
| †A goodly, formal saint | 93 | 5 |
| A gracious soul may fall from grace | 317 | 1 |
| A grateful song I'll raise | 657 | 10 |
| A great High-priest we have | 724 | 1 |
| †A guilty, weak, and helpless worm | 786 | 5 |
| A half-awakened child of man | 59 | 1 |
| A happiness beyond the view | 68 | 3 |
| A happy chosen band | 527 | 1 |
| A hardness o'er my heart | 110 | 4 |
| A heart from sin set free | 343 | 1 |
| †A heart in every thought renewed | 343 | 4 |

| | Hymn | Verse |
|---|---|---|
| †A heart resigned, submissive, meek | 343 | 2 |
| A heart that always feels thy blood | 343 | 1 |
| A heart that cannot faithless prove | 341 | 4 |
| A heart that no desire can move | 353 | 6 |
| †A heart thy joys and griefs to feel | 341 | 4 |
| A heart to mourn, a heart to pray | 99 | 5 |
| A heart where Christ alone may dwell | 341 | 4 |
| A heart with grief opprest | 102 | 1 |
| A heaven-born race of priests and kings | 439 | 2 |
| A helper of the helpless be | 163 | 7 |
| A helpless soul that comes to thee | 163 | 5 |
| †A helpless soul that looks to thee | 545 | 4 |
| A helpless worm that trusts in thee | 227 | 7 |
| †A hidden God indeed thou art | 130 | 3 |
| A holy boldness to desire | 805 | 2 |
| A holy, living sacrifice | 431 | 1 |
| †A house we call our own | 67 | 3 |
| A howling wilderness | 404 | 4 |
| A humble, contrite heart | 102 | 1 |
| A hundred-fold we here obtain | 286 | 7 |
| A jealous, just concern | 301 | 5 |
| A joy unspeakable | 500 | 5 |
| A keener appetite for thee | 100 | 3 |
| A kindly, gracious shower | 630 | 6 |
| A kingdom of heaven, A heaven below | 19 | 3 |
| A kingdom that never shall end | 220 | 3 |
| A kingdom without end | 586 | 5 |
| †A land of corn, and wine, and oil | 404 | 3 |
| A land of deepest shade | 43 | 1 |
| A land of sacred liberty | 800 | 6 |
| A large increase shall give | 734 | 1 |
| †A law shall soon from him proceed | 111 | 6 |
| A leper at thy feet | 135 | 3 |
| A life concealed in him | 125 | 1 |
| A life that never endeth | 923 | 3 |
| †A lifeless form we still retain | 454 | 4 |
| A light in every heart to shine | 129 | 3 |
| A light to shine upon the road | 787 | 1 |
| A Lion is in fight | 315 | 3 |
| A little point my life appears | 564 | 2 |
| A living, life-infusing word | 111 | 6 |
| A living sacrifice divine | 980 | 3 |
| A lot among the blest | 55 | 4 |
| A lot among the sanctified | 493 | 3 |
| A man! an heir of death! a slave | 279 | 4 |
| A man of griefs was seen | 215 | 3 |
| A man to stand before thy face | 985 | 5 |
| A mansion in the skies | 44 | 5 |
| A mansion with the blest | 943 | 1 |
| A medicine for my every wound | 138 | 9 |
| A meek and lowly mind | 243 | 4 |
| A messenger divine | 832 | 1 |
| A mind for all assaults prepared | 306 | 3 |

| | Hymn | Verse |
|---|---|---|
| A miracle of grace I stand | 230 | 2 |
| †A moment, and thine anger dies | 559 | 2 |
| A moment's misery, or joy | 44 | 4 |
| A mortal Son of man | 684 | 3 |
| †A mystical plurality | 256 | 2 |
| *A nation God delights to bless | 466 | 1 |
| A nation in a day | 450 | 4 |
| A never-dying soul to save | 318 | 1 |
| A never-fading crown | 21 | 6 |
| A new, a contrite heart | 354 | 3 |
| A new triumphant song | 605 | 1 |
| A pain to feel it near | 308 | 1 |
| A pardon bought with Jesu's blood | 656 | 3 |
| †A pardon written with his blood | 9 | 7 |
| A pardoned penitent | 778 | 3 |
| A passing stranger, has he skill | 695 | 2 |
| †A patient, a victorious mind | 353 | 6 |
| A pattern to my household give | 471 | 1 |
| A peace to sensual minds unknown | 500 | 5 |
| †A perfect confidence inspire | 805 | 2 |
| A perfect heart at home | 609 | 2 |
| A perfect rest from sin | 409 | 1 |
| †A perfect way in wisdom trod | 609 | 2 |
| A pillar in thy church above | 72 | 1 |
| A place than all beside more sweet | 825 | 2 |
| A pleasant vine did plant and train | 589 | 1 |
| A pledge of endless good we call | 62 | 5 |
| A pledge of liberty | 384 | 1 |
| A point my good, a drop my store | 374 | 2 |
| A point of time, a moment's space | 59 | 2 |
| A poor backsliding soul restore | 110 | 1 |
| †A poor blind child I wander here | 163 | 2 |
| A poor guilty worm am I | 164 | 1 |
| †A poor, unloving wretch, to thee | 145 | 2 |
| A poor wayfaring man | 68 | 5 |
| A portion of thy grief unknown | 106 | 2 |
| A potsherd of the earth | 164 | 1 |
| A power to turn and live | 86 | 5 |
| A Prophet who teaches Salvation by grace | 212 | 4 |
| A proverb of reproach—and love | 17 | 4 |
| A pure and a permanent light | 73 | 4 |
| A pure, believing multitude | 16 | 3 |
| A pure desire that all may learn | 301 | 5 |
| A quick-discerning eye | 301 | 3 |
| A quick-discerning eye | 311 | 4 |
| A ray of heavenly light appears | 832 | 1 |
| A refuge in distress | 573 | 3 |
| †A rest, where all our soul's desire | 403 | 2 |
| A rest where pure enjoyment reigns | 403 | 1 |
| A rock that cannot move | 250 | 5 |
| A sacrifice for guilty man | 708 | 1 |
| A sacrifice of nobler name | 703 | 2 |
| A sacrifice to thee | 979 | 5 |

| | Hymn | Verse |
|---|---|---|
| *A safe stronghold our God is still | 856 | 1 |
| A saint, a creature new | 18 | 2 |
| A saint indeed, I long to be | 472 | 3 |
| †A Saviour born, in love supreme | 689 | 2 |
| A Saviour every soul to save | 129 | 3 |
| A season of clear shining | 804 | 1 |
| A self-renouncing will | 301 | 2 |
| A sensibility of sin | 308 | 1 |
| A servant's form he meekly wears | 31 | 2 |
| †A servant's form he wore | 731 | 2 |
| †A shadow even in health | 565 | 3 |
| A sharper sense of hell within | 100 | 3 |
| A short-leased tenement | 942 | 3 |
| A sign of Jesus near | 62 | 5 |
| A sinful and impotent worm | 911 | 1 |
| A sinful world to save | 303 | 3 |
| A single, steady aim | 301 | 5 |
| A sinner believing in Jesus's name | 707 | 6 |
| A sinner born to die | 59 | 1 |
| A sinner, I am kept from sin | 366 | 3 |
| A sinner I, on mercy cast | 916 | 2 |
| A sinner in my last distress | 177 | 1 |
| A sinner in my sins I bow | 881 | 2 |
| A sinner o'erwhelmed with his load | 165 | 1 |
| A sinner of the Gentiles, I | 669 | 1 |
| A sinner, saved by grace, adore | 778 | 3 |
| †A sinner, saved myself from sin | 472 | 6 |
| †A sinner still, though saved, I am | 669 | 2 |
| A sinner weltering in his blood | 150 | 1 |
| A sinner whom thou cam'st to save | 164 | 2 |
| A slave redeemed from death and sin | 30 | 1 |
| A sober, vigilant mind bestow | 306 | 3 |
| A solemn darkness veils the skies | 712 | 1 |
| A solemn midnight song | 976 | 1 |
| A solemn reverence checks our songs | 316 | 5 |
| A song of holy praise | 566 | 3 |
| A soul inured to pain | 301 | 2 |
| A soul out of prison released | 49 | 1 |
| A soul that walks with Christ in light | 281 | 2 |
| A sovereign balm for every wound | 742 | 1 |
| †A spark of that ethereal fire | 513 | 4 |
| A spectacle to fiends and men | 439 | 1 |
| A spirit still prepared | 301 | 3 |
| A stiff-necked and hard-hearted race | 176 | 4 |
| †A stranger in the world below | 947 | 2 |
| †A stranger, Lord, with thee | 565 | 8 |
| A stranger to the blood which bought | 83 | 3 |
| A stranger to the gospel hope | 97 | 3 |
| †A stranger to the judge she was | 827 | 2 |
| A stranger to the world unknown | 68 | 6 |
| A strength that will not let thee go | 805 | 2 |
| A strict account to give | 318 | 2 |
| A strong desiring confidence | 865 | 3 |

| | Hymn | Verse |
|---|---|---|
| A stronger struggling to get free | 100 | 3 |
| A sudden trembling shakes the ground | 712 | 1 |
| A suffering life my Master led | 227 | 2 |
| A sun with healing in its wings | 957 | 2 |
| A sure and present aid | 217 | 2 |
| †A sure defence in thee | 602 | 4 |
| A sweeter sound than thy blest name | 680 | 2 |
| A temple built by God | 347 | 5 |
| A temple filled with God | 783 | 2 |
| A temple to the Lord | 989 | 3 |
| A tender, contrite heart receive | 341 | 3 |
| A thing from which we cannot part | 286 | 5 |
| A thought from thee I would not hide | 830 | 2 |
| †A thousand ages in thy sight | 41 | 4 |
| A thousand flowers between | 226 | 8 |
| A thousand herbs thy art displays | 226 | 8 |
| *A thousand oracles divine | 262 | 1 |
| A thousand promises declare | 250 | 5 |
| A thousand worlds my soul to shake | 269 | 2 |
| A token of his love he gives | 384 | 1 |
| †A touch, a word, a look from thee | 395 | 5 |
| A tower that stands for ever | 855 | 1 |
| A trembling homage pay | 136 | 4 |
| A trembling sinner, Lord, I cry | 795 | 1 |
| A triple light was given | 958 | 2 |
| A troubled heart that cannot rest | 102 | 1 |
| A trusty shield and weapon | 856 | 1 |
| A universal blessing gave | 129 | 3 |
| A vast, unfathomable sea | 250 | 3 |
| A vessel fitted for thy use | 472 | 4 |
| A vessel pure of love divine | 780 | 2 |
| †A vile, backsliding sinner, I | 365 | 8 |
| A warfare at thy charge I go | 439 | 1 |
| A way, a heart, a house, O God | 609 | 2 |
| A way no more expected | 276 | 3 |
| A week, a month, a year | 820 | 3 |
| *A widow, poor, forlorn, oppressed | 827 | 1 |
| A wisdom to discern and know | 805 | 2 |
| A wise and understanding heart | 320 | 2 |
| A whole eternity of love | 392 | 4 |
| A wonderful fashion of teaching he hath | 211 | 3 |
| A word, a gracious word of thine | 396 | 3 |
| A word of thine shall make me rise | 396 | 4 |
| A word of thy supporting breath | 555 | 3 |
| A word shall quickly slay him | 856 | 3 |
| A work so sweet, a theme so high | 658 | 6 |
| A world of righteousness and love | 536 | 7 |
| A worm, a leaf, a blast a shade | 38 | 6 |
| A worm exalt to God | 323 | 3 |
| A worm of earth, I cry | 59 | 1 |
| †Abba, Father! hear thy child | 390 | 2 |
| Abhor the pride that lurks within | 99 | 4 |
| Abhor the thing unclean | 340 | 1 |

| | Hymn | Verse |
|---|---|---|
| *Abide with me! fast falls the eventide | 972 | 1 |
| †Abide with me from morn till eve | 973 | 3 |
| Abide with me when night is nigh | 973 | 3 |
| Able thou art from sin to save | 356 | 6 |
| Abominable in thy sight | 454 | 5 |
| Above all earthly things shall soar | 836 | 6 |
| Above my troubles raise | 635 | 3 |
| Above the ground we tread | 610 | 8 |
| Above the hills, o'er all the land | 589 | 1 |
| Above the noblest songs | 232 | 4 |
| Above the reach of human thought | 616 | 5 |
| Above the skies | 855 | 2 |
| Above the stir of toil and care | 698 | 1 |
| Above the world, and Satan's power | 469 | 8 |
| Above what we can bear | 818 | 1 |
| Above yon angel powers | 65 | 5 |
| Above your scorn we rise | 21 | 3 |
| Abraham and Isaac there | 535 | 5 |
| *Abraham, when severely tried | 286 | 1 |
| Abroad thy healing influence shower | 236 | 2 |
| Abrogate or change thine own | 952 | 1 |
| †Absent, alas! from God | 74 | 4 |
| Absent from him I roam | 944 | 2 |
| Absent from our loving Lord | 50 | 4 |
| †Absent from thee, my exiled soul | 154 | 3 |
| Absolute God confessed | 583 | 1 |
| Abundant righteousness | 806 | 1 |
| †Abundant sweetness, while I sing | 437 | 6 |
| Acceptable through thy Son | 427 | 1 |
| †Acceptance through his only name | 394 | 3 |
| Accept a parent's vow | 893 | 1 |
| Accept each faithful vow | 991 | 3 |
| Accept his all-availing prayer | 298 | 5 |
| Accept my hallowed labour now | 321 | 2 |
| Accept my new-born cry | 193 | 1 |
| Accept our thanksgiving for creating grace | 199 | 2 |
| Accept the complicated wrong | 334 | — |
| Accept the evening sacrifice | 83 | 1 |
| Accept the gifts we offer | 988 | 3 |
| Accept the praise I bring | 679 | 4 |
| Accept the sacrifice we bring | 986 | 4 |
| Accept the tribute which we bring | 677 | 1 |
| Accept thy well-deserved renown | 677 | 1 |
| Accepted at thy throne of grace | 843 | 1 |
| †Accepted in the Well-beloved | 706 | 7 |
| Accepting our deliverance | 276 | 4 |
| Accepting salvation, Salvation by grace | 10 | 1 |
| Accompany the sign | 477 | 2 |
| Accomplished in the change of mine | 408 | 2 |
| Accomplished is the sacrifice | 706 | 1 |
| Accomplish now thy faithful word | 505 | 1 |
| Accomplish now thy work in me | 395 | 8 |
| According to his word | 335 | 1 |

| | Hymn | Verse |
|---|---|---|
| According to his word | 345 | 1 |
| †According to his word | 536 | 7 |
| According to his word | 862 | 1 |
| According to my faith to me | 152 | 4 |
| According to my will | 164 | 5 |
| †According to our faith in thee | 389 | 5 |
| According to thy will and word | 367 | 8 |
| According to thy word | 389 | 4 |
| Accounted worthy by thy grace | 985 | 4 |
| Accustomed daily to endure | 474 | 2 |
| Acknowledge for thy flesh and bone | 724 | 8 |
| Acknowledging how just thou art | 104 | 1 |
| Active faith that lives within | 521 | 8 |
| Actuate and fill the whole | 390 | 4 |
| †Adam descended from above | 33 | 2 |
| *Adam descended from above | 129 | 1 |
| †Adam's likeness now efface | 688 | 7 |
| Added to the chosen race | 735 | 8 |
| †Adopt me by thy grace | 888 | 4 |
| Adore their glorious Lord | 731 | 7 |
| Adore thy hand, from sin withheld | 130 | 4 |
| Adoring One in Persons Three | 256 | 2 |
| Adorned as a bride for her Lord | 73 | 2 |
| Adorned by their Redeemer's grace | 948 | 5 |
| Adorned with Christ, and meet for God | 536 | 8 |
| Adorn me with the robes of praise | 440 | 1 |
| Adorn the heavenly plains | 263 | 6 |
| Advocate with God, give ear | 517 | 1 |
| Affix thy blessed Spirit's seal | 901 | 2 |
| *Afflicted by a gracious God | 331 | 1 |
| Afford me a glimpse of thy face | 911 | 3 |
| Afraid the God of love to see | 425 | 2 |
| After all his waste of love | 8 | 1 |
| †After all that I have done | 182 | 8 |
| *After all that I have done | 185 | 1 |
| After all that I have done | 188 | 1 |
| After God we all shall rise | 400 | 5 |
| †After my lowly Lord to go | 17 | 8 |
| After the day's confusion, toil, and din | 967 | 5 |
| After thee we aspire | 488 | 7 |
| After thee we swiftly run | 538 | 1 |
| After thy lovely likeness, Lord | 169 | 1 |
| After thy righteousness | 834 | 1 |
| Again, and touch the skies | 452 | 4 |
| Again forgive my faithlessness | 909 | 2 |
| Again hath raised me up | 187 | 1 |
| †Again he comes! from place to place | 695 | 4 |
| Again he to his earth shall turn | 638 | 8 |
| Again in human darkness shine | 445 | 1 |
| Again in Jesu's praise we join | 478 | 1 |
| Again in thy Spirit descend | 220 | 3 |
| Again I say, Rejoice with me | 345 | 4 |
| Again preach peace to me | 799 | 4 |

| | Hymn | Verse |
|---|---|---|
| Again the stirring tones reply | 694 | 2 |
| †Again thou didst, in council met | 256 | 5 |
| Again through faith I stand | 587 | 4 |
| *Again we lift our voice | 52 | 1 |
| Against a child of thine | 359 | 3 |
| Against the face of sin | 271 | 1 |
| Against the fatal day | 44 | 2 |
| Against the Man thou lov'st so well | 917 | 2 |
| Against the spirit unclean | 409 | 1 |
| Against thy law, against thy grace | 574 | 2 |
| Ah, canst thou finally depart | 178 | 3 |
| †Ah, canst thou find it in thy heart | 178 | 8 |
| †Ah! do not of my goodness doubt | 31 | 4 |
| Ah, gather all thy living stones | 16 | 6 |
| Ah! give me, Lord (I still would say) | 99 | 3 |
| †Ah! give me, Lord, myself to feel | 99 | 5 |
| †Ah! give me, Lord, the tender heart | 186 | 6 |
| †Ah! give me this to know | 27 | 6 |
| †Ah! give to all thy servants, Lord | 190 | 9 |
| Ah, join me to thy secret ones | 16 | 6 |
| †Ah! leave us not to mourn below | 759 | 5 |
| †Ah! leave us not to venture | 818 | 2 |
| Ah, Lord! enlarge our scanty thought | 26 | 7 |
| †Ah, Lord! if thou art in that sigh | 134 | 4 |
| Ah, Lord! if thou hadst still been here | 184 | 7 |
| Ah, Lord, my soul is gone astray | 177 | 2 |
| Ah, Lord, thy depth of mercy show | 773 | 3 |
| *Ah! Lord, with trembling I confess | 317 | 1 |
| †Ah me! ah me! that I | 942 | 13 |
| Ah me! I'm loth to die | 931 | 4 |
| †Ah, no! I still may turn and live | 80 | 4 |
| †Ah no! ne'er will I backward turn | 344 | 7 |
| Ah, Shepherd, seek my soul, and find | 177 | 2 |
| †Ah, show me, Lord, my depth of sin | 773 | 3 |
| †Ah! show me that happiest place | 228 | 2 |
| Ah, soften, melt this rock, and may | 373 | 6 |
| †Ah! suffer not my foe to boast | 547 | 4 |
| Ah, tear it thence, and reign alone | 344 | 4 |
| †Ah, that day of tears and mourning | 933 | 18 |
| †Ah! then my spirit faints | 944 | 4 |
| †Ah! what avails my strife | 137 | 2 |
| †Ah! what avails superior light | 469 | 4 |
| *Ah, when shall I awake | 303 | 1 |
| Ah, when shall I wake up | 169 | 1 |
| †Ah! when shall we increase | 643 | 3 |
| †Ah, wherefore did I ever doubt | 163 | 5 |
| Ah! whither shall I fly | 109 | 1 |
| Ah! whither shall I go | 784 | 1 |
| Ah! whither should I go | 137 | 2 |
| *Ah! whither should I go | 152 | 1 |
| *Ah! why am I left to complain | 777 | 1 |
| Ah! why did I no sooner go | 210 | 2 |
| †Ah! why did I so late thee know | 210 | 2 |

| | Hymn | Verse |
|---|---|---|
| Ah! why do I delay | 152 | 1 |
| Ah, write the pardon on my heart | 44 | 6 |
| Aim at nothing great or high | 628 | 2 |
| Alarm me in this hour | 305 | 1 |
| Alarm their souls with humble fears | 461 | 5 |
| Alas! I all things want | 93 | 1 |
| Alas! I see their endless store | 155 | 4 |
| Alas! they all must flow in vain | 127 | 3 |
| Alike on all impartial power | 241 | 3 |
| Alike we glorify | 221 | 4 |
| Alive in him, my living Head | 201 | 5 |
| Alive in thee, my living Head | 196 | 1 |
| All adore thee | 748 | 6 |
| All, all at that last gasp are o'er | 638 | 3 |
| All, all is theirs, who righteous live | 590 | 5 |
| All, all I want is there | 138 | 9 |
| All, all may to their God draw nigh | 162 | 2 |
| All, all my happy hours | 229 | 4 |
| All, all my vileness may I feel | 351 | 3 |
| All, all that is in thee | 405 | 9 |
| †All are not lost or wandered back | 483 | 4 |
| All are safely gathered in | 987 | 4 |
| All are too mean delights for him | 225 | 5 |
| All are too mean to speak his worth | 675 | 1 |
| All around with praises ring | 348 | 2 |
| All at once to thee aspire | 538 | 1 |
| All before the throne it bringeth | 933 | 3 |
| All below and all above | 582 | 3 |
| All-blessing and all-blest | 586 | 6 |
| All clothed in pure array | 942 | 12 |
| All commerce with the world preclude | 828 | 3 |
| All creation is awaking | 933 | 4 |
| All creatures, praise the eternal name | 241 | 4 |
| All day long he spreads his hands | 8 | 3 |
| All discern him | 936 | 5 |
| All earth and heaven their King proclaim | 576 | 3 |
| All earthly things we scorn | 497 | 3 |
| All enquiring | 595 | 4 |
| All evil before His presence shall fly | 273 | 8 |
| All excellencies meet | 232 | 3 |
| All fulness dwells in thee alone | 332 | 4 |
| †All fulness of peace, All fulness of joy | 19 | 3 |
| All glory and power, All wisdom and might | 859 | 5 |
| All glory be to Christ my Lord | 393 | 3 |
| *All glory to God in the sky | 220 | 1 |
| *All glory to our gracious Lord | 616 | 1 |
| All glory to our gracious Lord | 616 | 12 |
| All good gifts around us | 988 | Cho. |
| All grace is now to sinners given | 706 | 8 |
| All hail, reproach, and welcome, pain | 279 | 8 |
| *All hail the power of Jesu's name | 681 | 1 |
| All have not left thy church and thee | 483 | 4 |
| All heaven is ready to resound | 9 | 5 |

| | Hymn | Verse |
|---|---|---|
| All heaven submits to his commands | 585 | 2 |
| All heaven's host their glorious Lord | 58 | 1 |
| All he has, and is, is mine | 197 | 3 |
| All he waters from above | 86 | 4 |
| All helplessness, all weakness, I | 141 | 6 |
| All her promises are sure | 572 | 3 |
| All his boasted pomp and show | 594 | 3 |
| All his care rejoice to prove | 13 | 2 |
| All his designs attend | 540 | 3 |
| All his drawings from above | 8 | 1 |
| All his enemies are gone | 407 | 4 |
| All his glorious power assumes | 605 | 7 |
| All his gracious works declare | 735 | 1 |
| All his heavenly charms survey | 295 | 5 |
| All his mind to us explain | 756 | 3 |
| All his paradise of love | 13 | 2 |
| All his people | 595 | 2 |
| All his sufferings, for mankind | 899 | 1 |
| All his various works declare | 661 | 1 |
| All his warfare now is o'er | 50 | 2 |
| All honour and blessing, with angels above | 859 | 5 |
| All honour and glory to Jesus alone | 219 | 1 |
| †All honour and praise | 231 | 10 |
| †All honour and praise, dominion and might | 869 | 6 |
| All I design, or do, or say | 964 | 7 |
| All I desired and wished below | 599 | 6 |
| All I have, and all I am | 430 | 3 |
| All I know, and all I feel | 430 | 4 |
| All I think, or speak, or do | 430 | 4 |
| All I want in him I have | 554 | 1 |
| All immersed and lost in love | 27 | 6 |
| All in cheerful green arrayed | 348 | 1 |
| All in Jesu's praise agree | 728 | 3 |
| All in milk-white robes arrayed | 75 | 1 |
| All in one thanksgiving join | 221 | 1 |
| All into thy holiness | 766 | 2 |
| All into thy nature turn | 766 | 2 |
| All Israel shall be saved at last | 451 | 2 |
| All Israel shall the Saviour own | 452 | 4 |
| All is safely gathered in | 987 | 1 |
| All its waves in glad commotion | 604 | 3 |
| All jubilant with song | 943 | 9 |
| All love we paid to thee | 785 | 5 |
| All mankind in righteous war | 748 | 2 |
| All may feel he died for all | 86 | 5 |
| †All may from him receive | 86 | 5 |
| All may glorify the Lamb | 748 | 6 |
| All may hear the effectual call | 86 | 5 |
| All may obey thy gracious word | 803 | 3 |
| All may we lose, so thee we gain | 494 | 5 |
| All men our fellowship shall see | 891 | 2 |
| All might, all majesty, all praise | 393 | 3 |
| All might and love they render thee | 647 | 5 |

| | Hymn | Verse |
|---|---|---|
| All might and majesty are thine | 800 | 12 |
| All my actions sanctify | 430 | 3 |
| †All my disease, my every sin | 397 | 7 |
| All my earthly dross consume | 766 | 1 |
| All my enemies control | 287 | 1 |
| All my Father's gracious will | 355 | 7 |
| All my goods and all my hours | 430 | 4 |
| All my help from thee I bring | 143 | 2 |
| All my inmost sins reveal | 101 | 2 |
| †All my promises renew | 910 | 3 |
| All my riches is thy love | 434 | 5 |
| All my Saviour asks above | 390 | 2 |
| All my shame with anguish owning | 933 | 12 |
| All my sins I now abjure | 910 | 2 |
| All my sins were laid on thee | 27 | 1 |
| †All my treasure is above | 434 | 5 |
| All my trust on thee is stayed | 143 | 2 |
| All my unbelief o'erthrow | 158 | 4 |
| All my wickedness eschew | 910 | 3 |
| All my words and thoughts receive | 430 | 3 |
| All nations must come in, and make | 460 | 3 |
| All nations shall adore him | 586 | 5 |
| All nature acknowledged thy birth | 220 | 2 |
| All nature rose to obey thy word | 788 | 1 |
| All nature trembles at thy voice | 666 | 2 |
| All number far above | 566 | 5 |
| All offences purge away | 987 | 3 |
| All of high and humble birth | 639 | 6 |
| All our blessings are divine | 233 | 2 |
| †All our desires to thee are known | 546 | 4 |
| All our fears and thoughts exceed | 60 | 1 |
| All our foes were forced to own | 623 | 3 |
| All our fresh springs shall be in thee | 595 | 6 |
| All our griefs to God display | 295 | 3 |
| All our heart dissolves in love | 350 | 7 |
| All our help and good, we own | 755 | 2 |
| All our joy, and all our peace | 399 | 2 |
| All our panting hearts desire | 995 | 3 |
| All our sins away hath done | 714 | 2 |
| All our sins on thee were laid | 722 | 2 |
| All our sins on thee were laid | 737 | 3 |
| All our soul's athirst for thee | 350 | 7 |
| †All our works in thee be wrought | 512 | 2 |
| All pain before thy presence flies | 373 | 3 |
| All partake the common bliss | 518 | 8 |
| All partake the glorious bliss | 218 | 1 |
| All pensive memories, as we journey on | 850 | 3 |
| *All people that on earth do dwell | 607 | 1 |
| All power and majesty are thine | 568 | 3 |
| †All power is thine in earth and heaven | 332 | 4 |
| †All power is to our Jesus given | 280 | 2 |
| All power to him is given | 267 | 2 |
| All power to him is given | 314 | 3 |

| | Hymn | Verse |
|---|---|---|
| †All power to our great Lord | 719 | 3 |
| All power to thee is given | 275 | 3 |
| All praise, all meekness, and all love | 341 | 4 |
| All praise, Blest Spirit, shall be thine | 770 | 7 |
| All praise to him belongs | 979 | 1 |
| *All praise to our redeeming Lord | 500 | 1 |
| †All praise to thee in light arrayed | 974 | 8 |
| †All praise to thee who safe hast kept | 964 | 5 |
| All praise to thy eternal merit | 751 | 3 |
| All prevalent for helpless man | 902 | 2 |
| All rapt up to heaven shall be | 58 | 2 |
| All receive the grace atoning | 899 | 2 |
| All refuge failed, and none vouchsafed | 634 | 2 |
| All salvation from him came | 75 | 2 |
| All sanctified by spotless love | 229 | 5 |
| All shall come to thee that live | 579 | 1 |
| All shall kneel, thy greatness telling | 580 | 1 |
| All sin, alas! thou know'st I am | 145 | 1 |
| All sorrow before thee shall fly | 220 | 4 |
| All souls are thine, teach, comfort all | 770 | 6 |
| All stained with hallowed blood | 314 | 2 |
| All subdue; through all my soul | 352 | 4 |
| All taken up by thee | 147 | 1 |
| All thanks, all might, all love, all praise | 524 | 1 |
| *All thanks be to God | 219 | 1 |
| All thanks, O Lord, to thee | 968 | 1 |
| *All thanks to the Lamb, Who gives us to meet | 481 | 1 |
| All that cut the air with wings | 639 | 5 |
| All that delights our eyes | 565 | 6 |
| All that feeds my knowing pride | 302 | 2 |
| All that now makes it hard to say | 841 | 6 |
| All that thou send'st to me | 848 | 3 |
| All the building rises fair | 516 | 1 |
| All the depths of humble love | 381 | 4 |
| All the depths of love express | 509 | 5 |
| All the dross of sin remove | 414 | 2 |
| All the fitness he requireth | 791 | 3 |
| All the forms that love could take | 194 | 1 |
| All the fruits of Paradise | 349 | 1 |
| All the heavenly host adore thee | 722 | 3 |
| All the heights of holiness | 381 | 4 |
| All the heights of holiness | 509 | 5 |
| All the joy and heaven of love | 156 | 2 |
| All the joy, and peace, and power | 390 | 2 |
| All the life and heaven of love | 390 | 2 |
| All the life of faith I prove | 156 | 2 |
| All the life of glorious love | 20 | 3 |
| All the light of life may see | 86 | 5 |
| All the Lord of hosts proclaim | 748 | 6 |
| All the mighty debt has paid | 737 | 3 |
| All the mind that was in thee | 355 | 5 |
| All the mountain flames with light | 728 | 5 |
| All the names that love could find | 194 | 1 |

| | Hymn | Verse |
|---|---|---|
| All the plenitude of God | 554 | 1 |
| All the power of Jesu's name | 151 | 8 |
| All the powers of music bring | 641 | 3 |
| All the promises are sure | 295 | 4 |
| All the reach of heavenly art | 641 | 3 |
| All the Saviour's dying merit | 899 | 1 |
| All the settled furrows fill | 578 | 2 |
| All the sins of all mankind | 463 | 1 |
| All the Spirit of his love | 218 | 4 |
| All the sprinkled blood receive | 899 | 2 |
| †All the struggle then is o'er | 407 | 4 |
| All the treasures of thy love | 723 | 3 |
| All the unbelief declare | 358 | 4 |
| All the vain things that charm me most | 700 | 2 |
| All the wants of all that live | 1022 | — |
| All the work of grace proclaim | 382 | 4 |
| All the world may unto thee | 166 | 1 |
| All their choirs thy glories sing | 737 | 6 |
| All their wants at once remove | 76 | 4 |
| All they who see these things, with fear | 566 | 3 |
| †All thine attributes we own | 242 | 2 |
| †All things are possible to God | 401 | 6 |
| *All things are possible to him | 401 | 1 |
| All things are possible to me | 401 | Cho. |
| All things are ready, come away | 9 | 1 |
| All things displeasing in thy sight | 666 | 5 |
| All things for him account but loss | 28 | 4 |
| All things for thee we count but loss | 286 | 6 |
| All things in Christ are ready now | 2 | 2 |
| †All things in earth, and air, and sea | 666 | 2 |
| All things in thee, live, move, and are | 241 | 3 |
| All things let me count but loss | 358 | 3 |
| All those that come to him | 402 | 3 |
| †All those that put their trust in thee | 543 | 7 |
| All thou hast, and all thou art | 530 | 4 |
| All thy blessed will be done | 914 | 8 |
| All thy counsel to fulfil | 430 | 2 |
| †All thy cures are mysteries | 698 | 2 |
| All thy delight in us fulfil | 655 | 3 |
| All thy faithful mercies crown | 385 | 1 |
| All thy foes shall melt away | 737 | 10 |
| All thy glorious joy is ours | 723 | 3 |
| All thy goodness waits to give | 158 | 2 |
| All thy grace on us bestow | 530 | 4 |
| All thy gracious sayings hear | 886 | — |
| All thy heavenly powers exert | 766 | 1 |
| All thy kind commands obey | 886 | — |
| All thy life was prayer and love | 529 | 2 |
| All thy mourning days below | 922 | 1 |
| All thy only love declare | 538 | 3 |
| All thy other gifts remove | 434 | 7 |
| All thy people are forgiven | 722 | 2 |
| All thy pleasures I forego | 809 | 1 |

| | Hymn | Verse |
|---|---|---|
| All thy power on me be shown | 158 | 1 |
| All thy Spirit's fulness shed | 424 | 1 |
| All thy thoughts are fathomless | 598 | 2 |
| All thy will on me be done | 112 | 7 |
| All thy words we would fulfil | 529 | 1 |
| All thy works shall praise thy name, in earth and sky and sea | 646 | 4 |
| All thy works to thee are known | 914 | 8 |
| All thy wrath aside is turned | 197 | 1 |
| All time, and toil, and care | 214 | 2 |
| All to each one assigned of tribulation | 850 | 3 |
| All tribes and tongues, shall flow | 740 | 2 |
| All triumphantly combine | 728 | 3 |
| All unprepared to meet him | 932 | 3 |
| All who groan beneath your load | 29 | 1 |
| †All who in their sins delight | 598 | 3 |
| All who on thy love depend | 999 | 4 |
| †All who read, or hear, are blessed | 885 | 2 |
| †All will I own unto my Lord | 561 | 5 |
| All with one sweet voice exclaim | 829 | 4 |
| All with shouts cry out, "'Tis he!" | 936 | 5 |
| All with the fire of love baptize | 524 | 2 |
| All ye sparkling eyes of night | 639 | 2 |
| *All ye that pass by | 707 | 1 |
| All ye who owe to him your birth | 235 | 3 |
| Alleluia! Alleluia! Alleluia! Amen | 663 | — |
| Alleluia to the Lord | 663 | — |
| Allow me, Lord, my heart's desire | 124 | 1 |
| Allow my humble claim | 764 | 1 |
| Allow no respite to our toil | 624 | 1 |
| Allow us even on earth to prove | 513 | 1 |
| Allures or tears me from my God | 154 | 1 |
| Almighty Advocate, to thine | 100 | 1 |
| Almighty, all-creating Lord | 234 | 1 |
| *Almighty God of love | 452 | 1 |
| Almighty God! receive | 259 | 4 |
| †Almighty God, to thee | 644 | 4 |
| Almighty King | 800 | 10 |
| Almighty Lord of all | 138 | 5 |
| †Almighty Lord of land and sea | 1003 | 2 |
| Almighty Love, stand by us | 818 | 2 |
| *Almighty Maker of my frame | 564 | 1 |
| Almighty! thy power Hath founded of old | 611 | 3 |
| Almighty to deliver | 276 | 1 |
| Almighty to deliver | 855 | 1 |
| Almighty to redeem | 665 | 4 |
| Almighty to renew | 301 | 1 |
| Alone consumed with pining want | 392 | 3 |
| Alone thou hast the winepress trod | 338 | 5 |
| †Already, Lord, I feel thy power | 366 | 2 |
| Already saved from self-design | 68 | 2 |
| Although, my gifts and comforts lost | 803 | 3 |
| Although the olive yield no oil | 803 | 2 |

| | Hymn | Verse |
|---|---|---|
| †Although the vine its fruit deny | 803 | 2 |
| Altogether like our Lord | 509 | 3 |
| Always even, always still | 355 | 6 |
| Always let us faithful prove | 516 | 2 |
| Always to pray I want | 301 | 4 |
| Always to watch and pray | 305 | 2 |
| Always unto Jesus look | 243 | 3 |
| Amazed, I still forgiveness found | 365 | 5 |
| Amazed, the wondrous tidings they proclaim | 691 | 4 |
| Amazing heights of boundless power | 1001 | 5 |
| Amazing love! how can it be | 201 | 1 |
| Amazing wisdom shines | 650 | 3 |
| Ambassadors to rebels sends | 11 | 1 |
| Ambushed lies the evil one | 829 | 3 |
| Amen! so let it be | 944 | 1 |
| Amen to what my Lord doth say | 127 | 10 |
| Am freely saved by grace | 115 | 1 |
| Amidst that general fire | 64 | 4 |
| Amidst the angelic multitude | 583 | 1 |
| Amidst their radiant orbs be found | 552 | 5 |
| Amid the blaze of gospel day | 163 | 2 |
| Among the justified is found | 616 | 4 |
| †Among the nations he shall judge | 740 | 4 |
| Among the saints have place | 540 | 5 |
| Among thy glorious saints to live | 72 | 4 |
| Among thy saints a seat | 558 | 2 |
| Ample dome to entertain | 862 | 1 |
| An adamantine heart | 361 | 6 |
| An alien from the life of grace | 547 | 1 |
| An angry thought I cannot know | 830 | 3 |
| An endless life with him to live | 833 | 3 |
| An end of all my sin | 410 | 1 |
| An end of all my troubles make | 410 | 1 |
| An entrance to the holiest give | 133 | 3 |
| An everlasting crown | 527 | 3 |
| An everlasting Father thou | 642 | 3 |
| An everlasting God | 642 | 3 |
| An everlasting life shall live | 4 | 9 |
| An everlasting ransom paid | 190 | 8 |
| An everlasting rest | 55 | 4 |
| An heir of endless bliss or pain | 59 | 1 |
| †An humble, lowly, contrite heart | 343 | 3 |
| An image of the Triune God | 256 | 6 |
| An immortal soul, designed | 18 | 1 |
| An interest in the Saviour's blood | 201 | 1 |
| An offering in the sinner's stead | 708 | 1 |
| †An offering to their God | 452 | 6 |
| An outcast from thy face | 110 | 2 |
| An understanding given | 673 | 1 |
| †An unregenerate child of man | 150 | 2 |
| Ancient Israel, the story | 606 | 2 |
| †Ancient of days! Thy name | 601 | 2 |
| †Ancient of days, why didst thou come | 772 | 4 |

| | Hymn | Verse |
|---|---|---|
| Ancient of endless days | 981 | 1 |
| Ancient of everlasting days | 800 | 1 |
| And " Abba, Father," humbly cry | 764 | 4 |
| And abide with thee in bliss | 753 | 10 |
| And a constant need for prayer | 842 | 7 |
| And a heart at leisure from itself | 842 | 2 |
| And a life of self-renouncing love | 842 | 8 |
| And a mind to blend with outward life | 842 | 5 |
| And a people prepared | 219 | 2 |
| And a work of lowly love to do | 842 | 4 |
| And add me to thy deathless choir | 881 | 2 |
| And admitted the harlots and publicans in | 219 | 3 |
| And admit to a sight of my face | 488 | 6 |
| And after death, in distant worlds | 657 | 9 |
| And after his image aspire | 371 | 1 |
| And agony is heaven | 336 | 1 |
| And aid my tongue to bless his name | 610 | 1 |
| And all a God can give | 874 | 2 |
| And all a solemn vigil keep | 977 | 2 |
| And all be equal in the grave | 470 | 10 |
| And all beside are serving him | 544 | 4 |
| And all eternity employ | 440 | 2 |
| And all eternity employ | 828 | 5 |
| And all eternity shall prove | 638 | 6 |
| And all fear of want remove | 594 | 2 |
| And all for wretched man | 136 | 6 |
| And all harmonious human tongues | 699 | 4 |
| And all heaven's eternal day | 737 | 10 |
| And all heaven's host adore their King | 338 | 6 |
| And all her flowery paths are peace | 14 | 5 |
| And all his greatness show | 572 | 1 |
| And all his greatness show | 641 | 1 |
| And all his great salvation prove | 731 | 4 |
| And all his hopeless mourners cheer | 111 | 2 |
| And all his name on us impress | 756 | 3 |
| And all his promises embrace | 614 | 9 |
| And all his saints restore | 761 | 6 |
| And all his steps attends | 245 | 2 |
| And all his wondrous love abuse | 695 | 6 |
| And all I am shall sink and die | 393 | 2 |
| And all I have, and all I am | 614 | 10 |
| And all I have is thine | 548 | 1 |
| And all I think or speak, or do | 322 | 2 |
| And all in air, or sea, or land | 241 | 3 |
| And all in all for ever live | 16 | 9 |
| And all in love together dwell | 630 | 2 |
| And all in smoke expire | 64 | 4 |
| And all its frantic ways | 526 | 3 |
| And all its fruits we show | 96 | 4 |
| And all its virtues spread | 402 | 3 |
| And all its wonders prove | 781 | 7 |
| And all mankind adore | 730 | 3 |
| And all mankind by this may see | 237 | 1 |

| | Hymn | Verse |
|---|---|---|
| And all mankind may enter in | 706 | 3 |
| And all mankind must stand before | 44 | 3 |
| And all may live by thee | 901 | 4 |
| And all may live from sin set free | 706 | 5 |
| And all my blessings, came | 229 | 2 |
| And all my faults to thee are known | 163 | 4 |
| And all my griefs at once shall cease | 150 | 4 |
| And all my heart be love | 361 | 11 |
| And all my life thy glory show | 378 | 3 |
| And all my passions, love | 788 | 7 |
| And all my passions sway | 188 | 2 |
| And all my paths with ease besets | 310 | 3 |
| And all my powers are thine | 903 | 3 |
| And all my powers shall join to bless | 574 | 13 |
| And all my sickness cure | 112 | 6 |
| And all my sighs, and griefs, and fears | 575 | 2 |
| And all my simple soul devour | 433 | 1 |
| And all my sins consume | 361 | 8 |
| And all my sins shall die | 150 | 4 |
| And all my soul be love | 346 | 4 |
| And all my soul renew | 340 | 1 |
| And all my spotless life be praise | 351 | 7 |
| And all my spotless life shall show | 342 | 6 |
| And all my spotless life shall tell | 363 | 2 |
| And all my steps to thee-ward tend | 344 | 3 |
| And all my thirst for creature-good | 332 | 2 |
| And all my vileness feel | 109 | 5 |
| And all my wants redressed | 657 | 2 |
| And all my work be praise | 555 | 5 |
| And all occasions fly | 811 | 4 |
| †And all, O Lord, crave perfect rest | 969 | 5 |
| And all our brethren greet | 535 | 4 |
| And all our consecrated powers | 979 | 5 |
| And all our faculties shall feel | 204 | 7 |
| And all our fear is lost in hope | 983 | 6 |
| And all our grief in praise | 983 | 6 |
| And all our land o'erspread | 453 | 1 |
| And all our salvation ascribe to his love | 212 | 5 |
| And all our sickness heal | 900 | 3 |
| And all our sins as smoke expire | 493 | 5 |
| And all our strength exert | 204 | 1 |
| And all our wants supply | 245 | 1 |
| And all our wants supply | 745 | 1 |
| And all our works be wrought in thee | 475 | 4 |
| And all physicians tried | 781 | 1 |
| And all renewed I am | 361 | 1 |
| And all shall own thou diedst for all | 39 | 6 |
| And all that now in bodies live | 48 | 1 |
| And all that to the end endure | 333 | 3 |
| And all the accuser's power | 482 | 1 |
| And all the attributes divine | 832 | 6 |
| And all the Deity is ours | 248 | 6 |
| And all the depths of Deity | 881 | 1 |

|  | Hymn | Verse |
|---|---|---|
| And all the earthly joys he grants | 624 | 2 |
| And all the enjoyment above | 73 | 5 |
| And all the fruits of Paradise | 404 | 2 |
| And all the fruits of righteousness | 466 | 2 |
| And all the glorious persons joined | 256 | 4 |
| And all the helps and hopes of man | 475 | 2 |
| And all the hosts above | 251 | 1 |
| And all the hours obedient run | 788 | 2 |
| And all the lore its scholars need | 662 | 1 |
| And all the martyr throng | 943 | 9 |
| And all the planets in their turn | 552 | 4 |
| And all the powers of language fail | 658 | 3 |
| And all the saints and prophets join | 647 | 3 |
| And all the saints of God | 535 | 5 |
| And all the saints of the Most High | 56 | 4 |
| And all the silent heaven of love | 9 | 10 |
| And all the solid ground | 603 | 2 |
| And all the sons of glory seal | 754 | 6 |
| And all the sons of God shall sing | 280 | 7 |
| And all the sons of want are blest | 585 | 10 |
| And all the wrongs thy people bear | 588 | 2 |
| And all their force defies | 278 | 1 |
| And all their happiness to know | 72 | 4 |
| And all their power defy | 315 | 2 |
| And all their work is praise and love | 592 | 2 |
| And all therein, are thine | 248 | 2 |
| And all thine image give | 900 | 4 |
| And all things are wanting, till Jesus is here | 200 | 1 |
| And all things, as they change, proclaim | 223 | 5 |
| And all things count but dung and loss | 982 | 3 |
| And all things inherit by coming to me | 10 | 2 |
| And all things inherit in virtue of one | 496 | 3 |
| And all things new become | 367 | 2 |
| And all things serve thy might | 831 | 6 |
| And all thou art in Christ is mine | 148 | 5 |
| And all thou art is mine | 358 | 5 |
| And all thou hast, and all thou art | 394 | 4 |
| And all thou hast for sinners done | 872 | 2 |
| And all thy death be mine | 772 | 6 |
| And all thy footsteps trace | 471 | 4 |
| And all thy fulness feel | 402 | 1 |
| And all thy glorious goodness show | 261 | 2 |
| And all thy glorious love proclaim | 510 | 4 |
| And all thy goodness know | 361 | 2 |
| And all thy goodness to partake | 545 | 4 |
| And all thy grace declare | 250 | 2 |
| And all thy heart is love | 112 | 3 |
| And all thy life restore | 806 | 2 |
| And all thy love to feel | 415 | 2 |
| And all thy lovingkindness show | 187 | 1 |
| And all thy merits, Lord, are mine | 706 | 7 |
| And all thy mighty wonders show | 511 | 2 |
| And all thy mind brought in | 282 | 4 |

| | Hymn | Verse |
|---|---|---|
| And all thy mind fulfil | 828 | 4 |
| And all thy pardoned people fill | 258 | 2 |
| And all thy righteous laws fulfil | 527 | 1 |
| And all thy saints the spirit breathe | 419 | 2 |
| And all thy sayings love | 887 | 1 |
| And all thy servants seal | 459 | 3 |
| And all thy state of suffering share | 330 | 4 |
| And all thy vast designs are one | 651 | 3 |
| And all thy words are truth | 637 | 3 |
| And all thy words fulfil | 857 | 3 |
| And all thy wounds to sinners cry | 35 | 8 |
| And all we have, and all we are | 241 | 2 |
| And all we taste be God | 108 | 8 |
| And all who seek, in him shall find | 360 | 3 |
| And all within me shout his praise | 246 | 2 |
| And all within me shouts thy name | 206 | 4 |
| And all, with one accord | 532 | 1 |
| And all with thankful hearts receive | 459 | 4 |
| And all your conflicts passed | 266 | 2 |
| And all your God, is doubly ours | 721 | 6 |
| And all your sin's forgiven | 36 | 3 |
| And always exercise your arms | 267 | 3 |
| And always feel thee near | 271 | 2 |
| And always see his face | 361 | 10 |
| And always shalt endure | 239 | 2 |
| And always sorrowful we live | 21 | 4 |
| And always watch and pray | 310 | 1 |
| *And am I born to die | 43 | 1 |
| *And am I only born to die | 44 | 1 |
| And angels beckon me away | 68 | 7 |
| And angels chant the solemn lay | 557 | 7 |
| And angels chant the solemn lay | 557 | 10 |
| And angels shout the harvest home | 935 | Cho. |
| And angels tremble while they gaze | 425 | 2 |
| And anger and hatred be o'er | 220 | 4 |
| And answer all his word | 172 | 3 |
| And answer all thy great design | 440 | 2 |
| And answer all thy righteous will | 419 | 3 |
| And answer every prayer | 697 | 8 |
| And answer me by fire | 119 | 6 |
| And antedate that day | 947 | 7 |
| And are we saved through him | 623 | 2 |
| *And are we yet alive | 478 | 1 |
| And armed with jealous care | 321 | 3 |
| And, armed with patience, run | 536 | 3 |
| And arm our souls with heavenly zeal | 655 | 6 |
| And art thou not pacified | 188 | 1 |
| †And art thou not the Saviour still | 397 | 3 |
| And art thou not well pleased with me | 121 | 4 |
| And as a bounding hart fly home | 141 | 7 |
| And as a guardian angel live | 471 | 1 |
| And as a tender child | 627 | 2 |
| And as thou wilt require | 432 | 4 |

| | Hymn | Verse |
|---|---|---|
| And as thyself endure | 601 | 5 |
| And ascertains our claim to heaven | 774 | 4 |
| And ask according to thy will | 17 | 9 |
| And ask and have whate'er we want | 295 | 1 |
| And ask that free from peril | 968 | 3 |
| And ask thee that offenceless | 968 | 2 |
| And ask the gift unspeakable | 95 | 2 |
| And asks our nobler strain | 262 | 3 |
| And at my tears relent | 144 | 2 |
| And at our Father's loved abode | 664 | 4 |
| And at thy decree are broken and gone | 869 | 2 |
| And at thy footstool fall | 333 | 7 |
| And back to the pure fountain flow | 513 | 2 |
| And bade her go in peace | 106 | 6 |
| And bade him rise again | 106 | 4 |
| And bade me trust his power to save | 810 | — |
| And bade the sinner live | 112 | 5 |
| And baffles our pursuers | 854 | 2 |
| And banishes thy fear | 618 | 4 |
| And bared thine arm in all our sight | 203 | 3 |
| And basely to the tempter yield | 803 | 1 |
| And bathe and wash them with my tears | 33 | 4 |
| And bear each other's pain | 510 | 3 |
| And bear me from the gulf beneath | 288 | 5 |
| And bear me through a sea of light | 550 | 3 |
| And bear me through the doubtful strife | 820 | 4 |
| And bear thine easy yoke | 504 | 2 |
| And bear thy witness with my heart | 765 | 3 |
| And be at peace with thee | 772 | 1 |
| And be by faith made whole | 162 | 4 |
| And be in spirit one | 415 | 1 |
| And be it with thy presence filled | 993 | 1 |
| And be my helper, and my friend | 559 | 3 |
| And be of paradise possest | 167 | 2 |
| And be parted in body no more | 491 | 6 |
| And be perfectly happy in thee | 488 | 7 |
| And be thy feast to us the token | 906 | 2 |
| And be whate'er thy will ordain | 836 | 5 |
| And be with Christ in God | 654 | 5 |
| And beat the pride of nature down | 467 | 7 |
| And, behold, I am spread into bands | 231 | 8 |
| And behold thee on thy throne | 709 | 3 |
| And believers increased | 219 | 4 |
| And better hopes above | 644 | 1 |
| And bidd'st me of thy strength lay hold | 772 | 1 |
| And bid his guilty conscience dread | 83 | 5 |
| And bid me, at the point to die | 117 | 4 |
| And bid me die in peace | 104 | 2 |
| And bid me live, for Jesus dies | 917 | 3 |
| And bid me not despair | 626 | 1 |
| And bid me sin no more | 110 | Cho. |
| And bid my doubts and terrors cease | 833 | 5 |
| And bid my heart be clean | 410 | 1 |

| | Hymn | Verse |
|---|---|---|
| And all thy mind fulfil | 828 | 4 |
| And all thy pardoned people fill | 258 | 2 |
| And all thy righteous laws fulfil | 527 | 1 |
| And all thy saints the spirit breathe | 419 | 2 |
| And all thy sayings love | 887 | 1 |
| And all thy servants seal | 459 | 3 |
| And all thy state of suffering share | 330 | 4 |
| And all thy vast designs are one | 651 | 3 |
| And all thy words are truth | 637 | 8 |
| And all thy words fulfil | 357 | 3 |
| And all thy wounds to sinners cry | 35 | 8 |
| And all we have, and all we are | 241 | 2 |
| And all we taste be God | 108 | 8 |
| And all who seek, in him shall find | 360 | 3 |
| And all within me shout his praise | 246 | 2 |
| And all within me shouts thy name | 206 | 4 |
| And all, with one accord | 532 | 1 |
| And all with thankful hearts receive | 459 | 4 |
| And all your conflicts passed | 266 | 2 |
| And all your God, is doubly ours | 721 | 6 |
| And all your sin's forgiven | 36 | 3 |
| And always exercise your arms | 267 | 3 |
| And always feel thee near | 271 | 2 |
| And always see his face | 361 | 10 |
| And always shalt endure | 239 | 2 |
| And always sorrowful we live | 21 | 4 |
| And always watch and pray | 310 | 1 |
| *And am I born to die | 43 | 1 |
| *And am I only born to die | 44 | 1 |
| And angels beckon me away | 68 | 7 |
| And angels chant the solemn lay | 557 | 7 |
| And angels chant the solemn lay | 557 | 10 |
| And angels shout the harvest home | 935 | Cho. |
| And angels tremble while they gaze | 425 | 2 |
| And anger and hatred be o'er | 220 | 4 |
| And answer all his word | 172 | 3 |
| And answer all thy great design | 440 | 2 |
| And answer all thy righteous will | 419 | 3 |
| And answer every prayer | 697 | 8 |
| And answer me by fire | 119 | 6 |
| And antedate that day | 947 | 7 |
| And are we saved through him | 623 | 2 |
| *And are we yet alive | 478 | 1 |
| And armed with jealous care | 321 | 3 |
| And, armed with patience, run | 536 | 3 |
| And arm our souls with heavenly zeal | 655 | 6 |
| And art thou not pacified | 188 | 1 |
| †And art thou not the Saviour still | 897 | 3 |
| And art thou not well pleased with me | 121 | 4 |
| And as a bounding hart fly home | 141 | 7 |
| And as a guardian angel live | 471 | 1 |
| And as a tender child | 627 | 2 |
| And as thou wilt require | 432 | 4 |

| | Hymn | Verse |
|---|---|---|
| And as thyself endure | 601 | 5 |
| And ascertains our claim to heaven | 774 | 4 |
| And ask according to thy will | 17 | 9 |
| And ask and have whate'er we want | 295 | 1 |
| And ask that free from peril | 968 | 3 |
| And ask thee that offenceless | 968 | 2 |
| And ask the gift unspeakable | 95 | 2 |
| And asks our nobler strain | 262 | 3 |
| And at my tears relent | 144 | 2 |
| And at our Father's loved abode | 664 | 4 |
| And at thy decree are broken and gone | 869 | 2 |
| And at thy footstool fall | 333 | 7 |
| And back to the pure fountain flow | 513 | 2 |
| And bade her go in peace | 106 | 6 |
| And bade him rise again | 106 | 4 |
| And bade me trust his power to save | 810 | — |
| And bade the sinner live | 112 | 5 |
| And baffles our pursuers | 854 | 2 |
| And banishes thy fear | 618 | 4 |
| And bared thine arm in all our sight | 203 | 3 |
| And basely to the tempter yield | 803 | 1 |
| And bathe and wash them with my tears | 33 | 4 |
| And bear each other's pain | 510 | 3 |
| And bear me from the gulf beneath | 288 | 5 |
| And bear me through a sea of light | 550 | 3 |
| And bear me through the doubtful strife | 820 | 4 |
| And bear thine easy yoke | 504 | 2 |
| And bear thy witness with my heart | 765 | 3 |
| And be at peace with thee | 772 | 1 |
| And be by faith made whole | 162 | 4 |
| And be in spirit one | 415 | 1 |
| And be it with thy presence filled | 993 | 1 |
| And be my helper, and my friend | 559 | 3 |
| And be of paradise possest | 167 | 2 |
| And be parted in body no more | 491 | 6 |
| And be perfectly happy in thee | 488 | 7 |
| And be thy feast to us the token | 906 | 2 |
| And be whate'er thy will ordain | 836 | 5 |
| And be with Christ in God | 654 | 5 |
| And beat the pride of nature down | 467 | 7 |
| And, behold, I am spread into bands | 231 | 8 |
| And behold thee on thy throne | 709 | 3 |
| And believers increased | 219 | 4 |
| And better hopes above | 644 | 1 |
| And bidd'st me of thy strength lay hold | 772 | 1 |
| And bid his guilty conscience dread | 83 | 5 |
| And bid me, at the point to die | 117 | 4 |
| And bid me die in peace | 104 | 2 |
| And bid me live, for Jesus dies | 917 | 3 |
| And bid me not despair | 626 | 1 |
| And bid me sin no more | 110 | Cho. |
| And bid my doubts and terrors cease | 833 | 5 |
| And bid my heart be clean | 410 | 1 |

| | Hymn | Verse |
|---|---|---|
| And bid my heart rejoice | 214 | 3 |
| And bid my heart rejoice | 358 | 1 |
| And bid my murmuring heart be still | 177 | 4 |
| And bid my soul the call obey | 25 | 5 |
| And bid my spirit rise | 166 | 4 |
| And bid my troubles end | 189 | 1 |
| And bid my unbelief depart | 341 | 1 |
| And bid our bliss, on earth begun | 535 | 6 |
| And bid our hearts arise | 62 | 3 |
| And bid our inmost souls rejoice | 485 | 3 |
| And bid our kindred rise | 929 | 4 |
| And bid our sin be gone | 413 | 1 |
| And bid our wanderings cease | 98 | 2 |
| And bid the dire enmity cease | 220 | 3 |
| And bid the fallen race arise | 441 | 4 |
| And bid the obedient waters flow | 131 | 1 |
| And bid the sinner live | 184 | 4 |
| And bid the sleeper rise | 83 | 5 |
| And bid the sun stand still | 138 | 3 |
| And bid the weak be strong | 586 | 2 |
| And bid the world's wide realms admire | 636 | 2 |
| And bid their guilty terrors cease | 462 | 3 |
| And bid us eat and live | 108 | 5 |
| And bid us eat and live | 1009 | — |
| And bid us freely drink and eat | 507 | 4 |
| And bid us go in peace | 900 | Cho. |
| And bid us to thy glory live | 511 | 1 |
| And bid us to thy glory live | 629 | 4 |
| And bids me weep no more | 809 | 3 |
| And bids the earth be glad | 277 | 1 |
| And bids us, each to each restored | 500 | 1 |
| And bids us take the prize | 815 | 4 |
| And bind thy gospel to my heart | 879 | 4 |
| And blameless in our Lord to abide | 531 | 3 |
| And blasphemies are turned to praise | 203 | 8 |
| And blasted every flower | 98 | 7 |
| And blaze through all eternity | 513 | 4 |
| And bled for Adam's helpless race | 201 | 3 |
| And bless and magnify thy name | 649 | 1 |
| And bless and praise thee evermore | 377 | 3 |
| And bless *his* mild command | 465 | 7 |
| And bless his works and bless his word | 599 | 3 |
| And bless in death a bond so dear | 912 | 5 |
| And bless me for the Saviour's sake | 909 | 2 |
| And bless me with a godly fear | 306 | 4 |
| And bless me with thy perfect love | 408 | 4 |
| And bless me, who believe thy word | 409 | 6 |
| And bless the day that I was born | 229 | 1 |
| And bless the day that I was born | 230 | 3 |
| And bless the light that leads to heaven | 111 | 7 |
| And bless the mighty Jesu's name | 575 | 1 |
| And bless the mighty Jesu's name | 575 | 3 |
| And bless the name to sinners given | 576 | 3 |

| AND BLESS | AND BREATHE |
|---|---|

| | Hymn | Verse |
|---|---|---|
| And bless the ordinance divine | 476 | 4 |
| And bless the sound of Jesu's name | 34 | 1 |
| And bless the welcome load | 295 | 3 |
| And bless thee in our prayer | 767 | 4 |
| And bless thee in the skies | 717 | 3 |
| And bless them all by blessing me | 861 | 4 |
| And bless us with the perfect power | 616 | 9 |
| And blessings from above | 801 | 2 |
| And blessings more than we can give | 678 | 3 |
| And blest in Jesus live | 738 | 4 |
| And blest Spirit, Three in One | 631 | 8 |
| And blest their weak endeavours | 736 | 2 |
| And blindly serve a God unknown | 118 | 2 |
| And bliss that ne'er shall end | 418 | 3 |
| And bloody sweat we pray | 900 | 2 |
| And blush at my own righteousness | 126 | 5 |
| And boast, as if their evil way | 546 | 2 |
| And bodies part no more | 534 | 6 |
| And boldly Abba, Father, cry | 97 | 4 |
| And boldly Abba, Father, cry | 827 | 4 |
| And boldness to fulfil | 756 | 3 |
| And bore the mild Immanuel's name | 685 | 2 |
| And born of God, I sin no more | 157 | 8 |
| And born of God, I sin no more | 159 | 3 |
| And born of God, through thee | 799 | 7 |
| And born unholy and unclean | 574 | 3 |
| And both fly up to heaven | 61 | 4 |
| And both the choirs ere long shall join | 259 | 5 |
| And both the witnesses are joined | 96 | 5 |
| And bow before thy throne | 15 | 3 |
| And bow myself before thy face | 127 | 1 |
| And bow our souls before thy throne | 647 | 1 |
| And bow them with your knees | 268 | 3 |
| And bow the whole world to thy sway | 220 | 3 |
| And bow to his command | 729 | 4 |
| And bow to thy command | 464 | 2 |
| And bow with rapture down to see | 713 | 1 |
| And bowed that sacred head | 122 | 3 |
| And bowed the heavens high | 551 | 3 |
| And, branches of the Vine, declare | 673 | 2 |
| And break, and fill the broken heart | 94 | 5 |
| And break my heart of stone | 106 | Cho. |
| And break my heart of stone | 145 | 4 |
| And break my stubborn heart | 105 | 1 |
| And break my stubborn heart | 122 | 2 |
| And break my stubborn heart | 982 | 2 |
| And break off every chain | 136 | 6 |
| And break these hearts of stone | 84 | 1 |
| And break this heart of stone | 102 | 2 |
| And breaks their dark designs | 650 | 3 |
| And breathe in tainted air | 1002 | 2 |
| And breathe our wishes to the throne | 441 | 1 |
| And breathe the life into our heart | 89 | 1 |

| | Hymn | Verse |
|---|---|---|
| And breathe the living word | 85 | 2 |
| And breathe the spirit of thy love | 505 | 5 |
| And brief is mercy's day | 792 | 3 |
| And brighter than the morning star | 431 | 5 |
| And brighter than the sun | 941 | 2 |
| And bright in all thine image wake | 576 | 1 |
| And bright in effulgence divine | 73 | 4 |
| And, bright with borrowed rays divine | 446 | 3 |
| And bright with many an angel | 943 | 9 |
| And brightly her builder displays | 73 | 3 |
| And bring all heaven before our eyes | 864 | 4 |
| And bring him from the sky | 192 | 1 |
| And bring his kingdom in | 719 | 5 |
| And bring it, Lord, to thee | 874 | 3 |
| And bring me again unto God | 174 | 2 |
| And bring me assurance and rest | 165 | 1 |
| And bring me back to God | 122 | 4 |
| And bring me down to nought | 188 | 2 |
| And bring me to the promised land | 161 | 6 |
| And bring my soul triumphant through | 126 | 4 |
| And bring our charge to land | 468 | 2 |
| And bring our child with us to meet | 469 | 11 |
| And bring our souls, with pardon blest | 686 | 2 |
| And bring salvation near | 164 | 6 |
| And bring salvation nigh | 625 | 1 |
| And bring the blind by ways unknown | 836 | 3 |
| And bring the glorious liberty | 367 | 1 |
| And bring the gospel-day | 625 | 4 |
| And bring the grand sabbatic year | 979 | 6 |
| And bring the heavenly nature in | 443 | 2 |
| And bring the perfect day | 449 | 2 |
| And bring the ransomed prisoners up | 462 | 3 |
| And bring the weary wanderer back | 177 | 2 |
| And bring their sheaves with vast increase | 120 | 2 |
| And bring them all to God | 893 | 2 |
| And bring them through their evil day | 894 | 1 |
| And bring thy feeblest children on | 458 | 1 |
| And bring us to a perfect man | 89 | 4 |
| And bring us to heaven whose trust is in him | 199 | 4 |
| And brings his wanderer home | 144 | 7 |
| And brings redemption near | 387 | 1 |
| And brings the monster down | 278 | 5 |
| And brings us now to God | 897 | 2 |
| And brings us salvation, and calls us his own | 211 | 5 |
| And, brooding o'er my nature's night | 121 | 1 |
| And brought back life, and hope, and strength again | 850 | 2 |
| And brought into distress | 93 | 6 |
| And brought me up from hell | 274 | 1 |
| And brought thee, Saviour of mankind | 772 | 5 |
| And bruise the serpent's head | 299 | Cho. |
| And bruise the serpent's head | 362 | 4 |
| And bruises Satan's head | 87 | 3 |
| And build me up in love | 436 | 9 |

| | Hymn | Verse |
|---|---|---|
| And build them up in holiest love | 89 | 5 |
| And build the temple of our God | 505 | 2 |
| And bulwarks of our land | 573 | 2 |
| And burdened, for the afflicted sigh | 441 | 2 |
| And burdened ones where'er he came | 694 | 3 |
| And burn with everlasting love | 328 | 2 |
| And burst the barriers of my tomb | 290 | 3 |
| And but at times could find access | 827 | 5 |
| And by him alone we live | 714 | 4 |
| And by his side sit down | 333 | 3 |
| And by losing his life he hath carried my cause | 707 | 7 |
| And by redemption thine | 614 | 11 |
| And by reiterated crimes | 122 | 1 |
| And by thee move, and in thee live | 26 | 3 |
| And by the joy of grace prepare | 734 | 2 |
| And, by the shining of thy grace | 121 | 2 |
| And by thine hallowing Spirit dwell | 97 | 6 |
| And by thy cross abide | 778 | 4 |
| And, by thy grace | 276 | 4 |
| And by thy love I live | 614 | 5 |
| And by thy manifested love | 122 | 4 |
| And by thy mercy live | 409 | 5 |
| And, by thy precious blood restored | 179 | 2 |
| And by thy sacred presence crown | 1014 | — |
| And by thy sprinkled blood | 122 | 4 |
| And called his rebels to a crown | 902 | 3 |
| And called us from darkness his glory to see | 869 | 6 |
| And call forth all his host to war | 30 | 4 |
| And call mankind to extol thy name | 616 | 12 |
| And call my darkness into day | 148 | 2 |
| And call upon his name | 614 | 13 |
| And call upon the Lord | 267 | 4 |
| And calls his wandering creatures home | 31 | 3 |
| And calls them heirs of heaven | 888 | 3 |
| And calm amid its rage didst sleep | 1004 | 2 |
| And calm, and purify my heart | 778 | 1 |
| And, calmly confident, I mourn | 144 | 4 |
| And calmly wait the end | 62 | 2 |
| And calms the roaring seas | 12 | 2 |
| And calms the troubled breast | 679 | 2 |
| *And can it be, that I should gain | 201 | 1 |
| †And can I yet delay | 137 | 7 |
| †And can my soul with hopes like these | 844 | 6 |
| *And can we forbear, in tasting our food | 1025 | 1 |
| And can no longer doubt | 417 | 3 |
| And cannot come to thee | 112 | 4 |
| And cannot fail, if God is love | 380 | 4 |
| And cannot share the praise with thee | 126 | 3 |
| And captivate my every thought | 188 | 2 |
| And careful less to serve thee much | 842 | 6 |
| And caring for the morrow | 1026 | — |
| And cast away his chains | 387 | 3 |
| And cast my shield away | 305 | 2 |

| | Hymn | Verse |
|---|---|---|
| And cast not out my languid prayer | 290 | 1 |
| And cast out every gracious soul | 94 | 8 |
| And cast their cords from our free hands | 541 | 1 |
| And cast the world and flesh behind | 163 | 3 |
| And cast thy foes with fury down | 386 | 1 |
| And cast us on thy sacrifice | 774 | 9 |
| And cast your bonds away | 983 | 1 |
| And catch, through openings in the skies | 838 | 6 |
| And cause the brightness of thy face | 581 | 1 |
| And cause the glories of thy face | 252 | 3 |
| And cause the world to know thy name | 749 | 5 |
| And cease at once to work and live | 45 | 3 |
| And ceaseless praise to thee is given | 203 | 5 |
| And, certified that thou art mine | 919 | 3 |
| And challenged thy beloved | 335 | 2 |
| And challenge them to sing | 262 | 3 |
| And charm into a beauteous frame | 16 | 7 |
| And charm their griefs to rest | 562 | 2 |
| And change, and make us all like thee | 754 | 6 |
| And change, and throughly purify | 875 | 5 |
| And change, and throughly sanctify | 523 | 6 |
| And change our faith to sight | 74 | 4 |
| And chase the murderer from our hearts | 442 | 3 |
| And cheer each languid heart | 901 | 3 |
| And cheer my drooping heart | 184 | 3 |
| And cheer our souls this day | 966 | 1 |
| And cheer the dark and silent night | 658 | 1 |
| And cheer the souls of death afraid | 686 | 3 |
| And cheer the world below | 578 | 1 |
| And cheer thy sons beneath | 88 | 1 |
| And cheerfully sing | 231 | 2 |
| And cherub and seraph adore | 946 | 1 |
| And children's children ever find | 610 | 11 |
| And children's voices echo, answer making, Alleluia | 663 | — |
| And Christ, and all with Christ, are mine | 376 | 2 |
| And Christ be all in all | 184 | 11 |
| And Christ by their rejection gain | 451 | 1 |
| And Christ in me shall live | 360 | 10 |
| And Christ is all in all | 414 | 1 |
| And Christ shall be our song | 682 | 4 |
| And Christ shall build me up | 382 | 5 |
| And Christ shall give you light | 1 | 9 |
| And Christ shall make thee whole | 305 | 1 |
| And Christ the whole creation made | 234 | 2 |
| And circumspectly tread | 311 | 1 |
| And claim a share in all my pain | 157 | 4 |
| And claim, in virtue of our birth | 21 | 6 |
| And claim me for thine own | 128 | 5 |
| And claim my heavenly rest | 68 | 8 |
| And claim my station in the skies | 72 | 1 |
| And claim the crown, through Christ my own | 201 | 5 |
| And claim the grace on all bestowed | 561 | 6 |
| And claim the kingdom of the earth | 863 | 3 |

# AND CLAIMED          AND CRY

| | Hymn | Verse |
|---|---|---|
| And claimed me for his own | 93 | 6 |
| And claimed the outcasts as thy right | 203 | 3 |
| And claps his wings of fire | 61 | 2 |
| And cleanse, and keep me clean | 846 | 2 |
| And closely walk with thee to heaven | 324 | 5 |
| And close the path to misery | 690 | 4 |
| And clothed in righteousness divine | 201 | 5 |
| And clothed in righteousness divine | 706 | 7 |
| And clothes the smiling fields with corn | 225 | 4 |
| And clothe us with our nobler house | 74 | 4 |
| And cold my warmest thought | 679 | 5 |
| And come at thy call, thy grace to receive | 10 | 3 |
| And come for the pardon God cannot deny | 707 | 5 |
| And come, in the spirit of prayer | 78 | 2 |
| And come to thee pure gold to buy | 455 | 1 |
| And comfort every heart | 905 | 1 |
| And comfort of my nights | 213 | 1 |
| And comforts them in their distresses | 595 | 2 |
| And command us to rise | 488 | 8 |
| And commune, Father, with thy child | 909 | 5 |
| And comprehend the whole | 872 | — |
| And, confident in strength divine | 616 | 2 |
| And conquering, I to conquer go | 293 | 7 |
| And conquering palms they bear | 948 | 5 |
| And conquering them, through Jesu's blood | 815 | 3 |
| And conquering them to conquer go | 511 | 2 |
| And conquer my rebellious will | 177 | 4 |
| And conquerors of the world, we dwell | 96 | 3 |
| And consciously believes | 85 | 4 |
| And consecrates the place | 630 | 4 |
| And constantly trample on pleasure and pain | 484 | 1 |
| And convoy us safe to our prosperous end | 760 | 4 |
| And cordially agree | 500 | 4 |
| †And couldst thou be delighted | 667 | 4 |
| And counts and treasures up my tears | 849 | 1 |
| And count thy choice the best | 560 | 2 |
| And count thy people's triumph mine | 612 | 4 |
| And, covered with the atoning blood | 917 | 4 |
| And cries in all thy banished ones | 16 | 8 |
| And cries, It shall be done | 360 | 9 |
| And criminals, with pardon blest | 11 | 4 |
| And crowds of wretched parents see | 467 | 3 |
| And, crowned with endless joy, return | 535 | 4 |
| And crown him Lord of all | 681 | Cho. |
| And crown my journey's end | 843 | 3 |
| And crown the whole with full success | 475 | 3 |
| And crown with living fire our head | 456 | 1 |
| And crowns upon our head | 537 | 10 |
| And crushed beneath our load | 701 | 3 |
| And cry aloud | 853 | 1 |
| And cry, "Behold he prays!" | 823 | 4 |
| And cry, in answer to thy call | 533 | 2 |
| And cry, O God, to thee | 469 | 6 |

27

| | Hymn | Verse |
|---|---|---|
| And cry out, "It is he!" | 491 | 8 |
| And cry, "Salvation to our God | 253 | 2 |
| And cry, with joy unspeakable | 85 | 2 |
| And curb my headstrong will | 138 | 3 |
| And cursed I am, till thou art mine | 132 | 2 |
| And curst I am, for God neglects my cry | 596 | 1 |
| And daily take up the pledge of our crown | 484 | 2 |
| And daily, through thy word, increase | 732 | 1 |
| And daily vows ascend | 586 | 5 |
| And dances his glad heart for joy | 84 | 4 |
| And dared to call thee God | 93 | 2 |
| And dark I am within | 135 | 8 |
| And dark is his path on the wings of the storm | 611 | 2 |
| And darkness into day | 750 | 2 |
| And David's royal fountain | 943 | 13 |
| And day and night be all my care | 873 | 4 |
| And day by day, whereby my soul may live | 794 | 5 |
| And days are dark, and friends are few | 849 | 1 |
| And dead to human praise | 204 | 4 |
| And deal to each his legacy | 754 | 4 |
| And death, and grief, and pain | 536 | 4 |
| And death-dews o'er the forehead creep | 961 | 6 |
| And death ungrasped his fainting prey | 335 | 2 |
| And death, when death shall be our lot | 1002 | 6 |
| And death's dark shadows put to flight | 690 | 3 |
| And declare thou hast died in thy murderer's stead | 160 | 1 |
| And deep and dark our fall | 626 | 5 |
| And deep beneath the burden groan | 99 | 4 |
| And deeper stamp thyself the seal | 374 | 5 |
| And deeply for acceptance groan | 176 | 2 |
| And deeply in the spirit groan | 311 | 3 |
| And deeply on my thoughtful heart | 59 | 8 |
| And deigns to approve | 495 | 1 |
| And delightfully join | 488 | 1 |
| And depth of perfect love | 136 | 10 |
| And depth, of perfect love | 870 | 4 |
| And depth of sovereign grace | 216 | 2 |
| And deserts blossom at the sight | 585 | 5 |
| And deserts learn the joy | 741 | 5 |
| And desperate souls to cure | 693 | 4 |
| And devils fear and fly | 37 | 1 |
| And did for succour flee | 614 | 4 |
| And died a cursed death | 137 | 6 |
| And died for us in love | 667 | 3 |
| And die, my fathers' God to meet | 45 | 1 |
| And die thyself to effect my cure | 816 | 1 |
| And die to all below | 88 | 4 |
| And die to make it known | 384 | 9 |
| And dies, and leaves them all behind | 564 | 3 |
| And disappoint his children's hope | 280 | 5 |
| And discord afflict us no more | 220 | 4 |
| And done despite to thee | 162 | 1 |
| And done thy loving Spirit despite | 176 | 8 |

| | Hymn | Verse |
|---|---|---|
| And do on earth thy perfect will | 119 | 5 |
| And do them good, and save them here | 622 | 8 |
| And do the will divine | 153 | 8 |
| And do thy will like those above | 524 | 3 |
| And do with faith whate'er we do | 1015 | — |
| And doth his spoils to all divide | 493 | 3 |
| And doth the mountain move | 85 | 4 |
| And doth till death endure | 162 | 5 |
| And, down the current borne | 469 | 7 |
| And doubts no longer mine | 882 | 1 |
| And draw, and sprinkle us, and seal | 261 | 2 |
| And draw me to his open side | 128 | 6 |
| And draw out all our souls in prayer | 441 | 2 |
| And draw their souls to God | 468 | 8 |
| And draw the wondering eyes | 740 | 1 |
| And, drawn by the power of his word | 78 | 1 |
| And dread to venture on | 471 | 2 |
| And drew their virtue from thy blood | 702 | 1 |
| And drink of the river of Jesus's love | 211 | 4 |
| And drink the living streams of bliss | 35 | 7 |
| And drive me to the blood again | 808 | 3 |
| And drive the alien armies back | 269 | 2 |
| And drive the evil spirit hence | 895 | 7 |
| And drives away his fear | 679 | 1 |
| And drop in blessings down | 578 | 2 |
| And drop in every listening heart | 801 | 2 |
| And drop into eternity | 918 | — |
| And drop salvation from thy wings | 462 | 5 |
| And dry up all the streams of sin | 412 | 3 |
| †And duly shall appear | 789 | 4 |
| And dwell for ever in my breast | 145 | 3 |
| And dwell in every breast | 756 | 2 |
| And dwell upon our tongues | 742 | 3 |
| And dwell upon thy love | 253 | 4 |
| And dwell within my heart | 172 | 4 |
| And dwells in us, we know | 96 | 4 |
| And dwelt among the dead | 699 | 3 |
| And dying drawn the sting of death | 648 | 3 |
| And, dying, find my latest foe | 421 | 1 |
| And dying sinners pray to live | 993 | 2 |
| And each a starry crown receive | 501 | 6 |
| And each chill night, its bourn | 838 | 3 |
| And each exalted seraph-flame | 665 | 2 |
| And each hath its distinct reward | 926 | 3 |
| And each hidden deed arraigneth | 933 | 6 |
| And each receives the crown of love | 590 | 8 |
| And each records the praise of him | 948 | 6 |
| And each regenerate soul restore | 528 | 2 |
| And each succeeding race remove | 997 | 4 |
| And each to each endeared | 504 | 1 |
| And, each to each in Jesus joined | 537 | 3 |
| And each wakes up a sinless saint | 295 | 4 |
| And eager long for our release | 949 | 4 |

| | Hymn | Verse |
|---|---|---|
| And eagerly to Zion run | 595 | 4 |
| And earth, and heaven, and all is ours | 1001 | 10 |
| And earth and heaven at once possess | 834 | 2 |
| And earth and heaven conspire to praise | 280 | 8 |
| And earth, and hell, and sin shall flee | 815 | 6 |
| And earth and hell at last prevail | 475 | 4 |
| And earth and hell withstand | 800 | 5 |
| And earth, and seas, with all their train | 224 | 2 |
| And earth is turned to heaven | 221 | 4 |
| And earth prolong the joyful strain | 585 | 12 |
| And earth, with her ten thousand tongues | 608 | 3 |
| And earthly comforts flee | 558 | 4 |
| †And earth's fields, with herbs and flowers | 604 | 4 |
| And earth's strong pillars bend | 22 | 2 |
| And eat his flesh, and drink his blood | 2 | 4 |
| And eat the bread of care | 624 | 1 |
| And eat the Paschal Lamb | 898 | 1 |
| And eat thy flesh, and drink thy blood | 507 | 5 |
| And echoes to the sky | 253 | 1 |
| And echo the joys of the skies | 946 | 4 |
| And echo to thy voice | 214 | 3 |
| And embrace the glad tidings of pardon and peace | 219 | 5 |
| And emulate the angel-choir | 420 | 4 |
| And emulate, with joy unknown | 658 | 5 |
| And endless praise | 800 | 12 |
| And endless rest | 800 | 6 |
| And end the apostasy | 447 | 2 |
| And envy and malice shall die | 220 | 4 |
| And envy rage in vain | 617 | 3 |
| And equal adoration be | 752 | 5 |
| And ere I speak thou know'st them all | 99 | 2 |
| And, ere my lips pronounce the word | 632 | 3 |
| And ere the darkness round us fell | 961 | 1 |
| And escort thee quick to heaven | 921 | 2 |
| And essence is I AM | 601 | 2 |
| And eternal redemption, in Jesus's name | 495 | 4 |
| And eternity seems as a day | 499 | 8 |
| And eternity spend | 488 | 8 |
| And ever bear us on your mind | 539 | 5 |
| And ever brings us nigher | 853 | 2 |
| And ever by thy Spirit guide | 473 | 6 |
| And ever dwell within | 820 | 1 |
| And ever dwell with me | 192 | 2 |
| And ever from the skies | 930 | 3 |
| And ever in thy bosom rest | 23 | 9 |
| And ever let there rise to thee | 1004 | 4 |
| And ever mightily defend | 649 | 2 |
| And ever move towards thee | 504 | 4 |
| And ever on thy people rain | 704 | 4 |
| And ever prays for me | 243 | 8 |
| And ever prays for me | 384 | 1 |
| And ever towards each other move | 504 | 4 |
| And ever-waking love | 618 | 3 |

| | Hymn | Verse |
|---|---|---|
| And everlasting joy | 985 | 3 |
| And everlasting love | 59 | 6 |
| And everlasting love | 139 | 4 |
| And everlasting love | 485 | 1 |
| And everlasting rest | 384 | 7 |
| And everlasting rest | 404 | 3 |
| And evermore shall be | 800 | 10 |
| And evermore, the same | 166 | 1 |
| And every beast and every tree | 788 | 4 |
| And every beating pulse we tell | 42 | 2 |
| And every bosom swell | 729 | 5 |
| And every comfort here | 243 | 2 |
| And every comfort here | 1018 | — |
| And every foe shall fall | 275 | 9 |
| And every grace bestow | 243 | 4 |
| And every grace, I own | 153 | 3 |
| And every grave becomes a bed | 715 | 5 |
| And every heart be filled with grace | 111 | 5 |
| And every heart his love | 268 | 1 |
| And every heart shall dance for joy | 977 | 3 |
| And every heart shall turn | 449 | 1 |
| And every hurtful snare | 814 | 2 |
| And every law of sin reverse | 457 | 2 |
| And every loving heart | 428 | 1 |
| And every moment, Lord, revive | 436 | 6 |
| And every moment watch and pray | 324 | 4 |
| And every night defend | 1003 | 4 |
| And every night, we feel | 630 | 5 |
| And every place is hallowed ground | 864 | 1 |
| And every place is hell; for God is gone | 596 | 1 |
| And every power find sweet employ | 599 | 6 |
| And every saint in earth and heaven | 559 | 4 |
| And every shape and every face | 930 | 4 |
| And every shining front displays | 948 | 5 |
| And every sin-sick soul to heal | 107 | 2 |
| And every solemn moment wait | 783 | 1 |
| And every soul displays thy love | 505 | 9 |
| And every soul that sheep might be | 144 | 7 |
| And every struggling soul release | 900 | 1 |
| And every tear be dry | 12 | 4 |
| And every thought of every heart | 239 | 4 |
| And every threatening danger ward | 985 | 2 |
| And every tongue confess | 730 | 3 |
| And every tongue proclaim | 472 | 5 |
| And every want supplies | 637 | 2 |
| And execute his will | 828 | 4 |
| And execute the vast design | 475 | 1 |
| And exercise thy power | 985 | 5 |
| And eye-sight to the blind | 109 | 6 |
| And face the Judge severe | 63 | 4 |
| And fain I would; but though my will | 344 | 2 |
| And fain I would to thee return | 130 | 1 |
| And faints, o'erpowered with strong desire | 590 | 1 |

| | Hymn | Verse |
|---|---|---|
| And faith desires no more | 659 | 6 |
| And faithfulness I give | 360 | 10 |
| And faithful to the end endure | 57 | 8 |
| And faithful unto death | 733 | 4 |
| And fall beneath his feet | 729 | 4 |
| And far above those nether skies | 977 | 5 |
| And, Father, Abba, Father, cry | 202 | 5 |
| And, Father, Abba, Father, cry | 303 | 4 |
| And fear gives place to filial love | 123 | 2 |
| And fear to launch away | 938 | 4 |
| And fearless pass the vale of death | 535 | 6 |
| And feast for ever there | 905 | 2 |
| And feast my hungry heart | 304 | 3 |
| And feasts his saints to-day | 956 | 2 |
| And fed by Christ their graces live | 868 | 8 |
| And feed their spirits now | 875 | 1 |
| And feel his blood applied | 96 | 2 |
| And feel his blood flow | 205 | 4 |
| And feel his brother's care | 503 | 3 |
| And feel his heavy hand | 106 | 5 |
| And feel his sprinkled blood | 622 | 1 |
| And feel that Christ is all in all | 393 | 4 |
| And feel the blood applied | 128 | 7 |
| And feel the indigence I see | 99 | 4 |
| And feel the influence of his eye | 550 | 1 |
| And feel the quickening spirit move | 901 | 2 |
| And feel the sprinkled blood | 982 | 3 |
| And feel thy warning eye | 309 | 3 |
| And fell, and kissed his bleeding feet | 721 | 4 |
| And fellowship with all we hold | 897 | 4 |
| And fervent zeal, and perfect love | 412 | 4 |
| And fierce diseases wait around | 42 | 4 |
| And fight against your God no more | 2 | 7 |
| And fight our passage through | 537 | 11 |
| And filled with all the life of God | 953 | 2 |
| And filled with love and lost in praise | 386 | 6 |
| And filled with love divine | 531 | 1 |
| And filled with perfect love | 368 | 4 |
| And filled with shouts the realms of light | 721 | 4 |
| And filled with thee be all our thought | 666 | 6 |
| And fillest every mouth with good | 235 | 1 |
| And fill his courts with songs of praise | 953 | 3 |
| And fill his heart with sacred grief | 83 | 4 |
| And fill me with the life divine | 148 | 3 |
| And fill me with thy perfect peace | 388 | 6 |
| And fill me with thy righteousness | 134 | 3 |
| And fill my soul with holy shame | 425 | 1 |
| And fill our hearts with heavenly peace | 861 | 3 |
| And fill our hearts with holy joy | 412 | 4 |
| And fill our souls with power divine | 754 | 5 |
| And fill the circle of my days | 577 | 5 |
| And fill the earth with purity | 731 | 5 |
| And fill the echoing courts above | 926 | 4 |

| | Hymn | Verse |
|---|---|---|
| And fill the illustrated abyss | 121 | 1 |
| And fill their hearts with sacred grief | 443 | 1 |
| And fill their souls with living bread | 629 | 6 |
| And fill them with thy love | 874 | 3 |
| And fill thy house with endless praise | 341 | 2 |
| And fill us now with watchful care | 55 | 1 |
| And fill us with rivers of water divine | 10 | 4 |
| And fill with all the life of God | 394 | 3 |
| And fill with all thy life below | 453 | 2 |
| And fill with godly jealousy | 309 | 2 |
| And fill with peace and joy | 303 | 4 |
| And fills it with divine perfumes | 630 | 4 |
| And fills their mouths with good | 637 | 3 |
| And fills them with divine perfumes | 902 | 4 |
| And fills the soul with joy divine | 644 | 3 |
| And fills with hallowed joy | 124 | 3 |
| And find a hiding-place, a rest, a home | 850 | 5 |
| And find annexed the vast reward | 440 | 2 |
| And find forgiveness at his feet | 11 | 2 |
| And find it ever new | 804 | 2 |
| And find its long-sought rest | 948 | 1 |
| And find my grace is free for all | 4 | 2 |
| And find my heaven in thee | 214 | 5 |
| And find my way to heaven | 320 | 2 |
| And find on earth the life, the home | 25 | 6 |
| And find prepared our heavenly place | 489 | 2 |
| And find that heaven and thou are one | 507 | 6 |
| And find the pearl of perfect love | 815 | 4 |
| And find with me their heaven below | 206 | 4 |
| And firm, as our Redeemer's love | 74 | 1 |
| And firm endures, while endless years | 802 | 3 |
| And fit for thy great service make | 474 | 1 |
| And fit it for the sky | 318 | 1 |
| And fit the creature of an hour | 833 | 3 |
| And fit us for thy will | 526 | 5 |
| And fitted by true holiness | 123 | 4 |
| And fixed it in the floating seas | 557 | 2 |
| And fix in every heart thy seat | 759 | 8 |
| And fix in me his loved abode | 376 | 3 |
| And fix in me thy lasting home | 155 | 7 |
| And fix in us the guest divine | 759 | 5 |
| And fix it ever there | 325 | 3 |
| And fix it in my heart | 187 | 3 |
| And fix my hope on thee alone | 564 | 4 |
| And fix on earth his heavenly throne | 927 | 1 |
| And fix on things above | 960 | — |
| And fix our thoughts on things divine | 955 | 2 |
| And fix thy Agent in our heart | 294 | 3 |
| And fix thy sacred presence there | 374 | 1 |
| And fix us in the golden mean | 468 | 2 |
| And flames around my head | 359 | 2 |
| And flames with the glory of God | 73 | 3 |
| And flourish unconsumed in fire | 272 | 7 |

| | Hymn | Verse |
|---|---|---|
| And flows through every faithful soul | 749 | 1 |
| And flow unto thee | 219 | 6 |
| And fly to the mountain of God | 70 | 1 |
| And fly up to acknowledge him there | 491 | 8 |
| And folds them in his arms | 889 | 1 |
| And follow after peace | 630 | 7 |
| And follow Christ, your Head, to heaven | 420 | 2 |
| And follow on to know as we are known | 850 | 6 |
| And follow thee where'er thou go | 338 | 4 |
| And followed with a heart sincere | 97 | 2 |
| And following our triumphant Head | 535 | 2 |
| And following their incarnate God | 940 | 4 |
| And forced thy mercy to remove | 180 | 1 |
| And force me to thy breast | 137 | 1 |
| And force the world into thy fold | 445 | 3 |
| And force your passage to the skies | 333 | 2 |
| And foremost of the Three | 642 | 2 |
| And for his help I tarry | 626 | 3 |
| And for his Israel cares | 622 | 2 |
| And for his sheep he doth us take | 607 | 2 |
| And for my hope of heaven | 248 | 2 |
| And for my hope of heaven | 1018 | — |
| †And for richer food than this | 631 | 7 |
| And for the love | 276 | 4 |
| And for thy mercy call | 245 | 1 |
| And for thy name's sake, Lord, my head | 635 | 3 |
| And for thy own possession take | 511 | 1 |
| And for thy second coming stay | 828 | 4 |
| And for thy servant fight | 465 | 2 |
| And for thyself prepare the place | 285 | 1 |
| And formed by power divine | 798 | 7 |
| And formed us man for this | 264 | 2 |
| And form my soul anew | 361 | 5 |
| And form my soul averse from sin | 574 | 8 |
| And fortify the whole | 266 | 4 |
| And foul with sins of deepest stain | 373 | 6 |
| And founded on a rock | 572 | 3 |
| And found salvation in thy name | 395 | 1 |
| And freed from its bodily chain | 49 | 1 |
| And freed me from the Egyptian yoke | 293 | 2 |
| And free from every spot of blame | 523 | 7 |
| And free from pain thy glories sing | 388 | 6 |
| And freely all accept their cure | 82 | 2 |
| And freely as Jesus hath given to give | 495 | 2 |
| And freely delight you in Jesus's love | 40 | 1 |
| And freely eat substantial food | 4 | 7 |
| And freely forgiven, receive | 79 | 2 |
| And freely give up all for thee | 378 | 4 |
| And freely give up all the rest | 285 | 8 |
| And freely my backslidings heal | 186 | 2 |
| And freely now be saved by grace | 2 | 8 |
| And, freely saved, thy grace declare | 365 | 7 |
| And freely talks with God | 325 | 4 |

| | Hymn | Verse |
|---|---|---|
| And freely then release | 84 | 4 |
| And fresh supplies of joy are shed | 599 | 5 |
| And friend holds fellowship with friend | 825 | 3 |
| And from defilement laved | 943 | 12 |
| And from his hand, his voice, his smile | 849 | 4 |
| And from our eyes for ever hide | 666 | 5 |
| And from the angel host | 966 | 6 |
| And from the iron furnace groan | 81 | 3 |
| And from the miry clay | 566 | 2 |
| And, from this moment, live or die | 426 | 2 |
| And from thy plenitude receive | 489 | 2 |
| And fruit unto perfection bear | 159 | 3 |
| And fruit unto perfection bear | 981 | 5 |
| And fruit we every hour shall bear | 492 | 5 |
| And full felicity | 949 | 4 |
| And full of love divine | 343 | 4 |
| And full of love thy tender heart | 568 | 2 |
| And full of power and love | 18 | 1 |
| And fully from this hour possess | 783 | 2 |
| And fully set my spirit free | 388 | 4 |
| And gain for Christ an entrance there | 770 | 4 |
| And gain the highest heaven of love | 977 | 5 |
| And gain the morning-star | 192 | 1 |
| And gain the mountain-top | 535 | 6 |
| And gasp and languish after home | 154 | 2 |
| And gasp for a drop of thy love | 165 | 5 |
| And gasp in thee to live | 92 | 4 |
| And gasps to be made whole | 109 | 2 |
| And Gath and Askelon shall mourn | 280 | 7 |
| And, gathered into one | 500 | 2 |
| And, gathered out of every land | 452 | 3 |
| And gather in the souls sincere | 459 | 1 |
| And gather with thy arm | 501 | 3 |
| And gave his Isaac back to God | 286 | 1 |
| And gavest light and life and peace | 1004 | 8 |
| And gay their silken leaves unfold | 46 | 1 |
| And gaze, transported at the sight | 128 | 8 |
| And gently bend their tender mind | 468 | 8 |
| And gently in thy bosom bear | 458 | 2 |
| And get thyself the victory | 122 | 4 |
| And gild our gloomy hemisphere | 686 | 1 |
| And give back all to thee | 432 | 3 |
| And give me a mansion above | 77 | 2 |
| And give me a mansion above | 79 | 2 |
| And give me, Lord, O give me love | 146 | 2 |
| And give me my pardon to feel | 165 | 3 |
| And give, O give us all one way | 505 | 1 |
| And give our inmost souls to feel | 1014 | -- |
| And give thee all the glory | 276 | 2 |
| And give thee all the glory | 736 | 1 |
| And give the glory, Lord, to thee | 526 | 6 |
| And give the praise to him | 115 | 2 |
| And give the Spirit of thy grace | 754 | 2 |

| | Hymn | Verse |
|---|---|---|
| And give their weary spirits rest | 107 | 4 |
| And give them victory o'er the grave | 690 | 2 |
| And give thyself unto our sight | 694 | 1 |
| And give thy servant to possess | 408 | 6 |
| And give thy triumphs o'er | 274 | 3 |
| And give to God | 853 | 1 |
| And give up all for thee | 137 | 4 |
| And give up all our hearts to him | 28 | 4 |
| And give us ears to hear | 88 | 3 |
| And give us eyes to see | 85 | 1 |
| And give us hearts to feel and know | 118 | 3 |
| And give us now to find in thee | 528 | 5 |
| And give us thrones above | 453 | 2 |
| And given me back at thy command | 289 | 3 |
| And given me back my hope | 187 | 1 |
| And gives glory to God and the Lamb | 231 | 9 |
| And gives the Comforter | 761 | 2 |
| And gives the purity divine | 705 | 4 |
| And gladden me with answers mild | 909 | 5 |
| And glad drink in the solar fire | 494 | 6 |
| And glad to act my part | 321 | 1 |
| And gladly bless | 736 | 1 |
| And gladly catch the healing stream | 28 | 4 |
| And gladly die their Lord to meet | 69 | 3 |
| And gladly linger out below | 356 | 4 |
| And gladly our loving Redeemer admire | 808 | 9 |
| And gladly reckon all things loss | 478 | 3 |
| And gladly reconciled to thee | 11 | 3 |
| And gladly sing thy praise | 654 | 1 |
| And gladly sing thy praise | 1020 | — |
| And gladly to resign | 772 | 6 |
| And gladly wander up and down | 948 | 2 |
| And glide to all my heaven above | 284 | 6 |
| And glory, and blessing, and honour, and praise | 481 | 6 |
| And glory crowns the mercy-seat | 825 | 4 |
| And glory decks the Saviour's face | 56 | 2 |
| And glory ends what grace begun | 236 | 1 |
| And glory end what grace begun | 196 | 3 |
| And glory give to God alone | 869 | 6 |
| And glory in his face appears | 919 | 3 |
| And glory in his grace | 345 | 7 |
| And glory in his grace | 605 | 5 |
| And glory in our guide | 829 | 3 |
| And glory in thy love | 357 | 2 |
| And glory in thy love | 387 | 2 |
| And glory shall be mine | 903 | 3 |
| And glory that he died for me | 803 | 3 |
| And glorify his name | 539 | 1 |
| And glorify the great I AM | 251 | 2 |
| And glorify thy grace | 801 | 5 |
| And glorious as your Head revealed | 420 | 6 |
| And glorious forests, sing Alleluia | 663 | — |
| And glorious with his saints in light | 800 | 7 |

| | Hymn | Verse |
|---|---|---|
| And go and sin no more | 166 | 4 |
| And God appeared below | 215 | 2 |
| And God beholds with gracious eyes | 423 | 3 |
| And God cries out, " Let me alone " | 298 | 1 |
| And God for ever see | 804 | 5 |
| And God hath quenched the wrath of God | 917 | 2 |
| And God himself is born | 684 | 2 |
| And God himself our Father is | 21 | 5 |
| And God is all in all | 275 | 9 |
| And God is all in all | 333 | 7 |
| And God is all my own | 150 | 5 |
| And God is all our own | 684 | 4 |
| And God is seen by mortal eye | 95 | 6 |
| And God of love | 800 | 1 |
| And God the Holy Ghost | 966 | 6 |
| And God the Holy Ghost declare | 647 | 5 |
| And godliness, with all its power | 464 | 1 |
| And going take thee to their home | 864 | 2 |
| And gold and incense bring | 586 | 5 |
| And gold is dross compared to her | 14 | 8 |
| And gospel salvation is preached to the poor | 40 | 5 |
| And got the victory | 605 | 1 |
| And govern all our race | 449 | 1 |
| And govern with a looser rein | 470 | 4 |
| And grace, and plentitude of power | 418 | 2 |
| And grace, sweet grace celestial | 943 | 13 |
| And grace to answer grace | 534 | 4 |
| And graciously receive us still | 396 | 1 |
| And graciously reply | 635 | 1 |
| And grant my heart's desire | 119 | 3 |
| And grant their hearts thy word to hear | 82 | 8 |
| And grant us each a seat | 761 | 5 |
| And grant what I require | 119 | 6 |
| And grants the prisoner sweet release | 224 | 3 |
| And grasp thee in the flaming skies | 536 | 4 |
| And grasp the Infinite | 384 | 6 |
| And grasp the sinner's friend | 299 | 2 |
| And grasp through death the glorious prize | 330 | 5 |
| And greater than my heart | 138 | 7 |
| And greater than our heart | 469 | 8 |
| And great in majesty | 249 | 3 |
| And great ones despise so vulgar a way | 212 | 2 |
| And great shall be the preachers' crowd | 744 | 4 |
| And greet the blood-besprinkled bands | 949 | 4 |
| And grief, and fear, and care shall fly | 337 | 4 |
| And grief shall, like a moth, consume | 565 | 6 |
| And griefs would tear my throbbing breast | 658 | 2 |
| And grieve thy gentleness no more | 170 | 1 |
| And grind us into dust | 61 | 1 |
| And groan, and bow with thee my head | 330 | 4 |
| And groan my nature's weight to feel | 100 | 2 |
| And groan to be renewed | 119 | 2 |
| And groan to feel his chastening now | 331 | 1 |

| | Hymn | Verse |
|---|---|---|
| And groaned the unspeakable groan | 165 | 3 |
| And grow more like him day by day | 961 | 4 |
| And guard and save us from them all | 968 | 4 |
| And guard in fierce temptation's hour | 272 | 4 |
| And guard me that I fall no more | 574 | 9 |
| And guard the gift thyself hast given | 291 | 2 |
| And guard us all our days below | 649 | 2 |
| And guard us through the coming night | 968 | 3 |
| And guardian care for all are free | 237 | 2 |
| And guided by his sacred word | 96 | 6 |
| And guided where I go | 842 | 3 |
| And guide into thy perfect peace | 161 | 6 |
| And guide into thy perfect will | 523 | 3 |
| And guide me to my journey's end | 602 | 4 |
| And guide my steps, that I, with thee | 38 | 4 |
| And guide my words aright | 270 | 1 |
| And guide our steps aright | 468 | 1 |
| And guide them through the dreadful shade | 686 | 3 |
| And guide us by the light of grace | 89 | 2 |
| And guides our giddy youth | 687 | 8 |
| And guilty in thy sight appear | 176 | 1 |
| And hail him their triumphant Lord | 56 | 3 |
| And hail me on the shore | 947 | 5 |
| And hail the sovereign Lord of all | 235 | 2 |
| And half o'erwhelm my sinking soul | 272 | 6 |
| And hallowed my whole heart to thee | 338 | 2 |
| And, hanging o'er the burning pit | 172 | 1 |
| And hang on a crucified God | 228 | 2 |
| And hang upon thy cross | 436 | 4 |
| And happy in the Spirit live | 525 | 1 |
| And harmony be found | 619 | 5 |
| And hasted to thy glorious day | 324 | 4 |
| And hasten through the vale of woe | 71 | 2 |
| And hasten to be swallowed up | 74 | 3 |
| And hasten to that day | 954 | 3 |
| And haste to better company | 482 | 2 |
| And haste to join those heavenly powers | 222 | 3 |
| And hast refreshed me whilst I slept | 964 | 5 |
| And hate the wisdom from above | 21 | 1 |
| †And hath bid the fruitful field | 631 | 5 |
| And have laid up their treasure above | 807 | 1 |
| And have thee all my own | 403 | 5 |
| And have their fruit to holiness | 120 | 2 |
| And have whate'er we ask of God | 860 | 2 |
| And, having thy whole counsel done | 438 | 2 |
| And headlong plunged in sin's abyss | 483 | 3 |
| And healed the bleeding wounds, and soothed the pain | 850 | 2 |
| And healed; ye never can be healed | 816 | 2 |
| And heal my soul of sin | 112 | 4 |
| And heal the sick, and raise the dead | 379 | 3 |
| And hear and feel thy sayings now | 881 | 2 |
| And hear a whisper, "Peace; be still" | 272 | 6 |
| And hear her final groan | 61 | 1 |

| | Hymn | Verse |
|---|---|---|
| And hear his speaking blood | 506 | 1 |
| And hear me feebly groan, "How long" | 547 | 3 |
| And hear me tell what thou hast done | 772 | 1 |
| And hear me when I prayed | 614 | 2 |
| And hear the blood speak that hath answered for me | 707 | 7 |
| And hear the blood that speaks above | 394 | 4 |
| And hear thee inly speak | 214 | 4 |
| And hear thee say, "Be still" | 92 | 2 |
| And heard it preached in vain | 91 | 1 |
| And hearest the young ravens cry | 236 | 3 |
| And hearest the young ravens cry | 1017 | 1 |
| And hearkened to my cry | 566 | 1 |
| And heathens all beside | 94 | 1 |
| And heaven bows down to Jacob's God | 223 | 4 |
| And heaven comes down our souls to greet | 825 | 4 |
| And heaven cry "Harvest home" | 739 | 6 |
| And heaven was opened on earth | 220 | 2 |
| And heaven with earth the strain prolong | 993 | 4 |
| And heavenly influences shed | 446 | 4 |
| And heavenly understanding gains | 14 | 2. |
| And heaven's high palace rings | 226 | 1 |
| And heaven's unutterable bliss | 490 | 6 |
| And heaven's whole orb with hallelujahs rang | 691 | 8 |
| And he can well secure | 811 | 3 |
| And he shall keep them still | 537 | 8 |
| And he shall save me to the end | 800 | 3 |
| And he that in thy statutes treads | 15 | 4 |
| And he who feeds the ravens | 804 | 3 |
| And he who would the Father seek | 671 | 1 |
| And he will make it plain | 845 | 3 |
| And he will soon appear | 384 | 2 |
| And height, of love divine | 91 | 3 |
| And hell's deep gloom, are open laid | 285 | 2 |
| And help a sinner to draw near | 365 | 1 |
| And help me to believe | 175 | 1 |
| And help our misery | 250 | 1 |
| And help us, this and every day | 965 | 7 |
| And henceforth live and die to him | 980 | 1 |
| And her crops with rich reward | 579 | 2 |
| And here confess my sin | 703 | 8 |
| And here the Holy Spirit rest | 993 | 5 |
| And here thy glory see | 325 | 5 |
| And here with God ourselves acquaint | 295 | 2 |
| And hide him in the silent grave | 467 | 5 |
| And hide our life with Christ above | 1005 | 2 |
| And hide their multitude of sin | 961 | 4 |
| And hide them in the rock | 459 | 1 |
| And hide them in thy breast | 893 | 1 |
| And hides our life above | 478 | 2 |
| And high on thine eternal throne | 248 | 8 |
| And high prerogative | 821 | — |
| And him my only Portion make | 800 | 2 |
| And him the Father always hears | 726 | 2 |

| | Hymn | Verse |
|---|---|---|
| And his Apostles' footsteps trace | 860 | 1 |
| And his blood that can for all atone | 794 | 4 |
| And his eternal praise | 617 | 1 |
| And his love by fragrance own | 769 | 3 |
| And his mercy fills our tongue | 580 | 4 |
| And his rapturous praises repeat | 491 | 7 |
| And his side | 793 | 2 |
| And his sun hath risen on all | 714 | 5 |
| And holds the powers of hell in chains | 280 | 2 |
| And holds the promises | 675 | 3 |
| And hold till I yield thee my heart | 165 | 2 |
| And, "Holy, Holy, Holy," cry | 222 | 4 |
| And, "Holy, Holy, Holy," cry | 647 | 2 |
| And, "Holy, Holy, Holy," cry | 800 | 10 |
| And homage to their King | 641 | 4 |
| And honour that descends from God | 14 | 4 |
| And hope in full supreme delight | 59 | 6 |
| And hope upon the way | 943 | 12 |
| And house, and friends above | 840 | 1 |
| And hovering hides me in his wings | 312 | 2 |
| And humbled into nothing own | 247 | 2 |
| And humbly ask for more | 614 | 8 |
| And humbly hope for more | 1002 | 5 |
| And humbly in a manger laid | 772 | 4 |
| And humbly own to thee | 42 | 1 |
| And humbly pour out our complaint | 295 | 3 |
| And humbly seek thy face | 323 | 1 |
| And humbly sue for saving grace | 395 | 2 |
| And humbly walk by faith with God | 127 | 4 |
| And hungry as I am, and faint | 437 | 2 |
| And hung upon the breast | 657 | 2 |
| And hurry, I withdraw | 358 | 2 |
| And hymns of glory sing | 603 | 1 |
| And hymn the great Three-One | 948 | 6 |
| And I also trust to see the glad hour | 198 | 4 |
| And I am chained to earth no more | 658 | 4 |
| And I am filled with God | 109 | 5 |
| And I am left alone with thee | 140 | 1 |
| And I am of thy promise sure | 112 | 6 |
| And I am thine | 851 | 2 |
| And I am thine by sacred ties | 577 | 2 |
| And I am white as snow | 410 | 3 |
| And I a parent there | 482 | 3 |
| And I his favoured son | 321 | 4 |
| And I hope, by thy good pleasure | 866 | 2 |
| And I receive the Comforter | 134 | 2 |
| And I shall be with him | 920 | 6 |
| And I shall conquer sin | 278 | 4 |
| And I shall do thy will on earth | 857 | 8 |
| And I shall never grieve thee more | 171 | 4 |
| And I shall praise thee evermore | 229 | 4 |
| And I shall see the perfect day | 365 | 9 |
| And I shall sin no more | 139 | 8 |

| | Hymn | Verse |
|---|---|---|
| And I shall sin no more | 356 | 10 |
| And I shall sin no more | 410 | 2 |
| And I shall then no longer rove | 354 | 4 |
| And I thy utmost word shall prove | 368 | 2 |
| And I trust thou wilt save to the end | 231 | 4 |
| And I was saved by grace | 93 | 7 |
| And I was with him then | 667 | 2 |
| And I, who dare thy word receive | 282 | 2 |
| And I will dare to call thee mine | 909 | 3 |
| And I with him shall reign | 274 | 8 |
| And if for thee on earth I live | 234 | 4 |
| And, if he can obtain thy leave | 281 | 5 |
| And if I fall, soon may I hear | 373 | 8 |
| And if I first attain | 947 | 5 |
| And if I pass before | 947 | 5 |
| And if I seal the truth with blood | 230 | 4 |
| †And if our fellowship below | 500 | 6 |
| And if our hope be fixed on thee | 1003 | 2 |
| And if our souls be hurried hence | 42 | 7 |
| †And if some things I do not ask | 842 | 6 |
| And if thou art well-pleased to hear | 532 | 4 |
| And if thou count us worthy | 853 | 4 |
| And if thy wisdom try us | 818 | 2 |
| And if to-morrow's care I see | 835 | 2 |
| And in all their leafy bowers | 604 | 4 |
| And in a manger lies | 684 | 3 |
| And in death finds happiness | 753 | 10 |
| And in earth's darkest place | 870 | 3 |
| And in full glory shine | 22 | 4 |
| And in God's house for evermore | 556 | 5 |
| And in heaven dwell ever near thee | 895 | 2 |
| And in her pleasant heritage | 549 | 3 |
| And in his arms expire | 125 | 2 |
| And in his body bore | 731 | 2 |
| And in his goodness trust | 626 | 3 |
| And in his mighty power | 266 | 1 |
| And in his saving grace | 627 | 4 |
| And in his sight appear | 478 | 1 |
| And in his Spirit lived | 65 | 4 |
| And in his steps who tread | 497 | 5 |
| And in his ways delight | 624 | 2 |
| And in its sevenfold light sublime | 957 | 3 |
| And in my heart reveal thy Son | 148 | 1 |
| And in my loving heart reside | 312 | 5 |
| And in our Lord rejoicing go | 954 | 4 |
| And in our hearts be love | 966 | 2 |
| And in our nature grow | 756 | 1 |
| And in our Priest we will rejoice | 682 | 2 |
| And in the clefts remain | 64 | 1 |
| And in the face of Jesus see | 673 | 2 |
| And in the fold remain | 897 | 4 |
| †And in the great decisive day | 994 | 3 |
| And, in the knowledge of my Lord | 369 | 2 |

| | Hymn | Verse |
|---|---|---|
| And in the new Jerusalem | 811 | 4 |
| And in the presence of our Lord | 342 | 2 |
| And in the ocean drowned | 63 | 3 |
| And in the Spirit down | 643 | 4 |
| And in the steps of Abraham's faith | 840 | 2 |
| And in their watchful hands they bear | 21 | 5 |
| And in their weakness show thy power | 462 | 6 |
| And in those brighter courts adore | 978 | 6 |
| And in thy arms of mercy take | 177 | 2 |
| And in thy blessed hands I am | 408 | 7 |
| And in thy cause expire | 428 | 3 |
| And in thy glories blest | 731 | 6 |
| And in thy house record thy praise | 590 | 2 |
| And in thy light our souls shall see | 563 | 5 |
| And in thy mercy heal us all | 969 | 7 |
| And in thy name we part | 537 | 2 |
| And in thy pleasure rest | 533 | 1 |
| And in thy praise combine | 737 | 6 |
| And in thy presence rest | 680 | 1 |
| And in thy right I claim thy heaven | 706 | 8 |
| And in thy sober, spotless mind | 419 | 4 |
| And, in thy Spirit given | 447 | 3 |
| And in thy strength rejoice | 733 | 1 |
| And in thy threatenings too | 242 | 3 |
| And in thy wounds I rest | 215 | 4 |
| And in whose death our sins are dead | 906 | 1 |
| And in your Captain's sight | 277 | 3 |
| And infant voices shall proclaim | 585 | 9 |
| And infinite in power | 243 | 1 |
| And innocently grieve | 482 | 2 |
| And inquire from what quarter they came | 231 | 9 |
| And intimately nigh | 537 | 5 |
| And into nothing fall | 184 | 11 |
| And into sin I cannot fall | 813 | — |
| And into thy protection take | 105 | 3 |
| And is at once made whole | 84 | 5 |
| And is from sin set free | 84 | 4 |
| †And is it not a dream | 623 | 2 |
| And is it not thy will | 820 | 2 |
| And Israel's ransomed tribes are free | 715 | 1 |
| And Israel's youngest born be saved | 589 | 7 |
| And Israel their joy partake | 595 | 5 |
| And Jacob's God is still our aid | 569 | 7 |
| And Jacob, shall receive | 535 | 5 |
| And Jesus begs us to be friends | 11 | 1 |
| And Jesus bids me come | 68 | 7 |
| And Jesus bids me come | 947 | 4 |
| And Jesus crucified | 809 | Cho. |
| And Jesus forces me to spare | 298 | 2 |
| And Jesus for ever shall reign in my heart | 273 | 8 |
| And Jesus is his name | 684 | 1 |
| And Jesus is our friend | 21 | 5 |
| And Jesus is the conqueror's name | 557 | 9 |

| | Hymn | Verse |
|---|---|---|
| And Jesus is the Prince of peace | 616 | 5 |
| And Jesus never knew | 94 | 2 |
| And Jesus, on the eternal throne | 823 | 7 |
| And Jesus prove to me | 139 | 2 |
| And Jesus rises in his heart | 467 | 9 |
| And join by thine atoning grace | 459 | 1 |
| And join in nobler worship there | 592 | 5 |
| And join in the catholic cry | 77 | 2 |
| And join me to the church above | 328 | 4 |
| And join, with mutual care | 510 | 5 |
| And join with the triumphant saints | 920 | 5 |
| And join with us to praise his love | 539 | 1 |
| And jointly glory in thy praise | 505 | 6 |
| And joy, and everlasting love | 209 | 2 |
| And joy and glory in my Lord | 545 | 1 |
| And joy, and happiness, and love | 524 | 3 |
| And joyful in the house of prayer | 619 | 3 |
| And joyfully sustain the cross | 539 | 3 |
| And Judah was his favourite throne | 223 | 1 |
| And judges grave, advice obey | 541 | 4 |
| And justice for the opprest | 610 | 4 |
| And keep an abject soul in awe | 103 | 1 |
| And keep for me in store | 549 | 7 |
| And keep him, till thy love takes place | 467 | 9 |
| And keep his kindest word | 897 | 1 |
| And keep me ever there | 112 | 7 |
| And keep me safe from sin | 998 | 1 |
| And keep me to the end | 820 | 4 |
| And keep in all our ways | 21 | 5 |
| And keep in perfect peace | 296 | 3 |
| And keep it shut against my foes | 828 | 3 |
| And keep it still awake | 308 | 2 |
| And keep it to that day | 537 | 7 |
| And keep it to the end | 487 | 1 |
| And keep our ransomed soul | 299 | 5 |
| And keep the issues of my heart | 309 | 1 |
| And keep the post assigned by thee | 470 | 8 |
| And keep the prize in view | 537 | 11 |
| And keep till he renews my heart | 312 | 3 |
| And keep till we can sin no more | 524 | 2 |
| And keep them to the end | 469 | 10 |
| And keep to that tremendous day | 648 | 6 |
| And keep us evermore | 252 | 2 |
| And keep us one in thee | 501 | 5 |
| And keep us pure from sin to-day | 649 | 2 |
| And keep us to that day | 532 | 6 |
| And keep us to the end | 258 | 1 |
| And keep us to the end | 1005 | 2 |
| And keeps his court below | 641 | 1 |
| And keeps his own in perfect peace | 404 | 3 |
| And keeps my happy soul above | 209 | 2 |
| And keeps our minds in perfect peace | 489 | 1 |
| And keeps the issues of my heart | 616 | 2 |

| | Hymn | Verse |
|---|---|---|
| And kept me safe, because he had | 551 | 5 |
| And kill, and make alive | 347 | 2 |
| And kindle life more pure and kind | 456 | 4 |
| And kindle my relentings now | 186 | 5 |
| And kindly continue to strive | 165 | 2 |
| And kindly dost relieve | 693 | 3 |
| And kindly each other embrace | 220 | 5 |
| And kindly for thy patient care | 112 | 7 |
| And kindly help each other on | 510 | 5 |
| And kindly think and speak the same | 489 | 1 |
| And kindly work in me to will | 153 | 3 |
| And kings and priests thy servants are | 590 | 4 |
| And kings their power and dignity | 248 | 4 |
| And kiss his late-returning son | 9 | 2 |
| And kiss my raptured soul away | 229 | 6 |
| And knit more close the sacred bands | 822 | 3 |
| And know as I am known | 550 | 3 |
| And know as we are known | 389 | 5 |
| And know myself thy child | 97 | 4 |
| And know my sins forgiven | 119 | 5 |
| And know no other will but thine | 332 | 3 |
| And know not how to shun | 471 | 2 |
| And know our prayer is heard | 504 | 1 |
| And know that I am born of God | 351 | 1 |
| And know that I am one with God | 351 | 8 |
| And know that Jesus is thy name | 366 | 2 |
| And know the things of God | 96 | 4 |
| And know their gracious hour | 85 | 2 |
| And know thou hear'st my prayer | 301 | 1 |
| And know thy hidden name | 297 | 3 |
| And knowing thee my Saviour prove | 782 | 3 |
| And knowledge empty prove | 767 | 5 |
| And knowledge of thy word | 789 | 1 |
| And, known by every nation | 736 | 3 |
| And knows her guilt was there | 703 | 4 |
| And labouring silence speaks my moans | 154 | 3 |
| And labouring while we time redeem | 858 | 2 |
| And labour on at thy command | 324 | 3 |
| And labour to be found | 536 | 8 |
| And labour to convert | 775 | 1 |
| And land us all in heaven | 949 | 5 |
| And languish thy descent to meet | 759 | 8 |
| And languish to conclude my race | 311 | 5 |
| And languish to return | 74 | 4 |
| And lasting as the mind | 880 | 2 |
| And late to rest repair | 624 | 1 |
| And laugh at danger near | 801 | 1 |
| And lay me down in peace | 998 | 5 |
| And lay our sins and sorrows at thy feet | 850 | 6 |
| And lay them at thy feet: thou knowest, Lord | 850 | 1 |
| And lay us up for heaven | 502 | 2 |
| And lays the giant low | 278 | 5 |
| And lead me in thyself the way | 548 | 6 |

| | Hymn | Verse |
|---|---|---|
| And lead me on from grace to grace | 180 | 7 |
| And lead me to the mount above | 317 | 2 |
| And lead me to thy holy hill | 339 | 5 |
| And lead my faithful family | 472 | 3 |
| And lead them to thy open side | 433 | 5 |
| And lead us in those paths of life | 771 | 2 |
| And leads me for his mercy's sake | 555 | 2 |
| And leap, ye lame, for joy | 1 | 6 |
| And learn, in meek humility | 801 | 2 |
| And leave a savour of thy name | 584 | 3 |
| And leave me not alone | 188 | 5 |
| And leave my bed of clay | 931 | 2 |
| And leave my fainting heart | 584 | 2 |
| And leave the world and sin behind | 803 | 4 |
| And leave thy creature in his blood | 178 | 3 |
| And led me in his way | 566 | 2 |
| And led me up to man | 657 | 5 |
| And led the monster death in chains | 712 | 3 |
| And led the vanquished host in chains | 731 | 3 |
| And led us safely over | 854 | 1 |
| And left his companions behind | 49 | 2 |
| And left me in my blood | 112 | 1 |
| And left the proud oppressor's land | 223 | 1 |
| And left with disdain, by Jesus are prized | 211 | 5 |
| And lend their youth a sacred clue | 468 | 4 |
| And lengthen out my days | 356 | 2 |
| And less beloved than God alone | 286 | 2 |
| And less than nothing in thine eye | 1001 | 7 |
| And, lest again we go astray | 752 | 4 |
| †And lest the flesh, profane and proud | 966 | 5 |
| And lest the purpose leave my thought | 799 | 6 |
| And let a worm prescribe to thee | 919 | 1 |
| And let a wretch come near thy throne | 574 | 10 |
| And let his praise be great | 573 | 1 |
| And let it droop and die | 948 | 1 |
| And let it now take place | 307 | 4 |
| And let it our full souls o'erflow | 492 | 2 |
| And let it swiftly run | 446 | 1 |
| And let me all thy Godhead prove | 413 | 2 |
| And let me all thy mercy prove | 159 | 1 |
| And let me always see thee near | 550 | 3 |
| And let me cease from sin | 403 | 3 |
| And let me feel thy love's constraint | 378 | 4 |
| And let me feel thy softening power | 110 | 4 |
| And let me find my all in thee | 163 | 7 |
| And let me in thy goodness trust | 323 | 1 |
| And let me into God | 117 | 5 |
| And let me live to preach thy word | 433 | 4 |
| And let me now be filled with God | 230 | 4 |
| And let me now the promise prove | 354 | 6 |
| And let me on a Father's loving heart | 967 | 6 |
| And let me pass my days below | 307 | 2 |
| And let me take my place above | 440 | 2 |

| | Hymn | Verse |
|---|---|---|
| And let me through thy Spirit know | 320 | 2 |
| And let me to thy glory live | 433 | 4 |
| And let me tremble at the word | 307 | 4 |
| And let me weep my life away | 308 | 3 |
| And let my eyes with tears o'erflow | 982 | 2 |
| And let my faith behold its Lord | 249 | 1 |
| And let my knowing zeal be joined | 270 | 2 |
| And let my soul on thee be cast | 114 | 1 |
| And let my soul, to health restored | 395 | 8 |
| And let my spirit cleave to thee | 391 | 5 |
| And let my sprinkled conscience know | 97 | 2 |
| And let on us thy Spirit fall | 412 | 1 |
| And let others both their sweetness | 882 | 7 |
| And let our all be lost in thee | 332 | 5 |
| *And let our bodies part | 535 | 1 |
| And let our gracious fruit | 981 | 5 |
| And let our gracious fruit remain | 492 | 4 |
| And let our ransomed spirits go | 947 | 8 |
| And let the captive go | 105 | 2 |
| And let the flames of pure desire | 490 | 5 |
| And let the gift unspeakable | 1005 | 2 |
| And let the plague be stayed | 986 | 4 |
| And let the priests themselves believe | 446 | 1 |
| And let the prince of ill | 856 | 3 |
| And let the sight affect, subdue | 122 | 2 |
| And let the soul-converting power | 734 | 2 |
| And let the vessel break | 947 | 8 |
| And let the waters flow | 778 | 2 |
| And let the world be filled with God | 448 | 4 |
| And let their lustre still increase | 446 | 6 |
| And let them feel the wrath they bear | 461 | 4 |
| And let them groan their want of thee | 461 | 4 |
| And let them in thine image rise | 474 | 1 |
| And let them now acceptance have | 35 | 2 |
| And let them see thee in thy vest | 35 | 4 |
| And let them sleep in sin no more | 461 | 5 |
| And let them speak thy word of power | 745 | 3 |
| And let there now be light | 87 | 3 |
| And let thine angel stand between | 986 | 3 |
| *And let this feeble body fail | 948 | 1 |
| And let this my adorning be | 431 | 5 |
| And let thy church on earth become | 771 | 5 |
| And let thy Father's nature shine | 72 | 3 |
| And let thy glorious Spirit, Lord | 804 | 7 |
| And let thy glorious Spirit reign | 448 | 4 |
| And let thy glorious toil succeed | 568 | 4 |
| And let thy happy child | 252 | 5 |
| And let thy healing grace abound | 112 | 3 |
| And let thy mercy find them out | 462 | 7 |
| And let thy mercy melt me down | 106 | 3 |
| And let thy mercy reach to me | 462 | 7 |
| And let thy precious word of grace | 828 | 4 |
| And let thy word, with power divine | 955 | 4 |

| | Hymn | Verse |
|---|---|---|
| And let us always kindly think | 504 | 3 |
| And let us die, to thee | 925 | 3 |
| And let us drink thy blood | 901 | 4 |
| And let us mercy find | 900 | 1 |
| And let us now thyself receive | 294 | 4 |
| And let us then our Saviour see | 423 | 4 |
| And let us to thy glory live | 428 | 3 |
| And let your joys be known | 12 | 1 |
| And let your souls delight in me | 4 | 8 |
| And lewdly sang the drunkard's songs | 203 | 7 |
| And life and everlasting joys | 880 | 4 |
| And life, and happiness, and heaven | 291 | 2 |
| And life, and liberty | 139 | 2 |
| And life eternal gain | 944 | 7 |
| And life into the dead | 37 | 3 |
| And lifted me up as I mourned | 165 | 4 |
| And lift it up in prayer | 135 | 5 |
| And lift me up to heaven | 669 | 2 |
| And lift my soul to heaven | 543 | 5 |
| And lift them from their low estate | 588 | 3 |
| And lift them up to heaven | 717 | 2 |
| And lift us up thy face to see | 258 | 2 |
| And lighten with celestial fire | 751 | 1 |
| And lighter than our guilt | 610 | 7 |
| And light there in our hearts shall be | 121 | 2 |
| And like a bulwark prove | 632 | 5 |
| And like the blessed spirits above | 858 | 3 |
| And linger, shivering on the brink | 938 | 4 |
| And lingers to remove | 775 | 3 |
| And listen to my cry | 635 | 1 |
| And live and die below | 128 | 4 |
| And live and die entirely thine | 261 | 4 |
| And live and die forgiven | 125 | 6 |
| And live and die wrapped up in thee | 533 | 4 |
| And live, eternal Life, in me | 668 | 2 |
| And live for God and die | 873 | 3 |
| And live for him who died for all | 2 | 9 |
| And live for this alone | 872 | 2 |
| And live from sinning free | 356 | 9 |
| And live, my heavenly Life, in me | 670 | 3 |
| And live the life they preach | 822 | 3 |
| And live this day as if thy last | 964 | 2 |
| And live to Christ, and die | 572 | 4 |
| And lived to the desires of men | 180 | 3 |
| And liveth again | 499 | 6 |
| And living water flowing | 958 | 4 |
| And lo! by reflection they shine | 73 | 4 |
| And lo! for thee I ever mourn | 134 | 2 |
| And lo! from sin, and grief, and shame | 209 | 1 |
| And lo! he saith, I quickly come | 406 | 5 |
| And lo! I come thy cross to share | 122 | 5 |
| And lo! I come to testify | 472 | 5 |
| And lo! I lay me at thy feet | 177 | 5 |

| | Hymn | Verse |
|---|---|---|
| And lo! I now begin to pray. | 982 | 2 |
| And lo! I plead the atoning blood. | 706 | 8 |
| And lo! I trust thy gracious power. | 779 | 3 |
| And lo! I wait on thee, my Lord. | 356 | 1 |
| And lo! in faith we pray for ours. | 985 | 1 |
| And lo! in thee | 736 | 2 |
| And lo! our hearts to heaven ascend | 827 | 4 |
| And lo! they fall beneath my feet. | 293 | 6 |
| And lo! thy offer I embrace | 162 | 3 |
| And lo! we fall before his feet | 333 | 6 |
| And lo! we reach you now. | 539 | 6 |
| And lo! we see another year | 981 | 4 |
| And lo! we see the vast reward | 535 | 2 |
| And lodged in the Eden of love | 49 | 1 |
| And lodge it, Saviour, in thy breast | 114 | 3 |
| And longed to be happy in thee | 165 | 3 |
| And longer live for this alone | 433 | 3 |
| And long hath languished at the pool | 396 | 4 |
| And long thy appearing to see | 488 | 7 |
| And long to be summoned away | 911 | 4 |
| And long to see that happy coast. | 949 | 3 |
| And long to see the perfect day | 313 | 4 |
| And longs, and labours to believe. | 545 | 4 |
| And look beyond this vale of tears. | 333 | 1 |
| And look down on the skies | 499 | 3 |
| And look for mercy now | 783 | 1 |
| And look my darkness into day | 154 | 3 |
| And look on him I pierced, and mourn | 982 | 3 |
| And looking for our Lord. | 55 | 4 |
| And looking up to thee | 305 | 2 |
| And looks and loves his image there | 225 | 6 |
| And looks to that alone | 360 | 9 |
| And loose a stammering infant's tongue | 440 | 1 |
| And loose my bands, and let me go | 290 | 4 |
| And Lord of all the worlds adore. | 689 | 3 |
| And Lord of his creation reigns | 638 | 4 |
| And loss shall be eternal gain | 286 | 7 |
| And, lost in endless raptures, prove. | 513 | 3 |
| And lost in following years | 41 | 5 |
| And lost in love divine | 368 | 1 |
| And lost in the ocean of God | 78 | 2 |
| And lost in thine immensity | 374 | 3 |
| And lost in thy immensity. | 1001 | 4 |
| And louder yet, and yet more dread | 934 | 2 |
| And loudly sing | 854 | 1 |
| And love, and life, and rest | 943 | 4 |
| And love, and praise, and pray | 956 | 2 |
| And love and save me to the end | 916 | 5 |
| And love and sorrow still to thee may come | 850 | 5 |
| And love, and wonder, and adore. | 86 | 6 |
| And love command my tongue | 263 | 7 |
| And love from God supreme | 892 | 5 |
| And love me to the end | 305 | 5 |

| | HYMN | VERSE |
|---|---|---|
| And love my loving God | 775 | 2 |
| And love shall never die | 789 | 4 |
| And love thee evermore | 943 | 11 |
| And love the faithless sinner still | 186 | 2 |
| And love them to the end | 622 | 3 |
| And love them with a zeal like thine | 433 | 5 |
| And love this sight so fair | 662 | 4 |
| And love with a passion like thine | 220 | 5 |
| And love, with softest pity joined | 23 | 8 |
| And loving Mary's heart | 825 | 1 |
| And low at his cross with astonishment fall | 707 | 3 |
| And lowly cottage cell | 692 | 3 |
| And lowly homage give | 942 | 9 |
| And lowly mind into my breast | 873 | 7 |
| And, lulled in worldly, hellish peace | 483 | 3 |
| And made me heir of heaven, the Father's child | 794 | 5 |
| And madly to folly returned | 165 | 4 |
| And magnify thy name | 243 | 5 |
| And magnify thy pardoning love | 298 | 4 |
| And magnify thy power | 329 | 1 |
| And make an end of fear and sin | 754 | 5 |
| And make an end of sin | 303 | 5 |
| And make an end of sin | 407 | 3 |
| And make an open way | 288 | 5 |
| And make a poor Lazarus whole | 174 | 3 |
| And make a thousand hearts thine own | 864 | 5 |
| And make her wilds a fruitful field | 111 | 3 |
| And make his wonders known | 814 | 4 |
| And make in thee their goings sure | 458 | 6 |
| And make it all divine | 145 | 3 |
| And make it soft, and make it new | 186 | 4 |
| And make me all like thee | 297 | 5 |
| And make me free within | 368 | 2 |
| And make me fully understand | 305 | 1 |
| And make me know thy name | 166 | 1 |
| And make me learn thy grace | 789 | 3 |
| And make me like thyself below | 309 | 5 |
| And make me live to thee | 843 | 2 |
| And make me love again | 146 | 4 |
| And make me meet for heaven | 139 | 3 |
| And make me, O Lord, in the world as thou art | 160 | 4 |
| And make me rich, for I am poor | 134 | 1 |
| And make me surely stand | 271 | 4 |
| And make me thy permanent home | 165 | 5 |
| And make me understand and live | 770 | 3 |
| And make my heart a house of prayer | 186 | 3 |
| And make my humble claim | 903 | 2 |
| And make our feeble footsteps sure | 469 | 9 |
| And make our hearts a house of prayer | 294 | 4 |
| And make our solemn service vain | 204 | 3 |
| And make the angry sea comply | 600 | 3 |
| And make the contrite heart thy heaven | 507 | 2 |
| And make the contrite sinner whole | 462 | 5 |

| | Hymn | Verse |
|---|---|---|
| And make the covenant peace mine own | 909 | 4 |
| And make the crown by suffering sure | 330 | 3 |
| And make the day entirely thine | 955 | 4 |
| And make the glad nations obey | 220 | 3 |
| And make the greedy sea restore | 57 | 1 |
| And make the happy sinners know | 461 | 3 |
| And make the helpless infants pass | 467 | 4 |
| And make the mountains fall | 138 | 5 |
| And make the mountains flow | 138 | 2 |
| And make the mountains flow | 361 | 7 |
| And make the sacrifice complete | 327 | 4 |
| And make the sea-bound earth thine own | 541 | 3 |
| And make the servant as his Lord | 523 | 7 |
| And make the sinner all like thee | 330 | 2 |
| And make the sinner whole | 112 | 7 |
| And make them patient to the end | 462 | 6 |
| And make this house thy home | 771 | 1 |
| And make thy faithful mercies known | 394 | 1 |
| And make thy gracious fulness mine | 782 | 4 |
| And make thy nature known | 901 | 2 |
| And make thy nature known | 905 | 1 |
| And make thy rest and gladness ours | 951 | 5 |
| And make thy richest mercy known | 441 | 3 |
| And make thy temples worthy thee | 752 | 1 |
| And make thy truth and goodness known | 576 | 2 |
| And make thy vanquished rebels find | 441 | 3 |
| And make to us the Godhead known | 85 | 1 |
| And make us all divine | 685 | 4 |
| And make us a pattern to all that believe | 219 | 7 |
| And make us of one heart | 459 | 2 |
| And make us of one heart and mind | 505 | 3 |
| And make us of one mind and heart | 16 | 8 |
| And make us strong in faith to die | 957 | 5 |
| And make us strong in faith to live | 957 | 5 |
| And makes a heaven of heaven | 941 | 3 |
| And makes his own | 854 | 2 |
| And makes his restless foes obey | 280 | 1 |
| And makes me for some moments feast | 404 | 1 |
| And makes me to salvation wise | 548 | 3 |
| And makes our hearts his home | 673 | 1 |
| And makes thee young again | 610 | 3 |
| And makes the host of aliens fly | 293 | 8 |
| And makes us priests and kings | 693 | 4 |
| And makes us see his goodness here | 980 | 1 |
| And manifest thy love | 118 | 2 |
| And man shall then be lost in God | 685 | 5 |
| And marched triumphant over | 276 | 3 |
| And mark each suppliant sigh | 991 | 3 |
| And mark the risings of desire | 313 | 2 |
| And mark who here keeps watch and ward | 595 | 1 |
| And mar our sacrifice | 204 | 3 |
| And match Omnipotence | 138 | 6 |
| And may meet him in the air | 720 | 9 |

| | Hymn | Verse |
|---|---|---|
| And may reign for ever there | 720 | 9 |
| And may sweet sleep mine eyelids close | 974 | 4 |
| And may that grace, once given | 991 | 4 |
| And may the music of thy name | 679 | 6 |
| And me among thy people bless | 861 | 3 |
| And me to walk doth make | 556 | 2 |
| And mean the thanks I cannot speak | 658 | 3 |
| And medicine in sickness | 943 | 4 |
| And meditates by night | 540 | 2 |
| And meekly agree to follow the Lamb | 484 | 1 |
| And meekly bear the load | 925 | 2 |
| And meet him in your heart | 54 | 1 |
| And meet our Captain in the skies | 71 | 6 |
| And meet our head in heaven | 487 | 4 |
| And meet the God of mercy there | 860 | 1 |
| And meet to part no more | 482 | 3 |
| And meet your instant doom | 55 | 3 |
| And melt at last, O melt me down | 103 | 3 |
| And melt it by thy dying love | 186 | 4 |
| And melt my hardness down | 102 | 2 |
| And melt the marble of our heart | 176 | 4 |
| And, melting at Messiah's feet | 697 | 3 |
| And melts at human woe | 343 | 5 |
| And mercy, mercy, I implore | 110 | 2 |
| And mercy shall be all my song | 440 | 1 |
| And met within thy holy place | 863 | 1 |
| And might, and majesty | 727 | 6 |
| And might and majesty are thine | 293 | 9 |
| And mightily shaken the kingdom of hell | 219 | 2 |
| And mightily striving, to save us by grace | 40 | 6 |
| And mighty works he showed | 693 | 1 |
| And milk and honey flow | 407 | 5 |
| And mine inheritance | 549 | 2 |
| And mine, the sons of men | 667 | 2 |
| And miracles of grace | 693 | 1 |
| And mix our friendly souls in thee | 510 | 2 |
| And mocked thee to thy face | 93 | 2 |
| And mock the sons of God | 21 | 1 |
| And more I joy to gain thy grace | 437 | 3 |
| And, more than conqueror, displayed | 583 | 2 |
| And more than conquers all | 281 | 2 |
| And more than mortal woe | 692 | 1 |
| And morning finds me glad | 838 | 5 |
| And mortal spirits tire and faint | 802 | 2 |
| And mortify their pride | 468 | 4 |
| And most the boldest suitor loves | 827 | 6 |
| And mould it into love | 145 | 2 |
| And mould it into love | 528 | 1 |
| And mount above the fiery void | 57 | 5 |
| And mount above the wreck | 61 | 2 |
| And mount our thrones encircling thine | 525 | 3 |
| And mount to our native abode | 73 | 1 |
| And mount with his spirit above | 49 | 1 |

# AND MOUNTAINS         AND NEVER

| | Hymn | Verse |
|---|---|---|
| And mountains are on mountains hurled | 57 | 4 |
| And mountains rise and ocean's roll | 537 | 4 |
| And move but to his praise | 641 | 2 |
| And moves at thy command | 788 | 1 |
| And multiply the faithful race | 734 | 1 |
| And murmur to contend so long | 140 | 5 |
| And music's charms bewitch and steal | 204 | 5 |
| And must I suddenly comply | 44 | 1 |
| And must my trembling spirit fly | 43 | 1 |
| And must these active limbs of mine | 930 | 1 |
| *And must this body die | 930 | 1 |
| And my abiding home | 68 | 7 |
| And my best robe thy righteousness | 431 | 4 |
| And my cup overflows | 556 | 4 |
| And my heart it doth dance at the sound of his name | 205 | 2 |
| And my iniquities | 566 | 7 |
| And my Redeemer know | 128 | 4 |
| And my Redeemer love | 243 | 1 |
| And my sole business be thy praise | 431 | 6 |
| And my whole head is faint | 109 | 2 |
| And myriads more | 736 | 3 |
| And myriads sink beneath the grave | 442 | 2 |
| And mystery divine | 667 | 4 |
| And nailed thee to a tree | 667 | 4 |
| And nailed thee to thy cross again | 176 | 3 |
| And nature's final hour | 62 | 4 |
| And nearest to thy throne | 724 | 3 |
| And near thine altar drew | 91 | 2 |
| †And need we, then, O Lord, repeat | 797 | 3 |
| And neither food nor feeder have | 82 | 2 |
| And neither knows measure nor end | 660 | — |
| And never again will he take him away | 760 | 2 |
| And never a moment depart | 228 | 3 |
| And never boast or murmur more | 126 | 6 |
| And never can itself forgive | 341 | 3 |
| And never can succeed | 526 | 1 |
| And never can remove | 345 | 6 |
| And never dare to offend thee more | 186 | 6 |
| And never doubt thy aid | 614 | 2 |
| And never enter more | 409 | 2 |
| And never grieve thee more | 105 | 4 |
| And never grieve thee more | 125 | 3 |
| And never grieve thee more | 182 | 1 |
| And never grieve thee more | 416 | 1 |
| And never grieve thee more | 625 | 3 |
| And never leave you more | 418 | 2 |
| And never let me go | 187 | Cho. |
| And never let me lose thy love | 649 | 3 |
| And never let us go | 812 | — |
| And never meet but in thy name | 524 | 1 |
| And never more depart | 311 | 4 |
| And never more my sins forgive | 917 | 1 |
| And never more to sin give place | 105 | 4 |

52

| | Hymn | Verse |
|---|---|---|
| And never, never cease | 221 | 2 |
| And never, never faint | 93 | 1 |
| And never, never faint | 295 | Cho. |
| And never, never faint | 301 | 4 |
| And never, never faint | 303 | 2 |
| And never, never, find it more | 317 | 1 |
| And never, never sin | 12 | 3 |
| And never, never thence depart | 177 | 1 |
| And never put to shame | 436 | 3 |
| And never sin again | 1005 | 1 |
| And never stand still till the Master appear | 47 | 1 |
| And never take the harsher way | 468 | 6 |
| And never-withering flowers | 938 | 2 |
| And new-discovered worlds arise | 460 | 2 |
| And night and day, thy power confess | 553 | 2 |
| And nightly to the listening earth | 552 | 3 |
| And no created thing remains | 64 | 5 |
| And no one bud of grace appear | 803 | 3 |
| And none may in this honour share | 656 | 2 |
| And none shall find his promise vain | 224 | 2 |
| And not a soul be left behind | 81 | 4 |
| And not one evil thought remain | 511 | 2 |
| And not regard the sin-sick soul | 397 | 6 |
| And not the God of Gentiles too | 444 | 2 |
| And nothing great or good can see | 21 | 2 |
| And nothing have to eat | 875 | 1 |
| And nothing know beside | 534 | 3 |
| And now absolve me from my sins | 97 | 5 |
| And now, as e'er. my voice attend | 909 | 5 |
| And now begin thy glorious reign | 445 | 1 |
| And now cry out—"It is the Lord" | 113 | 3 |
| And now he lives, and now he reigns | 644 | 2 |
| And now if more at length I see | 210 | 3 |
| And now into my heart inspire | 25 | 6 |
| And now it pleads before the throne | 675 | 7 |
| And now made willing to return | 186 | 1 |
| And now pronounce our sins forgiven | 121 | 5 |
| And now show forth his praise | 268 | 2 |
| And now supply the common want | 294 | 3 |
| And now the work of grace begin | 119 | 7 |
| And now triumphantly come down | 74 | 5 |
| And now we fight the battle | 943 | 2 |
| And now we inherit all fulness in thee | 19 | 2 |
| And now we live in hope | 943 | 3 |
| †And now we watch and struggle | 943 | 3 |
| And numbered with the saints above | 557 | 5 |
| And number with the blest | 982 | 4 |
| And O! can I possibly find | 174 | 1 |
| And O instruct us how to pray | 294 | 1 |
| And, O let a nation be born in a day | 219 | 6 |
| And, O my God, might I be one | 17 | 5 |
| And, O my God, shall I be there | 48 | 2 |
| And O! to crown my last desires | 916 | 6 |

| | Hymn | Verse |
|---|---|---|
| And O thy servant, Lord, prepare | 318 | 2 |
| †And O when I have safely passed | 849 | 5 |
| And o'er the creature strayed | 98 | 1 |
| And o'er the nations reign | 730 | 1 |
| And offer all my works to thee | 824 | 3 |
| And offers me his grace | 80 | 4 |
| And of himself enquire | 883 | 1 |
| And of his bounties may recall | 844 | 3 |
| And of my gracious acts below | 778 | 4 |
| And of the hearing ear | 887 | — |
| And oft endured the grief | 584 | 4 |
| And oft repeat before the throne | 944 | 8 |
| And oil and wine abound | 800 | 6 |
| And once I felt my sins forgiven | 365 | 3 |
| And once I knew him reconciled | 365 | 3 |
| And one into a thousand rise | 732 | 2 |
| And one long blast shattered the Canaanite's wall | 869 | 4 |
| And one thrice-holy God and Lord | 262 | 1 |
| And one with thee for ever reign | 72 | 5 |
| And on his only name rely | 669 | 1 |
| And on *his* soul the dews of grace | 896 | 4 |
| And on that ruined world look down | 57 | 6 |
| And on the eagle wings of love | 949 | 1 |
| And on the wings of all the winds | 551 | 4 |
| And on the wings of every hour | 263 | 2 |
| And on this we rely | 808 | 3 |
| And on thy grand oblation cast | 702 | 6 |
| And on thy milk and honey feed | 293 | 8 |
| And on thyself rely | 318 | 2 |
| And on to full perfection grow | 107 | 6 |
| And only breathe his praise and love | 953 | 4 |
| And only breathe, to breathe thy love | 433 | 3 |
| And only care my God to please | 833 | 2 |
| And only for his glory live | 638 | 1 |
| And only live to love and praise | 420 | 4 |
| And only love inspired the whole | 16 | 3 |
| And only man is vile | 747 | 2 |
| And only seek divine applause | 483 | 4 |
| And only thee to know | 222 | 2 |
| And only thee to obey | 352 | 3 |
| And opening now admit its Lord | 884 | — |
| And open, Lord, my soul | 372 | — |
| And open to thy piercing view | 240 | 4 |
| And open wide our heavenly home | 690 | 4 |
| And opens a fountain that washes us clean | 3 | 6 |
| And ope the portals of the skies | 648 | 3 |
| And our captive souls are free | 621 | 3 |
| And our defence is sure | 41 | 2 |
| And our devotion dies | 763 | 2 |
| And our eternal home | 41 | 1 |
| And our forgiveness seal | 705 | 3 |
| And our hearts rejoice to see | 714 | 5 |
| And our perpetual home | 41 | 7 |

| | Hymn | Verse |
|---|---|---|
| And our Saviour in glory adore | 491 | 6 |
| And our talents improve | 47 | 2 |
| And outfly all the arrows of death | 499 | 2 |
| And out of Egypt call thy son | 106 | 5 |
| And outwardly conformed to thee | 830 | 5 |
| And own all fulness dwells in thee | 568 | 2 |
| And own, as grateful sacrifice | 959 | 1 |
| And own him conqueror | 278 | 2 |
| And own how dreadful is this place | 494 | 1 |
| And own that love is heaven | 1 | 10 |
| And own thee conqueror | 137 | 8 |
| And own thee faithful to thy word | 507 | 1 |
| And own thy glorious ministry | 476 | 1 |
| And own thy peerless majesty | 247 | 8 |
| And own, when now the cloud's removed | 120 | 1 |
| And own your gracious God | 603 | 4 |
| And owns thy dreadful sentence just | 574 | 11 |
| And Paradise restored | 64 | 6 |
| And pardon a sinner once more | 174 | 2 |
| And pardon in thy mercy found | 206 | 2 |
| And pardon on my conscience seal | 180 | 4 |
| And pardon on my conscience seal | 395 | 4 |
| And pardon we claim | 495 | 4 |
| And pardoning love takes place | 184 | 8 |
| And pardons in his hands | 675 | 8 |
| And part are crossing now | 949 | 2 |
| And part exulting in thy name | 536 | 1 |
| And parting are no more | 536 | 4 |
| And passing through the fire | 853 | 2 |
| And passionless renown | 943 | 2 |
| And pass through death triumphant home | 386 | 4 |
| And pastors after thine own heart | 744 | 8 |
| And patience in all pain inspire | 666 | 4 |
| And pay thee back thy dying love | 378 | 4 |
| And peace o'erflows my heart | 123 | 2 |
| And peace on earth descend | 684 | 1 |
| And peace, the fruit of faith, bestow | 752 | 4 |
| And peace upon earth be restored | 220 | 1 |
| And pearly gates behold | 939 | 2 |
| And penitential pain | 83 | 4 |
| And Pentecostal grace | 771 | 6 |
| And perfect all our souls in one | 749 | 2 |
| And perfect holiness below | 17 | 8 |
| And perfect holiness in me | 891 | 2 |
| And perfect in a babe thy praise | 866 | 4 |
| And perfect it in holiness | 897 | 7 |
| And perfect liberty | 861 | 8 |
| And perfect me in love | 109 | 7 |
| And perfect me in love | 854 | Cho. |
| And perfect me in love | 360 | 11 |
| And perfect me in love | 674 | 1 |
| And perfect soundness give | 356 | 5 |
| And perfect us in love | 389 | 8 |

## AND PERFECT            AND PRAISE

| | HYMN | VERSE |
|---|---|---|
| And perfect us in love | 503 | 4 |
| And perfect us in one | 308 | 6 |
| And perfect us in one | 384 | 9 |
| And perfect you in love | 54 | 3 |
| And perfected in love | 295 | 5 |
| And perfected in love | 345 | 6 |
| And perfected in love | 368 | 2 |
| And perfected in love below | 523 | 5 |
| And perfected in one | 460 | 3 |
| And perfectly by faith made whole | 180 | 8 |
| And perfectly like thee | 502 | 5 |
| And, perfectly renewed | 323 | 3 |
| And perfectly restored | 622 | 3 |
| And perfects all our souls in one | 394 | 2 |
| And perfects them in love | 85 | 4 |
| And perish in extreme despair | 917 | 1 |
| And pestilence, with rapid stride | 986 | 2 |
| And Pharaoh's warriors strew the shore | 715 | 1 |
| And pine to quit this mean abode | 74 | 4 |
| And place her, enthroned at his side | 77 | 1 |
| And place me at thy feet | 136 | 3 |
| And plague of heart, thou, dost remove | 693 | 3 |
| And plant that guardian-angel here | 306 | 4 |
| And plant the kingdom of thy love | 447 | 2 |
| And plant thy nature in my heart | 364 | 8 |
| And pleads his death for me | 982 | 1 |
| And plead'st thy death for sinners now | 708 | 1 |
| And please my heavenly Lord | 828 | 1 |
| And pleasing in thy Father's sight | 429 | 8 |
| And pleasures banish pain | 938 | 1 |
| And pleasures, springing from the well | 21 | 4 |
| And plenuful pardon in Jesus's name | 219 | 3 |
| And plunge in eternal despair | 911 | 2 |
| And plunge into the flaming wave | 442 | 2 |
| And plunge into the glorious blaze | 284 | 2 |
| And plunge me, every whit made whole | 408 | 2 |
| And plunge the sinner there | 123 | 6 |
| And point them to the atoning Lamb | 439 | 3 |
| And poison while they feed | 108 | 2 |
| And portion evermore | 664 | 5 |
| And possess, in sweet communion | 1006 | — |
| And pour a ceaseless prayer | 803 | 4 |
| And pour contempt on all my pride | 700 | 1 |
| And pour in all our hearts | 822 | 1 |
| And pour out my complaint | 152 | 1 |
| And pour thyself into my heart | 131 | 4 |
| And poured his sacred blood | 731 | 2 |
| And poured out cries and tears | 940 | 2 |
| And pours the all-prevailing prayer | 127 | 9 |
| And power and wisdom too | 435 | 2 |
| And powers of hell unknown | 675 | 10 |
| And praise our common Lord | 497 | 1 |
| And praise sits silent on our tongues | 816 | 5 |

| | Hymn | Verse |
|---|---|---|
| And praise thee for ever, when time is no more | 1025 | 2 |
| And praise thee in a bolder strain | 877 | 4 |
| And praise thee in thy bright abode | 43 | 6 |
| And praise thy glorious name | 248 | 5 |
| And praise thy goodness all day long | 493 | 3 |
| And praise thy love for ever | 855 | 2 |
| And praises throng to crown his head | 585 | 8 |
| And pray, and weep for thee | 144 | 4 |
| And pray for Zion's peace | 268 | 3 |
| And pray that I no more may fall | 306 | 2 |
| And prayer, by thee inspired and taught | 863 | 3 |
| And prayer in endless praise | 297 | 6 |
| And preach the death by which we live | 474 | 4 |
| And preach the kingdom from above | 873 | 2 |
| And press to the skies | 495 | 1 |
| And press to our permanent place in the skies | 498 | 1 |
| And pride and rage prevail no more | 585 | 2 |
| And proffered mercy, we embrace | 11 | 3 |
| And promise, in this sacred hour | 532 | 2 |
| And props the house of clay | 44 | 2 |
| And prosper the work of my hands | 231 | 8 |
| And prostrate at thy feet adore | 583 | 2 |
| And prostrate in thy sight adore | 284 | 1 |
| And prove thee, verging on the grave | 636 | 4 |
| And prove the record true | 35 | 8 |
| And prove the work entirely thine | 475 | 5 |
| And prove thy acceptable will | 324 | 2 |
| And prove thy power to heal | 693 | 2 |
| And publish abroad his wonderful name | 859 | 1 |
| And publish to the sons of men | 96 | 1 |
| And publish with our latest breath | 831 | 15 |
| And publishes to every land | 552 | 2 |
| And pure, and happy too | 18 | 2 |
| And pure as those above | 389 | 3 |
| And pure as thou thyself art pure | 523 | 4 |
| And pure eternal love | 413 | 2 |
| And pure, ingenuous love | 468 | 7 |
| And pure in heart shall see his face | 616 | 3 |
| And pure unbounded love | 873 | 2 |
| And purge my conscience with thy blood | 397 | 8 |
| And purge my foul conscience, and bring me to God | 160 | 3 |
| And purifies the heart | 406 | 2 |
| And purify my heart | 414 | 1 |
| And purify the heart | 671 | 2 |
| And put a cheerful courage on | 802 | 1 |
| And put salvation on | 446 | 1 |
| And put your armour on | 266 | 1 |
| And quell the sinner's pride | 740 | 4 |
| And quenched in death those flaming eyes | 122 | 3 |
| And quenched with Jesu's blood | 267 | 1 |
| And quench the brands in Jesu's blood | 433 | 2 |
| And quench the kindling fire | 508 | 1 |
| And quiet sleep by night | 624 | 2 |

| | Hymn | Verse |
|---|---|---|
| And raiment fit provide | 664 | 3 |
| And raise a supplicating cry | 153 | 2 |
| And raise in death our triumph higher | 204 | 8 |
| And raise me from my fall | 150 | 2 |
| And raise my head, and cheer my heart | 339 | 4 |
| And raise the fallen up | 112 | 2 |
| And raise the poor that fall | 637 | 6 |
| And raise this individual me | 927 | 2 |
| And raise to glory all | 65 | 2 |
| And raised him from the dead | 717 | 1 |
| And raised him from the tomb | 750 | 4 |
| And, raised out of the earth, we live | 256 | 3 |
| And raised us into Abraham's sons | 203 | 1 |
| And ranks of shining thrones around | 316 | 2 |
| And ransom captive Israel | 690 | 1 |
| And ransom my soul from the grave | 174 | 2 |
| And rapture swells the solemn lay | 731 | 7 |
| And rapturous awe, and silent love | 369 | 4 |
| And ratified in death | 903 | 4 |
| And ravening wolves on every side | 458 | 3 |
| And ravening wolves, surround | 310 | 2 |
| And reaches out a starry crown | 315 | 4 |
| And reach the heavenly land | 949 | 3 |
| And read thee everywhere | 662 | 4 |
| And ready may I be | 805 | 2 |
| And ready utterance give | 733 | 4 |
| And real Christians live | 472 | 4 |
| And realms of endless day | 939 | 4 |
| And rectify their thought | 468 | 5 |
| And refuge in Jesus's righteousness take | 495 | 4 |
| And register our names on high | 532 | 6 |
| And regulate our ways | 846 | 1 |
| And reign above the sky | 501 | 6 |
| And reign in every heart alone | 568 | 4 |
| And reign in thy kingdom of grace | 220 | 1 |
| And reign within my heart | 275 | 5 |
| And reign without a rival there | 373 | 1 |
| And reign with thee above | 59 | 6 |
| And reigns a King for ever | 276 | 1 |
| And reigns eternal in the skies | 69 | 2 |
| And rejoice in the day thou wast born | 491 | 1 |
| And rejoice that I ever was born | 231 | 10 |
| And render him my heart | 80 | 5 |
| And render up my breath | 311 | 5 |
| And rescued from sin | 219 | 8 |
| And rescued me from passion's power | 178 | 2 |
| And rescue this poor soul of mine | 288 | 1 |
| And rest in thy redeeming love | 507 | 3 |
| And rest till my Redeemer come | 927 | 4 |
| And restless sing around thy seat | 222 | 4 |
| And, restless to behold thy face | 71 | 2 |
| And reverential love | 756 | 2 |
| And richer blood, than they | 703 | 2 |

| | Hymn | Verse |
|---|---|---|
| And rides upon the storm | 845 | 1 |
| And righteousness abound | 731 | 5 |
| And righteousness in fountains | 586 | 3 |
| And righteous word, is thine | 435 | 5 |
| And ripe in holiness appear | 775 | 4 |
| And rise again to fall no more | 953 | 2 |
| And rise in Christ a creature new | 616 | 3 |
| And rise in raptures higher | 18 | 3 |
| And rise prepared thy face to see | 74 | 5 |
| And rise renewed in perfect love | 510 | 3 |
| And rise to a share in thy throne | 946 | 3 |
| And rise to fall no more | 303 | 1 |
| And rise to purity of heart | 306 | 5 |
| And rise with filial fear divine | 96 | 6 |
| And rise with thee to reign | 311 | 5 |
| And risen, thy death for us to plead | 380 | 6 |
| And rose accepted in the skies | 702 | 4 |
| And rose again for me | 360 | 2 |
| And rose to sin anew | 697 | 6 |
| And rose triumphant from the dead | 953 | 1 |
| And round again till morn | 626 | 4 |
| And round it hath cast, like a mantle, the sea | 611 | 3 |
| And rounding years bring nigh the last | 961 | 5 |
| And rule in equity | 586 | 1 |
| And rule the lower world | 314 | 4 |
| And ruleth all things well | 831 | 11 |
| And run my course with even joy | 324 | 5 |
| And runs to this relief | 786 | 3 |
| And safe beneath thy wings to rest | 289 | 5 |
| And safe in his almighty hands | 622 | 2 |
| And safe in Jesus dwell | 738 | 4 |
| And saints and angels join to sing | 867 | 3 |
| And saints embodied give | 259 | 4 |
| And salvation in Jesus's name | 231 | 11 |
| And sanctified by grace | 685 | 5 |
| And sanctified by love divine | 340 | 1 |
| And sanctifying fear | 309 | 2 |
| And sanctify our humblest home | 997 | 2 |
| And sanctify the whole | 361 | 9 |
| And sanctify the whole | 453 | 2 |
| And Satan binds our captive souls | 786 | 1 |
| And Satan is their God | 447 | 1 |
| And Satan's works destroy | 761 | 3 |
| And satisfy the hungry poor | 629 | 6 |
| And satisfy their every need | 32 | 3 |
| And satisfy with endless peace | 134 | 3 |
| And save, by ways unknown | 801 | 1 |
| And save from all iniquity | 269 | 3 |
| And save from first to last | 818 | 2 |
| And save *him* to the end | 465 | 10 |
| And save me for his sake alone | 148 | 4 |
| And save me from my bosom sin | 395 | 5 |
| And save me to the end | 310 | 4 |

| | HYMN | VERSE |
|---|---|---|
| And save me, who for me hast died | 373 | 9 |
| And save the purchase of thy blood | 648 | 5 |
| And save the soul condemned to die | 574 | 11 |
| And save thy servants to the end | 649 | 2 |
| And save us by thy dying love | 774 | 1 |
| And save us through the coming night | 968 | 1 |
| And save us through the coming night | 968 | 2 |
| And, saved according to thy will | 816 | 2 |
| And saved by grace alone | 15 | 1 |
| And, saved from earth, appear | 738 | 6 |
| And saves whoe'er on Jesus call | 85 | 4 |
| And savingly believe | 886 | — |
| And saw the tongues of flame | 460 | 1 |
| And saw the wonders of thy hand | 460 | 1 |
| And say, from sin's remains | 345 | 2 |
| And say, in answer to my call | 164 | 5 |
| And say, was ever grief like his | 28 | 2 |
| And scale the mount of God | 333 | 2 |
| And scale the mount of heaven | 265 | 2 |
| And scan his work in vain | 845 | 3 |
| And 'scape from earth away | 925 | 1 |
| And scarce distinguish from a child | 470 | 5 |
| And scarce presume to pray | 93 | 1 |
| And scarcely can we turn aside | 863 | 1 |
| And scatter all their doubt and fear | 462 | 4 |
| And scatter peace on all around | 524 | 3 |
| And screened from the heat of the day | 228 | 1 |
| And screen me from my nature's power | 105 | 3 |
| And screen my naked head | 271 | 3 |
| And screen my naked head | 292 | 2 |
| And screen my naked head | 998 | 2 |
| And sealed it with thy blood | 162 | 4 |
| And sealed the grace with blood | 903 | 1 |
| And sealed the heir of heaven | 292 | 5 |
| And sealed the pardon with thy blood | 129 | 2 |
| And seal me all thine own | 383 | 3 |
| And seal me eternally thine | 165 | 5 |
| And seal me ever thine | 137 | 9 |
| And seal me for thine own | 188 | 5 |
| And seal me thine abode | 347 | 5 |
| And seal me thine abode | 403 | 8 |
| And seal the abode for ever thine | 655 | 4 |
| And seal the heirs of heaven | 765 | 2 |
| And seal us to that day | 761 | 4 |
| And seals the blessing sure | 888 | 2 |
| And search the heart of man | 244 | 3 |
| And search the oracles divine | 328 | 1 |
| And seat me by his side | 307 | 5 |
| And seat us on his glorious throne | 483 | 5 |
| And see but shadows of thy face | 651 | 5 |
| And see each other's face | 478 | 1 |
| And see his glorious face | 685 | 5 |
| And see his great salvation | 854 | 3 |

| | Hymn | Verse |
|---|---|---|
| And see his Maker face to face | 557 | 8 |
| And see its paradise restored | 443 | 3 |
| And see our Lord again | 58 | 2 |
| And see redemption near | 845 | 4 |
| And see the Bridegroom nigh | 54 | 1 |
| And see the Canaan that we love | 938 | 5 |
| And see the dazzling prize | 723 | 2 |
| And see the flaming skies | 43 | 2 |
| And see the Judge with glory crowned | 43 | 2 |
| And see the perfect day | 383 | 2 |
| And see the shadows fade | 217 | 1 |
| And see thee in glory appear | 946 | 3 |
| And see thee in the clouds appear | 311 | 5 |
| And see thee, Saviour, as thou art | 919 | 2 |
| And see thy glorious face | 325 | 5 |
| And see thy glorious face above | 254 | 3 |
| And see thy glory in thy Son | 452 | 2 |
| And see thy wonders in the deep | 1001 | 2 |
| And see your Lord appear | 387 | 1 |
| And seek a country out of sight | 68 | 6 |
| And seek an undiscovered land | 840 | 1 |
| And seek deliverance there | 573 | 4 |
| And seek thee in my heart, in vain | 547 | 2 |
| And seek the glorious things above | 420 | 2 |
| And seek thy face, and learn thy praise | 592 | 3 |
| And seek thy presence still | 546 | 1 |
| And seeks the things above | 68 | 2 |
| And seen on earth no more | 565 | 9 |
| And sees me to his will resigned | 331 | 2 |
| And sees the fruit of all his pains | 644 | 2 |
| And sees the smiling face of heaven | 561 | 1 |
| And sees the Tempter fly | 801 | 3 |
| And seize, and change, and fill my heart | 775 | 3 |
| And seize me for thine own | 138 | 1 |
| And self-deluding pride | 805 | 1 |
| And send a peaceful answer down | 298 | 5 |
| And send a peaceful answer down | 505 | 8 |
| And send the Promise down | 506 | 1 |
| And send us down the Comforter | 294 | 3 |
| And sends him in our hearts to plead | 827 | 8 |
| And sends it down to me | 435 | 4 |
| And sensibly believe | 901 | 2 |
| And sensualize his soul | 108 | 3 |
| And sent him down the world to save | 39 | 1 |
| And sent him from his throne above | 107 | 1 |
| And seraphs shout the Triune God | 647 | 2 |
| And serve and love thee all their days | 474 | 3 |
| And serve his pleasure still | 325 | 1 |
| And serve thee all my spotless days | 375 | 3 |
| And serve thee as thy hosts above | 877 | 3 |
| And serve the royal heirs of heaven | 17 | 8 |
| And serve thy pleasure still | 172 | 3 |
| And serve with heart sincere | 472 | 1 |

AND SET                                        AND SHOUT

| | Hymn | Verse |
|---|---|---|
| And set me faultless there before the throne | 794 | 4 |
| And set my heart at liberty | 408 | 5 |
| And set my longing spirit free | 285 | 2 |
| And set my soul at liberty | 125 | 4 |
| And set their feet upon the rock | 458 | 6 |
| And set thy plaintive prisoners free | 129 | 4 |
| And set up his kingdom of love in the heart | 760 | 3 |
| And set up in each of thine own | 220 | 3 |
| And set upon the rock my feet | 312 | 6 |
| And shadows pass away | 954 | 3 |
| And shake the gates of hell | 453 | 1 |
| And shall be till I die | 798 | 4 |
| And shall for ever fill | 407 | 5 |
| And shall for ever have | 874 | 1 |
| And shall for ever sit | 232 | 3 |
| And shall from age to age endure | 607 | 4 |
| And shall he bleed in vain | 36 | 1 |
| †And shall I slight my Father's love | 30 | 3 |
| †And shall my sins thy will oppose | 275 | 4 |
| And shall not we our joint request | 827 | 1 |
| And shall take his harvest home | 987 | 3 |
| And shall through endless ages live | 673 | 3 |
| †And shall we mourn to see | 52 | 3 |
| And shall we not sing | 219 | 4 |
| †And shall we then for ever live | 763 | 3 |
| And shall with him arise | 898 | 4 |
| And shared that better sacrifice | 721 | 5 |
| And share his sacrifice | 898 | 2 |
| And share in the gladness of all that believe | 198 | 6 |
| And share the everlasting throne | 57 | 6 |
| And share thy kingdom in the skies | 917 | 4 |
| And share thy majesty divine | 525 | 3 |
| And sharers of thy throne | 925 | 2 |
| And shed by his Spirit abroad | 911 | 2 |
| And shed his glory all abroad | 537 | 6 |
| And sheep-redeeming Shepherd art | 744 | 3 |
| And sheltered in thy wounds, I dwell | 561 | 7 |
| And shield me in the last alarms | 924 | 4 |
| And shield me in the threatening fight | 196 | 3 |
| And shield me with thy power | 292 | 8 |
| And shine as stars beyond the skies | 883 | 3 |
| And shine in every pagan heart | 444 | 3 |
| And shine like suns for ever there | 935 | 4 |
| And shortly receive us to banquet above | 1013 | 2 |
| And should I not with faith draw nigh | 97 | 4 |
| And shout above the fiery void | 536 | 5 |
| And shout, and wonder at his grace | 947 | 8 |
| And shout as we travel the wilderness through | 760 | 5 |
| And shout him welcome to the skies | 712 | 2 |
| And shout his praise in endless day | 731 | 7 |
| And shout Immanuel's name | 684 | 4 |
| And shout in universal song | 681 | 7 |
| And shout my all-sufficient grace | 629 | 7 |

|  | HYMN | VERSE |
|---|---|---|
| And shout our solemn joys | 52 | 1 |
| And shout the sons of God for joy | 629 | 3 |
| And shout to prove the Saviour mine | 272 | 3 |
| And shout to see our Captain's sign | 949 | 5 |
| And shout to see thy day | 983 | 7 |
| And shout to the Redeemer's praise | 976 | 1 |
| And shout to the trumpet of God | 946 | 4 |
| And shout, ye morning stars, for joy | 235 | 3 |
| And shouted our Deliverer's name | 483 | 2 |
| And show and seal us ever thine | 377 | 2 |
| And show forth all thy power | 187 | 2 |
| And show forth all thy power | 436 | 7 |
| And show his praise below | 534 | 2 |
| And show me all thy glorious love | 130 | 2 |
| And show me, all thy goodness show | 113 | 1 |
| And show me now the face of God | 124 | 2 |
| And show me the life-giving blood | 174 | 2 |
| And show me thy salvation now | 396 | 6 |
| And show me thy salvation now | 776 | 2 |
| And show me where the Christians live | 16 | 5 |
| And show my sins forgiven | 765 | 2 |
| And show that in the Father's love | 764 | 3 |
| And show that thou and I are one | 134 | 4 |
| And show the danger near | 309 | 2 |
| And show the mystery fulfilled | 452 | 6 |
| And show the world a nation born | 450 | 4 |
| And show them how believers true | 472 | 4 |
| And show them how the Christians live | 319 | 2 |
| And show thy grace to me | 242 | 4 |
| And show thy real presence here | 902 | 5 |
| And show thyself beyond the grave | 282 | 5 |
| And show thyself for ever mine | 130 | 4 |
| And show thyself his Lord and God | 861 | 1 |
| And show thyself the Comforter | 441 | 1 |
| And show thyself the Finisher | 812 | — |
| And show thyself the God of love | 283 | 4 |
| And show thyself to me | 124 | 1 |
| And showed our feet the way | 929 | 3 |
| And showed the Father in the Son | 493 | 1 |
| And showed the great Invisible | 902 | 3 |
| And shower his judgments down | 63 | 1 |
| And shows himself our friend | 684 | 1 |
| And shows that I am graven there | 127 | 9 |
| And shrink from my devoted head | 272 | 2 |
| And shrink to see a yawning hell | 57 | 2 |
| And shrivel as a parchment-scroll | 64 | 4 |
| And shun the paths of sin | 305 | 3 |
| And shut me up in God | 296 | 3 |
| And shy distrust remove | 528 | 1 |
| And sick, and poor I am | 136 | 5 |
| And sick of sin, implore a cure | 895 | 3 |
| And sighed from myself to get free | 165 | 3 |
| And sigheth for his rest | 942 | 2 |

| | Hymn | Verse |
|---|---|---|
| And sighing are no more | 941 | 2 |
| And sighs are unavailing | 932 | 3 |
| And sighs themselves expire | 942 | 4 |
| And signs us with his cross | 96 | 5 |
| And silence heightens heaven | 333 | 6 |
| And silence the blasphemer | 855 | 2 |
| And silent bow before his face | 494 | 1 |
| And sin against thy love | 184 | 6 |
| And sin and sorrow flies | 166 | 4 |
| And sin shall be no more | 413 | 1 |
| And sin shall give its raging o'er | 110 | 5 |
| And sin shall never enter there | 386 | 5 |
| And Sinai felt the incumbent God | 223 | 2 |
| And sing of the goodness I feel | 911 | 4 |
| And sing, in songs which never end | 800 | 9 |
| And sing my great Deliverer's praise | 561 | 8 |
| And sing the song of Moses | 853 | 3 |
| And sing the wonders of his grace | 800 | 4 |
| And sing thy perfect love | 409 | 4 |
| And sing thy power above | 930 | 5 |
| And sing, with all our friends in light | 377 | 4 |
| And sing with all the heavenly choir | 204 | 8 |
| And sing with cheerful melody | 543 | 7 |
| And sing with cheerful melody | 977 | 8 |
| And sink into eternal woe | 670 | 1 |
| And sink me to perfection's height | 216 | 9 |
| And sink the mountain to a plain | 433 | 1 |
| And sink unsaved among the dead | 776 | 1 |
| And sinned against the clearest light | 176 | 3 |
| And sinned against thy light and love | 365 | 5 |
| And sinners, plunged beneath that flood | .798 | 1 |
| And sit and sing herself away | 956 | 4 |
| And sitting at thy feet | 275 | 6 |
| And sleep in death, to rest with God | 959 | 5 |
| And slight and mock thee to thy face | 454 | 6 |
| And smile at toil and pain | 948 | 2 |
| And smile to see a burning world | 57 | 4 |
| And smile to see me feebly bring | 365 | 1 |
| And smiles have no alloy | 943 | 5 |
| And snatched from hell to heaven | 245 | 3 |
| And soar on angels' wings away | 69 | 2 |
| And soar to worlds on high | 948 | 1 |
| And softened by thy grace, repent | 983 | 5 |
| And softened every bed | 929 | 2 |
| And soften every clod | 578 | 2 |
| And soften my unyielding clay | 145 | 2 |
| And soft refreshing rain | 988 | 1 |
| And solemnize in songs divine | 947 | 6 |
| †And some have found the world is vain | 969 | 4 |
| And some have friends who give them pain | 969 | 4 |
| And some have lost the love they had | 969 | 3 |
| And some have never loved thee well | 969 | 3 |
| And Son proceeding; promised, sent | 770 | 1 |

| | Hymn | Verse |
|---|---|---|
| And soon avenge us of our foe | 280 | 3 |
| And soon my friends in Christ below | 939 | 5 |
| And soon my spirit, in his hands | 726 | 3 |
| And soon or later then translate | 367 | 3 |
| And soon the reaping time will come | 935 | Cho. |
| And soon with thee in glory reign | 590 | 6 |
| And soon with thee shall all receive | 286 | 7 |
| And sore the chastening rod | 838 | 4 |
| And sorrow and sin are no more | 49 | 2 |
| And sorrow fled away | 335 | 2 |
| And sorrow's waves around me roll | 272 | 6 |
| And sought, but never found | 741 | 3 |
| And sought from him relief | 634 | 1 |
| And souls beneath the altar groan | 749 | 2 |
| And sound his power abroad | 659 | 2 |
| And sound the unbelieving heart | 456 | 3 |
| And sound through all the worlds above | 800 | 11 |
| And sound, with all thy saints below | 87 | 4 |
| And so ye perish in the way | 541 | 5 |
| And spangled heavens, a shining frame | 552 | 1 |
| And spared the barren tree | 982 | 1 |
| And spares us yet another year | 981 | 1 |
| And spares us yet another year | 981 | 3 |
| And speak and sparkle in our eyes | 204 | 6 |
| And speak in every heart | 85 | 3 |
| And speak it to my heart | 128 | 2 |
| And speak me at last to the throne of thy love | 165 | 5 |
| And speak me in a moment whole | 396 | 4 |
| And speak my soul restored | 123 | 3 |
| And speak our sins forgiven | 84 | 7 |
| And speak our souls restored | 693 | 2 |
| And speak the answer to my heart | 17 | 9 |
| And speak the builder God | 226 | 11 |
| And speak the word of power, "Be clean". | 177 | 3 |
| And speak thy name into my heart | 113 | 2 |
| And speak us perfected in one | 438 | 1 |
| And speakest worlds from nought | 360 | 5 |
| And speaks me justified | 184 | 5 |
| And speaks salvation all around | 902 | 2 |
| And speaks thy glorious name | 259 | 2 |
| And speaks thy rebels up to heaven | 298 | 5 |
| And spend and be spent in assisting his saints | 495 | 3 |
| And spend the remnant to thy praise | 564 | 1 |
| And Spirit comprehend | 642 | 6 |
| And spirits enthroned on high | 815 | 1 |
| And spiritual bliss that never shall cloy | 19 | 3 |
| And spotless here below | 503 | 5 |
| And spotless love and peace | 417 | 6 |
| And spread before thy glorious eyes | 394 | 2 |
| And spread content and happiness | 471 | 1 |
| And spread its praise below | 92 | 3 |
| And spread the common Saviour's fame | 489 | 1 |
| And spread the truth from pole to pole | 552 | 4 |

| | Hymn | Verse |
|---|---|---|
| 'And spread the spark of living fire | 528 | 5 |
| And spread thy fame abroad | 637 | 11 |
| And spread thy mercy's praise below | 744 | 6 |
| And spread thy praise through earth and skies | 732 | 2 |
| And spread thy saving name abroad | 206 | 3 |
| And spread thy victory | 352 | 4 |
| And spread your hearts and hands abroad | 268 | 3 |
| And spreads for you his bleeding hands | 9 | 2 |
| And spreads through all the earth abroad | 277 | 2 |
| And sprinkle his heart with the blood | 165 | 1 |
| And sprinkles now the throne of grace | 202 | 2 |
| And square our useful lives below | 526 | 3 |
| And staff me comfort still | 556 | 3 |
| And stamped the day for ever his | 953 | 1 |
| And stamp me with thy Spirit's seal | 393 | 1 |
| And stamp thine image on my heart | 388 | 3 |
| And stamp thine image on my heart | 395 | 6 |
| And stamp thine image on our hearts | 752 | 3 |
| And stamp thy name on every face | 62 | 6 |
| And stamp us for thine own. | 901 | 2 |
| And stand against their open hate | 311 | 1 |
| And stand entire at last | 266 | 2 |
| And stand upon the mount of God | 557 | 3 |
| And standest now before the throne | 902 | 1 |
| And starred with sparkling gold | 226 | 2 |
| And starting cry from ruin's brink | 309 | 3 |
| And stayed on that alone | 335 | 4 |
| And still a den of thieves I made | 93 | 4 |
| And still extends his wounded hands | 947 | 3 |
| And still direct my paths to thee | 289 | 2 |
| And still for mercy, mercy, pray | 176 | 2 |
| And still he doth his help afford | 478 | 2 |
| And still he is nigh, his presence we have | 859 | 3 |
| And still he keeps our spirits one | 535 | 1 |
| And still he loves and guards his own | 272 | 1 |
| And still I hang upon thy word | 547 | 7 |
| And still I hear thy Spirit cry | 775 | 1 |
| And still in all my works maintain | 472 | 2 |
| And still in God confide | 618 | 2 |
| And still in him confide | 575 | 3 |
| And still in Jesu's footsteps tread | 534 | 2 |
| And still it guards and keeps thine own | 483 | 3 |
| And still my tempted soul stand by | 309 | 1 |
| And still prolongs my days | 229 | 1 |
| And still our wants declare | 295 | 4 |
| And still shook off my guilty fears | 161 | 2 |
| And still stir up thy gift in me | 327 | 3 |
| And still the conquest more than win | 456 | 5 |
| And still the pleasing task pursue | 204 | 2 |
| And still their own deny | 840 | 1 |
| And still they are talking of Jesus's grace | 198 | 2 |
| And still thy grace is free | 182 | 4 |
| And still thy healing power is here | 897 | 5 |

| | HYMN | VERSE |
|---|---|---|
| And still to higher glories rise | 284 | 6 |
| And still to thee all glory give | 524 | 1 |
| And still to things eternal look | 324 | 4 |
| And still we are seeking a country above | 498 | 2 |
| And still we by his death are blessed | 898 | 2 |
| And still we cry and wrestle on | 121 | 5 |
| And still we forego | 498 | 2 |
| And still, with thankful heart and voice | 559 | 2 |
| And stir desponding thought | 587 | 2 |
| And stir me up to pray | 309 | 1 |
| And stir them up to recognize | 871 | 1 |
| And stir us up to pray | 55 | 1 |
| And stir us up to seek thy face | 294 | 1 |
| And stir within our breast | 1014 | — |
| And stood thy chosen throne | 989 | 2 |
| And stoop, myself to save | 25 | 2 |
| And stoop to a poor virgin's womb | 648 | 2 |
| And stoop to a poor virgin's womb | 772 | 4 |
| And stoops beseeching from his throne | 770 | 4 |
| And stoops to ask my love | 137 | 3 |
| And stopped, my ruin to retrieve | 206 | 2 |
| And stopped us by crying, " Will ye also go " | 481 | 4 |
| And store with thoughts divinely true | 473 | 3 |
| And strangely suffered us to live | 980 | 2 |
| And strangely withheld from my sin | 165 | 2 |
| And streets of shining gold | 939 | 2 |
| And strength, and might, and earth, and heaven | 248 | 2 |
| And strength ascribe to Jesus | 276 | 1 |
| And strengthen my weakness, and bid me believe | 200 | 4 |
| And strike the wondering sight | 226 | 10 |
| And strive, and pant, and yearn | 943 | 6 |
| And strives, with those around the throne | 647 | 4 |
| And, strong in his protection | 587 | 4 |
| And strong ones will never their helplessness own | 212 | 2 |
| And strongly intercedes for me | 144 | 3 |
| And study war no more | 740 | 6 |
| And subjugate his rising will | 467 | 7 |
| And suffer all thy righteous will | 59 | 5 |
| And suffer for thy righteous cause | 304 | 7 |
| And suffered many things in vain | 781 | 1 |
| And, suffering all things for thy cause | 439 | 1 |
| And suits the will divine | 832 | 3 |
| And summon whom thou dost approve | 452 | 1 |
| And, sure as he hath died | 36 | 4 |
| And sure I taste thy love | 384 | 5 |
| And surely thou shalt make it whole | 897 | 6 |
| And surges swell no more | 984 | 4 |
| And swathed about the swelling | 667 | 2 |
| And swallow up my soul in thee | 379 | 1 |
| And sweeter than the virgin rose | 46 | 3 |
| And sweetly distils in the dew and the rain | 611 | 4 |
| And sweetly every moment draw | 340 | 3 |
| And sweetly join with one accord | 204 | 7 |

| | Hymn | Verse |
|---|---|---|
| And sweetly lose our will in thine | 510 | 1 |
| And sweetly prompt my heart to pray | 100 | 1 |
| And sweetly speak, the same | 504 | 3 |
| And sweetly steals the Sabbath rest | 957 | 1 |
| And sweet the sleep which follows pain | 957 | 1 |
| And swell and reach to heaven | 110 | 3 |
| And swell the growing fame | 800 | 9 |
| And swell the unutterable groan | 441 | 1 |
| And swells to make thee room | 506 | 3 |
| And swells unutterably full | 96 | 2 |
| And swift as the winds about the world go | 869 | 3 |
| And take away the stone | 117 | 3 |
| And take his exile home | 948 | 2 |
| And take his servants up | 729 | 6 |
| And take it as by storm | 265 | 1 |
| And take me home to God | 436 | 10 |
| And take me into heaven | 118 | 5 |
| And take me to thy breast | 167 | Cho. |
| And take my sins away | 984 | 2 |
| And take, O take, the veil away | 109 | 3 |
| And take our sins away | 84 | 3 |
| And take our souls to heaven | 74 | 5 |
| And take possession of my breast | 376 | 3 |
| And take the conquerors home | 268 | 4 |
| And take the glorious prize | 277 | 4 |
| And take the mould divine | 788 | 6 |
| And take the veil away | 152 | 3 |
| And take them all away | 97 | 5 |
| And take thine ancient people home | 749 | 3 |
| And take this seed of sin away | 816 | 1 |
| And take, through his blood, a power to draw near | 10 | 1 |
| And take to my heavenly home | 77 | 2 |
| And take to thee thy power divine | 568 | 3 |
| And take up all my heart | 356 | 7 |
| And take up all the place | 367 | 2 |
| And take up every thankful song | 428 | 1 |
| And take us up to heaven | 84 | 7 |
| And take us up to heaven | 459 | 4 |
| And talk of all thy truth at night | 599 | 1 |
| And taste, in holiness divine | 304 | 1 |
| And taste that I alone am good | 4 | 7 |
| And taste thy pardoning grace | 784 | 6 |
| And, taught by Jesus, own | 875 | 2 |
| And, taught by Jesus own | 1016 | 2 |
| And, taught by thee, we God revere | 255 | 3 |
| And, taught by thine apostle's word | 891 | 1 |
| And teach even us the spiritual song | 481 | 6 |
| And teach me the new song to sing | 436 | 8 |
| And teach my hands to fight | 270 | 1 |
| †And teach us erring souls to win | 961 | 4 |
| And tell its raptures all abroad | 912 | 1 |
| And tell mankind how good thou art | 545 | 1 |
| And tell me all thy name | 128 | 6 |

| | Hymn | Verse |
|---|---|---|
| And tell me, if I ever knew. | 97 | 1 |
| And tell me if thy name is Love | 141 | 1 |
| And tell me, Lord, shall I be there. | 59 | 4 |
| And tell me what by sin I am | 502 | 3 |
| And tell my infinite desire | 342 | 4 |
| And tell of the riches of Jesus's grace | 211 | 2 |
| And tell thee all my care | 303 | 4 |
| And tell the wonders he hath done. | 800 | 9 |
| And tells me I am born of God | 202 | 4 |
| And tells us our Head is exalted on high. | 760 | 1 |
| And temptations, and snares. | 231 | 5 |
| And testify to all mankind. | 85 | 3 |
| And thanked my Advocate above | 365 | 5 |
| And thankfully in Christ embrace. | 983 | 3 |
| And thanks for his redeeming grace | 616 | 4 |
| And thanks never-ceasing, and infinite love | 859 | 5 |
| And that I never more | 172 | 4 |
| And that shall kindle ours. | 763 | 4 |
| And that thou bidd'st me come to thee | 796 | 1 |
| And the burden is, "Mercy divine!" | 499 | 5 |
| And the changes that are sure to come | 842 | 1 |
| And the choirs that dwell on high | 663 | — |
| And the dark river to be crossed at last | 850 | 4 |
| And the eternal song begun. | 990 | 6 |
| And the Father's boundless love | 1006 | — |
| And the fugitive moment refuses to stay | 47 | 3 |
| And the full corn at length. | 739 | 4 |
| And the gifts we vowed in sorrow. | 580 | 3 |
| And the joys that eternally last | 488 | 2 |
| And the kings before him quail | 720 | 4 |
| And the mercies eternally new | 231 | 5 |
| And the mysterious One | 644 | 4 |
| And the performing God | 659 | 2 |
| And the prospect dark appears | 878 | 4 |
| And the portals high are lifted | 720 | 1 |
| And the servant of sin in a moment is free | 160 | 2 |
| †And the silver moon by night | 631 | 3 |
| And the Spirit of faith he imparts | 488 | 4 |
| And the sweet task of love. | 539 | 4 |
| And the universe filled with the glory of God | 219 | 7 |
| And the vast fabric still sustains | 600 | 1 |
| And the whole Trinity descends | 262 | 2 |
| And the wintry tempests blow | 672 | 3 |
| And the young ravens when they cry | 225 | 4 |
| And thee, my sanctifying Lord | 304 | 6 |
| And thee, of both, to be but One | 751 | 3 |
| And thee their utmost Saviour own | 17 | 2 |
| And their best wishes to fulfil | 637 | 9 |
| And their glad hearts with holy rapture burn | 691 | 4 |
| And their pride, like angry waters. | 621 | 2 |
| And their quickening virtue taste. | 882 | 7 |
| And then accept our prayer | 546 | 4 |
| And then by Gilead's balm restored | 89 | 3 |

| AND THEN | AND THINE |

|  | HYMN | VERSE |
|---|---|---|
| And then enrich the poor | 84 | 5 |
| And then fill up thy heavenly fold | 444 | 4 |
| And then from earth release | 998 | 5 |
| And then from the body set free | 70 | 3 |
| And then I joyfully depart | 913 | 4 |
| And then I raised my voice in prayer | 559 | 3 |
| And then I shall cleave unto thee | 911 | 3 |
| And then I shall love thee again | 911 | 4 |
| And then I shall never remove | 911 | 3 |
| And then I to thy arms ascend | 913 | 4 |
| And then in heaven our journey ends | 437 | 5 |
| And then my Resurrection be | 670 | 8 |
| And then my spotless soul receive | 436 | 10 |
| And then our sacrifice | 423 | 3 |
| And then remove the load | 84 | 6 |
| And then resign my breath | 167 | 4 |
| And then the heirs of glory take | 894 | 2 |
| And then the joys of heaven | 252 | 6 |
| And then the load remove | 105 | 2 |
| And then the pardoning God I know | 128 | 7 |
| And then the strife give o'er | 92 | 7 |
| And then their saving gospel seal | 871 | 2 |
| And then they preach and testify | 872 | 2 |
| And then to behold it above | 78 | 1 |
| And then to enjoy it above | 371 | 1 |
| And then to join the heavenly choir | 834 | 1 |
| And then to re-drink it above | 871 | 2 |
| And then to the city receive | 70 | 3 |
| And then transplant to Paradise | 474 | 1 |
| And then transport away | 510 | 6 |
| And then we give thee back thine own | 294 | 2 |
| And then we in thy Spirit groan | 294 | 2 |
| And then with sacred peace | 84 | 4 |
| And thence, on wings of angels, ride | 504 | 8 |
| And thence their pleasing savour took | 702 | 4 |
| And therefore now we thank our God | 248 | 5 |
| †And therefore our God the outcasts hath chose | 212 | 3 |
| And there for ever keep | 162 | 1 |
| And there for ever weep | 188 | 6 |
| And there, from care released | 943 | 10 |
| And there may I, though vile as he | 798 | 2 |
| And these dry bones shall live | 486 | 4 |
| And these rejoicing eyes | 956 | 1 |
| And they all are devoted to him | 231 | 12 |
| And they have robbed me of my God | 112 | 1 |
| And they seem to toil in vain | 878 | 6 |
| And they shall praise a pardoning God | 574 | 12 |
| And they that in thy house do dwell | 600 | 4 |
| And they that know and see him | 943 | 3 |
| And they that know thy name will trust | 545 | 2 |
| And they who fain would serve thee best | 969 | 5 |
| And they who with their Leader | 943 | 10 |
| And thine to us so great | 763 | 3 |

| | HYMN | VERSE |
|---|---|---|
| And think and speak the same | 630 | 2 |
| And think how soon my sway may end | 470 | 10 |
| And think ourselves sincere | 83 | 2 |
| And this is all my boast | 669 | 2 |
| †And this I shall prove | 205 | 6 |
| And this thy grace must give | 920 | 1 |
| And this (transporting thought!) shall be | 652 | — |
| And this will I require | 110 | 6 |
| And those who put their trust in thee | 671 | 3 |
| And thou art he that guards my lot | 249 | 2 |
| And thou art justified | 36 | 4 |
| And thou art loved alone | 403 | 1 |
| And thou art merciful to all | 249 | 6 |
| And thou by reverent love unite | 807 | 5 |
| And thou, descending, fill the place | 994 | 2 |
| And thou hast all my wanderings seen | 180 | 3 |
| And thou hast bid me always cry | 93 | 1 |
| And thou in me shalt live | 115 | 5 |
| And thou my rising sun | 213 | 2 |
| And thou shalt be our chosen God | 664 | 5 |
| And thou shalt call thine exile home | 177 | 5 |
| And thou shalt form my soul anew | 366 | 3 |
| And thou shalt give me power to pray | 282 | 4 |
| And thou shalt make me pure within | 366 | 3 |
| And thou shalt meet him there | 605 | 7 |
| And thou shalt reign with me | 315 | 4 |
| And thou shalt still prepare | 310 | 4 |
| And thou shalt there a husband meet | 482 | 3 |
| And thou shalt wear this glorious wreath | 315 | 4 |
| And thou wilt deign to call me thine | 909 | 3 |
| And thou wilt not quit thy right | 287 | 3 |
| And thou with judgment clad shalt come | 648 | 4 |
| And, though exalted, feels afresh | 725 | 3 |
| †And though it linger till the night | 626 | 4 |
| And though my body may not | 943 | 7 |
| And though the worms this skin devour | 927 | 2 |
| And though they take our life | 856 | 4 |
| And though thy face I cannot see | 130 | 3 |
| And though to worms my flesh he gives | 928 | 1 |
| And Three in nature One | 256 | 2 |
| And throng the downward road | 21 | 1 |
| And through eternity | 680 | 5 |
| And through heaven's vault resound thy praise | 241 | 1 |
| And through my Saviour's blood alone | 924 | 2 |
| And through the fire pursue my way | 272 | 3 |
| And through the howling wilderness | 800 | 5 |
| And through the ocean guides | 1003 | 1 |
| And through the paths of heavenly peace | 985 | 2 |
| And through the paths of pleasantness | 472 | 6 |
| And through the pleasing snares of vice | 657 | 6 |
| And through the shades of death unknown | 686 | 4 |
| And through this desert land | 675 | 5 |
| And through unnumbered years he reigns | 713 | 4 |

|  | Hymn | Verse |
|---|---|---|
| And throughly cleansed my heart | 166 | 8 |
| And throughly convert | 160 | 4 |
| And throughly purge thy floor | 502 | 1 |
| And thunder's voice appal | 1003 | 3 |
| And thus anticipate by faith | 907 | 3 |
| And thus from works I cease | 92 | 5 |
| And thus on thee most glorious | 958 | 2 |
| And thus prepare to meet him | 932 | 4 |
| And thus proclaim in joyful song | 991 | 2 |
| And thus to all mankind declare | 897 | 3 |
| And thus thy own new name obtain | 72 | 5 |
| And thy good Spirit impart | 243 | 3 |
| And thy holy will obey | 582 | 2 |
| And thy mercy manifold | 743 | 1 |
| And thy own work defend | 258 | 1 |
| And thy redeemed pass o'er | 587 | 6 |
| And thy redemption near | 558 | 6 |
| And thy refreshing grace | 567 | 1 |
| And thy salvation own | 581 | 2 |
| And thy saving health extend | 582 | 1 |
| And thy vicegerents reign | 985 | 1 |
| And time and sense seem all no more | 825 | 4 |
| And timely meet thee in thy way | 455 | 3 |
| And to adore the Lamb | 678 | 4 |
| And to be wholly free from sin | 969 | 5 |
| And to declare thy praise will prove | 437 | 4 |
| And to eternal life retain | 304 | 4 |
| And to him I with singing return | 231 | 1 |
| And to his cross in closest ties | 616 | 11 |
| And to his glory live | 614 | 9 |
| And to his house, we'll go | 740 | 2 |
| And to his testament of love | 903 | 5 |
| And to me a hope vouchsafest | 933 | 13 |
| And to my inmost soul make known | 97 | 6 |
| And to my inmost soul make known | 249 | 2 |
| And to my pardon join | 307 | 1 |
| And to my ransomed spirit show | 129 | 6 |
| And to my ways take heed | 103 | 2 |
| And to my ways take heed | 311 | 1 |
| And to our high abode | 497 | 8 |
| And to our Saviour turn | 84 | 2 |
| And to perfection grow | 424 | 2 |
| And to redeem us died | 692 | 2 |
| And to rivers of pleasure he leads | 499 | 7 |
| And to see, beyond the skies | 720 | 6 |
| And to the end endure | 59 | 5 |
| And to the friendless prove a friend | 924 | 3 |
| And to the healing leaves who come | 948 | 4 |
| And to the weary rest | 679 | 2 |
| And to thee, the one Foundation | 990 | 2 |
| And to thine arms my spirit take | 909 | 2 |
| And to thy arms return | 983 | 5 |
| And to thy bosom fly | 25 | 5 |

| | Hymn | Verse |
|---|---|---|
| And to thy bosom take | 724 | 3 |
| And to thy church the pattern give | 489 | 2 |
| And to thy glory die | 527 | 5 |
| And to thy glory live | 323 | 1 |
| And to thy glory live | 335 | 4 |
| And to thy glory live and die | 429 | 4 |
| And to thy gracious eye present | 102 | 1 |
| And to thy holy hill attain | 731 | 6 |
| And to thy love restored | 533 | 4 |
| And to thy people join | 94 | 5 |
| And to thy sceptre all subdue | 457 | 1 |
| And to thy temple come | 383 | 3 |
| And to thyself receive | 384 | 4 |
| And toil for precious souls, beloved | 871 | 2 |
| And told thy wondrous ways | 584 | 1 |
| And took their flight | 870 | 1 |
| And toss their troubled waves on high | 600 | 3 |
| And touch my lips with hallowed fire | 440 | 1 |
| And touch their hallowed lips with fire | 255 | 1 |
| And touch their lips with fire | 733 | 3 |
| And trace the providential way | 470 | 7 |
| And train us up in all thy ways | 89 | 4 |
| And trample death beneath their feet | 69 | 3 |
| And trample on thy richer love | 454 | 8 |
| And trampled on thy love | 182 | 2 |
| And transport you away | 488 | 6 |
| And treads the downward road | 788 | 3 |
| And treads the oppressor in the dust | 585 | 3 |
| And tread the tempter down | 675 | 9 |
| And treasure above | 491 | 2 |
| And treasure up our gracious tears | 507 | 3 |
| And trees of life for ever grow | 800 | 6 |
| And trees of paradise | 948 | 4 |
| And tremble at the trial near | 469 | 6 |
| And tremble on the brink of fate | 59 | 3 |
| And trembles at thy word | 104 | 1 |
| And trembling own the Almighty God | 38 | 7 |
| And trembling taste our food | 108 | 1 |
| And trembling to its source return | 327 | 2 |
| And tried, by the lure of thy love | 165 | 2 |
| And triumph evermore | 543 | 8 |
| And triumph evermore | 729 | 1 |
| And triumph in redemption found | 977 | 4 |
| And triumph in thy favour | 736 | 2 |
| And triumph in thy name | 482 | 1 |
| And triumph o'er a world of foes | 293 | 4 |
| And triumph o'er trouble and death | 49 | 3 |
| And triumph with your King | 605 | 5 |
| And trust him for all that's to come | 660 | — |
| And trust his bleeding love | 703 | 5 |
| And trust in him alone | 549 | 5 |
| And trust in thy defence | 281 | 5 |
| And trust on thee to feed | 901 | 1 |

| | HYMN | VERSE |
|---|---|---|
| And trust thee for a perfect cure | 408 | 7 |
| And trust thee though thou slay | 865 | 5 |
| And trust thou wilt not long delay | 134 | 6 |
| And trust upon the Lord | 786 | 2 |
| And truth, and holiness, and joy | 750 | 5 |
| And truth and love, let all men see | 473 | 5 |
| And try their choicest strains | 263 | 6 |
| And tuneful notes employ | 741 | 5 |
| And tune thy people's heart | 204 | 1 |
| And turn at once from every sin | 84 | 2 |
| And turn his sharpest dart aside | 458 | 5 |
| And turn our earth to paradise | 441 | 4 |
| And turn their joy to grief | 94 | 4 |
| And turn them to a pardoning God | 433 | 2 |
| And turn to God, and every sin | 83 | 7 |
| And turn, with zealous haste, and run | 455 | 4 |
| And turned the vengeful bolt aside | 980 | 2 |
| And turns their earth to heaven | 862 | 2 |
| And unbelief of heart | 382 | 2 |
| And underneath his feet he cast | 551 | 3 |
| And unlamented die | 21 | 2 |
| And use your every grace | 267 | 3 |
| And utter forth a glorious voice | 552 | 6 |
| And utterly contemned we live | 21 | 2 |
| And vain is help or hope from men | 961 | 6 |
| And valiantly the truth maintain | 445 | 3 |
| And vanquish my heart with the sense of thy love | 160 | 2 |
| And vexed, and urged thee to depart | 161 | 2 |
| And vibrate on our tongue | 204 | 6 |
| And vie with man's more favoured race | 721 | 2 |
| And view my Saviour there | 880 | 5 |
| And view thee bleeding on the tree | 708 | 3 |
| And view the landscape o'er | 938 | 6 |
| And vindicate *his* right | 465 | 2 |
| And vindicate thy gracious will | 270 | 2 |
| And visions of eternal day | 328 | 3 |
| And visit every nation | 613 | 3 |
| And wail their lost estate | 623 | 5 |
| And waited patiently | 566 | 1 |
| And wait, expecting to receive | 860 | 4 |
| And wait for all our inward heaven | 483 | 1 |
| And wait his grace to prove | 781 | 4 |
| And wait his heaven to share | 539 | 10 |
| And wait the healing grace | 166 | 2 |
| And wait the heavenly gift | 762 | 2 |
| And wait thy fulness to receive | 865 | 8 |
| And wait thy greatness to adore | 649 | 1 |
| And wait thy sanctifying word | 17 | 2 |
| And wait till all thou art is mine | 134 | 6 |
| And wait till Christ appear | 345 | 1 |
| And wait to be fully restored | 911 | 4 |
| And wait to be pardoned through Jesus's grace | 40 | 2 |
| And wait to taste how good thou art | 306 | 1 |

| | HYMN | VERSE |
|---|---|---|
| And wait to taste thy perfect grace | 230 | 1 |
| And wait unwearied all my days | 177 | 5 |
| And wait upon thy saints below | 17 | 8 |
| And wait with arms of faith to embrace | 415 | 2 |
| And waiting for thy blood to impart | 410 | 3 |
| And waits to prove thine utmost will | 408 | 3 |
| And waits to tear his sleeping prey | 310 | 2 |
| And wake to righteousness | 59 | 3 |
| And walk and talk himself with me | 328 | 2 |
| And walk in the light of the lamb | 946 | 2 |
| And walk unburned in fire | 329 | 2 |
| And walk with our God, till we fly to the skies | 760 | 5 |
| And walked unhurt in fire | 359 | 1 |
| And walking in the good | 320 | 1 |
| And, walking in the light of God | 740 | 7 |
| And wanders from her God | 788 | 3 |
| And want no other heaven | 528 | 3 |
| And want thine utmost power to save | 396 | 2 |
| And wars and fightings cease | 407 | 4 |
| And wash, and make us wholly clean | 523 | 6 |
| And wash and seal the sons of God | 9 | 3 |
| And wash me white as snow | 184 | 1 |
| And wash my nature white as snow | 397 | 8 |
| And wash the Æthiop white | 1 | 9 |
| And wash them white as snow | 35 | 7 |
| And watch against the power of sound | 204 | 5 |
| And watch a moment to secure | 55 | 4 |
| And watches to devour | 310 | 2 |
| And watchful troops of angels place | 465 | 4 |
| And watching to devour us | 856 | 3 |
| And watching unto prayer | 267 | 3 |
| And watching unto prayer | 301 | 3 |
| And watching unto prayer | 303 | 1 |
| And watching unto prayer | 998 | 3 |
| And watering our divine abode | 569 | 4 |
| And ways into his hands | 831 | 1 |
| And we are Christ's, and Christ is God's | 1001 | 10 |
| And we are just in him | 625 | 6 |
| And we are to the margin come | 949 | 3 |
| And we, even we | 276 | 3 |
| And we expect to die | 949 | 3 |
| And we in hymns below | 15 | 2 |
| And we shall all be lost in love | 490 | 7 |
| And we shall be where sons are not | 984 | 3 |
| And we shall be where tempests cease | 984 | 4 |
| And we shall be with those that rest | 984 | 1 |
| And we shall do the same | 469 | 5 |
| And we shall in thine image shine | 380 | 8 |
| And we shall reach the endless rest | 984 | 6 |
| And we shall then behold thee near | 450 | 7 |
| And we shall weep no more | 984 | 5 |
| And we the life of God shall know | 685 | 4 |
| And we will never end | 299 | 2 |

## AND WEAR — AND WHILE

| | Hymn | Verse |
|---|---|---|
| And wear it as my due | 405 | 8 |
| And wear our praises as thy crown | 677 | 1 |
| And weary, sinful days | 920 | 5 |
| And weep for their return in vain | 461 | 2 |
| And well-dissembled love | 311 | 1 |
| †And were this world all devils o'er | 856 | 3 |
| And wets his path with tears | 623 | 6 |
| And whatever I can be | 769 | 5 |
| And what for him will ye not do | 746 | 2 |
| And what he wills is best | 832 | 2 |
| And what I am by grace | 502 | 3 |
| And what my father's house to thee | 206 | 1 |
| And, what thou most desirest | 988 | 3 |
| And when absolved we live | 653 | 5 |
| And when created nature dies | 237 | 3 |
| And when created nature dies | 241 | 4 |
| And when his strokes are felt | 610 | 7 |
| And, when I fail on earth, secure | 44 | 5 |
| And when I have my Saviour's mind | 830 | 8 |
| And when I in thy person see | 124 | 4 |
| And when I lay this body down | 69 | 1 |
| And when I quit this cumbrous clay | 69 | 2 |
| And, when I would to sin return | 916 | 1 |
| And when in sins and sorrows sunk | 657 | 7 |
| And when life's short day is past | 970 | 2 |
| And when like wandering sheep we strayed | 608 | 2 |
| And when my all of strength shall fail | 140 | 5 |
| And when my voice is lost in death | 224 | 1 |
| And when my voice is lost in death | 224 | 4 |
| And when my voice is lost in death | 638 | 2 |
| And when our hearts are cold and dead | 696 | 2 |
| †And when, redeemed from sin and hell | 795 | 5 |
| And when the storms of life shall cease | 373 | 9 |
| And when thou didst thy face conceal | 180 | 2 |
| And when thou dost in glory come | 64 | 8 |
| And when thou hearest, Lord, forgive | 993 | 2 |
| †And when thy purity we share | 247 | 2 |
| And when to fight, and when to fly | 306 | 3 |
| And when to meet thee we prepare | 865 | 2 |
| And when we bring them to thy throne | 992 | 4 |
| †And when we rise in love renewed | 256 | 6 |
| And whensoe'er I hence depart | 44 | 6 |
| And where his love resolves to bless | 650 | 2 |
| And where is all his wisdom gone | 422 | 1 |
| And where the gospel-day | 870 | 1 |
| And where thou art appear no more | 955 | 2 |
| And where thou art is heaven | 415 | 5 |
| And where thou art is heaven | 548 | 6 |
| And, "Where's thy victory, boasting grave" | 712 | 8 |
| And while the bursting clouds come down | 62 | 2 |
| And while the truth of God remains | 250 | 6 |
| And, while to thy sweet yoke I bow | 471 | 5 |
| And while we do thy blessed will | 536 | 2 |

| | Hymn | Verse |
|---|---|---|
| And whispers I am his | 213 | 8 |
| And whoever hath found it hath paradise found | 205 | 3 |
| And who in heart approaches thee | 81 | 1 |
| And who our poverty retain | 874 | 2 |
| And who shall stay thy hand | 831 | 7 |
| And wholly lost in thee | 98 | 2 |
| And wholly sanctify | 761 | 4 |
| And why not then (let Satan say) | 820 | 3 |
| And why should hills or mountains shake | 223 | 3 |
| And why together brought | 510 | 2 |
| And wide diffuse the golden blaze | 333 | 5 |
| And wide his royal bounties flow | 868 | 1 |
| And wide unfold the ethereal scene | 557 | 8 |
| And will he write his name | 650 | 4 |
| And will in them for ever dwell | 629 | 5 |
| And will not let thee bless | 778 | 2 |
| And will not quit my claim | 361 | 1 |
| †And will this sovereign King | 650 | 4 |
| And wilt no more remove | 548 | 2 |
| And wilt thou not cherish the children of men | 1013 | 1 |
| And wilt thou now thy wrath retain | 178 | 2 |
| And wilt to all thy followers show | 668 | 2 |
| And, winters softened by thy care | 978 | 3 |
| And win the well-fought day | 268 | 4 |
| And wipe away his servant's tears | 948 | 2 |
| And wipe the latest tear away | 849 | 5 |
| And wipe the weeping eyes | 842 | 2 |
| And Wisdom is my name | 667 | 1 |
| And wisdom's ways approve | 469 | 4 |
| And wise from evil to depart | 306 | 5 |
| And wise to salvation he makes us through faith | 211 | 3 |
| And, wishing us to gain our cause | 827 | 2 |
| And with actions bold and meek | 769 | 1 |
| And with actions brotherly | 769 | 3 |
| And, with all majesty divine | 770 | 7 |
| And with a single heart | 321 | 1 |
| And with a thankful tongue | 605 | 1 |
| And with breathless expectation | 882 | 3 |
| And with especial grace approveth | 595 | 2 |
| And with gladness | 878 | 8 |
| And with him placed on my right hand | 548 | 4 |
| And with his angelic train | 720 | 7 |
| And with his daily bounties fed | 1023 | — |
| And with his glorious presence here | 947 | 7 |
| And with me let thy Spirit stay | 820 | 1 |
| And with me my reward I bring | 948 | 3 |
| And with my Saviour die | 122 | 5 |
| And with singing to Paradise go | 491 | 2 |
| And with singing to Zion return | 491 | 1 |
| And with the angels take thy part | 964 | 4 |
| And with the arms of faith embrace | 196 | 1 |
| And with the trump of God | 58 | 1 |
| And with these eyes my Saviour see | 931 | Cho. |

| | Hymn | Verse |
|---|---|---|
| And with thine ancients reign | 834 | 1 |
| And with thine own abide | 411 | 2 |
| And with those a covenant made | 989 | 1 |
| And with thy saints in glory seat | 648 | 6 |
| And with thyself my spirit fill | 964 | 6 |
| And with triumph declare | 231 | 7 |
| And with wisdom kind and clear | 769 | 2 |
| And with words that help and heal | 769 | 1 |
| And without a rival reign | 824 | 4 |
| And without end of days | 242 | 1 |
| And without praises die | 610 | 2 |
| And witness a heaven below | 79 | 2 |
| And witness all their sins forgiven | 82 | 8 |
| And witness, from all sin set free | 401 | 6 |
| And witness the power of his passion below | 219 | 2 |
| And witness thou hast died for me | 33 | 2 |
| And witness with the blood | 85 | 1 |
| And witness with the water now | 476 | 5 |
| And witnessing his mind to us | 770 | 7 |
| And wonder at his love | 34 | 3 |
| And wonder at thy boundless love | 206 | 1 |
| And, wondering, own thee for their God | 588 | 4 |
| And wondrous in our eyes | 617 | 4 |
| And words of peace reveal | 741 | 1 |
| And works his sovereign will | 845 | 1 |
| And worldly thoughts forget | 485 | 2 |
| And worlds created by thy nod | 642 | 5 |
| And worms have learned to lisp thy name | 316 | 4 |
| And worship at thy feet | 558 | 2 |
| And worship at thy feet | 948 | 7 |
| And worship only thee | 787 | 5 |
| And worship toward thy holy place | 543 | 5 |
| And worthily set forth his praise | 492 | 1 |
| And would be poorer still | 109 | 5 |
| And would not be made whole | 166 | 8 |
| And would not let him rest | 215 | 2 |
| And would thy word receive | 693 | 3 |
| And wounded mortality | 274 | 1 |
| And wrap me in thy crimson vest | 128 | 6 |
| And wrap me in thy love | 109 | 4 |
| And wrap thee in my clay | 772 | 3 |
| And wrestle for his friends with thee | 524 | 2 |
| And wrestle for thy love | 982 | 2 |
| And wrestle, Lord, with thee | 83 | 8 |
| And wrestle till the break of day | 140 | 1 |
| And write perfection on my heart | 369 | 1 |
| And write them on our faithful heart | 754 | 3 |
| And write thy law within | 139 | 5 |
| And write thy name upon my heart | 118 | 2 |
| And writ the blessing in thy word | 879 | 1 |
| And yawning whirlpools of despair | 272 | 5 |
| And yet bold in doing right | 882 | 5 |
| And yet from him I stay | 152 | 1 |

| | Hymn | Verse |
|---|---|---|
| And yet he called me still | 697 | 5 |
| And yet how unconcerned we go | 42 | 6 |
| And yet I hear a voice that bids me "Come" | 79 | 1 |
| And yet thou deign'st to come to me | 38 | 4 |
| And yet vouchsafes in Christian lands | 992 | 1 |
| And yield allegiance to its Lord | 448 | 2 |
| And yield my perfect will to approve | 561 | 10 |
| And yield thee all my heart | 575 | 4 |
| And yield them up to thee | 889 | 3 |
| And yields a free repast | 880 | 3 |
| And you, and Christ, are here | 539 | 7 |
| And you and I ascend at last | 333 | 4 |
| And you and I shall surely stand | 537 | 8 |
| And you in Jesu's name receive | 490 | 2 |
| And you, ye waters, roll | 747 | 4 |
| And zeal, and unity, and power | 456 | 2 |
| And Zion in her anguish | 943 | 3 |
| Angelical happiness prove | 79 | 2 |
| †Angel of gospel grace | 704 | 2 |
| †Angel powers the throne surround | 75 | 3 |
| Angel seemed to human sight | 768 | 8 |
| Angels and archangels all | 221 | 2 |
| †Angels and archangels join | 728 | 3 |
| Angels and men agree | 685 | 1 |
| Angels and men before it fall | 37 | 1 |
| Angels and men be joined | 34 | 1 |
| Angels, assist our mighty joys | 699 | 5 |
| †Angels catch the approving sound | 51 | 5 |
| Angels descend with songs again | 585 | 12 |
| Angels, joyful to attend | 921 | 2 |
| †Angels our servants are | 21 | 5 |
| †Angels rejoice in Jesu's grace | 721 | 2 |
| Angels shrink within their wings | 260 | 2 |
| Angels sing, "A child is born" | 51 | 3 |
| Angels that surround his throne | 53 | 1 |
| Angels to beckon me | 848 | 3 |
| Angels tremble as they gaze | 643 | 2 |
| Angels with both wings veil their eyes | 38 | 2 |
| †Angels your clear voices raise | 639 | 2 |
| *Angels your march oppose | 315 | 1 |
| †Anger and sloth, desire and pride | 417 | 4 |
| †Anger I no more shall feel | 355 | 6 |
| Anger, lust, and pride, thou art | 382 | 2 |
| Anguish, and sin, and dread, and pain | 614 | 3 |
| Anoint and cheer our soiled face | 751 | 2 |
| Anointed kings and priests to God | 16 | 4 |
| Anointed priests and kings | 423 | 2 |
| Apointed to declare his will | 107 | 2 |
| Another and another year | 981 | 2 |
| Another various year | 979 | 2 |
| Answered them in all their fear | 606 | 3 |
| Answer, if mine thou art | 184 | 3 |
| Answer me in dreams divine | 287 | 3 |

| | Hymn | Verse |
|---|---|---|
| Answer, O God, for me | 288 | 2 |
| †Answer on them the end of all | 473 | 2 |
| Answer our faith's effectual prayer. | 745 | 1 |
| †Answer that gracious end in me | 375 | 2 |
| Answer the deep unuttered groan | 134 | 4 |
| Answer the multitude's demand | 874 | 3 |
| Answer the universal "Come" | 749 | 3 |
| Answer, thou Man of grief and love | 128 | 2 |
| †Answer thy mercy's whole design | 686 | 4 |
| Answer to the Saviour's call | 29 | 1 |
| Answering his all-powerful prayer | 755 | 1 |
| Answers the beholder's face. | 824 | 5 |
| Antedate the joys above | 519 | 1 |
| Anticipate their heavenly rest | 493 | 2 |
| Anticipate your heaven below | 1 | 10 |
| Apace to death decline | 931 | 1 |
| Apollyon is their king, we know | 447 | 1 |
| †Apostles, martyrs, prophets there | 939 | 5 |
| Appear, and banish my complaint | 146 | 1 |
| Appear, and bid me turn again | 296 | 2 |
| †Appear, as when of old confest | 35 | 4 |
| Appear before thy awful face | 241 | 1 |
| Appear before thy sight | 543 | 2 |
| Appear, in my poor heart appear | 388 | 7 |
| Appear in the clouds of the sky | 77 | 2 |
| Appear my affliction to end | 911 | 3 |
| Appear, my confidence to abase | 126 | 5 |
| †Appear my sanctuary from sin | 124 | 2 |
| Appear our Advocate with God | 648 | 5 |
| Appear our omnipotent Lord | 220 | 1 |
| †Appear with clouds on Sion's hill | 62 | 6 |
| Appears, and hell is close behind | 181 | 5 |
| Appears, by grace forgiven | 528 | 3 |
| Appeased by the charms of thy grace | 220 | 5 |
| Apply thy blood to make us pure | 254 | 2 |
| *Appointed by thee, we meet in thy name | 484 | 1 |
| Appoint my soul a place | 811 | 4 |
| Approach his courts, besiege his throne | 268 | 1 |
| Approach with joy his courts unto | 607 | 3 |
| †Arabia's desert ranger | 586 | 4 |
| Ardent for thy coming o'er | 921 | 5 |
| Are all in Jesu's name | 314 | 3 |
| Are all in thee, the Truth, fulfilled | 702 | 5 |
| Are all laid up above | 325 | 4 |
| Are big with mercy, and shall break | 845 | 2 |
| Are blessings in disguise | 846 | 2 |
| Are both abhorred by thee | 543 | 3 |
| Are called his sovereign will to embrace | 840 | 1 |
| Are carried downward by the flood. | 41 | 5 |
| Are clad in robes of white | 943 | 10 |
| Are conscious most of wrong within | 969 | 5 |
| Are crowned with heavenly love | 624 | 2 |
| Are decked in glorious sheen | 943 | 9 |

| | Hymn | Verse |
|---|---|---|
| Are fed, on thy bosom reclined | 228 | 1 |
| Are full, thou source and life of all. | 494 | 5 |
| Are life, and light, and bliss | 696 | 5 |
| Are light, and majesty | 650 | 1 |
| Are like an evening gone | 41 | 4 |
| Are noted in thy book | 575 | 2 |
| Are not thy mercies large and free. | 574 | 1 |
| Are now at work for me | 832 | 6 |
| Are pages in that book, to show | 662 | 2 |
| Are possible to God | 138 | 4 |
| Are sent from heaven above | 988 | Cho. |
| *Are there not in the labourer's day. | 281 | 1 |
| Are to our Jesus given | 729 | 3 |
| Are we not met in thy great name. | 490 | 4 |
| Arise, and meet him in the sky | 55 | 3 |
| Arise, my love, make haste away | 948 | 3 |
| *Arise, my soul, arise | 194 | 1 |
| *Arise, my soul, arise | 202 | 1 |
| †Arise, O God, maintain thy cause | 39 | 6 |
| †Arise, O Lord, into thy rest | 629 | 2 |
| Arise resplendent from afar. | 445 | 1 |
| †Arise, stir up thy power | 737 | 12 |
| Arise, the woman's conquering Seed | 299 | 3 |
| Arise to administer thy grace | 449 | 1 |
| Armed in the arms of heavenly light | 266 | 3 |
| Armed with that adamant and gold | 267 | 1 |
| Armed with the unconquerable mind | 277 | 3 |
| Arm me in this fiery hour | 359 | 1 |
| †Arm me with jealous care | 318 | 2 |
| †Arm me with thy whole armour, Lord | 196 | 3 |
| Arm my soul with Jesu's name | 910 | 4 |
| Arm my weakness with thy power. | 271 | 1 |
| †Arm of God, thy strength put on | 158 | 4 |
| *Arm of the Lord, awake, awake | 386 | 1 |
| *Arm of the Lord, awake, awake | 443 | 1 |
| Arm our cautioned souls with patience | 60 | 1 |
| Arose the acceptable year | 220 | 1 |
| Around *his* sacred head | 465 | 4 |
| Around me clouds of darkness roll. | 154 | 3 |
| Around my Saviour stand | 939 | 5 |
| Around one common mercy-seat | 825 | 3 |
| Around the eternal throne | 61 | 3 |
| Around thy board, and round our own | 978 | 5 |
| Around thy throne of majesty | 592 | 2 |
| Around us all his glory shall display | 691 | 6 |
| Around us rolls the ceaseless tide | 863 | 1 |
| †Arrayed in glorious grace | 930 | 4 |
| †Arrayed in mortal flesh | 675 | 3 |
| Arrays in garments white and pure | 800 | 8 |
| Arrest the prisoner of thy love | 296 | 3 |
| Art able now our souls to save | 397 | 4 |
| Art always faithful to thy word | 157 | 5 |
| Art high above our thought | 244 | 1 |

| | Hymn | Verse |
|---|---|---|
| Art King from all eternity | 600 | 2 |
| Art not thou the sinner's friend | 116 | 1 |
| †Art thou not able to convert | 416 | 5 |
| Art thou not our living Head | 506 | 2 |
| †Art thou not touched with human woe | 157 | 4 |
| Art thou not willing too | 416 | 5 |
| Art thou sore distrest | 793 | 1 |
| †Art thou the God of Jews alone | 444 | 2 |
| †Art thou the Lamb of God | 883 | 2 |
| Art thou the man that died for me | 140 | 3 |
| *Art thou weary, art thou languid | 793 | 1 |
| Art willing to restore them now | 397 | 4 |
| Art with God the Father one | 257 | 7 |
| As a great rock extends its shade | 292 | 2 |
| As a maid her mistress' word | 620 | 2 |
| †As a servant marks his lord | 620 | 2 |
| As a thief in deepest night | 54 | 4 |
| As a thirsty land for showers | 156 | 1 |
| As angels do above | 275 | 7 |
| As angels do above | 528 | 4 |
| As angels do in heaven | 119 | 5 |
| As angels do in heaven | 229 | 5 |
| As angels do in heaven | 857 | 8 |
| As angels, who behold thy face | 857 | 3 |
| As at the beginning, free | 173 | 2 |
| †As beautiful as useful there | 72 | 2 |
| As best to thee may seem | 837 | 3 |
| As burning luminaries, chase | 446 | 5 |
| As by heavenly manna fed | 238 | 2 |
| As by heavenly manna fed | 1019 | 3 |
| As by the celestial host | 430 | 1 |
| As by the celestial host | 430 | 6 |
| As by the choirs above | 857 | 2 |
| As careless of the noontide heats | 46 | 1 |
| As children that have done amiss | 797 | 2 |
| As circling Sabbaths bless our eyes | 978 | 5 |
| As clouds before the mid-day sun | 337 | 4 |
| As crystal her buildings are clear | 73 | 3 |
| As days and months increase | 42 | 2 |
| As dust before the whirlwind flies | 502 | 4 |
| As earthen vessels, break their bones | 541 | 4 |
| As Eve thou gav'st to Adam | 996 | 4 |
| As far as hell from heaven | 93 | 3 |
| As far as hell from heaven | 150 | 1 |
| †As far from abjectness as pride | 470 | 8 |
| As far from danger as from fear | 326 | 2 |
| As far from God as hell from heaven | 180 | 6 |
| As fathers when their children cry | 245 | 1 |
| As fearless of the evening cold | 46 | 1 |
| †As flowers their opening leaves display | 494 | 6 |
| †As giants may they run their race | 446 | 5 |
| As God of God, and Light of Light | 668 | 1 |
| As guardians of his giddy youth | 467 | 8 |

| | HYMN | VERSE |
|---|---|---|
| As his head he on Calvary bowed | 488 | 5 |
| As his own lawful prey | 501 | 2 |
| As if filled with the fulness of God. | 807 | 4 |
| As I have heard of old | 697 | 7 |
| As incense in thy sight appear | 462· | 1 |
| As in heaven be here adored | 354 | 6 |
| As in heaven on earth adored | 641 | 4 |
| As in his ways abide | 551 | 6 |
| †As in the ancient days appear | 386 | 2 |
| As in thy sight to live | 318 | 2 |
| As Jesu's messenger. | 471 | 1 |
| As kind rebukes from thee | 334 | — |
| †As lightning launched from east to west | 444 | 4 |
| †As listed on Abaddon's side | 442 | 2 |
| As long as God shall live | 941 | 4 |
| As Lord and Master of the whole | 285 | 5 |
| As manna receive dropped down from the skies | 1025 | 2 |
| As man, our mortal weakness thou hast proved | 850 | 5 |
| As more of heaven in each we see | 965 | 5 |
| As Moses or Elijah prays | 298 | 1 |
| As mountains their foundations keep | 563 | 2 |
| As my guide, my guard, my friend. | 824 | 6 |
| As nothing in thine eye | 244 | 1 |
| As now for guilty sinners slain | 902 | 2 |
| As now it fills the choirs above | 656 | 4 |
| As only born to grieve | 21 | 2 |
| As on the margin of the grave | 919 | 1 |
| \*As pants the hart for cooling streams | 567 | 1 |
| As pillars, and go out no more | 492 | 6 |
| †As rain on meadows newly mown | 585 | 4 |
| †As round Jerusalem | 622 | 2 |
| As servants of the Lord most High | 319 | 1 |
| As set to form his tender mind | 467 | 8 |
| †As soon as in him we believe | 79 | 2 |
| As taught by thee, in faith I pray | 357 | 1 |
| As that which built the skies | 659 | 5 |
| †As the apple of an eye | 188 | 6 |
| †As the bright Sun of righteousness | 446 | 6 |
| As the great deep profound | 731 | 5 |
| †As the image in the glass | 824 | 5 |
| As the new-mown grass for rain | 743 | 2 |
| As the old Adam dies | 347 | 3 |
| As the publican distrest | 101 | 4 |
| As the stately cedars spread | 598 | 3 |
| As their stay thy promise taking | 878 | 2 |
| As they called they found him near | 606 | 3 |
| As thine in heaven to be | 696 | 6 |
| As thou art, so let us be | 350 | 1 |
| As thou art with the Father one | 459 | 3 |
| As thou art with thy Father one | 380 | 8 |
| As thou didst bind two natures | 996 | 5 |
| As thou for Christ the Bridegroom | 996 | 6 |
| As thou our prize wilt be | 680 | 5 |

| | Hymn | Verse |
|---|---|---|
| As thou wouldst have it done | 863 | 3 |
| As through the clouds riven the lightnings have shone | 869 | 2 |
| As to lay down his life to redeem us from hell | 808 | 4 |
| As travellers in thirsty lands | 577 | 3 |
| As vessels of thy richest grace | 438 | 2 |
| As when the dread trumpets went forth at thy word | 869 | 4 |
| As with them to partake | 945 | 2 |
| As workers with their God | 745 | 3 |
| As yesterday the same | 135 | 1 |
| As zealous for his glorious name | 319 | 1 |
| Ascending to the holiest place | 724 | 1 |
| Ascribe the everlasting praise | 438 | 2 |
| Ascribe their conquest to the Lamb | 940 | 3 |
| Ascribing salvation to God and the Lamb | 19 | 1 |
| Ascribing salvation to Jesus our King | 859 | 3 |
| †Ashamed I must for ever be | 425 | 2 |
| Ashamed, I sigh, and inly mourn | 210 | 2 |
| Ask, and ye shall all receive | 86 | 1 |
| Ask my Advocate above | 168 | 2 |
| Ask ye, Who is this same | 856 | 2 |
| Asks the work of his own hands | 6 | 1 |
| Asleep within the tomb | 984 | 1 |
| Aspiring to the plains of light | 71 | 3 |
| Assaulted by evil, I scorn to submit | 200 | 6 |
| Assault my faith with treacherous art | 879 | 4 |
| †Assembled here with one accord | 759 | 6 |
| Assembled in thy name | 485 | 1 |
| Assert the kingdom thine | 653 | 7 |
| †Assert thy claim, maintain thy right | 216 | 9 |
| Assert thy royalty divine | 445 | 1 |
| Assert thy worship and renown | 568 | 3 |
| Assist me, Saviour, to adore | 184 | 8 |
| Assist me still my course to run | 289 | 2 |
| Assist me to proclaim | 1 | 2 |
| Assist me with thy heavenly grace | 285 | 1 |
| Assist us to sing thy mercy and love | 199 | 1 |
| Assured, if I my trust betray | 318 | 2 |
| Assured that all who trust in thee | 64 | 2 |
| Assured that if to thee he live | 896 | 3 |
| Assured that thou our souls wilt keep | 524 | 3 |
| Assured that thou through life shalt save | 282 | 5 |
| Assure me now my soul is thine | 148 | 5 |
| Assure me of my great reward | 304 | 7 |
| †Assure my conscience of its part | 765 | 3 |
| †Astonished at thy frowning brow | 38 | 3 |
| Asunder put what God hath joined | 858 | 1 |
| At a marriage-feast like this | 995 | 2 |
| At eve hold not thine hand | 739 | 1 |
| *At even, ere the sun was set | 969 | 1 |
| At every solemn hour of prayer | 860 | 1 |
| At first to Salem came | 460 | 1 |
| At God's right hand | 853 | 4 |

| | Hymn | Verse |
|---|---|---|
| At his command | 800 | 5 |
| At his Redeemer's beck | 61 | 2 |
| At his right hand | 800 | 2 |
| †At Jesus's call | 498 | 2 |
| At Jesus's cries | 707 | 3 |
| At Jesu's everlasting word | 815 | 6 |
| At Jesu's feet abide | 307 | 5 |
| At Jesu's feet to lay it down | 388 | 1 |
| †At last I own it cannot be | 132 | 5 |
| At last, O Lord, let trouble cease | 924 | 1 |
| At my right hand the Lord doth stand | 549 | 5 |
| At once betrayed, denied, or fled | 849 | 3 |
| At once they strike the harmonious wire | 948 | 6 |
| At rest, till it finds rest in thee | 344 | 1 |
| At temptations darksome hour | 769 | 3 |
| At that transporting word | 213 | 4 |
| At that tremendous hour | 471 | 3 |
| At the fountains of the skies | 768 | 4 |
| At the great supper of the Lamb | 677 | 4 |
| At the great rising-day | 929 | 3 |
| At the last trumpet's sounding | 932 | 2 |
| At the point of death I lie | 112 | 4 |
| At this poor dying rate | 763 | 3 |
| At thy command I venture down | 584 | 5 |
| At thy command is still | 1002 | 4 |
| At thy command they sink and drop | 226 | 7 |
| At thy feet adoring fall | 593 | 3 |
| At thy feet their tribute pay | 582 | 2 |
| †At thy rebuke the bloom | 565 | 6 |
| At thy right hand in heaven | 469 | 11 |
| At thy throne I meekly bow | 620 | 1 |
| At times, to faith's foreseeing eye | 944 | 3 |
| At whose supreme command | 800 | 2 |
| At whose supreme decree | 264 | 1 |
| At whose most welcome call | 931 | 3 |
| At work for God, in loved employ | 957 | 4 |
| Athirst for salvation, salvation by grace | 3 | 4 |
| †Attended by the sacred dread | 306 | 5 |
| Attend me all my days | 555 | 5 |
| Attend the Almighty Father's name | 752 | 5 |
| Attend the blissful sound | 880 | 4 |
| Attend the promised Comforter | 376 | 2 |
| Attend the trumpet's sound | 314 | 1 |
| Attend thy feeblest follower's call | 294 | 1 |
| Attend with constant care | 267 | 3 |
| Attends the softest prayer | 831 | 4 |
| Attentive to the trumpet's sound | 55 | 4 |
| Attest that I am born again | 376 | 4 |
| Author and end of my desires | 773 | 1 |
| *Author of faith, appear | 852 | 1 |
| *Author of faith, eternal Word | 95 | 1 |
| Author of faith in me appear | 833 | 5 |
| *Author of faith, on me confer | 805 | 1 |

|  | Hymn | Verse |
|---|---|---|
| *Author of faith, to thee I cry | 118 | 1 |
| †Author of faith, to thee I lift | 784 | 4 |
| *Author of faith, we seek thy face | 458 | 1 |
| Author of my faith he is | 382 | 5 |
| Averse from good and prone to ill | 99 | 3 |
| Awaiting us below | 968 | 4 |
| Awake and bruise the serpent's head | 132 | 3 |
| Awake, and run the heavenly race | 802 | 1 |
| Awake, and sing out of the dust | 362 | 6 |
| Awake, and stir them up to pray | 81 | 3 |
| †Awake from guilty nature's sleep | 1 | 9 |
| Awake, my lute, and bear a part | 576 | 1 |
| *Awake, my soul, and with the sun | 964 | 1 |
| Awake my soul when sin is nigh | 308 | 2 |
| Awake, my voice, and sing | 659 | 1 |
| Awake, no more to sleep | 303 | 1 |
| *Awake, our souls, away, our fears | 802 | 1 |
| Awake out of the soothing dream | 461 | 5 |
| Awake the everlasting song | 241 | 4 |
| †Awake, the woman's conquering Seed | 132 | 3 |
| Awake them by the gospel call | 444 | 2 |
| Awake, ye nations under ground | 929 | 4 |
| Away my doubts and fears | 166 | 2 |
| *Away, my needless fears | 832 | 1 |
| *Away, my unbelieving fear | 803 | 1 |
| Away, sad doubt, and anxious fear | 189 | 4 |
| Away this soul-distracting care | 833 | 1 |
| Away to our eternal rest | 510 | 6 |
| Away to our Redeemer's breast | 510 | 6 |
| *Away with all our trouble | 1026 | — |
| *Away with our fears | 231 | 1 |
| *Away with our fears | 760 | 1 |
| *Away with our sorrow and fear | 73 | 1 |
| †Awed by a mortal's frown, shall I | 279 | 2 |
| Awed into a little child | 628 | 3 |
| Awhile forget your griefs and fears | 333 | 1 |
| †Awhile in flesh disjoined | 482 | 3 |
| Awhile my strength restore | 565 | 9 |
| Awhile show forth thy praise | 356 | 2 |
| Babes, though blind, may find the way | 349 | 2 |
| Back the closing waves shall roll | 672 | 10 |
| Back the flowing billows rolled | 580 | 2 |
| Back to my God at last I fly | 114 | 2 |
| Bade the glorious gospel shine | 605 | 2 |
| Bade the Jewish feast give place | 952 | 2 |
| Bade the waves roar, the planets shine | 651 | 2 |
| †Baffle the crooked serpent's skill | 458 | 5 |
| Baffle the sons of unbelief | 280 | 6 |
| Balm of all my grief and pain | 175 | 2 |
| Balm of my grief and care | 138 | 9 |
| Balm of the wounded conscience, come | 379 | 2 |
| Banquet with the Deity | 723 | 5 |

| | HYMN | VERSE |
|---|---|---|
| Baptized with heavenly fire | 527 | 2 |
| Baptize into thy name | 504 | 3 |
| Baptize this soul with blood | 892 | 4 |
| Baptizer of our spirits thou | 476 | 5 |
| Bare thine arm, and give the blow | 299 | 7 |
| †Barren although my soul remain | 803 | 3 |
| †Barren and withered trees | 981 | 2 |
| Be all cut off, and cast aside | 473 | 4 |
| Be all in Jesu's praise employed | 953 | 4 |
| †Be all my added life employed | 155 | 3 |
| Be all thy wonders showed | 135 | 2 |
| Be anger to my soul unknown | 851 | 4 |
| Be a pilgrimage to God | 995 | 4 |
| Be a true witness for my Lord | 279 | 1 |
| Be at rest | 793 | 1 |
| Be by all that live adored | 582 | 2 |
| Be cast into the crimson tide | 417 | 4 |
| Be cast this moment out | 417 | 3 |
| Be Christ in me, and I in him | 351 | 2 |
| Be clean, as thou, my Lord, art clean | 339 | 2 |
| Be conquered by my instant praye | 141 | 1 |
| Be done on earth, as 'tis in heaven | 366 | 5 |
| Be endless honours done | 644 | 4 |
| Be ever kept in mind | 532 | 3 |
| Be everlasting love | 208 | 4 |
| Be every heart a humble guest | 955 | 3 |
| Be every mourner's sleep to-night | 973 | 5 |
| Be every wish resigned | 846 | 3 |
| Be faithful unto death | 315 | 4 |
| Be fixed on thee alone | 323 | 2 |
| Be found—as, Lord, thou find'st us now | 65 | 6 |
| Be freely saved by grace | 182 | 2 |
| Be furthered, Lord, by thee | 966 | 4 |
| †Be grace from Christ our Lord | 892 | 5 |
| †Be heaven, even now, our soul's abode | 666 | 6 |
| Be heavenly and divine | 930 | 4 |
| Be her sure immortal friend | 915 | 3 |
| †Be he the only scope | 627 | 4 |
| Be in all alike resigned | 355 | 7 |
| Be in thy Spirit, Lord | 960 | — |
| †Be it according to thy will | 171 | 4 |
| Be it according to thy will | 389 | 4 |
| †Be it according to thy word | 118 | 5 |
| *Be it according to thy word | 362 | 1 |
| †Be it according to thy word | 362 | 8 |
| †Be it according to thy word | 395 | 8 |
| †Be it according to thy word | 406 | 6 |
| Be it I no longer now | 890 | 4 |
| Be it known to all mankind | 197 | 5 |
| *Be it my only wisdom here | 320 | 1 |
| †Be it so, they all reply | 75 | 4 |
| †Be it weariness and pain | 295 | 3 |
| Be it with thy presence blessed | 995 | 1 |

| | HYMN | VERSE |
|---|---|---|
| Be jealous for thy glorious name | 547 | 5 |
| Be justified by grace | 1 | 7 |
| *Be known to us in breaking bread | 908 | 1 |
| *Be known to us in breaking bread | 1024 | — |
| Be less than nothing in thy sight | 893 | 4 |
| Be living faith my costly dress | 431 | 4 |
| Be, Lord, for ever thine | 678 | 3 |
| Be, Lord, on me bestowed | 804 | 4 |
| Be mighty signs and wonders done | 993 | 3 |
| Be mindful of thy changeless word | 121 | 3 |
| Be mindful of thy gracious word | 155 | 7 |
| Be mindful of thy gracious word | 393 | 1 |
| Be mindful of thy youngest care | 458 | 2 |
| Be mine this better part | 147 | 3 |
| Be my last thought, How sweet to rest | 973 | 2 |
| Be my refuge and my rest | 292 | 1 |
| Be my safeguard and my tower | 271 | 1 |
| Be my shelter from the storm | 292 | 4 |
| Be no more to sin inclined | 355 | 12 |
| Be now omnipotently near | 386 | 2 |
| Be now the glorious earnest given | 366 | 5 |
| Be of sin the double cure | 709 | 1 |
| Be on his church bestowed | 1005 | 1 |
| Be our domestic altars raised | 997 | 2 |
| Be our immortal food | 908 | 2 |
| †Be present, awful Father | 996 | 4 |
| †Be present, gracious Saviour | 996 | 5 |
| †Be present, Holiest Spirit | 996 | 6 |
| Be registered above | 892 | 2 |
| Be saved from sin; in Jesus rest | 2 | 4 |
| Be saved to sin no more | 798 | 3 |
| Be set to hallow all we find | 965 | 4 |
| Be short our tunes, our words be few | 316 | 5 |
| Be sounding in our ears | 55 | 3 |
| †Be still! and know that I am God | 92 | 3 |
| †Be still, and learn that I am God | 569 | 10 |
| Be still my comforter and guide | 312 | 5 |
| Be straight, the rugged places plain | 836 | 5 |
| Be sullen, or repine | 844 | 6 |
| Be sure to win the field | 267 | 1 |
| Be taught thy precepts, and thy grace | 997 | 3 |
| Be tender of thy new-born lambs | 458 | 2 |
| Be that to others given | 167 | 3 |
| Be the pure flame of love | 300 | 2 |
| Be the wanderer's resting-place | 109 | 6 |
| Be these the friends in whom I trust | 609 | 3 |
| Be they many or few | 231 | 12 |
| Be this my happy choice | 147 | 4 |
| †Be this my one great business here | 59 | 5 |
| Be this night about my bed | 287 | 1 |
| Be this the cry of every heart | 297 | 4 |
| Be thou a cooling cloud by day | 704 | 3 |
| Be thou all our heart's desire | 399 | 2 |

| | Hymn | Verse |
|---|---|---|
| Be thou alone my constant flame | 373 | 1 |
| Be thou alone my one desire | 351 | 5 |
| †Be thou at my right hand | 944 | 6 |
| Be thou by all thy works adored | 494 | 3 |
| †Be thou exalted, Lord, above | 576 | 3 |
| Be thou for ever near | 880 | 5 |
| Be thou his father, Lord, be thou his friend | 596 | 3 |
| Be thou in them, and they in thee | 992 | 6 |
| Be thou in thy Spirit nigh | 517 | 1 |
| Be thou its finisher | 852 | 1 |
| †Be thou my Counsellor | 675 | 5 |
| Be thou my guide, be thou my way | 44 | 6 |
| Be thou my guide, my strength | 837 | 3 |
| Be thou my hope, my joy, my rest | 577 | 1 |
| †Be thou my joy, be thou my dread | 351 | 6 |
| Be thou my light, be thou my way | 339 | 3 |
| Be thou my strength and righteousness | 786 | 5 |
| Be thou my strength, my light, my way | 25 | 5 |
| Be thou my sure abode | 805 | 4 |
| Be thou, O Christ! the sinner's stay | 934 | 3 |
| †Be thou, O Love, whate'er I want | 379 | 3 |
| †Be thou, O Rock of ages, nigh | 337 | 4 |
| Be thou our everlasting peace | 258 | 3 |
| Be thou our guard while life shall last | 41 | 7 |
| †Be thou our soul's preserver | 968 | 4 |
| Be thou our strong salvation | 818 | 1 |
| Be thou still my help and shield | 839 | 2 |
| Be thou then in mercy near | 672 | 8 |
| Be thou with them | 878 | 1 |
| Be thou with them | 878 | 3 |
| Be thou with them | 878 | 4 |
| Be thy praise my highest aim | 672 | 2 |
| Be thy smile my chief delight | 672 | 2 |
| Be to all the nations told | 743 | 1 |
| Be to our Jesus given | 976 | 2 |
| Be to the churches given | 418 | 3 |
| Be to us what Adam lost | 514 | 4 |
| Be to us what Adam lost | 515 | 3 |
| Be unto the Lamb for ever | 742 | Cho. |
| Be wise, the erring soul to win | 857 | 5 |
| Be wise then, ye who sit on thrones | 541 | 4 |
| Be wise to know your gracious day | 9 | 1 |
| Be with me also in the silent night | 967 | 1 |
| Be with me when the daylight fades away | 967 | 1 |
| Be with us evermore | 991 | 4 |
| †Be with us this day to bless us | 882 | 2 |
| Beamed to still that raging sea | 621 | 3 |
| Bear a momentary pain | 922 | 4 |
| Bear him to the throne of love | 51 | 4 |
| Bear in our faithful minds the end | 537 | 11 |
| Bear me on eagles' wings above | 916 | 3 |
| Bear me, on thy bosom bear | 13 | 3 |
| Bear us to our thrones above | 238 | 4 |

| | Hymn | Verse |
|---|---|---|
| Bearer of our sin and shame | 722 | 1 |
| Bears all its sons away | 41 | 6 |
| Bear'st them through life's disparted wave | 386 | 3 |
| Beauty for ashes to confer | 107 | 5 |
| Because for me my Saviour prays | 982 | 1 |
| Because he first loved me | 43 | 6 |
| †Because I now can nothing do | 126 | 4 |
| Because thou didst for sinners die | 45 | 2 |
| †Because thou lov'dst and diedst for me | 772 | 6 |
| Because thy promise I believe | 796 | 5 |
| Beckoning on his martyr army | 720 | 6 |
| Becomes a sacrifice divine | 858 | 3 |
| Becomes the grandeur of a God | 316 | 1 |
| Before he filled the fountains | 667 | 1 |
| Before him, on the mountains | 586 | 3 |
| Before him prostrate fall | 681 | 7 |
| Before his face I dare not stand | 781 | 4 |
| Before his Father's face | 724 | 1 |
| Before his Father's face | 811 | 4 |
| Before his labourers lies | 535 | 2 |
| Before his people pay | 614 | 10 |
| Before I drew my breath | 784 | 2 |
| Before I hence remove | 325 | 4 |
| Before I hence remove | 436 | 9 |
| Before I read or hear | 887 | — |
| Before I wholly fall away | 309 | 4 |
| *Before Jehovah's awful throne | 608 | 1 |
| †Before me place, in dread array | 59 | 4 |
| Before me sickness, death, the tomb | 799 | 2 |
| †Before my eyes of faith confest | 128 | 6 |
| †Before my faith's enlightened eyes | 283 | 2 |
| Before my infant heart conceived | 657 | 4 |
| Before my ravished eyes | 124 | 4 |
| Before my ravished eyes | 948 | 4 |
| Before our faith they fall | 277 | 6 |
| Before our God appear | 979 | 2 |
| Before the birth of time | 256 | 1 |
| Before the blood we feel | 705 | 3 |
| Before the eternal throne | 958 | 1 |
| Before the evil come | 104 | 2 |
| Before the floods descend | 62 | 2 |
| Before the glory of his face | 814 | 3 |
| *Before the great Three-One | 800 | 9 |
| †Before the hills in order stood | 41 | 3 |
| Before the insufferable blaze | 38 | 2 |
| Before the morning watch I rise | 306 | 1 |
| Before the rising sun | 41 | 4 |
| †Before the Saviour's face | 800 | 11 |
| †Before the throne my Saviour stands | 726 | 2 |
| Before the throne my Surety stands | 202 | 1 |
| Before the throne of love | 724 | 2 |
| Before the whiteness of that throne appear | 794 | 2 |
| Before the world's foundation slain | 189 | 1 |

| | Hymn | Verse |
|---|---|---|
| Before the world's foundation slain | 237 | 1 |
| Before their Judge's face | 540 | 5 |
| Before they're formed within | 632 | 3 |
| Before thou as our Judge appear | 648 | 5 |
| Before thou dost my soul require | 124 | 1 |
| Before thy cross I lie | 982 | 4 |
| Before thy Father reign | 423 | 2 |
| †Before thy glorious eyes we spread | 513 | 2 |
| Before thy glorious face | 253 | 4 |
| Before thy glorious face | 309 | 5 |
| Before thy gracious throne | 982 | 1 |
| Before thy mind I know | 828 | 2 |
| Before thy shearers dumb | 883 | 2 |
| †Before thy sheep, great Shepherd, go | 523 | 3 |
| Before thy throne appear | 510 | 4 |
| Before thy throne of grace | 664 | 2 |
| Before us at the Father's throne | 827 | 7 |
| Before us in thy vesture stand | 901 | 1 |
| †Before us make thy goodness pass | 88 | 4 |
| Before we suffer in our turn | 951 | 3 |
| Before whose bar severe | 55 | 1 |
| Before your Saviour's face | 738 | 6 |
| *Begin, my soul, some heavenly theme | 659 | 1 |
| †Beguiled alas! by Satan's art | 461 | 2 |
| Beheld our helpless grief | 699 | 2 |
| Behind a frowning providence | 845 | 2 |
| Behind, the unpardoned past | 799 | 2 |
| Behold a cloud of incense rise | 523 | 1 |
| Behold, behold the Lamb | 37 | 6 |
| †Behold, for me the victim bleeds | 184 | 5 |
| †Behold him, all ye that pass by | 28 | 2 |
| Behold him present with his aid | 569 | 1 |
| Behold his life-blood stream | 665 | 4 |
| Behold his wrath prevailing | 932 | 3 |
| *Behold, how good a thing | 630 | 1 |
| †Behold, I fall before thy face | 574 | 4 |
| Behold in Christ thy glorious face | 121 | 2 |
| Behold me not with angry look | 574 | 7 |
| †Behold me waiting in the way | 135 | 10 |
| Behold the heavenly Bridegroom nigh | 65 | 1 |
| †Behold the Lamb of God, who bears | 31 | 2 |
| *Behold! the mountain of the Lord | 740 | 1 |
| *Behold the Saviour of mankind | 22 | 1 |
| *Behold the servant of the Lord | 429 | 1 |
| *Behold the sure foundation-stone | 617 | 1 |
| †Behold the violence, the scorn | 588 | 2 |
| †Behold the weary prodigal is come | 596 | 3 |
| Behold the works his hand hath wrought | 569 | 7 |
| Behold thy face and live | 117 | 4 |
| Behold thy open face | 297 | 6 |
| Behold thy servant in distress | 909 | 2 |
| †Behold, to thee our souls aspire | 759 | 8 |
| *Behold us, Lord, a little space | 863 | 1 |

| | Hymn | Verse |
|---|---|---|
| †Behold, with humble faith I bow | 820 | 5 |
| Behold, without a cloud between | 252 | 5 |
| Beholding thee with open face | 351 | 7 |
| Being every moment gives | 661ʳ | 2 |
| *Being of beings, God of love | 654 | 1 |
| *Being of beings, God of love | 1020 | — |
| †Being of beings! may our praise | 494 | 4 |
| Being thou art, and love, and power | 332 | 5 |
| Being's source begins to be | 684 | 2 |
| Believe, and all your sin's forgiven | 30 | 7 |
| Believe, and conquer all | 277 | 6 |
| Believe, and enter in | 403 | 3 |
| Believe, and feel him here | 54 | 2 |
| Believe, and feel thy sins forgiven | 439 | 3 |
| Believe, and I will give you rest | 31 | 3 |
| Believe, and who shall pluck you thence | 561 | 11 |
| Believe, believe in Jesu's name | 36 | 3 |
| Believe, believe the record true | 28 | 3 |
| "Believe," he cries, "believe" | 387 | 1 |
| Believe, hold fast your shield, and who | 267 | 2 |
| †Believe in him that died for thee | 36 | 4 |
| Believe myself to him | 406 | 4 |
| Believe that Jesus reigns | 267 | 2 |
| Believe the word which Christ hath said | 759 | 2 |
| Believe, till freed from sin's remains | 267 | 2 |
| Believe yourselves to heaven | 267 | 2 |
| Believing in their unbelief | 698 | 1 |
| †Believing on my Lord, I find | 217 | 2 |
| Believing, true, and clean | 343 | 3 |
| †Believing, we rejoice | 703 | 5 |
| †Beloved for Jesu's sake | 460 | 3 |
| Bend at thy mercy-seat | 619 | 3 |
| Bend by thy grace, O bend or break | 186 | 5 |
| †Bend the stubborn will to thine | 753 | 8 |
| Bending from thy throne on high | 710 | 1 |
| Beneath his cross I view the day | 932 | 4 |
| Beneath my Father's hand I bow | 331 | 1 |
| Beneath our curse he bowed his head | 127 | 8 |
| Beneath the heaviest load | 844 | 4 |
| Beneath the proud oppressor's frown | 637 | 7 |
| Beneath the shade of dying love | 64 | 1 |
| Beneath the shadow of thy wing | 437 | 8 |
| Beneath the spreading heavens | 804 | 3 |
| Beneath the weight I cannot move | 188 | 1 |
| Beneath thine anger move | 307 | 3 |
| Beneath thine eye we sail | 1003 | 2 |
| Beneath thine own almighty wings | 974 | 1 |
| †Beneath this mountain load of grief | 25 | 4 |
| Beneath thy bloody banner fight | 439 | 1 |
| Beneath thy command | 219 | 7 |
| Beneath thy contemplation | 943 | 8 |
| Beneath thy feet we lie afar | 651 | 5 |
| Beneath thy mercy's wings I rest | 836 | 2 |

| | Hymn | Verse |
|---|---|---|
| †Beneath thy shadow let us sit | 507 | 4 |
| Beneath thy shadow we abide | 326 | 1 |
| Beneath your feet we lie | 21 | 2 |
| †Bent to redeem a sinful race | 648 | 2 |
| Beset on every side | 632 | 4 |
| †Beside all waters sow | 739 | 2 |
| Beside the living stream | 555 | 1 |
| Beside my bed, my Saviour, stand | 923 | 1 |
| Besmeared with dust, and sweat, and blood | 23 | 1 |
| Bestow that peace unknown | 343 | 7 |
| Bestow thy promised rest | 982 | 4 |
| Bestrews the land with death | 986 | 2 |
| Bethel I'll raise | 848 | 4 |
| †Better a day thy courts within | 590 | 4 |
| Better than daughters or than sons | 68 | 4 |
| †Better than my boding fears | 335 | 2 |
| Better that we had never heard | 454 | 5 |
| †Better that we had never known | 454 | 6 |
| Between the cherubim he sits | 280 | 1 |
| Between the felons crucified | 774 | 7 |
| Betwixt the living and the dead | 81 | 2 |
| Betwixt the mount and multitude | 222 | 1 |
| Beyond his chain he cannot go | 280 | 3 |
| Beyond the bounds of time and space | 239 | 3 |
| †Beyond the bounds of time and space | 333 | 2 |
| Beyond the grave, beyond the power | 63 | 5 |
| Beyond the reach of earth or hell | 916 | 4 |
| †Beyond the reach of mortals, spread | 446 | 4 |
| Beyond the starry sky | 943 | 2 |
| Beyond thine other wonders shine | 656 | 1 |
| Beyond what angel minds can paint | 295 | 5 |
| Bid all his griefs and troubles cease | 985 | 2 |
| Bid all our fallen race arise | 448 | 1 |
| Bid all our simple souls be one | 527 | 2 |
| Bid every care be gone | 831 | 10 |
| Bid every creature help them on | 452 | 5 |
| Bid me bear the hallowed cross | 166 | 4 |
| Bid me be reconciled and blest | 799 | 7 |
| Bid me even in sleep go on | 287 | 3 |
| †Bid me in thy image rise | 18 | 2 |
| Bid me lay this body down | 877 | 4 |
| Bid me look on thee and mourn | 178 | 4 |
| Bid me look on thee, and weep | 101 | 3 |
| *Bid me of men beware | 311 | 1 |
| Bid me stretch out my withered hand | 135 | 5 |
| Bid me then in peace depart | 915 | 4 |
| Bid me to thy arms return | 173 | 4 |
| Bid me walk before thy face | 368 | 3 |
| Bid my anxious fears subside | 839 | 3 |
| Bid my inbred sin depart | 368 | 2 |
| Bid my quiet spirit hear | 358 | 1 |
| Bid my sins and sorrows end | 116 | 1 |
| Bid our jars for ever cease | 509 | 1 |

| | Hymn | Verse |
|---|---|---|
| Bid our unnatural discord end | 442 | 3 |
| Bid them come by faith to thee | 999 | 3 |
| Bid them to each other cleave | 999 | 3 |
| Bid them walk on life's rough sea | 999 | 3 |
| Bid the springing corn arise | 578 | 1 |
| Bid us find the food in thee | 531 | 1 |
| Bid us now depart in peace | 1007 | — |
| Bidd'st me come, as heretofore | 182 | 8 |
| Bidd'st me sit and feast with thee | 554 | 5 |
| Bids me go, and sin no more | 185 | 1 |
| Bids my freed heart in thee rejoice | 210 | 4 |
| Bids them bear us in their hands | 233 | 1 |
| Bids us take our seats above | 728 | 6 |
| Bids you all his promise prove | 54 | 3 |
| Big with woes and fiery trials | 60 | 1 |
| Binding all that lives in one | 990 | 6 |
| Bind my wandering heart to thee | 866 | 3 |
| Bind them with their own nature's chain | 461 | 6 |
| Bind the sinful inclination | 819 | 3 |
| †Bind up the wounds, assuage the aching smart | 967 | 6 |
| Bitterly as Peter mourn | 101 | 3 |
| Blameless before thy face to live | 119 | 4 |
| Blended and gathered into thee | 505 | 7 |
| Blended with my glorious end | 368 | 1 |
| Blend it with thine, and take away | 841 | 6 |
| †Blessed and holy Three | 870 | 4 |
| *Blessed are the pure in heart | 817 | 1 |
| Blessed, immortal, thou alone | 727 | 1 |
| Blessed, only Potentate | 606 | 1 |
| †Blessed Sun of grace! o'er all | 753 | 5 |
| Bless his love and sovereign grace | 639 | 9 |
| Bless his name and sing his praise | 941 | 4 |
| Bless his name, each farthest nation | 604 | 1 |
| Bless me; for I will prevail | 390 | 3 |
| Bless me with purity of heart | 804 | 5 |
| Bless the dark world with heavenly light | 553 | 5 |
| Bless the labourer's happy toil | 579 | 2 |
| †Bless the Lord, who ever liveth | 580 | 3 |
| Bless thy chastening, cheering rod | 554 | 4 |
| Bless to him the cleansing flood | 477 | 1 |
| †Bless us, that we may call thee blest | 616 | 10 |
| Bless us with that internal peace | 466 | 2 |
| Bless us with the spirit of grace | 756 | 1 |
| Bless with divine conformity | 528 | 5 |
| †Blessing and honour, and praise and love | 237 | 3 |
| †Blessing, and thanks, and love, and might | 976 | 2 |
| *Blessing, honour, thanks, and praise | 50 | 1 |
| Blessing, power, and majesty | 53 | 3 |
| *Blessing to God, for ever blest | 1023 | — |
| †Blessings abound where'er he reigns | 585 | 10 |
| Blessings every moment pours | 233 | 1 |
| Blessings implored, and sins to be confessed | 850 | 1 |
| Blessings more than we can give | 260 | 1 |

| | Hymn | Verse |
|---|---|---|
| †Blessings on all he pours | 86 | 4 |
| Blessings on his church below | 718 | 5 |
| Blessings on the babe bestowing | 895 | 4 |
| †Blest are the men whose hearts are set | 592 | 4 |
| †Blest are the saints that sit on high | 592 | 2 |
| †Blest are the souls that find a place | 592 | 3 |
| Blest as the church above | 771 | 5 |
| *Blest be our everlasting Lord | 248 | 1 |
| *Blest be the dear uniting love | 534 | 1 |
| Blest Comforter, with peace and joy | 785 | 4 |
| Blest day of God! we hail its dawn | 957 | 3 |
| Blest him for the sweet repose | 542 | 2 |
| Blest in Christ this moment be | 20 | 4 |
| *Blest is the man, supremely blest | 561 | 1 |
| †Blest is the man, to whom his Lord | 561 | 2 |
| †Blest, O Israel, art thou | 407 | 6 |
| Blest Saviour, I recline | 560 | 1 |
| Blest seats, through rude and stormy scenes | 939 | 3 |
| *Blest Spirit! from the eternal Sire | 770 | 1 |
| Blest to all eternity | 20 | 4 |
| Blest, unutterably blest | 51 | 1 |
| Blest with bliss that never ends | 53 | 4 |
| Blest with piety sincere | 464 | 2 |
| Blest with the scorn of finite good | 68 | 2 |
| Blest with this antepast of heaven | 30 | 2 |
| †Blind from my birth to guilt and thee | 135 | 8 |
| Blind unbelief is sure to err | 845 | 3 |
| Blind we were, but now we see | 348 | 5 |
| Bliss for every soul designed | 20 | 4 |
| Bliss to carnal minds unknown | 207 | 1 |
| Blood of Christ so rich, so free | 790 | 5 |
| Blood that washes white as snow | 76 | 2 |
| Bloom, and put forth fruits and flowers | 348 | 3 |
| Bloom as the garden of the Lord | 111 | 4 |
| Bloom, our infinite reward | 67 | 5 |
| Blot out my sins from thy record | 565 | 4 |
| Blots out our children's name | 888 | 4 |
| Blow soft o'er Ceylon's isle | 747 | 2 |
| *Blow ye the trumpet, blow | 738 | 1 |
| Body, soul, and spirit, join | 411 | 1 |
| Bold an unknown land to try | 1000 | 1 |
| Bold I approach the eternal throne | 201 | 5 |
| Bold I with thee, my Head, march up | 293 | 4 |
| *Bold in our Almighty Lord | 873 | 1 |
| †Bold shall I stand in thy great day | 190 | 2 |
| Bold shall they appear in the presence of God | 198 | 3 |
| Bold to scoff the Nazarene | 195 | 3 |
| Bold to take up, firm to sustain | 301 | 2 |
| Boldly we stand before thy seat | 1001 | 8 |
| Bondage ending | 715 | 3 |
| Borders on the shades of death | 687 | 1 |
| Bore all my sins upon the tree | 28 | 1 |
| Bore with me in defilement | 943 | 12 |

| | Hymn | Verse |
|---|---|---|
| Born a child and yet a king . | 688 | 2 |
| Born in thy family below . | 614 | 11 |
| †Born into the world above . | 51 | 4 |
| Born of God, to sin no more | 400 | 8 |
| Born only to lament and die | 913 | 2 |
| Born that man no more may die | 683 | 5 |
| †Born thy people to deliver . | 688 | 2 |
| Born to bruise the serpent's head . | 194 | 4 |
| Born to give them second birth | 683 | 5 |
| Born to raise the sons of earth | 683 | 5 |
| Born to redeem, and strong to save | 712 | 3 |
| Born to reign in us for ever | 688 | 2 |
| Born to set thy people free . | 688 | 1 |
| Borne by angels on their wings | 50 | 3 |
| Borne on angels' wings to heaven . | 1008 | 3 |
| Borne on contemplation's wing | 192 | 1 |
| Borne the Almighty's indignation . | 748 | 5 |
| Borrowed their whole effect from thee | 702 | 1 |
| Both day and night our suit may press | 827 | 5 |
| Both day and night their tents resound | 616 | 4 |
| Both loud and long, that glorious Name | 991 | 2 |
| Both man and beast thy bounty share | 563 | 3 |
| Both me and all mankind . | 118 | 4 |
| †Both now and ever, Lord, protect . | 992 | 6 |
| Both the nature and kingdom divine | 491 | 4 |
| Bought for us by Jesu's merit | 530 | 1 |
| Bound and oppressed, yet thine I am | 150 | 3 |
| †Bound down with twice ten thousand ties . | 139 | 6 |
| †Bound on the altar of thy cross | 412 | 2 |
| Boundless as ocean's tide | 870 | 4 |
| Boundless power his royal robe | 601 | 1 |
| †Boundless wisdom, power divine | 350 | 8 |
| Bow a nation to thy sway . | 463 | 1 |
| Bow, and bless the just award | 51 | 5 |
| Bow before the brightening vail | 817 | 3 |
| Bow down to Jesu's name . | 275 | 8 |
| Bow every knee to Jesu's name | 576 | 3 |
| Bow every soul and every knee | 444 | 4 |
| Bow the head and die like thee | 529 | 4 |
| Bow the heavens, and come down . | 158 | 4 |
| Bow thine ear, in mercy bow | 168 | 5 |
| †Bow thine ear, in mercy bow | 257 | 5 |
| Bow thine ear, in mercy bow | 257 | 6 |
| Bows down to wood and stone | 747 | 2 |
| Bows to Jesus every knee . | 195 | 1 |
| *Branch of Jesse's stem, arise | 756 | 1 |
| Bread of heaven . | 839 | 1 |
| *Bread of heaven ! on thee I feed | 904 | 1 |
| *Bread of the world, in mercy broken | 906 | 1 |
| †Break off the yoke of inbred sin | 388 | 4 |
| †Break off your tears, ye saints, and tell | 712 | 3 |
| Break the unbelieving heart· | 463 | 3 |
| Break this stony heart of mine | 27 | 2 |

| | Hymn | Verse |
|---|---|---|
| Break through them all | 853 | 3 |
| Break up the fallow ground | 981 | 5 |
| Break we (say they) their servile bands | 541 | 1 |
| Breathe life; and lo! divinely stirred | 799 | 5 |
| Breathe, Lord, and these dry bones shall live | 773 | 3 |
| Breathe my latest breath in prayer | 915 | 1 |
| †Breathe on us, Lord, in this our day | 486 | 4 |
| †Breathe on us, Lord! our sins forgive | 957 | 5 |
| Breathe their faith into my breast | 359 | 1 |
| Breathe the praise of silent love | 643 | 3 |
| Breathe thy Spirit, give thy peace | 520 | 2 |
| Breathe unutterable love | 260 | 2 |
| *Brethren in Christ, and well-beloved | 490 | 1 |
| *Brief life is here our portion | 943 | 1 |
| Brief sorrow, short-lived care | 943 | 1 |
| Brighter than the noon-day sun | 76 | 1 |
| Bright in all thine image shine | 368 | 3 |
| Bright in all thy glory shine | 852 | 1 |
| Bright, insufferably bright | 643 | 2 |
| Bright seraphs learn Immanuel's name | 263 | 6 |
| Bright with thy praise | 848 | 4 |
| Bring back the heavenly blessing, lost | 252 | 1 |
| Bring banished bliss to view | 587 | 2 |
| Bring forth out of this hellish pit | 129 | 5 |
| Bring forth the royal diadem | 681 | 1 |
| Bring him every tuneful strain | 605 | 4 |
| Bring his sheaves with vast increase | 623 | 6 |
| Bring into captivity | 358 | 4 |
| Bring I to gain thy grace | 175 | 4 |
| Bring me back, and lead, and keep | 13 | 3 |
| Bring me eyes thy book to read | 885 | 1 |
| Bring me not to nothing, Lord | 179 | 1 |
| Bring me, where I my heaven may find | 289 | 7 |
| Bring near, bring near, the joyful hour | 388 | 6 |
| Bring relief for all complaints | 975 | 5 |
| Bring the pride of sinners down | 463 | 4 |
| Bring the promised glory nearer | 878 | 5 |
| Bring thy heavenly kingdom in | 399 | 2 |
| Bring to every thankful mind | 899 | 1 |
| Bring us through the evil day | 653 | 6 |
| Bring with it what it may | 804 | 2 |
| Bring your sweetest, noblest lays | 722 | 4 |
| Broadcast it o'er the land | 739 | 1 |
| Broke off, and banished far from thee | 130 | 1 |
| Brood o'er our nature's night | 87 | 3 |
| Brother, friend, by Jesus freed | 50 | 5 |
| Brought back thy agonising pain | 176 | 3 |
| Brought my helper from the sky | 542 | 2 |
| Brought out of nothing by his word | 234 | 1 |
| Brought out their sick and deaf and lame | 695 | 3 |
| Brought through our sore temptation | 276 | 2 |
| Bruised and mangled by the fall | 791 | 4 |
| Bruise in us the serpent's head | 683 | 6 |

| | Hymn | Verse |
|---|---|---|
| Bud and blossom as the rose | 348 | 1 |
| †Build us in one body up | 515 | 2 |
| Build we each the other up | 480 | 2 |
| Built eternal in the skies | 67 | 3 |
| Built immovably secure | 67 | 3 |
| Built on his faithfulness and power | 569 | 5 |
| Built on the precious corner-stone | 992 | 2 |
| Built on thy strength we reach the skies | 670 | 1 |
| Burdened, and sick, and faint | 152 | 1 |
| †Burdened with a world of grief | 29 | 3 |
| Burdened with our sinful load | 29 | 3 |
| Burdened with the wrath of God | 29 | 3 |
| Burdened with this unbelief | 29 | 3 |
| †Buried in sin, thy voice I hear | 290 | 3 |
| Burn before him, quenched as tow | 570 | 5 |
| Burn up the dross of base desire | 361 | 7 |
| Burst every bond through which I groan | 408 | 5 |
| Burst our bonds, and set us free | 900 | 2 |
| Burst this Babylonish yoke | 368 | 2 |
| Burst thy shackles, drop thy clay | 921 | 3 |
| Bury me, Saviour, in thy grave | 347 | 3 |
| †But, above all, afraid | 311 | 3 |
| *But, above all, lay hold | 267 | 1 |
| †But, ah! how wide my spirit flies | 788 | 3 |
| But ah! the feebleness of man | 909 | 1 |
| †But all, before they hence remove | 48 | 2 |
| But all he hath for mine I claim | 269 | 4 |
| But all their joys are one | 678 | 1 |
| But all the powers of hell | 314 | 4 |
| But all things inherit through Jesus's right | 212 | 1 |
| †But all who truly righteous be | 935 | 4 |
| But all your heaven, ye glorious powers | 721 | 6 |
| But arm yourselves with all the mind | 266 | 4 |
| †But art thou not already mine | 184 | 3 |
| †But as for me, with humble fear | 543 | 4 |
| But, as palm-trees lift the head | 598 | 3 |
| But at the throne of sovereign grace | 303 | 3 |
| But basely from thy statutes roved | 176 | 3 |
| But bear me, till on eagles' wings | 365 | 2 |
| †But be it, Lord of mercy, all | 696 | 5 |
| But be my Saviour then | 877 | 4 |
| †But be the night-watch long | 838 | 4 |
| But blot their memory from thy book | 574 | 7 |
| †But both in Jesus join | 705 | 4 |
| But breathe unutterable praise | 369 | 4 |
| But bring me home to thee | 179 | 1 |
| But bring me through at last | 335 | 1 |
| But by believing thee | 410 | 3 |
| But by whatever means 'tis done | 331 | 3 |
| *But can it be that I should prove | 282 | 1 |
| But cannot, cannot pray | 153 | 2 |
| But cannot without thee | 153 | 1 |
| But, chiefly, Lord, the thanks receive | 239 | 8 |

| | Hymn | Verse |
|---|---|---|
| But chiefly we rejoice to know | 239 | 5 |
| But children more securely dear | 68 | 4 |
| But Christ be all the world to me | 361 | 11 |
| But Christ in me shall live | 362 | 7 |
| But Christ shall shortly root them up | 280 | 5 |
| †But Christ, the heavenly Lamb | 703 | 2 |
| But confident in self-despair | 141 | 1 |
| But conscious of my fall I mourn | 130 | 1 |
| But countless acts of pardoning grace | 656 | 1 |
| But day and night to feast on thee | 285 | 2 |
| But death itself there dies | 942 | 4 |
| But desperate wickedness is here | 803 | 3 |
| But didst thou not my Pattern die | 330 | 3 |
| But died without the sight | 741 | 4 |
| But do not from our hearts obey | 454 | 2 |
| But do not then depart | 908 | 1 |
| But do not then depart | 1024 | — |
| But dwell in perfect peace | 407 | 4 |
| But each, impelled by secret grace | 452 | 3 |
| But ever love thine own | 852 | 2 |
| But every soul assembled here | 81 | 1 |
| But faith, and heaven-born peace, be there | 353 | 5 |
| But faith puts forth a trembling hand | 781 | 4 |
| But faithful is my Lord | 360 | 8 |
| But far above the skies | 216 | 5 |
| But felt thee present in the flame | 483 | 2 |
| But fill our earth with glory | 736 | 3 |
| But first obedient to his word | 472 | 1 |
| But fix in me his constant home | 376 | 3 |
| But fix mine eyes on thee alone | 836 | 3 |
| †But, for the glory of thy name | 126 | 3 |
| †But, for thy truth and mercy's sake | 180 | 7 |
| But for true holiness | 304 | 6 |
| But for us fights the proper Man | 856 | 2 |
| But give the mourner rest | 565 | 7 |
| But give thyself to me | 415 | 4 |
| But God above can still their noise | 600 | 3 |
| But God cannot finally fail | 777 | 2 |
| †But God from his celestial throne | 541 | 2 |
| But God made flesh is wholly ours | 262 | 3 |
| But God our earnestness approves | 827 | 6 |
| But God with God is man with men | 31 | 2 |
| But, God with God, wast man with man | 353 | 2 |
| But greater is thy mercy's store | 110 | 3 |
| But guide our feet into the way | 503 | 2 |
| But guide thee with my gracious eye | 561 | 9 |
| But happier still are they | 925 | 1 |
| †But hark! a voice of sovereign grace | 786 | 2 |
| †But hast thou finally forsook | 451 | 2 |
| But hast thou not on earth prepared | 284 | 3 |
| But help me to believe thou *dost* | 780 | 1 |
| But help me to believe thou wilt | 780 | 2 |
| But he shall to the utmost save | 537 | 7 |

| | Hymn | Verse |
|---|---|---|
| But he shall tread them down | 719 | 5 |
| But he whom now we trust in | 943 | 3 |
| But he will bear us through | 804 | 3 |
| But how I may escape the death | 44 | 5 |
| But humbly lift them to the skies | 977 | 2 |
| But I am sick, and want thine aid | 396 | 2 |
| But I ask thee for a present mind | 842 | 1 |
| But I now my sins confess | 110 | 2 |
| †But I of means have made my boast | 91 | 6 |
| †But I shall share a glorious part | 599 | 5 |
| But I still refused thy love | 166 | 3 |
| But, if on thee we call | 118 | 3 |
| But if our works in thee be wrought | 526 | 1 |
| But if thou thy Spirit shed | 110 | 4 |
| But, if thou wilt, a gracious word | 135 | 4 |
| But if thy presence grace my humble board | 967 | 3 |
| But, if we trust our father's love | 624 | 2 |
| But if we trust thy providence | 874 | 1 |
| †But if you still his call refuse | 695 | 6 |
| But in behaviour mild | 627 | 2 |
| But in his pleasure rest | 832 | 5 |
| But inward holiness | 406 | 1 |
| †But is it possible that I | 342 | 5 |
| But it is fed and watered | 988 | 1 |
| But Jesus came the world to save | 34 | 2 |
| But Jesus crucified | 534 | 3 |
| But Jesus died for me | 115 | Cho. |
| But Jesus is my might | 278 | 3 |
| But joy returns when night is o'er | 559 | 2 |
| But know the truth and live | 118 | 1 |
| But let me all thy stamp receive | 429 | 4 |
| But let me all thy words obey | 429 | 4 |
| But let me feel applied | 778 | 4 |
| But let me feel thy blood applied | 125 | 6 |
| But let me rather prove | 249 | 4 |
| But let me rise | 855 | 2 |
| But let me still abide | 301 | 6 |
| But let them, Lord, the substance gain | 473 | 4 |
| †But let them still abide | 622 | 3 |
| But let us enter in | 797 | 1 |
| †But let us hasten to the day | 534 | 6 |
| But let us not be tempted | 818 | 1 |
| But life hath triumphed o'er his foe | 714 | 3 |
| But lift up your eyes | 707 | 3 |
| †But lo! a place he hath prepared | 227 | 3 |
| †But lo! I from thy justice, Lord | 917 | 2 |
| But lo! the burning Spirit of God | 493 | 5 |
| But lo! what sudden joys I see | 712 | 2 |
| But longing to triumph with thee | 946 | 3 |
| But long thy praises to proclaim | 767 | 2 |
| But love me to the end | 436 | 5 |
| But love thee with a constant heart | 357 | 6 |
| But make it all a pool | 405 | 7 |

| | Hymn | Verse |
|---|---|---|
| But make us of one mind and heart | 501 | 5 |
| But makes an end of sin | 251 | 4 |
| †But makes the perfect law of God | 540 | 2 |
| But man thou lov'st the best | 242 | 2 |
| But mark them, Lord, with thine | 894 | 2 |
| But may in him salvation find | 31 | 1 |
| But may return to thee | 303 | 3 |
| But meet the sons of night | 266 | 3 |
| But melt in the fountain that streams from thy side | 160 | 3 |
| But mine afflictions brought to mind | 558 | 5 |
| But mock their vain design | 266 | 3 |
| But more abundant life we claim | 394 | 3 |
| But more enjoy them there | 947 | 6 |
| But more than conquer through thy love | 171 | 3 |
| But mostly thou delight'st to bless | 239 | 7 |
| But my full soul shall still require | 392 | 4 |
| But neither can rejoice, nor grieve | 153 | 1 |
| But newly dipt in blood | 35 | 4 |
| But not a perfect sight obtain | 284 | 4 |
| †But nothing can obstruct thy way | 861 | 3 |
| But nothing is too hard for thee | 475 | 2 |
| But nothing like thyself appears | 651 | 2 |
| But nothing thou hast made | 270 | 4 |
| But now I find an aching void | 787 | 3 |
| But now the land possess | 404 | 4 |
| †But O! above all, Thy kindness we praise | 199 | 4 |
| †But, O almighty God of love | 475 | 5 |
| But O eternity's too short | 657 | 10 |
| †But O forgiveness is with thee | 625 | 3 |
| But O how dark and void | 117 | 1 |
| †But O, how soon thy wrath is o'er | 184 | 8 |
| But O, I cannot, cannot feel | 155 | 4 |
| But O! in tender mercy break | 176 | 4 |
| But O! the bliss to which I tend | 947 | 2 |
| But O! the glories of thy mind | 316 | 4 |
| †But O! the jealous God | 93 | 6 |
| But O the power impart | 982 | 2 |
| †But, O the power of grace divine | 203 | 8 |
| †But O! thou wouldst not have me live | 307 | 4 |
| But O thyself reveal | 485 | 3 |
| But O thyself reveal | 486 | 3 |
| †But O what gentle means | 675 | 2 |
| But O! when both shall end | 44 | 4 |
| †But O when that last conflict's o'er | 658 | 4 |
| But O! when thou shalt loose my tongue | 135 | 6 |
| But o'er them all thy blood doth flow | 923 | 2 |
| But of thorns | 793 | 3 |
| But on light that still shall blaze | 694 | 2 |
| But only thou canst make him known | 148 | 1 |
| But onward we move | 498 | 2 |
| But out of all the Lord | 478 | 2 |
| But own in fear thy grace hath wrought | 626 | 2 |
| But pity, and forgive me all | 178 | 4 |

| | Hymn | Verse |
|---|---|---|
| But he shall tread them down | 719 | 5 |
| But he whom now we trust in | 943 | 3 |
| But he will bear us through | 804 | 3 |
| But how I may escape the death | 44 | 5 |
| But humbly lift them to the skies | 977 | 2 |
| But I am sick, and want thine aid | 396 | 2 |
| But I ask thee for a present mind | 842 | 1 |
| But I now my sins confess | 110 | 2 |
| †But I of means have made my boast | 91 | 6 |
| †But I shall share a glorious part | 599 | 5 |
| But I still refused thy love | 166 | 3 |
| But, if on thee we call | 118 | 3 |
| But if our works in thee be wrought | 526 | 1 |
| But if thou thy Spirit shed | 110 | 4 |
| But, if thou wilt, a gracious word | 135 | 4 |
| But if thy presence grace my humble board | 967 | 3 |
| But, if we trust our father's love | 624 | 2 |
| But if we trust thy providence | 874 | 1 |
| †But if you still his call refuse | 695 | 6 |
| But in behaviour mild | 627 | 2 |
| But in his pleasure rest | 832 | 5 |
| But inward holiness | 406 | 1 |
| †But is it possible that I | 342 | 5 |
| But it is fed and watered | 988 | 1 |
| But Jesus came the world to save | 34 | 2 |
| But Jesus crucified | 534 | 3 |
| But Jesus died for me | 115 | Cho. |
| But Jesus is my might | 278 | 3 |
| But joy returns when night is o'er | 559 | 2 |
| But know the truth and live | 118 | 1 |
| But let me all thy stamp receive | 429 | 4 |
| But let me all thy words obey | 429 | 4 |
| But let me feel applied | 778 | 4 |
| But let me feel thy blood applied | 125 | 6 |
| But let me rather prove | 249 | 4 |
| But let me rise | 855 | 2 |
| But let me still abide | 301 | 6 |
| But let them, Lord, the substance gain | 473 | 4 |
| †But let them still abide | 622 | 3 |
| But let us enter in | 797 | 1 |
| †But let us hasten to the day | 534 | 6 |
| But let us not be tempted | 818 | 1 |
| But life hath triumphed o'er his foe | 714 | 3 |
| But lift up your eyes | 707 | 3 |
| †But lo! a place he hath prepared | 227 | 3 |
| †But lo! I from thy justice, Lord | 917 | 2 |
| But lo! the burning Spirit of God | 493 | 5 |
| But lo! what sudden joys I see | 712 | 2 |
| But longing to triumph with thee | 946 | 3 |
| But long thy praises to proclaim | 767 | 2 |
| But love me to the end | 436 | 5 |
| But love thee with a constant heart | 857 | 6 |
| But make it all a pool | 405 | 7 |

| | Hymn | Verse |
|---|---|---|
| But make us of one mind and heart | 501 | 5 |
| But makes an end of sin | 251 | 4 |
| †But makes the perfect law of God | 540 | 2 |
| But man thou lov'st the best | 242 | 2 |
| But mark them, Lord, with thine | 894 | 2 |
| But may in him salvation find | 31 | 1 |
| But may return to thee | 303 | 3 |
| But meet the sons of night | 266 | 3 |
| But melt in the fountain that streams from thy side | 160 | 3 |
| But mine afflictions brought to mind | 558 | 5 |
| But mock their vain design | 266 | 3 |
| But more abundant life we claim | 394 | 3 |
| But more enjoy them there | 947 | 6 |
| But more than conquer through thy love | 171 | 3 |
| But mostly thou delight'st to bless | 239 | 7 |
| But my full soul shall still require | 392 | 4 |
| But neither can rejoice, nor grieve | 153 | 1 |
| But newly dipt in blood | 35 | 4 |
| But not a perfect sight obtain | 284 | 4 |
| †But nothing can obstruct thy way | 861 | 3 |
| But nothing is too hard for thee | 475 | 2 |
| But nothing like thyself appears | 651 | 2 |
| But nothing thou hast made | 270 | 4 |
| But now I find an aching void | 787 | 3 |
| But now the land possess | 404 | 4 |
| †But O! above all, Thy kindness we praise | 199 | 4 |
| †But, O almighty God of love | 475 | 5 |
| But O eternity's too short | 657 | 10 |
| †But O forgiveness is with thee | 625 | 3 |
| But O how dark and void | 117 | 1 |
| †But O, how soon thy wrath is o'er | 184 | 8 |
| But O, I cannot, cannot feel | 155 | 4 |
| But O! in tender mercy break | 176 | 4 |
| But O! the bliss to which I tend | 947 | 2 |
| But O! the glories of thy mind | 316 | 4 |
| †But O! the jealous God | 93 | 6 |
| But O the power impart | 982 | 2 |
| †But, O the power of grace divine | 203 | 8 |
| †But O! thou wouldst not have me live | 307 | 4 |
| But O thyself reveal | 485 | 3 |
| But O thyself reveal | 486 | 3 |
| †But O what gentle means | 675 | 2 |
| But O! when both shall end | 44 | 4 |
| †But O when that last conflict's o'er | 658 | 4 |
| But O! when thou shalt loose my tongue | 135 | 6 |
| But o'er them all thy blood doth flow | 923 | 2 |
| But of thorns | 793 | 3 |
| But on light that still shall blaze | 694 | 2 |
| But only thou canst make him known | 148 | 1 |
| But onward we move | 498 | 2 |
| But out of all the Lord | 478 | 2 |
| But own in fear thy grace hath wrought | 626 | 2 |
| But pity, and forgive me all | 178 | 4 |

| | Hymn | Verse |
|---|---|---|
| But raise it to a flame | 725 | 4 |
| †But raise your eyes, and tune your songs | 713 | 3 |
| But rest in Jesus have | 25 | 2 |
| But rest in thy redeeming love | 436 | 4 |
| But sacred, high, eternal noon | 959 | 4 |
| †But saints are lovely in his sight | 225 | 6 |
| But saints are thy peculiar care | 563 | 3 |
| But saints our Immanuel sing | 946 | 1 |
| But saw thee on the floods appear | 483 | 2 |
| But seek a city out of sight | 71 | 3 |
| But sent the world his truth and grace | 610 | 5 |
| But servants of the heavenly King | 12 | 1 |
| But shall believers fear | 315 | 2 |
| But shall believers fly | 315 | 2 |
| †But shall he still devour | 447 | 2 |
| But shall I therefore let him go | 803 | 1 |
| But shower on *him* thy blessings down | 985 | 3 |
| But show thy power | 736 | 8 |
| But show us, Lord, is every one | 83 | 2 |
| But simply to my God display | 803 | 2 |
| But singing thy grace to thy paradise go | 808 | 6 |
| But sink beneath thy mighty hand | 176 | 1 |
| But sinners and the paths they tread | 540 | 6 |
| But snatch me from despair | 697 | 8 |
| †But soon he'll break death's envious chain | 22 | 4 |
| But soon he sends his pardoning word | 637 | 4 |
| But soon the reaping time will come | 935 | 3 |
| †But soon the Victor rose | 731 | 3 |
| But, spite of hell, shall have its course | 856 | 4 |
| But stand unshaken as thy love | 708 | 3 |
| But stand with constant care | 303 | 1 |
| But stay and love me to the end | 141 | 4 |
| But steadfastly to Jesus cleave | 172 | 3 |
| But still how weak my faith is found | 789 | 1 |
| But still in spirit joined | 536 | 2 |
| But still my watchful spirit keep | 306 | 4 |
| But still the sinner love | 270 | 4 |
| But still thy faithful servant keep | 310 | 4 |
| But still to adore, believe and love | 853 | 6 |
| But straitened in our own we are | 39 | 5 |
| But strangers and pilgrims ourselves we confess | 498 | 1 |
| But strength in thee I surely have | 805 | 5 |
| But sunk in guiltless shame adore | 869 | 3 |
| But sup with us, and let the feast | 208 | 4 |
| But sure a remedy to find | 136 | 5 |
| But sweeter far thy face to see | 680 | 1 |
| But sweet will be the flower | 845 | 3 |
| But take entire possession | 818 | 4 |
| But take, to arm you for the fight | 266 | 2 |
| †But, that my faith no more may know | 909 | 5 |
| But that thy blood was shed for me | 796 | 1 |
| But the blest volume thou hast writ | 553 | 2 |
| But the fruitful ears to store | 987 | 3 |

| | Hymn | Verse |
|---|---|---|
| But the last moment of my day | 776 | 2 |
| But the Lord is risen to-day | 714 | 1 |
| But the Lord will shortly pour | 218 | 4 |
| †But the mild glories of thy grace | 226 | 12 |
| †But the righteousness of faith | 192 | 3 |
| †But their Father God forgave them | 606 | 5 |
| †But their greatest happiness | 941 | 3 |
| But then shall wear the crown | 943 | 2 |
| But there no evil thing may find a home | 794 | 1 |
| But there's a nobler rest above | 959 | 2 |
| But they forget the mighty God | 802 | 2 |
| But thine essence | 748 | 3 |
| But this cannot suffice | 405 | 6 |
| But this is with burning and fuel of fire | 273 | 5 |
| †But this we can tell | 808 | 4 |
| But thou all pity art | 145 | 1 |
| But thou art, as yesterday | 183 | 2 |
| But thou art greater than my heart | 289 | 6 |
| But thou art merciful and good | 365 | 2 |
| But thou art my power, and holdest my hand | 273 | 3 |
| But thou didst turn thy face away | 559 | 3 |
| But thou dost all my anguish see | 795 | 3 |
| But thou hast all my wanderings known | 575 | 2 |
| †But thou hast given a loud alarm | 310 | 4 |
| But thou hast sent the Prince of peace | 148 | 4 |
| But thou must first bestow the power | 234 | 4 |
| But thou, O Christ, my wisdom art | 289 | 6 |
| †But thou, O Lord, art full of grace | 288 | 4 |
| But thou shalt flow down before | 382 | 3 |
| But thou the mighty Saviour art | 373 | 6 |
| †But thou, they say, art passing by | 135 | 9 |
| But thou, through whom I come to God | 136 | 8 |
| But thou wast nigh to hear my plaint | 559 | 1 |
| But thou wilt form thy Son in me | 360 | 11 |
| But thou, who gav'st the feeble will | 25 | 5 |
| But thou, whom we hasten to meet | 946 | 4 |
| †But though my life henceforth be thine | 127 | 5 |
| But though they grieve and wound me sore | 923 | 2 |
| But though they mourn awhile, his voice | 602 | 2 |
| †But thy compassions, Lord | 610 | 11 |
| But thy more abundant grace | 952 | 2 |
| But thy pure love within my breast | 285 | 8 |
| †But timorous mortals start and shrink | 938 | 4 |
| But 'tis enough that Christ knows all | 920 | 6 |
| But to a righteous Father we | 827 | 3 |
| But to my loving Saviour's breast | 289 | 5 |
| But to thy people join | 732 | 3 |
| But to thy right hand upraise me | 933 | 15 |
| But to thy wounds for refuge flee | 175 | 1 |
| But trust him for his grace | 845 | 2 |
| But turn their triumph into grief | 280 | 6 |
| But veiled before thy presence stand | 133 | 1 |
| But waiting at thy feet | 925 | 3 |

| | Hymn | Verse |
|---|---|---|
| But wait thy coming from above | 490 | 7 |
| But walk in all thy righteous ways | 306 | 2 |
| But watch with godly jealousy | 311 | 4 |
| But we a powerful spokesman find | 827 | 7 |
| But we God's chosen people are | 827 | 2 |
| But we turned from good to ill | 98 | 1 |
| †But we, who now our Lord confess | 57 | 3 |
| But we, who taste thy richer grace | 637 | 5 |
| †But what to those who find? Ah! this | 680 | 4 |
| †But when all in me is sin | 24 | 3 |
| But when all my care and pains | 24 | 1 |
| †But when he hath my patience proved | 331 | 2 |
| But when I see thee as thou art | 579 | 5 |
| But when, on thy bosom reclined | 70 | 2 |
| But when our eyes behold thy word | 553 | 1 |
| But when thou didst thy grace revoke | 180 | 2 |
| But when thou sendest, Lord, for me | 913 | 3 |
| But when thy hand has pressed me sore | 584 | 4 |
| †But when we view thy strange design | 263 | 4 |
| But when you raise your highest notes | 699 | 5 |
| But whence my sudden fear | 799 | 1 |
| †But while thou, my Lord, art nigh | 359 | 3 |
| †But while through pride I held my tongue | 561 | 3 |
| But who, I ask thee, who art Thou | 140 | 2 |
| But who is this that comes from far | 38 | 7 |
| †But who shall quit this low abode | 557 | 3 |
| *But who sufficient is to lead | 475 | 1 |
| †But will indeed Jehovah deign | 993 | 5 |
| But will not let thee go | 361 | 2 |
| But with their dying Head | 929 | 2 |
| But with thy kingdom in my breast | 834 | 2 |
| †But worse than all my foes I find | 310 | 3 |
| But yet to linger here is peace | 698 | 5 |
| †But yet with faith I venture | 943 | 12 |
| Build up thy rising church, and place | 526 | 5 |
| Build we each the other up | 521 | 1 |
| Buy wine, and milk, and gospel grace | 4 | 1 |
| By a bountiful God | 231 | 5 |
| By a look my soul recall | 168 | 6 |
| By a sudden light bewrayed | 633 | 4 |
| By actions show your sins forgiven | 420 | 2 |
| By actions, words, and tempers show | 472 | 1 |
| By all hell's host withstood | 315 | 3 |
| By all mankind and me | 252 | 1 |
| By all the hosts above | 262 | 1 |
| By all thou hast done for my sake | 174 | 4 |
| By all thy church below | 259 | 1 |
| By all thy hands have wrought | 244 | 1 |
| By all thy heavenly host adored | 259 | 1 |
| By all thy heavenly hosts adored | 247 | 3 |
| By all thy works be paid to thee | 237 | 3 |
| By all thy works on earth adored | 647 | 1 |
| By almighty love anointed | 722 | 2 |

| | Hymn | Verse |
|---|---|---|
| By angel-hosts adored | 719 | 3 |
| By an uncreated sun | 633 | 4 |
| By base desires I wronged thy love | 180 | 1 |
| By blotting out my sin | 674 | 1 |
| By characters divine | 894 | 2 |
| By creatures without end | 642 | 6 |
| By crystal walls protected | 276 | 3 |
| By day and by night | 760 | 4 |
| †By death and hell pursued in vain | 386 | 4 |
| By death I shall escape from death | 944 | 7 |
| By death prevent the second death | 467 | 5 |
| By each temptation tried | 692 | 2 |
| By earth and hell in vain withstood | 832 | 3 |
| By earth and heaven confest | 800 | 1 |
| By every scourge I feel | 548 | 3 |
| †By faith already there | 723 | 5 |
| By faith before my ravished eye | 240 | 1 |
| By faith behold Jehovah's face | 550 | 1 |
| By faith I always see him stand | 548 | 4 |
| †By faith I every moment stand | 366 | 3 |
| By faith I see thee passing now | 284 | 1 |
| By faith of his Spirit we take | 79 | 2 |
| †By faith of the upper choir we meet | 262 | 3 |
| By faith they enter in | 735 | 3 |
| †By faith we already behold | 73 | 3 |
| By faith we apprehend the power | 387 | 3 |
| †By faith we are come | 499 | 3 |
| *By faith we find the place above | 64 | 1 |
| †By faith we know thee strong to save | 95 | 3 |
| †By faith we now transcend the skies | 57 | 6 |
| †By faith we see the glory | 853 | 4 |
| †By faith we take the bread of life | 907 | 2 |
| By flaming vengeance hurled | 314 | 4 |
| By flourishing below | 756 | 1 |
| By frail, apostate man | 368 | 4 |
| By giving thee my heart | 998 | 4 |
| By God's almighty hand | 988 | 1 |
| By God, the eternal Word, than when | 950 | 2 |
| By heaven designed for me | 832 | 4 |
| By hiding it within my heart | 30 | 3 |
| By him redeemed of old | 460 | 3 |
| By him the birds are fed | 988 | 2 |
| By his beloved Son | 610 | 5 |
| By his blood and his prayer | 760 | 2 |
| By his cross he now hath led | 86 | 3 |
| By his death to life restored | 207 | 1 |
| By his disciples' hands conveyed | 875 | 3 |
| By his life your God hath sworn | 8 | 2 |
| By his pain he gives you ease | 20 | 2 |
| By holy, purifying hope | 539 | 4 |
| By hope we the rapture improve | 499 | 3 |
| By hymns of praise we learn to be | 950 | 1 |
| By ill advice to walk | 540 | 1 |

| | Hymn | Verse |
|---|---|---|
| By labouring for the rest of love | 466 | 2 |
| †By long experience have I known | 584 | 5 |
| By love above all height we rise | 57 | 6 |
| By love we still rise | 499 | 3 |
| By love's almighty power | 409 | 2 |
| By love's divine simplicity | 98 | 2 |
| †By me, O my Saviour, stand | 187 | 2 |
| By mercy gathered into thee | 62 | 2 |
| By mercy saved from first to last | 916 | 2 |
| By my kind protector kept | 542 | 2 |
| By our heavenly Father bestowed | 491 | 3 |
| By perfect holiness prepare | 84 | 7 |
| By perfect holiness, to appear | 309 | 5 |
| By perfect purity and love | 364 | 5 |
| By persevering prayer obtain | 827 | 1 |
| By principles of virtuous truth | 467 | 8 |
| By providential care | 258 | 1 |
| By putting on thy Son | 368 | 3 |
| By reason and by grace | 526 | 3 |
| By regal David's favoured son | 989 | 2 |
| By Satan long oppressed | 299 | 3 |
| *By secret influence from above | 775 | 1 |
| By self and Satan taught to paint | 93 | 5 |
| By self-consuming care | 831 | 4 |
| By shunning every evil way | 320 | 1 |
| By sin, alas! undone | 482 | 5 |
| By sin eternally undone | 441 | 3 |
| By sinners crucified below | 883 | 2 |
| By stormy clouds too quickly overcast | 850 | 4 |
| By sweet experience prove | 370 | 4 |
| By that unction from above | 676 | 1 |
| By the communing Spirit poured | 892 | 5 |
| By the dread mysterious hour | 710 | 2 |
| By the eternal Spirit made | 708 | 1 |
| By the Father's grace bestowed | 748 | 4 |
| By the gloom that veiled the skies | 710 | 4 |
| By the gracious tears that flowed | 710 | 3 |
| *By the holy hills surrounded | 595 | 1 |
| By the kingdom of God in our hearts | 488 | 4 |
| By the least of his servants, his savour of grace | 219 | 1 |
| By the marks received for me | 936 | 5 |
| By the mournful word that told | 710 | 3 |
| By the patience of hope, and the labour of love | 47 | 2 |
| By the purple robe of scorn | 710 | 4 |
| †By the sacred grief that wept | 710 | 3 |
| †By the same grace upheld, may we | 945 | 2 |
| By the sealed sepulchral stone | 710 | 5 |
| †By the Spirit of our Head | 423 | 2 |
| By the streams of comfort leads | 554 | 2 |
| By the tokens of his passion | 936 | 5 |
| By the vault whose dark abode | 710 | 5 |
| †By thee do we live, Thy daily supplies | 1025 | 2 |
| By thee on eagles' wings upborne | 977 | 5 |

| BY THEE | HYMN | VERSE |
|---|---|---|
| By thee the joyful news | 675 | 4 |
| By thee the reprobate repent | 770 | 1 |
| †By thee the victory is given | 248 | 2 |
| By thee, to exercise their grace | 325 | 5 |
| By thee to full perfection brought | 429 | 2 |
| By thee to heaven I'll go | 931 | 6 |
| By thee unsaved, we fall | 469 | 2 |
| By thee was to perfection brought | 240 | 3 |
| †By thine agonising pain | 900 | 2 |
| By thine agony of prayer | 710 | 4 |
| By thine all-sufficient merit | 688 | 2 |
| †By thine hour of whelming fear | 710 | 4 |
| By thine own eternal spirit | 688 | 2 |
| By thine own presence hide | 124 | 2 |
| †By thine unerring Spirit led | 326 | 2 |
| By those who shared his daily bread | 849 | 3 |
| By thousands through the skies | 263 | 1 |
| By thy all-piercing beam | 785 | 2 |
| By thy all-restoring merit | 687 | 3 |
| By thy bloody cross subdue | 463 | 3 |
| †By thy deep expiring groan | 710 | 5 |
| By thy depth of grief unknown | 151 | 5 |
| By thy dying love to man | 900 | 2 |
| By thy example taught | 468 | 5 |
| By thy fasting and distress | 710 | 2 |
| By thy forgiving love | 778 | 1 |
| †By thy helpless infant years | 710 | 2 |
| By thy judgment I am clear | 215 | 4 |
| By thy life of want and tears | 710 | 2 |
| By thy merits we find favour | 722 | 1 |
| By thy modulating skill | 538 | 2 |
| By thy mortal groans and sighs | 151 | 6 |
| †By thy own right hand of power | 717 | 2 |
| By thy own Spirit seal | 873 | 1 |
| By thy pains and consolations | 743 | 1 |
| By thy pangs and bloody sweat | 151 | 5 |
| By thy pardoning love compelled | 427 | 1 |
| By thy passion on the tree | 900 | 3 |
| By thy precious death I pray | 151 | 6 |
| †By thy reconciling love | 509 | 2 |
| †By thy Spirit, Lord, reprove | 101 | 2 |
| By thy Spirit's light revealed | 876 | 2 |
| By thy sufficient grace | 469 | 9 |
| By thy victorious blood cast down | 461 | 1 |
| By thy victorious love | 125 | 4 |
| By thy wounds, thy crown of thorn | 710 | 4 |
| By unfeigned humility | 192 | 2 |
| By vows and grates confined | 526 | 4 |
| By want, or affliction, or sickness opprest | 495 | 3 |
| By water and by blood | 705 | 1 |
| By which thy people seek thy face | 896 | 1 |
| By which we can salvation have | 34 | 2 |
| By whom our rightful Monarch reigns | 465 | 1 |

| | HYMN | VERSE |
|---|---|---|
| By whom the words of life were spoken | 906 | 1 |
| By whose almighty word | 731 | 1 |
| By whose arm upheld we stand | 580 | 3 |
| By whose strength ye faithful proved | 737 | 7 |
| By whose sufficient grace | 323 | 1 |
| By wondrous, unexhausted love | 642 | 4 |
| By word and by deed | 495 | 2 |
| By worldly thoughts opprest | 296 | 2 |
| By worlds on worlds destroyed | 61 | 3 |
| | | |
| Call back a wandering sheep | 106 | 1 |
| Call for songs of loudest praise | 866 | 1 |
| Call for the never-failing bread | 392 | 1 |
| Call forth the ray of heavenly love | 121 | 1 |
| Call forth thy living witnesses | 418 | 1 |
| Call home, call home thy banished ones | 462 | 2 |
| Call in the south, wake up the north | 746 | 3 |
| *Call Jehovah thy salvation | 597 | 1 |
| Call me forth thy witness, Lord | 402 | 2 |
| Call me, thou Son of God, that I | 136 | 1 |
| Call me, with thy saints surrounded | 933 | 16 |
| Call my little ones thine own | 915 | 2 |
| Call, O call us each by name | 520 | 4 |
| Call off my anxious heart | 296 | 2 |
| Call us hopeless and unblest | 51 | 3 |
| Call us, O Lord, to thine eternal peace | 962 | 4 |
| Call us thy friends, and love, and bride | 507 | 4 |
| Call us up thy face to see | 925 | 3 |
| Called forth this universal frame | 235 | 1 |
| Called in one high calling's hope | 515 | 2 |
| Called, I still refuse to rise | 173 | 2 |
| Called me still to seek thy face | 187 | 1 |
| Called the full power of faith to prove | 351 | 7 |
| Called together by his grace | 480 | 1 |
| †Called to sustain the hallowed cross | 804 | 7 |
| Called us to stand before his face | 203 | 1 |
| Called we are their joys to prove | 519 | 2 |
| Calling thy servants all in vain | 698 | 1 |
| Calls us back, from Eden driven | 480 | 3 |
| Calm and serene my frame | 787 | 6 |
| Calm I mark their vain design | 359 | 3 |
| Calm on tumult's wheel I sit | 325 | 3 |
| Calming the storms of dread and sin | 770 | 6 |
| Calmly for his coming stay | 142 | 1 |
| Calmly I sink among the dead | 917 | 4 |
| Calmly we wait the promised grace | 759 | 6 |
| Came at last our foe to smite | 714 | 2 |
| Came flying all abroad | 551 | 4 |
| Cam'st emptied of thy glory down | 666 | 3 |
| Canaanite, thy faith is great | 164 | 5 |
| Canaanite, thy faith is great | 164 | 6 |
| Can all our raging foes distress | 466 | 1 |
| Can do helpless sinners good | 791 | 5 |

| | Hymn | Verse |
|---|---:|---:|
| Can dust to distant years resound | 559 | 4 |
| Can for a single sin atone | 795 | 4 |
| Can, from afflictions, raise | 844 | 5 |
| Can guilt, and fear, and sorrow chase | 124 | 3 |
| Can hurt whom God delights to save | 337 | 6 |
| Can lead me forth, and make me free | 408 | 5 |
| Can my God his wrath forbear | 168 | 1 |
| Can sinful dust and ashes give | 155 | 1 |
| †Can these avert the wrath of God | 127 | 3 |
| Can these wash out my guilty stain | 127 | 3 |
| Can time his truth impair | 587 | 3 |
| Can turn my heart, and make it clean | 395 | 5 |
| Can violate our rest or stain | 482 | 6 |
| Can we make the fond request | 914 | 7 |
| Can we not watch one night for God | 977 | 2 |
| Can we to men benighted | 747 | 3 |
| Can we weep to see the tears | 52 | 3 |
| †Can we, whose souls are lighted | 747 | 3 |
| Can witness better things | 21 | 3 |
| †Can you doubt if God is love | 8 | 4 |
| Cannot pass from heir to heir | 67 | 4 |
| Canst, according to thy will | 952 | 1 |
| Canst thou be moved from hence | 382 | 3 |
| †Canst thou deny that love to me | 772 | 3 |
| Canst thou not accept my prayer | 151 | 3 |
| *Canst thou reject our dying prayer | 774 | 6 |
| Canst to the utmost save | 136 | 8 |
| †Captain, God of our salvation | 748 | 5 |
| *Captain of Israel's host, and guide | 326 | 1 |
| Captain of my salvation, thou | 293 | 1 |
| *Captain of our salvation, take | 474 | 1 |
| Captain, thy strength-inspiring eye | 298 | 8 |
| Captain, to thee I lift mine eyes | 293 | 6 |
| Captive—but happy sinners still | 461 | 3 |
| Captive lead captivity | 352 | 2 |
| Captive leads captivity | 758 | 2 |
| Captive our captivity | 86 | 3 |
| Captive thyself hast taken them | 583 | 1 |
| Care, anguish, sorrow, melt away | 373 | 3 |
| Care of my soul doth take | 566 | 10 |
| †Careful without care I am | 325 | 2 |
| Careless slumbers cannot steal | 618 | 3 |
| †Careless through outward cares I go | 322 | 3 |
| Cares of to-day, and burdens for to-morrow | 850 | 1 |
| Carmel's stores the heaven's dispense | 348 | 2 |
| Carnal desires control | 966 | 5 |
| Carried me through ten thousand snares | 916 | 1 |
| Carries me out with sweet constraint | 374 | 3 |
| Carrying on his victory | 728 | 3 |
| Carrying on his work within | 758 | 4 |
| Carry me in thy bosom, Lord | 916 | 4 |
| Carry on the earnest strife | 521 | 2 |
| Cast all your sins into the deep | 1 | 9 |

| | Hymn | Verse |
|---|---|---|
| Cast a look, and break my heart | 101 | 1 |
| Cast a look, and break my heart | 168 | 6 |
| Cast him out, by entering now | 299 | 5 |
| Cast it out by perfect love | 398 | 2 |
| Cast my besetting sin away | 775 | 2 |
| Cast off the weight, let fear depart | 831 | 10 |
| Cast off your doubts, disdain to fear | 380 | 5 |
| Cast on thee our every care | 29 | 2 |
| *Cast on the fidelity | 335 | 1 |
| Cast out and banished from thy sight | 574 | 9 |
| Cast out by perfect love | 403 | 2 |
| Cast out the cursed seed | 362 | 4 |
| †Cast out thy foes, and let them still | 136 | 3 |
| Cast out thy foes; the inbred sin | 404 | 5 |
| Cast your crowns before his throne | 727 | 3 |
| Cast thy dreams of ease away | 829 | 1 |
| Casting down their golden crowns around the glassy sea | 646 | 2 |
| Catch, my heart, the issuing blood | 27 | 2 |
| Caught into eternity | 52 | 5 |
| Caught them up thy face to see | 53 | 3 |
| Caught up on the clouds of heaven | 720 | 9 |
| Caught up to meet him in the skies | 932 | 2 |
| Caused thy wondrous incarnation | 933 | 9 |
| Cause me, my Saviour, to love thee | 772 | 6 |
| Cause of endless exultation | 66 | 3 |
| Cause of highest raptures this | 52 | 1 |
| †Cause us the record to receive | 486 | 6 |
| Cause us thy hallowed name to know | 523 | 3 |
| †Cautious the door of sense I close | 828 | 3 |
| Ceaseless, accepted sacrifice | 494 | 4 |
| Ceaseless influence derive | 193 | 2 |
| Ceaseless may, "Abba, Father," cry | 344 | 6 |
| Ceaseless to all thy glory show | 23 | 6 |
| †Cease, O man, thy worth to weigh | 24 | 2 |
| Ceases to preserve his own | 878 | 8 |
| Cedars, neighbours to the sky | 639 | 5 |
| †Celebrate the eternal God | 641 | 3 |
| Celebrate the feast of love | 519 | 1 |
| Celestial fruit on earthly ground | 12 | 4 |
| Celestial joys, or hellish pains | 44 | 1 |
| Cemented by love divine | 512 | 1 |
| *Centre of our hopes thou art | 512 | 1 |
| Change, and bid me die in peace | 287 | 6 |
| Change and decay in all around I see | 972 | 2 |
| Change into songs thy people's fears | 589 | 4 |
| Change it to that heavenly feast | 952 | 3 |
| Change my nature into thine | 390 | 4 |
| Changed from glory into glory | 385 | 3 |
| Changed, they exert a baneful power | 108 | 2 |
| Changing every hour I am | 183 | 2 |
| Chanters to the Lord most high | 260 | 1 |
| Chant, like them, the Lord most High | 643 | 3 |

| | Hymn | Verse |
|---|---|---|
| Chant the fulness of his praise | 604 | 3 |
| Chaos and darkness heard | 870 | 1 |
| Chariots he burns with heavenly flame | 569 | 9 |
| Charm, and melt, and change my will | 188 | 2 |
| Charmed to confess the voice divine | 912 | 3 |
| Chase all your fears away | 713 | 1 |
| Chase from our minds the infernal foe | 752 | 4 |
| Chase the evils of our mind | 693 | 2 |
| Chase this self-will through all my heart | 344 | 6 |
| Chasing all our fears, and cheering | 687 | 2 |
| Chaste, holy, spiritual delights | 14 | 5 |
| Chastise thine humbled son | 179 | 1 |
| †Cheered by a witness so divine | 764 | 4 |
| †Cheerful they walk with growing strength | 592 | 5 |
| Cheer it with hope, with love inflame | 431 | 2 |
| Cheer with thy presence every day | 1003 | 4 |
| Cheers us by his light and heat | 233 | 2 |
| Cherish us with kindest care | 518 | 4 |
| Cherubic choirs, Seraphic flames | 241 | 4 |
| Cherubic legions guard him home | 712 | 2 |
| Cherubim and seraphim falling down before the | 646 | 2 |
| Cherubs proclaim thy praise aloud | 647 | 2 |
| †Cherubs with seraphs join | 737 | 6 |
| Chiefly that I called my own | 910 | 3 |
| Chiefly those who on thee trust | 245 | 1 |
| Chief subject of the sacred book | 90 | 2 |
| Children, and wife, and servants seize | 472 | 6 |
| †Children of faithful Abraham these | 111 | 2 |
| Children's feebler voices there | 737 | 8 |
| †Chilled devotions, changed desires | 768 | 6 |
| Choose and cherish all things good | 769 | 5 |
| Choose out the path for me | 837 | 1 |
| Choose thou for me, my God | 837 | 2 |
| Choose thou my good and ill | 837 | 3 |
| †Chosen of God, to sinners dear | 617 | 2 |
| Christ again shall set it free | 275 | 2 |
| Christ and his cross my only plea | 794 | 2 |
| Christ, awhile to mortals given | 718 | 1 |
| Christ, be Lord, be King to me | 352 | 2 |
| †Christ, by highest heaven adored | 683 | 2 |
| Christ died; Christ "rose again," to save | 923 | 4 |
| *Christ, from whom all blessings flow | 518 | 1 |
| Christ hath brought the life to light | 605 | 2 |
| Christ hath brought us life again | 714 | 1 |
| Christ hath burst the bands of death | 519 | 4 |
| Christ hath burst the gates of hell | 716 | 3 |
| Christ hath gone before us | 715 | 10 |
| Christ hath opened Paradise | 716 | 3 |
| Christ hath risen! | 715 | 4 |
| Christ hath said it shall be so | 755 | 3 |
| †Christ hath the foundation laid | 382 | 5 |
| Christ, if thee our Lord we know | 516 | 2 |
| Christ in a pure and perfect heart | 379 | 5 |

| | Hymn | Verse |
|---|---|---|
| Christ, in whom thy glories shine | 348 | 3 |
| Christ is now gone up on high | 519 | 4 |
| *Christ is our corner stone | 991 | 1 |
| Christ is ready to impart | 192 | 3 |
| Christ Jesus is his name | 856 | 2 |
| †Christ leads me through no darker rooms | 920 | 3 |
| Christ my King is over all | 274 | 3 |
| †Christ, my Master and my Lord | 479 | 2 |
| *Christ, of all my hopes the ground | 672 | 1 |
| †Christ, our Brother and our Friend | 207 | 2 |
| *Christ, our Head, gone up on high | 517 | 1 |
| †Christ our Lord and God we own | 257 | 4 |
| Christ our Prophet, Priest, and King | 522 | 1 |
| Christ rose from depths of earth | 958 | 2 |
| †Christ shall bless thy going out | 618 | 5 |
| Christ shall come with dreadful noise | 58 | 1 |
| Christ shall in me appear | 405 | 1 |
| Christ shall suddenly come down | 54 | 4 |
| Christ, than earth-born monarchs higher | 727 | 2 |
| Christ, the everlasting Lord | 683 | 2 |
| Christ, the fathers' hope of old | 194 | 4 |
| Christ the Father's only Son | 257 | 4 |
| †Christ the head, the corner-stone | 382 | 4 |
| Christ, the incarnate Deity | 348 | 3 |
| Christ, the Lamb of God, was slain | 809 | 2 |
| *Christ, the Lord, is risen to-day | 716 | 1 |
| Christ, the mighty One, art thou | 352 | 1 |
| Christ the Saviour | 936 | 3 |
| †Christ the Saviour is come down | 728 | 6 |
| Christ, the Saviour long foretold | 194 | 4 |
| Christ, the Saviour of mankind | 142 | 3 |
| Christ, the Son, shall make us free | 86 | 3 |
| Christ, the spring of all my joy | 672 | 1 |
| *Christ, the true anointed seer | 676 | 1 |
| Christ, the true, the only Light | 963 | 1 |
| Christ, the woman's conquering Seed | 194 | 4 |
| Christ, the world's desire and hope | 730 | 1 |
| Christ, to all believers precious | 936 | 1 |
| Christ to every soul,—and mine | 899 | 2 |
| Christ to praise in hymns divine | 519 | 1 |
| Christ to praise let all conspire | 727 | 4 |
| Christ through death hath conquered death | 714 | 3 |
| Christ will be our food alone | 714 | 6 |
| Christ, who all your weakness sees | 348 | 4 |
| †Christ, who now gone up on high | 758 | 2 |
| *Christ, whose glory fills the skies | 531 | 1 |
| *Christ, whose glory fills the skies | 963 | 1 |
| Christ with all his church is there | 862 | 2 |
| Christ would quickly enter there | 192 | 2 |
| *Christians, awake, salute the happy morn | 691 | 1 |
| Christians, follow ye! | 715 | 10 |
| *Christian! seek not yet repose | 829 | 1 |
| Christian soldiers, onward go | 847 | 4 |

| | Hymn | Verse |
|---|---|---|
| †Circled round with angel-powers | 718 | 3 |
| Circling us with hosts of fire | 728 | 5 |
| City of God | 595 | 2 |
| Claim a crown in Jesu's right | 7 | 4 |
| Claim a ransomed world for thine | 937 | 4 |
| Claim, and seize me for thy own | 287 | 2 |
| Claim me for thy service, claim | 430 | 3 |
| Claim the heathen tribes for thine | 730 | 2 |
| Claim the kingdom for thine own | 66 | 4 |
| Claim the kingdoms in thy right | 449 | 1 |
| Claim the purchase of thy blood | 748 | 5 |
| Claim the Spirit for your own | 86 | 6 |
| Claim us for thy habitation | 530 | 2 |
| Clap our hands amidst the flame | 238 | 3 |
| Clap your hands, ye floods! Ye hills | 605 | 6 |
| *Clap your hands, ye people all | 571 | 1 |
| Cleanse by the water and the word | 523 | 7 |
| Cleanse from all unrighteousness | 522 | 3 |
| Cleanse me from every sinful thought | 391 | 4 |
| Cleanse me now from every sin | 350 | 2 |
| Cleanse this foul heart, and make it new | 139 | 5 |
| †Cleanse us, Lord, from sinful stain | 753 | 7 |
| Cleansed from all sin, and pure in heart | 926 | 2 |
| †Cleansed from sin's offensive stain | 817 | 2 |
| Clearly he sees, and wins his way | 281 | 2 |
| Cleaving the sky | 848 | 5 |
| †Close behind the tribulation | 936 | 2 |
| Close by the gates of death and hell | 281 | 4 |
| †Close by thy side still may I keep | 338 | 4 |
| †Close followed by their works they go | 926 | 3 |
| Close sheltered in thy bleeding side | 26 | 3 |
| Close sheltered in thy loving heart | 177 | 1 |
| †Close to thine own bright seraphim | 544 | 4 |
| Close to thy bleeding side | 346 | 1 |
| Closely in thy footsteps tread | 723 | 6 |
| †Closer and closer let us cleave | 534 | 4 |
| †Closer knit to Thee, our Head | 518 | 3 |
| Clothed in garments of salvation | 990 | 4 |
| Clothed in thy robe of righteousness complete | 850 | 6 |
| †Clothed with the spirit of holiness | 446 | 2 |
| †Clothe me with thy holiness | 109 | 7 |
| Clothe me with wisdom, patience, love | 431 | 5 |
| Clothe with salvation, through thy name | 431 | 4 |
| Clothe with thy righteousness, and heal | 136 | 3 |
| Clouds the treasured fatness bear | 578 | 2 |
| Clouds, thy chariots, from on high | 579 | 3 |
| Co-equal, co-eternal Three | 237 | 3 |
| Co-equal One and Three | 785 | 5 |
| Co-heir with the great Prince of peace | 304 | 2 |
| Cold, heat, and moist, and dry | 739 | 5 |
| Collect thy feeble flock | 459 | 1 |
| Collect thy flock, and give them food | 744 | 3 |
| Combined to seek the things above | 489 | 1 |

| | Hymn | Verse |
|---|---|---|
| Come all for help to me | 25 | 1 |
| Come, all the world; come, sinner, thou | 2 | 2 |
| *Come, all whoe'er have set | 497 | 1 |
| *Come, all who truly bear | 897 | 1 |
| †Come, all ye souls by sin opprest | 2 | 8 |
| †Come, almighty to deliver | 385 | 2 |
| †Come, and all our sorrows chase | 349 | 4 |
| Come, and baptize me now with fire | 376 | 4 |
| Come, and bring the gospel grace | 687 | 2 |
| Come, and by thy love's revealing | 687 | 1 |
| Come, and by thy presence chase | 413 | 1 |
| Come, and consume the sacrifice | 412 | 2 |
| †Come and hear the wondrous story | 580 | 2 |
| Come, and in me delight to rest | 374 | 1 |
| Come, and in thy temple stay | 390 | 5 |
| Come, and I will give you rest | 29 | 1 |
| Come, and I will save you all | 29 | 1 |
| *Come, and let us sweetly join | 519 | 1 |
| †Come, and maintain thy righteous cause | 568 | 4 |
| Come, and manifest the favour | 687 | 2 |
| Come, and my hallowed heart inspire | 351 | 1 |
| Come, and never leave us more | 86 | 7 |
| Come, and now reside in me | 18 | 1 |
| †Come, and partake the gospel feast | 2 | 4 |
| Come, and perfect us in one | 538 | 1 |
| †Come and possess me whole | 137 | 10 |
| Come, and Satan's works destroy | 413 | 2 |
| Come, and sit, and banquet there | 520 | 1 |
| Come, and spread thy banner hero | 509 | 2 |
| Come, and supply my only want | 146 | 1 |
| Come, and take us to thy side | 937 | 1 |
| Come, and thy sacred unction bring | 666 | 1 |
| Come, and thy sacred unction bring | 752 | 2 |
| Come and visit abject men | 520 | 1 |
| Come and with us, even us, abide | 71 | 1 |
| Come as a mighty rushing wind | 759 | 7 |
| †Come as the dew! and sweetly bless | 771 | 4 |
| †Come as the dove! and spread thy wings | 771 | 5 |
| †Come as the fire! and purge our hearts | 771 | 3 |
| †Come as the light! to us reveal | 771 | 2 |
| Come, as the people of his choice | 603 | 4 |
| †Come as the wind, with rushing sound | 771 | 6 |
| Come, ascend his holy hill | 606 | 6 |
| Come at thy creatures' call | 1014 | — |
| *Come away to the skies | 491 | 1 |
| Come back, and walk herein | 305 | 3 |
| Come back! this is the way | 305 | 3 |
| †Come, behold God's work of wonder | 570 | 5 |
| Come, behold him | 570 | 4 |
| Come, bow before the Lord | 603 | 3 |
| †Come, Desire of nations, come | 683 | 6 |
| *Come, Desire of nations, come | 937 | 1 |
| †Come, Divine and peaceful guest | 758 | 6 |

| | HYMN | VERSE |
|---|---|---|
| *Come, Divine Interpreter | 885 | 1 |
| Come down, and meet us now | 532 | 4 |
| †Come, each faithful soul, who fearest | 580 | 4 |
| Come, eternal King of glory | 60 | 4 |
| Come, exalt him all the living | 606 | 6 |
| Come exulting away | 491 | 1 |
| †Come, Father, in the Son | 643 | 4 |
| *Come, Father, Son, and Holy Ghost | 252 | 1 |
| *Come, Father, Son, and Holy Ghost | 261 | 1 |
| †Come, Father, Son, and Holy Ghost | 403 | 8 |
| *Come, Father, Son, and Holy Ghost | 473 | 1 |
| *Come, Father, Son, and Holy Ghost | 476 | 1 |
| †Come, glorious Lord, the rebels spurn | 280 | 7 |
| Come, gracious Lord, set up thy throne | 275 | 5 |
| Come, feel with me his blood applied | 28 | 2 |
| Come for his espoused below | 936 | 6 |
| Come, heavenly Comforter, come | 165 | 5 |
| *Come, holy celestial Dove | 165 | 1 |
| *Come, Holy Ghost, all quickening fire | 351 | 1 |
| †Come, Holy Ghost, all quickening fire | 351 | 8 |
| *Come, Holy Ghost, all quickening fire | 374 | 1 |
| Come, Holy Ghost, and fill the place | 759 | 6 |
| †Come, Holy Ghost, for moved by thee | 87 | 2 |
| Come, Holy Ghost, for thee I call | 361 | 8 |
| †Come, Holy Ghost, my heart inspire | 376 | 4 |
| *Come, Holy Ghost, our hearts inspire | 87 | 1 |
| *Come, Holy Ghost, our souls inspire | 751 | 1 |
| †Come, Holy Ghost, supply the want | 1005 | 3 |
| Come, Holy Ghost, their pardon seal | 476 | 6 |
| †Come, Holy Ghost, the Saviour's love | 654 | 5 |
| *Come, Holy Spirit, heavenly Dove | 763 | 1 |
| †Come, Holy Spirit, heavenly Dove | 763 | 4 |
| †Come, Holy Spirit, seal the grace | 764 | 3 |
| †Come in, come in, thou heavenly guest | 507 | 2 |
| Come in, my Lord, come in | 406 | 6 |
| †Come, in thee our toil is sweet | 753 | 4 |
| Come, in the house of God appear | 619 | 1 |
| †Come, in this accepted hour | 899 | 2 |
| Come in, this moment, at his call | 2 | 9 |
| †Come in thy pleading Spirit down | 294 | 5 |
| †Come, Jesus, and loose the stammerer's tongue | 481 | 6 |
| Come, Jesus, in thy name to join | 527 | 1 |
| Come, Jesus, while my head I bow | 776 | 2 |
| *Come, let us anew | 47 | 1 |
| *Come, let us anew | 498 | 1 |
| *Come, let us arise | 495 | 1 |
| *Come, let us ascend | 499 | 1 |
| *Come, let us join our cheerful songs | 678 | 1 |
| *Come, let us join our friends above | 949 | 1 |
| *Come, let us join with one accord | 954 | 1 |
| *Come, let us use the grace divine | 532 | 1 |
| *Come, let us, who in Christ believe | 208 | 1 |
| *Come, let us with our Lord arise | 953 | 1 |

| | Hymn | Verse |
|---|---|---|
| Come, Lord, and form my soul anew | 351 | 3 |
| †Come, Lord, and make me pure within | 230 | 4 |
| †Come, Lord, from the skies | 488 | 8 |
| Come, Lord of hosts, the waves divide | 949 | 5 |
| Come, Lord, the bride on earth replies | 749 | 2 |
| †Come, Lord! the drooping sinner cheer | 388 | 7 |
| †Come, Lord, thy glorious Spirit cries | 749 | 2 |
| †Come, Lord, thy Spirit bids thee come | 366 | 5 |
| †Come, Lord, when grace has made me meet | 920 | 4 |
| Come, my Saviour, come away | 156 | 1 |
| *Come, my soul, thy suit prepare | 824 | 1 |
| †Come near, and bless us when we wake | 973 | 6 |
| †Come, O come, all-glorious Lord | 299 | 7 |
| Come, O come, and in us be | 506 | 3 |
| †Come, O my comfort and delight | 379 | 4 |
| Come, O my God, my God | 405 | 8 |
| *Come, O my God, the promise seal | 417 | 1 |
| †Come, O my God, thyself reveal | 405 | 8 |
| †Come, O my guilty brethren, come | 30 | 6 |
| †Come, O my Saviour, come away | 403 | 7 |
| Come, O my soul's physician, thou | 396 | 6 |
| Come, O Redeemer, come away | 537 | 12 |
| *Come, O thou all-victorious Lord | 84 | 1 |
| *Come, O thou Prophet of the Lord | 90 | 1 |
| *Come, O thou Traveller unknown | 140 | 1 |
| †Come, O thou universal Good | 379 | 2 |
| *Come on, my partners in distress | 333 | 1 |
| Come, our life, and peace, and rest | 411 | 2 |
| Come pour thy joys on human kind | 752 | 1 |
| Come quickly, and kindly display | 174 | 4 |
| Come quickly from above | 216 | 9 |
| Come quickly from above | 343 | 8 |
| Come quickly, gracious Lord | 389 | 4 |
| †Come quickly, gracious Lord, and take | 216 | 8 |
| †Come quickly in, thou heavenly guest | 208 | 4 |
| †Come quickly, Lord, the veil remove | 124 | 4 |
| Come quickly, Lord! thy face display | 154 | 3 |
| Come quickly, Lord! thy own receive | 154 | 2 |
| Come quickly to help a lost soul | 174 | 3 |
| Come, Redeemer, come away | 52 | 6 |
| Come, Redeemer, come away | 852 | 3 |
| Come, Remembrancer Divine | 899 | 2 |
| Come, saints, and with your tears bedew | 712 | 1 |
| †Come, Saviour, come, and make me whole | 408 | 8 |
| Come, Saviour, come, thy wounds display | 861 | 3 |
| Come, Saviour, from above | 447 | 2 |
| *Come, Saviour, Jesus, from above | 285 | 1 |
| Come, see if there ever was sorrow like his | 707 | 1 |
| Come, see, ye worms, your Maker die | 28 | 2 |
| Come, shed abroad the Saviour's love | 763 | 4 |
| Come, sinners, and trust in Jesus's name | 5 | 3 |
| *Come, sinners, to the gospel feast | 2 | 1 |
| *Come, sound his praise abroad | 603 | 1 |

| | HYMN | VERSE |
|---|---|---|
| Come, taste the manna of my love | 4 | 8 |
| Come, ten thousand angels, come | 987 | 4 |
| †Come then, and claim me for thine own | 275 | 5 |
| Come then, and in thy people's eyes | 35 | 3 |
| †Come then, and loose my stammering tongue | 366 | 4 |
| †Come then, and to my soul reveal | 128 | 5 |
| †Come, then, divine Interpreter | 255 | 3 |
| Come then for Jesu's sake | 410 | 1 |
| †Come then from above | 160 | 2 |
| †Come then, my God, mark out thine heir | 374 | 5 |
| Come then, my Master, and my God | 375 | 4 |
| Come then, my Lord, and gather me | 144 | 7 |
| Come then, my Lord, thy right assert | 146 | 4 |
| †Come then, my Hope, my Life, my Lord | 155 | 7 |
| †Come, then, O house of Jacob! come | 740 | 7 |
| †Come then, O Lord, and deign to be my guest | 967 | 5 |
| †Come then, O Lord, thy light impart | 686 | 3 |
| †Come then, our heavenly Adam, come | 108 | 5 |
| *Come then, our heavenly Adam, come | 1009 | — |
| †Come, then, thou great Deliverer, come | 451 | 3 |
| †Come then to thy servants again | 220 | 4 |
| †Come, then, ye sinners, to your Lord | 9 | 6 |
| *Come, thou all-inspiring Spirit | 530 | 1 |
| *Come, thou Conquerer of the nations | 748 | 1 |
| *Come, thou everlasting Spirit | 899 | 1 |
| *Come, thou fount of every blessing | 866 | 1 |
| *Come, thou high and lofty Lord! | 520 | 1 |
| *Come, thou long-expected Jesus | 688 | 1 |
| *Come, thou omniscient Son of man | 502 | 1 |
| Come, thou righteous Judge of all | 299 | 8 |
| Come, thou Spirit of burning come | 766 | 1 |
| Come, thou universal Saviour | 687 | 2 |
| †Come, thou Witness of his dying | 899 | 2 |
| Come to God's own temple, come | 987 | 1 |
| Come to Jesus Christ and buy | 791 | 2 |
| Come to join us to his choir | 936 | 6 |
| Come to make our joys o'erflow | 936 | 6 |
| "Come to me," saith One, and coming | 793 | 1 |
| Come to my help, pronounce the word | 139 | 1 |
| †Come to the living waters, come | 4 | 2 |
| †Come to them who suffer dearth | 753 | 2 |
| Come unto thee, and rest from sin | 118 | 4 |
| Come up into the chariot of love | 499 | 1 |
| Come visit every waiting mind | 752 | 1 |
| Come, weary souls, to Jesus come! | 31 | 3 |
| *Come, wisdom, power, and grace divine | 527 | 1 |
| Come with thy Spirit's winnowing fan | 502 | 1 |
| †Come, worship at his throne | 603 | 3 |
| Come ye before him and rejoice | 607 | 1 |
| *Come, ye followers of the Lord | 295 | 1 |
| Come, ye guilty spirits oppressed | 29 | 1 |
| †Come, ye needy, come and welcome | 791 | 2 |
| *Come, ye sinners, poor and wretched | 791 | 1 |

| | Hymn | Verse |
|---|---|---|
| *Come, ye thankful people, come | 987 | 1 |
| *Come, ye that love the Lord | 12 | 1 |
| †Come, ye weary, heavy-laden | 791 | 4 |
| *Come, ye weary sinners, come | 29 | 1 |
| Comes to save a fallen race | 400 | 1 |
| Comes your favoured souls to bless | 418 | 2 |
| Comfort, and confirm, and heal | 188 | 5 |
| Comfort it brings, and power, and peace | 209 | 2 |
| Comfort my people, saith your God! | 120 | 1 |
| *Comfort, ye ministers of grace | 120 | 1 |
| Comforter through Jesus given | 766 | 1 |
| Comforts there, and blessings join | 407 | 5 |
| Coming, as at first I came | 175 | 4 |
| Commanded in thy steps to tread | 454 | 3 |
| Command me to be brought, and say | 135 | 10 |
| Command that mine may yield to thee | 884 | — |
| Command the blind thy rays to see | 129 | 4 |
| Command the crowd to sit | 875 | 1 |
| Command the light of faith to shine | 148 | 3 |
| Commands, we gladly do | 96 | 6 |
| Commemorate thee, our dying Lord | 901 | 1 |
| Commissioned from his Father's throne | 675 | 3 |
| Committed to thy faithful care | 893 | 2 |
| *Commit thou all thy griefs | 831 | 1 |
| Communicate his love | 875 | 3 |
| Communion with our Lord | 898 | 3 |
| Companions through the wilderness | 527 | 3 |
| Compassed round with songs of praise | 335 | 4 |
| Compasses with angel-bands | 233 | 1 |
| Compassion reigns alone | 152 | 4 |
| Compass my weakness round about | 998 | 1 |
| Compel the wanderer to come in | 857 | 5 |
| Complete in Jesu's name | 526 | 2 |
| Compose into a thankful frame | 204 | 1 |
| Concealed in the cleft of thy side | 228 | 3 |
| Concealed the word of God most high | 279 | 2 |
| Concealed, thou art a Saviour still | 130 | 3 |
| Concentred all, through Jesu's name | 500 | 4 |
| Concerning thee, O Christ, make known | 90 | 2 |
| Conclude them all in unbelief | 443 | 1 |
| †Conclude us first in unbelief | 84 | 4 |
| Conducted to the realms above | 258 | 1 |
| Conduct me to thy dazzling throne | 686 | 4 |
| Conduct them all to heaven | 472 | 6 |
| Conduct us by thy light | 704 | 3 |
| Conferred on them some gift unknown | 721 | 2 |
| Confer the grace unknown | 459 | 3 |
| Confessors undaunted here | 737 | 8 |
| Confess the Infinite unknown | 651 | 1 |
| Confess thine attributes divine | 235 | 2 |
| Confide in thee alone | 587 | 6 |
| Confident, divinely bold | 271 | 2 |
| Confident in thy defence | 542 | 1 |

| | HYMN | VERSE |
|---|---|---|
| †Confiding in thy only love | 432 | 8 |
| †Confiding in thy truth alone | 896 | 2 |
| Confined to neither court nor cell | 68 | 1 |
| Confirm and strengthen them in grace | 458 | 1 |
| Confirm the feeble knee | 831 | 14 |
| Confirm the prayer, the seal impart | 17 | 9 |
| Confirm the tidings as they roll | 552 | 4 |
| †Conflicts I cannot require | 819 | 4 |
| Conformed in all things to our Head | 523 | 4 |
| Conform me to thy death | 347 | 1 |
| Conform my heart to thine | 788 | 6 |
| Confound, abase me from this hour | 670 | 8 |
| †Confound, o'erpower me by thy grace | 893 | 8 |
| †Confound whoe'er *his* ruin seek | 465 | 6 |
| Confounds the powers of hell | 650 | 8 |
| Conquered all thy foes and ours | 757 | 1 |
| Conquering all with sovereign love | 60 | 2 |
| Conquering, and to conquer go | 852 | 4 |
| Conqueror of all adverse power | 737 | 4 |
| Conqueror of death with thee to rise | 72 | 1 |
| †Conqueror of hell, and earth, and sin | 347 | 2 |
| Conqueror over death and sin | 718 | 3 |
| Conqueror over sin proclaim | 278 | 7 |
| Conqueror through him I soon shall seize | 405 | 3 |
| Conquerors of the world, we tread | 423 | 2 |
| Conquers earth, and hell, and sin | 521 | 3 |
| Conquer sinners, comfort saints | 975 | 5 |
| Conquer thy worst foe in me | 158 | 4 |
| Conscious of my inveterate sin | 779 | 1 |
| Conscious of the blood applied | 735 | 4 |
| Consecrate my heart to thee | 287 | 2 |
| Consecrate to thee alone | 430 | 5 |
| Consecrating earthly love | 995 | 8 |
| Consists in the rapturous gaze | 73 | 5 |
| Conspire our rapture to complete | 333 | 6 |
| Conspire to raise the sound | 742 | 2 |
| Constancy to me impart | 183 | 2 |
| Constant joy, and lasting peace | 480 | 2 |
| Constant supplies of hallowing grace | 489 | 2 |
| Constrained by Jesu's love to live | 526 | 4 |
| Constrained by the grace of my Lord | 911 | 4 |
| †Consume our lusts as rotten wood | 412 | 8 |
| Consume our stony hearts within | 412 | 8 |
| Consume the dust, the serpent's food | 412 | 8 |
| Contending for our native heaven | 71 | 5 |
| Contending for thy heavenly home | 69 | 4 |
| Contending for your native place | 420 | 4 |
| †Contented now upon my thigh | 141 | 6 |
| Content if thou exalted be | 184 | 11 |
| Content to fill a little space | 842 | 5 |
| Continually adore | 243 | 1 |
| Continually ascend | 535 | 8 |
| Continually forsake | 88 | 7 |

| | Hymn | Verse |
|---|---|---|
| Continue to defend | 622 | 3 |
| Contracted to a span | 665 | 3 |
| Contracted to a span | 772 | 4 |
| Contrite grief, and pardoning grace | 757 | 2 |
| Control my every thought | 270 | 1 |
| †Convert, and send forth more | 745 | 3 |
| Convince and bring the wanderers back | 89 | 3 |
| †Convince him now of unbelief | 83 | 4 |
| Convinced that every perfect gift | 435 | 1 |
| Convinced we still are one in heart | 533 | 1 |
| Convulsions shake the solid world | 569 | 2 |
| Co-partner with my Lord | 304 | 2 |
| Correct me every night | 549 | 4 |
| Correct with kind severity | 179 | 1 |
| †Corruption, earth, and worms | 930 | 2 |
| Corrupts the race and taints us all | 574 | 3 |
| Could be merited by mine | 24 | 1 |
| Could give the guilty conscience peace | 703 | 1 |
| Could he more than shed his blood | 8 | 1 |
| Could I but my heart prepare | 192 | 2 |
| Could I but see thy face | 784 | 6 |
| Could I but touch his garment's hem | 781 | 3 |
| Could I hid from thee remain | 633 | 3 |
| †Could I of thy strength take hold | 271 | 2 |
| Could I the Omniscient leave | 633 | 3 |
| †Could my tears for ever flow | 709 | 2 |
| Could my zeal no languor know | 709 | 2 |
| Could never for one sin atone | 702 | 2 |
| Could so delight my ear | 764 | 2 |
| Could thy wisdom keep me there | 274 | 2 |
| †Could we but climb where Moses stood | 938 | 6 |
| Could weep, believe, and thrice reply | 147 | 5 |
| Courage, our fainting souls to keep | 865 | 5 |
| Courage, your Captain cries | 277 | 5 |
| Courteous, pitiful, and kind | 509 | 3 |
| Count her every precious shrine | 572 | 3 |
| †Countless as sands upon the shore | 923 | 2 |
| Countless, invisible | 315 | 1 |
| †Covered by the darkest shade | 633 | 4 |
| Covered is my unrighteousness | 189 | 3 |
| Covered my guilty face | 93 | 7 |
| Covered with meritorious scars | 726 | 1 |
| †Cover *his* enemies with shame | 985 | 3 |
| Cover me with thy hand | 271 | 4 |
| Cover me with thy mighty hand | 283 | 3 |
| Cover my defenceless head | 148 | 2 |
| Covers with the clothes we wear | 233 | 2 |
| Craving creaturely supplies | 768 | 4 |
| †Create all new; our wills control | 752 | 4 |
| †Create my nature pure within | 574 | 8 |
| Create our ruined frame anew | 666 | 5 |
| Created again | 491 | 4 |
| Created to share | 491 | 4 |

|   | Hymn | Verse |
|---|---|---|
| Creating and preserving grace | 229 | 2 |
| Creation rose in form complete | 731 | 1 |
| †Creation, varied by his hand | 223 | 5 |
| Creator of the seeing eye | 887 | — |
| *Creator Spirit, by whose aid | 752 | 1 |
| Creator, thee adore | 665 | 2 |
| Creatures capable of God | 7 | 2 |
| Creatures that never knew thy name | 788 | 5 |
| †Creatures with all their endless race | 637 | 5 |
| Credence to his word I give | 335 | 1 |
| Cried "Let it still alone" | 981 | 3 |
| Cries, "O my son, my son!" | 482 | 5 |
| Cries, "How shall I give thee up?" | 168 | 4 |
| Cries, Ye will not happy be | 8 | 3 |
| †Crimes of such horror to forgive | 656 | 2 |
| Crops of precious increase yield | 631 | 5 |
| Crowned with righteousness, arise | 349 | 3 |
| Crown *him* with grace, with glory crown | 985 | 3 |
| †Crown him, ye martyrs of our God | 681 | 3 |
| †Crown him, ye morning stars of light | 681 | 2 |
| Crown us with his heavenly love | 238 | 4 |
| Crown with joy this festive board | 995 | 2 |
| Crown with life beyond the grave | 597 | 3 |
| Crowns of glory on their head | 75 | 1 |
| Crowns of glory to bestow | 936 | 6 |
| Crucified before our eyes | 701 | 2 |
| Crucified to all below | 877 | 2 |
| Crucify your Lord again | 6 | 2 |
| Cry aloud in heavenly lays | 75 | 2 |
| Cry to every nation, cry | 197 | 5 |
| †Cursed for the sake of wretched man | 108 | 3 |
| Cut it short in righteousness | 287 | 6 |
| Cut it short in righteousness | 398 | 1 |
| Cut off and lost their last faint hope | 450 | 2 |
| Cut off for sins, but not his own | 706 | 1 |
| †Cut off our dependence vain | 508 | 3 |
| Cut off the entail of sin | 354 | 4 |
| Daily and hourly bid me die | 362 | 3 |
| Daily feels that Christ hath died | 522 | 2 |
| Daily I'm constrained to be | 866 | 3 |
| Daily thy salvation see | 238 | 2 |
| Daily thy salvation see | 1019 | 3 |
| Damned, till by Jesus saved, thou art | 439 | 3 |
| †Dangers stand thick through all the ground | 42 | 4 |
| Dare not in thy presence move | 358 | 2 |
| Dare not set thy God a time | 142 | 1 |
| Dare not think him insincere | 8 | 3 |
| Dare to behold thy awful throne | 133 | 2 |
| Dare to believe; on Christ lay hold | 380 | 5 |
| Dare we pray for a reprieve? | 914 | 7 |
| †Dark and cheerless is the morn | 963 | 2 |
| Darkened into endless night | 936 | 3 |

| | Hymn | Verse |
|---|---|---|
| Darkened the sun, and rent the veil | 902 | 3 |
| Darkly heaving | 570 | 1 |
| Darkness be over me | 848 | 2 |
| Dauntless, though rocks of pride be near | 272 | 5 |
| Dauntless to the high prize aspire | 873 | 4 |
| Dauntless, untired, I follow thee | 839 | 5 |
| Dawn on these realms of woe and sin | 959 | 5 |
| *Day after day I sought the Lord | 566 | 1 |
| Day and night they cry to thee | 350 | 1 |
| Day and night we'll speak our woe | 299 | 2 |
| Day by day his course to run | 631 | 2 |
| Day by day with strength supplied | 904 | 1 |
| Day of all the week the best | 975 | 1 |
| *Day of wrath! O day of mourning | 933 | 1 |
| Day-spring from on high, be near | 963 | 1 |
| Day-star, in my heart appear | 963 | 1 |
| †Dead, already dead within | 6 | 4 |
| Dead, by faith in Christ I live | 191 | 1 |
| Dead souls thou callest from their grave | 360 | 5 |
| Dead to God while here you breathe | 6 | 4 |
| Dead to the world and all its toys | 351 | 5 |
| Dead to the world and sin ye live | 420 | 5 |
| †Deafness to thy whispered calls | 768 | 3 |
| Deaf, we hearken now to thee | 348 | 5 |
| Dear Desire of every nation | 688 | 1 |
| *Dear is the day which God hath made | 951 | 1 |
| †Dear name! the Rock on which I build | 679 | 3 |
| Dearest fellowship we prove | 522 | 2 |
| Death and hell behind are cast | 50 | 2 |
| Death and the curse are known no more | 585 | 11 |
| Death dares never harm us more | 714 | 4 |
| †Death, hell, and sin are now subdued | 706 | 8 |
| Death, hell, are but the want of thee | 100 | 4 |
| Death in vain forbids his rise | 716 | 3 |
| Death is mocked, and set at nought | 714 | 3 |
| †Death is struck, and nature quaking | 933 | 4 |
| Death is swallowed up of life! | 50 | 3 |
| Death, like a narrow sea divides | 938 | 2 |
| Death of death, and hell's destruction | 839 | 3 |
| Death, only death, can cut the knot | 288 | 3 |
| Death, the latest foe, destroy | 349 | 4 |
| Death to thee, to us, is gain | 50 | 5 |
| *Deathless principle, arise! | 921 | 1 |
| Death's dark stream shall never more | 672 | 10 |
| Deceived by those I prized too well | 849 | 3 |
| Decked in the robes of joy and praise | 585 | 6 |
| Decked with a never-fading crown | 26 | 5 |
| Deck his mediatorial crown | 921 | 1 |
| Declare us reconciled in thee | 442 | 3 |
| Dedicate a house to him | 989 | 3 |
| Deeming our sad lives their prey | 621 | 1 |
| Deepens our imperfect groans | 758 | 5 |
| *Deepen the wound thy hands have made | 370 | 1 |

| | Hymn | Verse |
|---|---|---|
| Deeper sink, and higher rise | 424 | 2 |
| †Deeper than hell, it plucked me thence | 216 | 7 |
| Deeper than inbred sin | 216 | 7 |
| Deep founded in the truth of grace | 526 | 5 |
| Deep in a fleshly dungeon groans | 154 | 3 |
| Deep in the Father's bosom lies | 420 | 6 |
| Deep in unfathomable mines | 845 | 1 |
| Deep wounded by thy Spirit's sword | 89 | 3 |
| Deeply wailing | 66 | 2 |
| Defeat their every hostile aim | 985 | 3 |
| Defend *him*, Lord, defend | 465 | 10 |
| Defends his own | 276 | 1 |
| Defiance to the gates of hell | 569 | 11 |
| Deign to meet us, Saviour, here | 995 | 2 |
| Delay is endless death to me | 776 | 2 |
| Delighted with the wondrous theme | 636 | 2 |
| Delightful lesson of thy grace | 505 | 6 |
| Delightfully I prove | 834 | 2 |
| Delight in human blood | 447 | 1 |
| Delight in what thyself hast given | 507 | 2 |
| Delight to bless thy name | 637 | 5 |
| Delights our evil to remove | 250 | 1 |
| Deliverance in thy name | 818 | 3 |
| Deliverance he affords to all | 562 | 4 |
| †Deliverance to my soul proclaim | 139 | 2 |
| Deliver me from evil now | 820 | 5 |
| Demands and crowns eternity | 658 | 6 |
| Demands my soul, my life, my all | 700 | 4 |
| Demands our choicest songs | 979 | 1 |
| Demands our souls' collected powers | 955 | 1 |
| Demand successive songs of praise | 978 | 4 |
| Departed in thy faith and fear | 945 | 1 |
| Depends on every breath | 42 | 6 |
| Deprived of joy, and destitute of God | 596 | 3 |
| *Depth of mercy! can there be | 168 | 1 |
| Descend, and crown us now with fire | 457 | 4 |
| †Descend, and let thy lightning burn | 138 | 2 |
| Descend, and make me pure from sin | 391 | 3 |
| Descend in this accepted hour | 283 | 4 |
| †Descend, pass by me, and proclaim | 144 | 5 |
| Descend with all thy gracious powers | 771 | 1 |
| Descend with all thy gracious powers | 771 | 7 |
| Descending from above | 295 | 5 |
| Descending in a cloud | 249 | 1 |
| †Descending on his azure throne | 56 | 3 |
| Descending swift from Christ our Head | 630 | 3 |
| Descends from thee alone | 875 | 2 |
| Descends from thee alone | 1016 | 2 |
| Descends to make me whole | 870 | 1 |
| Desire in vain its depths to see | 147 | 2 |
| †Destroy me not by thy delay | 776 | 2 |
| Destroy the fiend that lurks within | 177 | 3 |
| Destroy the love of sin in me | 122 | 4 |

| | Hymn | Ver. |
|---|---|---|
| Destroy the works of self and pride | 453 | 1 |
| Destroy them all, destroy | 407 | 3 |
| †Determined all thy will to obey | 432 | 5 |
| Determined nought to know, beside | 439 | 1 |
| Determined thee alone to know | 773 | 1 |
| Detest and loathe myself and sin | 99 | 4 |
| Devoted solely to thy will | 431 | 3 |
| Devote its little all to thee | 395 | 8 |
| Devote our every hour to thee | 977 | 3 |
| Devotion shall be all my heart | 788 | 7 |
| Devoutly reads therein by day | 540 | 2 |
| Did e'er such love and sorrow meet | 700 | 3 |
| Did first our hearts unite | 535 | 1 |
| Did he not all their sickness heal | 32 | 3 |
| Did he reject his helpless clay | 32 | 3 |
| †Did not his word the fiends expel | 32 | 3 |
| Did not the prophet speak | 883 | 1 |
| Did not thy death my life procure | 157 | 3 |
| Did our creation plan | 256 | 4 |
| Did they know the Deity | 215 | 3 |
| Did they own him who he was | 215 | 3 |
| Didst all my griefs remove | 614 | 1 |
| Didst lead a suffering life below | 137 | 5 |
| Didst not abhor the virgin's womb | 353 | 2 |
| Didst quit thy throne with him to live | 544 | 3 |
| Didst stoop to redeem a lost race | 220 | 1 |
| †Didst thou not die that I might live | 375 | 4 |
| Didst thou not die the death for me | 145 | 4 |
| †Didst thou not in our flesh appear | 128 | 4 |
| †Didst thou not in the flesh appear | 375 | 3 |
| †Didst thou not make us one | 510 | 3 |
| Didst thou our sorrows bear | 883 | 3 |
| Died he for me, who caused his pain | 201 | 1 |
| Died himself, that ye might live | 6 | 2 |
| Die into the arms of God | 554 | 4 |
| Die, to live the life of glory | 922 | 4 |
| Dies at the opening day | 41 | 6 |
| Dies on the altar of thy cross | 286 | 6 |
| Diffuse thine image through my soul | 347 | 4 |
| Diffuse thy grace through every part | 453 | 2 |
| Diffusing life, and joy, and peace | 902 | 4 |
| Diffusive as thy sun's arise | 38 | 2 |
| Dipped in thy own sacred blood | 748 | 4 |
| Direct and govern all our ways | 475 | 4 |
| †Direct, control, suggest, this day | 964 | 7 |
| Direct my word, inspire my thought | 373 | 8 |
| Direct our wandering feet aright | 686 | 2 |
| Disburdened of her load | 96 | 2 |
| †Discerning thee, my Saviour, stand | 550 | 2 |
| Discern their every secret snare | 311 | 1 |
| Discharge the Christian parents' part | 467 | 9 |
| Disdain a Father's name | 764 | 1 |
| Disdain not, Lord, our meaner song | 494 | 2 |

# DISPARTED BY — DOST FOR

| | Hymn | Verse |
|---|---|---|
| Disparted by the wondrous rod | 223 | 2 |
| Dispel our darkness by thy light | 666 | 5 |
| Dispels my guilty fear | 764 | 2 |
| Disperse it by thy love | 502 | 4 |
| Disperse it with thine eyes | 733 | 2 |
| Disperse my sins as morning dew | 964 | 6 |
| Disperse the gloomy clouds of night | 690 | 3 |
| Display, our fallen souls to raise | 261 | 1 |
| Display the attributes divine | 656 | 1 |
| Display their Author's power | 665 | 2 |
| Display thy beams divine | 252 | 3 |
| Display thy glory from above | 393 | 2 |
| Display thy guardian power | 653 | 6 |
| Display thy salvation, And teach the new song | 40 | 7 |
| Display thy sanctifying power | 396 | 6 |
| Display thy sifting power | 502 | 1 |
| Display unto me | 160 | 2 |
| Dispose my heart by entering there | 132 | 4 |
| *Disposer Supreme, And Judge of the earth | 869 | 1 |
| Dispread the victory of thy cross | 568 | 4 |
| Dispread thy gracious kingdom here | 445 | 3 |
| Disquieted with pride | 565 | 3 |
| Dissipate the clouds beneath | 687 | 1 |
| Dissolve as liquid air | 64 | 3 |
| Dissolve, by raging flames destroyed | 57 | 5 |
| Distressed thee sore for my relief | 772 | 5 |
| Distribute now the heavenly bread | 875 | 1 |
| Disturb those peaceful years | 740 | 5 |
| Divers gifts to each divide | 518 | 5 |
| Divert thy vengeful thunder's aim | 298 | 4 |
| Divides me for a little while | 849 | 4 |
| Divide this consecrated soul | 285 | 5 |
| Divine, incarnate Word | 194 | 3 |
| †Divine Instructer, gracious Lord | 880 | 5 |
| Divine omnipotence | 382 | 3 |
| Divinely confident and bold | 144 | 1 |
| Divinely drawn to follow thee | 222 | 1 |
| Do as thou wilt with me | 851 | 1 |
| Do not in judgment rise | 635 | 1 |
| Do not let me turn again | 434 | 3 |
| Do this, he said,—and died | 897 | 1 |
| Do thou thy trembling servants stay | 767 | 5 |
| Do thus, O ye of Israel's seed | 626 | 4 |
| Docile, helpless, as a child | 302 | 3 |
| Does his Creator's power display | 552 | 2 |
| Doing or receiving good | 529 | 4 |
| Dominions, thrones, and powers | 727 | 3 |
| Done away death's power and right | 714 | 2 |
| Doomed to flames of woe unbounded | 933 | 16 |
| Doom him to infernal woe | 299 | 8 |
| Dooms them to everlasting death | 599 | 4 |
| Dost all my burdens bear | 325 | 3 |
| Dost for all incessant pray | 676 | 2 |

| | Hymn | Verse |
|---|---|---|
| Dost give the power to pray | 778 | 1 |
| Dost make thy gracious nature known | 121 | 3 |
| †Dost thou desire to know and see | 69 | 4 |
| Dost thou no longer chide | 188 | 1 |
| Dost thou not all my sorrows know | 157 | 4 |
| †Dost thou not dwell in all thy saints | 765 | 2 |
| Dost to each or bliss or woe | 242 | 3 |
| Dost to none thy fulness show | 242 | 1 |
| Dost with smiling plenty crown | 578 | 2 |
| Dost with thyself restore | 447 | 3 |
| Doth after God aspire | 368 | 1 |
| Doth all my inmost thoughts descry | 279 | 6 |
| Doth all their homage claim | 605 | 6 |
| Doth at thy bidding yield | 578 | 3 |
| Doth aught on earth my wishes raise | 279 | 6 |
| Doth bright in thy full image rise | 180 | 8 |
| Doth efficacious prove | 875 | 3 |
| Doth every secret thought explore | 955 | 2 |
| Doth his brethren's cause maintain | 724 | 2 |
| Doth his successive journeys run | 585 | 7 |
| Doth in my sorrows feel its part | 144 | 2 |
| Doth inwardly shine | 760 | 4 |
| Doth naked in thy sight appear | 81 | 1 |
| Doth now my table spread | 555 | 4 |
| Doth our Redeemer use | 675 | 2 |
| Doth through my conscience thrill | 799 | 5 |
| Double portion of his grace | 720 | 4 |
| Doubtful and insecure of bliss | 154 | 1 |
| Doubtless he shall soon return | 623 | 6 |
| †Down from the shining seats above | 699 | 3 |
| Down from thy throne above | 772 | 5 |
| Down to the deep, and buried there | 569 | 2 |
| †Downward I hasten to my destined place | 596 | 2 |
| Dragged to the judgment-seat | 80 | 3 |
| Dragged to the portals of the sky | 557 | 6 |
| Drag us from our trust in thee | 508 | 4 |
| Draw by the music of thy name | 16 | 7 |
| Draw me, Saviour, after thee | 27 | 1 |
| Draw nigh; thy pitying ear incline | 290 | 1 |
| Draw the Gentiles unto thee | 743 | 1 |
| Draw us by thy grace alone | 514 | 1 |
| Draw us to thyself again | 98 | 2 |
| Draw with stronger influence | 287 | 4 |
| Drawn by thee to seek thy face | 910 | 1 |
| Drawn by the lure of strong desire | 374 | 1 |
| Drawn by thy uniting grace | 538 | 1 |
| Drawn from Immanuel's veins | 798 | 1 |
| Dreams and visions of the night | 287 | 3 |
| Dried her tears, her pardon sealed | 106 | 6 |
| Dried up in a moment and gone | 777 | 2 |
| Drink comfort from the living well | 590 | 3 |
| Drink endless pleasures in | 12 | 3 |
| Drink into my Spirit, Who happy would be | 10 | 2 |

| | Hymn | Verse |
|---|---|---|
| Drink of the brook, then rise to sway | 613 | 3 |
| Drive all my fears away | 555 | 3 |
| Drive their terrors far away | 878 | 3 |
| *Drooping soul, shake off thy fears | 142 | 1 |
| †Drop down in showers of love | 86 | 6 |
| Drop from thy gracious eye | 106 | 3 |
| Drop in that holy choir | 942 | 4 |
| Drop it where thorns and thistles grow | 739 | 2 |
| Drops already from above | 218 | 4 |
| Drops of fatness, as they fly | 579 | 3 |
| Drunkards, your sins on him were laid | 36 | 2 |
| Dry corruption's fountain up | 354 | 4 |
| †Dry your tears, ye hearts nigh broken | 595 | 5 |
| Due from Adam's helpless race | 737 | 3 |
| †Dumb at thy feet I lie | 565 | 5 |
| Dumb, for thee our tongues employ | 348 | 5 |
| Dust and ashes is my name | 175 | 3 |
| †Dust and ashes though we be | 350 | 4 |
| Dwelling in an earthly clod | 684 | 3 |
| Dwelling in the midst of foes | 970 | 2 |
| Dwell in us, and we shall be | 517 | 4 |
| Dwell, nor ever be dismayed | 597 | 1 |
| Dwell on his love with sweetest song | 585 | 9 |
| Dwell with him above the sky | 7 | 1 |
| Dwell within our hallowed breast | 530 | 2 |
| Dwell within our single heart | 514 | 3 |
| Dwells on my lips, and fires my thought | 437 | 7 |
| Dying champions for their God | 519 | 2 |
| Dying, his soul an offering made | 750 | 4 |
| Dying, if thou still delay | 149 | 2 |
| Dying, I heard the welcome sound | 206 | 2 |
| †Dying Redeemer, to thy breast | 799 | 7 |
| Dying, risen, ascending for us | 720 | Dox. |
| Dying they shall not "see death" | 817 | 7 |
| | | |
| Each before his Saviour stands | 75 | 1 |
| Each evening shows thy tender love | 241 | 2 |
| †Each following moment as it flies | 677 | 4 |
| Each holy day Thy blessings pour | 991 | 3 |
| Each hour on earth we live | 696 | 1 |
| †Each moment applied | 160 | 5 |
| †Each moment draw from earth away | 344 | 8 |
| Each moment knit my soul to thee | 317 | 2 |
| Each moment may we feel | 497 | 4 |
| Each other's cross to bear | 503 | 3 |
| Each rising morn thy plenteous grace | 241 | 2 |
| Each the other's burden bear | 509 | 4 |
| Each to each, and all to thine | 515 | 1 |
| Each to each our tempers suit | 538 | 2 |
| Each to each unite, and bless | 514 | 2 |
| Each to each unite, endear | 509 | 2 |
| Each to each ye then shall say | 197 | 4 |
| Each toilsome duty, each foreboding fear | 850 | 3 |

| | Hymn | Verse |
|---|---|---|
| Each to love provoke his friend | 487 | 1 |
| Each true resolve, each solemn vow | 961 | 2 |
| Each upward glance of filial fear | 961 | 2 |
| Each wave a watery hill | 697 | 1 |
| †Eager for thee I ask and pant | 374 | 3 |
| Eager I ask, I pant for more | 374 | 2 |
| Early believing, ever blessed | 891 | 6 |
| Early in the morning our song shall rise to thee | 646 | 1 |
| †Early in the temple met | 529 | 3 |
| Earnest of love, and pledge of heaven | 374 | 4 |
| Ears that ear, and tongues that sing | 580 | 1 |
| Ears the mystic words to hear | 885 | 1 |
| Earth, air, and sea, before thy sight | 235 | 2 |
| Earth and heaven | 936 | 2 |
| Earth and heaven repeat the cry | 571 | 7 |
| Earth, and hell, and sin shall yield | 407 | 6 |
| Earth and hell their wars may wage | 359 | 3 |
| Earth and her sons beneath thee lie | 1001 | 7 |
| Earth, by thy soft dews prepared | 579 | 2 |
| Earth doth not open yet | 172 | 1 |
| †Earth from afar hath heard thy fame | 316 | 4 |
| Earth, hell, and heaven's strong pillars bow | 38 | 3 |
| Earth her hundred-fold increase | 578 | 3 |
| †Earth is thine; her thousand hills | 989 | 2 |
| Earth receives the wealthy rain | 579 | 2 |
| *Earth, rejoice, our Lord is king | 728 | 1 |
| Earth, repeat the glorious song | 727 | 4 |
| Earth shall then her fruits afford | 582 | 3 |
| Earth shall raise the glad acclaim | 580 | 1 |
| †Earth then a scale to heaven shall be | 108 | 8 |
| †Earth! tremble on, with all thy sons | 223 | 4 |
| Earth we shall view, and heaven destroyed | 536 | 5 |
| Earth with all thy nations wait | 606 | 1 |
| Earth, with all thy sons, rejoice | 605 | 4 |
| *Earth, with all thy thousand voices | 580 | 1 |
| Earthly passions far remove | 350 | 3 |
| Earthquakes, dearths, and desolations | 748 | 1 |
| Earth's basis shook confirms our hope | 62 | 3 |
| †Earth's but a sorry tent | 942 | 3 |
| Earth's fleeting treasures I resign | 564 | 4 |
| Earth's haughty potentates conspire | 541 | 1 |
| Earth's joys grow dim, its glories pass away | 972 | 2 |
| Earth's remotest bounds have seen | 605 | 3 |
| Earth's remotest bounds shall own | 572 | 2 |
| Earth's toys, for thee his constant flame | 344 | 7 |
| †Easy to be entreated, mild | 472 | 3 |
| Eat on earth the bread of heaven | 1012 | — |
| Echoing to the trump of God | 571 | 3 |
| Echoing thy eternal praise | 260 | 1 |
| Echo thy sacrificial prayer | 122 | 5 |
| Eden's door | 715 | 6 |
| Edom for thy possession take | 445 | 2 |
| E'en let the unknown to-morrow | 804 | 2 |

| | Hymn | Verse |
|---|---|---|
| E'en though it be a cross | 848 | 1 |
| E'er deemed the cross could, spell-like, save | 770 | 3 |
| †E'er since, by faith, I saw the stream | 798 | 4 |
| Effectually call | 219 | 6 |
| Effectuate now the sacred sign | 476 | 4 |
| †Effulgence of the light divine | 353 | 2 |
| †Eighteen, or eight and thirty, years | 396 | 5 |
| Else empty, barren darkness still | 240 | 3 |
| Else I must surely stray | 837 | 2 |
| Embalms the air, and paints the land | 978 | 2 |
| Emblem of eternal rest | 975 | 1 |
| Employ an endless rest | 950 | 1 |
| Employing a clod | 231 | 7 |
| Emptied himself of all but love | 201 | 3 |
| Emptied of all but love | 195 | 2 |
| Emptied of his majesty | 684 | 2 |
| Emptied of pride, and wrath, and hell | 351 | 3 |
| Empty my heart of earthly love | 285 | 1 |
| †Empty of him who all things fills | 117 | 2 |
| Empty, poor, and void of thee | 191 | 3 |
| Empty send me not away | 175 | 3 |
| Emulate the heavenly powers | 571 | 4 |
| Enable me to endure | 370 | 2 |
| Enable me to go | 840 | 2 |
| †Enable with perpetual light | 751 | 2 |
| Encouraged by the Saviour's word | 119 | 1 |
| Encouraged we, and sure to speed | 827 | 5 |
| Ended is the glorious strife | 50 | 3 |
| End, Jesus, end this war within | 773 | 3 |
| †End of my every action thou | 321 | 2 |
| End of our enlarged desires | 512 | 1 |
| Endless joys we may possess | 737 | 12 |
| †Endless scenes of wonder rise | 701 | 2 |
| Endless theme of earth and heaven | 645 | 2 |
| Endue me with thy patient love | 470 | 1 |
| Endue my soul with thee | 109 | 7 |
| †Endue the creatures with thy grace | 992 | 3 |
| Endue with heavenly graces | 736 | 3 |
| Engage the ear, and warm the heart | 955 | 4 |
| Engage to make me blest | 832 | 5 |
| †Engraved as in eternal brass | 659 | 4 |
| Engrave thy name on me | 854 | 6 |
| Engraving on our inmost parts | 438 | 2 |
| Engraving pardon on my heart | 374 | 4 |
| Enjoying the beams of his love | 946 | 2 |
| Enjoy the grace to angels given | 17 | 8 |
| Enjoy thy glorious infamy | 483 | 4 |
| Enlarge, and fill us all with God | 523 | 2 |
| †Enlarge, inflame, and fill my heart | 433 | 5 |
| Enlarge my heart to compass thee | 155 | 3 |
| †Enlarge my heart to make thee room | 289 | 8 |
| Enlarge my heart to understand | 370 | 3 |
| Enlightening, comforting and guiding | 595 | 3 |

|  | HYMN | VERSE |
|---|---|---|
| Enlisted under thy command | 293 | 1 |
| Enough for all, enough for each | 250 | 4 |
| Enough for evermore | 250 | 4 |
| Enough for us to trace thy will | 767 | 8 |
| *Enslaved to sense, to pleasure prone | 108 | 1 |
| †Entangled in the worldly snare | 836 | 2 |
| Enter, and find that God is here | 490 | 1 |
| Enter, and in me ever stay | 289 | 8 |
| Enter, and keep my heart | 137 | 12 |
| Enter, and make an end of sin | 616 | 9 |
| Enter, and make us free indeed | 299 | 4 |
| Enter, and receive thy crown | 51 | 4 |
| Enter and show yourselves approved | 490 | 1 |
| Enter every trembling heart | 385 | 1 |
| Enter in by thee to heaven | 13 | 4 |
| Enter into immediate rest | 926 | 1 |
| Enter into my joy, and sit down on my throne | 47 | 6 |
| Enter into my Master's joy | 214 | 5 |
| Enter into my Master's joy | 440 | 2 |
| Enter into my Master's joy | 828 | 5 |
| Enter into the promised rest | 391 | 7 |
| Enter into thy wise design | 510 | 1 |
| Enter my soul, and work within | 347 | 2 |
| Enter my soul, extirpate sin | 362 | 4 |
| Enter now thy poorest home | 149 | 2 |
| Enter our devoted breast | 758 | 6 |
| Enter thyself, and drive it hence | 367 | 2 |
| Enter with all thy mercy's power | 172 | 4 |
| Entered the grave in mortal flesh | 699 | 3 |
| *Entered the holy place above | 726 | 1 |
| †Entering into my closet, I | 119 | 2 |
| †Enthroned above yon sky | 737 | 5 |
| Enthroned at God's right hand | 275 | 2 |
| Enthroned in everlasting state | 256 | 1 |
| Enthroned, may reign in endless bliss | 38 | 4 |
| Enthrone, on Zion's sacred hill | 541 | 2 |
| Entirely all my sins remove | 408 | 8 |
| Entirely thine should be | 661 | 3 |
| Entranced, enwrapped, alone with thee | 698 | 4 |
| Entrusting thy riches, Which always endure | 869 | 1 |
| Equally be thou adored | 645 | 1 |
| †Equal with God most high | 194 | 2 |
| *Equip me for the war | 270 | 1 |
| Ere glowed with stars the ethereal blue | 240 | 2 |
| *Ere God had built the mountains | 667 | 1 |
| Ere I am summoned hence away | 565 | 9 |
| Ere I see the morning light | 287 | 6 |
| Ere rest, or light return | 838 | 3 |
| Ere rolling planets knew to shine | 353 | 2 |
| Ere shines the dawn of rising day | 437 | 1 |
| Ere stars were seen above | 667 | 3 |
| Ere that day of retribution | 933 | 11 |
| Ere the stars of morn be spent | 570 | 3 |

| | Hymn | Verse |
|---|---|---|
| Ere the winter storms begin | 987 | 1 |
| Ere through the world our way we take | 973 | 6 |
| Ere time began to be | 665 | 1 |
| Ere time its ceaseless course began | 353 | 2 |
| Ere we can offer our complaints | 569 | 1 |
| Ere yet my feeble thoughts had learned | 657 | 3 |
| Erring hearts to right incline | 753 | 8 |
| †Error and ignorance remove | 473 | 3 |
| Escaped to the mansions of light | 49 | 1 |
| Escapes or strikes the searching eye | 240 | 3 |
| †Essay your choicest strains | 727 | 2 |
| Essential life's unbounded sea | 240 | 2 |
| Established in our first estate | 256 | 5 |
| Established on the rock of peace | 247 | 4 |
| Esteem the scandal of the cross | 483 | 4 |
| †Eternal are thy mercies, Lord | 615 | 2 |
| *Eternal Beam of light divine | 337 | 1 |
| Eternal bliss to ensure | 59 | 5 |
| Eternal Comforter, to thee | 752 | 5 |
| *Eternal depth of love divine | 655 | 1 |
| *Eternal Father, strong to save | 1004 | 1 |
| Eternal glory be from man | 966 | 6 |
| Eternal happiness or woe | 43 | 2 |
| †Eternal life to all mankind | 360 | 3 |
| Eternal life with thee is given | 95 | 4 |
| Eternal light's co-eval beam | 351 | 2 |
| *Eternal Lord of earth and skies | 448 | 1 |
| Eternal Lord of heaven | 730 | 1 |
| Eternal mercy bears a part | 636 | 3 |
| *Eternal Power, whose high abode | 316 | 1 |
| Eternal praise be thine | 221 | 1 |
| Eternal praise to heaven's almighty King | 691 | 6 |
| *Eternal Source of every joy | 978 | 1 |
| *Eternal Spirit, come | 762 | 1 |
| †Eternal Spirit! descend from high | 476 | 5 |
| *Eternal, spotless Lamb of God | 237 | 1 |
| †Eternal Sun of righteousness | 252 | 3 |
| Eternal things impress | 59 | 3 |
| †Eternal, Triune Lord | 253 | 4 |
| Eternal truth attends thy word | 615 | 2 |
| †Eternal, undivided Lord | 785 | 5 |
| Eternal Wisdom is their guide | 1002 | 1 |
| *Eternal Wisdom! Thee we praise | 226 | 1 |
| Eternally fresh from the throne | 371 | 2 |
| Eternally held in thy heart | 228 | 3 |
| Eternally shall last | 947 | 2 |
| Eternally shall live | 948 | 4 |
| Eternally to reign | 1005 | 3 |
| †Eternity thy fountain was | 240 | 2 |
| Even crosses from his sovereign hand | 846 | 2 |
| Even for his own name's sake | 556 | 2 |
| Even from my infant days | 97 | 1 |
| Even from their infancy | 893 | 2 |

|  | Hymn | Verse |
|---|---|---|
| Even here thy walls discern | 943 | 6 |
| Even here to me fulfil | 944 | 5 |
| Even in this vale of woe | 593 | 2 |
| Even I should be made whole | 781 | 3 |
| Even me | 790 | Cho. |
| Even now by faith I see thee | 943 | 6 |
| Even now by faith we join our hands | 949 | 4 |
| Even now, my sins remove | 125 | 4 |
| †Even now our Lord doth pour | 630 | 6 |
| Even now we mournfully enjoy | 898 | 3 |
| †Even now we think and speak the same | 500 | 4 |
| Even tears in darkness, starlike, shine | 838 | 5 |
| Even then this shall be all my plea | 190 | 6 |
| Even those thy daily favours share | 241 | 3 |
| Even those whom death's sad fetters bound | 353 | 1 |
| Even to those in darkness sitting | 595 | 4 |
| Even when it seems that thou wouldst slay indeed | 851 | 1 |
| Even when my heart shall break, my God, my Life, my Lord | 851 | 3 |
| Ever apprised of danger nigh | 306 | 3 |
| Ever ask, "What shall we do?" | 529 | 1 |
| Ever by a mighty hope | 769 | 4 |
| *Ever fainting with desire | 354 | 1 |
| Ever faithful, ever sure | 631 | Cho. |
| Ever faithful to thy word | 348 | 1 |
| Ever flowing in bliss from the throne | 488 | 3 |
| Ever flows their thirst to assuage | 594 | 2 |
| Ever for us interceding | 722 | 3 |
| Ever fruitful, ever green | 598 | 3 |
| Ever gasping after rest | 109 | 1 |
| Ever gazing up to thee | 718 | 7 |
| Ever hasting to the day | 852 | 3 |
| Ever in thy Spirit live | 13 | 3 |
| Ever intimately near | 661 | 1 |
| Ever may my soul be fed | 904 | 1 |
| Ever merciful and just | 197 | 2 |
| Ever mighty to prevail | 218 | 2 |
| Ever near to allure and defend | 231 | 4 |
| Ever offering up my prayers | 193 | 7 |
| Ever ready was to save them | 606 | 5 |
| Ever suffered shipwreck there | 921 | 4 |
| †Ever upward let us move | 718 | 9 |
| Ever worship, praise, and fear | 990 | 1 |
| Everlasting God, come down | 66 | 4 |
| Everlasting life is this | 716 | 6 |
| Everlasting life is won | 521 | 4 |
| Everlasting righteousness | 86 | 4 |
| Every anxious thought repress | 999 | 2 |
| Every arm of flesh remove | 508 | 3 |
| Every burdened soul release | 687 | 3 |
| Every creature made by thee | 733 | 1 |
| †Every day the Lord of hosts | 278 | 7 |
| Every evil thought restrain | 287 | 1 |

| | Hymn | Verse |
|---|---|---|
| †Every eye shall now behold him | 66 | 2 |
| Every eye the Judge shall see | 605 | 7 |
| Every fainting soul inspire | 399 | 1 |
| Every faithful heart's desire | 538 | 1 |
| Every faithful soul's desire | 676 | 3 |
| †Every fresh alarming token | 60 | 3 |
| Every good in Jesus joined | 628 | 4 |
| Every grace that brings us nigh | 791 | 2 |
| Every high aspiring thought | 358 | 4 |
| Every knee to him shall bow | 728 | 2 |
| Every knee to thee shall bow | 449 | 1 |
| Every knee to thee shall bow | 730 | 3 |
| Every member feel its share | 518 | 7 |
| Every moment in our heart | 755 | 3 |
| Every moment, Lord, I want | 292 | 4 |
| Every moment springing up | 193 | 3 |
| Every mournful sinner cheer | 399 | 1 |
| Every one that asks shall have | 142 | 3 |
| †Every one that seeks shall find | 142 | 3 |
| Every passion's wild excess | 382 | 2 |
| Every poor benighted heart | 687 | 2 |
| Every secret thought is known | 819 | 1 |
| Every sickness and disease | 693 | 2 |
| Every soul and every heart | 245 | 4 |
| Every soul-infirmity | 693 | 3 |
| Every soul that moves and lives | 661 | 2 |
| Every stumbling-block remove | 398 | 2 |
| Every stumbling-block remove | 509 | 2 |
| Every tongue to thee confess | 727 | 5 |
| Every vile affection kill | 522 | 3 |
| Every weary, wandering spirit | 687 | 3 |
| Every word, and every thought | 512 | 2 |
| Every work I do below | 325 | 2 |
| Evil and danger turn away | 312 | 3 |
| Evil is ever with me day by day | 794 | 3 |
| Exacted is the legal pain | 706 | 4 |
| Exalted over all the lands | 569 | 10 |
| Exalt their great Creator's praise, and say Alleluia | 663 | — |
| Excellence of strength divine | 348 | 3 |
| Excellent his name we find | 197 | 5 |
| *Except the Lord conduct the plan | 526 | 1 |
| Excite our softest sympathy | 441 | 2 |
| Excluded is my every boast | 127 | 6 |
| Exert their baneful power | 315 | 2 |
| Exert thy all-subduing power | 528 | 2 |
| Exhaustless riches find | 880 | 2 |
| Exist, and live, and move in thee | 666 | 2 |
| †Expand thy wings, celestial Dove | 87 | 3 |
| *Expand thy wings, celestial Dove | 121 | 1 |
| Expectant waits the wished supply | 636 | 3 |
| Expect his fulness to receive | 534 | 4 |
| Expect not here nor there | 739 | 3 |
| Expect with joy thy face to see | 45 | 2 |

|  | Hymn | Verse |
|---|---|---|
| Expecting to receive. | 357 | 1 |
| Expecting to receive. | 486 | 1 |
| Expecting till the Bridegroom come | 154 | 2 |
| †Expel the fiend out of my heart | 409 | 2 |
| Experienced every human pain | 849 | 1 |
| Experienced in thy name | 872 | 1 |
| Experience will decide | 562 | 5 |
| Expires, in sweet confusion lost | 369 | 5 |
| Explain thine own transmitted word | 90 | 1 |
| Exposed to no temptation | 818 | 1 |
| Express the tempers of our Lord | 438 | 2 |
| *Extended on a cursed tree | 28 | 1 |
| Extend his power, exalt his throne | 585 | 1 |
| Extend the arms of mighty prayer | 268 | 3 |
| Extend thy ample shade | 271 | 3 |
| Extend thy mercy's arms to me | 649 | 3 |
| †Extend to me that favour, Lord | 612 | 3 |
| †Extend to these thy pardoning grace | 82 | 7 |
| Extends to all around | 630 | 4 |
| †Extol his kingly power | 277 | 2 |
| †Extol the Lamb of God | 738 | 3 |
| Extol the riches of thy grace | 206 | 3 |
| Extol to all eternity. | 232 | Cho. |
| Extolled above all thanks and praise | 545 | 1 |
| †Extort the cry, "What must be done | 83 | 6 |
| Exulting in their might | 446 | 5 |
| Exulting in their Saviour | 736 | 2 |
| Exult, O dust and ashes | 943 | 15 |
| Exults our rising soul | 96 | 2 |
| †Eye hath not seen, nor ear hath heard | 69 | 3 |
| Eyes that the beam celestial view | 965 | 1 |
| †Faded my virtuous show | 93 | 7 |
| Fading is the sinner's pleasure | 594 | 3 |
| Faint and dead no more I droop | 193 | 3 |
| †Faint and weary thou hast sought me | 933 | 10 |
| †Faint we were, and parched with drought | 348 | 6 |
| †Fainting soul, be bold, be strong | 142 | 2 |
| Fain we would on thee rely | 29 | 2 |
| Fain we would to thee return | 349 | 3 |
| Fain with them our souls would vie | 260 | 3 |
| Fain would I all my vileness own | 99 | 4 |
| †Fain would I all thy goodness feel | 119 | 5 |
| †Fain would I go to thee, my God | 290 | 5 |
| †Fain would I know, as known by thee | 99 | 4 |
| †Fain would I know my utmost ill | 100 | 2 |
| †Fain would I learn of thee, my God | 388 | 5 |
| *Fain would I leave the world below | 154 | 1 |
| †Fain would I the truth proclaim | 402 | 3 |
| †Fain would we cease from sinning | 818 | 3 |
| Fain would we his great name record | 492 | 1 |
| Fain would we leave this weary road | 959 | 5 |
| †Fairer than all the earth-born race | 568 | 2 |

| | Hymn | Verse |
|---|---|---|
| Fairer than spring the colours shine | 46 | 3 |
| †Fairer than the sons of men | 434 | 3 |
| Fairest among ten thousand fair | 853 | 1 |
| †Fair shall be thine earthly temple | 990 | 3 |
| Faith, and love, and joy increase | 520 | 3 |
| Faith cries out, " 'Tis He, 'tis He " | 701 | 3 |
| Faith his blood strikes on our door | 714 | 4 |
| Faith in every page descries | 876 | 2 |
| Faith in Jesu's conquering name | 278 | 5 |
| †Faith in the only sacrifice | 865 | 4 |
| †Faith in thy changeless name I have | 397 | 4 |
| Faith in thy name thou know'st I have | 548 | 1 |
| †Faith in thy power thou seest I have | 360 | 5 |
| †Faith lends its realising light | 95 | 6 |
| Faith, like its Finisher and Lord | 95 | 1 |
| Faith makes thy fulness all our own | 507 | 6 |
| †Faith, mighty faith, the promise sees | 360 | 9 |
| Faith no life but his will own | 714 | 6 |
| Faith on heathens hath bestowed | 735 | 2 |
| Faith only sees that God is here | 1001 | 3 |
| Faith our strong protection be | 464 | 1 |
| Faith renews the justified | 735 | 4 |
| Faith supports; by faith I stand | 193 | 8 |
| Faith these mountains would remove | 24 | 1 |
| Faith the word of power applies | 278 | 5 |
| †Faith to be healed thou know'st I have | 139 | 3 |
| †Faith to be healed thou know'st I have | 356 | 6 |
| Faith unfolds the gates of heaven | 735 | 4 |
| Faith which by our works is shown | 521 | 3 |
| Faith without thee I cannot have | 148 | 4 |
| Faith would make me ever thine | 24 | 1 |
| †Faithful and True, we now receive | 380 | 9 |
| Faithful hearts who on thee call | 753 | 5 |
| Faithful he is, and just | 345 | 3 |
| Faithful, if we our sins confess | 380 | 2 |
| Faithful in thy promises | 242 | 3 |
| Faithful is the promised word | 400 | 7 |
| Faithful let thy mercies prove | 29 | 2 |
| †Faithful, O Lord, thy mercies are | 250 | 5 |
| †Faithful soul, pray always; pray | 618 | 2 |
| Faithful to death I might endure | 330 | 3 |
| Faithful to my Lord's commands | 325 | 1 |
| Faithfully his gifts improve | 521 | 2 |
| Faith's effectual fervent prayer | 515 | 1 |
| Fall at their father's knee | 797 | 2 |
| Fall down at his feet And gladly believe | 5 | 5 |
| Fall down before his throne | 948 | 6 |
| Fall down on their faces, And worship the Lamb | 859 | 4 |
| Fall like them who dare not move | 643 | 3 |
| Fall o'erwhelmed with love, or soar | 260 | 3 |
| Fall prostrate, lost in wonder fall | 494 | 5 |
| Fall worshipping, and spread the ground | 316 | 2 |
| Fallen among thieves I am | 112 | 1 |

| | Hymn | Verse |
|---|---|---|
| Fallen, till in me thine image shine. | 132 | 2 |
| Falls plenteous from the sky | 115 | 3 |
| Falls soft and gentle as the evening shower | 967 | 2 |
| False and full of sin I am | 143 | 3 |
| False to thee, like Peter, I | 106 | 1 |
| Far above all earthly things | 325 | 4 |
| †Far above all earthly things | 508 | 8 |
| Far above these nether skies | 349 | 3 |
| †Far and wide, though all unknowing | 743 | 2 |
| *Far as creation's bounds extend | 636 | 1 |
| Far beneath his feet he views | 61 | 3 |
| Far distant from the living God | 150 | 1 |
| †Far, far above thy thought | 831 | 13 |
| Far from an evil world retreat | 526 | 3 |
| Far from a world of grief and sin | 65 | 5 |
| Far from earth our souls remove | 349 | 3 |
| Far from earth the spirit flies | 50 | 3 |
| Far from fear, from danger far | 349 | 2 |
| Far from my home, in life's rough way | 841 | 1 |
| Far from our hearts remove | 502 | 4 |
| Far from our souls be driven | 502 | 2 |
| Far from sorrow, sin, and fear | 538 | 4 |
| Far from the living Lord | 93 | 3 |
| Far from the path of peace | 21 | 1 |
| †Far from the paths of men, to thee. | 119 | 3 |
| †Far off I stand with tearful eyes | 795 | 3 |
| *Far off we need not rove | 661 | 1 |
| †Far off, yet at thy feet I lie | 180 | 6 |
| Far on the left with horror stand | 80 | 3 |
| Far wide my wandering thoughts were spread | 210 | 3 |
| Fast bound in sin and misery | 109 | 1 |
| Fast bound in sin and misery | 830 | 1 |
| Fast bound in sin and nature's night | 201 | 4 |
| Fast in his slavish chains | 786 | 1 |
| Fast in one mind and spirit stand | 505 | 2 |
| Fasted, and prayed, and read thy word | 91 | 1 |
| †Father, accept them through thy Son | 473 | 6 |
| Father, all thy name reveal | 477 | 2 |
| Father and Son to show | 258 | 3 |
| "Father," at the point to die | 106 | 7 |
| *Father, at thy footstool see | 514 | 1 |
| Father, before we taste | 875 | 2 |
| Father, before we taste | 1016 | 1 |
| †Father, behold thy dying Son | 894 | 4 |
| †Father, behold thy Son | 191 | 2 |
| †Father, behold, we claim | 86 | 7 |
| Father, bring the kingdom near | 653 | 2 |
| †Father, by right divine | 653 | 7 |
| Father, glorify thy Son | 506 | 1 |
| *Father, glorify thy Son | 755 | 1 |
| †Father, God, thy love we praise | 221 | 4 |
| †Father, God, to us impart | 717 | 3 |
| *Father, God, we glorify | 717 | 1 |

| | Hymn | Verse |
|---|---|---|
| *Father, how wide thy glory shines | 263 | 1 |
| *Father, I dare believe | 410 | 1 |
| *Father, I know that all my life | 842 | 1 |
| *Father, I stretch my hands to thee | 784 | 1 |
| †Father, if I may call thee so | 181 | 3 |
| *Father, if justly still we claim | 456 | 1 |
| *Father, if thou must reprove | 179 | 1 |
| Father, if 'tis thy will | 944 | 5 |
| Father, in Jesu's name I pray | 121 | 5 |
| †Father, in me reveal thy Son | 97 | 6 |
| *Father, in the name I pray | 336 | 1 |
| †Father, in these reveal thy Son | 476 | 3 |
| *Father, in whom we live | 253 | 1 |
| *Father, into thy hands alone | 432 | 1 |
| Father, leave me not alone | 819 | 1 |
| *Father, live, by all things feared | 645 | 1 |
| *Father, Lord of earth and heaven | 914 | 1 |
| Father, now accept of mine | 245 | 4 |
| *Father of all, by whom we are | 467 | 1 |
| *Father of all, in whom alone | 88 | 1 |
| *Father of all, thy care we bless | 997 | 1 |
| *Father of all! whose powerful voice | 235 | 1 |
| *Father of boundless grace | 460 | 1 |
| *Father of earth and heaven | 1011 | — |
| *Father of earth and sky | 653 | 1 |
| †Father of endless majesty | 647 | 5 |
| †Father of everlasting grace | 121 | 3 |
| *Father of everlasting grace | 377 | 1 |
| †Father of everlasting grace | 493 | 2 |
| †Father of everlasting love | 441 | 4 |
| *Father of faithful Abraham, hear | 451 | 1 |
| *Father of Jesus Christ, my Lord | 119 | 1 |
| *Father of Jesus Christ, my Lord | 360 | 1 |
| *Father of Jesus Christ the Just | 148 | 1 |
| *Father of lights, from whom proceeds | 99 | 1 |
| *Father of lights! thy needful aid | 469 | 1 |
| *Father of me, and all mankind | 251 | 1 |
| Father of mercies, glorify | 138 | 8 |
| *Father of mercies, in thy word | 880 | 1 |
| *Father of omnipresent grace | 81 | 1 |
| *Father of our dying Lord | 506 | 1 |
| †Father of the Fatherless | 915 | 4 |
| †Father, on me the grace bestow | 864 | 3 |
| *Father, our child we place | 892 | 1 |
| Father, our helplessness we own | 108 | 1 |
| Father, pardon through thy Son | 768 | 10 |
| Father, regard his sacrifice | 917 | 3 |
| †Father, regard thy pleading Son | 298 | 5 |
| *Father, see this living clod | 368 | 1 |
| †Father, Son, and Holy Ghost | 336 | 2 |
| †Father, Son, and Holy Ghost | 368 | 4 |
| *Father, Son, and Holy Ghost | 430 | 1 |
| †Father, Son, and Holy Ghost | 430 | 6 |

| | Hymn | Verse |
|---|---|---|
| *Father, Son, and Holy Ghost | 477 | 1 |
| Father, Son, and Holy Ghost | 479 | 3 |
| †Father, Son, and Holy Ghost | 514 | 4 |
| Father, Son, and Holy Ghost | 515 | 3 |
| †Father, Son, and Holy Ghost | 910 | 7 |
| Father, Son, and Holy Spirit | 990 | 1 |
| †Father, Son, and Spirit, come | 411 | 2 |
| Father, Son, and Spirit divine | 890 | 2 |
| Father, Son, and Spirit, hail | 643 | 1 |
| *Father, Son, and Spirit, hear | 515 | 1 |
| †Father, Son, and Spirit, send | 989 | 4 |
| *Father, supply my every need | 392 | 1 |
| †Father, the narrow path | 840 | 2 |
| †Father, thine everlasting grace | 189 | 2 |
| Father, this light, this breath we owe | 241 | 2 |
| *Father, through thy Son receive | 1022 | — |
| Father, thy ceaseless love | 831 | 5 |
| †Father, thy long-lost son receive | 785 | 4 |
| †Father, thy love in Christ reveal | 1005 | 2 |
| †Father, thy mercies past we own | 979 | 3 |
| Father, thy mercy never dies | 189 | 5 |
| †Father, 'tis thine each day to yield | 236 | 3 |
| *Father, 'tis thine each day to yield | 1017 | 1 |
| *Father, to thee I lift mine eyes | 306 | 1 |
| *Father, to thee my soul I lift | 435 | 1 |
| †Father, we ask in Jesu's name | 298 | 4 |
| *Father, whate'er of earthly bliss | 843 | 1 |
| Father, which thou to me hast showed | 30 | 2 |
| *Father, whose everlasting love | 39 | 1 |
| Favoured with God's peculiar smile | 404 | 3 |
| Fear and love thy awful name | 653 | 1 |
| Fear doth servile spirits bind | 355 | 8 |
| Fear even to ask thy grace | 93 | 2 |
| †Fear him, ye saints, and you will then | 562 | 6 |
| Fear not lest his truth should fail | 348 | 4 |
| Fear shall in me no more have place | 803 | 1 |
| Fear thou not the deadly quiver | 597 | 2 |
| Fear we not the world subsiding | 570 | 1 |
| Fear, ye fiends, for Christ is here | 728 | 4 |
| Fearful soul, be strong, be bold | 142 | 1 |
| †Fearless of hell and ghastly death | 213 | 5 |
| Fearless their violence dare | 272 | 2 |
| Fearless to his presence fly | 921 | 2 |
| Fed and guided by his hand | 975 | 2 |
| Fed with immortality | 531 | 1 |
| Federal Head of all mankind | 129 | 1 |
| Feeble, and faint, and blind, and poor | 395 | 3 |
| Feeble and unarmed I am | 278 | 3 |
| *Feeble in body and in mind | 836 | 1 |
| Feed me now and evermore | 839 | 1 |
| Feed this tender branch of thine | 193 | 2 |
| Feeds the young ravens when they cry | 99 | 1 |
| Feeds us with the food we eat | 233 | 2 |

| | HYMN | VERSE |
|---|---|---|
| Feel, my soul, the pangs divine | 27 | 2 |
| Feel our sins by grace forgiven | 463 | 2 |
| Feel our sins on earth forgiven | 487 | 4 |
| Feels the cleansing blood applied | 522 | 2 |
| Fellowship in Jesu's love | 522 | 2 |
| Fellowship with him they gain | 817 | 2 |
| Fiends, and men, and angels feel | 195 | 1 |
| Fiends and men exclaim aloud | 601 | 3 |
| Fiercely then his vengeance flowed | 606 | 4 |
| Fight, and I must prevail | 944 | 6 |
| Fight, nor think the battle long | 847 | 2 |
| Fight the fight, maintain the strife | 847 | 1 |
| Fight the good fight of faith with me | 277 | 3 |
| Fighting and fears, within, without | 796 | 3 |
| Fightings and wars shall cease | 447 | 3 |
| Fightings without, and fears within | 478 | 2 |
| Fill all my life with purest love | 328 | 4 |
| Fill all my soul with love | 146 | 1 |
| Fill all others with dismay | 878 | 3 |
| Fill all this mighty void | 405 | 8 |
| Fill each breast with consolation | 1007 | — |
| Fill every heart with mournful care | 441 | 2 |
| Fill every soul with sacred grief | 84 | 4 |
| Fill every want my spirit feels | 136 | 6 |
| Fill his soul, already full | 407 | 5 |
| Fill me, Radiancy Divine | 963 | 3 |
| †Fill me with all the life of love | 169 | 4 |
| Fill me with a sweet surprise | 287 | 4 |
| Fill me with pure, celestial fire | 323 | 3 |
| Fill me with pure desire | 110 | 6 |
| Fill me with righteousness divine | 773 | 1 |
| Fill my soul with love from heaven | 766 | 1 |
| Fill my whole soul with chaste desire | 210 | 1 |
| Fill my whole soul with filial fears | 186 | 5 |
| Fill our church with righteousness | 464 | 1 |
| Fill our hearts with joy and peace | 1008 | 1 |
| Fill our humbled hearts with prayer | 60 | 1 |
| Fill our mouths with food and praise | 1012 | — |
| Fill our spotless souls with God | 530 | 1 |
| Fill, satiate, with thy heavenly light | 210 | 5 |
| Fill the earth with golden fruit | 449 | 2 |
| Fill the wide earth with grateful praise | 656 | 4 |
| Fill thee with triumphant joy | 407 | 3 |
| Fill thy church with light divine | 582 | 1 |
| Fill thy consecrated shrine | 890 | 2 |
| Fill up every soul with love | 76 | 4 |
| Fill us now with heavenly fires | 512 | 1 |
| Fill us with immortal meat | 905 | 1 |
| †Fill us with the Father's love | 517 | 4 |
| Fill us with the glorious power | 399 | 2 |
| †Fill with inviolable peace | 114 | 4 |
| Fill with thyself the mighty void | 155 | 3 |
| Filled me with thy righteousness | 292 | 5 |

| | Hymn | Verse |
|---|---|---|
| Filled our hearts to overflowing | 895 | 4 |
| Filled with all the Deity | 27 | 6 |
| Filled with joy, and love, and peace | 400 | 5 |
| Filled with pangs unspeakable | 168 | 2 |
| Filled with peace, and heavenly joy | 413 | 2 |
| Filled with righteousness divine | 937 | 4 |
| Filled with the eternal Spirit's power | 689 | 3 |
| Filled with the glory of the Lord | 749 | 4 |
| Filled with wisdom, love, and power | 618 | 5 |
| Filling all the realms of light | 633 | 2 |
| Fills her furrows, smooths her soil | 579 | 2 |
| Fills the world with plenteous food | 1022 | — |
| Find, and love, and praise him there | 58 | 2 |
| †Find in Christ the way of peace | 20 | 2 |
| Find in Christ your all in all | 20 | 2 |
| Find in thee the way to heaven | 463 | 2 |
| Find light and life, if thou appear | 353 | 1 |
| Find, nor ever thence depart | 349 | 2 |
| Find on earth the life of heaven | 20 | 3 |
| Find our happy all in thee | 508 | 8 |
| Find our heaven of heavens in thee | 718 | 10 |
| Find our lasting quiet there | 29 | 2 |
| Find supplied, in Jesu's love | 487 | 4 |
| Find their heaven begun below | 325 | 5 |
| Find the pearl that Adam lost | 479 | 3 |
| Find the perfect holiness | 402 | 1 |
| Finds his God, and sits and sings | 50 | 3 |
| †Finish then thy new creation | 385 | 3 |
| Finish thy great work of grace | 398 | 1 |
| Finish thy great work of love | 287. | 6 |
| Firm as a rock thy truth shall stand | 608 | 4 |
| †Firm as his throne his promise stands | 811 | 3 |
| Firm as the mount of God | 622 | 1 |
| Firm fixed this universal chain | 240 | 8 |
| †Firm in the all-destroying shock | 63 | 6 |
| Firm on an everlasting seat. | 721 | 3 |
| Firmly grounded upon thee. | 355 | 1 |
| Firmly, singularly good | 737 | 9 |
| †Firmly trusting in thy blood | 672 | 9 |
| †First and last in me perform | 292 | 4 |
| First begotten from the dead | 418 | 1 |
| †First-born of many brethren thou | 26 | 8 |
| First let the birds, with painted plumage gay | 663 | — |
| First mine office to fulfil | 877 | 3 |
| First the blade, and then the ear | 987 | 2 |
| †First the dead in Christ shall rise | 58 | 2 |
| First the purchase of thy blood | 428 | 3 |
| Fitly framed in him we are | 516 | 1 |
| Fitly framed together lies | 990 | 6 |
| Fit me for the realms above | 287 | 6 |
| Fit us for perfect rest above | 965 | 7 |
| Fitted for our heavenly rest | 530 | 2 |
| Fitted here by perfect love | 601 | 5 |

| | Hymn | Verse |
|---|---|---|
| †Five bleeding wounds he bears | 202 | 3 |
| Fix a mighty gulf between | 508 | 6 |
| Fix in us thy humble dwelling | 385 | 1 |
| Fix in us thy humble home | 683 | 6 |
| †Fix my new heart on things above | 998 | 5 |
| †Fix, O fix my wavering mind | 350 | 3 |
| Fix on his work thy steadfast eye | 831 | 3 |
| Fix on thyself our single eye | 524 | 1 |
| Fix the Spirit in our soul | 348 | 6 |
| Fix with us thy glorious throne | 653 | 2 |
| Fixed as the throne which ne'er can move | 72 | 1 |
| Fixed on this blissful centre, rest | 912 | 4 |
| †Fixed on this ground will I remain | 189 | 6 |
| Fixed the Christian festival | 952 | 2 |
| Fixed to live and die for thee | 530 | 3 |
| Flame thine eyes with heavenly fire | 748 | 3 |
| Flee before the monster's face | 278 | 2 |
| Fleecy meads with gladness ring | 579 | 3 |
| Flesh of our flesh why wast thou made | 772 | 4 |
| Flesh, spirit, soul, to thee resign | 261 | 4 |
| Flesh thy vesture | 748 | 4 |
| Flocking round our heavenly King | 720 | 9 |
| Flock to the friend of human kind | 32 | 2 |
| Flow back the rivers to the sea | 332 | 5 |
| Flow from my heart, and fill my tongue | 328 | 4 |
| Flowers of Eden, fruits of grace | 348 | 3 |
| †Flowery hills and mountains high | 639 | 5 |
| Fly back to Christ, for sin is near | 312 | 4 |
| Fly, celestial inmate, fly | 921 | 3 |
| Fly on the rebel sons of men | 445 | 3 |
| Fly on wings of gospel light | 672 | 5 |
| Fly to earth's remotest bound | 633 | 3 |
| Fly to the shadow of thy wings | 563 | 4 |
| Fly to those dear wounds of his | 20 | 1 |
| Follow Christ in heart and mind | 521 | 2 |
| Follow, or be led by it | 910 | 4 |
| Follow your Captain, and be led | 314 | 3 |
| †Followed by their works, they go | 51 | 2 |
| Followers of our lamb-like Lord | 733 | 4 |
| Followers of the bleeding Lamb | 480 | 1 |
| Followers of the dying God | 76 | 1 |
| Followers of thy holiness | 529 | 1 |
| Following him where'er he goes | 554 | 2 |
| Following our exalted head | 716 | 5 |
| Following thee beyond the skies | 718 | 8 |
| Fondly call their lands their own | 67 | 1 |
| *Fondly my foolish heart essays | 291 | 1 |
| Fondly of their loss complain | 50 | 5 |
| Fond of created good | 108 | 1 |
| †Foolish, and impotent, and blind | 289 | 7 |
| †Foolish world, thy shouts forbear | 274 | 2 |
| †Fools and madmen let us be | 400 | 7 |
| †Fools never raise their thoughts so high | 599 | 4 |

| | Hymn | Verse |
|---|---|---|
| For all a full atonement made | 190 | 5 |
| For all, for all my Saviour died | 34 | 7 |
| For all he hath the atonement made | 39 | 4 |
| For all his depths of grace | 669 | 1 |
| For all his love | 988 | Cho. |
| For all his mercy's store | 614 | 8 |
| For all in Jesu's name | 136 | 5 |
| For all, it is open and free | 79 | 1 |
| For all mankind to atone | 413 | 1 |
| For all my Lord was crucified | 34 | 7 |
| For all my sins atonement made | 145 | 5 |
| For all our comforts here | 644 | 1 |
| For all our hopes on thee depend | 648 | 1 |
| For all that bear the sovereign sway | 985 | 1 |
| For all that I have done | 179 | 1 |
| For all the blessings of the light | 974 | 1 |
| For all the fallen race and me | 378 | 1 |
| For all the help that each conveys | 524 | 1 |
| For all the plenitude divine | 254 | 1 |
| For all the servants of our King | 949 | 1 |
| For all thine enemies | 757 | 4 |
| For all things bright and good | 988 | 3 |
| For all things serve thy sovereign will | 337 | 5 |
| For all thou hast, and art | 304 | 3 |
| For all thou hast in Christ prepared | 39 | 3 |
| For all thy hands have made | 245 | 2 |
| For all thy love imparts | 988 | 3 |
| For all thy mercies' store | 654 | 3 |
| For all thy saints, to memory dear | 945 | 1 |
| For all who feel thy work begun | 458 | 1 |
| For angels always love | 357 | 6 |
| For angels never sin | 357 | 5 |
| For a poor abject sinner's sake | 861 | 4 |
| For a sinner I am | 707 | 6 |
| For Christ hath risen, and man shall rise | 715 | 6 |
| For Christ hath won, and man shall win | 715 | 7 |
| For Christ our Lord | 1026 | — |
| For closer communion I pine | 228 | 1 |
| For constant power and grace | 471 | 4 |
| For counsel or for fight | 487 | 1 |
| †For countless sorrows hem me round | 566 | 7 |
| For dark and light are both alike to thee | 962 | 3 |
| For death is hallowed into sleep | 715 | 5 |
| †For dower of blessed children | 996 | 3 |
| For drops of finite happiness | 364 | 2 |
| For each assault prepared | 305 | 2 |
| For ever and ever shall last | 49 | 3 |
| For ever and ever, When time is no more | 199 | 5 |
| For ever and for ever | 943 | 10 |
| For ever and for ever reigns | 56 | 4 |
| For ever beginning what never shall end | 808 | 10 |
| For ever be thy name adored | 227 | 1 |
| For ever be thy name adored | 880 | 1 |

| | Hymn | Verse |
|---|---|---|
| For ever blest | 800 | 1 |
| For ever bruise his head | 299 | 8 |
| For ever cast thy own away | 451 | 2 |
| For ever cease from sin | 340 | 1 |
| For ever closed to all but thee | 26 | 2 |
| For ever doth for sinners plead | 190 | 4 |
| For ever drive it hence | 528 | 2 |
| For ever, ever rest | 18 | 2 |
| For ever faithful to thy love | 282 | 1 |
| For ever filled with God | 389 | 6 |
| †For ever firm thy justice stands | 563 | 2 |
| For ever fixed on me | 550 | 1 |
| For ever from our eyes | 482 | 6 |
| *For ever here my rest shall be | 346 | 1 |
| For ever in his heart | 477 | 2 |
| For ever in my heart | 97 | 6 |
| For ever in thy presence blessed | 72 | 2 |
| For ever let the archangel's voice | 55 | 3 |
| For ever like the God I see | 72 | 3 |
| For ever new | 800 | 11 |
| For ever on my Saviour's breast | 973 | 2 |
| For ever on your mind | 268 | 3 |
| For ever reigns | 800 | 7 |
| For ever singing as they shine | 552 | 6 |
| For ever standing on its guard | 301 | 3 |
| For ever standing on my guard | 305 | 2 |
| For ever subjected to thee | 448 | 2 |
| For ever to behold thy face | 558 | 2 |
| *For ever with the Lord | 944 | 1 |
| †For ever with the Lord | 944 | 5 |
| For ever with the Lord | 944 | 8 |
| For everlasting strength is thine | 139 | 4 |
| For evermore | 800 | 4 |
| For evermore draw nigh | 991 | 3 |
| For every child of Adam free | 171 | 1 |
| †For every fight is dreadful and loud | 273 | 5 |
| For every helpless soul | 781 | 3 |
| †For every sinful action | 818 | 4 |
| For every sinful soul | 162 | 4 |
| For every sinner free | 406 | 3 |
| For every soul atonement made | 860 | 2 |
| For every soul of man | 1 | 8 |
| For every soul of man hath died | 107 | 3 |
| For every soul of man is free | 365 | 7 |
| For every toil, if he enjoin | 858 | 3 |
| For faith and pardon at thy feet | 861 | 2 |
| For feeding famished souls we own | 874 | 3 |
| †For friends and brethren dear | 619 | 6 |
| For fuller joys above | 734 | 2 |
| For garners in the sky | 739 | 5 |
| †For God approves the just man's ways | 540 | 6 |
| For God hath bidden all mankind | 2 | 1 |
| For God hath spoke the word | 360 | 8 |

| | Hymn | Verse |
|---|---|---|
| For God hath spoke the word | 452 | 4 |
| For God is manifest below | 685 | 4 |
| For God is on my side | 575 | 3 |
| For God to live and die | 532 | 2 |
| For God, who all our days hath given | 858 | 2 |
| For God's all-seeing eye surveys | 964 | 3 |
| For good remember me | 336 | 2 |
| For grace and wisdom from above | 470 | 1 |
| For grace to guide what grace has given | 467 | 2 |
| For having grieved my God | 102 | 1 |
| For having grieved thy love | 308 | 3 |
| For heaven's superior praise | 262 | 4 |
| For he hath felt the same | 725 | 2 |
| For he hath spoke the word | 278 | 4 |
| For he was slain for us | 678 | 2 |
| For he whose blood is all our boast | 21 | 3 |
| For help against myself I flee | 145 | 2 |
| For here I will unwearied lie | 784 | 5 |
| For high mysterious union | 996 | 3 |
| For him and for his angels made | 299 | 8 |
| For him in pain to die | 544 | 3 |
| †For him shall endless prayer be made | 585 | 8 |
| For him shall prayer unceasing | 586 | 5 |
| For his glory I am | 231 | 1 |
| For his grace and power are such | 824 | 2 |
| For his heaven the bride prepare | 516 | 3 |
| For his mercies still endure | 631 | Cho |
| For his own pattern given | 940 | 5 |
| For his redeeming grace | 478 | 1 |
| For if thy work on earth be sweet | 920 | 4 |
| For I have much forgiven | 188 | 6 |
| For I have nought to pay | 110 | 1 |
| For I of him have need | 115 | 4 |
| For I, thou know'st, am poor | 175 | 3 |
| For it is seemly so to do | 607 | 3 |
| For Jesus crucified | 982 | 3 |
| For Jesus hath spoken the word | 70 | 2 |
| †For Jesus, my Lord, is now my defence | 198 | 5 |
| For Jesus takes my part | 575 | 4 |
| For Jesus to receive | 137 | 7 |
| For Jesus wept o'er Lazarus dead | 849 | 4 |
| For Jesu's sake alone | 103 | 3 |
| For Jesu's sake the gift send down | 119 | 6 |
| For Jesus's sake our enjoyments below | 498 | 2 |
| For, lo! the everlasting Rock | 63 | 6 |
| For, lo! the seventh angel pours | 63 | 2 |
| For love and faith's sweet sake | 996 | 3 |
| For love I sigh, for love I pine | 147 | 3 |
| For many long rebellious years | 161 | 2 |
| For many tedious years | 166 | 2 |
| For me a blood-bought free reward | 798 | 6 |
| For me and all thy hands have made | 190 | 8 |
| For me, even for my soul, was shed | 190 | 4 |

| | Hymn | Verse |
|---|---|---|
| For me, for me, thou hear'st it plead | 148 | 5 |
| For me, for me, thou know'st it flowed | 148 | 5 |
| For me let it plead | 160 | 1 |
| For me my elder brethren stay | 68 | 7 |
| †For me obtained he is | 757 | 4 |
| For me offered up | 160 | 1 |
| For me, on the accursed tree | 373 | 5 |
| For me the blood of sprinkling pleads | 184 | 5 |
| For me the Saviour died | 346 | 1 |
| For me to death was sold | 358 | 3 |
| For me to intercede | 202 | 2 |
| For me to receive from above | 165 | 5 |
| For me, who him to death pursued | 201 | 1 |
| For me, whom watchful angels keep | 227 | 3 |
| For mercy, Lord, is all our prayer | 797 | 3 |
| For messengers divine | 452 | 1 |
| For mine I humbly claim | 68 | 4 |
| For more than life on thee | 836 | 2 |
| †For more we ask; we open then | 654 | 4 |
| For mortals and for sinners | 943 | 1 |
| For my eternal rest | 123 | 4 |
| For my inmost soul is taught the truth | 842 | 8 |
| †For my life, and clothes, and food | 243 | 2 |
| *For my life, and clothes, and food | 1018 | — |
| †For my selfishness and pride | 110 | 2 |
| For my smallest spark of grace | 243 | 2 |
| For my smallest spark of grace | 1018 | — |
| For no man cares their souls to save | 82 | 2 |
| For O, my God, it found out me! | 201 | 3 |
| For O the storm is high | 292 | 1 |
| For O, the waters still are high | 114 | 2 |
| For O! the wolf is nigh | 501 | 1 |
| For one brief hour of prayer | 863 | 1 |
| For one who waits on thee | 182 | 1 |
| For our bridal day prepare | 207 | 2 |
| For our companion's good | 925 | 2 |
| For our glorious meeting there | 207 | 2 |
| For our God hath showed his grace | 714 | 5 |
| For our partnership in light | 207 | 2 |
| For our Redeemer's sake | 945 | 2 |
| For our sake himself did give | 714 | 4 |
| For our service doth call | 495 | 1 |
| For our wants to be supplied | 987 | 1 |
| For power I feebly pray | 410 | 2 |
| For righteous in thy spotless eyes | 635 | 1 |
| For salvation I depend | 116 | 4 |
| For sin and Satan plead | 345 | 2 |
| For sinners intercedes | 823 | 7 |
| For sins not his own | 707 | 4 |
| For some are sick, and some are sad | 969 | 3 |
| For soon the reaping time will come | 935 | 2 |
| For soon the reaping time will come | 935 | 4 |
| For sorrow and sadness I joy shall receive | 198 | 6 |

| | Hymn | Verse |
|---|---|---|
| For so the word of truth declares | 935 | 1 |
| For still his wrath delays | 80 | 4 |
| For still my throne in Zion stands | 569 | 10 |
| For still the more the servant hath | 696 | 3 |
| For surely thou canst tell | 797 | 2 |
| For that blissful sight I sigh | 877 | 2 |
| For that high prize | 853 | 4 |
| For that tremendous day | 55 | 1 |
| For the blessings numberless | 243 | 2 |
| For the blessings numberless | 1018 | — |
| For the blissful assurance of favour divine | 219 | 6 |
| For the brightness of thy face | 593 | 1 |
| For the converse of thy saints | 593 | 1 |
| For the country behind | 498 | 2 |
| For the great day thyself prepare | 964 | 2 |
| For the heaven of heavens is love | 499 | 3 |
| †For the joy he sets before thee | 922 | 4 |
| For the Lord on whom I wait | 842 | 4 |
| †For the Lord our God shall come | 987 | 3 |
| For the oil and the wine | 219 | 6 |
| For the riches of thy grace | 1022 | — |
| For the small and inward voice | 358 | 2 |
| For the whole world atonement made | 129 | 2 |
| For the work he hath done | 219 | 1 |
| For thee, and not thy foe | 863 | 3 |
| †For thee delightfully employ | 324 | 5 |
| For thee I cheerfully forego | 332 | 2 |
| For thee I long, to thee I look | 577 | 3 |
| †For thee, my God, the living God | 567 | 2 |
| †For thee my thirsty soul doth pant | 437 | 2 |
| For thee my thirsty soul doth pine | 338 | 1 |
| For thee, not without hope, I mourn | 186 | 1 |
| For thee, O Christ, I call | 854 | 1 |
| *For thee, O dear, dear country | 943 | 4 |
| †For thee our hearts we lift | 762 | 2 |
| For thee submit to die | 27 | 3 |
| For thee, the heavenly light | 135 | 10 |
| †For thee we leave our native shore | 1001 | 2 |
| For their guidance he hath made | 640 | 1 |
| For their Redeemer's sake | 871 | 2 |
| For them no further test remains | 926 | 1 |
| For these celestial lines | 880 | 1 |
| For thine immortal praise | 301 | 5 |
| For things by nature felt and seen | 68 | 3 |
| †For this alone I live below | 439 | 3 |
| †For this, as taught by thee, I pray | 417 | 3 |
| †For this I at thy footstool wait | 180 | 5 |
| †For this in faith we call | 74 | 3 |
| †For this in steadfast hope I wait | 356 | 10 |
| †For this let men revile my name | 279 | 8 |
| For this my cries shall never fail | 155 | 5 |
| †For this, no longer sons of night | 203 | 6 |
| †For this only thing I pray | 110 | 6 |

| | Hymn | Verse |
|---|---|---|
| For this our spirits groan | 108 | 6 |
| †For this shall every child of God | 561 | 6 |
| For this the hosts above rejoice | 203 | 5 |
| †For this the pleading Spirit groans | 16 | 8 |
| †For this the saints lift up their voice | 203 | 5 |
| †For this thou hast designed | 264 | 2 |
| For this to Jesus I look up | 406 | 1 |
| †For this we ask, in faith sincere | 468 | 7 |
| For this we weep and pray | 74 | 3 |
| For those in peril on the sea | 1004 | Cho. |
| For those perennial guerdons | 943 | 12 |
| For those that trample on thy blood | 23 | 8 |
| For those that will not come to him | 39 | 4 |
| For thou alone art King | 546 | 3 |
| For thou art always nigh | 281 | 3 |
| For thou art Love Divine | 560 | 1 |
| For thou art still by me, And holdest my hand | 200 | 3 |
| †For thou art their boast, Their glory and power | 198 | 4 |
| For thou art with me, and thy rod | 556 | 3 |
| For thou canst save thine own | 820 | 5 |
| For thou hast brought me low | 565 | 5 |
| For thou hast died that I may live | 815 | 3 |
| For thou hast made the sign of grace | 892 | 1 |
| For thou, O God, dost know | 968 | 4 |
| For thou, O Lord, and thou alone | 600 | 2 |
| For thou that faith hast given | 139 | 3 |
| For thou, the righteous Judge and King | 581 | 4 |
| For thou this faith hast wrought | 360 | 5 |
| For thou wilt crown thy choice | 549 | 6 |
| †For thou, within no walls confined | 864 | 2 |
| For thus I heard Jehovah say | 541 | 3 |
| For thy compassion, Lord, is great | 588 | 3 |
| For thy flesh is meat indeed | 904 | 1 |
| For thy fulness, God of grace | 593 | 1 |
| †For thy glory we are | 491 | 4 |
| For thy gospel's joyful sound | 1008 | 2 |
| For thy love and mercy's sake | 116 | 2 |
| †For thy loving-kindness, Lord | 572 | 2 |
| For thy name's sake, forbear to slay | 588 | 3 |
| †For thy own mercy's sake | 105 | 3 |
| For thy own truth and mercy's sake | 875 | 5 |
| For thy own truth and mercy's sake | 475 | 5 |
| For thy redeeming grace | 253 | 2 |
| For thy refreshing grace | 635 | 2 |
| For thy Spirit, new creating | 743 | 3 |
| For thy truth and mercy's sake | 402 | 2 |
| For thyself our hearts prepare | 520 | 1 |
| For thyself to thee I cry | 149 | 2 |
| For 'tis an holy day | 619 | 1 |
| For toil comes rest, for exile home | 857 | 6 |
| For 'twas to bless such souls as these | 889 | 2 |
| For us a bleeding victim made | 774 | 8 |
| For us he hath prayed, and the Comforter gained | 760 | 2 |

| | Hymn | Verse |
|---|---|---|
| For us he reigns above | 719 | 2 |
| For us his crown resigned | 262 | 4 |
| For us in heaven to intercede | 827 | 8 |
| For *us* suffice the season past | 977 | 1 |
| For us the blessing to receive | 759 | 1 |
| For us the Comforter receives | 827 | 8 |
| For us to groan, to bleed, to die | 666 | 3 |
| †For us wast thou not lifted up | 774 | 8 |
| For us, who his offers embrace | 79 | 1 |
| For us with prevailing prayer | 720 | 7 |
| For very joy I leap | 943 | 13 |
| For very love, beholding | 943 | 4 |
| For we are neither hot nor cold | 454 | 1 |
| For we have hope to rest in joy | 602 | 1 |
| †For weeping, wakeful eyes | 838 | 6 |
| For what are outward things to thee | 91 | 4 |
| For what my God refused to give | 126 | 2 |
| For what thou wouldst bestow to-day | 782 | 1 |
| †For what to thee, O Lord, we give | 286 | 7 |
| †For what you have done | 707 | 2 |
| For where thou art, there I shall be | 923 | 4 |
| For which our deathless spirits pine | 531 | 1 |
| For which thy precious life was given | 375 | 2 |
| For, while in him confiding | 804 | 4 |
| For who aught to my charge shall lay | 190 | 2 |
| †For who by faith your Lord receive | 420 | 5 |
| †For whom didst thou the cross endure | 157 | 3 |
| For whom thou sav'st, he ne'er shall fail | 437 | 9 |
| For whom was made whatever is | 467 | 1 |
| For whom we in thy Spirit plead | 81 | 4 |
| For whom we now lift up our voice | 204 | 1 |
| For why? His doom is writ | 856 | 3 |
| †For why? The Lord our God is good | 607 | 4 |
| For with me art thou, And shalt be within | 200 | 7 |
| For without thee I cannot live | 973 | 3 |
| For without thee I dare not die | 973 | 3 |
| For worldly hope, or worldly fear | 44 | 3 |
| For wretched, dying men | 659 | 3 |
| †For you and for me | 707 | 5 |
| For you he is pleading His merits and death | 5 | 4 |
| For you he suffered pain | 36 | 1 |
| For you in healing streams it rolls | 4 | 3 |
| For you the Prince of glory died | 30 | 7 |
| †For you the purple current flowed | 30 | 7 |
| †Forbid it, Lord, that I should boast | 700 | 2 |
| Forbids us to descry | 662 | 3 |
| Forced to acknowledge in thy sight | 633 | 4 |
| Forced to obey the tyrant's law | 106 | 5 |
| Force me, Lord, with all to part | 158 | 2 |
| Force me to be saved by grace | 158 | 4 |
| Force my violence to be still | 188 | 2 |
| Foremost of the sons of light | 76 | 1 |
| Forget my griefs, and find sweet rest at last | 967 | 6 |

| | Hymn | Verse |
|---|---|---|
| Forgive, and after God renew | 252 | 2 |
| Forgive, and bid me sin no more | 186 | 3 |
| †Forgive, and make my nature whole | 363 | 4 |
| Forgive, and take away my sin | 782 | 2 |
| "Forgive him, O forgive," they cry | 202 | 3 |
| †Forgive me, Lord, for thy dear Son | 974 | 2 |
| *Forgive my foes? it cannot be | 830 | 1 |
| Forgive them, Father, O forgive | 33 | 1 |
| *Forgive us, for thy mercy's sake | 511 | 1 |
| Forgiveness and holiness give | 70 | 3 |
| Forgiveness in his blood, we have | 394 | 3 |
| Forgiveness on my conscience seal | 982 | 4 |
| Forgiven greatly, how I greatly love | 794 | 8 |
| Forgotten in unthankfulness | 610 | 2 |
| Forlorn, forsaken, and exposed | 567 | 3 |
| Formed thee for his own abode | 594 | 1 |
| Forms the Saviour in the soul | 521 | 3 |
| Forsaken, and alone | 109 | 4 |
| Forth at thy call, though bound I come | 290 | 3 |
| *Forth in thy name, O Lord, I go | 324 | 1 |
| Forth to the river went the root | 589 | 2 |
| Forthwith my God heard my complaint | 551 | 2 |
| Fortified by power divine | 572 | 3 |
| †Forward they cast a faithful look | 702 | 4 |
| Fought the fight, the battle won | 716 | 2 |
| Fought the fight, the work is done | 50 | 3 |
| Found pleasures never wasting | 667 | 1 |
| Found the rest we toil to find | 52 | 2 |
| Fountain for guilt and sin | 846 | 2 |
| Fountain of all blessings, grant | 653 | 4 |
| Fountain of all blessings, grant | 1010 | — |
| †Fountain of all sufficient bliss | 290 | 8 |
| Fountain of being, and of power | 249 | 3 |
| †Fountain of good, all blessing flows | 38 | 5 |
| Fountain of grace, thyself make known | 525 | 2 |
| *Fountain of life and all my joy | 230 | 1 |
| Fountain of life eternal, him | 673 | 3 |
| Fountain of light and love | 87 | 1 |
| Fountain of light and love below | 236 | 2 |
| †Fountain of overflowing grace | 672 | 6 |
| †Fountain of unexhausted love | 170 | 3 |
| Fountain of unexhausted love | 337 | 1 |
| Fountain of unmingled bliss | 995 | 2 |
| Fount of pity, then befriend us | 933 | 8 |
| †Frail children of dust, And feeble as frail | 611 | 5 |
| Frankly the gift of God receive | 4 | 4 |
| Fraud and wrong shall then have ending | 604 | 4 |
| †Fraught with rich blessing, breathing sweet repose | 967 | 4 |
| Freedom, and life to win thy grace | 286 | 4 |
| Freedom, friends, and health, and fame | 430 | 5 |
| Freedom let me never find | 188 | 4 |
| †Freed from the power of cancelled sin | 290 | 6 |
| †Free from anger and from pride | 509 | 5 |

| | Hymn | Verse |
|---|---|---|
| Free from doubts, and griefs, and fears | 52 | 3 |
| Free from human miseries | 639 | 1 |
| Free from sin and servile fear | 13 | 2 |
| Free from sin, from sorrow free | 915 | 3 |
| Free from sorrow, free from sin | 987 | 4 |
| Free me indeed, repeat the word | 290 | 4 |
| Free we pass the upright wave | 580 | 2 |
| Freely all through faith forgiven | 735 | 4 |
| Freely and graciously forgiven | 71 | 5 |
| Freely as they receive to give | 474 | 4 |
| Freely flows from him alone | 755 | 2 |
| Freely from thy fulness give | 672 | 6 |
| Freely let me take of thee | 143 | 4 |
| Freely now to sinners given | 723 | 2 |
| Freely our backslidings heal | 179 | 2 |
| Freely shall his grace receive | 197 | 3 |
| Freely to all ourselves we give | 526 | 4 |
| Freely we are justified | 623 | 2 |
| Freely what I receive to give | 17 | 7 |
| Frequent the consecrated place | 860 | 1 |
| Fresh as these drops upon *his* face | 896 | 4 |
| Fresh grace shall still suffice for me | 835 | 2 |
| Friend of publicans,—and me | 195 | 4 |
| Friend of sinners, let me find | 109 | 1 |
| Friend of sinners, spotless Lamb | 175 | Cho. |
| Friend of sinners, why not now? | 149 | 1 |
| †Friends, and home, and all forsaking | 878 | 2 |
| From age to age endure | 888 | 2 |
| From age to age it never ends | 216 | 3 |
| From age to age more glorious | 586 | 6 |
| From all distraction free | 322 | 3 |
| From all earthly passions free | 530 | 3 |
| From all entanglements beneath | 296 | 2 |
| From all eternity | 750 | 1 |
| From all eternity | 750 | 6 |
| From all eternity his Son | 668 | 1 |
| From all indwelling sin | 356 | 6 |
| From all indwelling sin | 389 | 2 |
| †From all iniquity, from all | 406 | 4 |
| †From all iniquity redeem | 523 | 7 |
| From all iniquity release | 900 | 2 |
| From all my works I cease | 781 | 2 |
| From all our bands release | 299 | 3 |
| From all presumption free | 805 | 2 |
| *From all that dwell below the skies | 615 | 1 |
| From all that oppress us He rescues us all | 211 | 1 |
| From all the filth of self and pride | 391 | 4 |
| From all the guile of Satan free | 561 | 2 |
| From all the power of Satan save | 164 | 1 |
| From all their enemies | 622 | 2 |
| From all their sin and sorrow | 626 | 5 |
| From all their sins redeem | 625 | 6 |
| From all unrighteousness | 345 | 3 |

| | Hymn | Verse |
|---|---|---|
| From an evil world secure | 724 | 3 |
| From a suffering church beneath | 52 | 4 |
| From a tottering world remove | 67 | 4 |
| From Calvary's to Zion's height | 380 | 6 |
| From care, and sin, and sorrow free | 147 | 6 |
| From change to change the creatures run | 651 | 3 |
| †From Christ their varied gifts derive | 868 | 3 |
| From daily tasks set free | 863 | 1 |
| From death to save the helpless prey | 28 | 5 |
| from depths of hell thy people save | 690 | 2 |
| From doubt, and fear, and sorrow free | 391 | 5 |
| From earth, and death, and hell | 497 | 4 |
| From earth for heaven redeemed | 838 | 7 |
| From earth I rise, and seek the joys | 800 | 2 |
| From earth to things above | 958 | 3 |
| From earth we shall quickly remove | 73 | 1 |
| From East, and West, and South, and North | 452 | 5 |
| From endless misery | 43 | 5 |
| From everlasting thou art God | 41 | 3 |
| From everlasting woe | 644 | 2 |
| From every base desire | 818 | 3 |
| From every creature free | 533 | 2 |
| From every creature love | 68 | 2 |
| From every evil chance | 549 | 2 |
| From every evil to depart | 319 | 2 |
| From every murmur free | 843 | 2 |
| From every sin depart | 80 | 5 |
| From every sin I cease | 343 | 6 |
| From every sin set free | 502 | 5 |
| From every sinful snare | 103 | 2 |
| From every sinful stain | 732 | 2 |
| †From every sinful wrinkle free | 17 | 5 |
| *From every stormy wind that blows | 825 | 1 |
| From every swelling tide of woes | 825 | 1 |
| From every touch of ill | 820 | 2 |
| From every wish set free | 415 | 4 |
| From every work of mine | 402 | 1 |
| From faith and hope may grow | 12 | 4 |
| From faith to faith, from grace to grace | 196 | 3 |
| From false humility removed | 805 | 1 |
| From favoured Abraham's seed | 452 | 1 |
| From force and perfidy | 465 | 5 |
| From God obtained the grace | 981 | 4 |
| *From Greenland's icy mountains | 747 | 1 |
| From harm and danger keep thy children free | 962 | 3 |
| From heaven and thee removed so far | 290 | 1 |
| †From heaven angelic voices sound | 56 | 2 |
| †From heaven he shall once more | 761 | 6 |
| From heavenly wisdom's narrow way | 849 | 2 |
| From hell, the world, and sin secure | 458 | 6 |
| From hell to retrieve you he spreads out His hands | 3 | 1 |
| From hill to valley flow | 586 | 3 |
| From him I would no longer stray | 25 | 2 |

| | Hymn | Verse |
|---|---|---|
| From him that dwells within | 343 | 3 |
| From *his* anointed head | 985 | 2 |
| From his bounty, and live | 491 | 3 |
| From his field shall in that day | 987 | 3 |
| From his unsuspected wiles | 508 | 2 |
| From holy, humble souls | 591 | 5 |
| From humble faith to perfect love | 306 | 5 |
| From idols to the living God | 444 | 3 |
| From inbred sin to fly | 288 | 3 |
| From India's coral strand | 747 | 1 |
| From Jehovah I came | 231 | 1 |
| From Jehovah's Spirit fly | 633 | 1 |
| From Jesus Christ, the just, descend | 418 | 3 |
| †From lies, from slander, and deceit | 609 | 4 |
| From low desires set free | 785 | 3 |
| From many an ancient river | 747 | 1 |
| From many a palmy plain | 747 | 1 |
| From men of heart sincere | 637 | 10 |
| From mine inbred foes release | 676 | 3 |
| From my debt of sin set clear | 110 | 1 |
| From my earliest days | 231 | 4 |
| From my example comfort take | 562 | 2 |
| From nature's every path retreat | 312 | 6 |
| From nature's paths we turn aside | 485 | 2 |
| From open and from secret foes | 465 | 5 |
| From our fears and sins release us | 688 | 1 |
| From our graves we shall see | 491 | 8 |
| †From our own inventions vain | 98 | 2 |
| From our worldly cares set free | 975 | 3 |
| From out his head, his hands, his side | 809 | 3 |
| From rock and tempest, fire and foe | 1004 | 4 |
| †From sea to sea, through all their shores | 569 | 8 |
| From selfishness and pride to save | 467 | 5 |
| From sin and death | 595 | 6 |
| From sin and death we flee | 671 | 1 |
| From sin and dust to thee we cry | 316 | 3 |
| From sin and fear, from guilt and shame | 190 | 2 |
| From sin and from thrall Which saves the lost race | 199 | 4 |
| From sin and Satan let us flee | 237 | 2 |
| From sin and Satan's power | 35 | 2 |
| From sin and sorrow set me free | 379 | 1 |
| From sin and sorrow set us free | 752 | 1 |
| From sin for ever cease | 282 | 1 |
| From sin have set me free | 614 | 12 |
| From sin impatient to be free | 462 | 2 |
| From sin in its beginning | 818 | 3 |
| From sin preserve us free | 692 | 5 |
| †From sin, the guilt, the power, the pain | 136 | 9 |
| From sin, the world, and Satan's yoke | 493 | 4 |
| From sin to be made clean | 356 | 6 |
| From sin's alluring snare | 998 | 3 |
| From sin's soft-soothing power | 303 | 1 |

| FROM SINS | HYMN | VERSE |
|---|---|---|
| From sins of deepest dye | 786 | 4 |
| From sorrow, fear, and sin | 367 | 1 |
| From strength to strength advancing here | 590 | 3 |
| †From strength to strength go on | 268 | 4 |
| From strength to strength we still proceed | 497 | 3 |
| From strength to strength we travel on | 71 | 4 |
| From temptation's rage and heat | 271 | 4 |
| From that mysterious tree | 701 | 2 |
| From the blest footsteps of thy love | 344 | 7 |
| From the central point of bliss | 20 | 1 |
| From the dust of earth returning | 933 | 18 |
| From the flattering tempter's power | 508 | 2 |
| From the founded world prepared | 67 | 5 |
| From the guilt and power of sin | 623 | 4 |
| From the haven of his breast | 809 | 4 |
| From the heathen | 595 | 5 |
| From the house of bondage brought | 623 | 3 |
| From the insufferable beams | 737 | 10 |
| From the iron furnace take | 116 | 2 |
| From the living God depart | 355 | 2 |
| From the noisome pestilence | 597 | 2 |
| †From the oppressive power of sin | 110 | 5 |
| From the pillar of the cloud | 606 | 4 |
| From the poor manger to the bitter cross | 691 | 5 |
| From the sun's directer ray | 76 | 3 |
| †From the sword at noon-day wasting | 597 | 2 |
| †From the time that thee I know | 628 | 2 |
| †From the world of sin and noise | 358 | 2 |
| From the world's end shall come to own thee | 595 | 4 |
| From the world's pernicious smiles | 508 | 2 |
| From thee alone descends | 435 | 1 |
| †From thee, great God, while every eye | 636 | 3 |
| From thee, great Source of being, flow | 241 | 2 |
| From thee I ne'er shall part | 193 | 4 |
| From thee, like Pisgah's mountain | 958 | 3 |
| From thee, my Lord, to move | 188 | 4 |
| From thee, my Saviour, stray | 187 | 4 |
| From thee my strength I bring | 193 | 8 |
| From thee no more may I depart | 114 | 4 |
| †From thee no more shall I depart | 357 | 6 |
| From thee; no want thy fulness knows | 38 | 5 |
| †From thee our being we receive | 256 | 3 |
| †From thee the ever-flowing spring | 802 | 4 |
| From thee the waters burst | 595 | 6 |
| From thee their fountain flow | 750 | 5 |
| †From thee, through an eternal now | 642 | 3 |
| †From thee, through Jesus, we receive | 435 | 6 |
| From thee they spring; and by thy hand | 997 | 1 |
| From their tenderest infancy | 890 | 1 |
| From them that lowly lie | 797 | 1 |
| From thence our spirits rise | 15 | 4 |
| From thence to bring him up | 192 | 2 |
| From this bondage, Lord, release | 167 | 1 |

| | Hymn | Verse |
|---|---|---|
| From this hour together trod | 995 | 4 |
| From this national confusion | 60 | 3 |
| From this our day of rest | 958 | 5 |
| From this ruined earth and skies | 60 | 3 |
| From those his heart approves | 591 | 5 |
| From those that on my pleasure wait | 472 | 2 |
| From thrones of glory driven | 314 | 4 |
| From thy all-glorious Godhead streams | 974 | 8 |
| From thy gracious lips to hear | 882 | 1 |
| From thy high and holy place | 762 | 1 |
| From thy pursuing grace | 188 | 3 |
| From thy river in the skies | 578 | 1 |
| From thy seat above the sky | 710 | 3 |
| †From thy works my joy proceeds | 598 | 2 |
| From thy wounded side which flowed | 709 | 1 |
| From thyself to us proceed | 756 | 2 |
| From toil excepts but one in seven | 858 | 2 |
| *From trials unexempted | 818 | 1 |
| From us, adopted in their stead | 451 | 1 |
| From vice and wickedness restrain | 470 | 4 |
| From which I cannot part | 152 | 2 |
| From whom alone my birth | 229 | 2 |
| From whom I may assistance gain | 844 | 4 |
| From whom sorrow flieth fleet | 753 | 4 |
| From whom those comforts flowed | 657 | 4 |
| From worldly hope and fear | 68 | 1 |
| Fruit every month they give | 948 | 4 |
| †Fruit of a virgin's womb | 194 | 4 |
| †Fruit of thy gracious lips, on me | 343 | 7 |
| Fruit of thy gracious lips, restore | 180 | 5 |
| Fruit that grows from seed here sown | 878 | 8 |
| Fruit unto his praise to yield | 987 | 2 |
| Fruitful let thy sorrows be | 743 | 1 |
| †Fruitless, till thou thyself impart | 92 | 6 |
| Frustrate the determined deed | 244 | 2 |
| †Fulfil, fulfil my large desires | 405 | 9 |
| Fulfil in ours thy own design | 475 | 5 |
| Fulfil my heart's desire | 18 | 3 |
| Fulfil our faithful hearts' desire | 412 | 1 |
| Fulfil our hearts' desire | 428 | 3 |
| Fulfil the imperfect desire | 165 | 3 |
| †Fulfil thine own intense desire | 25 | 6 |
| Fulfil thy character | 704 | 2 |
| Fulfil thy love's redeeming plan | 89 | 4 |
| Fulfil thy sovereign counsel, Lord | 279 | 9 |
| Fuller joys ordained to know | 51 | 5 |
| Full for all of truth and grace | 519 | 3 |
| Full of goodness, full of thee | 520 | 3 |
| Full of grace and truth for me | 194 | 5 |
| Full of holy shame, adore | 185 | 1 |
| Full of immortal hope | 74 | 3 |
| Full of misery and sin | 116 | 3 |
| Full of pity joined with power | 791 | 1 |

| | Hymn | Verse |
|---|---|---|
| Full of providential love | 578 | 1 |
| Full of putrefying sores | 109 | 2 |
| Full of sin, alas! I am | 175 | 1 |
| Full of sin and misery | 350 | 4 |
| Full of thy praise is found | 737 | 10 |
| Full of unutterable grace | 25 | 1 |
| Full of zeal, and full of love | 672 | 4 |
| Full power the victory to win | 419 | 3 |
| Full relief from all my fear | 672 | 8 |
| Full royally he rode | 551 | 4 |
| Full soon were we down-ridden | 856 | 2 |
| †Full well the labour of our hands | 858 | 2 |
| Fully absolved through these I am | 190 | 2 |
| Fully and freely justified | 360 | 2 |
| †Fully in my life express | 381 | 4 |
| Fully in thee believe | 384 | 8 |
| Fully of the Spirit born | 623 | 6 |
| Fully on these my mission prove | 433 | 3 |
| Fulness of joy in thee there is | 290 | 8 |
| Fulness of joy with thee there is | 548 | 6 |
| Fulness of life eternal find | 369 | 2 |
| Fulness of love, of heaven, of God | 376 | 5 |
| Fulness of the Deity | 418 | 1 |
| Fulness of the gospel grace | 479 | 1 |
| †Furnished out of thy treasury | 89 | 5 |
| Furnished out with richest grace | 905 | 2 |
| Fury is not in thee | 182 | 4 |
| Future and past subsisting now | 95 | 3 |
| 'Gainst all the powers of Satan arm | 811 | 2 |
| 'Gainst every known or secret foe | 306 | 3 |
| 'Gainst God, and his Anointed King | 541 | 1 |
| Gales of holy aspirations | 720 | 8 |
| Galled with the tyrant's iron chain | 547 | 2 |
| Gasps in thee to live and move | 27 | 6 |
| Gasps my fainting soul for grace | 156 | 1 |
| Gathered into the fold | 231 | 6 |
| Gathered to the fold above | 13 | 4 |
| Gather God's children into one | 746 | 8 |
| Gather my wandering spirit home | 296 | 3 |
| †Gather the outcasts in, and save | 35 | 2 |
| Gave to our world below | 692 | 1 |
| Gav'st whatever is to be | 601 | 2 |
| Gaze we on those glorious scars | 66 | 3 |
| Gazing on that transfigured face | 698 | 4 |
| Gentle as the summer's eve | 921 | 4 |
| Gentle to him, and good, and mild | 470 | 5 |
| Gently lead me by thy side | 193 | 4 |
| †Gently the weak thou lov'st to lead | 290 | 2 |
| Gently touch the trembling strings | 538 | 2 |
| Get thyself the victory | 158 | 4 |
| Gifts for a rebellious race | 757 | 2 |
| Gifts he hath received for men | 86 | 2 |

| | Hymn | Verse |
|---|---|---|
| †Gigantic lusts come forth to fight | 293 | 5 |
| Gird on my thigh thy conquering sword | 196 | 3 |
| †Gird on thy thigh the Spirit's sword | 568 | 3 |
| †Gird thy heavenly armour on | 829 | 3 |
| Girt with equity and might | 449 | 1 |
| Girt with omnipotence and grace | 56 | 2 |
| †Give all thy saints to find in thee | 525 | 2 |
| Give, and my strength employ | 135 | 7 |
| Give a new, believing heart | 179 | 2 |
| †Give deep humility; the sense | 865 | 3 |
| Give, for the honour of thy name | 772 | 2 |
| Give, for thy mercy's sake | 772 | 2 |
| Give, give me all my soul requires | 405 | 9 |
| Give glory to his holy name | 559 | 2 |
| Give, herewith thy blessing give | 1012 | — |
| Give *him his* adversaries' neck | 465 | 6 |
| Give *him his* people's heart | 465 | 6 |
| Give him thanks, rejoice, and sing | 197 | 6 |
| Give him thanks, rejoice, and sing | 400 | 2 |
| Give him thanks, rejoice, and sing | 605 | 5 |
| †Give him then, and ever give | 233 | 3 |
| *Give him then, and ever give | 1021 | 1 |
| Give his angels charge at last | 987 | 3 |
| Give joy or grief, give ease or pain | 948 | 7 |
| Give, Lord, or take thy gifts away | 432 | 5 |
| †Give me a calm, a thankful heart | 843 | 2 |
| Give me a heart to find out thee | 662 | 4 |
| †Give me a new, a perfect heart | 391 | 5 |
| †Give me a sober mind | 311 | 4 |
| Give me a token from above | 177 | 4 |
| Give me back my peace and power | 173 | 1 |
| †Give me faith to hold me up | 183 | 3 |
| Give me faith to make me whole | 398 | 1 |
| Give me living bread to eat | 164 | 5 |
| †Give me, Lord, a holy fear | 187 | 3 |
| †Give me, Lord, the victory | 164 | 5 |
| Give me, my Lord, my life, my all | 353 | 6 |
| Give me now my sin to leave | 173 | 4 |
| Give me now to feel my sin | 173 | 4 |
| †Give me, O give me fully, Lord | 290 | 4 |
| Give me, O Lord, to find in thee | 147 | 6 |
| Give me on eagles' wings to fly | 284 | 2 |
| †Give me on thee to call | 305 | 2 |
| Give me on thee to wait | 301 | 1 |
| Give me perfect soundness, give | 183 | 1 |
| Give me the child-like praying love | 433 | 1 |
| *Give me the enlarged desire | 372 | — |
| Give me the faith that casts out sin | 406 | 2 |
| *Give me the faith which can remove | 433 | 1 |
| Give me the glorious liberty | 815 | 2 |
| †Give me the grace, the love I claim | 144 | 3 |
| *Give me the wings of faith to rise | 940 | 1 |
| Give me, through thy dying love | 106 | 2 |

| GIVE ME | HYMN | VERSE |
|---|---|---|
| Give me thy converting grace | 243 | 1 |
| Give me thy easy yoke to bear | 337 | 2 |
| Give me thy love, 'tis all I claim | 772 | 2 |
| Give me thy meek and lowly mind | 388 | 3 |
| Give me thy only love to know | 169 | 3 |
| †Give me thy strength, O God of power | 279 | 10 |
| Give me thyself, and take me home | 366 | 5 |
| Give me thyself, for ever give | 374 | 2 |
| †Give me thyself; from every boast | 415 | 4 |
| Give me thyself, I ask no more | 291 | 4 |
| Give me thyself, or else I die | 100 | 4 |
| †Give me to bear thy easy yoke | 324 | 4 |
| Give me to feel their solemn weight | 59 | 3 |
| Give me to prove the kingdom mine | 304 | 1 |
| Give me to trust in thee | 305 | 4 |
| Give me true simplicity | 302 | 1 |
| Give me with all the sanctified | 404 | 5 |
| Give my gasping soul to see | 101 | 5 |
| Give, O give us to thy Son | 514 | 1 |
| Give thanks to God on high | 253 | 1 |
| Give thanks to God on high | 800 | 12 |
| Give the knowledge of salvation | 687 | 3 |
| Give the needless contest o'er | 24 | 2 |
| Give the pardon of our sins | 687 | 3 |
| Give the praise to him alone | 878 | 8 |
| †Give the pure gospel word | 745 | 4 |
| †Give the pure word of general grace | 744 | 4 |
| Give the sweet relenting grace | 101 | 1 |
| Give the word, and of the preacher | 743 | 3 |
| Give them, all thy blessings give | 915 | 2 |
| Give them a trumpet-voice, to call | 744 | 5 |
| Give them the wisdom from above | 473 | 3 |
| Give them thy saving health to see | 462 | 7 |
| †Give then the bliss for which I pray | 782 | 4 |
| †Give these, and then thy will be done | 865 | 6 |
| Give thy gift of charity | 753 | 9 |
| Give thyself, the Comforter | 762 | 2 |
| Give to all the faithful race | 756 | 1 |
| Give to him who gave me thee | 769 | 5 |
| †Give to mine eyes refreshing tears | 186 | 5 |
| †Give to mine eyes refreshing tears | 210 | 6 |
| Give to my heart chaste, hallowed fires | 210 | 6 |
| Give to my soul, with filial tears | 210 | 6 |
| *Give to the winds thy fears | 831 | 8 |
| Give to us, the o'er-laden, rest | 753 | 3 |
| †Give up ourselves, through Jesu's power | 532 | 2 |
| Give us all thy mind to express | 531 | 3 |
| Give us back our paradise | 514 | 4 |
| Give us each day our daily bread | 664 | 3 |
| †Give us grace to bear our witness | 882 | 7 |
| Give us in faith to claim | 297 | 3 |
| Give us in heaven a happy lot | 503 | 6 |
| Give us living bread to eat | 905 | 1 |

| | Hymn | Verse |
|---|---|---|
| †Give us ourselves and thee to know | 84 | 3 |
| Give us quickness to discern | 756 | 3 |
| †Give us quietly to tarry | 530 | 3 |
| Give us that for which he prays | 506 | 1 |
| Give us the salvation Of all that believe | 481 | 5 |
| Give us thus to feel and know | 531 | 3 |
| Give us wings of faith and love | 720 | 8 |
| Give we all, with one accord | 519 | 1 |
| Give what I have long implored | 106 | 2 |
| †Giver and Lord of life, whose power | 237 | 2 |
| Giver, Lord of life divine | 762 | 2 |
| †Giver of peace and unity | 505 | 5 |
| †Giver of penitential pain | 982 | 4 |
| Gives me his grace of pardon, and will give | 794 | 5 |
| Gives us back our breath again | 661 | 2 |
| Givest us the victory | 50 | 1 |
| Giv'st me all I ask, and more | 554 | 5 |
| Glad hymns of praise from land and sea | 1004 | 4 |
| Glad is the hour, and loved the place | 799 | 1 |
| Glad my eyes, and warm my heart | 963 | 2 |
| Glad partakers of our hope | 53 | 4 |
| Glad the summons to obey | 1008 | 3 |
| Glad, thine attributes confess | 257 | 2 |
| Glad to fulfil all righteousness | 429 | 1 |
| Glad to pray and labour on | 529 | 4 |
| *Glad was my heart to hear | 619 | 1 |
| Gladly I all for thee resign | 291 | 4 |
| Gladly I thy promise plead | 915 | 1 |
| Gladly I would thy word believe | 153 | 1 |
| Gladly take up the hallowed cross | 439 | 1 |
| Gladly then from earth remove | 13 | 4 |
| †Gladly the toys of earth we leave | 494 | 3 |
| Gladly will we come to-day | 714 | 6 |
| Gladly would I now be clean | 350 | 2 |
| †Gladness and joy shall there be found | 111 | 5 |
| Gladness for mourning thou hast given | 559 | 4 |
| Gladness girds the mountain height | 579 | 3 |
| Gladness let us now obtain | 349 | 4 |
| Gladness shine o'er earth and sea | 604 | 3 |
| Gladsome hallelujahs sing | 348 | 2 |
| Glide imperceptibly away | 222 | 3 |
| Glide our happy hours along | 538 | 4 |
| Glide with down upon their feet | 538 | 4 |
| Glides swiftly away | 47 | 3 |
| Gloomy grief shall flee away | 349 | 4 |
| Gloomy pit of endless pains | 633 | 2 |
| Glorify my Saviour's name | 402 | 3 |
| Glorious all, and numberless | 257 | 2 |
| Glorious and unspeakable | 207 | 1 |
| Glorious ecstasy is given | 941 | 3 |
| *Glorious God, accept a heart | 242 | 1 |
| Glorious in thy saints appear | 852 | 3 |
| Glorious in thy saints appear | 937 | 5 |

| | Hymn | Verse |
|---|---|---|
| †Glorious is the Lord most High | 571 | 2 |
| Glorious joys ordained to know | 941 | 1 |
| Glorious Lord of earth and heaven | 430 | 1 |
| Glorious Lord of earth and heaven | 430 | 6 |
| Glorious on thy heavenly throne | 423 | 4 |
| *Glorious Saviour of my soul | 215 | 1 |
| *Glorious things of thee are spoken | 594 | 1 |
| Glorious thy perfections shine | 572 | 2 |
| Glorious Trinity | 870 | 4 |
| Glorious Triune Majesty | 643 | 4 |
| Glory and praise to Jesus give | 478 | 1 |
| Glory ascribe to glory's King | 719 | Cho. |
| Glory begun below | 12 | 4 |
| Glory begun in grace | 834 | 2 |
| Glory be to Christ alone | 382 | 4 |
| *Glory be to God above | 480 | 1 |
| Glory be to God most High | 571 | 7 |
| *Glory be to God on high | 53 | 1 |
| *Glory be to God on high | 257 | 1 |
| *Glory be to God on high | 684 | 1 |
| †Glory be to God the Father | 720 | Dox. |
| Glory be to God the Son | 720 | Dox. |
| Glory both in earth and heaven | 720 | Dox. |
| Glory divine is risen on thee | 134 | 5 |
| Glory doth to God belong | 75 | 2 |
| Glory, endless glory be. Amen | 720 | Dox. |
| Glory give to Jesu's name | 238 | 3 |
| Glory, honour, praise, and power | 742 | Cho. |
| Glory, honour, praise receive | 727 | 6 |
| Glory in dissolution near | 351 | 6 |
| Glory in thy perfect love | 385 | 2 |
| Glory in thy perfect love | 390 | 1 |
| Glory let creation sing | 631 | 8 |
| Glory of the elect | 943 | 6 |
| Glory to God be given | 232 | 4 |
| †Glory to God belongs | 232 | 4 |
| *Glory to God, whose sovereign grace | 203 | 1 |
| †Glory to his name belongs | 197 | 5 |
| †Glory to our bounteous King | 631 | 8 |
| Glory to our common Lord | 519 | 1 |
| Glory to our heavenly King | 221 | 1 |
| Glory to the bleeding Lamb | 75 | 2 |
| Glory to the Father, Son | 631 | 8 |
| Glory to the Holy Spirit | 720 | Dox. |
| Glory to the Lamb be sung | 743 | 3 |
| Glory to the new-born King | 683 | 1 |
| *Glory to thee, my God, this night | 974 | 1 |
| Glory to their Maker give | 641 | 4 |
| Glory to their Saviour King | 582 | 2 |
| Glory, wisdom, thanks, and power | 75 | 4 |
| Glorying thy cross to bear | 737 | 9 |
| Glows our heart to find thee near | 506 | 3 |
| Go, by angel guards attended | 922 | 1 |

| | Hymn | Verse |
|---|---|---|
| Go forth, for he hath ransomed all | 107 | 8 |
| Go forth into the world's highway | 857 | 5 |
| Go forth then everywhere | 739 | 3 |
| Go forth to glorious war | 314 | 1 |
| Go forth with joy to meet your Lord | 65 | 2 |
| Go, get thee up, and die | 948 | 3 |
| Go, his triumph to adorn | 921 | 1 |
| *Go labour on; spend, and be spent | 857 | 1 |
| †Go labour on; 'tis not for nought | 857 | 2 |
| †Go labour on, while it is day | 857 | 3 |
| †Go, meet him in the sky | 65 | 3 |
| Go mourning all their days | 765 | 1 |
| Go on;—we'll meet you there | 539 | 10 |
| Go spread your trophies at his feet | 681 | 6 |
| Go to his temple, go | 268 | 1 |
| Go to shine before his throne | 921 | 1 |
| †Go up with Christ your Head | 314 | 3 |
| Go ye forth to meet your Lord | 54 | 1 |
| God alone deserves the praise | 243 | 5 |
| God and his Messiah fall | 75 | 3 |
| God and sinners reconciled | 683 | 1 |
| God appears on earth to reign | 66 | 1 |
| God, be merciful to me | 101 | 4 |
| God by heaven and earth adored | 643 | 1 |
| God, by sense unseen, to see | 817 | 1 |
| God comes down, he bows the sky | 684 | 1 |
| God comes down; the God and Lord | 618 | 1 |
| God counts the living dead | 822 | 2 |
| God delights in man to dwell | 197 | 6 |
| †God did in Christ himself reveal | 686 | 2 |
| God doth in his saints delight | 76 | 2 |
| God ever blest! we bow the knee | 568 | 2 |
| God for a guilty world hath died | 706 | 2 |
| God for them hath wonders wrought | 623 | 3 |
| God from all eternity | 598 | 2 |
| God from whom all blessings flow | 480 | 1 |
| God has been merciful to me | 795 | 5 |
| God hath brought us on our way | 975 | 1 |
| God hath for our ransomed race | 687 | 2 |
| God hath made his saints victorious | 640 | 2 |
| God hath made their footsteps sure | 349 | 2 |
| God hath said it shall be so | 278 | 4 |
| God hears thy sighs, and counts thy tears | 831 | 8 |
| God his blessings shall dispense | 521 | 1 |
| God if over all thou art | 158 | 1 |
| God inaccessible, unknown | 150 | 1 |
| †God in Christ is all forgiving | 606 | 6 |
| God in every thought require | 287 | 3 |
| God in man for ever dwell | 757 | 4 |
| †God in the flesh below | 719 | 2 |
| God in the flesh, my God, to see | 927 | 2 |
| †God, in this dark vale of tears | 215 | 3 |
| God in Three Persons, blessed Trinity | 646 | 1 |

| | HYMN | VERSE |
|---|---|---|
| God in Three Persons, blessed Trinity | 646 | 4 |
| God in whom we live and die | 53 | 1 |
| God, incline thy gracious ear | 260 | 2 |
| God incomprehensible | 515 | 2 |
| God incomprehensible | 633 | 1 |
| God incomprehensible | 643 | 1 |
| *God is a name my soul adores | 651 | 1 |
| *God is gone up on high | 719 | 1 |
| God is his own interpreter | 845 | 3 |
| †God is in heaven, and men below | 316 | 5 |
| *God is in this and every place | 117 | 1 |
| God is in us; for God is love | 237 | 1 |
| God is light, and God is here | 633 | 4 |
| God is love! I know, I feel | 168 | 4 |
| †God is our sun and shield | 591 | 4 |
| God is their strength, and through the road | 592 | 4 |
| †God is the Lord that shows us light | 616 | 11 |
| *God is the refuge of his saints | 569 | 1 |
| God is there, a strong salvation | 570 | 3 |
| †God is thine; disdain to fear | 407 | 3 |
| God is where our hosts assemble | 570 | 4 |
| God it is who justifies | 521 | 3 |
| *God moves in a mysterious way | 845 | 1 |
| †God, my Redeemer, lives | 930 | 3 |
| *God of all consolation, take | 537 | 1 |
| God of all-creating grace | 233 | 3 |
| God of all-creating grace | 1021 | 2 |
| God of all grace | 736 | 3 |
| *God of all grace and majesty | 307 | 1 |
| *God of all power, and truth, and grace | 391 | 1 |
| *God of all-redeeming grace | 427 | 1 |
| †God of all-sufficient grace | 368 | 3 |
| *God of almighty love | 323 | 1 |
| *God of eternal truth and grace | 342 | 1 |
| †God of everlasting grace | 53 | 2 |
| †God of goodness, from thy store | 579 | 2 |
| God of heaven, on earth appear | 653 | 2 |
| *God of Israel's faithful three | 359 | 1 |
| God of Jacob | 570 | 6 |
| †God of love, in this my day | 149 | 2 |
| *God of love, that hear'st the prayer | 508 | 1 |
| God of love, the doubt explain | 24 | 3 |
| *God of mercy, God of grace | 582 | 1 |
| *God of my childhood and my youth | 584 | 1 |
| *God of my life through all my days | 658 | 1 |
| *God of my life, to thee | 229 | 1 |
| *God of my life, what just return | 155 | 1 |
| *God of my life, whose gracious power | 289 | 1 |
| *God of my salvation, hear | 175 | 1 |
| †God of my strength, how long shall I | 567 | 3 |
| God of my unguarded hours | 287 | 1 |
| God of our fathers, be the God | 664 | 2 |
| God of power, and God of love | 257 | 3 |

| | Hymn | Verse |
|---|---|---|
| God of spotless purity | 287 | 2 |
| *God of that glorious gift of grace | 896 | 1 |
| †God of the patriarchal race | 647 | 3 |
| *God of truth and power and grace | 910 | 1 |
| *God of unexampled grace | 701 | 1 |
| *God of unspotted purity | 454 | 1 |
| God only can declare | 883 | 3 |
| †God only knows the love of God | 147 | 3 |
| *God only wise, almighty, good | 468 | 1 |
| God only wise and true | 838 | 1 |
| God on us, in gracious showers | 233 | 1 |
| God our hearts doth still unite | 522 | 2 |
| *God, our Hope and Strength abiding | 570 | 1 |
| God our Maker doth provide | 987 | 1 |
| God our souls and bodies made | 233 | 1 |
| God over all, for ever blessed | 557 | 11 |
| God over all, for ever blessed | 629 | 2 |
| God send his people peace | 619 | 6 |
| God shall be thy sure defence | 597 | 2 |
| God shall crown his ordinance | 521 | 1 |
| God shall his angels send | 535 | 6 |
| God shall in thy flesh appear | 407 | 3 |
| God shall lift up thy head | 831 | 8 |
| God shall thrust him out, and say | 407 | 3 |
| God so good, so true, so kind | 355 | 11 |
| God spake out, earth melts away | 570 | 4 |
| God refreshes in the air | 233 | 2 |
| †God reigns on high, but not confines | 637 | 2 |
| God resides among his own | 76 | 2 |
| †God ruleth on high, Almighty to save | 859 | 3 |
| †God, the Almighty God, hath made | 605 | 2 |
| God, the Almighty God, is thine | 407 | 1 |
| God, the blest, the Great I AM | 684 | 1 |
| God, the bounteous God, is here | 661 | 1 |
| God, the Comforter, receive | 260 | 1 |
| †God, the everlasting God | 758 | 3 |
| God the Father, and the Word | 260 | 1 |
| *God the Father! be thou near | 971 | 1 |
| God, the giver of all grace | 238 | 1 |
| God, the giver of all grace | 1019 | 1 |
| God, the glorious Saviour, praise | 75 | 2 |
| God the invisible appears | 684 | 1 |
| *God the Lord is King; before him | 606 | 1 |
| †God the Lord is King of glory | 606 | 2 |
| God the man of sin shall slay | 407 | 3 |
| *God, the offended God, most high | 11 | 1 |
| †God the Saviour! be our peace | 971 | 2 |
| God, the Spirit, asks you why | 6 | 3 |
| God, the universal God | 735 | 2 |
| God their Saviour to possess | 941 | 3 |
| God through endless ages blest | 643 | 4 |
| †God, through himself, we then shall know | 87 | 4 |
| God to all that ask shall give | 86 | 1 |

| | Hymn | Verse |
|---|---|---|
| God to man his blessing give | 582 | 3 |
| God to you his Son hath given | 20 | 3 |
| God vouchsafed a worm to appear | 195 | 2 |
| God was man, and served below | 413 | 3 |
| †God we absolutely trust | 914 | 8 |
| *God! who didst so dearly buy | 411 | 1 |
| God, who did your being give | 6 | 1 |
| God, who did your souls retrieve | 6 | 2 |
| God, who guides us by his love | 53 | 1 |
| God whose glory fills the sky | 257 | 1 |
| God, whose mercies are bestowed | 238 | 1 |
| God, whose mercies are bestowed | 1019 | 1 |
| God will aid her | 570 | 3 |
| God will count but vain and nought | 753 | 6 |
| †God will not always chide | 610 | 7 |
| God will provide for sacrifice | 965 | 4 |
| God with God wast man with man | 737 | 2 |
| God with us, we cannot fear | 728 | 4 |
| †God, your God, shall surely come | 348 | 5 |
| God, your Maker, asks you why | 6 | 1 |
| God, your Saviour, asks you why | 6 | 2 |
| God's bounteous love doth thee restore | 614 | 6 |
| God's free bounty glorify | 791 | 2 |
| God's great gift to all mankind | 20 | 4 |
| God's hands or bound or open are | 298 | 1 |
| God's highest glory was their anthem still | 691 | 3 |
| †God's image, which our sins destroy | 750 | 5 |
| God's kingdom fixed below | 737 | 4 |
| God's original promise this | 20 | 4 |
| God's own radiance through it hail | 817 | 3 |
| God's own word saith | 595 | 6 |
| God's watchful eye surveys | 846 | 1 |
| God's witness of celestial things | 957 | 2 |
| God's wondrous love in saving lost mankind | 691 | 5 |
| †God's word, for all their craft and force | 856 | 4 |
| Gone, that we might all pursue | 723 | 6 |
| Gone, that we might follow too | 723 | 6 |
| Good and faithful as thou art | 755 | 3 |
| Good and faithful servant thou | 51 | 4 |
| Good as thou art, and strong to save | 272 | 5 |
| Good Physician of mankind | 693 | 2 |
| Good Physician, show thy art | 463 | 3 |
| Good Physician, speak the word | 112 | 4 |
| *Good thou art, and good thou dost | 245 | 1 |
| †Good, when he gives, supremely good | 846 | 2 |
| †Goodness and mercy all my life | 556 | 5 |
| Goods, honour, children, wife | 856 | 4 |
| Gospel grace unsearchable | 952 | 2 |
| Governed by thy only will | 529 | 1 |
| Grace and glory flow from thee | 593 | 3 |
| Grace and mercy | 595 | 3 |
| Grace can subdue each fond desire | 666 | 4 |
| Grace did much more than sin abound | 365 | 5 |

| | Hymn | Verse |
|---|---|---|
| Grace divinely free for all | 430 | 2 |
| †Grace every morning new | 630 | 5 |
| Grace every sickness knows to heal | 666 | 4 |
| Grace for every soul is free | 86 | 5 |
| Grace hath opened mercy's door | 51 | 2 |
| †Grace, in answer to his prayer | 243 | 4 |
| Grace is the anchor of the soul | 666 | 4 |
| Grace, love, and might | 870 | 4 |
| Grace of God so strong and boundless | 790 | 5 |
| Grace that gave thine only Son | 245 | 3 |
| Grace, that God with man may live | 758 | 2 |
| †Grace, the fountain of all good | 418 | 2 |
| Grace to cover all my sin | 143 | 4 |
| Grace to help in time of need | 424 | 1 |
| †Grace we implore; when billows roll | 666 | 4 |
| Grace which, like the Lord, the giver | 594 | 2 |
| Gracious dew his heavens distil | 407 | 5 |
| †Gracious God, my sins forgive | 243 | 3 |
| Gracious, merciful, benign | 727 | 5 |
| *Gracious Redeemer, shake | 305 | 1 |
| Gracious Redeemer, take, O take | 137 | 9 |
| *Gracious Spirit, dwell with me | 769 | 1 |
| Grafted in thee, the living Vine | 923 | 3 |
| Grafted into thee I live | 193 | 2 |
| *Granted is the Saviour's prayer | 758 | 1 |
| Grant in death my sole desire | 877 | 4 |
| Grant, Lord, when I from death shall wake | 964 | 5 |
| Grant me, Lord, my heart's desire | 27 | 4 |
| Grant me, Lord, my heart's desire | 287 | 6 |
| Grant me my sins to feel | 105 | 2 |
| †Grant me now the bliss to feel | 354 | 6 |
| Grant me power to watch and pray | 173 | 5 |
| Grant me the purchase of thy blood | 815 | 2 |
| †Grant me within thy courts a place | 558 | 2 |
| †Grant my importunate request | 171 | 3 |
| Grant my importunate request | 283 | 1 |
| Grant, O harvest Lord, that we | 987 | 2 |
| *Grant, O Saviour, to our prayers | 826 | — |
| Grant our hearts may thither rise | 718 | 8 |
| †Grant that all we, who here to-day | 992 | 2 |
| †Grant that every moment I | 355 | 4 |
| Grant that every soul may feel | 179 | 2 |
| Grant the grace for which we pine | 762 | 2 |
| †Grant this, and then from all below | 504 | 7 |
| †Grant this, O holy God and true | 457 | 4 |
| †Grant, though parted from our sight | 718 | 8 |
| Grant thy gift of absolution | 933 | 11 |
| Grant us a forgiving heart | 653 | 5 |
| Grant us and all our race | 1011 | — |
| †Grant us, Lord, who cry to thee | 753 | 9 |
| Grant us that Way to know | 671 | 4 |
| Grant us thine eternal rest | 933 | 19 |
| †Grant us thy peace, Lord, through the coming night | 962 | 3 |

| | Hymn | Verse |
|---|---|---|
| †Grant us thy peace throughout our earthly life | 962 | 4 |
| †Grant us thy peace upon our homeward way | 962 | 2 |
| Grasp we our high calling's prize | 487 | 4 |
| Grateful, accepted sacrifice | 523 | 1 |
| Gratefully my God adore | 355 | 11 |
| Gratefully thy sway to own | 727 | 7 |
| Graven on my heart for ever be | 23 | 7 |
| Great, and marvellous, and high | 197 | 5 |
| Great builder of thy church below | 17 | 1 |
| Great builder of thy church below | 989 | 1 |
| Great Comforter, descend, and bring | 765 | 1 |
| Great David's greater son | 586 | 1 |
| †Great God! create my soul anew | 788 | 6 |
| *Great God, indulge my humble claim | 577 | 1 |
| Great God of universal love | 33 | 2 |
| *Great God of wonders! all thy ways | 656 | 1 |
| †Great God! on what a slender thread | 42 | 5 |
| *Great God, this sacred day of thine | 955 | 1 |
| †Great God! thy sovereign aid impart | 789 | 3 |
| *Great God, thy watchful care we bless | 994 | 1 |
| *Great God! to me the sight afford | 249 | 1 |
| †Great God, unknown, invisible | 126 | 5 |
| *Great God! what do I see and hear | 932 | 1 |
| †Great God! what do I see and hear | 932 | 4 |
| *Great God, whose universal sway | 585 | 1 |
| Great grace be now upon us all | 759 | 7 |
| Great he is, and dwells in thee | 197 | 6 |
| *Great is our redeeming Lord | 572 | 1 |
| *Great is the Lord our God | 573 | 1 |
| †Great object of our growing love | 492 | 2 |
| Great, O God, thy saving grace | 579 | 1 |
| †Great Prophet of my God | 675 | 4 |
| †Great Searcher of the mazy heart | 830 | 2 |
| †Great Shepherd of thy chosen few | 864 | 3 |
| †Great Sun of righteousness, arise | 553 | 5 |
| Great your strength if great your need | 847 | 3 |
| Greater than my sinful heart | 158 | 1 |
| Greater things we soon shall see | 623 | 4 |
| Greatest of gifts thy love impart | 16 | 8 |
| Greatness unspeakable is thine | 240 | 2 |
| Greatness, whose undiminished ray | 240 | 2 |
| Greedy of eternal pain | 6 | 4 |
| Grief and suffering are no more | 50 | 2 |
| Grieved him by a thousand falls | 168 | 1 |
| Grievous to feeble flesh and blood | 331 | 1 |
| Groaning beneath your load of sin | 30 | 6 |
| Groan the sinner's only plea | 101 | 4 |
| Grounded in the holy place | 723 | 4 |
| Ground of our communion this | 515 | 3 |
| Grovelling aims in work sublime | 768 | 5 |
| †Grovelling on earth we still must lie | 108 | 4 |
| Guarded by almighty power | 975 | 2 |
| †Guard *him* from all who dare oppose | 465 | 5 |

| | Hymn | Verse |
|---|---|---|
| Guard my first springs of thought and will | 964 | 6 |
| Guard thou the lips from sin, the hearts from shame | 962 | 2 |
| Guard thou thine own, possess it whole | 431 | 2 |
| Guards are scattered | 715 | 4 |
| Guards from all impending harms | 618 | 4 |
| Guards securing | 715 | 4 |
| Guide and guard my erring heart | 593 | 3 |
| Guide, and nourish me, and keep | 183 | 1 |
| Guide into thy perfect peace | 687 | 3 |
| *Guide me, O thou great Jehovah | 839 | 1 |
| †Guide of my life hast thou not been | 178 | 2 |
| Guide us through the watery way | 999 | 1 |
| Guided by thee, through all I go | 281 | 3 |
| Guides into the paths of peace | 554 | 3 |
| Guile nor violence can harm thee | 597 | 1 |
| †Guilty I stand before thy face | 127 | 7 |
| †Guilty now I pour my moaning | 933 | 12 |
| | | |
| Had engulfed our struggling soul | 621 | 2 |
| Had held his unmolested reign | 240 | 3 |
| †Had not thy help been nigh | 602 | 3 |
| Had stole my heart away | 93 | 4 |
| Hail, Abraham's God, and mine | 800 | 12 |
| Hail, apostles of the Lamb | 737 | 7 |
| †Hail, by all thy works adored | 257 | 3 |
| *Hail, co-essential Three | 643 | 1 |
| Hail, derided Majesty | 195 | 4 |
| †Hail! everlasting Lord | 194 | 3 |
| *Hail! Father, Son, and Holy Ghost | 239 | 1 |
| Hail, Father, Son, and Holy Ghost | 800 | 12 |
| *Hail! Father, Son, and Spirit great | 256 | 1 |
| *Hail, Father, whose creating call | 642 | 1 |
| †Hail, Galilean King | 195 | 4 |
| *Hail, God the Son, in glory crowned | 665 | 1 |
| Hail him who saves you by his grace | 681 | 4 |
| †Hail him, ye heirs of David's line | 681 | 5 |
| *Hail, Holy Ghost, Jehovah, Third | 750 | 1 |
| †Hail, Holy Ghost, Jehovah, Third | 750 | 6 |
| *Hail! holy, holy, holy Lord | 259 | 1 |
| †Hail! holy, holy, holy Lord | 259 | 6 |
| Hail, in the time appointed | 586 | 1 |
| Hail, Lord, almighty to create | 665 | 4 |
| †Hail, Saviour, Prince of peace | 731 | 5 |
| *Hail the day that sees him rise | 718 | 1 |
| Hail the Cause, the Lord of all | 727 | 3 |
| Hail, the everlasting Lord | 257 | 3 |
| †Hail the heaven-born Prince of peace | 68 | 4 |
| Hail the heir with glory crowned | 51 | 5 |
| Hail the incarnate Deity | 683 | 3 |
| Hail the Sun of righteousness | 683 | 4 |
| Hail, thou agonizing Saviour | 722 | 1 |
| Hail, thou Galilean King | 722 | 1 |

|  | Hymn | Verse |
|---|---|---|
| *Hail, thou once despised Jesus | 722 | 1 |
| *Hail to the Lord's Anointed | 586 | 1 |
| †Hail, venerable train | 737 | 7 |
| †Hail, with essential glory crowned | 665 | 6 |
| †Hail your dread Lord and ours | 727 | 3 |
| Hallelujah | 66 | 1 |
| Hallelujah | 595 | 1 |
| Hallelujah | 595 | 6 |
| Hallelujah | 714 | Cho. |
| Hallelujah | 1007 | — |
| Hallelujah again | 491 | 7 |
| Hallelujah, Praise the Lord | 742 | Cho. |
| †Hallelujah, they cry | 499 | 6 |
| Hallelujah to God and the Lamb | 499 | 6 |
| †Hallelujah, we sing | 491 | 7 |
| †Hallow, and make thy servants meet | 648 | 6 |
| Hallow each thought; let all within | 339 | 2 |
| Hallow in me thy glorious name | 375 | 5 |
| Hallow our food, reverse our doom | 108 | 5 |
| Hallow our food, reverse our doom | 1009 | — |
| Hallow thy great and glorious name | 391 | 2 |
| Hallowed and made meet for heaven | 51 | 2 |
| Hallowed be his name beneath | 641 | 4 |
| Hallowed by the present grace | 862 | 2 |
| Hallowed let this union be | 995 | 1 |
| †Hallowed thus their every breath | 817 | 7 |
| Hand in hand we seek thy face | 538 | 1 |
| Hands, and hearts, and voices raise | 519 | 1 |
| Hang everlasting things | 42 | 5 |
| Hang fruitful showers around | 226 | 7 |
| Hang on thy arm alone | 311 | 3 |
| Hang upon thine accents sweet | 882 | 3 |
| Hanging, bursting o'er our head | 60 | 1 |
| Hanging on the arm of God | 238 | 3 |
| Hangs my helpless soul on thee | 143 | 2 |
| Hangs o'er all the thirsty land | 218 | 4 |
| Happier souls that find a rest | 593 | 2 |
| Happier still if thine I die | 430 | 5 |
| Happier we each other keep | 487 | 2 |
| Happy are the faithful dead | 51 | 1 |
| Happy at the Saviour's feet | 530 | 3 |
| †Happy beyond description he | 14 | 2 |
| †Happy birds that sing and fly | 593 | 2 |
| †Happy he whom Christ shall find | 54 | 5 |
| †Happy if, watching to the end | 828 | 5 |
| †Happy, if with my latest breath | 37 | 6 |
| †Happy in thy glorious love | 53 | 4 |
| Happy in thyself alone | 242 | 2 |
| *Happy man whom God doth aid | 233 | 1 |
| †Happy morrow | 715 | 3 |
| Happy souls! their praises flow | 593 | 2 |
| *Happy soul that free from harms | 13 | 1 |
| *Happy soul, thy days are ended | 922 | 1 |

| | Hymn | Verse |
|---|---|---|
| *Happy soul who sees the day | 197 | 1 |
| *Happy the man that finds the grace | 14 | 1 |
| †Happy the man whose hopes rely | 224 | 2 |
| †Happy the man who wisdom gains | 14 | 6 |
| †Happy the men to whom 'tis given | 590 | 2 |
| Happy the race | 595 | 1 |
| *Happy the souls that first believed | 16 | 1 |
| *Happy the souls to Jesus joined | 15 | 1 |
| †Happy they who never rest | 260 | 3 |
| †Happy they whose joys abound | 115 | 2 |
| †Happy we live, when God doth fill | 858 | 3 |
| Happy while on earth we breathe | 58 | 3 |
| *Happy who in Jesus live | 925 | 1 |
| Harbinger of human race | 718 | 6 |
| Hardly now at last I yield | 166 | 3 |
| Hard toiling to make the blest shore | 49 | 2 |
| *Hark! a voice divides the sky | 51 | 1 |
| Hark, his gracious lips bestow | 718 | 4 |
| Hark how he calls the tender lambs | 889 | 1 |
| †Hark, how he groans! while nature shakes | 22 | 2 |
| Hark, how my silence speaks, and cries | 133 | 5 |
| *Hark, how the watchmen cry | 314 | 1 |
| Hark on earth the doleful cry | 936 | 4 |
| Hark, the choirs of angel-voices | 720 | 1 |
| *Hark! the herald-angels sing | 683 | 1 |
| †Hark! the wastes have found a voice | 348 | 2 |
| Hark! we now our voices raise | 538 | 3 |
| Hark! what shouts the air are rending | 595 | 6 |
| Harlots, and publicans, and thieves | 30 | 5 |
| Harmony's full concert raise | 641 | 2 |
| Harping on harps of gold | 942 | 11 |
| Has broken every barrier down | 796 | 6 |
| Has learnt Messiah's name | 747 | 3 |
| Has wrought to spoil our sacrifice | 961 | 3 |
| Hast all our fathers led | 664 | 1 |
| Hast died to bear their sins away | 82 | 5 |
| Hast leaped the bounds of time | 52 | 5 |
| Hast made the reprobates thine own | 203 | 3 |
| Hast multiplied the faithful race | 493 | 2 |
| Hast never left a soul distressed | 545 | 2 |
| Hast raised my head in triumph high | 559 | 1 |
| Hast ransomed every soul of man | 444 | 1 |
| Hast saved us from grief, Hast saved us from sin | 19 | 2 |
| Hast set the captive free | 215 | 1 |
| Hast snatched me from the gates of hell | 365 | 6 |
| †Hast thou been with me, Lord, so long | 113 | 2 |
| Hast thou forgot thy gracious skill | 397 | 3 |
| Hast thou not a gracious word | 182 | 1 |
| †Hast thou not died to purge our sin | 380 | 6 |
| †Hast thou not made me willing, Lord | 362 | 5 |
| Hast thou not received him now | 506 | 2 |
| Hast, with thy own precious blood | 423 | 1 |
| Haste, for him the robe prepare | 191 | 4 |

| | Hymn | Verse |
|---|---|---|
| Haste, my Lord, no more delay | 156 | 1 |
| †Haste, O haste, to my relief | 116 | 2 |
| Haste thee, O Lord, I pray | 635 | 2 |
| Haste to my aid, thine ear incline | 288 | 1 |
| Haste to the supper of my Lord | 9 | 1 |
| Haste, work in me to do | 799 | 6 |
| Hastening to infernal pain | 151 | 1 |
| Hastening to the happy dead | 915 | 1 |
| Hasten, Lord, the general doom | 937 | 1 |
| †Hasten, Lord, the perfect day | 400 | 8 |
| Hasten not to cut him down | 168 | 3 |
| †Hasten the joyful day | 367 | 2 |
| Hasten the long-expected hour | 408 | 4 |
| Hasten to your pardoning God | 29 | 1 |
| Hastens homeward to return | 51 | 3 |
| Hate, envy, jealousy, be gone | 351 | 4 |
| Hath animated senseless stones | 203 | 1 |
| Hath begotten me these | 231 | 9 |
| Hath bound me fast to thee | 614 | 12 |
| Hath brought us by his love | 478 | 2 |
| Hath cleared this guilty soul of mine | 330 | 2 |
| Hath drawn thee from above | 112 | 5 |
| Hath from the dead our Shepherd brought | 616 | 8 |
| Hath full atonement made | 738 | 2 |
| †Hath God cast off for ever | 587 | 3 |
| Hath grace through him and blessing given | 721 | 1 |
| †Hath he diadem as monarch | 793 | 3 |
| Hath he his loving-kindness | 587 | 3 |
| †Hath he marks to lead me to him | 793 | 2 |
| Hath he our sinful Israel spared | 980 | 2 |
| Hath his truth and mercy showed | 605 | 3 |
| Hath made and called his own | 954 | 1 |
| Hath made it prevail | 219 | 2 |
| Hath made us priests and kings | 21 | 3 |
| Hath pity left the Son of man | 157 | 4 |
| Hath prospered his word | 219 | 2 |
| Hath raised him from the dead | 360 | 1 |
| Hath risen with purpose fell | 856 | 1 |
| Hath rose with healing in his wings | 141 | 5 |
| Hath saved us from the world and sin | 482 | 1 |
| Hath spoke the word | 1026 | — |
| Hath stablished it fast By a changeless decree | 611 | 3 |
| Hath stood, and shall for ever last | 612 | 1 |
| Hath surely died for me | 85 | 1 |
| Hath taught me better things | 192 | 3 |
| Hath wrought a perfect cure | 370 | 2 |
| Have conquered in the fight | 943 | 10 |
| †Have I not heard, have I not known | 157 | 5 |
| Have I not vowed and wept in vain | 909 | 1 |
| Have lifted up their voice | 601 | 3 |
| Have my Jesus ever near | 13 | 2 |
| Have nothing else to fear | 562 | 6 |
| Have passed the sea | 276 | 3 |

|  | Hymn | Verse |
|---|---|---|
| Have pierced a thousand thousand times | 122 | 1 |
| †Have pity on my fears | 565 | 7 |
| Have sealed this call my last | 799 | 2 |
| Have seen a glorious gospel day | 203 | 2 |
| Have spurned to-day the voice divine | 973 | 4 |
| Haven to take the shipwrecked in | 379 | 2 |
| Having known it "Christ to live" | 672 | 11 |
| Head of the church he lives and reigns | 616 | 7 |
| †Head of the martyrs' noble host | 647 | 4 |
| *Head of thy church triumphant | 853 | 1 |
| *Head of thy church, whose Spirit fills | 749 | 1 |
| Head, thy living member make *him* | 895 | 3 |
| Healed by thy stripes I am | 215 | 4 |
| Healing and sight | 870 | 2 |
| He all day long spreads out his hands | 31 | 3 |
| †He all his foes shall quell | 729 | 5 |
| †He all shall break through; His truth and his grace | 273 | 7 |
| He all thy promises shall gain | 590 | 6 |
| He alone the fight hath fought | 605 | 1 |
| He alone the work hath wrought | 218 | 3 |
| He, and no other one | 856 | 2 |
| †He answered for all | 707 | 3 |
| He awes the trembling world to peace | 569 | 8 |
| He bade us arise, An impotent throng | 212 | 4 |
| He bears the righteous sway | 719 | 4 |
| He beckons from the skies | 315 | 4 |
| He bids the blind their Saviour see | 638 | 5 |
| †He bids us build each other up | 500 | 2 |
| He bore it home, upon his shoulders laid | 850 | 2 |
| He bore our sins upon the tree | 127 | 8 |
| He bore the cross for all | 314 | 2 |
| He bows his head and dies | 22 | 3 |
| †He breaks the bow, he cuts the spear | 569 | 9 |
| †He breaks the power of cancelled sin | 1 | 4 |
| He brings his kingdom in | 761 | 3 |
| †He brings my wandering spirit back | 555 | 2 |
| He brings salvation near | 384 | 2 |
| †He brought me forth in open place | 551 | 5 |
| He brought us to his fold again | 608 | 2 |
| He by death has spoiled his foes | 720 | 2 |
| †He by himself hath sworn | 800 | 4 |
| †He called me in the time of dread | 697 | 6 |
| †He called me when my thoughtless prime | 697 | 5 |
| He calls a worm his friend | 800 | 3 |
| He calls himself my God | 800 | 3 |
| He calls the weary burdened race | 25 | 1 |
| He calls the weary sinner home | 152 | 1 |
| He calls you now, invites you home | 30 | 6 |
| He calls you to receive | 387 | 1 |
| †He came from above | 808 | 2 |
| He came the lost to seek and save | 30 | 5 |
| He can create, and he destroy | 608 | 1 |
| He cannot himself deny | 142 | 2 |

| | Hymn | Verse |
|---|---|---|
| He cannot turn away | 202 | 4 |
| He claims the kingdoms for his own | 56 | 3 |
| He claims these mansions as his right | 557 | 8 |
| He comes, and bids you hope | 54 | 2 |
| *He comes! he comes! the Judge severe | 56 | 1 |
| †He comes, he comes, to call | 65 | 2 |
| He comes his people to redeem | 689 | 2 |
| He comes in man to live | 761 | 1 |
| †He comes, of hellish malice full | 501 | 2 |
| He comes our fallen souls to raise | 689 | 2 |
| He comes to break oppression | 586 | 1 |
| He comes to meet us from the sky | 25 | 1 |
| †He comes, with succour speedy | 586 | 2 |
| He counts their numbers, calls their names | 225 | 2 |
| †He deigns in flesh to appear | 685 | 4 |
| He descends on the luminous cloud | 488 | 5 |
| He died for all mankind | 262 | 4 |
| He died to save my soul from death | 378 | 2 |
| *He dies! the friend of sinners dies | 712 | 1 |
| †He dies to atone | 707 | 4 |
| He disarms the wrath of God | 168 | 3 |
| He doth still in life maintain | 661 | 2 |
| He doth with nightly pains chastise | 548 | 3 |
| He drew me, and I followed on | 912 | 3 |
| †He drew me from the fearful pit | 566 | 2 |
| He dwelt with sinful men | 215 | 3 |
| He enters, condescends to stay | 695 | 4 |
| He enters heaven with prayer | 823 | 5 |
| †He ever lives above | 202 | 2 |
| †He ever lives for me to pray | 127 | 10 |
| He ever reigns the same | 314 | 3 |
| He falls to rise on earth no more | 638 | 3 |
| He feeds his flock, he calls their names | 675 | 6 |
| He fights alone | 854 | 2 |
| He fights his peoples' battles | 854 | 2 |
| He fills them with his choicest store | 630 | 8 |
| †He fills the poor with good | 610 | 4 |
| He flew to our relief | 699 | 2 |
| He for all hath risen again | 86 | 2 |
| He for every man hath died | 86 | 2 |
| He for us the fight hath won | 50 | 1 |
| †He formed the deeps unknown | 603 | 2 |
| †He formed the stars, those heavenly flames | 225 | 2 |
| He formed us by his word | 603 | 3 |
| He freely doth forgive | 144 | 6 |
| He gave the seas their bound | 603 | 2 |
| He gently clears thy way | 831 | 9 |
| He gives our daily bread | 988 | 2 |
| He gives them life for evermore | 630 | 8 |
| He gives the sufferers rest | 610 | 4 |
| He gives us needful food by day | 624 | 2 |
| He goes and seeks the one lost sheep | 144 | 7 |
| He governs all our race | 731 | 4 |

| | Hymn | Verse |
|---|---|---|
| He grants the soul again | 804 | 1 |
| He guards them by his side | 800 | 8 |
| He had not where to lay his head | 227 | 2 |
| He hangs on yonder cross | 215 | 3 |
| He harms us not a whit | 856 | 3 |
| He has gained the victory | 720 | 2 |
| He has none to lift him up | 487 | 2 |
| †He has raised our human nature | 720 | 5 |
| He has vanquished sin and Satan | 720 | 2 |
| He hath all the storms outrode | 52 | 2 |
| He hath filled the garner floor | 631 | 6 |
| He hath given the word of grace | 218 | 3 |
| He hath left his mates behind | 52 | 2 |
| He hath loved, he hath loved us, because he would love | 808 | 2 |
| He hath loved, he hath loved us, we cannot tell why | 808 | 3 |
| He hath loved me, I cried | 807 | 3 |
| He hath loved us so well | 808 | 4 |
| He hath made me to do | 231 | 10 |
| He hath on us bestowed | 96 | 4 |
| †He hath opened a door | 219 | 3 |
| †He hath our salvation wrought | 400 | 3 |
| †He hath ransomed our race | 808 | 5 |
| He hath reconciled to God | 400 | 3 |
| He hath suffered, and died | 807 | 3 |
| He hath washed us in his blood | 400 | 3 |
| He heaps up treasures, mixed with woe | 564 | 3 |
| He heard those accents mild | 697 | 3 |
| He heareth the prayer, And he will provide | 496 | 2 |
| He hears; he smiles; and all the choir | 948 | 6 |
| He hears the blood of sprinkling now | 726 | 2 |
| He helps his poor afflicted one | 545 | 3 |
| He helps my soul's infirmity | 144 | 3 |
| He helps the stranger in distress | 224 | 3 |
| He hides a smiling face | 845 | 2 |
| He hides his face behind his wings | 316 | 2 |
| He hides the brightness of his face | 803 | 1 |
| He himself has bid thee pray | 824 | 1 |
| He himself prepares the fane | 862 | 1 |
| He hindered our flying (His goodness to show) | 481 | 4 |
| He his conquering grace affords | 278 | 6 |
| He his sovereign sway maintains | 571 | 2 |
| †He in sickness makes me whole | 554 | 3 |
| †He in the days of feeble flesh | 725 | 3 |
| He is able | 791 | 1 |
| He is a sure defence to such | 551 | 6 |
| He is become my joyful song | 616 | 3 |
| He is become the corner-stone | 616 | 7 |
| He is full of grace for all | 197 | 3 |
| He is gathered into God | 50 | 2 |
| He is holy | 606 | Cho. |
| He is Israel's sure defence | 618 | 3 |
| He is mine, and I am his | 554 | 1 |

| | Hymn | Verse |
|---|---|---|
| He is my own wickedness | 278 | 2 |
| He is my tower, my rock, my shield | 626 | 3 |
| He is my triumphal song | 197 | 3 |
| He is parted from his friends | 720 | 3 |
| He is the God of hallowing grace | 412 | 6 |
| He is the God of saving power | 412 | 6 |
| He is the Truth, the Life, the Way | 616 | 6 |
| He is willing; doubt no more | 791 | 1 |
| He its finisher shall be | 382 | 5 |
| †He justly claims us for his own | 428 | 2 |
| †He keeps his own secure | 800 | 8 |
| He knows my wants, allays my fears | 849 | 1 |
| He knows our feeble frame | 610 | 9 |
| He knows our feeble frame | 725 | 2 |
| He knows what sore temptations mean | 725 | 2 |
| He laid his glory by | 194 | 2 |
| †He laid his glory by | 685 | 2 |
| †He left his Father's throne above | 201 | 3 |
| †He left his throne above | 195 | 2 |
| He lights the evening star | 988 | 2 |
| He like a victim stood | 731 | 2 |
| He lives, and on the earth shall stand | 928 | 1 |
| He lives who died for me, I know | 927 | 1 |
| He loves the injured to redress | 638 | 5 |
| He made by Moses known | 610 | 5 |
| He makes his churches his abode | 573 | 1 |
| He makes me down to lie | 556 | 1 |
| †He makes the grass the hills adorn | 225 | 4 |
| He makes the noise of battle cease | 569 | 8 |
| He maketh fast her bolts and bars | 595 | 2 |
| He may his Prince and Saviour own | 670 | 2 |
| †He met that glance so thrilling sweet | 697 | 3 |
| He mildly rules the hosts of heaven | 280 | 2 |
| †He now stands knocking at the door | 208 | 2 |
| He now vouchsafes a kind reprieve | 80 | 4 |
| He obtained for our race | 488 | 4 |
| He offers you pardon; he bids you be free | 5 | 3 |
| He on his throne shall rest | 586 | 6 |
| †He only can the words apply | 754 | 4 |
| He only chastened whom he loved | 120 | 1 |
| He only is the Maker | 988 | 2 |
| He only sojourns here | 68 | 1 |
| He our captive souls hath bought | 400 | 3 |
| He, our Enoch, is translated | 720 | 3 |
| He our faithful guide shall be | 572 | 4 |
| He our guide will be | 715 | 10 |
| He our loving Saviour is | 207 | 1 |
| He owns, and shall for ever own | 14 | 6 |
| He owns me for his child | 202 | 5 |
| He paid my ransom with his blood | 917 | 2 |
| He paints the wayside flower | 988 | 2 |
| He pauses at our threshold, nay | 695 | 4 |
| He placed my feet upon a rock | 566 | 2 |

| | Hymn | Verse |
|---|---|---|
| He plants his footsteps in the sea | 845 | 1 |
| He pleads his passion on the tree | 726 | 1 |
| He poured out cries and tears for you | 712 | 1 |
| He prayed on the tree | 707 | 5 |
| He prays that I with him may reign | 127 | 10 |
| He prevents his creatures' call | 238 | 1 |
| †He prevents his creatures' call | 1019 | 2 |
| He promises to bless | 680 | 7 |
| He purchased the grace | 707 | 6 |
| He reigns above the skies | 724 | 2 |
| He reigns and triumphs here | 741 | 2 |
| He reigns supreme in heaven | 719 | 3 |
| He relieves my grief and pain | 809 | 3 |
| He removes the flaming sword | 480 | 3 |
| He revives my fainting soul | 554 | 3 |
| He rides upon the sky | 407 | 1 |
| He rises, who mankind has bought | 950 | 2 |
| He rose, the Prince of life and peace | 953 | 1 |
| He rules o'er earth and heaven | 729 | 3 |
| He said; and gave his soul to death | 903 | 1 |
| He saith, who cannot lie | 405 | 2 |
| He saves the opprest, he feeds the poor | 224 | 2 |
| He saw, and—O amazing love | 699 | 2 |
| He sees their hope, he knows their fear | 225 | 6 |
| He seizes every straggling soul | 501 | 2 |
| He sends the labouring conscience peace | 224 | 3 |
| He sends the snow in winter | 988 | 1 |
| †He sends them from the skies | 86 | 3 |
| He sent his own eternal Son | 644 | 1 |
| He sets the mournful prisoners free | 638 | 5 |
| He sets the prisoner free | 1 | 4 |
| He shakes his future home | 405 | 5 |
| He shakes the centre with his nod | 223 | 4 |
| He shall accepted be | 162 | 3 |
| He shall all their sorrows chase | 76 | 4 |
| He shall be saved eternally | 162 | 5 |
| He shall bestow Upon our race | 591 | 4 |
| He shall both grace and glory give | 590 | 5 |
| He shall come and save you too | 348 | 5 |
| †He shall come down like showers | 586 | 3 |
| He shall destroy each idol-king | 613 | 3 |
| He shall direct thy wandering feet | 831 | 2 |
| He shall his pitying aid bestow | 849 | 3 |
| He shall lift your hands cast down | 348 | 4 |
| He shall my soul redeem | 406 | 4 |
| †He shall obtain the starry crown | 557 | 5 |
| He shall, on his victorious way | 613 | 3 |
| He shall prepare thy way | 831 | 2 |
| He shall prop your feeble knees | 348 | 4 |
| He shed for you his precious blood | 712 | 1 |
| He shook and bound the strong man armed | 93 | 6 |
| He shows himself to God for me | 726 | 1 |
| He shows his prints of love | 800 | 11 |

| | Hymn | Verse |
|---|---|---|
| †He sits at God's right hand | 729 | 4 |
| He slumbers not, nor sleeps | 595 | 1 |
| He smooths my bed, and gives me sleep | 227 | 3 |
| He sojourns in a house of clay | 31 | 2 |
| He spake, and all was still | 697 | 1 |
| †He spake; and straightway the celestial choir | 691 | 3 |
| †He spake the word, and it was done | 234 | 2 |
| †He speaks, and, listening to his voice | 1 | 5 |
| He speaks the almighty word | 64 | 6 |
| He spreads his arms to embrace you all | 30 | 5 |
| He spread the skies abroad | 667 | 2 |
| He still our soul secures | 854 | 2 |
| †He still respects thy sacrifice | 902 | 4 |
| He still shall flourish, and success | 540 | 3 |
| He still supplies | 800 | 8 |
| He surely shall fulfil | 384 | 8 |
| He takes our children to his arms | 888 | 3 |
| He tasted death for me | 809 | 2 |
| †He taught my soul a new-made song | 566 | 3 |
| He teaches me his will | 548 | 8 |
| †He that believes in thee | 162 | 5 |
| He that hath ears, now let him hear | 935 | 4 |
| He that into God's kingdom comes | 920 | 3 |
| †He that on the throne doth reign | 76 | 4 |
| He that was born upon this joyful day | 691 | 6 |
| He the atonement now receives | 350 | 5 |
| He the door hath opened wide | 218 | 8 |
| He the door hath opened wide | 735 | 2 |
| He, the eternal God, was born | 194 | 2 |
| He the fatal cause demands | 6 | 1 |
| †He then is blest, and only he | 638 | 4 |
| †He this flowery carpet spread | 233 | 2 |
| He threw their empire down | 731 | 3 |
| He thy feeble steps shall stay | 618 | 2 |
| He thy quiet spirit keeps | 618 | 2 |
| He to all the sons of men | 605 | 3 |
| †He to Israel's chosen race | 605 | 3 |
| He to my rescue came | 562 | 3 |
| He, to rescue me from danger | 866 | 2 |
| He took his seat above | 729 | 2 |
| He treasures up his bright designs | 845 | 1 |
| He turns and looks, and cries, " 'Tis done" | 106 | 7 |
| He undertakes our cause | 277 | 2 |
| He upon the clouds ascends | 720 | 3 |
| He utters a cry, Ye sinners, give ear | 3 | 1 |
| He utters his almighty voice | 569 | 6 |
| He views his children with delight | 225 | 6 |
| He views with gracious eyes | 321 | 3 |
| †He visits now the house of clay | 405 | 5 |
| He vouchsafes to dwell in man | 758 | 3 |
| He walks and cannot fall | 281 | 2 |
| He weareth in this hour | 856 | 1 |
| He who all creation saves | 605 | 6 |

| | Hymn | Verse |
|---|---|---|
| He who all your lives hath strove | 6 | 3 |
| He who found the wandering sheep | 13 | 1 |
| He who from the grave arose | 720 | 2 |
| He who is, and was, in peace | 418 | 2 |
| He who on the cross did suffer | 720 | 2 |
| He, who set the world so fast | 604 | 2 |
| He, who still its state sustaineth | 604 | 2 |
| He who walked with God, and pleased him | 720 | 3 |
| He, whose word cannot be broken | 594 | 1 |
| He who would all the world receive | 8 | 2 |
| He who would have you turn and live | 8 | 2 |
| He will hearken, he will save | 597 | 3 |
| †He will his to glory raise | 639 | 9 |
| †He will present our souls | 814 | 3 |
| He will send down his heavenly powers | 12 | 2 |
| He will shield thee from above | 597 | 3 |
| He wills that all the fallen race | 144 | 6 |
| †He wills that I should holy be | 384 | 3 |
| *He wills that I should holy be | 408 | 1 |
| He with joy beholds thy face | 350 | 5 |
| He with the harsh command complied | 286 | 1 |
| He wrapped him in our clay | 685 | 2 |
| He wrought by weight and measure | 667 | 2 |
| He'll help us clear from all the ill | 856 | 1 |
| He'll make your wants his care | 562 | 6 |
| †He'll never quench the smoking flax | 725 | 4 |
| Heal me of my grief and pain | 167 | 1 |
| Heal my bruises, and bind up | 112 | 3 |
| Heal the diseased, and cure the blind | 397 | 2 |
| Heal the sick, and lead the blind | 143 | 3 |
| Heal the wounded of its pain | 753 | 7 |
| Heal'st whoe'er apply to thee | 693 | 3 |
| Health to the sick in mind | 870 | 2 |
| Health, wisdom, joy in thee they find | 770 | 2 |
| Heap ill on ill | 851 | 1 |
| †Hear, above all, hear thy Lord | 829 | 5 |
| Hear an apostate spirit groan | 130 | 1 |
| Hear, and all the graces shower | 390 | 2 |
| Hear, and fulfil thine own request | 17 | 1 |
| Hear, and my weak petitions join | 100 | 1 |
| Hear, and our petitions seal | 515 | 1 |
| †Hear, for thou, O Christ, alone | 257 | 7 |
| Hear from thy dwelling-place in heaven | 121 | 5 |
| †Hear him, ye deaf; his praise, ye dumb | 1 | 6 |
| Hear, Holy Ghost, our joint request | 441 | 1 |
| Hear in my heart thy Spirit's cry | 134 | 4 |
| Hear in this solemn evening hour | 969 | 7 |
| Hear, Lord, my feeble cries | 587 | 1 |
| Hear me then for pardon call | 242 | 4 |
| Hear my Advocate divine | 390 | 3 |
| Hear my dying spirit's cries | 151 | 6 |
| Hear our solemn litany | 710 | Cho. |
| Hear, rejoicing while thou hearest | 580 | 4 |

|  | HYMN | VERSE |
|---|---|---|
| Hear their sighs, and count their tears | 878 | 4 |
| Hear the Spirit and the bride | 937 | 1 |
| †Hear the victors who o'ercame | 829 | 4 |
| Hear, the world's atonement, thou | 257 | 5 |
| Hear, the world's atonement, thou | 257 | 6 |
| Hear thou in heaven, thy dwelling-place | 993 | 2 |
| *Hear thou my prayer, O Lord | 635 | 1 |
| Hear us, architect divine | 989 | 1 |
| Hear us now, and save thine own | 937 | 3 |
| Hear us, we humbly pray | 870 | 1 |
| Hear us, who thy nature share | 518 | 1 |
| Hear, well-pleased, the joyous sound | 191 | 1 |
| Heard me cry out of the deep | 274 | 1 |
| †Hearken to me with earnest care | 4 | 7 |
| Hearken to my dying cry | 112 | 2 |
| Hearken to my request | 565 | 7 |
| *Hearken to the solemn voice | 54 | 1 |
| Hearts that with rising morn arise | 965 | 1 |
| Hearts, voices, and lyres | 499 | 5 |
| Heart to heart, as lute to lute | 538 | 2 |
| †Heathens rage, dominions tremble | 570 | 4 |
| Heathens sing their Saviour's praise | 735 | 3 |
| Heaven already is begun | 521 | 4 |
| Heaven and earth, and all creation | 640 | 2 |
| Heaven and earth to ashes burning | 933 | 1 |
| Heaven, earth, and hell, stand all displayed | 240 | 4 |
| Heaven is my home, my friends | 942 | 2 |
| Heaven is thine, and earth, and sea | 733 | 1 |
| Heaven of heavens, his praise declare | 639 | 3 |
| Heaven on earth in Jesu's face | 542 | 3 |
| Heaven thy awful presence fills | 989 | 2 |
| †Heavenly Adam, Life divine | 390 | 4 |
| †Heavenly, all-alluring Dove | 514 | 3 |
| Heavenly bodies they put on | 941 | 2 |
| Heavenly Comforter divine | 757 | 3 |
| *Heavenly Father, sovereign Lord | 348 | 1 |
| Heavenly mansions to prepare | 720 | 7 |
| †Heaven's glory is thy awful throne | 240 | 4 |
| Heaven's host their noblest praises bring | 494 | 2 |
| Heaven's morning breaks, and earth's vain shadows flee | 972 | 5 |
| Heaven's still my song, my praise | 942 | 3 |
| †Heavenward our every wish aspires | 654 | 3 |
| Heavenward take the burdened sigh | 895 | 4 |
| *Heavy on me, O Lord, thy judgments lie | 596 | 1 |
| Heir of the promises is given | 689 | 1 |
| Held in vain the rising God | 710 | 5 |
| Hell, and death, and sin control | 352 | 4 |
| Hell, and earth, and nature's powers | 287 | 1 |
| Hell assails the throne of God | 601 | 3 |
| Hell at his command is still | 601 | 4 |
| Hell, earth, and sin, with ease o'ercome | 141 | 7 |
| Hell is nigh, but God is nigher | 728 | 5 |

| | HYMN | VERSE |
|---|---|---|
| Hell is ready to devour | 819 | 1 |
| Hell without a veil appears | 359 | 2 |
| †Hell's armies tremble at thy nod | 38 | 7 |
| Hell's horrid language filled our tongues | 203 | 7 |
| Help a feeble child of man | 151 | 1 |
| Help can come alone from thee | 621 | 3 |
| Help for all on thee is laid | 352 | 1 |
| *Help, Lord! the busy foe | 296 | 1 |
| *Help, Lord, to whom for help I fly | 309 | 1 |
| Help me at thy feet to lie | 188 | 6 |
| Help me in all thy paths to go | 909 | 5 |
| Help me in my last condition | 933 | 17 |
| Help me, Jesus, show thy grace | 164 | 3 |
| Help me, Lord; to thee I look | 27 | 1 |
| Help me, Saviour, speak the word | 354 | Cho. |
| Help me thy benefits to own | 772 | 1 |
| Help me thy benefits to sing | 365 | 1 |
| Help me to tear it from thy throne | 787 | 5 |
| Help me to watch and pray | 318 | 2 |
| Help of the helpless, O abide with me | 972 | 1 |
| Help, O help, attend my call | 352 | 2 |
| Help to chant Immanuel's praise | 722 | 4 |
| Help to gain our calling's hope | 521 | 1 |
| Help to live, and help to die | 971 | 4 |
| Help to sing our Saviour's merits | 722 | 4 |
| Help us in thought, and word, and deed | 696 | 1 |
| Help us thee to glorify | 411 | 1 |
| †Help us thy mercy to extol | 39 | 2 |
| †Help us to build each other up | 503 | 4 |
| †Help us to help each other, Lord | 503 | 3 |
| Help us to look on thee and mourn | 122 | 1 |
| Help us to look up with Stephen | 720 | 6 |
| †Help us to make our calling sure | 523 | 4 |
| Help us to obtain the prize | 737 | 12 |
| Help us well to close our race | 737 | 12 |
| Help, while yet I ask, is given | 618 | 1 |
| Help, ye angel-choirs, to bless | 194 | 3 |
| Help, ye bright, angelic spirits | 722 | 4 |
| †Helpless howe'er my spirit lies | 396 | 4 |
| Henceforth, and evermore | 618 | 5 |
| †Henceforth may no profane delight | 285 | 5 |
| Hence is my heart dismayed | 566 | 8 |
| †Hence may all our actions flow | 522 | 4 |
| Hence my doubts, away my fears | 197 | 2 |
| †Hence our hearts melt, our eyes o'erflow | 26 | 6 |
| †Hence sprung the Apostles' honoured name | 868 | 2 |
| Her bulwarks who can shock | 572 | 3 |
| Her calm waters | 570 | 2 |
| †Her hands are filled with length of days | 14 | 4 |
| Her heavenly Founder's praise resounds | 647 | 4 |
| Her heavenly Lord to descend | 77 | 1 |
| Her only law his sovereign word | 223 | 4 |
| Her priests, and clothe with robes of praise | 629 | 7 |

| | Hymn | Verse |
|---|---|---|
| Her saints their joy aloud shall speak | 629 | 7 |
| Her temple on Moriah stand | 452 | 4 |
| †Her vehemence did the judge provoke | 827 | 6 |
| Her walls are of jasper and gold | 78 | 3 |
| Her waste and desolate places build | 111 | 3 |
| Her ways are ways of pleasantness | 14 | 5 |
| †Hereafter none can take away | 432 | 2 |
| Hereafter shall in glory live | 557 | 4 |
| †Here as in their due succession | 990 | 2 |
| †Here, as in the lion's den | 238 | 3 |
| Here at thy feet for ever lie | 155 | 6 |
| Here babes thy grace proclaim | 544 | 1 |
| Here babes thy grace proclaim | 544 | 5 |
| Here enjoy the earnest given | 512 | 3 |
| Here for a season, then above | 796 | 7 |
| Here for ever let it flow | 348 | 6 |
| Here for grief reward thee double | 597 | 3 |
| Here for three and thirty years | 215 | 3 |
| †Here, gracious God, do thou | 991 | 3 |
| Here in an ampler, purer air | 698 | 1 |
| †Here in due and solemn order | 990 | 5 |
| †Here in the body pent | 944 | 2 |
| †Here, in thine own appointed ways | 92 | 2 |
| †Here in thy house shall incense rise | 978 | 5 |
| †Here I raise my Ebenezer | 866 | 2 |
| Here is my hope, my joy, my rest | 189 | 4 |
| Here is yet one quiet rill | 570 | 2 |
| Here let me over, ever stay | 330 | 6 |
| Here let me give my wanderings o'er | 170 | 1 |
| Here let me give my wanderings o'er | 998 | 4 |
| Here let me wash my spotted soul | 786 | 4 |
| Here let the mountains thunder forth sonorous Alleluia | 663 | — |
| Here let thy light for ever shine | 431 | 3 |
| Here may strains of holy gladness | 990 | 5 |
| †Here may the wretched sons of want | 880 | 2 |
| †Here may we gain from heaven | 991 | 4 |
| †Here may we prove the power of prayer | 864 | 4 |
| Here on the holy mount with thee | 698 | 6 |
| Here, on the steps of Jesu's throne | 896 | 2 |
| Here prepare to meet our Lord | 512 | 3 |
| Here regain our paradise | 512 | 3 |
| Here set up thy gracious throne | 676 | 3 |
| Here shall find a still retreat | 990 | 3 |
| Here the bread of heaven be broken | 990 | 5 |
| Here the careless passer-by | 990 | 3 |
| Here the child of God be sealed | 990 | 5 |
| †Here the fair tree of knowledge grows | 880 | 3 |
| †Here the Redeemer's welcome voice | 880 | 4 |
| †Here the whole Deity is known | 263 | 5 |
| Here the word of life be spoken | 990 | 5 |
| Here then I cast them all behind | 781 | 2 |
| †Here then I doubt no more | 832 | 5 |

|   | Hymn | Verse |
|---|---|---|
| †Here then, my God, vouchsafe to stay | 214 | 3 |
| Here then to thee I all resign | 131 | 2 |
| Here then to thee I all resign | 132 | 5 |
| †Here then to thee thy own I leave | 429 | 4 |
| Here they behold thy gentler rays | 592 | 3 |
| Here they find their trials o'er | 76 | 3 |
| Here they knew their sins forgiven | 51 | 2 |
| Here they laid their burden down | 51 | 2 |
| Here thy faithful love record | 572 | 2 |
| Here thy mean abode take up | 413 | 2 |
| Here to abide, no transient guest | 993 | 5 |
| Here to our waiting hearts proclaim | 864 | 3 |
| Here to The Absolver's feet | 990 | 3 |
| Here we in the Spirit breathe | 423 | 3 |
| Here we may sit, and see him here | 956 | 2 |
| Here we raise our voices higher | 238 | 3 |
| †Here, when thy messengers proclaim | 993 | 3 |
| †Here, when thy people seek thy face | 993 | 2 |
| Here, where on eagles' wings we move | 698 | 3 |
| Here, where the apostle's heart of rock | 698 | 3 |
| Here, where the son of thunder learns | 698 | 3 |
| †Here will I ever lie | 303 | 4 |
| Here will I my spirit hide | 175 | 5 |
| †Here will I set up my rest | 809 | 4 |
| Here will the world's Redeemer reign | 993 | 5 |
| Here with prayer its deep foundations | 990 | 1 |
| †Hereby we sweetly know | 533 | 2 |
| Hereby your faith approve | 897 | 1 |
| †Here's love and grief beyond degree | 712 | 2 |
| Here's pardon, comfort, rest, and home | 695 | 5 |
| Hid be our life with Christ in God | 666 | 6 |
| Hid from the general scourge we are | 466 | 1 |
| Hid in our Saviour's hand we lie | 801 | 1 |
| Hide, and bring us safe to land | 999 | 1 |
| Hide from their eyes the devilish ill | 458 | 5 |
| Hide in the hollow of thy hand | 272 | 4 |
| Hide in the place where Moses stood | 124 | 2 |
| Hide me, earth, the sinner hide | 185 | 1 |
| Hide me, Jesus, till o'erpast | 292 | 1 |
| Hide me, O my Saviour, hide | 143 | 1 |
| Hide me, Saviour, with thine hand | 292 | 2 |
| Hide not thy face: I droop as they | 635 | 2 |
| Hide thou thy face, yet, Help in time of need | 851 | 1 |
| Hide us, hide us | 936 | 4 |
| Hide within thy heart his word | 829 | 5 |
| *High above every name | 195 | 1 |
| High above yon azure height | 718 | 8 |
| High as heaven aspires thy brow | 382 | 1 |
| †High as the heavens are raised | 610 | 8 |
| High as the heavens our voices raise | 608 | 3 |
| †High heaven, that heard the solemn vow | 912 | 5 |
| *High in the heavens, eternal God | 563 | 1 |
| High is thy power above all height | 240 | 3 |

| | Hymn | Verse |
|---|---|---|
| High o'er its branches springs the thorn | 589 | 3 |
| †High o'er the angelic bands he rears | 713 | 4 |
| High on his everlasting throne | 616 | 7 |
| High on his Father's throne | 277 | 2 |
| †High on his holy seat | 719 | 4 |
| †High on Immanuel's land | 67 | 4 |
| High on the broken wave | 1002 | 3 |
| High on the mountain here with thee | 698 | 1 |
| High on thy eternal throne | 66 | 4 |
| †High on thy Father's throne | 352 | 2 |
| †High on thy great white throne | 67 | 7 |
| High over all is thy right hand | 293 | 9 |
| High praise to the eternal King | 964 | 4 |
| High thine everlasting throne | 727 | 1 |
| †High throned on heaven's eternal hill | 38 | 4 |
| Higher than the angels place | 724 | 3 |
| Higher than the highest star | 639 | 8 |
| Hills and vales with praises ring | 578 | 3 |
| Him and his works destroy below | 443 | 2 |
| Him a sign by all blasphemed | 195 | 3 |
| †Him beholding face to face | 941 | 4 |
| Him, by highest heaven adored | 572 | 1 |
| †Him eye to eye we there shall see | 537 | 9 |
| Him, for our offences slain | 717 | 1 |
| Him from whom all good proceeds | 641 | 1 |
| †Him have I set before my face | 548 | 4 |
| Him I evermore shall praise | 382 | 4 |
| Him I now rejoice to see | 383 | 1 |
| Him in heavenly glory see | 243 | 3 |
| Him in our eye of faith we keep | 493 | 3 |
| Him in outward works pursue | 325 | 1 |
| Him in Three Persons magnify | 255 | 3 |
| †Him, in whom they move and live | 641 | 4 |
| Him let all our hearts adore | 571 | 7 |
| Him let all our orders praise | 75 | 4 |
| Him let Israel still adore | 628 | 4 |
| †Him let us tend, severely kind | 467 | 8 |
| †Him Prophet, and King, And Priest we proclaim | 211 | 2 |
| Him serve with fear, his praise forth tell | 607 | 1 |
| Him that did for sinners die | 75 | 4 |
| †Him the angels all adored | 684 | 2 |
| Him the Judge of all mankind | 54 | 5 |
| Him the mighty waves obey | 601 | 4 |
| Him, the promised Comforter | 86 | 7 |
| Him, the Spirit of truth and grace | 755 | 2 |
| Him they all a madman deemed | 195 | 3 |
| †Him they beheld our conquering God | 721 | 4 |
| †Him they still through busier life | 817 | 6 |
| †Him though highest heaven receives | 718 | 4 |
| Him thou hast for sinners given | 717 | 2 |
| Him thou hast received for me | 757 | 3 |
| Him thou lovest to obey | 829 | 5 |
| Him Three in One, and One in Three | 232 | Cho. |

| | Hymn | Verse |
|---|---|---|
| Him we called not ours, but thine | 914 | 2 |
| Him we claim, and rest in him | 572 | 4 |
| Him we promised to resign | 914 | 2 |
| Him we trembled to receive | 914 | 2 |
| Him who fills the eternal throne | 580 | 4 |
| Him, who reigns enthroned on high | 75 | 2 |
| Him who spake a world from nought | 218 | 3 |
| Him whose dying love and power | 921 | 4 |
| †Him with lute and harp record | 605 | 5 |
| Him with quiet joy adore | 1000 | 2 |
| Him would I tenderly entreat | 470 | 5 |
| Him ye heavenly armies praise | 639 | 2 |
| Himself doth all our burdens bear | 827 | 2 |
| Himself hath caused to put your trust | 380 | 2 |
| Himself to worms impart | 128 | 2 |
| †His adorable will | 47 | 2 |
| His agents all their powers employ | 458 | 4 |
| His all-redeeming love | 202 | 2 |
| His anger newly but begun | 541 | 5 |
| His are the hands stretched out to draw me near | 794 | 4 |
| His arm he hath bared | 219 | 2 |
| His attributes and name | 232 | 2 |
| His beauty of holiest love | 70 | 1 |
| His be righteousness divine | 191 | 4 |
| His bleeding heart shall make you room | 30 | 6 |
| His blood alone can sanctify | 438 | 1 |
| His blood atoned for all our race | 202 | 2 |
| His blood availed for me | 1 | 4 |
| His blood can make the foulest clean | 1 | 4 |
| †His blood demands the purchased grace | 435 | 4 |
| His blood for me did once atone | 272 | 1 |
| His blood must atone | 707 | 2 |
| His blood to all our souls apply | 438 | 1 |
| His blood which once for all atones | 897 | 2 |
| His blood's availing plea | 435 | 4 |
| His bosom bears the tender lambs | 675 | 6 |
| His boundless love proclaim | 947 | 6 |
| His bounty to the skies | 637 | 2 |
| His bowels yearn with love | 725 | 1 |
| ✦His burden who bear | 495 | 2 |
| His calling's work pursue | 281 | 1 |
| His changeless name of Love | 586 | 6 |
| His chariot will not long delay | 62 | 5 |
| His child who on his care relies | 833 | 4 |
| His choicest graces to bestow | 630 | 7 |
| His church below sustains | 665 | 5 |
| His church on earth doth praise | 572 | 1 |
| His comforts impart | 760 | 3 |
| His conquering love consent to feel | 2 | 7 |
| His constant love shall keep secure | 810 | — |
| His counsels and his care | 814 | 2 |
| His counsel shall appear | 831 | 13 |
| His covenant remove | 586 | 6 |

| | Hymn | Verse |
|---|---|---|
| His dear Anointed One | 202 | 4 |
| His dear, his sacred burden lay | 465 | 9 |
| His dear peculiar ones | 897 | 2 |
| †His death is my plea | 707 | 7 |
| His deserved praise record | 639 | 3 |
| His desperate state explain | 83 | 4 |
| His dire apostasy to show | 467 | 6 |
| His everlasting word | 144 | 5 |
| †His every word of grace is strong | 659 | 5 |
| His faith by his obedience showed | 286 | 1 |
| His faithful people stand secure | 622 | 1 |
| His favoured path is trod | 544 | 4 |
| His fiat is obeyed! 'tis done | 64 | 6 |
| †His foes and ours are one | 719 | 5 |
| His foes beneath his feet | 719 | 4 |
| His foes compelled to own | 781 | 3 |
| His foes overturning, Till all shall expire | 273 | 5 |
| His free and everlasting grace | 619 | 1 |
| His friends and confessors to own | 483 | 5 |
| His fury canst control | 299 | 5 |
| His gifts I will for him improve | 638 | 1 |
| His glories shine with beams so bright | 650 | 1 |
| His glorious appearing to see | 78 | 1 |
| His glorious Godhead to reveal | 668 | 2 |
| His glory come to see | 586 | 4 |
| His glory in his Son | 605 | 2 |
| His glory is no longer seen | 31 | 2 |
| His glory our design | 96 | 6 |
| His glory pouring from my breast | 72 | 3 |
| His glory to show | 219 | 2 |
| His golden sceptre, not his rod | 120 | 1 |
| His goodness elected, The foolish and base | 212 | 3 |
| His grace for needy sinners free | 827 | 3 |
| His grace is the fountain, His peace is the stream | 496 | 1 |
| His grace on fainting souls distils | 585 | 4 |
| His grace shall set me free | 382 | 4 |
| His gracious compassion We thankfully prove | 212 | 5 |
| His gracious creation In us he makes known | 211 | 5 |
| His great decrees and sovereign will | 650 | 3 |
| His great salvation known | 605 | 2 |
| His guardian hand doth hold, protect | 801 | 1 |
| His hand hath writ the sacred word | 659 | 3 |
| His hand no good withholds | 591 | 5 |
| His heart is made of tenderness | 725 | 1 |
| His heavy hand and rod removed | 331 | 2 |
| His help and comfort still afford | 574 | 10 |
| His helping mercy hath no bounds | 626 | 5 |
| His holy footsteps we can trace | 695 | 4 |
| His image visibly exprest | 72 | 3 |
| His ineffable name | 499 | 8 |
| His instrument if he ordain | 331 | 3 |
| †His Israel himself shall clear | 625 | 6 |
| His joy is to bless us, And free us from thrall | 211 | 1 |

## HIS JUDGMENTS — HIS NAME

| | Hymn | Verse |
|---|---|---|
| His judgments truth shall guide | 740 | 4 |
| His justice shall avenge the poor | 585 | 2 |
| His kind invitation Ye sinners embrace | 10 | 1 |
| †His kingdom cannot fail | 729 | 3 |
| His kingdom is glorious, and rules over all | 859 | 1 |
| His kingdom over all maintains | 277 | 1 |
| His kingdom over all maintains | 616 | 7 |
| His kingdom receives | 760 | 3 |
| His kingdom still increasing | 586 | 5 |
| His kingdom still maintains | 800 | 7 |
| His kingdom stretch from shore to shore | 585 | 7 |
| His last mysterious supper share | 897 | 1 |
| His late repentance is not vain | 162 | 3 |
| His laud and benediction | 943 | 5 |
| His life and death,—that God is love | 31 | 1 |
| His life, and his joy's everlasting increase | 760 | 3 |
| His lightnings flash, his thunders roll | 56 | 1 |
| His Lord's unutterable peace | 754 | 4 |
| His lot shall be below | 407 | 5 |
| His love all-victorious Shall conquer for me | 273 | 6 |
| His love and hate, esteem and scorn | 638 | 3 |
| His love and truth who hath wrought this | 595 | 5 |
| His love be by his church adored | 616 | 1 |
| His love can ne'er be told | 699 | 5 |
| His love condescends By titles so dear | 40 | 1 |
| His love eternally the same | 616 | 1 |
| †His love is mighty to compel | 2 | 7 |
| His love let Aaron's sons confess | 616 | 1 |
| His love surpasseth all | 626 | 5 |
| †His love surpassing far | 96 | 8 |
| His love we proclaim, His praises repeat | 481 | 1 |
| His loved, his everlasting home | 759 | 3 |
| His mansion of despair | 697 | 2 |
| His meanest task is all divine | 590 | 4 |
| His meaning to my heart explain | 883 | 1 |
| His mercy and his power | 725 | 5 |
| †His mercy he will cause to rest | 111 | 7 |
| His mercy is for ever sure | 607 | 4 |
| His mercy now implore | 268 | 2 |
| His mercy unbought We freely receive | 212 | 5 |
| His messengers his place supply | 11 | 1 |
| His method so plain, So easy his way | 211 | 4 |
| His mighty power displays | 278 | 7 |
| His militant embodied host | 949 | 3 |
| His miracles of grace | 268 | 2 |
| His most delightful seat | 573 | 1 |
| His name be praised, his love adored | 616 | 12 |
| His name eternally confessed | 612 | 5 |
| His name is all my trust | 811 | 2 |
| *His name is Jesus Christ the Just | 669 | 1 |
| His name like sweet perfume shall rise | 585 | 8 |
| His name shall stand for ever | 586 | 6 |
| †His name the sinner hears | 34 | 4 |

| | HIS SOUL | |
|---|---:|---:|
| | HYMN | VERSE |
| His name to glorify . . . . . | 532 | 2 |
| His nature and his works invite . . . | 225 | 1 |
| His nature, life, and mind to prove . . . | 525 | 2 |
| His needful aid impart . . . . | 153 | 2 |
| His oath to sinners given . . . . | 536 | 7 |
| His offered benefits embrace . . . | 2 | 8 |
| †His offering pure we call to mind . . . | 860 | 2 |
| His once dishonoured head . . . . | 713 | 4 |
| His one sufficient sacrifice . . . . | 724 | 2 |
| His only, his for ever . . . . | 943 | 15 |
| †His only righteousness I show . . . | 37 | 5 |
| His onsets to repel . . . . . | 311 | 2 |
| His open side shall take you in . . . | 30 | 6 |
| †His own on earth he sought . . . | 195 | 3 |
| His own received him not . . . . | 195 | 3 |
| His pardoning grace for all is free . . | 144 | 6 |
| His pardoning love hath showed . . . | 623 | 4 |
| His pardoning voice I hear . . . . | 202 | 5 |
| His pardon on the tree . . . . | 83 | 3 |
| His passion alone . . . . . | 495 | 4 |
| His phial in the air . . . . . | 63 | 2 |
| His power and his peace . . . . | 760 | 3 |
| His powerful blood did once atone . . . | 675 | 7 |
| His praise all people sing . . . . | 586 | 5 |
| His praise let all his saints proclaim . . | 559 | 2 |
| His praise shall tune my voice . . . | 804 | 4 |
| His precious blood to plead . . . | 202 | 2 |
| His presence makes me free indeed . . | 384 | 2 |
| His presence sheds eternal day . . . | 932 | 2 |
| His prevalence with God declare . . | 726 | 3 |
| His proffered benefits embrace . . . | 9 | 6 |
| His promise hath fulfilled . . . . | 605 | 3 |
| †His providence hath brought us through . | 979 | 2 |
| †His purposes will ripen fast . . . | 845 | 3 |
| His reign on earth begun . . . . | 586 | 1 |
| His rest he hath sooner obtained . . . | 49 | 2 |
| His resurrection's power declare . . . | 420 | 1 |
| †His right arm is o'er us . . . . | 715 | 10 |
| His righteousness divine . . . . | 605 | 2 |
| His righteousness showed to heathens like us . | 212 | 3 |
| †His sacred unction from above . . . | 312 | 5 |
| His saving grace, and glory too . . . | 591 | 4 |
| His saving health revealed . . . . | 605 | 3 |
| His saving name record . . . . | 989 | 3 |
| His saving truth proclaim . . . . | 37 | 5 |
| His saying we receive . . . . | 897 | 3 |
| His sceptre shall protect the just . . . | 740 | 4 |
| His sinless nature to impart . . . | 616 | 10 |
| His sins on earth forgiven . . . . | 96 | 1 |
| †His son the father offered up . . . | 286 | 2 |
| His sorrows all he bears in mind . . . | 545 | 3 |
| His soul disdains on earth to dwell . . | 68 | 1 |
| His soul was once an offering made . . | 1 | 8 |

| | HYMN | VERSE |
|---|---|---|
| †His sovereign power, without our aid | 608 | 2 |
| His sovereign right assert | 428 | 1 |
| His Spirit answers to the blood | 202 | 4 |
| His Spirit doth my heart assure | 810 | — |
| His Spirit hath shed | 760 | 2 |
| His Spirit in our hearts hath shone | 493 | 1 |
| †His Spirit revives | 219 | 5 |
| His Spirit send into our hearts | 438 | 2 |
| His Spirit, to reside | 761 | 2 |
| His Spirit to us he gave | 96 | 4 |
| His spotless bride | 800 | 8 |
| His standard-bearer, I | 314 | 2 |
| His standard to bear | 231 | 7 |
| His steps I at a distance see | 115 | 2 |
| His strokes are fewer than our crimes | 610 | 7 |
| His study and delight | 540 | 2 |
| His sufferings to record | 898 | 3 |
| His summons cheerfully obey | 267 | 4 |
| His tender mercy never | 587 | 3 |
| His thoughts, and words, and actions prove | 31 | 1 |
| His throne is built on high | 650 | 1 |
| His tokens below | 219 | 5 |
| His tribute of glory to raise | 231 | 7 |
| His tribute of immortal praise | 612 | 2 |
| His truth at all times firmly stood | 607 | 4 |
| His truth confirms and seals the grace | 650 | 2 |
| His truth for ever stands secure | 224 | 2 |
| His unspeakable riches of grace | 231 | 7 |
| His utmost salvation, his fulness of love | 481 | 2 |
| His vacant tomb survey | 713 | 5 |
| His victory o'er a child of thine | 547 | 4 |
| His voice behind me may I hear | 312 | 4 |
| His wanderer to the fold | 697 | 7 |
| His watchful eye shall keep | 675 | 6 |
| His watchword at the gates of death | 823 | 5 |
| His way to Canaan find | 452 | 3 |
| His, who made you by his word | 639 | 3 |
| His wisdom's vast, and knows no bound | 225 | 2 |
| His wonders of grace | 219 | 5 |
| His wonders plagued the sinful race | 693 | 1 |
| His wonders to perform | 845 | 1 |
| †His wondrous works and ways | 610 | 5 |
| †His word did out of nothing call | 557 | 2 |
| His Word is his eternal Son | 234 | 2 |
| His word is truly tried | 551 | 6 |
| His work completes the great design | 644 | 3 |
| His work in our lives | 219 | 5 |
| His worship and his fear shall last | 585 | 3 |
| His wounds are opened wide | 184 | 5 |
| His wounds for me stand open wide | 809 | 4 |
| His wrath and justice stand | 650 | 2 |
| His wrath in their confusion shown | 541 | 2 |
| His zeal inspired their breast | 940 | 4 |

| | Hymn | Verse |
|---|---|---|
| His Zion cannot move | 622 | 1 |
| Hither by thine help I'm come | 866 | 2 |
| Hither, when hell assails, I flee | 189 | 4 |
| Hitherto thou hast been | 231 | 4 |
| †Ho! all ye heavy-laden, come | 695 | 5 |
| *Ho! every one that thirsts draw nigh | 4 | 1 |
| Ho, ye despairing sinners, come | 786 | 2 |
| Hoar frost and summer glow | 663 | — |
| Hold me till I apprehend | 156 | 3 |
| Hold me with thy powerful hand | 839 | 1 |
| Hold their licentious spirits fast | 461 | 6 |
| Holiness unto the Lord | 427 | 2 |
| Holiness without alloy | 418 | 3 |
| Holy and just are all thy ways | 637 | 8 |
| Holy, and pure, and perfect here | 401 | 5 |
| Holy and pure is God alone | 247 | 2 |
| *Holy, and true, and righteous Lord | 393 | 1 |
| Holy, angelical, divine | 380 | 8 |
| Holy, angelical, divine | 513 | 2 |
| Holy are all thy ways | 587 | 4 |
| *Holy as thou, O Lord, is none | 247 | 1 |
| Holy faith, and heavenly might | 756 | 2 |
| Holy Ghost, before thy face | 633 | 1 |
| Holy Ghost, Eternal Lord | 645 | 1 |
| *Holy Ghost, Illuminator | 720 | 6 |
| *Holy Ghost! my Comforter | 753 | 1 |
| †Holy Ghost, no more delay | 390 | 5 |
| Holy Ghost, renew and dwell | 477 | 2 |
| †Holy Ghost, the Comforter | 506 | 3 |
| Holy Ghost, to make thee room | 411 | 2 |
| †Holy, holy, holy! all the saints adore thee | 646 | 2 |
| "Holy, holy, holy," cry | 643 | 3 |
| Holy, holy, holy Lord | 221 | 1 |
| *Holy, holy, holy Lord | 260 | 1 |
| *Holy, holy, holy, Lord God Almighty | 646 | 1 |
| †Holy, holy, holy, Lord God Almighty | 646 | 4 |
| Holy, holy, holy, merciful and mighty | 646 | 1 |
| Holy, holy, holy, merciful and mighty | 646 | 4 |
| †Holy, holy, holy! though the darkness hide thee | 646 | 8 |
| Holy influence from above | 995 | 3 |
| Holy is his awful name | 606 | 2 |
| Holy joy and peace divine | 873 | 2 |
| *Holy Lamb, who thee confess | 529 | 1 |
| *Holy Lamb, who thee receive | 350 | 1 |
| †Holy, like thyself, and pure | 724 | 3 |
| Holy, pure, and perfect, now | 618 | 5 |
| Holy, purifying hope | 183 | 3 |
| Holy souls alone can see | 601 | 5 |
| †Holy Spirit! deign to come | 971 | 3 |
| †Holy Spirit, dwell with me | 769 | 5 |
| *Holy Spirit! pity me | 768 | 1 |
| †Holy Trinity! be nigh | 971 | 4 |
| Home of my soul! how near | 944 | 3 |

| | Hymn | Verse |
|---|---|---|
| Honour and love thine image here | 465 | 7 |
| †Honour, and might, and thanks, and praise | 206 | 3 |
| Honour and power divine | 678 | 3 |
| †Honour and praise to Jesus pay | 953 | 4 |
| †Honour, glory, and salvation | 748 | 7 |
| Honour, majesty, and might | 75 | 4 |
| Honour the means ordained by theo | 476 | 1 |
| Honour thy triumphant Son | 653 | 2 |
| Honoured if one member is | 518 | 8 |
| Hope, and be undismayed | 831 | 8 |
| Hope, and joy, and peace begin | 715 | 7 |
| Hope for all the promised grace | 876 | 3 |
| Hope of all the earth thou art | 688 | 1 |
| Hope of earth's extremest race | 579 | 1 |
| Hope of ocean's utmost bound | 579 | 1 |
| Hope still, and thou shalt sing | 567 | 4 |
| Hope to the end, in Jesus hope | 880 | 4 |
| Hosanna! let their angels sing | 993 | 4 |
| †Hosanna! to their heavenly King | 993 | 4 |
| Hosannas languish on our tongues | 763 | 2 |
| Hosts on high his powers proclaim | 640 | 2 |
| Hourly within my soul renew | 373 | 4 |
| Hourly with lifted hands I'll pay | 437 | 5 |
| Hours of sweet fellowship and parting sadness | 850 | 4 |
| †Hours spent with pain—and thee | 838 | 7 |
| Hover around us while we pray | 965 | 3 |
| Hovering over me, with eyes | 112 | 5 |
| Hovering round thy pillows bend | 921 | 2 |
| *How are the Gentiles all on fire | 541 | 1 |
| *How are thy servants blest, O Lord | 1002 | 1 |
| †How august the hallowed place | 862 | 2 |
| How base the noblest pleasures there | 590 | 4 |
| *How beauteous are their feet | 741 | 1 |
| How beautiful they stand | 573 | 2 |
| †How blessed are our ears | 741 | 3 |
| †How blessed are our eyes | 741 | 4 |
| How blessed they are, and only they | 562 | 5 |
| †How blest are they who still abide | 26 | 3 |
| *How blest is he who ne'er consents | 540 | 1 |
| How bright has his salvation shone | 573 | 3 |
| How bright their glories be | 940 | 1 |
| How bright thy beaming glories shine | 655 | 1 |
| *How can a sinner know | 96 | 1 |
| How can I be true to my word | 911 | 1 |
| How can I from my nature run | 288 | 2 |
| How can I my destruction shun | 288 | 2 |
| How can I thy grace obtain | 24 | 3 |
| †How can it be, thou heavenly King | 26 | 5 |
| How can my gracious Saviour show | 96 | 1 |
| How can one be warm alone | 487 | 1 |
| How can our arduous toil succeed | 475 | 1 |
| †How cheering is their voice | 741 | 2 |
| How Christians lived in days of old | 17 | 4 |

| | Hymn | Verse |
|---|---|---|
| †How cold and feeble is my love | 789 | 2 |
| How could I thy good Spirit grieve | 184 | 6 |
| How deep thy counsels, how divine | 599 | 3 |
| How do her citizens increase | 595 | 5 |
| *How do thy mercies close me round | 227 | 1 |
| How easy his yoke | 495 | 2 |
| How far above these earthly things | 439 | 2 |
| How feeble is our mortal frame | 42 | 1 |
| How few affections there | 789 | 2 |
| How firm our hope and comfort stands | 879 | 3 |
| How frail, at best, is dying man | 564 | 2 |
| How frail my best estate | 565 | 1 |
| How free from every anxious thought | 68 | 1 |
| How glorious to behold | 226 | 2 |
| How God builds Zion up, and ponder | 595 | 5 |
| How God himself is found | 662 | 2 |
| *How good and pleasant 'tis to see | 489 | 1 |
| †How good thou art! how large thy grace | 614 | 5 |
| How good to those who seek | 680 | 3 |
| How great salvation, who can tell | 269 | 4 |
| How great the weakest child of thine | 590 | 4 |
| How happy all thy servants are | 439 | 2 |
| *How happy are the little flock | 62 | 1 |
| *How happy are they | 807 | 1 |
| *How happy are we | 488 | 1 |
| *How happy every child of grace | 947 | 1 |
| *How happy, gracious Lord! are we | 222 | 1 |
| *How happy is the pilgrim's lot | 68 | 1 |
| †How happy the man whose heart is set free | 198 | 2 |
| †How happy the people that dwell | 70 | 3 |
| †How happy then are we | 67 | 2 |
| How happy we live | 499 | 4 |
| †How have I thy Spirit grieved | 182 | 2 |
| How he brake the warrior's bow | 570 | 5 |
| How he knapped the spear in sunder | 570 | 5 |
| How high thy wonders rise | 263 | 1 |
| How high your great Deliverer reigns | 712 | 3 |
| How I ask not,—ever thine | 24 | 3 |
| How I triumph in thy deeds | 598 | 2 |
| How in heaven they live | 488 | 4 |
| How in thy purer eyes appear | 127 | 1 |
| How intimately one with God | 439 | 2 |
| How Jehovah's presence shun | 633 | 1 |
| †How kind are thy compassions, Lord | 637 | 4 |
| *How large the promise, how divine | 888 | 1 |
| †How long, great God, have we appeared | 454 | 5 |
| How long pollute thy holy shrine | 588 | 1 |
| †How long shall I inquire within | 547 | 2 |
| †How long shall Satan's rage prevail | 547 | 3 |
| How long shall they invade thy fold | 588 | 1 |
| How long the time since Christ began | 697 | 4 |
| *How long wilt thou forget me, Lord | 547 | 1 |
| *How lovely are thy tents, O Lord | 590 | 1 |

| | Hymn | Verse |
|---|---|---|
| How low my hope of joys above | 789 | 2 |
| How make mine own election sure | 44 | 5 |
| How many are the perils | 968 | 4 |
| *How many pass the guilty night | 977 | 1 |
| How marvellous thy works of grace | 545 | 1 |
| How merciful thou art | 97 | 6 |
| How much more our God above | 233 | 3 |
| How much more our God above | 1021 | 1 |
| How negligent my fear | 789 | 2 |
| †How often when his arm was bared | 980 | 2 |
| How our mighty God of old | 580 | 2 |
| How pay the mighty debt I owe | 23 | 6 |
| How pleasant and how fair | 591 | 1 |
| †How pleasant and sweet | 488 | 2 |
| *How pleasant, how divinely fair | 592 | 1 |
| How pleasing to our King | 630 | 1 |
| How poor a lot was thine | 692 | 4 |
| How presume thyself to win | 24 | 3 |
| How pure, when washed in Jesu's blood | 439 | 2 |
| How ready to forgive | 614 | 5 |
| †How sad and cold if thou be absent, Lord | 967 | 3 |
| *How sad our state by nature is | 786 | 1 |
| How safe in thy sweet keeping | 923 | 1 |
| *How shall a lost sinner in pain | 174 | 1 |
| How shall a sinful worm appear | 184 | 10 |
| †How shall a sinner find | 151 | 3 |
| How shall a trembling sinner shun | 83 | 6 |
| How shall he meet that dreadful day | 934 | 1 |
| How shall I all to heaven aspire | 30 | 1 |
| How shall I equal triumphs raise | 30 | 1 |
| †How shall I find the living way | 177 | 2 |
| How shall I in his sight appear | 779 | 1 |
| †How shall I leave my tomb | 43 | 3 |
| How shall I love that word | 944 | 8 |
| †How shall I thank thee for the grace | 365 | 9 |
| †How shall I thank thee for the grace | 378 | 3 |
| *How shall I walk my God to please | 471 | 1 |
| †How shall polluted mortals dare | 651 | 5 |
| How shall sin an entrance find | 355 | 9 |
| †How shall weak eyes of flesh, weighed down | 133 | 2 |
| How shouldst thou, Lord, thy grace restrain | 133 | 6 |
| How slow thine anger moves | 637 | 4 |
| How sovereign is thy hand | 788 | 1 |
| †How sure established is thy throne | 600 | 2 |
| How sure is their defence | 1002 | 1 |
| How swiftly didst thou move | 34 | 6 |
| How sweet that is | 595 | 3 |
| How sweet the abode | 595 | 2 |
| How sweet the joys, the crown how bright | 241 | 4 |
| *How sweet the name of Jesus sounds | 679 | 1 |
| How sweet the tidings are | 741 | 2 |
| How sweet their memory still | 787 | 3 |
| How the good Shepherd followed, and how kindly | 850 | 2 |

| | Hymn | Verse |
|---|---|---|
| How the mighty debt repay | 27 | 3 |
| How then before thee shall I dare | 279 | 2 |
| †How then ought I on earth to live | 44 | 2 |
| How to make our calling sure | 480 | 2 |
| How unspeakably happy am I | 231 | 6 |
| How vain are all his hopes and fears | 564 | 2 |
| How vast the love that him inclined | 22 | 1 |
| How vast thy love, how great thy grace | 655 | 2 |
| *How weak the thoughts, and vain | 67 | 1 |
| How welcome to the faithful soul | 56 | 1 |
| †How well thy blessed truths agree | 879 | 3 |
| How wide thy healing streams are spread | 655 | 1 |
| How wise and holy thy commands | 879 | 3 |
| How wise, how strong his hand | 831 | 12 |
| How wonderful the grace | 595 | 2 |
| How wondrous things thy love hath wrought | 873 | 8 |
| †How would my fainting soul rejoice | 784 | 6 |
| Howe'er impatient, to his sway | 280 | 1 |
| Howe'er life's various current flow | 338 | 4 |
| Howe'er rebellious nature swell | 666 | 4 |
| However dark it be | 837 | 1 |
| However late, I turn | 182 | 5 |
| Human hearts in thee would rest | 743 | 2 |
| Human prophet like divine | 193 | 6 |
| Human tears for thee are flowing | 743 | 2 |
| Humble, and break this stubborn heart | 670 | 3 |
| †Humble, and teachable, and mild | 351 | 4 |
| Humble fear, and purest love | 757 | 2 |
| Humble, O humble to the dust | 270 | 3 |
| Humbled to the dust he is | 684 | 3 |
| Humbly and confidently wait | 313 | 4 |
| Humbly ask, that as my day | 336 | 1 |
| Humbly come to meet thee here | 910 | 1 |
| Humbly I pass my trial here | 775 | 4 |
| Humbly met, may boldly claim | 862 | 1 |
| Humbly receive thy warning word | 310 | 1 |
| Humbly stoop to earth again | 520 | 1 |
| Humbly we our seal set to | 348 | 1 |
| Humbly we trust thy faithful love | 1005 | 2 |
| Hunger now and thirst no more | 76 | 3 |
| Hungry, and sorrowful, and poor | 134 | 6 |
| Hungry, sick, and faint, and blind | 191 | 3 |
| Hung the issue of the day | 829 | 6 |
| Husband of the widow prove | 915 | 4 |
| †Husband of thy church below | 516 | 2 |
| Hymn his grace, and truth, and power | 605 | 5 |
| Hymns of adoration sing | 631 | 1 |
| I aim at thee, yet from thee stray | 344 | 2 |
| I all his truth and grace shall know | 815 | 5 |
| I all on earth forsake | 800 | 2 |
| I all their goods despise | 68 | 6 |
| †I all thy holy will shall prove | 357 | 7 |

| | Hymn | Verse |
|---|---|---|
| I am a God to thee and thine | 888 | 1 |
| †I am all unclean, unclean | 109 | 2 |
| I am all unrighteousness | 143 | 3 |
| I am condemned, but thou art clear | 574 | 2 |
| I am his, and he is mine | 274 | 2 |
| I am longing for thy favour | 790 | 3 |
| I am my Lord's, and he is mine | 912 | 3 |
| †I am never at one stay | 183 | 2 |
| I am not gone to my own place | 172 | 1 |
| I am not proud of heart | 627 | 1 |
| I am not yet in hell | 172 | 1 |
| I am thy love, thy God, thy all | 344 | 8 |
| I am weak, but thou art mighty | 839 | 1 |
| *I and my house will serve the Lord | 472 | 1 |
| I ask, desire, and trust in thee | 417 | 2 |
| †I ask in confidence the grace | 357 | 3 |
| I ask in faith his promised aid | 272 | 2 |
| I ask no higher state | 867 | 3 |
| †I ask not aught whereof to boast | 778 | 4 |
| I ask not for my merit | 943 | 11 |
| †I ask not how or when | 877 | 4 |
| I ask not life, but let me love | 998 | 5 |
| †I ask the blood-bought pardon sealed | 416 | 2 |
| I ask, the chief of sinners I | 380 | 3 |
| *I ask the gift of righteousness | 416 | 1 |
| I ask the mercy of my Lord | 778 | 1 |
| †I ask thee for a thoughtful love | 842 | 2 |
| I ask thee with a faltering tongue | 547 | 3 |
| †I ask them whence their victory came | 940 | 3 |
| I at thy feet for mercy groan | 106 | 6 |
| I, a weak, sinful worm | 357 | 7 |
| I, a wretch undone and lost | 115 | 1 |
| I believe in Jesu's name | 142 | 4 |
| †I believe thy pardoning grace | 173 | 2 |
| †I bid you all my goodness prove | 4 | 8 |
| I bless the day that I was born | 230 | 1 |
| I bless the day that I was born | 230 | 2 |
| I bless thee from my heart | 549 | 1 |
| I bless thee, Saviour, for thy grace | 575 | 4 |
| I blush and tremble to draw near | 779 | 1 |
| I blush in all things to abound | 227 | 1 |
| I bow and bless the sacred name | 800 | 1 |
| I bow before thee in the dust | 924 | 2 |
| I bring good tidings of a Saviour's birth | 691 | 2 |
| I bring my children now | 893 | 1 |
| I bring my heaven for thee | 948 | 3 |
| I build not there, but on his word | 626 | 3 |
| †I call that legacy my own | 903 | 4 |
| *I call the world's Redeemer mine | 927 | 1 |
| †I call to recollection | 587 | 4 |
| I calmly sojourn here | 947 | 2 |
| I calmly wait for this | 406 | 1 |
| I can hold out no more | 25 | 3 |

| | Hymn | Verse |
|---|---|---|
| I can hold out no more | 137 | 8 |
| I can, I do believe in thee | 401 | 1 |
| I can no longer fear | 202 | 5 |
| I can repent; I will | 799 | 5 |
| I can to none myself deny | 31 | 4 |
| I cannot but rejoice | 804 | 4 |
| I cannot change a single hair | 833 | 1 |
| I cannot draw the envenomed dart | 830 | 2 |
| I cannot fall, upheld by thee | 550 | 2 |
| I cannot find it nigh | 109 | 1 |
| I cannot from his praise forbear | 568 | 1 |
| I cannot give up my hope | 115 | 4 |
| I cannot lengthen out my span | 833 | 1 |
| †I cannot live without thy light | 574 | 9 |
| I cannot love my God | 146 | 3 |
| I cannot, no, I will not rest | 134 | 2 |
| I cannot of my cross complain | 369 | 5 |
| I cannot of my goodness boast | 369 | 5 |
| †I cannot praise thee as I would | 865 | 2 |
| I cannot raise my eyes | 566 | 7 |
| I cannot render pain for pain | 830 | 3 |
| I cannot rest in sins forgiven | 376 | 4 |
| †I cannot rest till in thy blood | 136 | 8 |
| I cannot rest till pure within | 388 | 4 |
| †I cannot see thy face, and live | 284 | 2 |
| I cannot speak a word unkind | 830 | 3 |
| I cannot, till thy Spirit blow | 131 | 1 |
| †I cannot wash my heart | 410 | 3 |
| I claim the blessing now | 417 | 5 |
| I claim the promise now | 288 | 1 |
| I claim thee with a faltering tongue | 113 | 2 |
| †I come, I come at thy command | 924 | 4 |
| I come my family to win | 472 | 6 |
| I come, to find them all again | 948 | 7 |
| I come to meet thee in the skies | 68 | 8 |
| †I come, thy servant, Lord, replies | 68 | 8 |
| I consecrate my lengthened days | 155 | 2 |
| I consecrate to thee | 229 | 4 |
| I consecrate to thee | 426 | 1 |
| I could not then the mastery gain | 126 | 2 |
| I daily see and feel | 310 | .1 |
| I dare believe in Jesu's name | 269 | Cho. |
| †I dare not choose my lot | 837 | 2 |
| †I deprecate that death alone | 181 | 6 |
| †I do believe thy blood was spilt | 780 | 2 |
| I do it to the Lord | 325 | 2 |
| I do it unto thee | 321 | 2 |
| I do not fear to see | 842 | 1 |
| I do, return to thee | 410 | 2 |
| †I do the thing thy laws enjoin | 92 | 7 |
| I, ere I sleep, at peace may be | 974 | 2 |
| I, even I, shall see his face | 405 | 1 |
| I, even I, shall then proclaim | 159 | 2 |

| | Hymn | Verse |
|---|---|---|
| I ever into ruin run | 289 | 6 |
| †I every hour in jeopardy stand | 273 | 3 |
| I every moment tread | 359 | 2 |
| I faint beneath thy blow | 565 | 5 |
| I fain would now obey the call | 137 | 4 |
| I faithfully commend | 282 | 5 |
| I fear no denial, No danger I fear | 273 | 2 |
| †I fear no foe, with thee at hand to bless | 972 | 4 |
| I feel he spake of thee alone | 883 | 4 |
| †I feel thee willing, Lord | 303 | 3 |
| I feel, through all my soul I feel | 781 | 5 |
| †I feel what then shall raise me up | 928 | 3 |
| I fell on the atoning Lamb | 93 | 7 |
| I find again in thee | 362 | 8 |
| †I find brought in a better hope | 781 | 3 |
| †I find him lifting up my head | 384 | 2 |
| I find in perfect love | 548 | 2 |
| I find his name | 855 | 1 |
| I find his service my reward | 325 | 2 |
| I find, I find thee strong to save | 366 | 2 |
| I find my paradise | 124 | 4 |
| I first found in the blood of the Lamb | 807 | 2 |
| I follow on to apprehend | 144 | 1 |
| †I forced thee first to disappear | 184 | 7 |
| I from my grave shall rise | 43 | 2 |
| I from sin shall be set free | 142 | 3 |
| I from the sovereign Lord receive | 470 | 3 |
| I full redemption have | 136 | 8 |
| I gain that perfect love unknown | 368 | 3 |
| I gasp for the Spirit of love | 78 | 1 |
| I gasp for the stream of thy love | 371 | 2 |
| I give thee victory | 948 | 3 |
| I give up every plea beside | 132 | 6 |
| I glorify thy name | 229 | 2 |
| I glory in his sprinkled blood | 422 | 2 |
| †I glory in redemption found | 781 | 6 |
| I glory in salvation near | 547 | 6 |
| I go on to conquer, Till sin is no more | 200 | 7 |
| I groan to be set free | 137 | 4 |
| I halt, till life's short journey end | 141 | 6 |
| I hang upon a God who came | 669 | 2 |
| I harden it no more, but pray | 788 | 1 |
| I hate it, Lord, and yet I love | 177 | 3 |
| I hate the sins that made thee mourn | 787 | 4 |
| I hate the tyrant's chain | 150 | 4 |
| I have a fellowship with hearts | 842 | 4 |
| I have a shield shall quell their rage | 269 | 2 |
| I have all in having thee | 620 | 3 |
| I have an Advocate above | 186 | 1 |
| I have broke from thy embrace | 182 | 2 |
| I have, but still I ask for more | 284 | 1 |
| I have declared thy heavenly truth | 584 | 1 |
| I have finished the work thou didst give me to do | 47 | 5 |

| | Hymn | Verse |
|---|---|---|
| I have fought my way through | 47 | 5 |
| I have long withstood his grace | 168 | 1 |
| I have my all restored | 432 | 1 |
| I have neither will nor power | 158 | 1 |
| †I have no babes to hold me here | 68 | 4 |
| I have no part in thee | 184 | 2 |
| †I have no skill the snare to shun | 289 | 6 |
| I have not believed in vain | 382 | 3 |
| I have not thee put on | 109 | 4 |
| I have now obtained the power | 400 | 8 |
| I have o'ercome for you | 277 | 5 |
| I have sinned against the light | 182 | 2 |
| †I have spilt his precious blood | 168 | 2 |
| I have the faith maintained | 421 | 2 |
| I have the hope within me | 943 | 14 |
| I have the words of endless life | 4 | 6 |
| I hear, and bow me to the rod | 186 | 1 |
| I hear his Spirit cry | 948 | 3 |
| I hear his Spirit's cry | 405 | 2 |
| I hear, I feel, he died for me | 34 | 5 |
| I hear the voice that calls me home | 924 | 1 |
| I hear the voice that calls me home | 924 | 5 |
| I hear thy whisper in my heart | 141 | 2 |
| I hearken to the gospel sound | 470 | 7 |
| I here shall in thine image shine | 401 | 4 |
| I hide me, Jesus, in thy name | 209 | 1 |
| †I hold thee with a trembling hand | 361 | 2 |
| †I hope at last to find | 172 | 2 |
| I hope thee, wish thee, sing thee | 943 | 11 |
| I hope to see thy glorious face | 172 | 2 |
| I humbly seek thy face | 119 | 1 |
| I humbly seek to touch my Lord | 779 | 1 |
| I hunger now, I thirst for God | 134 | 3 |
| †I, I alone, have done the deed | 23 | 3 |
| I in faith on Jesus call | 142 | 3 |
| I in thy temple wait | 92 | 1 |
| I join the heavenly lays | 800 | 12 |
| †I knew not that the Lord was gone | 180 | 3 |
| I know—I feel it now | 193 | 3 |
| †I know in thee all fulness dwells | 136 | 6 |
| *I know in whom I have believed | 810 | — |
| I know it shall be mine | 832 | 3 |
| I know not, O I know not | 943 | 8 |
| *I know that my Redeemer lives | 384 | 1 |
| *I know that my Redeemer lives | 928 | 1 |
| I know that thou wouldst give | 303 | 2 |
| I know thee good, I know thee just | 560 | 2 |
| †I know thee, Saviour, who thou art | 141 | 4 |
| †I know the work is only thine | 118 | 3 |
| I know thine eye is fixed on me | 130 | 3 |
| †I know thou canst not but be good | 133 | 6 |
| I know thou canst this moment cleanse | 395 | 7 |
| I know thou never wilt despise | 157 | 7 |

| | Hymn | Verse |
|---|---|---|
| I know thou never wilt despise | 365 | 2 |
| I know thou wilt deliver | 855 | 2 |
| I know, with healing in his wings | 157 | 7 |
| I know within thine arms is room | 166 | 1 |
| I labour night and day | 943 | 12 |
| I languish and sigh to be there | 70 | 1 |
| I lean upon my Saviour's breast | 227 | 5 |
| I leap for joy, pursue my way | 141 | 7 |
| †I leave the world without a tear | 924 | 3 |
| I lift it up to thee | 215 | 1 |
| †I lift my eyes to thee | 436 | 3 |
| I lift my heart to things above | 323 | 1 |
| I lift my soul to thee | 635 | 3 |
| †I, like Gideon's fleece, am found | 115 | 3 |
| †I loathe myself when God I see | 184 | 11 |
| I lodge awhile in tents below | 68 | 5 |
| I long appeared in sight | 93 | 5 |
| I long for a glimpse of thy face | 78 | 1 |
| I long for all who long for me | 629 | 5 |
| *I long to behold him arrayed | 70 | 1 |
| †I long to know and to make known | 378 | 2 |
| I long to reside where thou art | 228 | 1 |
| I long to see thy face | 674 | 2 |
| I long with Paul to share | 421 | 1 |
| I look at heaven and long to enter in | 794 | 1 |
| I look for all from thee | 92 | 8 |
| I look for mercy at thy throne | 924 | 2 |
| I look into my Saviour's breast | 189 | 4 |
| I look—till thou my peace create | 783 | 1 |
| I look to find thee in thy word | 92 | 1 |
| †I looked, but found no friend | 634 | 2 |
| I love his name, I love his word | 650 | 4 |
| †I love my Shepherd's voice | 675 | 6 |
| I mark, disdain, and all break through | 293 | 5 |
| I mark the thoughts that thence proceed | 828 | 2 |
| I may be still forgiven | 110 | 3 |
| I may but gasp his name | 37 | 6 |
| I may from every evil cease | 125 | 3 |
| I may of endless light partake | 964 | 5 |
| I may the appointed charge fulfil | 470 | 2 |
| I may the welcome word receive | 45 | 3 |
| I may, with all my skill and might | 828 | 1 |
| I may with confidence proceed | 471 | 4 |
| I may with joy appear | 43 | 5 |
| I might with joy behold | 942 | 11 |
| I muse on all thy hands have wrought | 437 | 7 |
| I must be born again, or die | 83 | 8 |
| †I must for faith incessant cry | 83 | 8 |
| I must from God be driven | 43 | 4 |
| I must myself appear | 472 | 1 |
| †I must the fair example set | 472 | 2 |
| †I must this instant now begin | 83 | 7 |
| I my own wickedness eschew | 366 | 3 |

| | Hymn | Verse |
|---|---|---|
| I myself would gracious be | 769 | 1 |
| I myself would holy be | 769 | 5 |
| I myself would mighty be | 769 | 4 |
| I myself would tender be | 769 | 3 |
| I myself would truthful be | 769 | 2 |
| †I need not tell thee who I am | 140 | 2 |
| †I need thy presence every passing hour | 972 | 3 |
| I neither have nor want | 68 | 3 |
| I never fail to find | 602 | 4 |
| I never shall remove | 548 | 4 |
| I never shall remove | 550 | 2 |
| I never will depart | 175 | 5 |
| I never will give up my shield | 803 | 1 |
| I never will unloose my hold | 140 | 3 |
| I nothing have, I nothing am | 127 | 6 |
| I nothing want beside | 834 | 2 |
| †I now believe in thee | 152 | 4 |
| †I now beneath their fury groan | 575 | 2 |
| I now bespeak thy power to save | 919 | 1 |
| I now exult to see | 405 | 4 |
| †I now from all my sins would turn | 982 | 3 |
| I now should feel thy power | 784 | 3 |
| I now the cross sustain | 948 | 2 |
| I on his oath depend | 800 | 4 |
| I only for his glory burn | 361 | 10 |
| I only give thee back thine own | 127 | 5 |
| I only live for this | 27 | 4 |
| I only live my sin to mourn | 155 | 1 |
| I only live to watch and pray | 828 | 4 |
| I only yield thee what was thine | 841 | 3 |
| I onward press to you | 939 | 3 |
| I own his power, accept the sign | 272 | 3 |
| †I pant to feel thy sway | 352 | 3 |
| I passed from folly on to crime | 697 | 5 |
| I pine for thee with lingering smart | 379 | 1 |
| I plead thy word for more | 806 | 2 |
| I plead what thou hast done | 145 | 4 |
| I poured my care and grief | 634 | 1 |
| I praise thee evermore | 432 | 5 |
| I praise thee, Lord; my heart was faint | 559 | 1 |
| "I praise thee, Lord, who o'er my foes | 559 | 1 |
| I pray thee, in a feeble groan | 113 | 2 |
| I pray thee to remove | 778 | 1 |
| I prove the strength of Jesus mine | 230 | 2 |
| I prove thine utmost power to save | 916 | 4 |
| I reach my heavenly home | 840 | 2 |
| I render thee the glory | 855 | 2 |
| I render to my pardoning God | 206 | 3 |
| †I rest beneath the Almighty's shade | 227 | 6 |
| †I rest in thine almighty power | 282 | 3 |
| I rest me, till the storm is passed | 288 | 4 |
| I rest secure from sin and hell | 561 | 7 |
| †I rest upon thy word | 301 | 6 |

| | Hymn | Verse |
|---|---|---|
| †I rested in the outward law . | 91 | 8 |
| †I right early shall awake . | 388 | 2 |
| I rise superior to my pain . | 140 | 5 |
| I rose, went forth, and followed thee | 201 | 4 |
| I run to meet my foe . | 278 | 5 |
| I sacrifice them to his blood . | 700 | 2 |
| I said; and felt the pardoning word | 561 | 5 |
| †I said sometimes with tears . | 931 | 4 |
| I say in love to thee . | 851 | 3 |
| I seal the engagement to my Lord . | 903 | 2 |
| †I see an open door of hope . | 293 | 4 |
| I see an open door of hope . | 365 | 8 |
| †I see a world of spirits bright . | 948 | 5 |
| I see cast down on every side . | 293 | 7 |
| I see from far thy beauteous light . | 344 | 1 |
| I see my business here . | 877 | 3 |
| I see my natal hour return . | 229 | 1 |
| I see my sin, but cannot feel . | 131 | 1 |
| †I see stretched out to save me . | 855 | 2 |
| I see the bar to heaven removed . | 706 | 7 |
| †I see the exceeding broad command | 370 | 3 |
| †I see the perfect law requires . | 91 | 5 |
| I see thee face to face, and live . | 141 | 3 |
| I see thee gloriously descend . | 828 | 5 |
| I see thy mercies rise . | 216 | 5 |
| I seek my place in heaven . | 947 | 1 |
| I seek not to deny . | 948 | 11 |
| I seek redemption through thy blood | 815 | 1 |
| †I seek the faithful and the just . | 609 | 3 |
| *I seek the kingdom first . | 834 | 1 |
| I seek, where thou wilt come . | 609 | 2 |
| *I seem desirous to repent . | 153 | 1 |
| I seem with heavenly manna to be fed | 967 | 3 |
| I set my worthless name . | 903 | 2 |
| †I set the Lord before my face . | 549 | 5 |
| I set to my seal That Jesus is true. | 5 | 2 |
| I shall as my Master be . | 628 | 1 |
| †I shall, a weak and helpless worm . | 356 | 9 |
| I shall be by grace redeemed . | 383 | 1 |
| I shall be free indeed . | 136 | 7 |
| I shall be holy here . | 405 | 1 |
| I shall be pure within . | 357 | 5 |
| I shall be safe; for Christ displays. | 675 | 10 |
| I shall be thine for ever . | 923 | 3 |
| I shall behold his face . | 800 | 4 |
| I shall feel thy death applied . | 115 | 5 |
| I shall for ever die . | 318 | 2 |
| I shall from him receive the prize . | 928 | 4 |
| †I shall fully be restored . | 355 | 13 |
| I shall hang upon my God . | 292 | 5 |
| I shall have no power to sin. | 355 | 9 |
| I shall his power adore . | 800 | 4 |
| I shall his salvation see . | 142 | 8 |

| | Hymn | Verse |
|---|---|---|
| I shall his salvation see | 335 | 1 |
| I shall in Christ, in that glad hour | 360 | 10 |
| I shall in thy temple spend | 554 | 6 |
| I shall into thy hands resign | 919 | 3 |
| †I shall my ancient strength renew | 356 | 8 |
| I shall not be o'erthrown | 549 | 5 |
| I shall not in thy presence move | 369 | 4 |
| I shall not lose my friends above | 947 | 6 |
| †I shall nothing know beside | 355 | 10 |
| I shall, on eagles' wings upborne | 800 | 4 |
| I shall receive the gracious power | 815 | 4 |
| I shall shout my Saviour's name | 382 | 4 |
| †I shall suffer and fulfil | 355 | 7 |
| I shall, the helpless creature I | 815 | 5 |
| I shall thy life receive | 115 | 5 |
| I shall to the end endure | 355 | 12 |
| †I shall triumph evermore | 355 | 11 |
| I shall with the God-man prevail | 140 | 5 |
| I share a filial part | 764 | 3 |
| I should be called a child of God | 30 | 2 |
| I should never yield to ill | 910 | 5 |
| I simply follow thee | 806 | 2 |
| †I sing of thy grace | 231 | 4 |
| I sing, O Lord, to thee | 609 | 1 |
| †I sing the goodness of the Lord | 547 | 7 |
| I sink beneath my sin | 135 | 4 |
| I sink, by dying love compelled | 137 | 8 |
| I sink, I die for want of rest | 25 | 4 |
| †I sink, if thou longer delay | 174 | 4 |
| I sink in blissful dreams away | 328 | 3 |
| I sink in welcome sleep | 838 | 2 |
| †I smite upon my troubled breast | 795 | 2 |
| I solemnly retire | 119 | 3 |
| I soon may view thy open face | 304 | 5 |
| *I soon shall hear thy quickening voice | 366 | 1 |
| I sought, and will pursue | 558 | 1 |
| I sought thee, yet from thee I roved | 210 | 3 |
| I sought thy comforts, and found rest | 602 | 3 |
| I spend in his praise | 231 | 12 |
| †I stand, and admire Thine outstretched arm | 200 | 6 |
| I stand, and from the mountain-top | 404 | 2 |
| I stay me on thy faithful word | 375 | 1 |
| I steadfastly believe | 384 | 4 |
| I steadfastly rely | 335 | 3 |
| I still am forced to hope | 172 | 1 |
| I still shall tell to all around | 561 | 8 |
| I still would choose the better part | 325 | 1 |
| †I stretch my longing hands | 635 | 2 |
| I strive, and see my fruitless pain | 92 | 5 |
| I suffered this for you | 35 | 8 |
| I suffer out my threescore years | 948 | 2 |
| I surely shall behold him near | 928 | 2 |
| I take my last triumphant flight | 330 | 6 |

| | Hymn | Verse |
|---|---|---|
| I take the blessing from above | 206 | 1 |
| I taste salvation in thy name | 196 | 1 |
| I taste unutterable bliss | 384 | 7 |
| I testify that thou art near | 781 | 7 |
| †I thank thee for that gracious taste | 365 | 3 |
| I thank thee for the blessed hope | 282 | 1 |
| †I thank thee, uncreated Sun | 210 | 4 |
| I thank thee, who hast overthrown | 210 | 4 |
| I thank thee, whose enlivening voice | 210 | 4 |
| †I thank the Lord who teacheth me | 549 | 4 |
| I thank with heart sincere | 243 | 2 |
| I thank with heart sincere | 1018 | — |
| I the chief of sinners am | 115 | Cho. |
| *I the good fight have fought | 421 | 1 |
| I then shall turn my steady face | 351 | 6 |
| †I thirst for a life-giving God | 371 | 2 |
| I thirst for the streams of thy grace | 78 | 1 |
| I thirst, I faint, I die to prove | 147 | 1 |
| *I thirst, thou wounded Lamb of God | 26 | 1 |
| I thy perfect strength shall find | 335 | 4 |
| I too shall gather up my feet | 45 | 1 |
| †I too with thee shall walk in white | 136 | 10 |
| I to thee my children leave | 915 | 2 |
| I touch him now! by faith even I | 781 | 5 |
| I trample on their whole delight | 68 | 6 |
| I trample on thy wealth and pride | 809 | 1 |
| I tread him down with holy scorn | 230 | 3 |
| I tread them down in Jesu's might | 293 | 5 |
| I tread the world beneath my feet | 439 | 1 |
| I tremble at what I have done | 911 | 1 |
| †I tremble lest the wrath divine | 181 | 4 |
| I trembled on my feverish bed | 697 | 6 |
| I triumph in the love divine | 422 | 2 |
| I triumph still, if thou abide with me | 972 | 4 |
| I triumph through his mighty grace | 616 | 3 |
| I trust him now to clothe and feed | 833 | 4 |
| †I trust in him who stands between | 92 | 8 |
| I trust in his word, None plucks me from thence | 198 | 5 |
| I trust in means no more | 92 | 7 |
| I trust in thee, whose powerful word | 360 | 1 |
| †I trust in thy unbounded grace | 543 | 5 |
| I trust my great Physician's skill | 816 | 2 |
| I trust the all-creating voice | 659 | 6 |
| I trust thee still | 851 | 1 |
| I trust to recover thy love | 371 | 1 |
| I trust thy truth, and love, and power | 69 | 1 |
| I turned thy face aside | 184 | 7 |
| I urge my way to heaven | 281 | 4 |
| †I view the Lamb in his own light | 128 | 8 |
| I wait for hallowing grace | 543 | 1 |
| †I wait my vigour to renew | 92 | 4 |
| I wait the moving of the pool | 131 | 3 |
| I wait the truth to know | 150 | 3 |

| | Hymn | Verse |
|---|---|---|
| I wait the word that speaks me whole | 131 | 3 |
| I wait thy coming from above | 354 | 1 |
| I wait thy faithfulness to prove | 432 | 3 |
| I wait thy guiding eye to feel | 429 | 1 |
| I wait thy perfect will to prove | 229 | 5 |
| †I wait thy will to do | 229 | 5 |
| †I wait, till he shall touch me clean | 406 | 2 |
| I wait to feel thy blood applied | 779 | 3 |
| I wait to hear thy quickening voice | 548 | 5 |
| I wait to learn thy will | 92 | 2 |
| I wait to prove thy perfect will | 393 | 1 |
| I wait to see thy glorious face | 815 | 1 |
| I wait with humble awe | 358 | 2 |
| I wake from my long sleep | 931 | 2 |
| I walk in pilgrimage | 565 | 8 |
| I walk on hostile ground | 310 | 2 |
| I walk through the fire, And suffer no harm | 200 | 6 |
| I want a calmly-fervent zeal | 433 | 2 |
| I want a constant liberty | 409 | 1 |
| †I want a godly fear | 301 | 3 |
| †I want a heart to pray | 301 | 4 |
| *I want a principle within | 308 | 1 |
| †I want a sober mind | 301 | 2 |
| I want a sun, a sea of light | 284 | 3 |
| I want a thousand lives to employ | 366 | 4 |
| †I want a true regard | 301 | 5 |
| I want, and thee alone | 403 | 5 |
| †I want an even strong desire | 433 | 2 |
| I want, do thou enrich the poor | 163 | 6 |
| I want my God, my all | 354 | 1 |
| I want the first approach to feel | 308 | 1 |
| *I want the Spirit of power within | 376 | 1 |
| †I want the witness, Lord | 367 | 3 |
| †I want thy life, thy purity | 417 | 2 |
| I want thy love to know | 343 | 5 |
| I was, but now defy its power | 230 | 3 |
| I was perfectly blest | 807 | 4 |
| I wash my garments in the blood | 217 | 3 |
| I weep, or try to weep | 943 | 13 |
| I went over the brook | 231 | 8 |
| I, who yet am not in hell | 168 | 2 |
| †I will accept his offers now | 80 | 5 |
| I will approach thy gate | 543 | 4 |
| I will be known and feared abroad | 569 | 10 |
| I will come in that day | 488 | 6 |
| I will ever give to thee | 839 | 3 |
| I will glory in the shame | 594 | 3 |
| *I will hearken what the Lord | 182 | 1 |
| †I will improve what I receive | 80 | 6 |
| †I will increase their gracious store | 629 | 6 |
| I will in no wise cast him out | 31 | 4 |
| †I will instruct thy child-like heart | 561 | 9 |
| I will lean upon his word | 197 | 2 |

| | Hymn | Verse |
|---|---|---|
| I will not fear what flesh can do | 575 | 4 |
| I will not fear what men can do | 575 | 1 |
| †I will not let thee go | 151 | 4 |
| I will not let thee go | 164 | 3 |
| I will not let thee go | 297 | 4 |
| I will not let thee go | 851 | Cho. |
| †I will not let thee go, my God, my Life, my Lord | 851 | 3 |
| †I will not let thee go. Should I forsake my bliss | 851 | 2 |
| *I will not let thee go, thou Help in time of need | 851 | 1 |
| †I will not let thee go, unless | 297 | 5 |
| I will not, till my suit prevail | 155 | 5 |
| I will on his promise trust | 197 | 2 |
| †I will, through grace, I will | 410 | 2 |
| I will with thanks receive | 614 | 9 |
| I with the monster fight | 278 | 3 |
| I woke, the dungeon flamed with light | 201 | 4 |
| †I work, and own the labour vain | 92 | 5 |
| I would be by myself abhorred | 393 | 3 |
| †I would be thine, thou know'st I would | 403 | 5 |
| I would be treated as a child | 842 | 3 |
| I would believe thy promise, Lord | 786 | 3 |
| †I would; but thou must give the power | 388 | 6 |
| I would have my spirit filled the more | 842 | 6 |
| †I would, more sensibly distressed | 153 | 2 |
| †I would not have the restless will | 842 | 3 |
| I would not, if I might | 837 | 2 |
| I would not, Lord, my soul deceive | 97 | 3 |
| †I would not to thy foe submit | 150 | 4 |
| †I would the precious time redeem | 433 | 3 |
| I would thy will obey | 310 | 1 |
| †I wrestle not now, But trample on sin | 200 | 7 |
| I yet will cling to thee | 851 | 1 |
| I yield my spirit to thy hand | 924 | 4 |
| I yield to be renewed | 783 | 2 |
| I yield with all my sins to part | 166 | 3 |
| I'd break through every foe | 213 | 5 |
| I'd call them vanity and lies | 879 | 4 |
| I'll bid this world of noise and show | 285 | 3 |
| I'll call upon thee while I live | 614 | 2 |
| I'll lead them to my Saviour's blood | 574 | 12 |
| †I'll lift my hands, I'll raise my voice | 577 | 5 |
| †I'll praise him while he lends me breath | 224 | 4 |
| *I'll praise my Maker while I've breath | 224 | 1 |
| I'll praise thee as I ought | 679 | 5 |
| I'll sing thy power to save | 798 | 5 |
| I'll sing upon a happier shore | 841 | 7 |
| I'll take the gifts he hath bestowed | 614 | 8 |
| I'll walk o'er life's tempestuous sea | 272 | 5 |
| †I'll weary thee with my complaint | 155 | 6 |
| *I'm not ashamed to own my Lord | 811 | 1 |
| I've Canaan's goodly land in view | 939 | 4 |
| †If all long-suffering thou hast shown | 171 | 2 |
| If all the world through thee may live | 33 | 2 |

| | Hymn | Verse |
|---|---|---|
| If all thy promises are sure | 134 | 1 |
| †If any man thirst, And happy would be | 3 | 2 |
| †If aught should tempt my soul to stray | 849 | 2 |
| †If but my fainting heart be blest | 841 | 5 |
| *If but one faithless soul be here | 861 | 1 |
| †If down I turn my wondering eyes | 226 | 4 |
| †If, drawn by thine alluring grace | 148 | 2 |
| If each should have its rightful meed | 626 | 1 |
| †If e'er to forms of truth I gave | 770 | 3 |
| If even now I find thy power | 188 | 3 |
| †If every one that asks may find | 759 | 7 |
| If faith surround your heart | 267 | 1 |
| If firm the word of God remains | 46 | 6 |
| If for Jesus it pine | 499 | 1 |
| If for thy truth they may be spent | 279 | 9 |
| If found one moment from their guide | 458 | 3 |
| †If gaily clothed and proudly fed | 692 | 3 |
| If God my strength depart | 584 | 2 |
| If haply I may feel thee near | 163 | 2 |
| If haply they may feel thee near | 462 | 1 |
| If heaven must recompense our pains | 46 | 6 |
| If he be my guide | 793 | 2 |
| †If his life a snare would prove | 914 | 9 |
| †If his life would matter raise | 914 | 10 |
| †If I ask him to receive me | 793 | 6 |
| If I begin to wake | 162 | 1 |
| †If I find him, if I follow | 793 | 4 |
| †If I have begun once more | 188 | 3 |
| If I have mercy found with thee | 307 | 1 |
| †If I have only known thy fear | 97 | 2 |
| †If I have tasted of thy grace | 312 | 2 |
| If I rightly read thy heart | 168 | 5 |
| †If I still hold closely to him | 793 | 5 |
| †If in the night I sleepless lie | 974 | 5 |
| †If in this darksome wild I stray | 339 | 3 |
| †If in this feeble flesh I may | 356 | 2 |
| If Jesus hath bought thee with blood | 165 | 5 |
| If Jesus shows his mercy mine | 213 | 3 |
| †If life be long, I will be glad | 920 | 2 |
| If life so soon is gone | 44 | 3 |
| If, Lord, thou count me meet | 948 | 7 |
| If mercy cannot draw | 103 | 1 |
| †If mercy is indeed with thee | 307 | 2 |
| If my heart to thee incline | 274 | 2 |
| †If my obduracy impede | 778 | 2 |
| †If near the pit I rashly stray | 309 | 4 |
| If nothing is too hard for thee | 401 | 2 |
| If now, accepted in thy sight | 513 | 1 |
| If now at last I see | 162 | 1 |
| If now for me prevails thy prayer | 100 | 1 |
| If now I find thee pleading there | 100 | 1 |
| †If now I lament after God | 165 | 5 |
| If now in thee begin to live | 374 | 2 |

| | Hymn | Verse |
|---|---|---|
| If now o'er me thy bowels yearn | 177 | 4 |
| If now o'er me thy mercies move | 354 | 3 |
| If now the Judge is at the door | 44 | 3 |
| †If now the witness were in me | 97 | 4 |
| If now thine eye with pity sees | 919 | 2 |
| †If now thou talkest by the way | 113 | 3 |
| †If now thy influence I feel | 374 | 2 |
| If now thy Spirit moves my breast | 17 | 1 |
| If of parents I came | 231 | 3 |
| If one sharp blast sweep o'er the field | 610 | 10 |
| †If on our daily course our mind | 965 | 4 |
| If on the margin of the grave | 776 | 1 |
| †If on thy promised grace alone | 469 | 10 |
| *If our God had not befriended | 621 | 1 |
| †If pressed by poverty severe | 692 | 4 |
| †If pure essential love thou art | 527 | 2 |
| If risen indeed with him ye are | 420 | 1 |
| †If rough and thorny be the way | 339 | 6 |
| If saints and prophets hide their face | 425 | 2 |
| If short, yet why should I be sad | 920 | 2 |
| If sin be your burden, O come unto me | 5 | 3 |
| †If some poor wandering child of thine | 973 | 4 |
| †If so poor a worm as I | 430 | 3 |
| If still thou art able to save | 174 | 2 |
| If still thou dost on sinners fall | 759 | 7 |
| †If still thou goest about to do | 135 | 2 |
| If still to me thy bowels move | 216 | 1 |
| †If, strangers to thy fold, we call | 696 | 4 |
| †If such a worm as I can spread | 356 | 3 |
| If the Lord had not defended | 621 | 1 |
| †If the morning's wings I gain | 633 | 3 |
| If this vile house of clay | 74 | 1 |
| If thou all compassion art | 168 | 5 |
| If thou art good, if thou art true | 356 | 8 |
| †If thou art rigorously severe | 625 | 2 |
| If thou art truth and love | 150 | 5 |
| If thou before thy servant go | 836 | 4 |
| If thou be glorified | 842 | 5 |
| If thou be with me when my labours close | 967 | 4 |
| If thou bring into the fire | 819 | 4 |
| If thou canst so greatly bow | 149 | 1 |
| If thou claim thine own again | 914 | 3 |
| †If thou direct my path aright | 836 | 4 |
| †If thou gav'st the enlarged desire | 530 | 2 |
| †If thou hast willed me to return | 178 | 4 |
| †If thou impart thyself to me | 136 | 7 |
| If thou, my God, art here | 214 | 2 |
| If thou rememberest each misdeed | 626 | 1 |
| If thou reverse the creature's doom | 154 | 4 |
| †If thou shouldst call me to resign | 841 | 3 |
| If thou, the God, the Saviour come | 154 | 4 |
| If thou the secret wish convey | 100 | 1 |
| If thou, the Son, shalt make me free | 136 | 7 |

| | Hymn | Verse |
|---|---|---|
| If thou withdraw thyself from me | 784 | 1 |
| If thou within us shine | 87 | 4 |
| If thou whose eyelids never sleep | 828 | 2 |
| If thy command ordain | 732 | 2 |
| †If thy dreadful controversy | 60 | 2 |
| †If thy grace for all is free | 164 | 6 |
| If thy heart be as mine | 499 | 1 |
| If thy plain commands we do | 885 | 2 |
| If thy providence forsake me | 819 | 1 |
| If to all his bowels move | 8 | 4 |
| †If to heaven I take my flight | 633 | 2 |
| If to hell I could retire | 633 | 2 |
| †If to the right or left I stray | 308 | 3 |
| If unlamented crimes forbid | 778 | 2 |
| If veiled it makes me sad | 838 | 5 |
| If weeping at thy feet I fall | 178 | 4 |
| If we our sins confess | 345 | 3 |
| †If what I wish is good | 832 | 3 |
| †If when I had put thee to grief | 165 | 4 |
| If with a faithful heart | 806 | 2 |
| If with love thy heart is stored | 354 | 3 |
| If with me now thy Spirit stays | 312 | 2 |
| †If wounded love my bosom swell | 849 | 3 |
| If your death were his delight | 8 | 2 |
| If you tarry till you're better | 791 | 4 |
| Ignorant of all below | 381 | 2 |
| Ills have no weight, and tears no bitterness | 972 | 4 |
| Illuminate my soul | 361 | 9 |
| Illustrious as the sun | 446 | 3 |
| Immeasurably far from God | 100 | 2 |
| Immeasurably filled with God | 443 | 3 |
| Immeasurably kind | 846 | 3 |
| Immeasurably shed on thee | 756 | 1 |
| Immense and unconfined | 216 | 3 |
| Immense, immovable | 382 | 1 |
| Immense, unfathomed, unconfined | 39 | 2 |
| Immortal glory too | 644 | 2 |
| †Immortal honours, endless fame | 752 | 5 |
| Immortal worship give | 644 | 3 |
| Immovably founded in grace | 73 | 3 |
| Impartial I to all may give | 470 | 3 |
| Impassive, he suffers; immortal, he dies | 707 | 3 |
| Impatient to be freed | 416 | 4 |
| Impending o'er my head | 103 | 2 |
| Imperceptibly supply | 156 | 3 |
| Implant, and root it deep within | 186 | 6 |
| Implant it deep within | 340 | 2 |
| Imploring at thy feet | 696 | 4 |
| Implunged in the crystal abyss | 78 | 2 |
| Importunate her suit could gain | 827 | 1 |
| Impossibilities perform | 356 | 9 |
| †Impotent, dumb, and deaf, and blind | 136 | 5 |
| †Impoverish, Lord, and then relieve | 84 | 5 |

| | Hymn | Verse |
|---|---|---|
| Impressed the image of its God | 241 | 1 |
| In a believer's breast | 1000 | 2 |
| In a believer's ear | 679 | 1 |
| In a believing heart | 383 | 2 |
| †In a dry land, behold, I place | 437 | 3 |
| In a father's bosom move | 914 | 6 |
| In a heavenly Father's breast | 593 | 2 |
| †In a land of corn and wine | 407 | 5 |
| In a milder clime they dwell | 76 | 3 |
| In a new world his truth to prove | 536 | 7 |
| In a perpetual covenant join | 532 | 1 |
| In a perpetual stream | 892 | 5 |
| In a rapture of heavenly love | 488 | 8 |
| †In a rapture of joy | 231 | 11 |
| †In a service which thy will appoints | 842 | 8 |
| In a vile house of clay | 537 | 7 |
| In a world of waters drowned | 633 | 3 |
| In Abraham's footsteps tread | 360 | 4 |
| In accents hushed the throng reply | 695 | 1 |
| In active faith and humble prayer | 919 | 2 |
| *In age and feebleness extreme | 918 | — |
| In all commotions rest | 62 | 1 |
| In all godly quietness | 826 | — |
| In all his Father's majesty | 420 | 3 |
| In all his majesty appear | 928 | 2 |
| In all his members here | 537 | 6 |
| In all his members here | 761 | 2 |
| In all his soldiers, "Come" | 268 | 4 |
| †In all I do I feel thine aid | 437 | 8 |
| In all I think, or speak, or do | 324 | 1 |
| In all its depth and height | 384 | 6 |
| In all my troubles nigh | 335 | 3 |
| *In all my vast concerns with thee | 632 | 1 |
| In all my ways | 800 | 3 |
| †In all my ways thy hand I own | 289 | 2 |
| In all my works thy presence find | 324 | 2 |
| In all our bosoms reign | 251 | 3 |
| In all our hearts abide | 1005 | 2 |
| In all our intercourse below | 524 | 1 |
| In all our temptation He keeps us to prove | 481 | 2 |
| In all the attributes divine | 648 | 4 |
| In all the confidence of hope | 417 | 5 |
| In all the depths of love divine | 408 | 2 |
| In all the hellish rage of war | 442 | 1 |
| In all the image of his Lord | 670 | 2 |
| In all the marks of death appear | 290 | 3 |
| In all the omnipotence of prayer | 524 | 2 |
| In all the paths of righteousness | 180 | 7 |
| In all their Captain's steps to tread | 474 | 4 |
| In all things nothing may I see | 344 | 5 |
| In all things thee I see | 821 | 2 |
| In all things to depend | 436 | 5 |
| In all thy footsteps tread | 270 | 4 |

| IN ALL | IN DEATHS | |
|---|---:|---:|
| | Hymn | Verse |
| In all thy gifts and graces grant | 1005 | 3 |
| In all thy glorious self reveal | 524 | 2 |
| In all thy people live | 418 | 1 |
| In all thy pleasant ways | 536 | 3 |
| In all thy saving power | 359 | 1 |
| In all thy works, and thee alone | 210 | 1 |
| In all we do and know | 863 | 3 |
| In all who here expect thy grace | 474 | 3 |
| In ancient times didst give the law | 690 | 5 |
| In an hour to us unknown | 54 | 4 |
| In answer to my Friend above | 178 | 4 |
| †In answer to ten thousand prayers | 125 | 5 |
| In anxious want we pine | 692 | 4 |
| In any arm but thine | 270 | 3 |
| †In assurance of hope | 491 | 8 |
| In battle cover thou my head | 351 | 6 |
| In blessings on your head | 845 | 2 |
| †In blessing thee with grateful songs | 437 | 5 |
| In bliss improved, in glory higher | 721 | 3 |
| In bliss returns to reign | 747 | 4 |
| In bondage, grief, or pain | 307 | 4 |
| In bonds my perfect liberty | 209 | 4 |
| In bonds no power can sever | 923 | 3 |
| In bonds of perfect charity | 16 | 9 |
| In brazen armour strong | 278 | 1 |
| In ceaseless songs of praise | 537 | 1 |
| In childhood, youth, and trembling age | 916 | 2 |
| In choral symphonies | 221 | 2 |
| In Christ abundantly forgiven | 216 | 5 |
| In Christ a creature new | 229 | 5 |
| In Christ a hearty welcome find | 2 | 3 |
| In Christ I am thy own | 191 | 2 |
| In Christ, our Redeemer, we see | 79 | 1 |
| In Christ the glorious Deity | 284 | 5 |
| In Christ to endless ages mine | 422 | 2 |
| In Christ to paradise restored | 9 | 6 |
| In close and firm array | 266 | 3 |
| In cloud, and majesty, and awe | 690 | 5 |
| In co-eternal Three | 259 | 6 |
| In comforts and in griefs agree | 524 | 2 |
| In concert with the blest | 950 | 1 |
| In copious shower On all who pray | 991 | 3 |
| In council join again | 368 | 4 |
| †In creation him they own | 817 | 5 |
| †In daily prayer to God commend | 470 | 10 |
| In dangerous wealth we dwell | 692 | 3 |
| †In darkest shades, if thou appear | 213 | 2 |
| †In darkness willingly I strayed | 210 | 3 |
| In death as life be thou my guide | 373 | 9 |
| In death my guide and Saviour be | 916 | 6 |
| In death the wicked and the just | 61 | 1 |
| In deathless triumph end | 535 | 6 |
| In death's triumphant hour | 229 | 6 |

| | Hymn | Verse |
|---|---|---|
| *In deep distress, to God | 634 | 1 |
| †In deepest hell, or heaven's height | 750 | 3 |
| In doing and bearing The will of our Lord | 484 | 2 |
| In doubtful things grant liberty | 822 | 4 |
| In dreadful majesty severe | 648 | 5 |
| In dreadful pomp arrayed | 605 | 7 |
| In dust and ashes lies | 184 | 10 |
| In each approach of sin alarm | 309 | 2 |
| In each believing soul | 303 | 6 |
| In each the Triune God adore | 255 | 3 |
| In earth and heaven, are one | 949 | 1 |
| In earth below, and heaven above | 237 | 3 |
| In earth-enriching rain | 578 | 1 |
| In earth, in heaven, in all thou art | 241 | 1 |
| In earth, in paradise, in heaven | 504 | 9 |
| In ecstasies of love | 828 | 5 |
| In endless plenty grow | 404 | 2 |
| In England's pastures fed | 897 | 4 |
| In eternal safety there | 597 | 1 |
| In everlasting lays | 222 | 3 |
| In everlasting pomp to reign | 420 | 3 |
| In every age the same | 732 | 1 |
| In every bosom fix thy throne | 993 | 6 |
| In every clime, from sun to sun | 746 | 3 |
| In every dark unguarded hour | 916 | 5 |
| In every day's deliverance | 854 | 1 |
| In every drooping sinner's ears | 33 | 4 |
| In every evangelic call | 770 | 6 |
| †In every fiery hour | 653 | 6 |
| In every heart of man | 447 | 2 |
| In every heart of man | 653 | 2 |
| In every heart reign thou alone | 236 | 1 |
| In every longing heart | 531 | 1 |
| In every new, believing heart | 616 | 10 |
| †In every new distress | 573 | 4 |
| In every place and age the same | 397 | 3 |
| In every solid truth abide | 473 | 4 |
| In every sorrow of the heart | 636 | 3 |
| In every star thy wisdom shines | 553 | 1 |
| In every time and place | 221 | 1 |
| *In every time and place | 840 | 1 |
| In every trying hour | 105 | 3 |
| In every waiting heart | 506 | 2 |
| In faith's sincerity | 873 | 3 |
| In faith your foes assail | 314 | 4 |
| *In fellowship alone | 268 | 1 |
| In fellowship are given | 630 | 8 |
| In fellowship divine | 731 | 7 |
| In finished holiness renewed | 443 | 3 |
| In fervent flames of strong desire | 666 | 1 |
| In flames of joy, and praise, and love | 290 | 6 |
| ⁋In flesh we part awhile | 536 | 2 |
| †In foreign realms, in lands remote | 1002 | 2 |

| | Hymn | Verse |
|---|---|---|
| In form of God distinctly seen | 916 | 6 |
| In fulness of majesty come | 77 | 2 |
| In gathering in thy lambs and sheep | 524 | 3 |
| In gloomy despair of relief | 777 | 1 |
| In glorious, heavenly love | 62 | 6 |
| In glorious joy to live | 65 | 5 |
| In glorious strength arrayed | 277 | 1 |
| In glory that never shall end | 77 | 1 |
| In God incarnate sealed | 460 | 1 |
| †In God I trust, the good, the true | 575 | 4 |
| †In God we put our trust | 845 | 3 |
| In God's garner to abide | 987 | 4 |
| In goodness infinite | 242 | 2 |
| In grasping all mankind | 268 | 3 |
| *In grief and fear, to thee, O Lord | 986 | 1 |
| In grief determined to remain | 982 | 4 |
| In grief my joy unspeakable | 209 | 4 |
| In guilt and misery | 792 | 1 |
| In heart and in voice | 760 | 5 |
| In heart, in mind, in speech | 822 | 3 |
| In heaven above, and earth below | 187 | 4 |
| In heaven above, to give | 169 | 3 |
| In heaven and earth the same | 544 | 1 |
| In heaven and earth the same | 544 | 5 |
| †In heaven thou reign'st enthroned in light | 235 | 2 |
| In heaven, who dwell in love | 96 | 3 |
| In heaven's eternal rest | 304 | 7 |
| In hell, or earth, or sky | 37 | 1 |
| In highest joy and glory stand | 647 | 3 |
| In him alone I put my trust | 669 | 1 |
| In him a pure river Of life shall arise | 3 | 3 |
| In him eternal life receive | 415 | 1 |
| In him the tribes of Adam boast | 585 | 11 |
| †In him we have peace, In him we have power | 481 | 2 |
| In him, we live, and move, and are | 673 | 2 |
| †In him when brethren join | 680 | 7 |
| In him who bears their sins away | 616 | 8 |
| In him who died for all | 34 | 7 |
| In him who lived and died for me | 148 | 1 |
| In his Father's glory bright | 936 | 3 |
| In his feet and hands are wound-prints | 793 | 2 |
| In his garner evermore | 987 | 3 |
| †In his great name alone | 232 | 3 |
| In his heavenly citadel | 720 | 8 |
| In his high praise agree | 641 | 3 |
| In his holy mount below | 572 | 1 |
| In his inner court they bow | 817 | 3 |
| In his members distrest | 495 | 3 |
| In his name when we meet | 488 | 2 |
| In his providential care | 661 | 1 |
| In his secret habitation | 597 | 1 |
| In his self-righteousness | 93 | 6 |
| In his various gifts sent down | 418 | 3 |

| | HYMN | VERSE |
|---|---|---|
| In holiness arrayed, shall they | 613 | 2 |
| In holiness show forth thy praise | 875 | 3 |
| †In holy contemplation | 804 | 2 |
| In honour of his bleeding love | 178 | 4 |
| In honour of his name | 605 | 6 |
| In honour of my great High-priest | 161 | 4 |
| In honour of our Spokesman there | 298 | 5 |
| In honour of thy Son | 982 | 1 |
| †In hope, against all human hope | 860 | 7 |
| In hope believing against hope | 150 | 3 |
| †In hope, believing against hope | 803 | 4 |
| In hope of perfect love | 485 | 3 |
| †In hope of that ecstatic pause | 833 | 7 |
| †In hope of that immortal crown | 948 | 2 |
| In humble love and fear | 311 | 5 |
| In humble prayer and fervent praise | 827 | 2 |
| In humbleness and fear | 807 | 2 |
| In hymns around the throne | 954 | 1 |
| In hymns of joy, unknown before, conspire | 691 | 3 |
| In hymns we now our voices raise | 203 | 8 |
| In instant prayer display | 267 | 4 |
| In isles and continents to spread | 452 | 1 |
| In Israel's camp appear | 704 | 2 |
| In Jesus approved, No goodness have we | 212 | 1 |
| In Jesus believes, His God and his Lord | 3 | 3 |
| In Jesus be so sweet | 500 | 6 |
| In Jesus Christ to prove | 1011 | — |
| In Jesus crucified | 897 | 1 |
| In Jesus, God with us, displayed | 655 | 1 |
| In Jesus I believe, and shall | 406 | 4 |
| In Jesus, in heaven they live | 73 | 5 |
| In Jesus let us meet | 497 | 1 |
| In Jesus let us still go on | 497 | 1 |
| In Jesus reconciled | 97 | 4 |
| In Jesus's power, In Jesus's love | 19 | 1 |
| In Jesu's breast | 854 | 3 |
| In Jesu's compassion The sick find a cure | 40 | 5 |
| In Jesu's guardian love | 622 | 1 |
| In Jesu's lovely face displayed | 203 | 2 |
| In Jesu's love we know | 21 | 4 |
| In Jesu's mighty love | 277 | 1 |
| †In Jesu's name behold we meet | 526 | 3 |
| In Jesu's name I lift it up | 314 | 2 |
| In Jesu's power and spirit pray | 298 | 4 |
| In Jesu's powerful name | 274 | 4 |
| In Jesu's service join | 295 | 1 |
| In Jesu's work below | 535 | 2 |
| In joy, and peace, and thee | 939 | 1 |
| In joy that none can take away | 364 | 2 |
| In Kedar's tents here stay | 942 | 13 |
| In knowledge pure their minds renew | 473 | 3 |
| In largest characters of blood | 365 | 4 |
| In latter days shall rise | 740 | 1 |

| | Hymn | Verse |
|---|---|---|
| In life and death confess | 304 | 6 |
| In life and death declare | 872 | 2 |
| In life and death, O Lord, abide with me | 972 | 5 |
| In life and death the same | 531 | 2 |
| In life and heart entirely clean | 782 | 3 |
| In life which shall for ever stay | 364 | 2 |
| In life's dry dreary sand | 958 | 3 |
| In life's worst anguish close to thee | 698 | 5 |
| In light thou dwellest; light that no shade | 240 | 4 |
| †In light unsearchable enthroned | 642 | 2 |
| In love be every wish resigned | 338 | 2 |
| In love create thou all things new | 351 | 4 |
| In love's benign command | 527 | 1 |
| In loveliness excel | 549 | 3 |
| In lowlier forms before our eyes | 868 | 2 |
| In lowly awe and loving zeal | 306 | 4 |
| In lowly meekness may I rest | 338 | 3 |
| In majesty come down | 138 | 1 |
| In majesty supreme | 583 | 1 |
| †In manifested love explain | 128 | 3 |
| †In many a soul, and mine | 732 | 3 |
| In me abundantly increase | 392 | 2 |
| In me all the hindrance lies | 173 | 2 |
| In me, from everlasting | 667 | 1 |
| In me is all my woe | 943 | 7 |
| In me is all the bar | 152 | 4 |
| In me, Lord, thyself reveal | 287 | 4 |
| In me no longer let it stay | 391 | 6 |
| In me, O Lord, fulfil again | 340 | 3 |
| †In me thine utmost mercy show | 309 | 5 |
| In me thy bowels move | 300 | 2 |
| In me thy servant reign | 275 | 4 |
| †In me thy Spirit dwell | 300 | 2 |
| In me thy strengthening grace be shown | 338 | 5 |
| In me, till all my life be love | 431 | 3 |
| In me, who died for you | 486 | 6 |
| In memory of my dying love | 897 | 1 |
| *In memory of the Saviour's love | 907 | 1 |
| In mercy establish below | 220 | 4 |
| In mercy given | 848 | 3 |
| In mercy haste to me | 112 | 4 |
| In mercy, Lord, incline | 581 | 1 |
| In mercy receive | 219 | 7 |
| In mercy to us speak | 682 | 2 |
| †In midst of dangers, fears, and deaths | 1002 | 5 |
| In mighty phalanx joined | 277 | 3 |
| In mildest majesty | 25 | 1 |
| In mine anointed Son shall shine | 629 | 8 |
| In my behalf appears | 202 | 1 |
| In my behalf came down | 93 | 6 |
| In my cup of blessing be | 842 | 6 |
| In my deepest darkness shine | 766 | 1 |
| In my hand no price I bring | 709 | 2 |

|  | Hymn | Verse |
|---|---|---|
| In my necessity | 551 | 1 |
| In my own froward will went on | 180 | 3 |
| In my Redeemer's breast | 948 | 1 |
| In my utter helplessness | 292 | 8 |
| In mystic fellowship of love | 16 | 1 |
| In mystic union join | 169 | 4 |
| In mystic Unity | 643 | 1 |
| In nature's acts thy will pursue | 1015 | — |
| In nature's slippery ways | 469 | 9 |
| †In nature's strength I sought in vain | 126 | 2 |
| In never-ceasing prayer | 297 | 2 |
| In never-ceasing showers | 86 | 4 |
| In number, weight, and measure still | 38 | 4 |
| †In old times when dangers darkened | 606 | 8 |
| In one great chorus join | 719 | 6 |
| In order of the Three | 750 | 1 |
| In order of the Three | 750 | 6 |
| In other climes thy works explore | 1001 | 2 |
| In our deepest darkness rise | 687 | 1 |
| In our hearts and lives abound | 1008 | 2 |
| In our hearts prepare thy home | 971 | 3 |
| In our journey below | 808 | 6 |
| In our Redeemer's praise | 411 | 1 |
| In pain, and weariness, and want | 744 | 2 |
| In panoply divine | 311 | 2 |
| In pardon, Lord, my cure begin | 397 | 7 |
| In pardons from his wounded side | 30 | 7 |
| †In part we only know thee here | 490 | 7 |
| In pastures fresh he makes me feed | 555 | 1 |
| In pastures green; he leadeth me | 556 | 1 |
| In paths of truth and grace | 555 | 2 |
| In peace and joy abide | 566 | 9 |
| In peerless majesty | 601 | 1 |
| In perfect harmony | 459 | 2 |
| In perfect harmony | 500 | 4 |
| In perfect holiness | 74 | 5 |
| In perfect holiness and love | 525 | 2 |
| In perfect holiness renewed | 536 | 8 |
| In perfect righteousness renewed | 953 | 2 |
| In perfect sacrifice | 996 | 8 |
| †In pity of the soul thou lov'st | 909 | 3 |
| In pity yet thy servant spare | 559 | 3 |
| In power, and truth, and grace | 572 | 1 |
| In praise, and ecstacy, and love | 440 | 2 |
| In praise your every hour employ | 235 | 3 |
| In presence of my foes | 556 | 4 |
| In presence of thy awful Lord | 223 | 4 |
| In proof that such we are | 897 | 3 |
| †In prosperous times I dared to say | 559 | 3 |
| In publishing the sinner's friend | 433 | 4 |
| In publishing the sounds of joy | 366 | 4 |
| In pure consummate love | 458 | 2 |
| In purest streams of love | 500 | 3 |

| | Hymn | Verse |
|---|---|---|
| In rapturous awe on him to gaze | 947 | 8 |
| †In reason's ear they all rejoice | 552 | 6 |
| In revellings and frantic mirth | 977 | 1 |
| †In reverent homage kiss the Son | 541 | 5 |
| In righteousness divine | 719 | 6 |
| In righteousness hast sworn | 449 | 1 |
| In robes of white arrayed | 537 | 10 |
| In ruinous decay | 74 | 1 |
| In sacred peace our souls abide | 569 | 3 |
| †In safety lead thy little flock | 458 | 6 |
| In Satan's hellish triumph join | 547 | 4 |
| In Scripture's sacred lore | 767 | 3 |
| †In search of empty joys below | 4 | 6 |
| In search of fame and wealth we live | 454 | 3 |
| In secret prayer for mercy cry | 119 | 2 |
| In setting forth thy love | 204 | 8 |
| In shame, in want, in pain, hast showed | 373 | 5 |
| In shame my glory and my crown | 209 | 3 |
| In shining characters displayed | 239 | 6 |
| In shouts, or silent awe, adore | 268 | 2 |
| In showers of heavenly love | 424 | 1 |
| In sin and error's deadly shade | 203 | 2 |
| †In sin and Satan's onsets | 854 | 2 |
| In sin conceived, of woman born | 38 | 6 |
| In sin conceived, to trouble born | 913 | 2 |
| In singleness of heart | 537 | 2 |
| In soft Laodicean ease | 454 | 2 |
| In solemn hymns proclaim their Lord | 612 | 5 |
| In solemn power come down | 477 | 1 |
| In some unguarded hour | 310 | 2 |
| In song before the Lord rejoice | 559 | 2 |
| In songs of joy and wonder | 854 | 1 |
| In songs of loudest praise | 731 | 8 |
| In sore temptation's hour | 187 | 2 |
| In soul and body clean | 452 | 6 |
| †In souls unholy and unclean | 543 | 2 |
| In sounds of glory sing | 637 | 1 |
| In spirit and in truth adore | 159 | 3 |
| In spirit joined to thee the Son | 380 | 8 |
| †In spite of our resolves we fear | 469 | 6 |
| In splendid triumph o'er his foes | 868 | 1 |
| In storms and hurricanes abide | 622 | 1 |
| In streams of pure perennial peace | 364 | 2 |
| In such a clod of earth as mine | 772 | 3 |
| In such a frame as this | 956 | 4 |
| †In suffering be thy love my peace | 373 | 9 |
| In sure and certain hope rejoice | 208 | 3 |
| In sweet consent unite your Alleluia | 663 | — |
| †In tears who sowed, in joy we reap | 493 | 3 |
| In tempers far as hell from thee | 467 | 3 |
| In ten thousand objects sought | 98 | 1 |
| In thanks and praises give | 229 | 8 |
| In thanks we endeavour Thy gifts to restore | 1025 | 2 |

| | Hymn | Verse |
|---|---|---|
| In that eternal day | 482 | 6 |
| In that eternal day | 948 | 7 |
| In that eternal house above | 48 | 2 |
| In that eternal world of joy | 599 | 6 |
| In that immortal song | 263 | 7 |
| In that inheritance above | 731 | 8 |
| †In that revealing Spirit come down | 249 | 2 |
| In that thrice happy place | 761 | 5 |
| In the arms of my best friend | 942 | 5 |
| In the atoning blood | 84 | 6 |
| In the beauty of your spring | 639 | 7 |
| In the believing soul | 453 | 2 |
| In the Beloved accepted make | 629 | 4 |
| In the blood of yonder Lamb | 76 | 2 |
| *In the bonds of death he lay | 714 | 1 |
| In the bonds of duty joined | 522 | 2 |
| In the celestial road | 472 | 3 |
| In the city of our God | 572 | 1 |
| In the clear light of endless day | 951 | 4 |
| In the clouds to God's right hand | 720 | 5 |
| In the dark and stormy day | 878 | 3 |
| In the dark unguarded hour | 819 | 1 |
| In the darkness be our light | 971 | 1 |
| In the depth of midnight blasting | 597 | 2 |
| †In the devouring lion's teeth | 23 | 5 |
| In the distressing hour | 725 | 5 |
| In the faith of Christ we lay | 990 | 1 |
| †In the feebleness of nature | 819 | 2 |
| In the fire the tares to cast | 987 | 3 |
| In the general ruin sure | 67 | 3 |
| In the great Redeemer's name | 975 | 3 |
| In the haven of the skies | 52 | 3 |
| †In the heavenly Lamb | 205 | 2 |
| In the hollow of his hand | 1000 | 2 |
| In the hollow of thy hand | 999 | 1 |
| In the land of light and love | 593 | 1 |
| In the Lord who sweetly die | 51 | 1 |
| In the midnight of your grief | 54 | 2 |
| In the midst do thou appear | 520 | 2 |
| †In the midst of opposition | 878 | 7 |
| In the midst of thee abiding | 595 | 3 |
| *In the name which earth and heaven | 990 | 1 |
| In the new Jerusalem | 67 | 7 |
| In the new, the joyful song | 50 | 4 |
| In the palace of God the great King | 499 | 4 |
| In the path of righteousness | 349 | 1 |
| In the praise of his excellent love | 488 | 1 |
| In the pure glory of that holy land | 794 | 2 |
| In the rapturous sound | 205 | 3 |
| In the Redeemer's blood | 765 | 3 |
| In the Redeemer's love | 605 | 4 |
| In the same age and place | 510 | 2 |
| In the savage wilderness | 710 | 2 |

| | Hymn | Verse |
|---|---|---|
| In the spirit of harmony join | 499 | 5 |
| †In the strength of God I rise | 278 | 5 |
| †In the strength of Jesu's name | 278 | 3 |
| In the terrors of his glory | 580 | 2 |
| †In the time of my distress | 292 | 3 |
| †In the wilderness I stray | 109 | 3 |
| In thee, all-gracious Lord | 622 | 3 |
| In thee do we trust, Nor find thee to fail | 611 | 5 |
| In thee eternal life we know | 490 | 6 |
| †In thee I place my trust | 560 | 2 |
| In thee is all I want | 109 | 6 |
| In thee is all my glory | 943 | 7 |
| In thee is all my hope | 112 | 2 |
| In thee let all my thoughts unite | 431 | 6 |
| In thee let every sinner find | 129 | 1 |
| In thee may all my wanderings cease | 114 | 4 |
| In thee may I my Eden find | 109 | 6 |
| †In thee, O Lord, I put my trust | 282 | 2 |
| In thee our endless bliss | 264 | 2 |
| In thee our Head, we are | 723 | 5 |
| In thee rejoice | 276 | 2 |
| In thee their covenant | 164 | 2 |
| In thee, the Life, the Truth, the Way | 528 | 4 |
| In thee to walk and live | 169 | 3 |
| †In thee we move; all things of thee | 494 | 5 |
| In thee, who to thy promise just | 545 | 2 |
| In their divinest forms | 263 | 4 |
| In their flesh shall saints see him | 817 | 8 |
| In their own lies confide | 94 | 1 |
| In their promised resting-place | 720 | 4 |
| †In them let all mankind behold | 17 | 4 |
| In these cold hearts of ours | 763 | 1 |
| In these, for whom we seek thy face | 476 | 3 |
| In these reviving words | 58 | 3 |
| In these thy Spirit's gospel-days | 395 | 2 |
| In thine almighty favour | 853 | 2 |
| In thine arms of love embraced | 271 | 4 |
| In thine arms may we repose | 970 | 2 |
| In thine eternal bands | 996 | 5 |
| In thine eternal Son | 460 | 3 |
| In thine only will delight | 427 | 2 |
| In things or great or small | 837 | 3 |
| †In this barren wilderness | 905 | 2 |
| In this cold heart of mine | 145 | 3 |
| †In this identic body I | 927 | 3 |
| In this land of sin and woe | 593 | 1 |
| In this my evil day | 271 | 1 |
| In this our evil day | 297 | 1 |
| In this our gracious day | 84 | 3 |
| In this polluted breast | 249 | 5 |
| In this poor stony heart | 147 | 3 |
| †In this re-animated clay | 928 | 2 |
| In this, the accepted hour | 784 | 3 |

# IN THIS — IN VAIN

| | Hymn | Verse |
|---|---|---|
| In this weak, helpless soul | 370 | 1 |
| In those whom up to thee we give | 473 | 5 |
| In thought and word and deed | 818 | 3 |
| In thy blessed service join | 427 | 2 |
| In thy cross, and by thy side | 737 | 4 |
| In thy fatherly choice | 231 | 3 |
| In thy gracious hands I am | 116 | 4 |
| In thy great temple here below | 902 | 1 |
| †In thy members here beneath | 423 | 3 |
| In thy mouth, and in thy heart | 192 | 3 |
| In thy presence to live | 488 | 7 |
| In thy sole glory may unite | 210 | 6 |
| In thy sole glory may unite | 964 | 7 |
| †In thy spotless people show | 531 | 3 |
| In thy sufficient love | 834 | 2 |
| In thy temple we present | 890 | 1 |
| In thy wrath remember mercy | 60 | 2 |
| In time and eternity thine | 491 | 4 |
| In time and in eternity | 227 | 7 |
| In time and in eternity | 380 | 9 |
| *In time of tribulation | 587 | 1 |
| In times of need their Help is near | 545 | 2 |
| In tribute at his feet | 586 | 4 |
| In trouble and in joy | 562 | 1 |
| In truth and patience wrought | 863 | 2 |
| In truth I will love thee | 551 | 1 |
| In unexhausted grace | 460 | 2 |
| In us a quickening Spirit be | 33 | 2 |
| In us be all thy goodness showed | 237 | 2 |
| In us eternally to dwell | 1005 | 3 |
| In us, even us, fulfil | 342 | 1 |
| In us, even us, fulfil | 459 | 3 |
| In us the work of faith fulfil | 95 | 2 |
| In us the work of faith fulfil | 236 | 2 |
| In us vouchsafe to be | 901 | 4 |
| In vain all hell its powers engage | 353 | 3 |
| In vain does the old dragon rage | 353 | 3 |
| †In vain doth Satan rage his hour | 280 | 3 |
| †In vain for redemption I look | 777 | 2 |
| In vain he died, and rose on high | 770 | 4 |
| In vain I have not wept and strove | 141 | 3 |
| In vain my soul would try | 632 | 1 |
| In vain our march opposes | 853 | 3 |
| †In vain our trembling conscience seeks | 879 | 2 |
| In vain the first-born seraph tries | 201 | 2 |
| In vain the snare we see | 469 | 3 |
| †In vain thou strugglest to get free | 140 | 3 |
| †In vain, till thou the power bestow | 461 | 3 |
| In vain to urge "It cannot be" | 816 | 2 |
| *In vain we build, unless the Lord | 624 | 1 |
| In vain we rise before the day | 624 | 1 |
| In vain we strive to rise | 763 | 2 |
| †In vain we tune our formal songs | 763 | 2 |

| | Hymn | Verse |
|---|---|---|
| In vain with lavish kindness | 747 | 2 |
| In vehement expectation | 854 | 3 |
| In vehement love To sinners he cries | 10 | 2 |
| In verdure, beauty, strength | 739 | 4 |
| †In want my plentiful supply | 209 | 4 |
| In war my peace, in loss my gain | 209 | 3 |
| In weakness be thy love my power | 373 | 9 |
| In weakness my almighty power | 209 | 4 |
| In whatsoe'er estate | 842 | 4 |
| In what their various states demand | 89 | 5 |
| In which my Saviour's footsteps shine | 285 | 4 |
| In which the sowers came to sow | 935 | 1 |
| In which thou dost thy name record | 121 | 3 |
| In whom I now believe | 357 | 1 |
| In whom I still confide | 575 | 1 |
| In whom the Father's glories shine | 337 | 1 |
| In whom thou art well-pleased with me | 394 | 1 |
| In whom thy smiling face we see | 394 | 1 |
| In whom we all agree | 487 | 3 |
| In whom we are, and move | 253 | 1 |
| In whom we are, and move, and live | 435 | 6 |
| In willing bonds before thy feet | 675 | 8 |
| †In wisdom infinite thou art | 239 | 4 |
| In wisdom, righteousness, and love | 731 | 4 |
| In wisdom thou hast made us | 667 | 3 |
| In woe they rise, but all their tears | 932 | 3 |
| †In wonder lost, with trembling joy | 656 | 3 |
| In wonder, love, and praise | 657 | 1 |
| In word, and deed, and mind | 823 | 6 |
| In worlds unknown pursue the song | 978 | 6 |
| In yonder blest abode | 535 | 5 |
| In yon thrice-happy seat | 482 | 3 |
| In your unexhausted song | 604 | 2 |
| †In Zion God is known | 573 | 3 |
| Incapable of woe | 482 | 4 |
| †Incarnate Deity | 253 | 2 |
| Incarnate God, I fly | 786 | 4 |
| †Incarnate Word! by every grief | 692 | 2 |
| Incessant blessings down distils | 241 | 3 |
| Incline a gracious ear to me | 626 | 1 |
| Incomprehensibly made man | 685 | 1 |
| Increase in us the kindled fire | 95 | 2 |
| Increase our faith, confirm our hope | 503 | 4 |
| Increase thy praise, improve our joys | 677 | 4 |
| Increase thy saints' felicity | 861 | 4 |
| Indissolubly joined | 266 | 4 |
| Indissolubly sure | 74 | 2 |
| Indulged another kind reprieve | 980 | 2 |
| Indulge me at thy feet to weep | 778 | 3 |
| Indulge me but in this | 367 | 3 |
| Indulge me in my fond request | 919 | 1 |
| Indulge us, Lord, in this request | 294 | 5 |
| Ineffable delight | 673 | 3 |

| | Hymn | Verse |
|---|---|---|
| Infant of days he here became | 685 | 2 |
| Infected nature heal | 108 | 4 |
| †Inferiors as a sacred trust | 470 | 3 |
| Infinite day excludes the night | 938 | 1 |
| *Infinite God, thy greatness spanned | 1001 | 6 |
| *Infinite God, to thee we raise | 647 | 1 |
| †Infinite joy, or endless woe | 42 | 6 |
| Infinite lengths beyond the bounds | 316 | 1 |
| Infinite my sin's increase | 110 | 3 |
| *Infinite Power, eternal Lord | 788 | 1 |
| †Infinite strength and equal skill | 226 | 11 |
| Infinite thy mercies are | 188 | 1 |
| *Infinite, unexhausted Love | 216 | 1 |
| Infinite, unsearchable | 434 | 5 |
| Infinitely good, and greater | 819 | 2 |
| Infinitely great, and more | 244 | 2 |
| Inflame our hearts with perfect love | 236 | 2 |
| Infuse the principle divine | 474 | 3 |
| Infuse the softest social care | 527 | 4 |
| Inhabitest the humble mind | 864 | 2 |
| Inheritor of heaven above | 896 | 5 |
| Inly I sigh for thy repose | 344 | 1 |
| Inmate of an humble heart | 758 | 4 |
| Inscribed with Jesu's name | 68 | 4 |
| Inscribe the living name | 989 | 4 |
| †Inscribing with the city's name | 72 | 4 |
| Insensibly remove | 504 | 7 |
| Inseparably joined in heart | 535 | 1 |
| Inseparably one with thee | 881 | 1 |
| Inspire a feeble worm | 265 | 1 |
| Inspire, and then accept, my prayer | 312 | 1 |
| †Inspire the living faith | 85 | 4 |
| Inspire me with thy power and peace | 395 | 4 |
| Inspire with wisdom from above | 756 | 2 |
| Inspired by thee we pray | 423 | 4 |
| Inspired with humble love | 464 | 2 |
| *Inspirer of the ancient seers | 89 | 1 |
| Instinctive look above | 838 | 6 |
| Intensely for thy glory burn | 513 | 4 |
| Intent on pleasing thee | 842 | 1 |
| Intercedes in silence there | 758 | 5 |
| Interposed his precious blood | 866 | 2 |
| Into a fruitful field | 578 | 3 |
| Into a saint exalt a **worm** | 323 | 3 |
| †Into a world of ruffians sent | 310 | 2 |
| Into a world unknown | 43 | 1 |
| Into all our spirits pour | 86 | 7 |
| Into all those that seek | 303 | 5 |
| Into all truth our spirit guide | 666 | 5 |
| Into every longing heart | 530 | 1 |
| Into himself he all receives | 95 | 4 |
| Into its darkest corner shine | 152 | 3 |
| Into life eternal rise | 193 | 3 |

| | Hymn | Verse |
|---|---|---|
| Into me thy kingdom bring | 676 | 3 |
| Into me thy Spirit inspire | 676 | 3 |
| Into my being come | 362 | 2 |
| Into my soul bring in | 303 | 5 |
| Into my soul descend | 403 | 7 |
| Into our faithful hearts | 262 | 2 |
| Into our lower world didst come | 648 | 2 |
| Into our souls bring in | 251 | 4 |
| Into peace and mirth | 715 | 3 |
| Into the ark of love receive | 114 | 3 |
| Into the depths of God | 477 | 1 |
| Into the mould of love | 103 | 3 |
| Into the outstretched arms of God | 455 | 4 |
| Into the wealthy place | 436 | 8 |
| Into their paradise | 504 | 8 |
| Into their simple hearts is given | 862 | 2 |
| Into thine hands my all resign | 134 | 6 |
| Into thy arms of mercy take | 162 | 1 |
| Into thy blessed hands receive | 433 | 4 |
| Into thy church abroad | 745 | 3 |
| Into thy family | 883 | 4 |
| Into thy glorious liberty | 171 | 4 |
| *Into thy gracious hands I fall | 196 | 1 |
| Into thy hands I fall | 786 | 5 |
| Into thy hands I will commend | 923 | 1 |
| Into thy hands receive | 472 | 4 |
| Into thy hands the matter take | 475 | 5 |
| Into thy holy church receive | 893 | 2 |
| Into thy love direct our heart | 686 | 3 |
| Into thy meanest home | 762 | 1 |
| Into thy perfect love | 301 | 6 |
| Into thy perfect love | 414 | 2 |
| Into thy protection take | 915 | 3 |
| Into thy temple come | 405 | 5 |
| Into thy way of perfect peace | 686 | 3 |
| Into your faithful hearts | 539 | 8 |
| †Inured to poverty and pain | 227 | 2 |
| Inured to toil and patient pain | 474 | 2 |
| †Invited by him | 488 | 3 |
| Invites us to a heavenly feast | 955 | 3 |
| Invite the longing taste | 880 | 3 |
| " Inward turn thine eyes," it saith | 192 | 3 |
| Irradiant with a light divine | 698 | 4 |
| Is a life of liberty | 842 | 8 |
| Is all the sacrifice I bring | 574 | 6 |
| Is as a flood come in | 296 | 1 |
| Is as a thousand years to thee | 776 | 2 |
| Is by the Father given | 719 | 3 |
| Is by thy inspiration given | 255 | 2 |
| Is cleft to take us in | 63 | 6 |
| Is comfort, life, and fire of love | 751 | 1 |
| †Is crucified for me and you | 28 | 3 |
| Is dust and vanity | 565 | 2 |

| | Hymn | Verse |
|---|---|---|
| Is ever new and ever young | 802 | 3 |
| Is ever to his promise just | 380 | 2 |
| Is every man or wheat or tare | 935 | 2 |
| Is every moment stayed | 217 | 2 |
| Is fixed on things above | 403 | 2 |
| Is fixed to triumph in thy grace | 576 | 1 |
| Is found no living man | 635 | 1 |
| Is found on earth no more | 767 | 3 |
| Is fully known to thee | 239 | 4 |
| Is governing by love | 471 | 5 |
| Is happy anywhere | 842 | 7 |
| Is heard the joyful sound | 595 | 3 |
| †Is here a soul that knows thee not | 83 | 3 |
| Is his fruit to our spiritual taste | 488 | 2 |
| Is joined with holy fear | 637 | 10 |
| Is kindled at Jesus's face | 73 | 5 |
| Is made a welcome guest | 907 | 1 |
| Is manifested here below | 673 | 1 |
| Is mercy there, is sweet forgiveness found | 596 | 2 |
| Is more than conqueror | 266 | 1 |
| Is music in a sinner's ear | 397 | 1 |
| Is nerved against temptation's shock | 698 | 3 |
| Is not all thy nature love | 168 | 5 |
| Is one great sacrifice | 322 | 2 |
| Is ours, a drop derived from thee | 247 | 1 |
| Is plain and naked to thy sight | 240 | 4 |
| Is portioned out for me | 842 | 1 |
| Is ready with their shining host | 9 | 5 |
| Is sent from the sky | 760 | 1 |
| Is still the same | 855 | 1 |
| Is subject to thy sway | 952 | 1 |
| Is such as tender parents feel | 610 | 9 |
| Is sure at last thy face to see | 545 | 4 |
| Is sweet, and life or death is gain | 26 | 1 |
| Is sweeter than ten thousand days | 956 | 3 |
| Is, that I e'er from sin should cease | 401 | 2 |
| Is, that we ask for more | 654 | 3 |
| †Is there a thing beneath the sun | 344 | 4 |
| †Is there a thing than life more dear | 286 | 5 |
| †Is there a thing too hard for thee | 138 | 5 |
| Is thine; so let the way | 837 | 2 |
| †Is thy earthly house distressed | 921 | 3 |
| Is to feel your need of him | 791 | 3 |
| Is to taste thy love divine | 995 | 3 |
| Is unction to the breast | 943 | 4 |
| Is very darkness in thy sight | 974 | 9 |
| Is weary, and cannot forbear | 77 | 1 |
| Israel all his care shall prove | 618 | 3 |
| Israel is his first-born son | 407 | 1 |
| Israel now shall dwell alone | 407 | 4 |
| Israel then shall sin no more | 407 | 4 |
| Israel, what hast thou to dread? | 407 | 2 |
| Israel's God let all below | 278 | 7 |

| | Hymn | Verse |
|---|---|---|
| Israel's HOLY ONE is he | 197 | 6 |
| Israel's strength and consolation | 688 | 1 |
| It bears on eagles' wings | 404 | 1 |
| It bids them rejoice in Jesus their Lord | 40 | 4 |
| It bore in every season fruit | 589 | 2 |
| It breathes in the air, it shines in the light | 611 | 4 |
| It brings to life the dead | 333 | 4 |
| It brought the Saviour from above | 686 | 1 |
| It calls me still to seek thy face | 137 | 3 |
| †It can bring with it nothing | 804 | 3 |
| It cannot in my Saviour be | 146 | 3 |
| It cannot seal the sinner's doom | 298 | 2 |
| It caused the springing day to shine | 686 | 1 |
| It charms the hosts above | 34 | 3 |
| †It cost thy blood my heart to win | 146 | 4 |
| It could not, Lord, my life devour | 289 | 3 |
| It gently cleared my way | 657 | 6 |
| It gives me back my peace | 282 | 1 |
| It gives my ravished soul a taste | 404 | 1 |
| It hath not passed away | 996 | 1 |
| †It is not exile, rest on high | 715 | 8 |
| It is not my desire, but thine | 171 | 8 |
| It is not night if thou be near | 978 | 1 |
| It is not sadness, peace from strife | 715 | 8 |
| It is not thus that souls are won | 857 | 3 |
| It is the blood-stained mercy-seat | 825 | 2 |
| *It is the Lord! enthroned in light | 844 | 1 |
| †It is the Lord! should I distrust | 844 | 2 |
| †It is the Lord! who can sustain | 844 | 4 |
| †It is the Lord! who gives me all | 844 | 3 |
| It is the Lord! who rises | 804 | 1 |
| †It is the Lord! whose wondrous skill | 844 | 5 |
| †It is the voice of Jesus that I hear | 794 | 4 |
| It is the way the Master went | 857 | 1 |
| It is to dwell in peace | 630 | 1 |
| It lifts me up to things above | 404 | 1 |
| It lifts my drooping spirits up | 282 | 1 |
| It lifts the fainting spirits up | 333 | 4 |
| It lives, and moves, and is from thee | 240 | 2 |
| †It makes the wounded spirit whole | 679 | 2 |
| It must be good for me | 560 | 4 |
| It now comes streaming from the sky | 759 | 1 |
| It passes away like a brook | 777 | 2 |
| It reaches all mankind | 216 | 3 |
| It saves me from falling, Or plucks me from hell | 273 | 3 |
| It scatters all their guilty fear | 37 | 2 |
| It shall speak, and shall not lie | 142 | 2 |
| It soothes his sorrows, heals his wounds | 679 | 1 |
| It sought the sun, and drank the rain | 589 | 1 |
| It spreads from pole to pole. | 747 | 4 |
| †It stands securely high | 74 | 2 |
| It streams from the hills, It descends to the plain. | 611 | 4 |
| It touched and glanced on every land | 553 | 3 |

| | Hymn | Verse |
|---|---|---|
| It turns their hell to heaven | 37 | 2 |
| It wants not now the power to save | 386 | 3 |
| It will be still the best | 837 | 1 |
| It withers in an hour | 610 | 10 |
| Its ancient conqueror | 277 | 6 |
| Its atmosphere the air of heaven | 951 | 1 |
| †Its body totally destroy | 412 | 4 |
| †Its boughs like goodly cedars spread | 589 | 2 |
| Its cities' fall but lifts us up | 62 | 3 |
| †Its energy exert | 453 | 2 |
| Its evils cure, its wants supply | 841 | 1 |
| Its evils in a moment end | 947 | 2 |
| Its glorious matter to declare | 568 | 1 |
| Its God to glorify | 122 | 5 |
| Its grateful honours to our King | 585 | 12 |
| Its hallowed issues, tell | 838 | 8 |
| Its hardness remove. | 160 | 2 |
| Its idle pomp, and fading joys | 351 | 5 |
| Its joys as soon are past | 947 | 2 |
| Its light the rainbow of the seven | 951 | 1 |
| †Its limit, its relief | 838 | 8 |
| Its mouth for its enormous prey | 442 | 2 |
| Its nature with its guilt and power. | 413 | 1 |
| Its own appointed limits keep | 1004 | 1 |
| Its richer energy declare | 457 | 3 |
| Its riches are unsearchable | 147 | 2 |
| Its saving benefits partake | 702 | 6 |
| Its savour sweet doth always please | 902 | 4 |
| Its shoots low in the dust are laid | 589 | 3 |
| †Its streams the whole creation reach | 250 | 4 |
| †Its Surety, thou alone hast paid | 129 | 2 |
| Its utmost virtue show | 453 | 2 |
| Its virtue below | 160 | 4 |
| Its wisdom, fame, and power | 800 | 2 |
| Itself a gift from thee | 874 | 2 |
| Itself with work be one | 863 | 3 |
| Jacob's God, our rock, and stay | 570 | 4 |
| Jacob's well is in his soul | 407 | 5 |
| Jah, Jehovah | 66 | 4 |
| JAH, JEHOVAH, great I AM | 355 | 3 |
| JAH, JEHOVAH, is my Lord | 197 | 2 |
| Jehovah, and his conquering Son | 280 | 8 |
| †Jehovah, Christ, I thee adore | 249 | 3 |
| Jehovah, comprehending all | 642 | 1 |
| Jehovah crucified | 128 | 7 |
| JEHOVAH, ELOHIM | 256 | 1 |
| Jehovah, Father, Great I AM | 800 | 10 |
| Jehovah for her sovereign Lord | 557 | 1 |
| *Jehovah, God the Father, bless | 258 | 1 |
| †Jehovah, God the Son, reveal | 258 | 2 |
| †Jehovah, God the Spirit, shine | 258 | 3 |
| Jehovah, Great I AM | 800 | 1 |

| | Hymn | Verse |
|---|---|---|
| Jehovah himself doth invite | 79 | 1 |
| †Jehovah in Three Persons, come | 261 | 2 |
| †Jehovah in thy person show | 128 | 7 |
| JEHOVAH is his name | 555 | 1 |
| Jehovah is the sovereign God | 603 | 1 |
| Jehovah on his shining seat | 262 | 3 |
| Jehovah reigns! be glad, O earth | 235 | 3 |
| *Jehovah reigns on high | 601 | 1 |
| Jehovah's changeless sign despise | 951 | 2 |
| *Jehovah's Fellow, and his Son | 670 | 1 |
| Jehovah's glorious majesty | 124 | 4 |
| Jehovah's smiling face | 673 | 2 |
| Jehovah's Son confess | 673 | 2 |
| Jehovah's will be done | 61 | 1 |
| Jerusalem above | 944 | 4 |
| Jerusalem, a true complaint | 32 | 4 |
| Jerusalem breaks forth in songs | 741 | 5 |
| *Jerusalem divine | 731 | 6 |
| *Jerusalem, exulting | 943 | 11 |
| *Jerusalem, my happy home | 939 | 1 |
| †Jerusalem, my happy home | 939 | 6 |
| *Jerusalem on high | 942 | 6 |
| Jerusalem shall rise | 452 | 4 |
| †Jerusalem the glorious | 943 | 6 |
| *Jerusalem the golden | 943 | 8 |
| †Jerusalem, the only | 943 | 7 |
| Jerusalem, the saints' abode | 71 | 3 |
| Jerusalem, who shedd'st his blood | 32 | 4 |
| †Jesu, attend, thyself reveal | 490 | 4 |
| *Jesu, at whose supreme command | 901 | 1 |
| †Jesu, be endless praise to thee | 190 | 8 |
| Jesu, be thou our glory now | 680 | 5 |
| Jesu, build us up in grace | 990 | 2 |
| Jesu, cast a pitying eye | 166 | 2 |
| Jesu, come with my distress | 336 | 1 |
| Jesu, dear redeeming Lord | 354 | 1 |
| *Jesu, friend of sinners, hear | 110 | 1 |
| *Jesu, if still the same thou art | 134 | 1 |
| *Jesu, if still thou art to-day | 135 | 1 |
| Jesu, in mercy hear my cry | 135 | 9 |
| *Jesu, in whom the weary find | 114 | 1 |
| †Jesu, let my nature feel | 355 | 3 |
| *Jesu, let thy pitying eye | 106 | 1 |
| Jesu, Lord, restore my sight | 109 | 3 |
| *Jesu, Lover of my soul | 143 | 1 |
| *Jesu, my Advocate above | 100 | 1 |
| †Jesu, my all in all thou art | 209 | 3 |
| *Jesu, my God and King | 727 | 1 |
| †Jesu, my heart's desire obtain | 100 | 3 |
| †Jesu, my Lord, mighty to save | 275 | 2 |
| *Jesu, my Saviour, Brother, Friend | 312 | 1 |
| Jesu, my single eye | 323 | 2 |
| *Jesu, my Truth, my Way | 436 | 1 |

| | Hymn | Verse |
|---|---|---|
| †Jesu, our only joy be thou | 680 | 5 |
| *Jesu! Redeemer, Saviour, Lord | 139 | 1 |
| Jesu, remember Calvary | 145 | 4 |
| †Jesu, seek thy wandering sheep | 101 | 3 |
| †Jesu, see my panting breast | 350 | 2 |
| *Jesu, shall I never be | 355 | 1 |
| *Jesu, Shepherd of the sheep | 183 | 1 |
| Jesu, Son of David, hear | 711 | Cho. |
| Jesu, support the tottering clay | 356 | 2 |
| *Jesu, take my sins away | 166 | 1 |
| †Jesu, the hindrance show | 152 | 3 |
| *Jesu, the Life, the Truth, the Way | 357 | 1 |
| *Jesu, the sinner's friend, to thee | 132 | 1 |
| *Jesu, the very thought of thee | 680 | 1 |
| †Jesu, the weary wanderer's rest | 337 | 2 |
| *Jesu, the word of mercy give | 446 | 1 |
| Jesu, thou art all compassion | 385 | 1 |
| †Jesu, thou art my King | 193 | 8 |
| Jesu, thou great eternal Mean | 92 | 8 |
| *Jesu, thou great redeeming Lord | 525 | 1 |
| *Jesu, thou hast to hoary hairs | 916 | 1 |
| *Jesu, thou sovereign Lord of all | 294 | 1 |
| *Jesu, thy blood and righteousness | 190 | 1 |
| Jesu, thy blood and righteousness | 190 | 11 |
| Jesu, thy blood is drink indeed | 507 | 5 |
| *Jesu, thy boundless love to me | 373 | 1 |
| †Jesu, thy chosen servant guard | 985 | 2 |
| *Jesu, thy far-extended fame | 397 | 1 |
| Jesu, thy flesh is angels' food | 507 | 5 |
| Jesu, thy timely aid impart | 339 | 4 |
| *Jesu, thy wandering sheep behold | 744 | 1 |
| *Jesu, to thee our hearts we lift | 483 | 1 |
| *Jesu, we look to thee | 485 | 1 |
| *Jesu, whose glory's streaming rays | 133 | 1 |
| Jesu's is a *constant* mind | 355 | 12 |
| Jesu's is a *gentle* mind | 355 | 6 |
| Jesu's is a *loving* mind | 355 | 10 |
| Jesu's is a *noble* mind | 355 | 8 |
| Jesu's is a *patient* mind | 355 | 7 |
| Jesu's is a *perfect* mind | 355 | 13 |
| Jesu's is a *quiet* mind | 355 | 5 |
| Jesu's is a *spotless* mind | 355 | 9 |
| Jesu's is a *thankful* mind | 355 | 11 |
| Jesu's love the nations fires | 218 | 1 |
| †Jesu's name in Satan's hour | 238 | 4 |
| †Jesu's praise be all our song | 538 | 4 |
| †Jesu's tremendous name | 315 | 3 |
| Jesu's word is glorified | 218 | 3 |
| †Jesus, accept our sacrifice | 286 | 6 |
| *Jesus, accept the praise | 536 | 1 |
| *Jesus, all-atoning Lamb | 434 | 1 |
| Jesus all our wants relieves | 402 | 3 |
| †Jesus all the day long | 807 | 3 |

| | HYMN | VERSE |
|---|---|---|
| Jesus, all thy name impart | 477 | 2 |
| Jesus alone | 276 | 1 |
| Jesus, and all in him, is mine | 201 | 5 |
| Jesus, and him crucified | 355 | 10 |
| Jesus, and him crucified | 508 | 7 |
| Jesus and love are one | 216 | 1 |
| †Jesus, answer from above | 168 | 5 |
| Jesus assembled with thine own | 861 | 1 |
| Jesus, be thou my power | 805 | 4 |
| Jesus bids your hearts be clean | 54 | 3 |
| Jesus calls his wanderers home | 29 | 1 |
| †Jesus Christ, God's only Son | 714 | 2 |
| Jesus Christ is our Redeemer | 742 | Cho. |
| Jesus Christ, our dying Lord | 50 | 1 |
| Jesus Christ, the good, the just | 185 | 1 |
| Jesus comes to cast out sin | 54 | 3 |
| Jesus comes to lift us up | 400 | 1 |
| *Jesus comes with all his grace | 400 | 1 |
| †Jesus, confirm my heart's desire | 327 | 3 |
| Jesus crucified for me | 101 | 5 |
| Jesus, dear expected guest | 520 | 1 |
| *Jesus descended from the sky | 881 | 1 |
| Jesus died the sheep to save | 554 | 1 |
| Jesus, do all the work alone | 126 | 4 |
| Jesus doth for you appear | 278 | 6 |
| Jesus doth his mourners cheer | 54 | 2 |
| Jesus doth his own defend | 238 | 4 |
| Jesus doth his spirit bear | 13 | 1 |
| *Jesus, faithful to his word | 58 | 1 |
| Jesus, for thee distressed I am | 343 | 5 |
| †Jesus, for this we still attend | 448 | 3 |
| †Jesus, friend of human kind | 514 | 2 |
| *Jesus, from thy heavenly place | 464 | 1 |
| *Jesus, from whom all blessings flow | 17 | 1 |
| †Jesus, fulfil our one desire | 528 | 5 |
| †Jesus, full of truth and grace | 109 | 6 |
| Jesus, full of truth and grace | 221 | 4 |
| †Jesus, full of truth and love | 29 | 2 |
| Jesus gives the sacred word | 295 | 1 |
| *Jesus, great Shepherd of the sheep | 501 | 1 |
| Jesus, God's eternal Son | 724 | 1 |
| †Jesus hail! enthroned in glory | 722 | 3 |
| Jesus hail! the sinner's friend | 195 | 4 |
| †Jesus, harmonious name | 34 | 3 |
| †Jesus hath died for you | 267 | 2 |
| Jesus hath died for you and me | 277 | 6 |
| *Jesus hath died that I might live | 415 | 1 |
| Jesus hath lived, hath died, for me | 190 | 6 |
| †Jesus, hear thy Spirit's call | 299 | 8 |
| Jesus himself imparts | 761 | 1 |
| Jesus himself the stronger showed | 93 | 6 |
| *Jesus, I believe thee near | 173 | 1 |
| †Jesus, I bless thy gracious power | 206 | 4 |

| | Hymn | Verse |
|---|---|---|
| *Jesus, I fain would find | 300 | 1 |
| †Jesus, I fain would walk in thee | 312 | 6 |
| †Jesus, I hang upon thy word | 384 | 4 |
| *Jesus I humbly seek | 883 | 1 |
| Jesus, I make thy word my guide | 470 | 8 |
| †Jesus, if we aright confess | 874 | 2 |
| Jesus, in death remember me | 45 | 2 |
| *Jesus, in earth and heaven the same | 893 | 1 |
| Jesus in himself hath joined | 194 | 1 |
| Jesus, in me display | 409 | 3 |
| Jesus, in our children dwell | 890 | 2 |
| Jesus, in that important hour | 373 | 9 |
| †Jesus, in the sacred book | 876 | 2 |
| †Jesus, in thy great name I go | 69 | 2 |
| Jesus, in thy name we pray | 257 | 5 |
| Jesus is become my peace | 197 | 2 |
| Jesus is come, your common Lord | 32 | 1 |
| Jesus is come your souls to save | 32 | 1 |
| †Jesus is glorified | 761 | 2 |
| †Jesus is gone up on high | 571 | 3 |
| Jesus is good, and strong, and true | 575 | 1 |
| *Jesus is lifted up on high | 616 | 7 |
| Jesus is our atoning Lamb | 705 | 1 |
| Jesus is our brother now | 684 | 4 |
| *Jesus is our common Lord | 207 | 1 |
| Jesus is the corner-stone | 487 | 3 |
| Jesus is their endless rest | 51 | 1 |
| Jesus is their great reward | 51 | 1 |
| Jesus is thy flaming sword | 407 | 6 |
| Jesus is thy seven-fold shield | 407 | 6 |
| Jesus is unchangeable | 348 | 4 |
| †Jesus is worthy to receive | 678 | 3 |
| *Jesus, Jehovah, God | 583 | 1 |
| Jesus, let all my work be thine | 429 | 3 |
| †Jesus, let all thy lovers shine | 446 | 3 |
| †Jesus, let our faithful mind | 999 | 2 |
| †Jesus, let thy kingdom come | 423 | 4 |
| Jesus, look to thy faithfulness | 401 | 2 |
| Jesus, Lord, I cry to thee | 151 | 1 |
| *Jesus, Lord, thy servants see | 895 | 1 |
| *Jesus, Lord, we look to thee | 509 | 1 |
| Jesus, Lord, what hast thou done | 701 | 2 |
| †Jesus loves and guards his own | 554 | 2 |
| Jesus loves to answer prayer | 824 | 1 |
| *Jesus, Master of the feast | 905 | 1 |
| Jesus, Master, seal my peace | 167 | Cho. |
| Jesus, mighty to redeem | 218 | 3 |
| †Jesus, mighty to redeem | 349 | 3 |
| Jesus, mighty to redeem | 402 | 3 |
| †Jesus, mighty to renew | 158 | 3 |
| †Jesus, my God! I know his name | 811 | 2 |
| †Jesus, my great High-priest | 675 | 7 |
| *Jesus, my King, to thee I bow | 293 | 1 |

| | Hymn | Verse |
|---|---|---|
| †Jesus, my life, appear within | 362 | 4 |
| *Jesus, my Life! thyself apply | 347 | 1 |
| Jesus my Lord and God I claim | 803 | 4 |
| Jesus, my Lord and God, look round | 781 | 6 |
| *Jesus, my Lord, I cry to thee | 409 | 1 |
| Jesus, my Lord, remember me | 774 | 9 |
| *Jesus, my Master and my Lord | 810 | 1 |
| Jesus! my only hope thou art | 918 | — |
| †Jesus, my redeeming Lord | 672 | 8 |
| Jesus my salvation is | 197 | 2 |
| †Jesus, my Shepherd, Husband, Friend | 679 | 4 |
| *Jesus, my strength, my hope | 801 | 1 |
| †Jesus, my Strength, my Life, my Rest | 217 | 4 |
| Jesus my strength shall lift me up | 803 | 4 |
| Jesus now is glorified | 86 | 2 |
| †Jesus, now our hearts inspire | 414 | 2 |
| †Jesus, now teach our hearts to know | 868 | 5 |
| Jesus now to heaven restored | 758 | 1 |
| Jesus of Nazareth *has passed by* | 695 | 6 |
| Jesus of Nazareth passeth by | 695 | Cho. |
| †Jesus, on me bestow | 102 | 2 |
| †Jesus, on thine only name | 116 | 4 |
| Jesus, on thy word and name | 335 | 3 |
| †Jesus, our great High-priest | 738 | 2 |
| Jesus, our Immanuel here | 683 | 3 |
| Jesus our Lord! accept them now | 961 | 2 |
| Jesus our Lord! forgive us now | 961 | 3 |
| Jesus our Lord! receive us then | 961 | 6 |
| Jesus, our reproach remove | 531 | 2 |
| Jesus, our Shepherd great and good | 438 | 1 |
| †Jesus, our tendered souls prepare | 527 | 4 |
| Jesus, Power of God, subdue | 653 | 7 |
| †Jesus protects; my fears, be gone | 227 | 4 |
| Jesus ready stands to save you | 791 | 1 |
| Jesus, regard our vows | 74 | 4 |
| †Jesus, regard the joint complaint | 294 | 3 |
| Jesus reigns, adored by angels | 720 | 5 |
| Jesus, remember Calvary | 157 | 1 |
| Jesus, remember Calvary | 774 | 6 |
| †Jesus, roll away the stone | 463 | 3 |
| †Jesus, seek thy wandering sheep | 13 | 3 |
| Jesus shall bruise the Serpent's head | 280 | 4 |
| Jesus shall claim you for his bride | 65 | 4 |
| †Jesus shall his great arm reveal | 280 | 4 |
| Jesus, shall re-appear below | 927 | 1 |
| *Jesus shall reign where'er the sun | 585 | 7 |
| Jesus, show thine open face | 413 | 1 |
| Jesus smiles, and says, "Well done" | 51 | 4 |
| *Jesus, soft, harmonious name | 538 | 1 |
| Jesus, Son of God and man | 185 | 2 |
| Jesus sought me when a stranger | 866 | 2 |
| Jesus, speak my pardon sealed | 414 | 1 |
| Jesus, speak our souls restored | 98 | 2 |

JESUS SPEAKS · · · JESUS, THOU

| | Hymn | Verse |
|---|---|---|
| Jesus speaks, and pleads his blood | 168 | 3 |
| Jesus still delights to keep | 13 | 1 |
| Jesus, stir up thy glorious power | 447 | 2 |
| †Jesus take all the praise | 482 | 2 |
| Jesus takes his every care | 13 | 1 |
| Jesus takes our sins away | 516 | 1 |
| Jesus takes up all the room | 383 | 2 |
| *Jesus, the all-restoring Word | 169 | 1 |
| †Jesus the ancient faith confirms | 888 | 3 |
| *Jesus, the conquerer, reigns | 277 | 1 |
| Jesus, the corner-stone | 535 | 1 |
| †Jesus, the crowning grace impart | 304 | 5 |
| Jesus, the crucified | 486 | 5 |
| Jesus, the dead, revives again | 712 | 2 |
| Jesus, the feeble sinner's friend | 141 | 4 |
| *Jesus, the first and last | 674 | 1 |
| Jesus the foundation is | 516 | 1 |
| *Jesus, the gift divine I know | 864 | 1 |
| *Jesus the good Shepherd is | 554 | 1 |
| Jesus, the grace bestow | 410 | 3 |
| Jesus, the great I AM | 195 | 1 |
| *Jesus, the infinite I AM | 668 | 1 |
| Jesus the Judge shall come | 729 | 6 |
| Jesus the King, the conquerer, reigns | 275 | 8 |
| †Jesus, the Lamb of God hath bled | 127 | 8 |
| †Jesus, the Lord and God most high | 234 | 3 |
| Jesus, the meek, the angry Lamb | 315 | 3 |
| Jesus the Messiah reigns | 728 | 1 |
| *Jesus! the name high over all | 37 | 1 |
| †Jesus! the name that charms our fears | 1 | 3 |
| †Jesus! the name to sinners dear | 37 | 2 |
| *Jesus, the needy sinner's friend | 875 | 1 |
| †Jesus! the prisoner's fetters breaks | 37 | 3 |
| †Jesus the Saviour reigns | 729 | 2 |
| Jesus the Saviour takes my part | 616 | 2 |
| Jesus, the second time appear | 861 | 4 |
| Jesus, the sinner's friend, proclaim | 30 | 4 |
| Jesus the wheat, Satan the tares | 935 | 1 |
| Jesus, the woman's conquering Seed | 280 | 4 |
| *Jesus, the word bestow | 458 | 1 |
| *Jesus, thee thy works proclaim | 693 | 1 |
| †Jesus, thine all-victorious love | 361 | 4 |
| †Jesus, thine own at last receive | 428 | 3 |
| Jesus, this mean oblation join | 321 | 3 |
| *Jesus, thou all-redeeming Lord | 35 | 1 |
| *Jesus, thou art our King | 352 | 1 |
| Jesus, thou canst not pray in vain | 127 | 10 |
| *Jesus, thou everlasting King | 677 | 1 |
| †Jesus, thou for me hast died | 115 | 5 |
| *Jesus, thou hast bid us pray | 299 | 1 |
| *Jesus, thou know'st my sinfulness | 177 | 1 |
| Jesus, thou our guardian be | 970 | 1 |
| †Jesus, thou precious corner-stone | 489 | 2 |

| | Hymn | Verse |
|---|---|---|
| *Jesus, thou soul of all our joys | 204 | 1 |
| Jesus, thou the giver art | 757 | 4 |
| Jesus, through thy free grace alone | 1005 | 1 |
| Jesus, thy creature see | 25 | 4 |
| Jesus, thy flock we feed | 874 | 1 |
| †Jesus, thy killing, quickening power | 670 | 3 |
| †Jesus, thy loving Spirit alone | 408 | 5 |
| Jesus, thy mercies I embrace | 230 | 1 |
| *Jesus, thy servants bless | 872 | 1 |
| Jesus, thy sovereign skill display | 816 | 1 |
| †Jesus, thy speaking blood | 981 | 4 |
| Jesus, thyself in me reveal | 113 | 1 |
| Jesus, thyself in us reveal | 204 | 7 |
| Jesus, till I thy Spirit receive | 830 | 2 |
| †Jesus! 'tis he who once below | 695 | 3 |
| Jesus, to me be given | 320 | 2 |
| Jesus, to me impart | 340 | 2 |
| Jesus to our rescue ran | 215 | 2 |
| Jesus, to sinners still the same | 30 | 4 |
| Jesus, to thee for help I fly | 471 | 4 |
| †Jesus, to thee I bow | 194 | 5 |
| *Jesus, to thee I now can fly | 217 | 1 |
| Jesus, to thee I plight my vows | 290 | 7 |
| Jesus, to thee my heart aspires | 773 | 1 |
| †Jesus, to thee my soul aspires | 290 | 7 |
| Jesus, to thee my soul looks up | 91 | 7 |
| *Jesus, to thee we fly | 723 | 1 |
| †Jesus, to thee we look | 387 | 3 |
| †Jesus, to thy dear wounds we flee | 64 | 2 |
| *Jesus, to whom alone we live | 1015 | — |
| †Jesus, transporting sound | 34 | 2 |
| *Jesus, united by thy grace | 504 | 1 |
| Jesus, upheld by thy right hand | 230 | 2 |
| †Jesus, vouchsafe a pitying ray | 44 | 6 |
| Jesus weeps, and loves me still | 168 | 4 |
| Jesus weeps! believe his tears | 8 | 4 |
| Jesus, we dare require | 818 | 3 |
| Jesus, we now sustain the cross | 333 | 7 |
| *Jesus, we on the word depend | 754 | 1 |
| *Jesus, we steadfastly believe | 812 | — |
| †Jesus, we thy members are | 518 | 4 |
| †Jesus, we thy promise claim | 520 | 2 |
| Jesus, when I lowest fell | 274 | 1 |
| †Jesus, when this light we see | 350 | 7 |
| *Jesus, where'er thy people meet | 864 | 1 |
| Jesus, who on the serpent treads | 380 | 1 |
| Jesus will not tarry long | 348 | 4 |
| Jesus, with humble faith and fear | 919 | 1 |
| Jesus with joy we witness | 276 | 1 |
| *Jesus, with kindest pity see | 513 | 1 |
| †Jesus! with us thou always art | 476 | 4 |
| Jesus's love my heart shall cleanse | 216 | 7 |
| Join all my powers to praise the Lord | 650 | 4 |

| | Hymn | Verse |
|---|---|---|
| Join all on earth, rejoice and sing | 719 | Cho. |
| Join all the glad choirs | 499 | 5 |
| *Join all the glorious names | 675 | 1 |
| *Join, all ye ransomed sons of grace | 976 | 1 |
| †Join every soul that looks to thee | 16 | 9 |
| Join in a song with sweet accord | 12 | 1 |
| Join in creation's hymn, and cry again Alleluia | 663 | — |
| Join in the everlasting song | 681 | 8 |
| Join our new-born spirits, join | 515 | 1 |
| Join our praying pattern there | 529 | 3 |
| Join the happy few whose love | 167 | 4 |
| Join the longing choir above | 921 | 5 |
| Join to extol his sacred name | 737 | 7 |
| Join to thyself, our common Lord | 459 | 8 |
| †Join us, in one spirit join | 518 | 2 |
| Join we then our hearts and hands | 487 | 1 |
| †Join we then, with one accord | 50 | 4 |
| Join we then with sweet accord | 221 | 1 |
| Joined by the unction from above | 16 | 1 |
| †Joined in one spirit to our Head | 534 | 2 |
| Joined in spirit all agree | 538 | 3 |
| Joined to all thy hosts above | 53 | 4 |
| Joined to God, in spirit one | 516 | 3 |
| Joined to his, it cannot fail | 390 | 3 |
| Jointly let us rise, and sing | 522 | 1 |
| Jordan past | 793 | 5 |
| Jordan ran backward to its head | 223 | 2 |
| Joshua now is come to Canaan | 720 | 4 |
| Joy, and perfect love impart | 530 | 4 |
| Joy ascends to heaven above | 578 | 3 |
| Joy cometh with thy light | 851 | 2 |
| Joy of every longing heart | 688 | 1 |
| †Joy of God's abode, the station | 570 | 3 |
| Joy of heaven, to earth come down | 385 | 1 |
| Joy that earth cannot afford | 995 | 2 |
| Joy through my swimming eyes shall break | 658 | 3 |
| Joy unuttered we possess | 58 | 3 |
| Joyful all his praise rehearse | 605 | 6 |
| Joyful all your voices raise | 727 | 2 |
| Joyful at God's right hand appear | 80 | 2 |
| Joyful consentaneous sound | 538 | 3 |
| Joyful from my own works to cease | 429 | 1 |
| Joyful hallelujahs sing | 720 | 1 |
| †Joyful in hope, my spirit soars | 384 | 5 |
| Joyful in thine arms expire | 877 | 4 |
| Joyful in tribulation | 855 | 1 |
| Joyful that we ourselves are thine | 889 | 3 |
| Joyful thus my faith to show | 325 | 2 |
| Joyful tidings to proclaim | 463 | 2 |
| Joyful to meet, willing to part | 533 | 1 |
| Joyfully his deeds record | 605 | 1 |
| Joyless is the day's return | 963 | 2 |
| Joys begun which ne'er shall end | 67 | 7 |

| | Hymn | Verse |
|---|---|---|
| Joys which earth cannot afford | 1006 | — |
| Judge and conquer | 748 | 2 |
| Judge not the Lord by feeble sense | 845 | 2 |
| Judged here unfit to live | 942 | 9 |
| Judgment is at thy house begun | 176 | 1 |
| Just and good is thy decree | 914 | 4 |
| Just and holy is thy name | 143 | 3 |
| Just and holy thou alone | 194 | 5 |
| †Just as I am, and waiting not | 796 | 2 |
| †Just as I am, of that free love | 796 | 7 |
| †Just as I am, poor, wretched, blind | 796 | 4 |
| †Just as I am, though tossed about | 796 | 3 |
| †Just as I am, thou wilt receive | 796 | 5 |
| †Just as I am, thy love unknown | 796 | 6 |
| *Just as I am, without one plea | 796 | 1 |
| Just as the port is gained | 421 | 2 |
| Just at the point to die | 151 | 1 |
| Just in righteousness divine | 197 | 3 |
| Just now the stony to remove | 9 | 3 |
| Justice and truth before thee stand | 241 | 2 |
| †Justice and truth maintain | 727 | 7 |
| Justice awakes its flaming sword | 917 | 2 |
| Justice divine is satisfied | 706 | 2 |
| Justice lingers into love | 168 | 3 |
| Justice pursue, and mercy love | 127 | 4 |
| Justified through faith alone | 51 | 2 |
| Justify us by thy blood | 257 | 6 |
| Justly they claim the softest prayer | 451 | 1 |
| *Justly thou might'st, in helpless age | 917 | 1 |
| Justly we are abhorred by thee | 454 | 1 |
| | | |
| Keep far our foes, give peace at home | 751 | 2 |
| Keep me from earthly, base desires | 290 | 7 |
| Keep me, keep me, gracious Lord | 187 | Cho. |
| Keep me, lest I turn again | 188 | 2 |
| Keep me, O keep me, King of kings | 974 | 1 |
| Keep me, or from thee I fly | 156 | 3 |
| Keep our souls in perfect peace | 999 | 2 |
| Keep silence, all the earth, and hear | 569 | 9 |
| Keep the Christian festival | 52 | 1 |
| †Keep the souls whom now we leave | 999 | 3 |
| Keep the wide world in awe | 650 | 2 |
| Keep them while on earth they breathe | 915 | 2 |
| Keep this branch in thee abiding | 895 | 3 |
| Keep this feeble, trembling heart | 185 | 2 |
| Keep thy fear before my sight | 672 | 2 |
| Keep us, and every seeking soul | 536 | 3 |
| Keep us from the world unspotted | 530 | 3 |
| Keep us little and unknown | 508 | 6 |
| Keep us still in perfect peace | 514 | 2 |
| Keeps his appointed way | 788 | 2 |
| Keeps with most distinguished care | 245 | 2 |
| Kept by the power of grace divine | 421 | 2 |

| | Hymn | Verse |
|---|---|---|
| Kept by the strength of Jesus | 855 | 1 |
| Kept by watchful providence | 618 | 3 |
| Kept in an obedient heart | 885 | 1 |
| Kept in peace by Jesu's name | 325 | 2 |
| Kind and merciful to all | 238 | 1 |
| Kind and merciful to all | 1019 | 2 |
| Kindle a flame of sacred love | 327 | 1 |
| Kindle a flame of sacred love | 763 | 1 |
| Kindle higher joy in heaven | 921 | 5 |
| Kindle in each the living fire | 759 | 8 |
| Kindle now the heavenly fire | 414 | 2 |
| †Kindle the flame of love within | 119 | 7 |
| Kindled by a spark of grace | 218 | 1 |
| †Kindled his relentings are | 168 | 4 |
| Kindled in some hearts it is | 218 | 1 |
| Kindles in each a secret fire | 493 | 5 |
| Kindly commands us to draw nigh | 827 | 4 |
| Kindly compass thee about | 618 | 5 |
| †Kindly do the showers distil | 578 | 2 |
| Kindly for each other care | 518 | 7 |
| Kindly for thy people care | 508 | 1 |
| King o'er all the earth he reigns | 571 | 2 |
| King of all, with pitying eye | 737 | 11 |
| King of glory, Lord of all | 352 | 2 |
| †King of glory! Soul of bliss! | 716 | 6 |
| King of kings, for ever live! | 748 | 7 |
| †King of majesty tremendous | 933 | 8 |
| King of righteousness and peace | 676 | 3 |
| King of saints, and Prince of peace | 717 | 2 |
| King of saints, let all conspire | 727 | 7 |
| King of saints, thine empire spread | 418 | 1 |
| †Kings shall fall down before him | 586 | 5 |
| Kings through all eternity | 936 | 7 |
| Kiss the exalted Son | 277 | 2 |
| Knees and hearts to him we bow | 684 | 4 |
| Knit us in like unity | 517 | 2 |
| Knit us in the bond of peace | 515 | 1 |
| †Knowing as I am known | 944 | 8 |
| Knowledge and vital piety | 473 | 5 |
| Knowledge, love divine, impart | 302 | 4 |
| Known is the Father to thy sight | 750 | 3 |
| Known through the earth by thousand signs | 263 | 1 |
| Know salvation in thy name | 463 | 2 |
| Know that the Lord is God alone | 608 | 1 |
| | | |
| Labour is rest, and pain is sweet | 214 | 2 |
| *Lamb of God, for sinners slain | 167 | 1 |
| Lamb of God for sinners slain | 257 | 4 |
| *Lamb of God, who bear'st away | 463 | 1 |
| *Lamb of God, whose bleeding love | 900 | 1 |
| Lame, and, lo! we leap for joy | 348 | 5 |
| †Lame as I am, I take the prey | 141 | 7 |
| †Lame at the pool I still am found | 135 | 7 |

| | HYMN | VERSE |
|---|---|---|
| Lamenting all my days | 354 | 2 |
| Lamenting sore their sinful life | 797 | 1 |
| Landed in the arms of God | 52 | 2 |
| Land me safe on Canaan's side | 839 | 3 |
| Land us on the heavenly shore | 999 | 4 |
| Languished for you the eternal God | 80 | 7 |
| †Large and abundant blessings shed | 896 | 4 |
| Large as infinity | 405 | 9 |
| Large petitions with thee bring | 824 | 2 |
| Late in Jesus reconciled | 390 | 2 |
| Late in time behold him come | 683 | 2 |
| Late may *he* reach that high abode | 985 | 4 |
| Late partakers of our hope | 925 | 2 |
| Late to *his* heaven remove | 985 | 4 |
| Laud and magnify his name | 640 | 2 |
| Laughs at impossibilities | 360 | 9 |
| Laugh the harvesters, and sing | 578 | 9 |
| Launched on the floods this solid ball | 557 | 2 |
| †Laws divine to them were spoken | 606 | 4 |
| Laws, that never shall be broken | 640 | 1 |
| Lay claim to my merit, and take for his own | 3 | 2 |
| Lay my reasonings at thy feet | 802 | 2 |
| Lay on them, Lord, thy gracious hands | 893 | 1 |
| Lay the aspiring mountain low | 158 | 4 |
| Lay their honours at thy feet | 508 | 5 |
| Lay thy hand upon my soul | 287 | 1 |
| *Lay to thy hand, O God of grace | 159 | 1 |
| Lay to thy mighty hand | 805 | 1 |
| Lead captive their captivity | 462 | 2 |
| Lead me all my journey through | 839 | 2 |
| Lead me a way I have not known | 289 | 7 |
| Lead me by thine own hand | 837 | 1 |
| †Lead me in all thy righteous ways | 543 | 6 |
| Lead me in thyself, the Way | 27 | 3 |
| *Lead me not into temptation | 819 | 1 |
| Lead me to my journey's end | 824 | 6 |
| Lead them safely by the hand | 878 | 2 |
| Lead us in the way of peace | 349 | 1 |
| Lead us through the paths of peace | 512 | 2 |
| *Leader of faithful souls, and guide | 71 | 1 |
| Leading on millennial days | 672 | 5 |
| Leading to eternal day | 350 | 6 |
| Lean on thy Redeemer's breast | 618 | 2 |
| Leaped desperate from their guardian Rock | 483 | 3 |
| Learning and holiness combined | 473 | 5 |
| †Learning's redundant part and vain | 473 | 4 |
| †Least of all thy creatures, we | 238 | 2 |
| †Least of all thy creatures, we | 1019 | 3 |
| Leave, ah! leave me not alone | 143 | 2 |
| Leave all our soaring thoughts behind | 316 | 4 |
| Leave all you have and are behind | 4 | 4 |
| Leave it, leave it all to him | 142 | 9 |
| Leave me not to reprobation | 933 | 1 |

| | HYMN | VERSE |
|---|---|---|
| Leave me, out of thy presence cast | 178 | 3 |
| Leave me to breathe my slighted prayer | 917 | 1 |
| Leave me to faint in life's last stage | 917 | 1 |
| Leave me unchanged, and unrestored | 547 | 1 |
| †Leave not thy work undone | 852 | 2 |
| †Leave no unguarded place | 266 | 4 |
| Leave the fountain-head of bliss | 434 | 3 |
| †Leave to his sovereign sway | 831 | 12 |
| Leave us not below to mourn | 349 | 3 |
| Leave us not comfortless | 503 | 2 |
| Leaves but the number less | 42 | 2 |
| Leaving lands and seas behind | 633 | 3 |
| Lebanon is hither come | 348 | 2 |
| Led by the multitude | 883 | 2 |
| Left in my bosom from the day just past | 967 | 6 |
| Left me long to wander wide | 110 | 2 |
| Legions of dire malicious fiends | 315 | 1 |
| Legions of sins in vain oppose | 293 | 4 |
| Legions of wily fiends oppose | 266 | 3 |
| Lend *him* for ever, Lord, to thee | 896 | 3 |
| Lent to be all laid out for thee | 835 | 1 |
| †Lent to us for a season, we | 896 | 3 |
| †Less grievous will the judgment-day | 454 | 8 |
| Less guilty if, with those of old | 454 | 7 |
| Less numerous than thy mercies are | 655 | 5 |
| Less than the least of all thy store | 351 | 3 |
| Less than thyself cannot suffice | 304 | 3 |
| Lest haply sense should damp our zeal | 204 | 5 |
| Lest he his wrathful looks display | 541 | 5 |
| Lest I into temptation fall | 305 | 2 |
| †Lest that my fearful case should be | 317 | 2 |
| Lest we from our God depart | 653 | 5 |
| Let Adam's sons and daughters | 587 | 6 |
| Let age to age thy righteousness | 637 | 1 |
| Let all be lost in God | 403 | 8 |
| Let all be wrought in love | 270 | 1 |
| Let all cry aloud, And honour the Son | 859 | 4 |
| Let all earth's sons thy mercy prove | 236 | 1 |
| Let all his saints with full accord | 612 | 5 |
| †Let all hold fast the truths whereby | 822 | 4 |
| Let all I am in thee be lost | 403 | 8 |
| Let all I am in thee be lost | 415 | 4 |
| Let all I have, and all I am | 23 | 6 |
| Let all in thee redemption find | 81 | 4 |
| *Let all men rejoice; By Jesus restored | 211 | 1 |
| Let all my fruit be found of thee | 429 | 2 |
| Let all my hallowed heart be love | 351 | 7 |
| Let all my powers thine entrance feel | 374 | 5 |
| Let all my works in thee be wrought | 270 | 1 |
| Let all my works in thee be wrought | 429 | 2 |
| Let all obey the gospel word | 749 | 4 |
| Let all on earth bow down to thee | 247 | 3 |
| Let all on earth fulfil | 653 | 3 |

| | Hymn | Verse |
|---|---|---|
| Let all our actions tend | 108 | 7 |
| Let all our griefs and troubles cease | 900 | 3 |
| Let all our hearts agree | 504 | 4 |
| Let all our hearts receive | 532 | 5 |
| Let all our spirits cleave | 504 | 5 |
| Let all our works in thee be wrought | 666 | 6 |
| *Let all that breathe Jehovah praise | 234 | 1 |
| Let all that fear the Lord proclaim | 616 | 1 |
| Let all that is within me praise | 229 | 2 |
| Let all the angel-throng | 253 | 1 |
| Let all the heathen know thy name | 444 | 3 |
| Let all the heavenly offspring know | 894 | 2 |
| Let all the hosts above | 253 | 4 |
| †Let all the nations join | 581 | 3 |
| Let all the nations know | 719 | 2 |
| Let all the nations know | 738 | 1 |
| Let all the nations meet | 452 | 6 |
| Let all the nations now behold | 741 | 6 |
| Let all the ransomed race | 253 | 2 |
| Let all the saints below the skies | 814 | 1 |
| Let all the saints terrestrial sing | 949 | 1 |
| Let all the sons of Adam raise | 637 | 11 |
| Let all the sons of men, record | 253 | 4 |
| Let all the wanderers come | 452 | 5 |
| Let all the world proclaim | 232 | 2 |
| Let all their bleeding Saviour know | 749 | 4 |
| Let all things praise the Lord | 641 | 4 |
| Let all thy bleeding grace adore | 236 | 1 |
| †Let all thy converse be sincere | 964 | 3 |
| Let all thy followers perceive | 525 | 1 |
| Let all thy love, and all thy grief | 23 | 7 |
| Let all thy saints adore | 253 | 3 |
| Let all to Jesu's cross draw nigh | 314 | 2 |
| †Let all who love the Lord join hands | 822 | 3 |
| *Let all who truly bear | 898 | 1 |
| Let all within me join | 610 | 1 |
| Let all within us feel his power | 494 | 1 |
| Let all with thankful joy receive | 465 | 8 |
| Let angel-minds inquire no more | 201 | 2 |
| Let angels prostrate fall | 681 | 1 |
| Let angels sing thy glorious love | 576 | 3 |
| Let a repenting rebel live | 574 | 1 |
| Let cheerful anthems fill his house | 912 | 2 |
| Let each his friendly aid afford | 503 | 3 |
| Let each improve the grace bestowed | 474 | 3 |
| Let each soon recognise thy voice | 770 | 6 |
| Let each the common burden bear | 524 | 2 |
| Let each the double blessing know | 524 | 2 |
| Let earth and heaven adore | 641 | 1 |
| *Let earth and heaven agree | 34 | 1 |
| *Let earth and heaven combine | 685 | 1 |
| Let earth and heaven his power confess | 234 | 1 |
| †Let earth no more my heart divide | 351 | 5 |

| | Hymn | Verse |
|---|---|---|
| †Let earth's remotest bound | 727 | 4 |
| *Let everlasting glories crown | 879 | 1 |
| †Let every act of worship be | 677 | 2 |
| †Let every creature rise and bring | 585 | 12 |
| Let every creature sing | 232 | 2 |
| Let every creature sing | 641 | 4 |
| Let every house his worship know | 268 | 1 |
| Let every soul be Jesu's guest | 2 | 1 |
| *Let every tongue thy goodness speak | 637 | 6 |
| Let every trembling thought be gone | 802 | 1 |
| †Let every tribe and every tongue | 681 | 7 |
| Let every understanding mind | 251 | 1 |
| *Let God, who comforts the distrest | 441 | 1 |
| †Let good or ill befall | 560 | 4 |
| †Let heaven and earth's stupendous frame | 665 | 2 |
| Let him as he listeth blow | 381 | 3 |
| Let *him* feel thy tender chastening | 895 | 2 |
| Let him fix his mansion here | 86 | 7 |
| Let him no more lie down in sin | 973 | 4 |
| Let him on the altar lie | 914 | 5 |
| *Let Him to whom we now belong | 428 | 1 |
| Let him who raised thee from the dead | 356 | 3 |
| Let in us thy bowels sound | 520 | 3 |
| †Let Israel's captive sons be free | 588 | 4 |
| Let Israel's consolation hear | 441 | 1 |
| †Let Israel's God be ever blessed | 612 | 5 |
| Let it hallow my heart | 160 | 4 |
| Let it not my Lord displease | 167 | 4 |
| Let it now be done to me | 164 | 5 |
| Let it once more be proved in me | 171 | 1 |
| Let it opposers all o'errun | 457 | 2 |
| Let it over me be cast | 271 | 3 |
| †Let it still my heart constrain | 188 | 2 |
| Let it still to heaven ascend | 368 | 1 |
| Let it thy blood impart | 901 | 3 |
| Let it to a temple rise | 516 | 1 |
| Let it to us be done | 389 | 5 |
| Let it wash me, and I shall be whiter than snow | 160 | 4 |
| †Let me according to thy word | 341 | 3 |
| *Let me alone another year | 982 | 1 |
| †Let me alone, that all my wrath | 298 | 2 |
| Let me be by grace restored | 106 | 1 |
| Let me be still and murmur not | 841 | 2 |
| Let me be wronged, reviled, abhorred | 304 | 6 |
| †Let me cast my reeds aside | 802 | 2 |
| Let me choose the better part | 434 | 2 |
| Let me depart in peace | 44 | 6 |
| Let me desire what thou approv'st | 909 | 3 |
| Let me die to thee, and live | 287 | 2 |
| Let me die with thee to reign | 358 | 3 |
| Let me do thy perfect will | 402 | 1 |
| Let me enforce thy call | 270 | 2 |
| Let me ever cleave to thee | 434 | 2 |

| | HYMN | VERSE |
|---|---|---|
| Let me find it "gain to die" | 672 | 11 |
| Let me from strength to strength proceed | 306 | 5 |
| †Let me gain my calling's hope | 354 | 4 |
| Let me give thee all my heart | 434 | 2 |
| Let me hear the welcome sound | 151 | 4 |
| Let me hide myself in thee | 709 | 1 |
| Let me hide myself in thee | 709 | 3 |
| Let me in the cleft be placed | 271 | 4 |
| Let me in thy image rise | 287 | 4 |
| Let me into nothing fall | 398 | 4 |
| Let me know my Shepherd's voice | 13 | 3 |
| Let me live and cling to thee | 790 | 3 |
| Let me never be confounded | 819 | 3 |
| Let me never grieve thee, Lord | 185 | 2 |
| †Let me no more, in deep complaint | 392 | 3 |
| Let me now my fall lament | 168 | 6 |
| †Let me of thy life partake | 287 | 5 |
| Let me peace with God regain | 676 | 2 |
| Let me see, and let me feel | 101 | 2 |
| Let me sink into the dust | 185 | 1 |
| Let me sleep to thee, and wake | 287 | 2 |
| Let me taste my liberty | 390 | 1 |
| Let me thee when waking feel | 287 | 4 |
| Let me then obtain the grace | 167 | 2 |
| Let me thy forerunner be | 479 | 2 |
| †Let me thy power and truth proclaim | 584 | 3 |
| Let me thy salvation see | 402 | 1 |
| †Let me thy witness live | 436 | 10 |
| Let me to every creature cry | 439 | 3 |
| Let me to righteousness awake | 306 | 2 |
| Let me to thy bosom fly | 143 | 1 |
| Let men exclaim, and fiends repine | 401 | 4 |
| Let Moses in the Spirit groan | 298 | 1 |
| †Let mountains from their seats be hurled | 569 | 2 |
| Let my life declare thy power | 402 | 2 |
| Let my Lord be all in all | 398 | 4 |
| Let my soul be fully healed | 166 | 3 |
| Let my widow trust in thee | 915 | 3 |
| Let no foe our peace molest | 970 | 1 |
| Let no ill dreams disturb my rest | 974 | 5 |
| Let no ill power find place | 996 | 7 |
| Let no other trust intrude | 791 | 5 |
| †Let not conscience make you linger | 791 | 3 |
| Let not fears your course impede | 847 | 3 |
| †Let not sorrow dim your eye | 847 | 3 |
| Let not these thy people join | 508 | 4 |
| *Let not the wise his wisdom boast | 422 | 1 |
| †Let others hug their chains | 345 | 2 |
| Let our faith and love increase | 1007 | — |
| Let our lot be cast with them | 349 | 3 |
| Let our whole soul an offering be | 771 | 3 |
| Let Satan pluck me thence | 281 | 5 |
| ⁑Let sickness blast, let death devour | 46 | 6 |

| | Hymn | Verse |
|---|---|---|
| Let sin no more thy people shame . | 531 | 2 |
| Let some drops now fall on me . | 790 | 1 |
| †Let sprinkled water seal them now | 891 | 5 |
| Let that grace, Lord, like a fetter . | 866 | 3 |
| *Let the beasts their breath resign . | 7 | 1 |
| Let the blessing now take place . | 479 | 1 |
| Let the Creator's praise arise . | 615 | 1 |
| †Let the earth his praise resound . | 639 | 4 |
| Let the fiery, cloudy pillar . | 839 | 2 |
| Let the final trump proclaim . | 67 | 7 |
| Let the fragments be my meat . | 164 | 4 |
| †Let the fruits of grace abound . | 520 | 3 |
| Let the healing streams abound . | 143 | 4 |
| Let the heathen fall before thee . | 748 | 2 |
| Let the isles thy power declare . | 748 | 2 |
| Let the least and greatest know . | 464 | 2 |
| †Let the living stones cry out . | 400 | 2 |
| Let the manner be unknown . | 381 | 3 |
| Let the morning stars reply . | 75 | 2 |
| Let the nations shout and sing . | 582 | 2 |
| Let the new-made world appear . | 67 | 6 |
| †Let the path our friends pursue . | 995 | 4 |
| †Let the people praise thee, Lord . | 582 | 2 |
| †Let the people praise thee, Lord . | 582 | 3 |
| †Let the promised inward grace . | 477 | 2 |
| Let the purer flame revive . | 519 | 2 |
| Let the pure seraphic joy . | 418 | 3 |
| *Let the redeemed give thanks and praise . | 123 | 1 |
| Let the Redeemer's name be sung . | 615 | 1 |
| Let the shadows flee away . | 67 | 6 |
| Let the sons of Abraham shout . | 400 | 2 |
| †Let the Spirit before his throne . | 418 | 1 |
| Let the Spirit now come down . | 479 | 3 |
| †Let the Spirit of grace o'erflow . | 464 | 2 |
| †Let the Spirit of our Head . | 756 | 2 |
| †Let the sweet hope that thou art mine . | 843 | 3 |
| Let the trumpet's martial sound . | 641 | 2 |
| Let the unbelievers mourn . | 50 | 5 |
| Let the unknown peace of God . | 479 | 1 |
| Let the utmost grace be given . | 116 | 4 |
| Let the victim live, or die . | 914 | 5 |
| Let the virgin choir advance . | 641 | 2 |
| Let the water and the blood . | 709 | 1 |
| Let the whole world thy mercy prove . | 190 | 10 |
| †Let the world bewail their dead . | 50 | 5 |
| Let the world deride or pity . | 594 | 3 |
| Let the world our influence feel . | 424 | 1 |
| *Let the world their virtue boast . | 115 | 1 |
| Let the world, who know us not . | 51 | 3 |
| Let their lives resemble thine . | 873 | 2 |
| Let their souls the witness know . | 873 | 2 |
| Let their spirit downward go . | 7 | 1 |
| Let their zeal revive again . | 878 | 6 |

| | Hymn | Verse |
|---|---|---|
| "Let them alone," his mercy cried | 980 | 2 |
| Let them believe, and therefore speak | 744 | 6 |
| Let them be still my stay | 566 | 6 |
| Let them boil—each dark-browed hill | 570 | 2 |
| †Let them roar, his awful surges | 570 | 2 |
| Let them see that peaceful shore | 878 | 5 |
| Let them see thee in thy glory | 743 | 1 |
| Let them trust, O Lord, in thee | 878 | 7 |
| Let there be light | 870 | Cho. |
| †Let there be light, again command | 121 | 2 |
| Let there in my dark soul be light | 121 | 1 |
| Let thine awful counsel stand | 733 | 2 |
| Let thine emanations flow | 515 | 3 |
| Let thine image be restored | 109 | 7 |
| Let this barren soul alone | 168 | 3 |
| Let this earth dissolve, and blend | 61 | 1 |
| †Let this my every hour employ | 214 | 5 |
| Let this petition rise | 843 | 1 |
| Let those ponderous orbs descend | 61 | 1 |
| Let those refuse to sing | 12 | 1 |
| Let those who love thy grace still say | 566 | 9 |
| †Let those who seek thee faithfully | 566 | 9 |
| †Let thy blood, by faith applied | 900 | 3 |
| Let thy blood for sinners spilt | 824 | 3 |
| †Let thy dying love constrain | 463 | 4 |
| Let thy every servant say | 400 | 8 |
| †Let thy face upon me shine | 620 | 3 |
| Let thy goodness be displayed | 109 | 4 |
| Let thy good Spirit lead | 635 | 3 |
| Let thy good Spirit ne'er depart | 574 | 8 |
| Let thy life-giving blood | 160 | 3 |
| Let thy life in mine appear | 769 | 2 |
| Let thy light and solace fall | 753 | 5 |
| †Let thy love my heart inflame | 672 | 2 |
| Let thy love my spirit cheer | 824 | 6 |
| Let thy mercy-beaming eye | 672 | 3 |
| Let thy mercy light on me | 790 | 2 |
| Let thy salvation visit me | 612 | 3 |
| Let thy servants humbler be | 878 | 7 |
| Let thy smile of love afford | 672 | 8 |
| Let thy sovereign will be done | 914 | 1 |
| Let thy strongest joys be given | 336 | 1 |
| Let thy will on earth be done | 430 | 1 |
| Let thy will on earth be done | 430 | 6 |
| †Let thy will on me be done | 18 | 3 |
| Let thy word richly in me dwell | 196 | 2 |
| Let thy word richly in us dwell | 492 | 4 |
| Let us all our work fulfil | 518 | 5 |
| Let us all thy goodness prove | 852 | 2 |
| Let us all thy grace receive | 385 | 2 |
| †Let us all together rise | 512 | 3 |
| Let us daily growth receive | 518 | 3 |
| Let us each, thy love possessing | 1008 | 1 |

| | Hymn | Verse |
|---|---|---|
| Let us exult, give thanks, and sing | 977 | 4 |
| Let us feel thy power, applying | 899 | 2 |
| Let us find our rest in thee | 688 | 1 |
| †Let us, for conscience' sake, revere | 465 | 7 |
| †Let us for each other care | 509 | 4 |
| †Let us for this faith contend | 521 | 4 |
| Let us give thanks, and sing | 345 | 7 |
| Let us gladly fulfil | 47 | 2 |
| Let us groan thine inward groaning | 899 | 2 |
| Let us herewith receive | 901 | 3 |
| Let us his command obey | 295 | 1 |
| Let us in all things grow | 503 | 5 |
| Let us in due season yield | 424 | 2 |
| Let us in hymns employ | 954 | 4 |
| Let us in Jesus see thy face | 88 | 4 |
| †Let us in life, in death | 831 | 15 |
| †Let us in patience wait | 303 | 6 |
| Let us in the flesh remain | 925 | 2 |
| Let us in thine image rise | 514 | 4 |
| Let us in thy name agree | 509 | 1 |
| Let us in thy name be joined | 514 | 2 |
| Let us in thy Spirit rise | 717 | 3 |
| Let us join our hearts and hands | 521 | 1 |
| *Let us join, ('tis God commands) | 521 | 1 |
| Let us keep high festival | 714 | 5 |
| Let us lean upon thy breast | 520 | 4 |
| †Let us never, never rest | 479 | 3 |
| Let us never, never rest | 480 | 3 |
| Let us now a blessing seek | 975 | 1 |
| Let us now the answer feel | 515 | 1 |
| Let us our voices raise | 204 | 4 |
| †Let us patiently endure | 295 | 4 |
| Let us see thy great salvation | 385 | 3 |
| Let us still our Saviour greet | 529 | 3 |
| Let us still receive of thine | 518 | 2 |
| †Let us still to thee look up | 508 | 7 |
| Let us take up the cross | 478 | 3 |
| Let us thankfully embrace | 463 | 1 |
| †Let us then as brethren love | 521 | 2 |
| †Let us then rejoice in hope | 400 | 6 |
| †Let us then sweet counsel take | 480 | 2 |
| †Let us then with joy remove | 509 | 6 |
| Let us thine influence prove | 87 | 1 |
| Let us thus in God abide | 509 | 5 |
| Let us thy mercy prove | 737 | 11 |
| Let us thy presence feel | 486 | 3 |
| †Let us, to perfect love restored | 342 | 2 |
| Let us to the end believe | 852 | 2 |
| Let us walk with him in white | 207 | 2 |
| Let us without ceasing Give thanks for thy grace | 481 | 6 |
| Let what I ask be given | 118 | 5 |
| †Let your drooping hearts be glad | 847 | 2 |
| *Let Zion in her King rejoice | 569 | 6 |

| | Hymn | Verse |
|---|---|---|
| Lets the lifted thunder drop | 168 | 4 |
| Levelled at one common aim | 512 | 2 |
| Lie mouldering in the clay | 930 | 1 |
| Lies silent in the grave | 798 | 5 |
| Life, and all, descend from God | 233 | 1 |
| Life and death together fought | 714 | 3 |
| Life, and happiness, and love | 106 | 3 |
| Life, and health, and rest, and food | 554 | 1 |
| Life and joy thy beams impart | 687 | 2 |
| Life and salvation bring | 785 | 1 |
| Life by his expiring groan | 20 | 2 |
| Life could no lasting bliss afford | 577 | 4 |
| Life divine in us renew | 758 | 6 |
| Life eternal, to my heart | 302 | 4 |
| Life from the dead for all mankind | 451 | 3 |
| Life from the dead is in that word | 944 | 1 |
| Life-giving, holy Dove | 870 | 3 |
| Life is given through thy name | 722 | 1 |
| †Life, like a fountain rich and free | 563 | 5 |
| Life, love, and joy still gliding through | 569 | 4 |
| Life of all that live below | 515 | 3 |
| Life of every dying soul | 723 | 1 |
| *Life of the world, come down | 1014 | — |
| †Life or death depend on thee | 914 | 4 |
| Life to all, for life who sigh | 192 | 3 |
| Life to all thy limbs impart | 506 | 2 |
| †Life's best joy, to see thy praise | 672 | 5 |
| Lifted up their voice on high | 601 | 3 |
| Lift her heart above the skies | 990 | 5 |
| Lift my heart to things above | 325 | 3 |
| Lift to heaven my heart and hand | 910 | 2 |
| Lift up a standard, and o'erthrow | 296 | 1 |
| †Lift up, lift up your voices now | 715 | 2 |
| Lift up the standard of thy cross | 39 | 6 |
| †Lift up thy countenance serene | 252 | 5 |
| Lift up your heads! at last | 595 | 5 |
| Lift up your heads, ye heavenly gates | 557 | 7 |
| Lift up your heads, ye heavenly gates | 557 | 10 |
| Lift up your heart, lift up your voice | 277 | 1 |
| Lift up your heart, lift up your voice | 729 | Cho. |
| *Lift up your hearts to things above | 539 | 1 |
| *Lift your eyes of faith, and see | 75 | 1 |
| Lift your heads, eternal gates | 718 | 2 |
| *Lift your heads, ye friends of Jesus | 936 | 1 |
| Lift your hearts and voices up | 522 | 1 |
| Lift your voice, and shout his praise | 571 | 1 |
| Light and joy his looks impart | 54 | 1 |
| Light and life to all he brings | 683 | 4 |
| Light as a hart I then shall bound | 135 | 7 |
| Light in thy light I then shall see | 134 | 5 |
| †Light in thy light O may I see | 252 | 4 |
| Light in thy light still may I see | 351 | 7 |
| *Light of life, seraphic fire | 399 | 1 |

# LIGHT OF — LIVE TILL

| | Hymn | Verse |
|---|---|---|
| †Light of the Gentile world, appear | 129 | 4 |
| Light of the world, illumine all | 444 | 2 |
| †Light of the world, thy beams I bless | 281 | 3 |
| *Light of those, whose dreary dwelling | 687 | 1 |
| Lighten all our darkness, Lord | 971 | 4 |
| Lighten all who dwell on earth | 753 | 2 |
| Lighten my eyes with faith, my heart | 785 | 2 |
| Lightened of his fleshly load | 50 | 2 |
| Lighter than dust within thy scale | 1001 | 7 |
| Lightnings swift, and thunders loud | 58 | 1 |
| Lights in a benighted land | 519 | 3 |
| Like brutes they live, like brutes they die | 599 | 4 |
| Like chaff before the wind | 540 | 4 |
| †Like clouds are they borne To do thy great will | 869 | 3 |
| Like David's harp of solemn sound | 599 | 2 |
| Like flame, o'er nature's funeral pyre | 61 | 2 |
| Like grass they flourish, till thy breath | 599 | 4 |
| Like heavenly dew on thirsty hills | 585 | 4 |
| Like holy oil to cheer my head | 599 | 5 |
| Like humble Mary, lo! I sit | 353 | 4 |
| Like infant's slumbers, pure and light | 973 | 5 |
| Like Israel saved in Midian's day | 493 | 4 |
| Like Jordan's swelling stream | 115 | 2 |
| Like Mary's gift, let my devotion prove | 794 | 8 |
| †Like mighty winds, or torrents fierce | 457 | 2 |
| Like Moses' bush, I'll mount the higher | 272 | 7 |
| Like Moses to thyself convey | 229 | 6 |
| Like one forgotten, mourn | 567 | 3 |
| Like our espousals, Lord, to thee | 677 | 2 |
| Like sacrificial flame | 771 | 3 |
| †Like some fair tree which, fed by streams | 540 | 3 |
| Like that my Saviour showed | 701 | 3 |
| Like the blind beside the way | 694 | 1 |
| Like the glad hour when from above | 677 | 2 |
| Like theirs with glory crowned | 949 | 5 |
| Like thy spotless Master, thou | 618 | 5 |
| Like us assembled here | 983 | 2 |
| Like us, rejoice to see | 983 | 3 |
| Like us thou hast a mourner been | 692 | 5 |
| Listening for the call divine | 61 | 4 |
| Listen, listen to the cry | 710 | 5 |
| Listen to a wailing heart | 768 | 1 |
| Listen to our humble cry | 710 | 4 |
| Listen to thy speaking blood | 182 | 5 |
| Little as a human hand | 218 | 4 |
| Live happy in my Saviour's love | 125 | 2 |
| Live in glorious liberty | 402 | 1 |
| Live in thy sight, and gladly prove | 511 | 1 |
| Live out in cheerful hope | 535 | 6 |
| Live the life of heaven above | 20 | 3 |
| Live the Son, alike revered | 645 | 1 |
| †Live, till all thy life I know | 18 | 4 |
| †Live till the Lord in glory come | 589 | 10 |

| | Hymn | Verse |
|---|---|---|
| Live to declare I'm saved from sin | 230 | 4 |
| Live we all as angels here | 538 | 4 |
| †Lives again our glorious King | 716 | 4 |
| Living in the flesh, but thou | 390 | 4 |
| Lo! abundantly they bloom | 348 | 2 |
| Lo! all we are to thee we give | 655 | 3 |
| Lo! an Advocate is found | 168 | 3 |
| Lo! at thy word our Isaac dies | 286 | 6 |
| Lo! for us the wilds are glad | 348 | 1 |
| †Lo! from their seats the mountains leap | 63 | 3 |
| †Lo! God is here! him day and night | 494 | 2 |
| *Lo! God is here! let us adore | 494 | 1 |
| †Lo, he beckons from on high | 921 | 2 |
| Lo! he brings you sure relief | 54 | 2 |
| Lo! he comes to keep his word | 54 | 1 |
| *Lo! He comes with clouds descending | 66 | 1 |
| †Lo! he comes with clouds! he comes | 605 | 7 |
| Lo! he dwells with his own | 499 | 7 |
| Lo! he holds thee by thy hand | 618 | 4 |
| Lo! he sets in blood no more | 716 | 2 |
| Lo! he spreads his wings abroad | 407 | 1 |
| "Lo, here is Christ!" or, "Christ is there" | 16 | 5 |
| †Lo! here thy wondrous skill arrays | 226 | 8 |
| †Lo! his triumphal chariot waits | 557 | 10 |
| Lo! I answer to thy call | 430 | 2 |
| Lo! I cast on thee my care | 915 | 1 |
| Lo! I come to do thy will | 430 | 2 |
| *Lo! I come with joy to do | 325 | 1 |
| †Lo! I cumber still the ground | 168 | 3 |
| Lo! I in thy courts appear | 910 | 1 |
| Lo! I my King have crowned, and will | 541 | 2 |
| †Lo! I take thee at thy word | 182 | 5 |
| †Lo! in the arms of faith and prayer | 465 | 3 |
| Lo! in the hollow of thy hand | 1001 | 6 |
| †Lo! on a narrow neck of land | 59 | 2 |
| †Lo! on dangers, deaths, and snares | 359 | 2 |
| Lo! on the wings of love he flies | 387 | 1 |
| Lo! Salem's daughters weep around | 712 | 1 |
| †Lo, the Book, exactly worded | 933 | 5 |
| Lo! the heavenly spirit towers | 61 | 2 |
| †Lo! the incarnate God, ascended | 791 | 5 |
| Lo! the pain of life is past | 50 | 2 |
| †Lo! the prisoner is released | 50 | 2 |
| Lo! the promise of a shower | 218 | 4 |
| Lo! the Saviour stands above | 922 | 2 |
| Lo! the snare is rent and broken | 621 | 3 |
| Lo! the sun's eclipse is o'er | 716 | 2 |
| †Lo! the tall sons of Anak rise | 293 | 6 |
| Lo! this infant comes to thee | 895 | 1 |
| †Lo! 'tis he! our hearts' desire | 936 | 6 |
| †Lo! to faith's enlightened sight | 728 | 5 |
| Lo! to his my suit I join | 390 | 3 |
| Lo! to thee I all resign | 24 | 3 |

| | Hymn | Verse |
|---|---|---|
| †Lo! to the hills I lift mine eye | 138 | 8 |
| Lo! we answer thy demand | 914 | 3 |
| Lo! we come to thee for ease | 29 | 3 |
| Lo! we now rejoice for thee | 52 | 5 |
| †Lo! we to our promise stand | 914 | 3 |
| †Loathsome, and vile, and self-abhorred | 185 | 4 |
| Lodge there in Abraham's breast | 942 | 2 |
| Lonely deserts now rejoice | 348 | 2 |
| Long as a deathless soul shall live | 658 | 6 |
| Long as eternal ages roll | 181 | 4 |
| †Long as I live beneath | 229 | 3 |
| †Long as my God shall lend me breath | 638 | 2 |
| †Long as our fiery trials last | 297 | 2 |
| Long as the cross we bear | 297 | 2 |
| †Long as the guilt of sin shall last | 461 | 6 |
| †Long hath thy good Spirit strove | 166 | 3 |
| Long hath felt thee fixed within | 382 | 1 |
| *Long have I lived in grief and pain | 781 | 1 |
| *Long have I sat beneath the sound | 789 | 1 |
| *Long have I seemed to serve thee, Lord | 91 | 1 |
| Long have I wandered to and fro | 114 | 2 |
| Long may they echo to thy praise | 994 | 2 |
| Long may we work the works of God | 524 | 3 |
| †Long my imprisoned spirit lay | 201 | 4 |
| Long provoked him to his face | 168 | 1 |
| Long-suffering, merciful, and kind | 144 | 5 |
| †Long we have our burden borne | 531 | 2 |
| Longing, gasping after home | 718 | 9 |
| Longings for vanished smiles, and voices gone | 850 | 3 |
| Look, and be saved through faith alone | 1 | 7 |
| Look, and with thy flaming eyes | 383 | 3 |
| †Look, as when thine eye pursued | 106 | 4 |
| †Look, as when thy grace beheld | 106 | 6 |
| †Look, as when thy languid eye | 106 | 7 |
| †Look, as when thy pity saw | 106 | 5 |
| Look down, O Lord, with pitying eye | 574 | 11 |
| Look forward to that heavenly place | 333 | 2 |
| Look grim as e'er he will | 856 | 3 |
| Look on him we pierced, and grieve | 899 | 2 |
| †Look on the heart by sorrow broken | 906 | 2 |
| Look on the tears by sinners shed | 906 | 2 |
| Look on thy hands, and read it there | 140 | 2 |
| †Look through us with thy eyes of flame | 502 | 3 |
| Look to the rock from whence ye came | 111 | 1 |
| †Look unto him, ye nations, own | 1 | 7 |
| Look unto me, the pardoning God | 387 | 1 |
| Look up, for thou shalt weep no more | 134 | 5 |
| Look we down on earthly kings | 508 | 8 |
| Looking for God my soul to keep | 303 | 1 |
| Looking when our Lord shall come | 718 | 9 |
| Looks down, and watches all my dust | 930 | 3 |
| Looks through the cloud | 854 | 2 |
| Looks to Jesus, help implores | 109 | 2 |

| | Hymn | Verse |
|---|---|---|
| †Loose all your bars of massy light . | 557 | 8 |
| †Loose me from the chains of sense | 287 | 4 |
| †Loosed from my God, and far removed | 114 | 2 |
| Lord, all-pitying, Jesu blest | 933 | 19 |
| *Lord, and is thine anger gone | 188 | 1 |
| Lord, appear! appear to glad us | 60 | 4 |
| †Lord, arm me with thy Spirit's might | 481 | 6 |
| †Lord, at thy feet I fall | 137 | 4 |
| *Lord, dismiss us with thy blessing | 1007 | — |
| *Lord, dismiss us with thy blessing | 1008 | 1 |
| †Lord, endue thy word from heaven | 882 | 6 |
| Lord, for thy servant do | 558 | 1 |
| Lord, from each far-peopled dwelling | 580 | 1 |
| †Lord God of hosts, thine ear incline | 589 | 4 |
| Lord God! O hear my prayer | 626 | 1 |
| *Lord, I adore thy gracious will | 334 | — |
| †Lord, I am blind, be thou my sight | 163 | 7 |
| Lord, I am damned, but thou hast died | 132 | 6 |
| †Lord, I am sick, my sickness cure . | 163 | 6 |
| Lord, I am sin, but thou art love | 132 | 6 |
| †Lord I am vile, conceived in sin | 574 | 3 |
| Lord, I am weak, be thou my might | 163 | 7 |
| Lord, I believe, and not in vain | 136 | 9 |
| *Lord, I believe a rest remains | 403 | 1 |
| †Lord, I believe the promise sure | 134 | 6 |
| †Lord, I believe thou hast prepared . | 798 | 6 |
| *Lord, I believe thou *wilt* forgive | 780 | 1 |
| *Lord, I believe thy every word | 356 | 1 |
| *Lord, I believe thy mercy's power . | 813 | — |
| †Lord, I believe thy power the same | 408 | 7 |
| †Lord, I believe thy precious blood . | 190 | 4 |
| †Lord, I believe, were sinners more . | 190 | 5 |
| †Lord, I come to thee for rest | 824 | 4 |
| *Lord, I despair myself to heal | 131 | 1 |
| *Lord, I hear of showers of blessing | 790 | 1 |
| Lord, I my unbelief confess | 833 | 5 |
| †Lord, I my vows to thee renew | 964 | 6 |
| Lord, I no more thy truth blaspheme | 401 | 1 |
| †Lord, I will not let thee go . | 390 | 3 |
| *Lord, if at thy command | 734 | 1 |
| †Lord, if I now thy drawings feel | 17 | 9 |
| †Lord, if I on thee believe | 354 | 3 |
| Lord, if on thee I dare rely . | 342 | 5 |
| †Lord, if thou didst the wish infuse . | 472 | 4 |
| †Lord, if thou didst thyself inspire . | 526 | 2 |
| †Lord, if thou from me hast broke . | 368 | 2 |
| †Lord, if thou hast bestowed . | 172 | 4 |
| *Lord, if thou the grace impart | 628 | 1 |
| †Lord, if thou wilt, I do believe | 395 | 6 |
| †Lord, if thy grace I have | 806 | 2 |
| *Lord, in the strength of grace | 426 | 1 |
| Lord, in thy arms I will entrust | 974 | 6 |
| Lord, in thy name my work I do | 321 | 1 |

| | Hymn | Verse |
|---|---|---|
| *Lord, it belongs not to my care | 920 | 1 |
| *Lord! it is good for us to be | 698 | All. |
| Lord Jesu Christ, attend me | 923 | 1 |
| *Lord, let me know mine end | 565 | 1 |
| Lord, meet us by the way | 865 | 2 |
| †Lord, my time is in thine hand | 142 | 4 |
| †Lord, my time is in thy hand | 358 | 5 |
| Lord, no long tarrying make | 566 | 10 |
| *Lord of all, thy creatures see | 1012 | — |
| *Lord of all, with pure intent | 890 | 1 |
| Lord of battles, God of armies | 720 | 2 |
| *Lord of earth, and air, and sea | 1000 | 1 |
| Lord of glory | 621 | 3 |
| Lord of glory, Son of man | 195 | 2 |
| †Lord of grace! to thee we cry | 895 | 4 |
| Lord of hell, and earth, and heaven | 728 | 2 |
| *Lord of hosts, our God and Lord | 733 | 1 |
| Lord of hosts, we know thee nigh | 570 | 6 |
| Lord of lords, shall soon appear | 936 | 1 |
| †Lord, of thee we fain would learn | 756 | 3 |
| †Lord of the hallowed day | 952 | 3 |
| *Lord of the harvest, hear | 745 | 1 |
| *Lord of the Sabbath, hear our vows | 959 | 1 |
| †Lord of the Sabbath, 'tis thy will | 951 | 5 |
| *Lord of the wide, extensive main | 1001 | 1 |
| *Lord of the worlds above | 591 | 1 |
| †Lord over all, and God most high | 471 | 4 |
| *Lord over all, if thou hast made | 444 | 1 |
| †Lord over all, sent to fulfil | 353 | 4 |
| Lord, receive my happy soul | 941 | 4 |
| *Lord, regard my earnest cry | 164 | 1 |
| Lord, remove this load of sin | 824 | 3 |
| Lord, should thy judgment be severe | 574 | 2 |
| Lord, silence thou those fears | 931 | 4 |
| †Lord, spare them till their lives and tongues | 891 | 6 |
| Lord! teach us how to pray | 823 | 8 |
| *Lord teach us how to pray aright | 865 | 1 |
| *Lord, that I may learn of thee | 802 | 1 |
| Lord, that we belong to thee | 522 | 4 |
| †Lord, the cause belongs to thee | 733 | 2 |
| Lord, they go at thy command | 878 | 2 |
| Lord, thou art most great, most high | 598 | 2 |
| *Lord, thou hast bid thy people pray | 985 | 1 |
| †Lord, thou hast joined my soul to thine | 923 | 3 |
| †Lord, thou hast seen; arise and save | 546 | 3 |
| Lord, thou hear'st the praying sigh | 925 | 1 |
| Lord, thou know'st my simple heart | 434 | 6 |
| Lord, thou stay'st for my consent | 910 | 6 |
| Lord, thou read'st the panting heart | 925 | 1 |
| Lord, to my humble suit attend | 559 | 3 |
| Lord, to thy dying love | 930 | 5 |
| †Lord, we are few, but thou art near | 864 | 5 |
| Lord, we ask no other heaven | 522 | 4 |

| | Hymn | Verse |
|---|---|---|
| †Lord, we believe, and wait the hour | 380 | 7 |
| Lord, we believe the promise sure | 254 | 2 |
| †Lord, we believe to us and ours | 759 | 4 |
| †Lord, we do not ask to gaze | 694 | 2 |
| Lord, we pray, this house adorn | 990 | 4 |
| *Lord! we sit and cry to thee | 694 | 1 |
| *Lord, we thy will obey | 533 | 1 |
| Lord, we will not let thee go | 530 | 4 |
| †Lord, what shall earth and ashes do | 316 | 3 |
| Lord, when I die, I die to thee | 923 | 3 |
| *Lord, who hast taught to us on earth | 822 | 1 |
| Lord, who shall stand before thee | 626 | 1 |
| *Lord, whom winds and seas obey | 999 | 1 |
| *Lord, with open heart and ear | 886 | — |
| Lords are we of the lands and floods | 1001 | 10 |
| Lose all their guilty stains | 798 | 1 |
| Lose thy pardoning grace again | 653 | 5 |
| Lost, and confused, and dark, and blind | 177 | 2 |
| Lost and undone, for aid I flee | 182 | 1 |
| †Lost are they now, and scattered wide | 744 | 2 |
| Lost hours have never seemed | 838 | 7 |
| Lost in astonishment and love | 393 | 2 |
| Lost in wonder, love, and praise | 385 | 3 |
| Lost, I now in Christ am found | 191 | 1 |
| Lost is thy reason's feeble ray | 240 | 4 |
| Loud and strong their voices be | 193 | 6 |
| †Loud may the troubled ocean roar | 569 | 3 |
| Loud they sang his power to save | 580 | 2 |
| Loudest praises without ceasing | 722 | 4 |
| Loudly in strange hosannas join | 203 | 8 |
| Loudly of his strength he boasts | 278 | 1 |
| Love, and save us to the end | 238 | 4 |
| Love be all my paradise | 434 | 6 |
| Love be there our endless feast | 520 | 4 |
| †Love can bow down the stubborn neck | 361 | 6 |
| Love descending | 715 | 3 |
| *Love divine, all loves excelling | 385 | 1 |
| †Love divine shall still embrace | 554 | 6 |
| Love divine, thyself impart | 399 | 1 |
| Love fills up my whole desire | 434 | 7 |
| Love, for ever love thine own | 518 | 4 |
| †Love in me intensely burn | 766 | 2 |
| Love inordinate and blind | 382 | 2 |
| Love joy and hope like flowers | 586 | 3 |
| †Love, like death, hath all destroyed | 518 | 10 |
| Love made my God a man of grief | 772 | 5 |
| Love me freely, seal my peace | 110 | Cho. |
| Love mine inmost essence seize | 766 | 2 |
| †Love moved him to die | 808 | 3 |
| †Love of God so pure and changeless | 790 | 5 |
| †Love only can the conquest win | 361 | 5 |
| †Love, only love, thy heart inclined | 772 | 5 |
| Love, our full reward shall be | 936 | 7 |

| | Hymn | Verse |
|---|---|---|
| Love shall crown us | 936 | 7 |
| Love shall keep me to the end | 554 | 6 |
| Love shall make us persevere | 238 | 4 |
| Love so amazing, so divine | 700 | 4 |
| Love that gave thy Son to die | 717 | 1 |
| Love that made thee condescend | 423 | 1 |
| Love that o'erwhelms the saints in light | 440 | 1 |
| Love, the earnest of our heaven | 936 | 7 |
| Love the mystic union be | 516 | 3 |
| Love the proof that Christ we know | 522 | 4 |
| Love, the sealing grace, impart | 514 | 3 |
| Love, thine image, love impart | 522 | 4 |
| Love unspeakable are thine | 350 | 8 |
| Love us, save us to the end | 508 | 1 |
| †Love us, though far in flesh disjoined | 539 | 5 |
| Loved with an everlasting love | 114 | 4 |
| Loved with an everlasting love | 189 | 6 |
| †Lover of souls! thou know'st to prize | 35 | 3 |
| †Lover of souls, to rescue mine | 122 | 3 |
| *Lovers of pleasure more than God | 36 | 1 |
| Love's all-sufficient sea to raise | 291 | 1 |
| Love's pure flame, and wisdom's light | 743 | 3 |
| †Love's redeeming work is done | 716 | 2 |
| Loves me still,—I know not why | 554 | 3 |
| Lov'st whate'er thy hands have made | 242 | 2 |
| Low at thy feet they bow | 875 | 1 |
| †Low I kneel, with heart-submission | 933 | 17 |
| Low we bow the adoring knee | 710 | 1 |
| Lower if our voices sound | 221 | 3 |
| Lowly and gentle may I be | 353 | 5 |
| Lowly and meek in heart, I see | 471 | 5 |
| Lowly as thine shall be my mind | 366 | 1 |
| Lowly both my heart and eye | 628 | 2 |
| Lowly I wept, and strongly vowed | 909 | 1 |
| †Lowly, loving, meek, and pure | 355 | 12 |
| Lowly, meek, incarnate Word | 520 | 1 |
| Lowly, meek, in thought and word | 509 | 3 |
| Lulled with the transporting sound | 75 | 3 |
| | | |
| Made, and preserved, and saved by thee | 654 | 2 |
| †Made apt, by thy sufficient grace | 468 | 3 |
| Made by him, and purchased, why | 7 | 3 |
| Made for God, to God return | 921 | 1 |
| Made his own life the seal | 903 | 5 |
| Made like him, like him we rise | 716 | 5 |
| Made perfect first in love | 504 | 7 |
| †Made perfect first in love | 685 | 5 |
| Made ready for your full reward | 65 | 2 |
| Made ready in thy powerful day | 416 | 3 |
| Made the earth on which we tread | 233 | 2 |
| Made the new way to heaven appear | 902 | 3 |
| Made them of thy favour sure | 245 | 3 |
| Made thy pleasure to fulfil | 952 | 1 |

| | Hymn | Verse |
|---|---|---|
| Made us of clay, and formed us men | 608 | 2 |
| Made you with himself to live | 6 | 1 |
| Madly raging | 621 | 1 |
| †Madness and misery | 21 | 2 |
| Magnify it all in me | 790 | 5 |
| Magnify thy name for ever | 819 | 4 |
| Maintains our unity | 487 | 3 |
| Maintain the honour of his word | 811 | 1 |
| Make all thy gracious goodness pass | 283 | 2 |
| Make all thy pastors one, O Lord | 822 | 3 |
| Make a lost world thy home | 771 | 7 |
| †Make a loud and cheerful noise | 605 | 4 |
| Make and keep me pure within | 143 | 4 |
| Make even me a creature new | 158 | 2 |
| Make even me a creature new | 158 | 3 |
| Make good our apostolic boast | 476 | 1 |
| Make haste to bring thy nature in | 389 | 3 |
| †Make *him* and keep *him* thine own child | 896 | 5 |
| Make *him*, Lord, thy child below | 895 | 2 |
| Make in me thy mean abode | 149 | 1 |
| Make me faithful to the end | 156 | 3 |
| Make me just and good, like thee | 18 | 1 |
| Make me Lord—I ask not why | 24 | 3 |
| Make me restless to return | 101 | 3 |
| Make me rich, for I am poor | 109 | 6 |
| Make me steadfastly believe | 183 | 1 |
| Make me still thy tender care | 193 | 4 |
| Make me thy duteous child, that I | 344 | 6 |
| Make me willing to be clean | 158 | 2 |
| Make me willing to be free | 173 | 3 |
| Make me willing to receive | 158 | 2 |
| Make my infected nature pure | 131 | 4 |
| Make, O make my heart thy seat | 352 | 3 |
| Make, O make us meet for thee | 522 | 3 |
| Make our darkened souls to see | 694 | 1 |
| †Make our earthly souls a field | 424 | 2 |
| Make our feast a feast of love | 520 | 2 |
| Make our hearts a watered garden | 530 | 1 |
| Make safe the way that leads on high | 690 | 4 |
| Make slaves the partners of thy throne | 26 | 5 |
| Make the fruits of grace abound | 975 | 5 |
| Make the harmony of love | 538 | 2 |
| Make the thirsty land a pool | 348 | 6 |
| Make their heart the house of God | 890 | 2 |
| †Make this the acceptable hour | 396 | 6 |
| Make this the acceptable hour | 616 | 9 |
| Make thy healing virtue known | 463 | 3 |
| Make thy priestly office known | 676 | 2 |
| Make us all for glory meet | 520 | 4 |
| †Make us all in thee complete | 520 | 4 |
| Make us all thy children dear | 971 | 1 |
| Make us faithful to the end | 653 | 6 |
| †Make us gentle, meek, and humble | 882 | 5 |

| | Hymn | Verse |
|---|---|---|
| †Make us into one spirit drink | 504 | 3 |
| Make us meet for our reward | 937 | 2 |
| Make us meet thy face to see | 643 | 4 |
| †Make us of one heart and mind | 509 | 3 |
| Make us, O uniting Son | 517 | 2 |
| Make us thy eternal home | 479 | 2 |
| Make us trees of paradise | 424 | 2 |
| Make we mention of his love | 480 | 1 |
| Make you his service your delight | 562 | 6 |
| Maker of all mankind and me | 234 | 8 |
| Maker of the earth and skies | 990 | 6 |
| *Maker, Saviour of mankind | 18 | 1 |
| Makes all my heart and nature pure | 124 | 3 |
| Makes his sun on sinners rise | 238 | 1 |
| Makes his sun on sinners rise | 1019 | 2 |
| Makes his sun on us to shine | 233 | 2 |
| Makes me quietly lie down | 554 | 2 |
| Makes the dead sinner live | 644 | 3 |
| Makes with mortals his abode | 758 | 3 |
| Mak'st my cup of joy run o'er | 554 | 5 |
| Male nor female, Lord, in thee | 518 | 9 |
| Man for judgment must prepare him | 933 | 18 |
| Man, in his highest honour, man | 565 | 2 |
| Man, the well-beloved of heaven | 257 | 1 |
| Man to God devoted live | 582 | 3 |
| Man to save from endless death | 737 | 2 |
| Man we for his kindness love | 233 | 3 |
| Man we for his kindness love | 1021 | 1 |
| Man with God is on the throne | 720 | 5 |
| Man with men he deigned to appear | 194 | 2 |
| Man's pathway trod, 'mid pain and woe | 695 | 3 |
| Manifest thy presence here | 520 | 2 |
| Manifest thyself within | 299 | 4 |
| Manna feeds them from the skies | 593 | 2 |
| Manna that from heaven comes down | 905 | 1 |
| †Many are we now and one | 518 | 9 |
| Many a sorrow, many a labour | 793 | 4 |
| Many a tear | 793 | 4 |
| Many crowns upon thy head | 748 | 3 |
| Many though its days, or few | 995 | 4 |
| March in heavenly armour clad | 847 | 2 |
| March on, nor fear to win the day | 675 | 9 |
| Marked as thine own,—and bid the name | 892 | 2 |
| Marks the new, the living way | 350 | 6 |
| Mark the toil, the pains we feel | 737 | 11 |
| Mark the tokens | 936 | 1 |
| Mark what my labouring soul would say | 134 | 4 |
| *Master, I own thy lawful claim | 332 | 1 |
| *Master supreme, I look to thee | 470 | 1 |
| *Master, thy grace vouchsafe to me | 828 | 1 |
| Master, thy right maintain | 757 | 7 |
| †Master, (will we ever say) | 263 | 7 |
| Matter eternity to fill | 844 | 5 |

| | Hymn | Verse |
|---|---|---|
| Matter of all our lays | 536 | 1 |
| Matter of eternal praise | 701 | 1 |
| May all our hearts with love o'erflow | 483 | 1 |
| May all thy people prove | 446 | 2 |
| May barrenness rejoice to own | 771 | 4 |
| May be in very deed thine own | 992 | 2 |
| May be the garment of thy righteousness | 794 | 6 |
| May believe, and feel thee nigh | 355 | 4 |
| May drink of my Spirit, Excepted is none | 3 | 2 |
| May dwell, but thy pure love alone | 373 | 2 |
| May every ear the call obey | 955 | 3 |
| May fall and weep, like me | 303 | 3 |
| May feel his resurrection's power | 953 | 2 |
| May find eternal life in thee | 190 | 9 |
| May follow thee, and never rest | 373 | 7 |
| May from thy ways depart | 172 | 4 |
| May gladly give up all to thee | 286 | 3 |
| May hear thy voice and live | 136 | 1 |
| May hear thy whisper in thy word | 884 | — |
| May her ceaseless prayer arise | 990 | 5 |
| May her proper work pursue | 826 | — |
| May he with all his gifts impart | 1023 | — |
| †May I but find the grace | 731 | 8 |
| May I feel a kindred flame | 672 | 4 |
| May I in sight of heaven rejoice | 974 | 7 |
| May I obedient prove | 307 | 2 |
| May I prove it "Christ to live" | 672 | 6 |
| May I that weight of glory bear | 72 | 2 |
| May I their help enjoy | 609 | 3 |
| *May I throughout this day of thine | 960 | — |
| May in thee have peace and power | 182 | 1 |
| May it before the world appear | 994 | 3 |
| May it be found a dwelling meet | 609 | 4 |
| May know my steps no more | 799 | 3 |
| May learn of Jews to adore | 452 | 2 |
| May mansions for themselves prepare | 48 | 2 |
| May not a sinner trust in thee | 574 | 1 |
| May now be saved, whoever will | 82 | 1 |
| May now thy truth and mercy feel | 476 | 6 |
| May our brief Sabbaths melt away | 951 | 4 |
| May peace and pardon have | 303 | 3 |
| May quicken and convert us all | 81 | 2 |
| May raise the top-stone in its day | 992 | 5 |
| May ready help be found | 966 | 3 |
| May receive the glad word | 47 | 6 |
| May rise and wash away their sin | 476 | 6 |
| May rise, no more by guilt opprest | 111 | 7 |
| May rise the wicked to consume | 298 | 2 |
| May self-constraining temperance | 966 | 5 |
| May serve me while I live below | 935 | 3 |
| May so peaceably advance | 826 | — |
| May speak their joys abroad | 12 | 1 |
| May strive to shut, but strive in vain | 492 | 4 |

| | Hymn | Verse |
|---|---|---|
| May taste the grace that found out me | 33 | 5 |
| May the fruits of thy salvation | 1008 | 2 |
| *May the grace of Christ our Saviour | 1006 | — |
| May they be found with God | 42 | 7 |
| May through the world be known | 581 | 2 |
| May thy glory meet our eyes | 975 | 4 |
| †May thy gospel's joyful sound | 975 | 5 |
| May thy presence | 1008 | 2 |
| May to thy great glory live | 430 | 3 |
| May view the final scene | 63 | 6 |
| May we ever | 1008 | 3 |
| May we feel thy presence near | 975 | 4 |
| †May we live in holiness | 753 | 10 |
| May we rejoice with thee | 692 | 5 |
| May we rest this night with thee | 975 | 3 |
| May we the worth of Sabbaths learn | 951 | 3 |
| May with my much-loved Master part | 188 | 4 |
| May work on from hour to hour | 882 | 6 |
| Meanest follower of the Lamb | 115 | 2 |
| Meanest of all thy creatures, me | 429 | 2 |
| Meanest vessel of thy grace | 430 | 2 |
| Meanly clothed in human nature | 748 | 4 |
| Me and mine persist to bless | 915 | 4 |
| Me, a sinner, pass not by | 112 | 2 |
| †Me, behold! thy mercy spares | 197 | 2 |
| Me, for Jesu's sake forgiven | 242 | 4 |
| Me for thine own this moment take | 375 | 5 |
| †Me for thine own thou lov'st to take | 227 | 7 |
| Me from his care | 851 | 3 |
| Me from the flames below | 931 | 6 |
| Me from the gospel hope shall move | 815 | 4 |
| Me from this evil world to free | 269 | 3 |
| Me he now delights to spare | 168 | 4 |
| †Me if thy grace vouchsafe to use | 429 | 2 |
| †Me in my blood thy love passed by | 206 | 2 |
| Me in verdant pastures feeds | 554 | 2 |
| †Me, me, who still in darkness sit | 129 | 5 |
| Me now a creature new | 402 | 2 |
| Me, of sinners chief, forgive | 116 | 3 |
| Me receive, thy favoured child | 242 | 4 |
| Me, the chief of sinners, spare | 168 | 1 |
| Me, the farthest from thy face | 116 | 3 |
| †Me, the vilest of the race | 116 | 3 |
| Me, the worst of rebels, me | 173 | 2 |
| Me thou dost every moment prove | 775 | 1 |
| Me thou hast made to glorify | 234 | 3 |
| Me, through mercy reconciled | 242 | 4 |
| Me thy bowels yearned to see | 191 | 3 |
| Me thy living member, flow | 193 | 5 |
| Me thy mercy ran to find | 191 | 3 |
| Me thy mercy's witness make | 173 | 3 |
| †Me to retrieve from Satan's hands | 269 | 3 |
| Me to save from endless woe | 809 | 2 |

| | Hymn | Verse |
|---|---|---|
| Me to thine image now restore | 229 | 4 |
| Me to thy Father's grace restore | 170 | 2 |
| Me to thyself, and let me prove | 169 | 4 |
| Me, weary of forbearing, see | 378 | 4 |
| Me, who life to none deny | 8 | 3 |
| Me, whom thou hast caused to trust | 336 | 2 |
| Me, with all my sins, I cast | 182 | 5 |
| Me with arms of love receive | 116 | 3 |
| †Me with that restless thirst inspire | 304 | 3 |
| Me with the chords of love | 188 | 4 |
| Meek and lowly let us be | 520 | 3 |
| Meek follower of the Undefiled | 896 | 5 |
| Meek Lamb! which was in thee | 270 | 2 |
| †Meek, simple followers of the Lamb | 16 | 2 |
| †Meeken my soul, thou heavenly Lamb | 304 | 2 |
| Meekly on my God reclined | 355 | 6 |
| †Meekly we our vow repeat | 914 | 5 |
| Meet again our heavenly friends | 53 | 4 |
| *Meet and right it is to praise | 238 | 1 |
| *Meet and right it is to praise | 1019 | 1 |
| *Meet and right it is to sing | 221 | 1 |
| Meet at the marriage of the Lamb | 510 | 4 |
| Meet him in its haunts alone | 817 | 5 |
| Meet in his appointed ways | 521 | 1 |
| †Meet it is, and just, and right | 427 | 2 |
| Meet it is for us to give | 722 | 4 |
| Meet our happy brother there | 50 | 4 |
| Meet, through consecrated pain | 336 | 2 |
| Meet to appear before thy sight | 520 | 4 |
| Meets the God of Israel's hosts | 278 | 1 |
| Melt before the Judge's face | 936 | 2 |
| Melt down my will, and let it flow | 788 | 6 |
| Melt me into gracious tears | 173 | 5 |
| Melt my hardness into love | 27 | 3 |
| Melt our spirits down, and mould | 414 | 2 |
| Melt the cold with fire divine | 753 | 8 |
| Melt the rebels with thy blood | 463 | 4 |
| †Men die in darkness at your side | 857 | 4 |
| Men heed thee, love thee, praise thee not | 857 | 2 |
| †Men of worldly, low design | 508 | 4 |
| Men on rocks and mountains calling | 936 | 4 |
| Men shall see with fear and wonder | 595 | 5 |
| Men walk safely in the light | 882 | 5 |
| Men who, fixed to earth alone | 67 | 1 |
| Men with minds angelic vie | 653 | 3 |
| †Mercies multiplied each hour | 975 | 2 |
| Merciful Father! grant us this | 945 | 2 |
| †Merciful God, how shall we raise | 980 | 3 |
| †Merciful God, thyself proclaim | 249 | 5 |
| Mercy and free salvation buy | 4 | 1 |
| †Mercy and grace are thine alone | 435 | 2 |
| *Mercy and judgment will I sing | 609 | 1 |
| ⊥Mercy and peace your portion be | 539 | 9 |

| | Hymn | Verse |
|---|---|---|
| Mercy first and last be shown | 60 | 2 |
| Mercy for all in Jesu's blood | 440 | 1 |
| Mercy for all who know not God | 440 | 1 |
| Mercy, free, boundless mercy, cries | 189 | 3 |
| †Mercy he doth for thousands keep | 144 | 7 |
| †Mercy I ask to seal my peace | 125 | 3 |
| Mercy is above the skies | 110 | 3 |
| Mercy is all that's written there | 189 | 4 |
| Mercy is thy distinguished name | 249 | 5 |
| Mercy, mercy upon me | 164 | 1 |
| Mercy, mercy upon me | 164 | 2 |
| Mercy, mercy upon me | 164 | 3 |
| †Mercy o'er thy works presides | 245 | 2 |
| Mercy, O Lord! mercy we ask | 797 | 3 |
| Mercy shall thy soul deliver | 597 | 2 |
| Mercy still reserved for me | 168 | 1 |
| Mercy, that earth and heaven transcends | 440 | 1 |
| †Mercy then there is for me | 166 | 2 |
| Mercy, thou God of mercy, show | 133 | 5 |
| Mercy, thy own supreme delight | 364 | 3 |
| Mercy to my rescue flew | 335 | 2 |
| †Mercy who show shall mercy find | 304 | 4 |
| Mercy will not let him die | 914 | 10 |
| Mercy will not let him stay | 914 | 9 |
| Mercy with him remains | 625 | 5 |
| †Mercy, with love and endless grace | 239 | 7 |
| Mercy withholds thy lifted hand | 241 | 2 |
| Mercy's full power I then shall prove | 189 | 6 |
| Messenger from the most High | 676 | 1 |
| *Messiah, full of grace | 450 | 1 |
| *Messiah, joy of every heart | 648 | 1 |
| †Messiah on my throne shall sit | 629 | 9 |
| †Messiah, Prince of peace | 303 | 5 |
| *Messiah, Prince of peace | 447 | 1 |
| Messiah's praise let all repeat | 731 | 1 |
| Methinks he should not call in vain | 697 | 7 |
| Met in thy name, we look to thee | 486 | 1 |
| Midst all the rage of hell they stand | 868 | 3 |
| Midst busy multitudes alone | 325 | 3 |
| †Midst danger's blackest frown | 737 | 9 |
| Midst flaming worlds in these arrayed | 190 | 1 |
| Midst means and ministries of grace | 770 | 5 |
| Midst the banded powers of hell | 737 | 11 |
| Midst the snares of death we lie | 737 | 11 |
| Mid this sweet stillness while we bow | 961 | 3 |
| Might blameless in thy sight appear | 261 | 4 |
| Might body, soul, and spirit give | 375 | 4 |
| Might follow, and partake thy throne | 648 | 3 |
| Might from thy ways depart | 998 | 4 |
| Might his salvation see | 124 | 1 |
| †Might I in thy sight appear | 101 | 4 |
| Might like the Man of sorrows grieve | 330 | 4 |
| Might live to God alone | 415 | 1 |

| | Hymn | Verse |
|---|---|---|
| Might lose my life for thee | 362 | 1 |
| Might now begin to glow | 361 | 7 |
| Might now their brethren bring | 452 | 3 |
| Might proclaim how good thou art | 427 | 2 |
| †Might we now with pure desire | 179 | 3 |
| Might with an even flame aspire | 313 | 2 |
| Mightier bliss ordained to know | 58 | 3 |
| Mighty, and merciful, and just | 282 | 2 |
| Mighty God, ascended Lord | 710 | 5 |
| Mighty Lord, eternal King | 737 | 6 |
| Mighty Lord, in thine ascension | 720 | 5 |
| Mighty so as to prevail | 769 | 4 |
| †Mighty Spirit, dwell with me | 769 | 4 |
| Mighty their envious foes to move | 17 | 4 |
| †Mild he lays his glory by | 683 | 5 |
| †Millions more thou ready art | 245 | 4 |
| Millions of transgressors poor | 245 | 3 |
| Mindful of his mercies past | 278 | 3 |
| Mindful of his word of grace | 605 | 3 |
| †Mindful of thy chosen race | 937 | 3 |
| Mindful of thy place above | 529 | 2 |
| Mine age as nought with thee | 565 | 2 |
| Mine, and yours, whoe'er believe | 197 | 3 |
| Mine eyes their vigils keep | 943 | 4 |
| Mine eyes with tears kept waking | 587 | 1 |
| Mine heart of unbelief convince | 97 | 5 |
| *Mine hour appointed is at hand | 923 | 1 |
| Mine inmost soul expose to view | 97 | 1 |
| Mine only is the present hour | 835 | 1 |
| †Mine own and not another's eyes | 928 | 4 |
| Mine the life won, and thine the life laid down | 794 | 7 |
| Mine thou art! while thus I say | 24 | 2 |
| †Mine utter helplessness I feel | 25 | 5 |
| Mingled with his blood, they cry | 8 | 4 |
| Minister of wrath divine | 693 | 1 |
| †Misers, for you his life he paid | 36 | 2 |
| Misery we exchange for bliss | 207 | 1 |
| Mistakes and lesser faults pass by | 470 | 4 |
| Mistrustful of ourselves, afraid | 469 | 1 |
| Mixed with those beyond the sky | 260 | 1 |
| †Mollify our harsher will | 538 | 2 |
| Money ye need not bring, nor price | 4 | 3 |
| Monstrous whales, and seas profound | 639 | 4 |
| Monuments of Jesu's grace | 522 | 1 |
| More and more in Jesus live | 518 | 3 |
| More and more in thee rejoice | 13 | 3 |
| More and more it spreads and grows | 218 | 2 |
| †More and more let love abound | 480 | 3 |
| More and more of thee receive | 13 | 8 |
| More and more thyself display | 963 | 3 |
| More and more thyself reveal | 188 | 5 |
| More blessings than their father lost | 585 | 11 |
| More confirms the faithful word | 60 | 3 |

| | Hymn | Verse |
|---|---|---|
| †More dear than life itself, thy love | 437 | 4 |
| †More favoured than the saints of old | 284 | 5 |
| More firmly to believe | 696 | 3 |
| More full of grace than I of sin | 186 | 2 |
| More gifts we shall receive | 874 | 2 |
| †More hard than marble is my heart | 373 | 6 |
| More his Saviour glorify | 914 | 10 |
| †More of thy life, and more, I have | 347 | 3 |
| More sensibly within me live | 874 | 5 |
| More shouldst thou have, if I had more | 431 | 1 |
| More than all in thee I find | 143 | 3 |
| More than all we pant to give | 727 | 6 |
| More than conquered in our stead | 757 | 1 |
| More than conqueror now I am | 274 | 4 |
| †More than conquerors at last | 76 | 3 |
| More than conquerors in his love | 728 | 6 |
| More than conquerors ye shall prove | 847 | 4 |
| More than he hath done for you | 8 | 1 |
| More than I can request | 303 | 2 |
| More than now our hearts conceive | 238 | 2 |
| †More than outward wonder show | 873 | 2 |
| More than tongue can e'er express | 941 | 1 |
| More than we could know, and live | 238 | 2 |
| More there are with us than them | 728 | 4 |
| More to be feared than they | 657 | 6 |
| Morning and night present its vows | 997 | 3 |
| Morning light and evening balm | 817 | 5 |
| Mortals cry, "A man is dead" | 51 | 3 |
| Mortals, give thanks, and sing | 729 | 1 |
| †Moses thy backward parts might view | 284 | 4 |
| Moses thy forerunner came | 693 | 1 |
| Most amidst its Sabbath calm | 817 | 5 |
| Most awful thou art seen | 602 | 1 |
| †Most awful truth! and is it so | 935 | 2 |
| Most beautiful, most bright | 958 | 1 |
| †Most blessed is the man whose hope | 566 | 4 |
| Most chiefly show in thy delight | 821 | — |
| Most graciously forgiven | 229 | 5 |
| Most holy God, come in | 818 | 4 |
| Most pitiful Spirit of grace | 165 | 4 |
| Most unholy, most unclean | 116 | 3 |
| Most vigorous when the body dies | 376 | 1 |
| †Mother thou of every nation | 595 | 6 |
| Motion, virtue, strength, to me | 193 | 5 |
| Mould as thou wilt thy passive clay | 429 | 4 |
| †Mountains, alas! on mountains rise | 475 | 2 |
| Mountains, and stars, and skies | 536 | 6 |
| Mount, their transports to improve | 921 | 5 |
| Mount to Christ, my glorious Head | 192 | 1 |
| Mounting high on wings of love | 921 | 3 |
| Mourn for God in every groan | 287 | 3 |
| †Move, and actuate, and guide | 518 | 5 |
| Move and spread throughout my soul | 390 | 4 |

| | Hymn | Verse |
|---|---|---|
| Move on the waters' face | 870 | 3 |
| Move round this dark terrestial ball | 552 | 5 |
| Much more to us, his children | 988 | 2 |
| Much of love I ought to know | 188 | 6 |
| Multiplied grace and blessings gain | 874 | 2 |
| Multiplied our wandering thought | 98 | 1 |
| Murmur not at his delay | 142 | 1 |
| Music for the King of kings | 538 | 2 |
| Must all my efforts prove | 92 | 6 |
| Must all the world that harvest know | 935 | 2 |
| Must be suddenly restored | 60 | 3 |
| Must bow to thy command | 733 | 1 |
| Must come at his command to heaven | 43 | 4 |
| Must enter by this door | 920 | 3 |
| Must I not for ever die | 149 | 2 |
| Must seek him, Lord, by thee | 671 | 1 |
| Must still in holiness excel | 600 | 4 |
| Must surely lurk within | 152 | 2 |
| Must take the path thy word hath showed | 127 | 4 |
| Must then my portion be | 43 | 2 |
| Mustering their unseen array | 829 | 2 |
| Mutual love the token be | 522 | 4 |
| My aching breast inspire | 102 | 2 |
| My acts of faith and love repeat | 327 | 4 |
| My Advocate at God's right hand | 550 | 2 |
| My Advocate prove | 160 | 5 |
| My Advocate see | 707 | 7 |
| My Advocate with God | 669 | 1 |
| My Æthiop-soul shall change her skin | 159 | 2 |
| My all in earth and heaven | 167 | 3 |
| My all is sin and misery | 175 | 3 |
| My all of happiness below | 283 | 1 |
| My all thy property I own | 432 | 1 |
| My all to my Redeemer give | 335 | 4 |
| My author and my end | 403 | 7 |
| My base ingratitude I feel | 178 | 1 |
| My beauty are, my glorious dress | 190 | 1 |
| My beloved, arise | 491 | 1 |
| My bleeding Sacrifice expired | 330 | 3 |
| My blooming hopes cut off I see | 803 | 3 |
| My boast, and confidence, and might | 379 | 4 |
| My body in the tomb | 104 | 2 |
| My body, spirit, soul | 112 | 7 |
| My body with my charge lay down | 45 | 3 |
| My bones till that sweet day | 931 | 2 |
| My bones were wasted all day long | 561 | 3 |
| My bounding heart shall own thy sway | 214 | 3 |
| *My brethren beloved, Your calling ye see | 212 | 1 |
| My burden cast upon the Lord | 833 | 2 |
| My burden of guilt to remove | 165 | 1 |
| My business this, my only care | 99 | 5 |
| My calling to fulfil | 318 | 1 |
| My Captain leads me forth | 675 | 9 |

| | Hymn | Verse |
|---|---|---|
| My chains fell off, my heart was free | 201 | 4 |
| My cheerful soul I raise | 229 | 1 |
| My chief and sole desire | 834 | 1 |
| My child-like heart to thee | 307 | 5 |
| My children's sins remove | 894 | 1 |
| My chosen 'midst ten thousand, thou | 133 | 4 |
| My comfort thou wilt give me back | 180 | 7 |
| My companion and friend | 499 | 1 |
| My company before is gone | 140 | 1 |
| My comrades through the wilderness | 333 | 1 |
| My confidence is all in thee | 282 | 3 |
| My Conqueror and my King | 675 | 8 |
| My consecrated heart | 323 | 3 |
| My consecrated heart inspire | 351 | 8 |
| My consent through grace I give | 910 | 6 |
| My constant need of watchful prayer | 310 | 1 |
| My Councillor thou art | 436 | 2 |
| My covetous and vain desires | 332 | 2 |
| My cup with blessings overflows | 555 | 4 |
| My daily labour to pursue | 324 | 1 |
| My daily thanks employ | 657 | 8 |
| My dawning is begun | 213 | 2 |
| My days and nights alternate tell | 838 | 1 |
| My days are his due | 231 | 12 |
| †My days are shorter than a span | 564 | 2 |
| My days, how brief their date | 565 | 1 |
| My days of praise shall ne'er be past | 224 | 1 |
| My days of praise shall ne'er be past | 224 | 4 |
| My dear Redeemer know | 153 | 1 |
| My delegated power | 471 | 3 |
| My depth of desperate wickedness | 561 | 4 |
| My drooping soul exults to hear | 397 | 1 |
| My dust again, even mine | 931 | 1 |
| My dust lies numbered in his hand | 928 | 1 |
| My dwelling place shall be | 556 | 5 |
| My dwelling shall be free | 609 | 4 |
| My dying bed—for thou hast died | 849 | 5 |
| †My dying Saviour, and my God | 346 | 2 |
| My earnest suit present, and gain | 100 | 3 |
| †My earth thou waterest from on high | 405 | 7 |
| My eternal Life is near | 554 | 4 |
| My everlasting Friend | 282 | 5 |
| My everlasting rest | 147 | 6 |
| My everlasting rest from sin | 379 | 2 |
| My every act, word, thought, be love | 373 | 2 |
| My every care and want | 303 | 2 |
| My every pulse shall beat for him | 638 | 2 |
| My every sacred moment spend | 433 | 4 |
| †My every weak, though good design | 429 | 3 |
| My exceeding great Reward | 187 | 4 |
| My exceeding great Reward | 354 | 5 |
| My eyes from tears of dark despair | 246 | 1 |
| †My eyes no longer drowned in tears | 614 | 7 |

| | Hymn | Verse |
|---|---|---|
| My eyes on his perfections gaze | 246 | 2 |
| My failing heart to save | 635 | 2 |
| My faint desires receive | 323 | 1 |
| My fair inheritance thou art | 548 | 2 |
| My fainting soul in silence owns | 25 | 3 |
| My fainting soul on Christ is stayed | 917 | 3 |
| My faith desires to see | 635 | 3 |
| My faith hath fixed its eye | 281 | 3 |
| My faith shall make me whole | 136 | 9 |
| †My faith would lay her hand | 703 | 3 |
| My faith's integrity maintain | 364 | 5 |
| My faithlessness again I mourn | 909 | 2 |
| My faithfulness to prove | 147 | 5 |
| My fallen soul renew | 410 | 1 |
| My fallen spirit's hope | 169 | 1 |
| My fallen spirit to restore | 186 | 3 |
| My Father and my Friend | 650 | 4 |
| †"My Father God!" that gracious sound | 764 | 2 |
| My Father knows, let that suffice | 833 | 4 |
| †My Father knows the things I need | 833 | 4 |
| My Father must forgive | 184 | 4 |
| *My Father, my God, I long for thy love | 200 | 1 |
| My Father pacified | 124 | 2 |
| My Father, still I strive to say | 841 | 4 |
| My Father, thee I sing | 191 | 1 |
| My Father's goodness see | 334 | — |
| My Father's hand prepares the cup | 832 | 2 |
| †My Father's house on high | 944 | 3 |
| My faults are not concealed from thee | 177 | 1 |
| My fearful doom to meet | 80 | 3 |
| †My feeble heart's extreme desire | 919 | 2 |
| My feeble mind sustain | 296 | 2 |
| My feeble mind transform | 323 | 3 |
| My feeble, sin-sick mind | 188 | 5 |
| My feeble voice I cannot raise | 123 | 1 |
| My feet from falling free | 614 | 7 |
| My feet from falling into hell | 246 | 1 |
| My feet in righteous ways | 635 | 3 |
| My feet were sinking to the grave | 559 | 1 |
| My fellow-prisoners now | 345 | 5 |
| My fellow-soldiers, fight | 277 | 3 |
| My flesh exults in hope | 548 | 5 |
| My flesh in tranquil hope shall rest | 549 | 6 |
| My flesh shall be thy care | 584 | 6 |
| †My flesh, which cries, "It cannot be" | 815 | 6 |
| My fluctuating heart | 809 | 4 |
| My foes, and healed my wounded mind | 210 | 4 |
| My foes dost control, And quiet their strife | 200 | 5 |
| My foes, I know, shall fear and fly | 575 | 3 |
| My foes with cordial love embrace | 830 | 1 |
| My fond pursuits I all give o'er | 332 | 3 |
| My foolish heart is blind | 109 | 3 |
| My foolishness I mourn | 182 | 5 |

| | Hymn | Verse |
|---|---|---|
| My form without the power | 93 | 7 |
| My fortress and my tower | 305 | 4 |
| My frailties there should end | 942 | 5 |
| My Friend and Advocate appears | 726 | 2 |
| My Friend and Advocate with God | 145 | 5 |
| My Friend and Advocate with God | 815 | 2 |
| My Friend and Advocate with thee | 148 | 1 |
| My friend before the throne of love | 100 | 1 |
| My friends, my all resign | 137 | 9 |
| My friends, my beloved, and hasten away | 495 | 1 |
| My full heart it replies | 231 | 9 |
| My fulness of corruption show | 100 | 3 |
| My fulness of rapture I find | 70 | 2 |
| My glory, and my God | 838 | 4 |
| My glory is to sing thy praise | 576 | 1 |
| My glory swallowed up in shame | 127 | 6 |
| *My God, and Father! while I stray | 841 | 1 |
| †My God and my Lord! Thy call I obey | 8 | 4 |
| My God, be thou my guide | 543 | 6 |
| My God, forbid the blasphemy | 547 | 5 |
| My God for ever pacified | 869 | 6 |
| My God for me resigned his breath | 378 | 2 |
| My God! here find, here grant thy rest | 770 | 5 |
| †My God, how excellent thy grace | 563 | 4 |
| *My God, I am thine | 205 | 1 |
| My God, I bow before thy throne | 564 | 4 |
| *My God! I know, I feel thee mine | 361 | 1 |
| My God I will proclaim | 614 | 13 |
| *My God, if I may call thee mine | 290 | 1 |
| My God incarnated for me | 686 | 4 |
| My God in Christ thou art | 368 | 3 |
| †My God, in Jesus pacified | 123 | 6 |
| †My God is my guide; Thy mercies abound | 200 | 4 |
| †My God is reconciled | 202 | 5 |
| *My God, my God, to thee I cry | 184 | 1 |
| My God, my heavenly King | 637 | 1 |
| My God, my Saviour, and my Spouse | 290 | 7 |
| My God, my Saviour, come away | 388 | 7 |
| My God, that suffers there | 701 | 3 |
| *My God, the spring of all my joys | 213 | 1 |
| My God through all eternity | 916 | 6 |
| My God, thyself declare | 123 | 6 |
| My God, to thee I leave the rest | 841 | 5 |
| My God, who dies for me, for me | 708 | 3 |
| †My God will add the rest | 834 | 2 |
| My God will think on me | 558 | 4 |
| My God, with thee, To see thy face | 942 | Cho. |
| My good cannot to thee extend | 548 | 1 |
| My good did first from thee descend | 548 | 1 |
| My gospel hope, my calling's prize | 379 | 4 |
| My grace is free for all | 164 | 5 |
| *My gracious, loving Lord | 93 | 1 |
| †My gracious Master and my God | 1 | 2 |

| MY GRATEFUL | MY HOPE | |
|---|---:|---:|
| | HYMN | VERSE |
| My grateful powers shall sound thy praise . | 658 | 1 |
| My grave shall be unbound | 931 | 3 |
| My great Deliverer, and my God | 353 | 3 |
| My great Deliverer thou | 288 | 1 |
| My great Preserver I proclaim | 366 | 2 |
| My great Redeemer's praise | 1 | 1 |
| My great Redeemer's throne | 343 | 2 |
| My griefs expire, my troubles cease | 227 | 6 |
| My guard, the presence of my Lord | 577 | 4 |
| My guilty conscience seeks | 675 | 7 |
| †My hairs in number they surpass | 566 | 8 |
| My hands are but engaged below | 322 | 3 |
| My hands, my head, my heart | 346 | 3 |
| My happy life shall glide away | 437 | 5 |
| My happy soul to thee | 340 | 3 |
| My head thou dost with oil anoint | 556 | 4 |
| My heart and soul are there | 947 | 3 |
| My heart and tongue employ | 562 | 1 |
| My heart and tongue shall still employ | 437 | 4 |
| *My heart and voice I raise | 731 | 1 |
| My heart ever fainting He only can cheer | 200 | 1 |
| My heart from every sin release | 388 | 6 |
| *My heart is fixed, O God my heart | 576 | 1 |
| *My heart is full of Christ and longs | 568 | 1 |
| My heart is pained nor can it be | 344 | 1 |
| My heart is still with thee | 322 | 3 |
| My heart no longer gives the lie | 357 | 4 |
| My heart shall ne'er mistrust thy might | 626 | 4 |
| My heart shall then confess | 883 | 4 |
| †My heart shall triumph in the Lord | 599 | 3 |
| My heart, that lowly waits thy call | 344 | 8 |
| †My heart, thou know'st, can never rest | 343 | 6 |
| †My heart, thy meanest house, I keep | 828 | 2 |
| My heart was full of sin | 93 | 3 |
| †My heart, which now to thee I raise | 395 | 7 |
| My heart with grief is breaking | 587 | 1 |
| My heart with purity | 410 | 2 |
| My heart would leap for joy, and say | 558 | 3 |
| My heart would now receive thee, Lord | 406 | 6 |
| My heart would then with love o'erflow | 378 | 3 |
| My heart's desire fulfil | 164 | 5 |
| My heart's extreme desire | 125 | 2 |
| My heaven of heavens in thee | 70 | 2 |
| My heaven on earth, my heaven above | 354 | 5 |
| My help and refuge from my foes | 209 | 1 |
| My help and refuge in distress | 305 | 4 |
| My help is all laid up above | 141 | 5 |
| My help, my all, in thee | 109 | 1 |
| My helper is for ever near | 616 | 2 |
| My helpless soul defend | 820 | 4 |
| My highest heaven in Jesu's love | 284 | 6 |
| My home whene'er I die | 942 | 6 |
| My hope in a Saviour unknown | 777 | 2 |

| | Hymn | Verse |
|---|---|---|
| My hope is all centred in thee | 371 | 1 |
| My hope is full (O glorious hope) | 405 | 4 |
| My hope is in thy Name | 565 | 4 |
| My Hope, my heavenly treasure, now | 137 | 12 |
| My hopes of happiness below | 332 | 2 |
| My horn, and rock, and buckler be | 305 | 4 |
| †My humbled soul, when thou art near | 184 | 10 |
| My humble praise and love | 614 | 1 |
| My humble sacrifice of praise | 365 | 1 |
| My hundred-fold reward | 304 | 2 |
| My idols all be cast aside | 391 | 4 |
| My immortality | 193 | 2 |
| My inbred malady remove | 363 | 4 |
| My inbred sin away | 383 | 2 |
| My Jesus and him crucified | 439 | 1 |
| My Jesus, quickly come | 144 | 7 |
| †My Jesus to know | 205 | 4 |
| My Jesus's love The battle shall win | 273 | 6 |
| My joy, my glory, and my crown' | 379 | 4 |
| My joy, my heaven on earth, be this | 147 | 4 |
| My joy, my treasure, and my crown | 373 | 2 |
| My joy, the sense of pardoning love | 577 | 4 |
| My joy thy sayings to repeat | 328 | 1 |
| My joy to endure and do thy will | 196 | 2 |
| My Judge's anger dare | 103 | 2 |
| My kind, long-suffering Lord | 172 | 3 |
| My King and my Saviour Shall make me anew | 198 | 5 |
| †My knowledge of that life is small | 920 | 6 |
| "My leanness, O my leanness!" cry | 392 | 3 |
| My life and death attend | 843 | 3 |
| My life and soul, my heart and flesh | 903 | 3 |
| My life be all with thine the same | 772 | 6 |
| My life I employ | 231 | 11 |
| My life in death, my heaven in hell | 209 | 4 |
| My life in premature decay | 841 | 4 |
| †My life is but a span | 565 | 2 |
| My life, my all, for them to give | 364 | 4 |
| †My life, my blood, I here present | 279 | 9 |
| My life, my every breath, be prayer | 99 | 5 |
| My life, my only heaven thou art | 100 | 4 |
| †My Life, my Portion thou | 137 | 12 |
| My life, or goods, or fame | 432 | 2 |
| *My life's a shade, my days | 931 | 1 |
| My life's with thee on high | 931 | 4 |
| My light and full salvation be | 686 | 4 |
| My light in Satan's darkest hour | 209 | 4 |
| My light, my life, my God, is come | 919 | 3 |
| My Light, my Life, my Lord, my all | 131 | 3 |
| My lips shall bless thy name | 675 | 4 |
| †My lips shall dwell upon thy praise | 637 | 11 |
| My lips were all unclean | 93 | 3 |
| †My lips with shame my sins confess | 574 | 2 |
| My little all to give | 137 | 7 |

| | Hymn | Verse |
|---|---|---|
| My longing eyes, and restless heart | 306 | 1 |
| My longing heart implores thy grace | 338 | 1 |
| My longing heart is all on fire | 415 | 3 |
| My longing heart vouchsafe to make | 216 | 8 |
| My longing soul and thee | 169 | 5 |
| My Lord and God from heaven he came | 269 | 3 |
| †My Lord and God I then could see | 365 | 4 |
| †My Lord his angels shall | 931 | 3 |
| My Lord his death shall save | 931 | 8 |
| †My Lord in my behalf appears | 293 | 6 |
| My Lord is life, he'll raise | 931 | 1 |
| My Lord, lay hold on thee | 781 | •5 |
| My Lord, my Life, my Way, my End | 679 | 4 |
| My Lord, my Love is crucified | 26 | 6 |
| My Lord, my Love is crucified | 28 | Cho. |
| My Lord, remember me | 64 | 8 |
| My love entire on thee | 785 | 3 |
| My Love is crucified | 27 | 2 |
| †My loving God, the hindrance show | 775 | 3 |
| My loving God to praise | 216 | 2 |
| My lowly Master's steps pursue | 351 | 4 |
| My manners and my burdens borne | 916 | 1 |
| My merciful High-priest | 947 | 3 |
| My merit is destruction | 943 | 11 |
| †My message as from God receive | 2 | 6 |
| My midnight into day | 109 | 3 |
| †My mind, by thy all-quickening power | 785 | 3 |
| My mind to seek her peace in thee | 344 | 3 |
| My misery and sin declare | 140 | 2 |
| My misery mark, attend my prayer | 625 | 1 |
| My mountain-sins depart | 123 | 2 |
| My mountain stands for ever sure | 559 | 3 |
| My mouth as in the dust I hide | 369 | 6 |
| My mouth I in the dust may lay | 126 | 6 |
| My mouth was stopped, and shame | 93 | 7 |
| My much-offended God | 103 | 1 |
| †My name be on the children? no | 894 | 2 |
| My name inscribed in heaven | 96 | 1 |
| My name is graven on his hands | 726 | 2 |
| My name is written on his hands | 202 | 1 |
| My nature every moment waits | 310 | 3 |
| †My nature I obeyed | 93 | 4 |
| My never-failing treasury, filled | 679 | 3 |
| My offerings all be offered through | 323 | 2 |
| My offspring to be blessed | 893 | 1 |
| †My old affections mortify | 362 | 3 |
| My old companions say | 619 | 1 |
| †My one desire be this | 137 | 11 |
| My only care, delight, and bliss | 147 | 4 |
| My only refuge is thy grace | 574 | 4 |
| My own besetting sin | 278 | 2 |
| My own desires pursued | 93 | 4 |
| My own in all things to resign | 832 | 3 |

| | Hymn | Verse |
|---|---|---|
| My own insidious sin | 310 | 3 |
| My own obduracy | 153 | 1 |
| My own unconquerable sin | 361 | 5 |
| †My pardon I claim | 707 | 6 |
| My pardoning Lord embrace | 669 | 1 |
| My pattern, and my guide | 675 | 5 |
| My peace, and bid me sin no more! | 180 | 5 |
| My peace, my glory, and my joy | 437 | 4 |
| †My peace, my life, my comfort thou | 374 | 4 |
| †My peaceful grave shall keep | 931 | 2 |
| My plague is gone, my heart is free | 396 | 5 |
| My poor desponding soul to cheer | 130 | 2 |
| My poor expiring soul | 34 | 5 |
| My Portion here below | 354 | 5 |
| My portion in the land of life | 634 | 3 |
| My portion thou, my treasure art | 291 | 2 |
| My powerful sighs thou canst not bear | 144 | 2 |
| †My prayer hath power with God; the grace | 141 | 3 |
| My prayer omnipotent | 144 | 2 |
| My precious pearl, my present heaven | 379 | 5 |
| My present help in time of need | 288 | 1 |
| My present Saviour thou! | 417 | 5 |
| My preserver from sin | 231 | 4 |
| My pride and passion slay | 409 | 3 |
| My promised pardon seal | 783 | 1 |
| My promises empty as air | 911 | 2 |
| My promises for all are free | 4 | 8 |
| My Prophet, Priest, and King | 679 | 4 |
| My public walks, my private ways | 632 | 2 |
| My Ransom and my Peace | 145 | 5 |
| My ransom he was | 707 | 7 |
| My raptured song shall ever be | 795 | 5 |
| My ready tongue makes haste to sing | 568 | 1 |
| My Redeemer and King | 231 | 2 |
| †My remnant of days | 231 | 12 |
| My rest a stone | 848 | 2 |
| My rest in toil, my ease in pain | 209 | 3 |
| My richest gain I count but loss | 700 | 1 |
| My rich inheritance possess | 304 | 2 |
| My rising and my rest | 632 | 2 |
| My rising soul surveys | 657 | 1 |
| My Sabbath scenes be o'er | 799 | 3 |
| †My Sabbath suns may all have set | 799 | 3 |
| My sad afflicted state | 112 | 1 |
| My saving grace for all is free | 31 | 4 |
| My Saviour, and my all | 786 | 5 |
| My Saviour, and my God | 305 | 4 |
| My Saviour, and my Head | 360 | 1 |
| My Saviour, and my Prince above | 170 | 3 |
| My Saviour and salvation too | 616 | 3 |
| My Saviour, and the world's to praise | 378 | 1 |
| My Saviour bids me come | 152 | 1 |
| My Saviour died for all | 215 | 1 |

| | Hymn | Verse |
|---|---|---|
| My Saviour doth not yet appear | 803 | 1 |
| My Saviour gasped "forgive!" | 106 | 7 |
| My Saviour hangs on yonder tree | 706 | 6 |
| †My Saviour how shall I proclaim | 23 | 6 |
| My Saviour in distresses past | 335 | 1 |
| My Saviour marks the tears I shed | 849 | 4 |
| †My Saviour thou, not yet revealed | 130 | 4 |
| †My Saviour, thou thy love to me | 373 | 5 |
| My Saviour to the utmost, thou | 365 | 6 |
| My Saviour to the utmost thou | 547 | 7 |
| My Saviour, who hath died for me | 365 | 4 |
| My Saviour's mean, but constant home | 783 | 2 |
| My selfish ends and creature-loves | 93 | 4 |
| My senses' and my passions' food | 332 | 2 |
| My shadow from the sun | 292 | 4 |
| My shame I will no longer hide | 561 | 4 |
| *My Shepherd will supply my need | 555 | 1 |
| My shield, and hiding-place | 679 | 3 |
| My Shield and Tower | 800 | 2 |
| My simple, upright heart prepare | 270 | 1 |
| My sinking footsteps stay | 169 | 2 |
| My sins and troubles end | 125 | 5 |
| My sins are numberless, I know | 923 | 2 |
| My sins are swallowed up in thee | 189 | 3 |
| My sins are thronging round me | 923 | 2 |
| My sins have caused thee, Lord, to bleed | 23 | 3 |
| My sins I will at large confess | 561 | 4 |
| My sins o'erturn, o'erturn, o'erturn | 138 | 2 |
| My sin shall all depart | 406 | 5 |
| †My sin's incurable disease | 395 | 4 |
| My smile beneath the tyrant's frown | 209 | 3 |
| My sole concern, my single care | 44 | 2 |
| †My solemn engagements are vain | 911 | 2 |
| My song and city is | 942 | 6 |
| My song shall wake with opening light | 658 | 1 |
| My son, give me thy heart | 775 | 1 |
| My Son is in my servant's prayer | 298 | 2 |
| My soul adores | 855 | 1 |
| †My soul and all its powers | 229 | 4 |
| My soul and flesh, O Lord of might | 210 | 5 |
| My soul, and let me put on thee | 431 | 4 |
| My soul and spirit part | 105 | 1 |
| My soul a sudden calm shall feel | 272 | 6 |
| My soul away from thee | 296 | 1 |
| My soul before thy throne | 820 | 5 |
| †My soul breaks out in strong desire | 415 | 3 |
| My soul delights to dwell | 549 | 3 |
| My soul disdains to fear | 359 | 3 |
| My soul, disdain to fear | 558 | 6 |
| †My soul draws nigh and cleaves to thee | 437 | 9 |
| My soul encompassed round | 614 | 3 |
| †My soul, escaped the fowler's net | 836 | 6 |
| My soul for all assaults, and arm | 310 | 4 |

| | Hymn | Verse |
|---|---|---|
| My soul for all thy fulness cries | 304 | 3 |
| My soul for all thy presence cries | 284 | 1 |
| My soul for ever fill | 372 | — |
| My soul for that great day | 984 | 2 |
| My soul forgets the heavenly prize | 788 | 3 |
| My soul from endless death | 784 | 2 |
| My soul, from out the body torn | 230 | 4 |
| My soul hath called thee mine | 548 | 1 |
| †My soul he doth restore again | 556 | 2 |
| My soul hell, earth, and sin defies | 820 | 6 |
| My soul in confidence shall rise | 139 | 6 |
| My soul in Jesu's wounded side | 283 | 3 |
| *My soul, inspired with sacred love | 638 | 1 |
| My soul into his hands received | 810 | — |
| My soul into thy hands I give | 281 | 5 |
| My soul is all an aching void | 109 | 5 |
| My soul is lightened of its load | 68 | 2 |
| My soul is more than conqueror | 230 | 3 |
| My soul its life and succour brings | 141 | 5 |
| †My soul lies humbled in the dust | 574 | 11 |
| †My soul looks back to see | 703 | 4 |
| †My soul obeys the almighty's call | 786 | 3 |
| My soul of evil near | 305 | 3 |
| My soul O lighten and inflame | 974 | 9 |
| My soul on thee depends | 435 | 1 |
| †My soul on thee, O Lord, relies | 820 | 6 |
| My soul on thy word Of promise I stay | 3 | 4 |
| My soul outflies the angel-choir | 590 | 1 |
| *My soul, repeat his praise | 610 | 6 |
| My soul shall in all things obey | 911 | 4 |
| My soul shall live for God alone | 246 | 2 |
| My soul shall quit the mournful vale | 948 | 1 |
| My soul shall then, like thine | 340 | 1 |
| My soul shall then outstrip the wind | 803 | 4 |
| My soul still pants for thee | 939 | 6 |
| My soul the glorious sight to bear | 283 | 4 |
| My soul the second death defies | 69 | 2 |
| My soul the Spirit feels | 618 | 1 |
| *My soul, through my Redeemer's care | 246 | 1 |
| My soul to love its God again | 122 | 5 |
| My soul to perfect rest | 303 | 2 |
| My soul to swallow up | 172 | 1 |
| My soul to thee alone | 305 | 5 |
| My soul to thee convert | 358 | 5 |
| My soul to thy continual care | 282 | 5 |
| My soul upon thy love I cast | 288 | 4 |
| †My soul, when I shake off this dust | 974 | 6 |
| †My soul, while still to him it flies | 625 | 4 |
| My soul with heavenly thoughts supply | 974 | 5 |
| My soul, with joy and wonder see | 675 | 2 |
| My soul with saints above | 409 | 4 |
| †My soul with thy whole armour arm | 309 | 2 |
| My soul without it dies | 784 | 4 |

| | HYMN | VERSE |
|---|---|---|
| †My soul would leave this heavy clay | 213 | 4 |
| My soul would scorn to fear | 271 | 2 |
| My soul's infirmity sustain | 916 | 3 |
| My soul's new creation, A life from the dead | 198 | 4 |
| My spirit after God renew | 303 | 4 |
| My spirit, calm and undismayed | 919 | 3 |
| My spirit be alarmed | 93 | 6 |
| My spirit hide with saints above | 104 | 2 |
| My spirit in holiness raise | 165 | 4 |
| †My spirit, Lord, alarm | 311 | 2 |
| My spirit make thy radiant shrine | 686 | 4 |
| My spirit meek, my will resigned | 366 | 1 |
| *My spirit on thy care | 560 | 1 |
| My spirit seeks thee fain | 943 | 7 |
| My spirit shall rejoice | 549 | 6 |
| My spirit shall resume the theme | 638 | 2 |
| My spirit, soul, and flesh receive | 431 | 1 |
| My spirit, soul, and flesh restore | 171 | 4 |
| My spirit to Calvary bear | 228 | 2 |
| My spirit to thyself unite | 550 | 3 |
| My spirit's every wound | 112 | 3 |
| †My steadfast soul, from falling free | 361 | 11 |
| My stiff-necked will obey | 136 | 4 |
| My strength and health, my shield and sun | 379 | 4 |
| My strength consumed with pining grief | 561 | 3 |
| My strength proportion to my day | 339 | 6 |
| My strict observer see | 307 | 5 |
| My strict observer see | 550 | 1 |
| My struggling spirit free | 110 | 5 |
| †My struggling will by grace control | 697 | 9 |
| My stubborn unbelief remove | 861 | 3 |
| My succour and salvation, Lord | 301 | 6 |
| *My sufferings all to thee are known | 157 | 1 |
| My suffering strength may prove | 336 | 1 |
| My sure, unerring light | 436 | 1 |
| †My table thou hast furnished | 556 | 4 |
| †My talents, gifts, and graces, Lord | 433 | 4 |
| My Teacher saith, for ever nigh | 561 | 9 |
| My thirst for creature happiness | 180 | 1 |
| My thirsty soul doth pine | 567 | 2 |
| †My thoughts lie open to thee, Lord | 632 | 3 |
| My thoughts, nor soar too high | 627 | 2 |
| My tomb, my nature, white | 93 | 5 |
| My total misery reveal | 99 | 5 |
| My tower of refuge art | 549 | 1 |
| My treasure, and my all thou art | 374 | 4 |
| My treasure and my heart are there | 68 | 7 |
| My tree of life, my paradise | 379 | 4 |
| My trembling soul at my last end | 923 | 1 |
| †My trespass was grown up to heaven | 216 | 5 |
| My true and living Way | 187 | 4 |
| My trust is in thy bleeding Son | 917 | 3 |
| †My trust is in thy gracious power | 547 | 6 |

| | Hymn | Verse |
|---|---|---|
| My tuneful voice I'll raise | 731 | 8 |
| My utter helplessness I feel | 916 | 4 |
| My utter helplessness reveal | 313 | 1 |
| My unbelief and troubles end | 150 | 5 |
| My unfettered soul to thee | 287 | 4 |
| My unopposing heart | 783 | 2 |
| †My vehement soul cries out opprest | 416 | 4 |
| My vile affections crucify | 344 | 5 |
| My vile affections crucify | 347 | 1 |
| My voice I cannot raise | 135 | 6 |
| My vows, I shall break them again | 911 | 2 |
| †My vows I will to his great name | 614 | 10 |
| My wandering soul among | 675 | 6 |
| My wandering to and fro | 137 | 2 |
| My want of living faith I feel | 148 | 2 |
| †My want of thankfulness and love | 153 | 3 |
| My way pursue | 800 | 5 |
| My weak distempered soul | 136 | 2 |
| My weakness bends beneath the weight | 240 | 1 |
| My weakness to hide | 160 | 5 |
| My wealth, my friends, my ease | 844 | 3 |
| My wearied eyelids gently steep | 973 | 2 |
| My weary, longing eyes | 784 | 4 |
| My well-instructed soul | 308 | 3 |
| My whole desire on thee, O Lord | 437 | 3 |
| My whole heart is sick of sin | 109 | 2 |
| My whole of sin remove | 270 | 1 |
| †My will be swallowed up in thee | 851 | 7 |
| My will perverse, my passions blind | 100 | 2 |
| My willing heart I bow | 783 | 1 |
| †My willing soul would stay | 956 | 4 |
| My wisdom, and my all | 837 | 3 |
| †My Wisdom and my guide | 436 | 2 |
| My words believingly receive | 4 | 9 |
| My work he then shall own | 321 | 4 |
| My works I count but dust | 626 | 3 |
| My worthless affections to win | 165 | 2 |
| †My worthless heart to gain | 137 | 6 |
| My wounds compassionately see | 112 | 2 |
| My Zerubbabel is near | 382 | 3 |
| My Zion every moment feed | 629 | 6 |
| Myself I cannot keep | 305 | 5 |
| †Myself I cannot save | 305 | 5 |
| Myself in all things to deny | 332 | 1 |
| Myself, my residue of days | 426 | 1 |
| Myself the chief of sinners know | 778 | 4 |
| Myself the Father's pleasure | 667 | 2 |
| Mysteries of grace reveal | 676 | 1 |
| Mysterious Deity | 731 | 9 |
| †Mysterious gifts unseen | 757 | 2 |
| Mysterious One and Seven | 418 | 3 |
| Mystery of love adored | 971 | 4 |

| | Hymn | Verse |
|---|---|---|
| Nailed to the shameful tree | 22 | 1 |
| Nail my affections to the cross | 339 | 2 |
| Nail to the cross my will | 362 | 3 |
| Naked, and poor, and void of thee | 99 | 2 |
| Naked at the noon of night | 633 | 4 |
| †Naked of thine image, Lord | 109 | 4 |
| Naked, sick, and poor, and blind | 109 | 1 |
| Name ever dear to me | 939 | 1 |
| Names, and sects, and parties fall | 518 | 10 |
| †Nations that have never known thee | 595 | 4 |
| Nature and grace, with all their powers | 651 | 1 |
| Nature answers from within | 278 | 2 |
| Nature (for its Lord hath spoken) | 60 | 3 |
| †Nature is subject to thy word | 275 | 3 |
| Nature shall to grace submit | 914 | 5 |
| Nature's end we wait to see | 61 | 1 |
| Nature's expanse beneath thee spread | 235 | 2 |
| †Nay, and when we remove | 808 | 7 |
| Nay, but he uttered over thee | 32 | 4 |
| †Nay, but his bowels yearned to see | 32 | 4 |
| †Nay, but I yield, I yield | 137 | 8 |
| Nay, but whence'er my soul ascends | 947 | 4 |
| †Nearer, and nearer still | 497 | 2 |
| *Nearer, my God, to thee | 848 | 1 |
| Nearer, my God, to thee | 848 | Cho. |
| †Nearer than the seraphim | 817 | 8 |
| Nearer to save thou art | 138 | 7 |
| Nearer to thee | 848 | Cho. |
| Nearest the eternal throne | 76 | 1 |
| Near himself prepares our place | 718 | 6 |
| Near in our temptation stay | 653 | 6 |
| Nearness, likeness to their Lord | 817 | 2 |
| Needful to each other prove | 518 | 6 |
| Need neither sin nor fear | 801 | 1 |
| Need we ask that he may live | 914 | 7 |
| Ne'er from my defence remove | 271 | 4 |
| Neglect, betray, my charge divine | 471 | 3 |
| Neglect their heavenly business too | 858 | 1 |
| †Neither passion nor pride | 160 | 3 |
| †Neither sin, nor earth, nor hell | 618 | 3 |
| Never by the sinner trod | 349 | 1 |
| Never by thy work abide | 355 | 1 |
| Never fails from age to age | 594 | 2 |
| Never from my Saviour fly | 182 | 1 |
| †Never from our office move | 518 | 6 |
| Never from our souls remove | 517 | 4 |
| Never from the rock remove | 521 | 4 |
| Never from thy charge depart | 819 | 2 |
| Never give the creature part | 516 | 2 |
| Never in the whirlwind found | 858 | 1 |
| Never in thy wounds reside | 855 | 1 |
| Never leave them | 878 | 7 |
| †Never let me me leave thy breast | 187 | 4 |

|  | Hymn | Verse |
|---|---|---|
| †Never let the world break in | 508 | 6 |
| Never lose thy gracious power | 910 | 5 |
| †Never love nor sorrow was | 701 | 3 |
| Never more our duty leave | 295 | 2 |
| Never more resist, or fly | 188 | 3 |
| Never more, thy temples leave | 385 | 2 |
| †Never more will I commit | 910 | 4 |
| Never mortal spake like thee | 193 | 6 |
| Never need our footsteps slip | 487 | 2 |
| Never, never quit thy hold | 142 | 1 |
| Never, never to remove | 18 | 1 |
| Never rob thee of our heart | 516 | 2 |
| Never shall his promise fail | 640 | 2 |
| †Never shall I want it less | 292 | 5 |
| Never shall my triumphs end | 195 | 4 |
| Never shall our triumphs end | 207 | 2 |
| Never sin or grieve thee more | 910 | 5 |
| Never to be broke off again | 169 | 5 |
| Never to murmur at thy stay | 301 | 4 |
| Never turn to sin again | 185 | 2 |
| †Never will he thence depart | 758 | 4 |
| †Never will I remove | 436 | 4 |
| †Never will we hence depart | 900 | 4 |
| †New every morning is the love | 965 | 2 |
| †New graces ever gaining | 958 | 5 |
| New life the dead receive | 1 | 5 |
| †New mercies each returning day | 965 | 3 |
| New mercies from on high | 544 | 3 |
| New perils past, new sins forgiven | 965 | 3 |
| †New rising in this gospel time | 957 | 3 |
| New songs do now his lips employ | 34 | 4 |
| New they every morning are | 245 | 1 |
| New thoughts of God, new hopes of heaven | 965 | 3 |
| New treasures still of countless price | 965 | 4 |
| Next the saints in glory they | 75 | 3 |
| Nightly to the mount repair | 529 | 3 |
| †Nigh with my lips I drew | 93 | 3 |
| †Nipt by the wind's unkindly blast | 46 | 2 |
| No anger may'st thou ever find | 353 | 5 |
| No anxious doubt, no guilty gloom | 919 | 3 |
| No balm is in Gilead found | 777 | 1 |
| No base ingratitude above | 482 | 4 |
| No cares to break the long repose | 959 | 4 |
| No charms but those to thee are dear | 353 | 5 |
| No clouds nor tempests rise | 482 | 6 |
| No condemnation now I dread | 196 | 1 |
| †No condemnation now I dread | 201 | 5 |
| No cottage in this wilderness | 68 | 5 |
| No creature but is fed | 804 | 3 |
| No cross I shun, I fear no shame | 279 | 8 |
| No cross, no sufferings I decline | 773 | 4 |
| †No, dear companion, no | 52 | 4 |
| No devouring beast is there | 349 | 2 |

# NO END                                                      NO MORE

| | HYMN | VERSE |
|---|---|---|
| No end of oppression and pain | 777 | 1 |
| No excessive heat they feel | 76 | 8 |
| No father can he find, no friend abroad | 596 | 3 |
| No father there in passion loud | 482 | 5 |
| No foes, no violence I fear | 339 | 3 |
| †No foot of land do I possess | 68 | 5 |
| No formal hypocrite shall then | 540 | 5 |
| No fraud, while thou, my God, art near | 339 | 3 |
| No friendly physician I see | 777 | 1 |
| No fruit of all my toil and pain | 803 | 3 |
| No fruits of holiness | 981 | 2 |
| No gloom of affliction or sin | 73 | 2 |
| No gloomy fears their souls dismay | 932 | 2 |
| No good thing in me resides | 109 | 5 |
| †No good word, or work, or thought | 175 | 4 |
| No, gracious God, take what thou please | 844 | 6 |
| No guile hath in thy lips been found | 23 | 2 |
| No guilt thy spotless heart hath known | 23 | 2 |
| †No heavenly harpings soothe our ear | 767 | 4 |
| †No help can I from these receive | 781 | 2 |
| †No horrid alarum of war | 220 | 5 |
| No ill can come nigh me, By faith while I stand | 200 | 3 |
| No ill-requited love | 482 | 4 |
| No, in the strength of Jesus, no | 803 | 1 |
| No, I would not, when I might | 182 | 2 |
| No lasting root shall find | 540 | 4 |
| No longer from thy creature stay | 403 | 7 |
| †No longer hosts, encountering hosts | 740 | 6 |
| No longer let me be opprest | 167 | 1 |
| No longer, Lord, delay | 449 | 2 |
| No longer, Lord, my own, but thine | 775 | 4 |
| No longer mine, but thine I am | 431 | 2 |
| †No longer must the mourners weep | 715 | 5 |
| No longer now an exile roam | 792 | 1 |
| No longer now delay | 299 | 7 |
| †No longer then my heart shall mourn | 361 | 10 |
| No longer to myself, but thee | 375 | 4 |
| No longer trample on thy blood | 170 | 1 |
| †No longer we join While sinners invite | 19 | 4 |
| No longing we find | 498 | 2 |
| †No man can truly say | 85 | 2 |
| †No matter how dull The scholar whom he | 211 | 3 |
| No matter what cheer | 498 | 3 |
| †No matter which my thoughts employ | 44 | 4 |
| No merits or good works, to plead | 774 | 2 |
| No midnight shade, no clouded sun | 959 | 4 |
| No moon by silent night | 942 | 8 |
| No more a face of horror wear | 978 | 3 |
| No more, but Christ in me, may live | 344 | 5 |
| †No more fatigue, no more distress | 959 | 3 |
| No more forsaken and forlorn | 230 | 1 |
| No more imputes iniquity | 561 | 2 |
| No more is needed to complete my rest | 967 | 4 |

| | Hymn | Verse |
|---|---|---|
| †No more I stagger at thy power | 408 | 4 |
| No more on this side Jordan stop | 404 | 4 |
| No more thy goodness grieve | 508 | 2 |
| No more thy lingering anger move | 170 | 1 |
| No more unfaithful prove | 857 | 6 |
| No more your captive now | 274 | 4 |
| No mortal cares disturb my breast | 599 | 2 |
| No mortal eye can bear the sight | 650 | 1 |
| No music's like thy charming name | 682 | 1 |
| No, my God, I cannot doubt | 167 | 2 |
| No mystic dreams we share | 767 | 4 |
| No need of a physician have | 896 | 2 |
| No need of him the righteous have | 80 | 5 |
| †No need of the sun in that day | 73 | 4 |
| No one ever asked in vain | 287 | 1 |
| No one object of his care | 921 | 4 |
| No other good below | 187 | 11 |
| No other good I need | 186 | 7 |
| No other good will I pursue | 285 | 3 |
| No other help I know | 784 | 1 |
| No other help is found | 84 | 2 |
| No other name but thine | 798 | 7 |
| No other name is given | 84 | 2 |
| No other portion know | 533 | 4 |
| †No other right have I | 162 | 2 |
| No outward form can make me clean | 574 | 4 |
| No pain the inhabitants feel | 70 | 8 |
| No peace my wandering soul shall see | 844 | 3 |
| No period lingers unemployed | 222 | 2 |
| No place like this on high | 942 | 13 |
| No power can make us twain | 537 | 4 |
| No powers of darkness me molest | 974 | 5 |
| No pride, in my unruffled mind | 353 | 5 |
| †No profit canst thou gain | 831 | 4 |
| No promise of mercy for me | 777 | 1 |
| No real good they e'er shall want | 590 | 5 |
| No respite, or ease of my grief | 777 | 1 |
| No rest my spirit e'er shall know | 773 | 3 |
| No riches or merit, No wisdom or might | 212 | 1 |
| †No room for mirth or trifling here | 44 | 3 |
| †No rude alarms of raging foes | 959 | 4 |
| No Sabbath save eternity | 951 | 4 |
| No sacrifice beside | 675 | 7 |
| No shadow of evil is there | 73 | 2 |
| No sickness or sorrow shall prove | 70 | 3 |
| No sighs shall mingle with the songs | 959 | 3 |
| No sin in heaven is found | 482 | 4 |
| No sorrow can breathe in the air | 73 | 2 |
| No sound of the trumpet is there | 220 | 5 |
| †No strife shall rage, nor hostile feuds | 740 | 5 |
| †No sun by day shines there | 942 | 8 |
| †No tears from any eyes | 942 | 4 |
| No; this is mine own blindness | 587 | 3 |

| | Hymn | Verse |
|---|---|---|
| No! those are lost, which but might be | 838 | 7 |
| No, thou art mine | 851 | 2 |
| No thought can reach, no tongue declare | 373 | 1 |
| †No! though the ancient dragon rage | 30 | 4 |
| †No unexamined thought or word | 828 | 4 |
| No variation, ever knew | 240 | 4 |
| No weakness of the soul | 266 | 4 |
| No word from thee can fruitless fall | 969 | 7 |
| No, ye will not come to me | 8 | 3 |
| Noblest of his creatures, why | 7 | 2 |
| Nobly for their Master stood | 76 | 1 |
| Nobly scorned to bow the knee | 359 | 1 |
| None but Christ in earth or heaven | 398 | 3 |
| None but Christ on earth we know | 876 | 3 |
| None but Christ to me be given | 398 | 3 |
| None but Christ to others show | 876 | 3 |
| None but his loved ones know | 680 | 4 |
| None but Jesus | 791 | 5 |
| None but thy Wisdom knows thy might | 651 | 6 |
| None but thy Word can speak thy name | 651 | 6 |
| None but Zion's children know | 594 | 3 |
| None can ever ask too much | 824 | 2 |
| None can withstand thy conquering blood | 353 | 3 |
| None can with thyself compare | 244 | 1 |
| None envy nor despise | 627 | 1 |
| None, except thyself can read | 748 | 3 |
| *None is like Jeshurun's God | 407 | 1 |
| None of thy mercy need despair | 365 | 7 |
| None shall in thy mount destroy | 730 | 3 |
| None shall rend her walls asunder | 595 | 1 |
| None thy majesty can tell | 242 | 1 |
| None without holiness shall see | 543 | 1 |
| Nor all the saints in heaven | 421 | 2 |
| †Nor alms, nor deeds that I have done | 795 | 4 |
| Nor among the goats abase me | 933 | 15 |
| Nor aught shall the loved stamp efface | 373 | 5 |
| Nor bleed nor die in vain | 146 | 4 |
| Nor call departed Christians dead | 715 | 5 |
| Nor can her firm foundation move | 569 | 5 |
| Nor can I doubt its power divine | 909 | 4 |
| Nor can I, Lord, nor will I rest | 416 | 4 |
| Nor can its happiness or woe | 947 | 2 |
| Nor can the memory find | 680 | 2 |
| Nor can the powers of darkness rase | 659 | 4 |
| Nor can the sign deceive | 764 | 4 |
| Nor can thy grace procure | 175 | 3 |
| Nor can we pray in vain | 985 | 1 |
| Nor can we suffer shame | 617 | 2 |
| Nor can your hungry soul sustain | 4 | 5 |
| Nor canst thou it to me deny | 380 | 3 |
| Nor cast my easy yoke away | 561 | 10 |
| Nor cast the sinner quite away | 161 | 1 |
| Nor cast the souls away | 602 | 2 |

| | Hymn | Verse |
|---|---|---|
| Nor checked by fear, nor charmed by love | 99 | 3 |
| Nor count itself forlorn | 626 | 4 |
| Nor curse me with this want of love | 161 | 5 |
| Nor dare provoke his rod | 603 | 4 |
| Nor dare tumultuous foes invade | 994 | 1 |
| Nor dare uplift them to the skies | 795 | 3 |
| Nor dares a creature guess | 263 | 5 |
| Nor death nor hell shall harm | 671 | 3 |
| Nor dread the Almighty's frown | 63 | 1 |
| Nor earth nor hell I then shall fear | 351 | 6 |
| Nor earth nor hell shall pluck me thence | 272 | 4 |
| Nor e'er abuse my liberty | 307 | 2 |
| Nor envy the swine Their brutish delight | 19 | 4 |
| Nor ever from thy footsteps move | 171 | 3 |
| Nor ever from thy Lord depart | 912 | 4 |
| Nor ever hence remove | 208 | 4 |
| Nor ever, in my Judge's eye | 103 | 2 |
| Nor ever let me hunger more | 392 | 2 |
| Nor ever let the wanderers rest | 461 | 6 |
| Nor ever love thy child again | 178 | 2 |
| Nor ever may we parted be | 373 | 7 |
| Nor faint to bear the glorious sight | 927 | 3 |
| Nor fear the coming storm | 560 | 3 |
| Nor fear the ruin spread below | 281 | 3 |
| Nor feel my happy toil | 325 | 2 |
| Nor feels his want of thee | 88 | 3 |
| Nor flocks, nor herds be there | 804 | 4 |
| Nor flowed thy cleansing blood in vain | 373 | 6 |
| Nor fold, nor place of refuge near | 82 | 2 |
| Nor for a moment's space depart | 812 | 3 |
| Nor found whereon to rest below | 114 | 2 |
| Nor from his altar move | 268 | 1 |
| Nor from my hope remove | 301 | 6 |
| Nor from the promise of thy grace | 888 | 4 |
| Nor give me up to shame | 565 | 4 |
| Nor half so sweet can be | 682 | 1 |
| Nor have I power from thee to move | 141 | 6 |
| Nor hear the trumpet's sound | 466 | 1 |
| Nor hence again remove | 137 | 10 |
| Nor hide thy presence from my heart | 574 | 8 |
| Nor human hearts can e'er conceive | 721 | 6 |
| Nor impotent to save | 1002 | 3 |
| Nor in thy righteous anger swear | 161 | 4 |
| Nor is the least a thankful heart | 657 | 8 |
| Nor joy, nor grief, nor time, nor place | 584 | 5 |
| Nor knew its deep design | 91 | 3 |
| Nor knew my want of power within | 126 | 1 |
| Nor knew the omnipotence of grace | 126 | 1 |
| Nor know the name we take in vain | 454 | 4 |
| Nor know they their Redeemer nigh | 82 | 4 |
| Nor know what faith and duty mean | 858 | 1 |
| Nor leave a single moment void | 953 | 4 |
| Nor leave me in my lost estate | 161 | 5 |

| | Hymn | Verse |
|---|---|---|
| Nor leave the least remains behind | 412 | 5 |
| Nor less when he denies | 840 | 2 |
| Nor let his mercies lie | 616 | 2 |
| Nor let me cry in vain | 150 | 4 |
| Nor let me ever grieve thee more | 170 | 2 |
| Nor let me in my sins expire | 181 | 3 |
| Nor let my hope be lost | 811 | 2 |
| Nor let one darling lust survive | 844 | 5 |
| Nor let our faith forsake its hold | 677 | 3 |
| Nor let that ransomed sinner die | 202 | 8 |
| Nor let thee from my paths depart | 561 | 9 |
| Nor let the greedy grave devour | 178 | 2 |
| Nor let the proud Philistines' host | 547 | 4 |
| Nor let the rapid current bear | 296 | 1 |
| Nor let the tempting fiend intrude | 828 | 3 |
| Nor let thy chariot-wheels delay | 388 | 7 |
| Nor let thy former gifts be vain | 376 | 4 |
| Nor let thy whole displeasure rise | 298 | 3 |
| Nor lets the drops descend in vain | 225 | 3 |
| Nor life nor death can move | 877 | 2 |
| Nor life, nor death can part | 534 | 5 |
| Nor looked to be forgiven | 98 | 3 |
| Nor look with lofty eyes | 627 | 1 |
| Nor long permit them to rejoice | 280 | 6 |
| Nor man, nor fiends, nor flesh I fear | 616 | 2 |
| †Nor me alone instruct, rejoice | 770 | 6 |
| Nor men nor means can e'er relieve | 781 | 2 |
| Nor men nor means my soul can heal | 781 | 1 |
| Nor miss our providential way | 326 | 2 |
| Nor my affections rove | 788 | 7 |
| Nor of fitness fondly dream | 791 | 3 |
| Nor owned my helpless unbelief | 561 | 3 |
| †Nor prayer is made on earth alone | 823 | 7 |
| Nor quench the smoking flax in me | 290 | 2 |
| †Nor quite displayed to worlds above | 642 | 4 |
| Nor quite on earth concealed | 642 | 4 |
| Nor rove, nor seek the crooked way | 675 | 5 |
| Nor scorns the meanest name | 725 | 4 |
| Nor scorn their humble name | 889 | 2 |
| Nor see the bloody waste of war | 466 | 1 |
| Nor shall they, while unsaved from sin | 543 | 2 |
| †Nor shall thy spreading gospel rest | 553 | 4 |
| Nor short thine arm, nor deaf thine ear | 864 | 5 |
| Nor sin in deed, or word, or thought | 357 | 5 |
| Nor sin in deed, or word, or thought | 401 | 4 |
| Nor sin nor hell shall reach the place | 959 | 3 |
| Nor sin nor Satan can I fear | 281 | 1 |
| Nor sin nor sorrow know | 939 | 3 |
| †Nor slightest touch of pain | 482 | 6 |
| Nor slow to hear, nor weak to save | 636 | 4 |
| Nor sorrow's least alloy | 482 | 6 |
| Nor spot of guilt remains on me | 189 | 3 |
| Nor stands in sinners' ways, nor sits | 540 | 1 |

NOR STAND NOT ONE

| | Hymn | Verse |
|---|---|---|
| Nor stand the violence of my prayer | 144 | 2 |
| Nor start from the trial, While Jesus is near | 273 | 2 |
| Nor stop thine ears against my love | 561 | 10 |
| Nor struggle out of thine embrace | 188 | 3 |
| Nor suffer him to die in vain | 2 | 6 |
| Nor suffer him to take their crown | 461 | 1 |
| Nor suffer me again to stray | 210 | 5 |
| Nor suffer me to die | 106 | 3 |
| Nor suffer me to slide | 543 | 6 |
| Nor suffer thee to slide | 618 | 2 |
| Nor swift to flee, nor strong to oppose | 269 | 1 |
| Nor take thine everlasting flight | 161 | 1 |
| Nor take thy light from me away | 196 | 2 |
| Nor tire along the heavenly road | 802 | 5 |
| Nor tongue nor pen can show | 680 | 4 |
| †Nor to vain pomp apply | 627 | 2 |
| Nor visit as a transient guest | 376 | 3 |
| †Nor voice can sing, nor heart can frame | 680 | 2 |
| Nor, while unworthy I draw nigh | 764 | 2 |
| Nor will he put my soul to shame | 811 | 2 |
| Nor will I hear, nor will I speak | 285 | 4 |
| Nor will the mountains e'er remove | 153 | 3 |
| Nor will we fear | 853 | 3 |
| Nor will we think of aught beside | 26 | 6 |
| Nor wilt thou with the night depart | 141 | 4 |
| Nor zeal need droop, nor hope decay | 838 | 3 |
| †Not all the archangels can tell | 946 | 2 |
| *Not all the blood of beasts | 703 | 1 |
| Not all the bolts and bars of death | 713 | 3 |
| Not all the harmony of heaven | 764 | 2 |
| †Not all the powers of hell can fright | 281 | 2 |
| †Not angel-tongues can e'er express | 721 | 6 |
| Not angel-tongues can tell | 253 | 3 |
| Not bestow the grace I claim | 151 | 3 |
| †Not by human might or power | 382 | 3 |
| Not deaf to my desponding cry | 559 | 1 |
| Not death can tear | 851 | 3 |
| †Not for my fault or folly's sake | 304 | 6 |
| *Not from a stock of ours but thine | 874 | 1 |
| Not in anger, but in love | 179 | 1 |
| †Not in mine innocence I trust | 924 | 2 |
| Not in the dark monastic cell | 526 | 4 |
| †Not in the name of pride | 485 | 2 |
| †Not in the tombs we pine to dwell | 526 | 4 |
| Not Jordan's stream, nor death's cold flood | 938 | 6 |
| Not labouring after more | 806 | 1 |
| †Not like the warring sons of men | 493 | 5 |
| Not made with mortal hands | 74 | 1 |
| Not mine, not mine the choice | 837 | 3 |
| Not one be left behind | 452 | 3 |
| †Not one, but all our days below | 954 | 4 |
| Not one of all the apostate race | 31 | 1 |
| Not one of all the race | 303 | 3 |

276

| | Hymn | Verse |
|---|---|---|
| Not one shall pass into a deed | 828 | 2 |
| †Not only for ourselves we claim | 891 | 3 |
| Not only vast but numberless | 612 | 2 |
| Not seraphs view with open face | 133 | 1 |
| Not slow to mark my secret woes | 559 | 1 |
| Not the righteous | 791 | 4 |
| Not they can overpower us | 856 | 3 |
| Not till earth, and not till heaven | 793 | 6 |
| Not to man, but God submit | 302 | 2 |
| Not worthy to be called thy son | 178 | 1 |
| Not wrestling against flesh and blood | 314 | 4 |
| †Nothing am I in thy sight | 164 | 4 |
| Nothing beside my God I want | 403 | 6 |
| Nothing but sin I call my own | 332 | 4 |
| Nothing desire, nothing esteem | 534 | 3 |
| Nothing desire or seek, but thee | 844 | 5 |
| Nothing desire, or seek, but thee | 873 | 3 |
| Nothing do I know; the way | 109 | 3 |
| †Nothing else can I require | 434 | 7 |
| †Nothing else will we know | 808 | 6 |
| Nothing felt but doubts and fears | 878 | 4 |
| †Nothing hath the just to lose | 61 | 3 |
| †Nothing have I, Lord, to pay | 175 | 3 |
| Nothing have I to plead | 164 | 4 |
| †Nothing I ask or want beside | 125 | 6 |
| Nothing in earth or heaven | 403 | 6 |
| †Nothing is worth a thought beneath | 44 | 5 |
| Nothing know, or seek, beside | 508 | 7 |
| †Nothing less will I require | 398 | 3 |
| Nothing more can I desire | 398 | 3 |
| Nothing more can we require | 399 | 2 |
| †Nothing on earth do I desire | 285 | 8 |
| †Nothing on earth I call my own | 68 | 6 |
| Nothing seen but toils and dangers | 878 | 4 |
| Nothing shall I seek below | 628 | 2 |
| Nothing shall my heart confound | 672 | 9 |
| Nothing should my firmness shock | 271 | 2 |
| Nothing unavenged remaineth | 933 | 6 |
| Nothing would I seek but thee | 354 | 5 |
| †Nothing ye in exchange shall give | 4 | 4 |
| Nought by me thy fulness gains | 24 | 1 |
| †Nought can I bring thee, Lord, for all I owe | 794 | 8 |
| Nourished I, and fed by thee | 193 | 5 |
| Nourish us, O Christ, and feed | 518 | 3 |
| Nourish us with social grace | 521 | 1 |
| †Now admit my bold appeal | 910 | 8 |
| Now affix thy Spirit's seal | 910 | 8 |
| Now all my wants thou wouldst relieve | 784 | 3 |
| Now and evermore the same | 183 | 2 |
| Now assume thy royal power | 730 | 1 |
| Now, as yesterday, the same | 175 | 2 |
| †Now as yesterday the same | 335 | 3 |
| Now as yesterday the same | 519 | 3 |

| | Hymn | Verse |
|---|---|---|
| †Now at last | 715 | 7 |
| Now avenge us of our foe | 299 | 8 |
| Now before my face ye fly | 274 | 4 |
| Now before the throne of grace | 168 | 2 |
| Now be manifested here | 413 | 1 |
| Now bid the new creation be | 148 | 3 |
| Now bid the sin thou hat'st expire | 909 | 3 |
| Now bid thy banished ones rejoice | 190 | 11 |
| Now descend, and take thy bride | 60 | 4 |
| Now destroy the envious root | 449 | 2 |
| †Now destroy the man of sin | 937 | 4 |
| Now discern the Deity | 701 | 3 |
| Now, even now, I see thy face | 112 | 5 |
| *Now, even now, I yield, I yield | 414 | 1 |
| Now, even now, your Saviour stands | 8 | 3 |
| Now exert thy power to heal | 733 | 3 |
| Now, Father, let the gracious shower | 891 | 3 |
| Now, Father, to thy servant give | 123 | 5 |
| Now for good some token give | 173 | 4 |
| Now for my Lord and God I own | 190 | 3 |
| Now, for the honour of thy cause | 412 | 2 |
| Now, from all men be out-poured | 663 | — |
| Now from highest heaven appear | 753 | 1 |
| Now give the kingdom to thy Son | 585 | 1 |
| Now hail the strength of Israel's might | 681 | 2 |
| Now he plants the tribes of Israel | 720 | 4 |
| Now his heavenly birth declare | 701 | 3 |
| †Now if thy gracious will it be | 125 | 4 |
| Now I give thee back thine own | 430 | 5 |
| Now I glory in thine aid | 542 | 1 |
| Now I hate, renounce, disown | 910 | 3 |
| *Now I have found the ground wherein | 189 | 1 |
| Now in bitterness for thee | 768 | 10 |
| Now in every waiting heart | 717 | 3 |
| Now in heavenly places sit | 723 | 5 |
| Now in majesty descend | 989 | 4 |
| Now in my gasping soul reveal | 417 | 1 |
| †Now in thy strength I strive with thee | 815 | 2 |
| Now incline me to repent | 168 | 6 |
| Now it spreads along the skies | 218 | 4 |
| Now it wins its widening way | 218 | 2 |
| †Now, Jesus, now, the Father's love | 117 | 5 |
| †Now, Jesus, now the veil remove | 90 | 3 |
| †Now, Jesus, now thy love impart | 526 | 5 |
| †Now, Jesus, let thy powerful death | 362 | 2 |
| Now let all the members groan | 518 | 8 |
| Now let it all on me be shown | 170 | 2 |
| Now let it pass the years between | 708 | 3 |
| Now let me find my pardoning Lord | 118 | 5 |
| Now let me find thee in my heart | 364 | 1 |
| †Now let me gain perfection's height | 393 | 4 |
| Now let me hear thy quickening voice | 784 | 6 |
| Now let me in thine image shine | 171 | 3 |

| | Hymn | Verse |
|---|---|---|
| Now let me into nothing fall | 893 | 4 |
| Now let me see thy face, and live | 154 | 2 |
| Now let me serve and please my God | 835 | 1 |
| †Now let my soul arise | 675 | 9 |
| †Now let our darkness comprehend | 88 | 3 |
| Now let the pilgrim's journey end | 68 | 8 |
| †Now let thy chosen ones appear | 445 | 3 |
| †Now let thy dying love constrain | 122 | 5 |
| Now let thy salvation come | 479 | 2 |
| Now let thy servant die in peace | 924 | 1 |
| Now let thy servant die in peace | 924 | 5 |
| †Now let thy Spirit bring me in | 408 | 6 |
| Now let thy word o'er all prevail | 190 | 10 |
| Now let us from thyself receive | 1015 | — |
| †Now, Lord, if thou art power, descend | 150 | 5 |
| Now, Lord, in ours exert | 732 | 1 |
| Now, Lord, in us, even us, fulfil | 754 | 2 |
| Now, Lord, let every bounding heart | 485 | 3 |
| Now, Lord, my gasping spirit receive | 284 | 2 |
| Now, Lord, my soul restore | 856 | 10 |
| †Now, Lord, my weary soul release | 161 | 6 |
| Now, Lord, on us thy flesh bestow | 901 | 4 |
| Now, Lord, the Comforter bestow | 759 | 5 |
| Now, Lord, the glorious fulness give | 16 | 9 |
| Now, Lord, the gracious work begin | 973 | 4 |
| Now, Lord, throughout my darkness shine | 130 | 4 |
| †Now, Lord, to thee our all we leave | 286 | 4 |
| †Now, Lord, to whom for help I call | 135 | 3 |
| Now, may grateful Israel say | 621 | 1 |
| Now make thy loving-kindness known | 171 | 2 |
| Now my fallen soul restore | 173 | 1 |
| Now my Father's bowels move | 168 | 3 |
| Now my foul revolt deplore | 168 | 6 |
| Now my guilty conscience clear | 173 | 1 |
| Now my treasure and my heart | 325 | 4 |
| Now, my utmost Saviour, come | 149 | 2 |
| Now my whole heart renew | 799 | 6 |
| Now, now command him to depart | 409 | 2 |
| Now, now let it touch me, and make | 174 | 4 |
| Now, now let me find thee Almighty to save | 273 | 1 |
| †Now, now let me know | 160 | 4 |
| Now, now the further grace bestow | 97 | 2 |
| Now, now to receive you, He graciously stands | 3 | 1 |
| †Now, O God, thine own I am | 430 | 5 |
| Now, O my God, let trouble cease | 924 | 5 |
| †Now, O my Joshua, bring me in | 404 | 5 |
| Now, O my Saviour, Brother, Friend | 68 | 8 |
| †Now once more | 715 | 6 |
| †Now, only now, against that hour | 63 | 5 |
| Now on the brink of death we stand | 947 | 5 |
| Now on thy white horse appear | 748 | 1 |
| Now our cancelled sin reveal | 530 | 2 |
| Now our great Elijah offers | 720 | 4 |

| | Hymn | Verse |
|---|---|---|
| Now our groaning souls release | 29 | 3 |
| †Now our heavenly Aaron enters | 720 | 4 |
| Now our joyful souls are free | 623 | 4 |
| †Now our Paschal Lamb is he | 714 | 4 |
| Now our panting souls inspire | 530 | 2 |
| Now, partakers of thy throne | 423 | 2 |
| Now prepare, and take us now | 52 | 6 |
| Now received into the fold | 735 | 3 |
| Now receive thy meanest guest | 905 | 1 |
| Now rejoicing with his Lord | 51 | 5 |
| †Now rest, my long-divided heart | 912 | 4 |
| Now returning from above | 952 | 3 |
| Now reveal his great salvation | 899 | 1 |
| Now righteous through thy wounds I am | 196 | 1 |
| †Now, Saviour, now appear, appear | 550 | 3 |
| Now, Saviour, now on me bestow | 397 | 8 |
| Now, Saviour, now the power bestow | 403 | 3 |
| †Now, Saviour, now thyself reveal | 901 | 2 |
| Now, Saviour, now thy servant bless | 783 | 2 |
| Now, Saviour, with thy grace endowed | 835 | 1 |
| †Now shall my fainting heart rejoice | 659 | 6 |
| Now supply our bodies' want | 653 | 4 |
| Now supply our bodies' want | 1010 | — |
| Now sustain our souls with love | 653 | 4 |
| Now sustain our souls with love | 1010 | — |
| Now take the spoils of death and hell | 190 | 10 |
| Now the all-conquering Spirit give | 171 | 2 |
| †Now the full glories of the Lamb | 263 | 6 |
| Now the gracious word repeat | 164 | 6 |
| †Now the gracious work begin | 173 | 4 |
| Now the Holy Ghost impart | 757 | 4 |
| Now the living faith impart | 899 | 1 |
| Now the manna from above | 653 | 4 |
| Now the manna from above | 1010 | — |
| Now the new heavens and earth create | 356 | 10 |
| Now the power from high be given | 910 | 8 |
| Now the revealing Spirit send | 88 | 3 |
| Now the stone to flesh convert | 168 | 6 |
| Now the word doth swiftly run | 218 | 2 |
| †Now then, my God, thou hast my soul | 431 | 2 |
| †Now then the ceaseless shower | 734 | 2 |
| Now therefore I commend | 305 | 5 |
| Now they go to free the slaves | 878 | 1 |
| Now thine ancient flock bring in | 937 | 4 |
| Now thine inward witness bear | 390 | 5 |
| Now thou know'st I love thee, Lord | 101 | 3 |
| Now thou liftest up my head | 542 | 1 |
| Now thy all-cleansing blood apply | 410 | 3 |
| Now thy blissful self impart | 530 | 1 |
| Now thy Father's name reveal | 757 | 4 |
| Now thy gracious kingdom bring | 688 | 2 |
| Now thy kind relief afford | 112 | 4 |
| Now thy love almighty show | 158 | 2 |

| | Hymn | Verse |
|---|---|---|
| Now thy love almighty show | 158 | 3 |
| Now thy power almighty show | 299 | 3 |
| Now to be thine, yea, thine alone | 796 | 6 |
| Now to my soul thyself reveal | 351 | 1 |
| Now triumphantly descend | 67 | 7 |
| Now upon this cheerful morrow | 580 | 3 |
| Now upon thy servants shine | 989 | 1 |
| Now we reign with thee above | 723 | 3 |
| Now we taste the heavenly powers | 723 | 3 |
| Now, with willing heart entire | 179 | 3 |
| Now write on this accepted stone | 989 | 4 |
| ‡Numbered among thy people, I | 45 | 2 |
| †Numbered with the transgressors thou | 774 | 7 |
| Number me with salvation's heirs | 125 | 5 |
| O add them to thy chosen race | 82 | 7 |
| O all-atoning Lamb of God | 815 | 1 |
| *O all-creating God | 264 | 1 |
| O all-redeeming God, come down | 568 | 3 |
| O all-redeeming grace | 34 | 6 |
| *O all that pass by, To Jesus draw near | 3 | 1 |
| *O Almighty God of love | 271 | 1 |
| †O arm me with the mind | 270 | 2 |
| O avenge us of our foe | 299 | Cho. |
| O balm of care and sadness | 958 | 1 |
| †O be a nobler portion mine | 564 | 4 |
| †O be merciful to me | 768 | 10 |
| O be mindful of thy word | 187 | 2 |
| O be mindful of thy word | 479 | 2 |
| O be not faithless, but believe | 486 | 6 |
| O be with them | 878 | 2 |
| †O believe the record true | 20 | 3 |
| O bid it all depart | 503 | 1 |
| O bid the wretched sons of need | 955 | 3 |
| *O blessed, blessed sounds of grace | 799 | 1 |
| †O blessed word of gospel grace | 298 | 3 |
| O bless my coming in | 998 | 1 |
| *O bless the Lord, my soul | 610 | 1 |
| †O bless the Lord, my soul | 610 | 2 |
| O break not then a bruised reed | 290 | 2 |
| O burst these bonds, and set it free | 339 | 1 |
| O by all thy pains and woe | 710 | 1 |
| †O call to mind thy earnest prayers | 157 | 2 |
| O cast a pitying look on me | 779 | 2 |
| O Christians, to their rescue fly | 746 | 1 |
| O Christ, thou art my Head | 193 | 5 |
| O Christ, thy Spirit give | 506 | 2 |
| O claim them for thy ransomed ones | 82 | 6 |
| O cleanse, and keep us ever clean | 237 | 1 |
| O come and consecrate my breast | 374 | 1 |
| *O come, and dwell in me | 367 | 1 |
| O come, and righteousness divine | 376 | 2 |
| O come at his call | 707 | 3 |

| | HYMN | VERSE |
|---|---|---|
| O come, great Spirit, come | 771 | 1 |
| O come, great Spirit, come | 771 | 7 |
| *O come, O come, Immanuel | 690 | 1 |
| †O come, O come, thou Lord of might | 690 | 5 |
| †O come, thou Day-spring, come and cheer | 690 | 3 |
| †O come, thou Key of David, come | 690 | 4 |
| *O come, thou radiant morning Star | 445 | 1 |
| †O come, thou rod of Jesse, free | 690 | 2 |
| †O come to a mourner in pain | 911 | 4 |
| O come to bring me peace, and joy, and rest | 967 | 5 |
| O come to my Saviour, His grace is for all | 5 | 2 |
| O conclude this mortal story | 60 | 4 |
| †O confirm the gracious word | 185 | 2 |
| †O conquer this rebellious will | 146 | 2 |
| †O could I always know thee near | 770 | 5 |
| †O could I always pray | 303 | 2 |
| O could I catch one smile from thee | 918 | — |
| †O could I emulate the zeal | 470 | 9 |
| †O could I lose myself in thee | 184 | 9 |
| †O could we make our doubts remove | 938 | 5 |
| *O crucified, triumphant Lord | 891 | 1 |
| †O cut short the work, and make | 402 | 2 |
| O dark! dark! dark! I still must say | 163 | 2 |
| O day of joy and light | 958 | 1 |
| *O day of rest and gladness | 958 | 1 |
| O deafer than the sea | 697 | 4 |
| O dear and future vision | 943 | 6 |
| O descend on me, and bring | 292 | 2 |
| †O death! where is thy sting? Where now | 337 | 6 |
| *O disclose thy lovely face | 156 | 1 |
| †O do not let me trust | 270 | 8 |
| †O do not suffer him to part | 501 | 5 |
| O do not suffer me to sleep | 310 | 4 |
| O do not then in wrath chastise | 298 | 3 |
| †O do thou always warn | 305 | 8 |
| O dying Lamb for me | 772 | 1 |
| †O dying Lamb, thy precious blood | 798 | 3 |
| †O enter then his gates with praise | 607 | 3 |
| O ever-blessed Trinity | 992 | 6 |
| †O Father, glorify thy Son | 119 | 6 |
| O Father, glorify thy Son | 148 | 4 |
| *O Father of all, Who fillest with good | 1013 | 1 |
| O Father, Son, and Holy Spirit | 751 | 3 |
| O Father, thou know'st he hath died in my place | 707 | 6 |
| O feed us with thy grace, and give | 236 | 3 |
| O feed us with thy grace, and give | 1017 | 2 |
| *O filial Deity | 193 | 1 |
| O first prepare our hearts to pray | 546 | 4 |
| O fix thy sacred presence there | 655 | 4 |
| *O for a closer walk with God | 787 | 1 |
| †O for a faith like his, that we | 286 | 3 |
| *O for a heart to praise my God | 343 | 1 |
| *O for a thousand tongues to sing | 1 | 1 |

| | Hymn | Verse |
|---|---|---|
| †O for a trumpet voice | 34 | 7 |
| *O for that tenderness of heart | 104 | 1 |
| †O for this love let rocks and hills | 699 | 4 |
| O for those humble, contrite tears | 104 | 1 |
| †O for thy love, thy Jesu's sake | 629 | 4 |
| O! for thy truth and mercy's sake | 186 | 3 |
| †O for thy truth and mercy's sake | 749 | 5 |
| O from earth to heaven restored | 710 | 5 |
| O from his heart's o'erflowing font | 892 | 4 |
| O fulfil his faithful word | 506 | 1 |
| O gather every halting soul | 462 | 5 |
| O give me love or else I die | 155 | 6 |
| †O give me, Saviour, give me more | 155 | 4 |
| O give me sickness, want, or woe | 697 | 8 |
| *O glorious hope of perfect love | 404 | 1 |
| O glorious seat! Thou God, our King | 591 | 3 |
| *O God, at thy command we rise | 652 | — |
| O God! be merciful to me | 795 | Cho. |
| †O God, how faithful are thy ways | 888 | 4 |
| *O God! how often hath thine ear | 909 | 1 |
| *O God, if thou art love indeed | 171 | 1 |
| O God! I hear thee now | 697 | 9 |
| O God, let all my life declare | 439 | 2 |
| O God, let there be faith in me | 148 | 3 |
| †O God, mine inmost soul convert | 59 | 3 |
| *O God, most merciful and true | 369 | 1 |
| O God, my conscience make | 308 | 2 |
| O God, my God, my all thou art | 437 | 1 |
| *O God, my hope, my heavenly rest | 283 | 1 |
| O God, my strength and fortitude | 551 | 1 |
| O God of all grace | 808 | 1 |
| O God of Bethel, by whose hand | 664 | 1 |
| *O God of God, in whom combine | 666 | 1 |
| *O God, of good the unfathomed sea | 38 | 1 |
| ⁑O God, of good the unfathomed sea | 38 | 8 |
| ‖O God of my salvation, hear | 365 | 1 |
| *O God of our forefathers, hear | 394 | 1 |
| †O God of our life, We hallow thy name | 199 | 2 |
| *O God of peace and pardoning love | 438 | 1 |
| *O God! our help in ages past | 41 | 1 |
| †O God! our help in ages past | 41 | 7 |
| O God, the billows saw | 587 | 5 |
| *O God, the help of all thy saints | 546 | 1 |
| O God, the work is worthy thee | 159 | 1 |
| *O God, thou bottomless abyss | 240 | 1 |
| *O God, thy faithfulness I plead | 288 | 1 |
| †O God! thy record I believe | 360 | 4 |
| *O God, thy righteousness we own | 176 | 1 |
| *O God, to whom, in flesh revealed | 395 | 1 |
| *O God, to whom the faithful dead | 945 | 1 |
| *O God, what offering shall I give | 431 | 1 |
| O God, what tongue aright can tell | 655 | 2 |
| O God, who bidd'st my heart be glad | 437 | 8 |

| | Hymn | Verse |
|---|---|---|
| *O God, who dost thy sovereign might | 821 | — |
| †O grant that nothing in my soul | 373 | 2 |
| O grant us power to pray | 865 | 2 |
| O gratefully sing His power and his love | 611 | 1 |
| †O great absolver, grant my soul may wear | 794 | 6 |
| *O great mountain, who art thou | 382 | 1 |
| O grief too heavy to endure | 559 | 3 |
| †O happy bond that seals my vows | 912 | 2 |
| *O happy day that fixed my choice | 912 | 1 |
| †O happy, happy day | 536 | 5 |
| †O happy, happy place | 535 | 4 |
| O happy men that pay | 591 | 2 |
| O happy place! When shall I be | 942 | Cho |
| O happy retribution | 943 | 1 |
| †O happy souls that pray | 591 | 2 |
| †O hasten the hour! Send down from above | 3 | 5 |
| O hasten to my aid | 566 | 8 |
| O heavenly Father, grant us this | 822 | 2 |
| *O heavenly King, Look down from above | 199 | 1 |
| O height immense! What words suffice | 240 | 1 |
| O hear us when we cry to thee | 1004 | Cho. |
| O help my unbelief | 786 | 3 |
| O help, that I may never move | 344 | 7 |
| †O help us, Jesu, from on high | 696 | 6 |
| *O help us, Lord! each hour of need | 696 | 1 |
| O help us, Lord, the more | 696 | 2 |
| O help us so to live and die | 696 | 6 |
| †O help us, through the prayer of faith | 696 | 3 |
| †O help us when our spirits bleed | 696 | 2 |
| †O hide this self from me, that I | 344 | 5 |
| †O hope of every contrite heart | 680 | 3 |
| *O how blest the hour, Lord Jesus | 882 | 1 |
| O how great! how excellent | 639 | 8 |
| †O how lightly have I slept | 768 | 7 |
| O how quickly doth my heart | 355 | 2 |
| *O how shall a sinner perform | 911 | 1 |
| O how shall I, most gracious Lord | 363 | 1 |
| †O how shall I the goodness tell | 30 | 2 |
| O how shall we praise | 808 | 5 |
| O how sweet with heart and tongue | 598 | 1 |
| O how swiftly didst thou move | 292 | 3 |
| †O how wavering is my mind | 355 | 2 |
| O in what divers pains they met | 969 | 1 |
| O Israel, adore | 627 | 3 |
| O Jesu, keep us in thy sight | 968 | 1 |
| O Jesu, keep us in thy sight | 968 | 3 |
| O Jesu, lover of mankind | 38 | 1 |
| O Jesu, lover of mankind | 38 | 8 |
| O Jesu, make their darkness light | 968 | 2 |
| O Jesu, nothing may I see | 373 | 3 |
| *O Jesu, source of calm repose | 853 | 1 |
| †O Jesus, appear! No longer delay | 484 | 3 |
| *O Jesus, at thy feet we wait | 389 | 1 |

| | Hymn | Verse |
|---|---|---|
| †O Jesus, could I this believe | 784 | 3 |
| O Jesus, exalted on high | 220 | 1 |
| †O Jesus, full of grace! the sighs | 133 | 5 |
| †O Jesus, full of truth and grace | 186 | 2 |
| *O Jesus, full of truth and grace | 815 | 1 |
| O Jesus, I confess | 894 | 1 |
| †O Jesus! in pity draw near | 174 | 3 |
| O Jesus, in triumph appear | 77 | 2 |
| *O Jesus, let me bless thy name | 145 | 1 |
| *O Jesus, let thy dying cry | 341 | 1 |
| *O Jesus my Hope | 160 | 1 |
| †O Jesus! of thee I inquire | 174 | 2 |
| O Jesus, quickly come | 537 | 12 |
| †O Jesus! ride on Till all are subdued | 40 | 7 |
| O Jesus, to be filled with thee | 179 | 3 |
| O Jesus, we receive | 418 | 1 |
| *O joyful sound of gospel grace | 405 | 1 |
| O joy of all the meek | 680 | 3 |
| O keep it always here | 172 | 4 |
| O keep us faithful to the end | 483 | 5 |
| O King of glory, hear my call | 196 | 1 |
| †O King of glory, thy rich grace | 655 | 5 |
| O King of saints, come down | 67 | 7 |
| O knit my thankful heart to thee | 373 | 1 |
| O Lamb of God for sinners slain | 145 | 4 |
| O Lamb of God, I come | 796 | Cho. |
| O Lamb of God! was ever pain | 22 | 4 |
| O let his love your hearts constrain | 2 | 6 |
| O let it, Lord, be done | 152 | 4 |
| O let it make me whole | 136 | 2 |
| O let it never more steal in | 204 | 3 |
| †O let it now make haste to die | 362 | 7 |
| O let it speak us up to God | 774 | 5 |
| O let me cheerfully fulfil | 324 | 2 |
| †O let me commend My Saviour to you | 5 | 4 |
| O let me find thee near | 135 | 9 |
| O let me gain my Saviour's mind | 369 | 2 |
| †O let me kiss thy bleeding feet | 33 | 4 |
| O let me now be saved by grace | 171 | 1 |
| O let me now receive that gift | 784 | 4 |
| O let me now the gift embrace | 171 | 1 |
| O let me see thy gathering frown | 309 | 3 |
| O let me sin no more | 402 | 2 |
| †O let me still the promise plead | 916 | 2 |
| O let me then be found in peace | 919 | 2 |
| O let me tremble at thy word | 103 | 2 |
| O let me turn again and live | 170 | 3 |
| O let me walk before thy sight | 635 | 3 |
| O let my feet ne'er run astray | 675 | 5 |
| O let my stubborn spirit bow | 136 | 4 |
| O let not thy usurping foes | 275 | 4 |
| O let our deed begin and end | 526 | 2 |
| †O let our faith and love abound | 526 | 6 |

| | Hymn | Verse |
|---|---|---|
| O let our glorious joy be full | 977 | 4 |
| †O let our heart and mind | 535 | 3 |
| O let our lives to all around | 526 | 6 |
| O let our souls on thee be cast | 297 | 2 |
| †O let the dead now hear thy voice | 190 | 11 |
| O let the messenger be love | 913 | 3 |
| *O let the prisoners' mournful cries | 462 | 1 |
| O let the vessels of thy grace | 411 | 1 |
| O let their hearts with love o'erflow | 744 | 6 |
| †O let their sins be washed away | 588 | 3 |
| †O let them all thy mind express | 17 | 3 |
| †O let them shout and sing | 581 | 4 |
| †O let them spread thy name | 745 | 5 |
| O let thy hand support me still | 339 | 5 |
| †O let thy love my heart constrain | 33 | 5 |
| O let thy mercy come | 797 | 3 |
| O let thy pity answer me | 157 | 3 |
| †O let thy sacred presence fill | 285 | 2 |
| O let thy Spirit from thee proceed | 89 | 2 |
| †O let thy Spirit shed abroad | 145 | 3 |
| O let thy terrors and his anguish end | 596 | 3 |
| O let us all be saints indeed | 523 | 4 |
| †O let us all join hand in hand | 505 | 2 |
| O let us all our lives employ | 204 | 8 |
| O let us all receive | 901 | 2 |
| O let us all thy praise declare | 981 | 5 |
| †O let us on thy fulness feed | 507 | 5 |
| *O let us our own works forsake | 455 | 1 |
| †O let us put on thee | 74 | 5 |
| †O let us still proceed | 535 | 2 |
| O let us (still we pray) possess | 504 | 6 |
| †O let us stir each other up | 539 | 4 |
| †O let us take a softer mould | 505 | 7 |
| †O let us thus go on | 536 | 8 |
| O lift the abject sinner up | 163 | 6 |
| O lift thou up the sinking hand | 831 | 14 |
| †O long-expected day begin | 959 | 5 |
| O look with pity down | 852 | 2 |
| †O look with pity on the scene | 986 | 3 |
| O Lord arise, and let thy beams control | 596 | 1 |
| *O Lord, how good, how great art thou | 544 | 1 |
| †O Lord, how good, how great art thou | 544 | 5 |
| *O Lord, how long shall heathens hold | 588 | 1 |
| †O Lord, if I at last discern | 177 | 4 |
| †O Lord, if mercy is with thee | 170 | 2 |
| O Lord, I'll live to thee | 614 | 7 |
| O Lord, in darkness, in despair I groan | 596 | 1 |
| O Lord, my soul had died | 602 | 3 |
| †O Lord of hosts, almighty King | 569 | 11 |
| †O Lord of hosts, how blest is he | 590 | 6 |
| O Lord of hosts, thy dwellings are | 592 | 1 |
| O Lord of hosts, thy glorious name | 144 | 5 |
| *O Lord of hosts, whose glory fills | 992 | 1 |

| | Hymn | Verse |
|---|---|---|
| †O Lord, O God of love | 737 | 11 |
| O Lord, rebuke our sullen night | 694 | 1 |
| O Lord, resorb it into thee | 513 | 3 |
| *O Lord, thy faithful servant save | 548 | 1 |
| *O Lord, turn not thy face away | 797 | 1 |
| †O Lord, what wonders hast thou wrought | 566 | 5 |
| *O Lord, who by thy presence hast made light | 967 | 1 |
| *O Lord, with vengeance clad | 602 | 1 |
| *O Love divine, how sweet thou art | 147 | 1 |
| *O Love divine! what hast thou done | 28 | 1 |
| †O Love, how cheering is thy ray | 373 | 3 |
| *O Love, I languish at thy stay | 379 | 1 |
| †O Love, our stubborn will subdue | 666 | 5 |
| †O Love, thou bottomless abyss | 189 | 3 |
| †O Love, thy sovereign aid impart | 291 | 2 |
| †O Love, thy sovereign aid impart | 344 | 6 |
| O love unsearchable | 172 | 1 |
| †O Lover of sinners, extend | 911 | 3 |
| O loving Jesu, hear our call | 968 | 4 |
| †O madder than the raving man | 697 | 4 |
| †O magnify the Lord with me | 562 | 3 |
| †O make but trial of his love | 562 | 5 |
| †O make me all like thee | 436 | 9 |
| O make me glorious all within | 347 | 5 |
| O make me in thy likeness shine | 338 | 1 |
| O make me thy peculiar care | 974 | 6 |
| O make my longings and thy mercy sure | 596 | 2 |
| O make the sinner clean | 354 | 4 |
| †O may I always ready stand | 974 | 7 |
| O may I, as a little child | 351 | 4 |
| †O may I bear some humble part | 263 | 7 |
| O may I calmly wait | 311 | 1 |
| O may I conquer through thy blood | 338 | 5 |
| O may I hearken and obey | 305 | 3 |
| O may I learn from thee, my God | 23 | 8 |
| O may I learn the art | 270 | 4 |
| †O may I love like thee | 270 | 4 |
| O may I never grieve | 172 | 3 |
| O may I set my face | 311 | 2 |
| †O may I still from sin depart | 320 | 2 |
| O may I still lament | 778 | 3 |
| O may I to the utmost prove | 216 | 6 |
| O may I triumph so | 421 | 1 |
| †O may I worthy prove to see | 612 | 4 |
| O may it all my powers engage | 318 | 1 |
| O may it ever with us stay | 677 | 3 |
| O may my heart in tune be found | 599 | 2 |
| †O may my soul on thee repose | 974 | 4 |
| O may no earth-born cloud arise | 973 | 1 |
| †O may no sin our hands defile | 966 | 2 |
| †O may our more harmonious tongue | 978 | 6 |
| †O may the gracious words divine | 328 | 2 |
| O may the least omission pain | 308 | 3 |

| | Hymn | Verse |
|---|---|---|
| O may the reconciling word | 328 | 3 |
| O may they illumine Our spirits within | 869 | 5 |
| O may thine house be mine abode | 555 | 5 |
| †O may this strange, this matchless grace | 656 | 4 |
| O may thy grace our hearts refine | 955 | 2 |
| †O may thy love inspire my tongue | 574 | 13 |
| O may thy love possess me whole | 873 | 2 |
| *O may thy powerful word | 265 | 1 |
| O may thy quickening voice | 485 | 3 |
| †O may thy Spirit seal | 510 | 6 |
| O may thy Spirit whisper near | 692 | 4 |
| †O may we all improve | 265 | 2 |
| O may we all the loving mind | 504 | 5 |
| O may we all the time redeem | 980 | 1 |
| †O may we all triumphant rise | 977 | 5 |
| O may we always ready stand | 89 | 5 |
| O may we bless thy grace below | 930 | 5 |
| †O may we ever hear thy voice | 682 | 2 |
| †O may we ever walk in him | 534 | 3 |
| †O! may we keep and ponder in our mind | 691 | 5 |
| O may we still retain | 1005 | 1 |
| †O may we thus be found | 55 | 4 |
| O may we thus ensure | 55 | 4 |
| O may we to his day remain | 254 | 2 |
| †O measureless Might! Ineffable Love | 611 | 6 |
| O might he now descend, and rest | 145 | 3 |
| O might he now to us bring in | 754 | 5 |
| O might I feel thee in my heart | 100 | 4 |
| O might I now embrace | 105 | 4 |
| O might I now my Saviour meet | 881 | 2 |
| O might I see thy smiling face | 283 | 2 |
| *O might I this moment cease | 402 | 1 |
| O might I thy form express | 368 | 4 |
| †O might it now from thee proceed | 448 | 4 |
| O might it now my Lord proclaim | 425 | 1 |
| †O might my lot be cast with these | 17 | 6 |
| †O might our every work and word | 488 | 2 |
| O might the tabernacle fall | 74 | 3 |
| †O might the universal friend | 442 | 3 |
| †O might they at last With sorrow return | 19 | 5 |
| O might thy Spirit the blood apply | 363 | 3 |
| O might we all again be joined | 459 | 2 |
| †O might we, Lord! the grace improve | 466 | 2 |
| †O might we quickly find | 67 | 6 |
| O might we 'scape away | 74 | 3 |
| †O might we see in this our day | 455 | 3 |
| †O might we, through thy grace, attain | 455 | 2 |
| †O might we with believing eyes | 774 | 9 |
| †O mighty God, thy matchless power | 802 | 3 |
| †O multiply the sower's seed | 492 | 5 |
| O my bleeding, loving Lord | 106 | 7 |
| *O my God, what must I do | 158 | 1 |
| O my Life, my Righteousness | 112 | 6 |

| | Hymn | Verse |
|---|---|---|
| *O my offended God | 162 | 1 |
| *O my old, my bosom foe | 274 | 1 |
| O! my spirit longs and faints | 593 | 1 |
| †O my threefold enemy | 274 | 4 |
| O mystery of love | 772 | 5 |
| O nail my willing heart | 188 | 4 |
| †O never in these veils of shame | 431 | 4 |
| O never let me leave thy side | 436 | 2 |
| †O never suffer me to sleep | 306 | 4 |
| O no! these needless are | 942 | 8 |
| †O nought of gloom and nought of pride | 957 | 4 |
| O now for refuge flee | 792 | 2 |
| O now to all mankind | 870 | 2 |
| †O one, O only mansion | 943 | 5 |
| †O! on that day, that awful day | 934 | 3 |
| O paradise of joy! | 943 | 5 |
| O plunge me in thy mercy's sea | 240 | 1 |
| †O powerful Love, to thee we bow | 666 | 3 |
| O preserve in perfect peace | 188 | 5 |
| †O put it in our inward parts | 511 | 3 |
| †O put me in the cleft; empower | 283 | 4 |
| O raise me, heal me, by thy grace | 196 | 1 |
| O reach me out thy gracious hand | 312 | 7 |
| O receive my soul at last | 143 | 1 |
| O refresh us | 1008 | 1 |
| O rejoice to see his day | 197 | 4 |
| O remember Calvary | 900 | Cho. |
| †O remember me for good | 101 | 5 |
| *O render thanks to God above | 612 | 1 |
| O rend the heavens, come quickly down | 864 | 5 |
| O righteous Lord for thee | 609 | 4 |
| O rise and save me from eternal night | 596 | 1 |
| †O Sacred Spirit! who didst brood | 1004 | 3 |
| †O satisfy their soul in drought | 462 | 7 |
| O save, and give me to thy Son | 181 | 6 |
| O save (in my distress I said) | 614 | 4 |
| O save me, or I die | 309 | 3 |
| O save me yet, while on the brink I stand | 596 | 2 |
| O save, or I sink into hell | 174 | 3 |
| O save them from the demon, pride | 458 | 5 |
| O save us from our own | 108 | 6 |
| *O Saviour, cast a gracious smile | 528 | 1 |
| †O Saviour Christ, our woes dispel | 969 | 3 |
| †O Saviour Christ, thou too art man | 969 | 6 |
| O Saviour, do not now disdain | 614 | 1 |
| †O Saviour of all, Thy word we believe | 10 | 3 |
| O Saviour of mankind | 680 | 2 |
| O Saviour take our sins away | 648 | 5 |
| O Saviour, thou hast wept, and thou hast loved | 850 | 5 |
| *O Saviour, whom this holy morn | 692 | 1 |
| †O Saviour, whose almighty word | 1004 | 2 |
| O send me thy help from above | 911 | 1 |
| O send us now thy saving grace | 616 | 9 |

| | Hymn | Verse |
|---|---|---|
| O set up thy kingdom there | 352 | 3 |
| O shed it abroad; Send Christ from above | 200 | 1 |
| O shed it in my heart abroad | 376 | 5 |
| O shield us, lest we die | 986 | 1 |
| O shut them not against us, Lord | 797 | 1 |
| O Son of man, I fly | 292 | 1 |
| O source of life, live, dwell, and move | 431 | 3 |
| †O source of uncreated heat | 752 | 2 |
| †O sovereign love to thee I cry | 100 | 4 |
| †O spare me yet, I pray | 565 | 9 |
| O speak, and I shall live | 784 | 5 |
| †O speak a word of blessing, gracious Lord | 967 | 2 |
| †O spread thy covering wings around | 664 | 4 |
| †O spread thy pure wings o'er them | 996 | 7 |
| O sprinkle all their hearts with blood | 82 | 7 |
| O Sun of righteousness, arise | 462 | 4 |
| *O Sun of righteousness, arise | 785 | 1 |
| †O sweet and blessed country | 943 | 14 |
| O take away this heart of stone | 391 | 6 |
| O take it not away | 566 | 6 |
| O take me, seize me, from above | 155 | 8 |
| O take my sins away | 167 | 1 |
| O take, O seal them for thine own | 494 | 3 |
| †O take this heart of stone away | 391 | 6 |
| O taste the goodness of your God | 2 | 4 |
| O teach me from my heart to say | 841 | 1 |
| †O teach me my first lesson now | 471 | 5 |
| O tell me, tell me, Yes | 943 | 14 |
| †O tell of his might, O sing of his grace | 611 | 2 |
| O that all his salvation may see | 807 | 3 |
| O that all I am might cease | 898 | 4 |
| O that all men might know | 219 | 5 |
| O that all might catch the flame | 218 | 1 |
| †O that all might seek and find | 628 | 4 |
| †O that all the art might know | 825 | 5 |
| O that all the earth might know | 278 | 7 |
| †O that all with us might prove | 487 | 4 |
| †O that each from his Lord | 47 | 6 |
| †O that each in the day | 47 | 5 |
| O that earth and heaven might join | 653 | 1 |
| O that even now thy powerful call | 81 | 2 |
| O that every work and word | 427 | 2 |
| O that his mercy's beams would rise | 625 | 4 |
| †O that I, as a little child | 373 | 7 |
| O that I at last may stand | 13 | 4 |
| O that I could at last submit | 388 | 1 |
| O that I could believe | 105 | 1 |
| O that I could but stand in fear | 103 | 1 |
| †O that I could for ever sit | 147 | 4 |
| *O that I could, in every place | 550 | 1 |
| *O that I could my Lord receive | 125 | 1 |
| *O that I could repent | 102 | 1 |
| *O that I could repent | 105 | 1 |

|  | Hymn | Verse |
|---|---|---|
| \*O that I could revere | 103 | 1 |
| †O that I could the blessing prove | 125 | 2 |
| †O that I could with favoured John | 147 | 6 |
| \*O that I, first of love possessed | 124 | 1 |
| †O that I might at once go up | 404 | 4 |
| O that I might but faithful prove | 439 | 3 |
| O that I might know thee mine | 287 | 5 |
| †O that I might now decrease | 398 | 4 |
| †O that I might so believe | 13 | 2 |
| O that I might sweetly wake | 287 | 5 |
| O that I might thee receive | 287 | 5 |
| †O that I never, never more | 998 | 4 |
| †O that I now, from sin released | 391 | 7 |
| O that I now, my gracious Lord | 362 | 1 |
| †O that I now the rest might know | 403 | 3 |
| †O that in me the sacred fire | 361 | 7 |
| †O that it now from heaven might fall | 361 | 8 |
| O that it now might kindled be | 115 | 4 |
| O that it now were shed abroad | 147 | 3 |
| O that my every breath were praise | 378 | 3 |
| O that my heart were filled with God | 378 | 3 |
| \*O that my load of sin were gone | 388 | 1 |
| O that my Lord would count me meet | 17 | 6 |
| †O that my tender soul might fly | 313 | 3 |
| O that my voice could reach you all | 2 | 5 |
| †O that our faith may never move | 708 | 3 |
| O that our hearts were all a heaven | 389 | 6 |
| †O that our life might be | 852 | 3 |
| †O that the chosen band | 452 | 3 |
| †O that the Comforter would come | 376 | 3 |
| †O that the fire from heaven might fall | 412 | 5 |
| †O that the perfect grace were given | 389 | 6 |
| †O that the souls baptized therein | 476 | 6 |
| O that the word were given | 949 | 5 |
| †O that the world might know | 85 | 3 |
| †O that the world might taste and see | 37 | 4 |
| \*O that thou wouldst the heavens rent | 138 | 1 |
| †O that, to thee my constant mind | 313 | 2 |
| †O that we all might now begin | 84 | 2 |
| O that we all thy face might see | 389 | 5 |
| †O that we now in love renewed | 261 | 4 |
| O that we now might grasp our guide | 949 | 5 |
| †O that we now the power might feel | 528 | 4 |
| †O that with all thy saints I might | 370 | 4 |
| †O that with humbled Peter I | 147 | 5 |
| †O that with yonder sacred throng | 681 | 8 |
| †O that without a lingering groan | 45 | 3 |
| O the blessings bestowed | 231 | 5 |
| †O the fathomless love | 231 | 8 |
| †O the goodness of God | 231 | 7 |
| O the grace unsearchable | 197 | 6 |
| †O the infinite cares | 231 | 5 |
| †O the rapturous height | 807 | 4 |

|  | Hymn | Verse |
|---|---|---|
| O the vast, the boundless treasure . | 866 | 1 |
| †O ! then with hymns of praise | 991 | 2 |
| O think on Calvary . | 151 | 6 |
| †O thou almighty Lord | 675 | 8 |
| †O thou by whom we come to God . | 823 | 8 |
| *O thou eternal victim, slain . | 708 | 1 |
| *O thou faithful God of love . | 915 | 1 |
| *O thou God who hearest prayer | 579 | 1 |
| †O thou good Samaritan | 112 | 2 |
| †O thou jealous God ! come down | 287 | 2 |
| †O thou meek and gentle Lamb | 182 | 4 |
| O thou mild, pacific Prince . | 687 | 3 |
| O thou my Sun ; should I forsake my bliss. | 851 | 2 |
| *O thou, our Husband, Brother, Friend | 523 | 1 |
| †O thou that every thought canst know | 697 | 8 |
| *O thou that hangedst on the tree . | 774 | 1 |
| *O thou that hear'st when sinners cry | 574 | 7 |
| †O thou that wouldst not have . | 43 | 5 |
| *O thou to whose all-searching sight | 339 | 1 |
| *O thou who camest from above | 327 | 1 |
| O thou who changest not, abide with me . | 972 | 2 |
| *O thou who hast our sorrows borne | 122 | 1 |
| *O thou who hast redeemed of old . | 772 | 1 |
| †O thou who seest and know'st my grief | 117 | 3 |
| *O thou who, when I did complain . | 614 | 1 |
| *O thou whom fain my soul would love | 113 | 1 |
| *O thou, whom once they flocked to hear | 396 | 1 |
| *O thou, whose offering on the tree . | 702 | 1 |
| *O timely happy, timely wise | 965 | 1 |
| O 'tis better to depart | 925 | 1 |
| *O 'tis enough, my God, my God | 170 | 1 |
| O 'tis more than I can bear . | 188 | 1 |
| O 'tis more than tongue can tell | 207 | 1 |
| †O to grace how great a debtor | 866 | 3 |
| †O Trinity of love and power | 1004 | 4 |
| O turn thy threatening wrath away | 298 | 4 |
| *O unexhausted grace | 172 | 1 |
| †O unexampled love | 34 | 6 |
| O wash me in thy precious blood . | 984 | 2 |
| O were it now expelled by thee | 816 | 1 |
| O were we all caught up to share | 74 | 2 |
| O were we entered there | 74 | 2 |
| †O what a blessed hope is ours | 947 | 7 |
| O what a choice, peculiar race | 16 | 4 |
| O what a glorious company | 537 | 9 |
| O what a happiness is this | 285 | 7 |
| †O what a joyful meeting there | 537 | 10 |
| †O ! what a mighty change . | 482 | 4 |
| †O what an age of golden days | 16 | 4 |
| †O what are all my sufferings here . | 948 | 7 |
| O what could hope and confidence afford . | 850 | 4 |
| †O what fear man's bosom rendeth . | 933 | 2 |
| †O what hath Jesus bought for me . | 948 | 4 |

292

| | Hymn | Verse |
|---|---|---|
| O what is man! I wondering cry | 544 | 2 |
| *O what shall I do My Saviour to praise | 198 | 1 |
| †O what shall we do Our Saviour to love? | 481 | 5 |
| O what sweet surprise we found | 623 | 1 |
| O when shall all my wanderings end | 344 | 3 |
| O when shall I behold thy face | 567 | 2 |
| O when shall I declare | 421 | 1 |
| †O when shall my tongue Be filled with thy praise. | 200 | 2 |
| O when shall we enter our rest | 946 | 1 |
| O when shall we meet in the air | 70 | 1 |
| *O when shall we sweetly remove | 946 | 1 |
| O when wilt thou descend and bring | 609 | 1 |
| O where shall I appear? | 63 | 4 |
| †O who can explain This struggle for life | 273 | 4 |
| O who so wise to choose our lot | 846 | 1 |
| †O why did I my Saviour leave | 184 | 6 |
| O with what joy they went away | 969 | 1 |
| O wondrous grace! O boundless love! | 26 | 4 |
| †O wondrous knowledge, deep and high! | 632 | 4 |
| *O wondrous power of faithful prayer! | 298 | 1 |
| *O worship the King, all glorious above | 611 | 1 |
| †O would he more of heaven bestow | 947 | 8 |
| †O wouldst thou again be made known | 220 | 3 |
| †O wouldst thou break the fatal snare | 461 | 4 |
| †O wouldst thou end the storm | 459 | 2 |
| O wouldst thou, Lord, on this glad day | 405 | 5 |
| †O wouldst thou, Lord, reveal their sins | 94 | 4 |
| †O wouldst thou, Lord, thy servant guard | 306 | 3 |
| O write it in my heart | 340 | 2 |
| O ye dying sinners, why | 6 | 4 |
| †O ye of fearful hearts, be strong! | 380 | 4 |
| O Zion, yet on earth shalt be | 595 | 6 |
| †Obedient faith, that waits on thee | 360 | 11 |
| Obedient to his love | 65 | 4 |
| Obedient to his word | 55 | 4 |
| Obedient to thy gospel-call | 983 | 4 |
| Obedient to thy gracious word | 901 | 1 |
| Obedient to thy will | 43 | 6 |
| Obedient to thy will | 1002 | 4 |
| Obedient unto death for me | 330 | 1 |
| Obey thy strong command | 226 | 9 |
| Object of all his joy and hope | 286 | 2 |
| Object of all our wishes thou | 666 | 3 |
| Object of his creatures' scorn | 194 | 2 |
| Object of our glorious hope | 400 | 1 |
| Object of our joy and dread | 748 | 3 |
| Object of the heathen's scorn | 531 | 2 |
| Obstinately disbelieved | 182 | 2 |
| Obtained the help for all our race | 435 | 4 |
| †Occasion from my slowness take | 861 | 4 |
| Ocean owns his sovereign sway | 601 | 4 |
| †Ocean, roar, with all thy waves | 605 | 6 |
| O'er all beneath my care | 471 | 1 |

| | Hymn | Verse |
|---|---|---|
| O'er all my bright humanity | 72 | 3 |
| O'er all our hearts to reign | 447 | 2 |
| O'er all the earth abroad | 296 | 3 |
| O'er all the great Messiah reigns | 731 | 3 |
| O'er all the nations let it flow | 236 | 2 |
| O'er all the ransomed race | 418 | 1 |
| O'er all thy glory reigns | 989 | 2 |
| O'er all thy works doth reign | 239 | 7 |
| O'er a parched and weary land | 292 | 2 |
| O'er death, who now has lost his sting | 948 | 3 |
| O'er earth and hell victorious | 854 | 2 |
| O'er earth in endless circles roved | 114 | 2 |
| O'er earth's rebellious sons he reigns | 280 | 2 |
| †O'er every foe victorious | 586 | 6 |
| O'er hill and dale, by plots 'tis found | 739 | 3 |
| O'er men and angels reign | 248 | 3 |
| O'er the dreadful sacrifice | 710 | 4 |
| O'er the earth | 715 | 3 |
| O'er the grave where Lazarus slept | 710 | 3 |
| O'er the heathen throned am I | 570 | 6 |
| O'er the parched heart O rain | 753 | 7 |
| O'er the poor fallen sons of men | 315 | 2 |
| †O'er the vast howling wilderness | 293 | 3 |
| O'er the wide earth wars allay | 570 | 4 |
| O'er these dark hills of time | 984 | 3 |
| O'er us dominion have | 387 | 3 |
| O'er us had been seen to roll | 621 | 2 |
| O'erawed by majesty divine | 1001 | 4 |
| O'erflow my eyes, and heave my breast | 23 | 9 |
| †O'erlook them with a guardian eye | 470 | 4 |
| O'erpowered I sink, I faint, I die | 240 | 1 |
| O'errule, or change, as seems thee meet | 429 | 3 |
| O'ertake our kindred in the skies | 489 | 2 |
| O'erwhelmed at his almighty grace | 800 | 11 |
| O'erwhelmed before thy throne | 221 | 2 |
| O'erwhelmed beneath their load of sins | 81 | 3 |
| †O'erwhelmed with blessings from above | 875 | 2 |
| *O'erwhelmed with blessings from above | 1016 | 1 |
| †O'erwhelmed with justest fear again | 469 | 2 |
| O'erwhelmed with mountain-loads of care | 836 | 2 |
| †O'erwhelmed with thy stupendous grace | 369 | 4 |
| Of a departed friend | 482 | 5 |
| Of a saint in Christ deceased | 51 | 3 |
| Of a sick heart with pity view | 133 | 5 |
| Of a soul in its earliest love | 807 | 1 |
| Of all, alas! whom I have known | 80 | 1 |
| Of all good gifts the giver | 1026 | — |
| Of all in earth and heaven | 243 | 5 |
| Of all in earth or heaven | 125 | 6 |
| Of all in earth or heaven | 232 | 4 |
| Of all my Father's children, I | 392 | 3 |
| Of all my works be thou the aim | 431 | 6 |
| Of all that travel to the sky | 71 | 1 |

| | Hymn | Verse |
|---|---|---|
| Of all the ancient race | 452 | 3 |
| Of all things, near and far | 988 | 2 |
| †Of all thou hast in earth below | 169 | 3 |
| Of all thou hast in earth or heaven | 163 | 3 |
| Of all thy gifts we ask but one | 294 | 5 |
| Of all thy new creation | 736 | 3 |
| Of all thy saints and me | 1005 | 3 |
| Of all thy tempted followers here | 294 | 3 |
| Of all who e'er thy grace received | 161 | 3 |
| Of all who seek the land above | 326 | 1 |
| Of an expiring Deity | 254 | 1 |
| Of any other love but thine | 285 | 4 |
| Of bleeding love unfold | 358 | 3 |
| Of blind idolatry | 469 | 3 |
| Of bruises, and of wounds, my soul | 109 | 2 |
| Of business, toil, and care | 863 | 1 |
| Of carnal self-security | 461 | 4 |
| Of Christian brotherhood | 822 | 3 |
| Of Christian man and maid | 996 | 2 |
| Of damning unbelief | 94 | 4 |
| Of dark mortality | 767 | 1 |
| Of each I an account must give | 471 | 3 |
| Of empyrean light | 74 | 4 |
| Of everlasting life | 74 | 3 |
| Of everlasting light | 333 | 5 |
| Of everlasting love | 271 | 4 |
| Of everlasting love | 548 | 4 |
| Of everlasting peace | 503 | 2 |
| Of every heart thou hast the key | 884 | — |
| Of every hope my hold | 558 | 5 |
| Of every sinful heart | 503 | 1 |
| Of every sinner's heart | 208 | 2 |
| Of every soul that cleaves to thee | 629 | 1 |
| Of exceeding sinfulness | 768 | 2 |
| Of fancied happiness | 98 | 2 |
| Of fellowship to you we give | 490 | 2 |
| Of filial fear, Of knowledge and grace | 3 | 5 |
| Of formless waters lay | 750 | 2 |
| Of forms without the power | 25 | 3 |
| Of full and everlasting | 943 | 2 |
| Of glory and of God | 96 | 2 |
| Of glory condescend | 650 | 4 |
| Of glory shall appear | 345 | 4 |
| Of glory that no period knows | 437 | 6 |
| Of glory was displayed | 950 | 2 |
| Of God incarnate and the Virgin's son | 691 | 1 |
| Of godly sorrow give | 865 | 3 |
| Of gospel blessings send | 734 | 2 |
| Of gospel hope, of humble fear | 130 | 2 |
| Of guilt and desperate unbelief | 25 | 4 |
| Of having all in thee | 560 | 4 |
| Of health, that pain and death defies | 376 | 1 |
| Of hearts opprest with doubt and grief | 698 | 1 |

|  | Hymn | Verse |
|---|---|---|
| Of heart-reviving love | 680 | 6 |
| Of heaven a larger earnest give | 374 | 5 |
| †Of heaven the sign, of earth the calm | 957 | 2 |
| Of heavenly birth | 498 | 1 |
| Of hell, and earth, and heaven | 275 | 3 |
| Of hell, our spirits hide | 63 | 5 |
| Of hell subdued, and peace with heaven | 675 | 4 |
| Of him I make my loftier songs | 568 | 1 |
| Of him in spotless peace | 586 | 8 |
| Of him that sits upon the throne | 280 | 8 |
| Of him that sits upon the throne | 678 | 4 |
| Of him who fills the sky | 862 | 2 |
| Of his anger, did lay | 707 | 2 |
| Of his coming may say | 47 | 5 |
| Of his dazzling glories shorn | 684 | 2 |
| †Of his deliverance I will boast | 562 | 2 |
| Of his faithfulness proclaim | 606 | 2 |
| Of his heavenly kingdom near | 936 | 1 |
| Of his redeeming power | 478 | 3 |
| Of his sting he is bereft | 714 | 2 |
| Of holiness and love | 960 | — |
| Of holiness the spirit shower | 456 | 2 |
| Of immortality | 405 | 4 |
| Of infinite compassions, hear. | 170 | 3 |
| Of jealous, godly fear | 308 | 1 |
| Of Jesse's stem extol the Rod | 681 | 3 |
| Of Jesus and his word | 787 | 2 |
| Of joy unspeakable possest | 493 | 2 |
| †Of judgment now the world convince | 443 | 2 |
| Of judgments, and our sins confess | 455 | 8 |
| Of justified believers | 736 | 2 |
| Of liberty and love | 307 | 3 |
| Of life, and the white stone | 343 | 7 |
| Of life, and the white stone | 539 | 9 |
| Of life our souls o'erflow | 21 | 4 |
| †Of life the fountain thou | 193 | 3 |
| †Of life thou art the tree | 193 | 2 |
| Of light thou form'st thy dazzling robe | 651 | 4 |
| Of living thus to thee | 325 | 5 |
| Of love, and of a healthful mind | 376 | 1 |
| Of love divine, which never ends | 440 | 1 |
| Of love, this shall be all my plea | 115 | 5 |
| Of love, to thee and all mankind | 376 | 1 |
| Of love unspeakable | 413 | 3 |
| Of man, short-sighted man, can find | 288 | 3 |
| Of man thou wouldst receive | 245 | 4 |
| Of man's vain beauty flies | 565 | 6 |
| Of means an idol made | 91 | 6 |
| Of mercies always new | 838 | 1 |
| Of mercies, I myself abhor | 351 | 3 |
| †Of my boasted wisdom spoiled | 302 | 3 |
| Of my life and felicity here | 231 | 2 |
| Of my Lord's unchanging love | 866 | 1 |

| | Hymn | Verse |
|---|---|---|
| Of my own bosom-foe | 311 | 3 |
| Of my Redeemer's blood | 417 | 4 |
| Of my redeeming Lord | 335 | 1 |
| Of my Saviour possessed | 807 | 4 |
| Of my state and condition below | 231 | 3 |
| Of never-failing skill | 845 | 1 |
| Of nothing think or speak beside | 28 | 4 |
| Of ocean's mighty flood | 667 | 2 |
| Of old, O God, thine own right hand | 589 | 1 |
| Of omnipresent love | 550 | 2 |
| Of our crucified Lord | 488 | 6 |
| Of our eternal King | 659 | 1 |
| Of our everlasting feast | 975 | 4 |
| Of our flesh and of our bone | 684 | 4 |
| Of our full redemption here | 67 | 6 |
| Of our High-priest above | 725 | 1 |
| Of our own treacherous heart | 469 | 1 |
| Of our paradise possest | 480 | 3 |
| Of our salvation came | 675 | 4 |
| Of our solemn litany | 710 | 5 |
| Of our unworthy race | 667 | 3 |
| Of pain and sin the dark abode | 154 | 1 |
| Of paradise possest | 384 | 7 |
| Of peace I cannot find | 109 | 3 |
| Of perfect holiness possessed | 72 | 2 |
| Of pitying tenderness divine | 686 | 1 |
| Of pleasurable sin | 956 | 3 |
| Of power demonstrative, impart | 456 | 3 |
| Of power, sobriety, and love | 419 | 2 |
| Of power, to conquer inbred sin | 376 | 1 |
| Of prayers, and hopes, complaints, and groans | 25 | 3 |
| Of present grace And joys above | 991 | 1 |
| Of pride, or fond desire | 308 | 1 |
| Of purging fires and torturing pains | 926 | 1 |
| Of rage and malice on | 675 | 10 |
| Of reconciling grace | 307 | 4 |
| Of righteousness divine | 266 | 3 |
| Of sadness and of dread | 986 | 3 |
| Of saints, and make our joys abound | 977 | 4 |
| Of sanctifying grace | 382 | 4 |
| Of second death is past | 112 | 6 |
| Of self-deluding men | 67 | 1 |
| Of Shimei's hand and Shimei's tongue | 334 | — |
| Of sin, and earth, and hell | 310 | 1 |
| Of sin, your heads lift up | 54 | 2 |
| Of sojourning beneath | 311 | 5 |
| Of souls entrusted to my care | 470 | 9 |
| Of spotless majesty | 942 | 1 |
| Of tenderness and love | 112 | 5 |
| Of the atoning Lamb | 217 | 3 |
| Of the holier house on high | 990 | 3 |
| Of the holy delight | 807 | 4 |
| Of the last tremendous days | 936 | 2 |

| | Hymn | Verse |
|---|---|---|
| Of the sad heart that comes to thee for rest | 850 | 1 |
| Of the subtle tempter's power | 710 | 2 |
| Of the three witnesses above | 261 | 3 |
| Of thee possessed, in thee we prove | 154 | 4 |
| Of thee, the world's Desire | 883 | 1 |
| Of thee they justly make their boast | 647 | 4 |
| Of thee we make our joyful boast | 239 | 1 |
| Of their succeeding race | 664 | 2 |
| Of thine can make me clean | 135 | 4 |
| Of thine elect attend | 299 | 6 |
| Of thine everlasting praise | 914 | 10 |
| Of thine unseen decree | 871 | 1 |
| Of this we make our empty boast | 454 | 4 |
| Of those that are in thee | 354 | 6 |
| Of those that basely pant | 68 | 3 |
| Of those who to thy love aspire | 241 | 4 |
| Of thy afflicting rod | 103 | 1 |
| Of thy creating love | 253 | 1 |
| Of thy cross the wondrous story | 743 | 1 |
| Of thy flesh and of thy bone | 518 | 4 |
| Of thy free unbounded grace | 877 | 3 |
| †Of thy great unbounded power | 244 | 2 |
| Of thy incarnate Love | 336 | 1 |
| Of thy kingdom here possessed | 885 | 2 |
| Of thy promised strength secure | 910 | 2 |
| Of thy prophetic word | 460 | 2 |
| Of thy redeeming grace | 245 | 3 |
| Of thy reward lay hold | 723 | 3 |
| Of thy rich blessing here descend | 589 | 5 |
| Of thy salvation, Lord | 789 | 1 |
| Of thy unfainting hope | 627 | 4 |
| Of unanimity divine | 489 | 2 |
| Of unexhausted love | 184 | 9 |
| Of vast eternity | 665 | 1 |
| Of virtues full, and happy days | 985 | 4 |
| Of whole eternity | 665 | 6 |
| Of wisdom and prayer, Of joy and of praise | 3 | 5 |
| Of wisdom, grace, and power | 21 | 4 |
| Of wisdom, love, and power | 675 | 1 |
| Of wisdom's costly merchandise | 14 | 3 |
| Of wise discernment, humble love | 456 | 2 |
| Of Zion it shall yet be spoken | 595 | 5 |
| Offered his blood and died | 675 | 7 |
| Offering here obedience willing | 895 | 1 |
| Offer my sacrifice of praise | 575 | 4 |
| Offer the sacrifice of praise | 614 | 13 |
| Offer up our all to God | 423 | 3 |
| Offers all his joy and peace | 86 | 4 |
| Offspring of a virgin's womb | 683 | 2 |
| †Oft as I lay me down to rest | 328 | 3 |
| Oft as they meet for worship here | 619 | 6 |
| †Oft did I with the assembly join | 91 | 2 |
| †Oft from the margin of the grave | 289 | 4 |

| | Hymn | Verse |
|---|---|---|
| †Oft had I fainted and resigned | 558 | 5 |
| †Oft hath the sea confessed thy power | 289 | 3 |
| †Oft have I heard thy threatenings roar | 584 | 4 |
| *Oft I in my heart have said | 192 | 1 |
| †Oft I in my heart have said | 192 | 2 |
| *Oft in danger, oft in woe | 847 | 1 |
| Oft observed my silent tears | 335 | 2 |
| Often made returns of sin | 975 | 2 |
| Ofttimes thou hast laid me low | 274 | 1 |
| Oil in your vessels take | 65 | 1 |
| †Old friends, old scenes, will lovelier be | 965 | 5 |
| Old men and children praise | 232 | 1 |
| Old things past | 715 | 7 |
| *Omnipotent Lord, my Saviour and King | 273 | 1 |
| †Omnipotent Redeemer | 276 | 2 |
| *Omnipotent Redeemer | 736 | 1 |
| Omnipotent to save | 724 | 1 |
| Omnipotently glorious | 854 | 2 |
| Omnipotently good | 693 | 1 |
| Omnipotently near | 618 | 4 |
| *Omnipresent God! whose aid | 287 | 1 |
| Omniscient Lord, thy piercing eye | 955 | 2 |
| On all created things | 423 | 2 |
| On all his enemies | 86 | 3 |
| On all his works again hath smiled | 721 | 1 |
| On all mankind to turn and live | 744 | 5 |
| On all our assemblies, and glow in our breast | 760 | 4 |
| On all that hunger after thee | 134 | 3 |
| *On all the earth thy Spirit shower | 457 | 1 |
| On all the kings of earth | 21 | 6 |
| On all the members rest | 756 | 2 |
| On all the powers of darkness tread | 299 | 5 |
| On all the ransomed race bestowed | 448 | 4 |
| On all the world below | 446 | 4 |
| On all the world to call | 34 | 7 |
| On all their goods my soul looks down | 439 | 2 |
| On all thy creatures writ | 263 | 3 |
| On all thy glorious beauties gaze | 304 | 5 |
| On all thy saints to shine | 581 | 1 |
| On all thy works; thy mercy's beams | 38 | 2 |
| On angelical cheer | 488 | 2 |
| On a poor abject worm exert | 670 | 3 |
| On a poor sojourner | 307 | 2 |
| On ashes, husks, and air ye feed | 4 | 5 |
| †On cherub and on cherubim | 551 | 4 |
| On Christ, my Life, in death rely | 927 | 4 |
| On Christ, on Christ alone | 865 | 4 |
| On clouds and storms below | 226 | 4 |
| On clouds of glory seated | 932 | 1 |
| On clouds of glory seated | 932 | 4 |
| On earth as pilgrims rove | 840 | 1 |
| On earth is not his fellow | 856 | 1 |
| †On earth the usurpers reign | 315 | 2 |

| | HYMN | VERSE |
|---|---|---|
| On earth thou shalt give us A taste of thy love | 1013 | 2 |
| On earth thy salvation to see | 371 | 1 |
| On earth with purest sympathies o'erflowing | 850 | 5 |
| On earthly good look down | 539 | 3 |
| On everlasting strength our weakness staying | 850 | 6 |
| On every listening heart | 871 | 2 |
| On every loyal heart | 465 | 9 |
| On every side | 595 | 4 |
| On every side Are gathered to him | 40 | 2 |
| On every side he stands | 622 | 2 |
| On every side I found | 614 | 3 |
| On every side They compass me round | 200 | 4 |
| On faith's strong eagle-pinions rise | 333 | 2 |
| On faith's victorious shield | 267 | 1 |
| On her firm base securely founded | 595 | 1 |
| On her men look with fear and wonder | 595 | 1 |
| On her place she towers unbent | 570 | 3 |
| On him alone we build | 991 | 1 |
| On him I lean, who not in vain | 849 | 1 |
| On him they pierced, and weep, and pray | 451 | 2 |
| On his all-seeing eyes | 618 | 3 |
| On his great love Our hopes we place | 991 | 1 |
| On his name whoe'er shall call | 197 | 3 |
| On *his* new-born soul impress | 477 | 2 |
| On his only love rely | 13 | 2 |
| On his promise I rely | 278 | 4 |
| On his redeeming love | 278 | 3 |
| On his sword and spear relies | 278 | 1 |
| On his word my soul I cast | 142 | 2 |
| On homeliest work thy blessing falls | 863 | 2 |
| On Israel's God; he made the sky | 224 | 2 |
| †On Jesus, my power, Till then I rely | 273 | 8 |
| On Jewish altars slain | 703 | 1 |
| On me and all mankind bestowed | 378 | 3 |
| On me be all long-suffering shown | 106 | 1 |
| On me I feel thy wrath abide | 127 | 7 |
| †On me that faith divine bestow | 342 | 6 |
| On me, that I thy praise may show | 135 | 2 |
| On me that others may believe | 171 | 2 |
| On me, the chief of sinners, me | 170 | 2 |
| On me, the chief of sinners, me | 206 | 1 |
| On me this gracious fear | 172 | 4 |
| On me, through grace forgiven | 252 | 6 |
| On me thy Spirit pour | 409 | 6 |
| On mercy's wings I swiftly fly | 364 | 4 |
| On mountain-tops above the hills | 740 | 1 |
| On multitudes confer | 734 | 2 |
| On my atoning God | 182 | 5 |
| On my expanding heart | 764 | 3 |
| On no support but thine | 533 | 3 |
| On our dead souls were found | 981 | 2 |
| On our dim and earthly sun | 694 | 2 |
| On our disordered spirits move | 87 | 3 |

| | Hymn | Verse |
|---|---|---|
| On princes desolation | 613 | 3 |
| On soul-reviving dainties feed | 955 | 3 |
| On such a worm as me | 781 | 6 |
| On that meek head of thine | 703 | 3 |
| On that securest shore | 943 | 11 |
| On the approaching Sabbath-day | 975 | 1 |
| On the clouds will come again | 720 | 7 |
| On the cross of suffering bought me | 933 | 10 |
| On the dark mountains the lost wanderer strayed | 850 | 2 |
| On the eternal shore | 949 | 4 |
| On the evil and the good | 238 | 1 |
| On the evil and the good | 1019 | 1 |
| On the help of feeble man | 508 | 3 |
| On the living and the dead | 53 | 2 |
| On the mean altar of my heart | 327 | 1 |
| On the poor heart worn out with toil, thy word | 967 | 2 |
| On the Rock of ages founded | 594 | 1 |
| On the Rock of heavenly love | 67 | 2 |
| †On the thin air, without a prop | 226 | 7 |
| On the union witnessed now | 995 | 1 |
| On the wings of angels fly | 509 | 6 |
| On thee, all faith, all hope be placed | 785 | 5 |
| On thee, almighty to create | 301 | 1 |
| On thee alone for strength depend | 141 | 6 |
| On thee alone I rest | 627 | 3 |
| On thee alone my constant mind | 217 | 2 |
| On thee alone our spirits stay | 71 | 1 |
| †On thee, at the creation | 958 | 2 |
| On thee, bright Sun of righteousness | 281 | 3 |
| On thee for daily food | 637 | 3 |
| On thee for help rely | 723 | 1 |
| On thee for our salvation | 958 | 2 |
| On thee I calmly rest | 560 | 2 |
| On thee I cast my care | 301 | 1 |
| †On thee I ever call | 151 | 2 |
| On thee, importunate, I call | 164 | 3 |
| On thee in Jesu's name we call | 412 | 1 |
| On thee my feeble steps I stay | 436 | 1 |
| †On thee, my Priest, I call | 193 | 7 |
| On thee, my Saviour and my God | 912 | 1 |
| On thee my soul is cast | 112 | 6 |
| On thee my soul is cast | 674 | 1 |
| †On thee, O God, my soul is stayed | 408 | 3 |
| *On thee, O God of purity | 543 | 1 |
| On thee, O never, Lord, depart | 436 | 5 |
| On thee our Lord victorious | 958 | 2 |
| On thee the high and lowly | 958 | 1 |
| On thee we cast our care; we live | 236 | 3 |
| †On thee we cast our care, we live | 1017 | 2 |
| †On thee we depend Our wants to supply | 1013 | 2 |
| †On thee we humbly wait | 745 | 2 |
| On thee whom we have slain | 122 | 1 |
| On thee will I depend | 217 | 4 |

| | Hymn | Verse |
|---|---|---|
| On them, recovered from their fall | 473 | 2 |
| †On they go from strength to strength | 593 | 3 |
| On thine every work impressed | 242 | 2 |
| †On this day, most blest of days | 714 | 5 |
| On this festival day | 491 | 1 |
| †On this glad day a brighter scene | 950 | 2 |
| On this my steadfast soul relies | 189 | 5 |
| On this thy day, in this thy house | 959 | 1 |
| On this wild rocky shore | 984 | 4 |
| On those prepared to meet him | 982 | 2 |
| On those that humbly hear | 873 | 2 |
| On thy approaching sacrifice | 702 | 4 |
| On thy eternal throne | 258 | 2 |
| On thy own gifts and graces feast | 507 | 2 |
| On thy redeeming wing | 870 | 2 |
| †On thy thigh and vesture written | 748 | 6 |
| On to perfect holiness | 512 | 2 |
| On us a longer space | 981 | 4 |
| On us let all thy grace be shown | 394 | 4 |
| On us, poor ransomed worms, look down | 262 | 4 |
| On which such blessings are bestowed | 595 | 2 |
| On which the Prince of glory died | 700 | 1 |
| On whom for all things I depend | 312 | 1 |
| On whom I cast my every care | 312 | 1 |
| On whom my help is laid | 217 | 1 |
| On whose sentence all dependeth | 933 | 2 |
| On wings of love mount up on high | 803 | 4 |
| On wings of love our souls shall fly | 802 | 5 |
| On your triumphant brow | 345 | 5 |
| On Zion it doth sweetly fall | 630 | 5 |
| On Zion's sacred height | 800 | 7 |
| Once for favoured sinners slain | 66 | 1 |
| Once he died our souls to save | 716 | 4 |
| Once more in my behalf appear | 170 | 3 |
| *Once more the sun is beaming bright | 966 | 1 |
| Once more thy power display | 952 | 3 |
| †Once more 'tis eventide, and we | 969 | 2 |
| Once more to God we pray | 966 | 1 |
| Once more to thy creatures return | 220 | 1 |
| Once offered up, a spotless Lamb | 902 | 1 |
| †Once they were mourners here below | 940 | 2 |
| *Once thou didst on earth appear | 413 | 1 |
| One army of the living God | 949 | 2 |
| One, as Thou and He are one | 517 | 2 |
| One bright celestial ray dart down | 88 | 1 |
| One chorus of perpetual praise | 636 | 1 |
| One church, above, beneath | 949 | 2 |
| †One day amidst the place | 956 | 3 |
| One drop of thy blood I implore | 174 | 4 |
| †One family we dwell in him | 949 | 2 |
| One God, in Persons Three | 239 | 1 |
| One God in Persons Three | 251 | 2 |
| One God in Persons Three | 252 | 1 |

| | Hymn | Verse |
|---|---|---|
| One grain of living faith impart | 150 | 5 |
| One holy thought conceive | 435 | 3 |
| One in every time and place | 519 | 3 |
| One in joy and light and love | 582 | 3 |
| One in Three, and Three in One | 430 | 1 |
| One in Three, and Three in One | 430 | 6 |
| †One, inexplicably Three | 260 | 2 |
| One looking up to thee | 852 | 3 |
| One moment will not linger | 856 | 4 |
| †One only gift can justify | 422 | 2 |
| One only thing resolved to know | 526 | 3 |
| †One only way the erring mind | 288 | 3 |
| One spirit and one mind | 459 | 2 |
| One supreme, almighty Lord | 643 | 1 |
| One supreme, eternal THREE | 257 | 7 |
| One the faith, and common Lord | 515 | 2 |
| †One the Father is with thee | 517 | 2 |
| One the Father lives adored | 515 | 2 |
| One the Holy Ghost with thee | 257 | 7 |
| One the pure baptismal flame | 515 | 2 |
| One the Spirit whom we claim | 515 | 2 |
| *One thing with all my soul's desire | 558 | 1 |
| One undivided Christ proclaim | 505 | 6 |
| One undivided fold | 460 | 3 |
| †One undivided Trinity | 259 | 2 |
| One wide-extended field of blood | 442 | 1 |
| †One with God, the source of bliss | 515 | 3 |
| One with thine almighty Sire | 727 | 7 |
| One wretched sinner die | 43 | 5 |
| Only believe, and yours is heaven | 30 | 7 |
| Only by faith in thee I stand | 312 | 7 |
| Only can by him be told | 24 | 2 |
| Only faith the grace applies | 521 | 3 |
| Only for thy love I pant | 167 | 3 |
| Only grant the grace I claim | 910 | 4 |
| Only guided by thy light | 381 | 2 |
| †Only have faith in God | 314 | 4 |
| Only in thy wisdom wise | 381 | 1 |
| Only Jesus I pursue | 809 | 1 |
| Only Jesus will I know | 809 | Cho. |
| Only let all my heart be thine | 773 | 4 |
| Only let thy servants live | 925 | 3 |
| Only let us persevere | 521 | 4 |
| Only live the life divine | 287 | 5 |
| Only love to us be given | 522 | 4 |
| Only mighty in thy might | 381 | 2 |
| †Only my gracious look obey | 561 | 10 |
| †Only, O Lord, in thy great love | 965 | 7 |
| Only on thee for help I call | 312 | 7 |
| Only seeing in thy light | 302 | 3 |
| Only sing, and praise, and love | 538 | 4 |
| †Only tell me I am thine | 287 | 3 |
| †Only thee content to know | 381 | 2 |

| | Hymn | Verse |
|---|---|---|
| Only the form of death is left | 714 | 2 |
| Only thou art holy, there is none beside thee | 646 | 3 |
| Only thou canst set us free | 299 | 3 |
| Only thou canst succour man | 112 | 2 |
| Only thou possess the whole | 434 | 1 |
| Only thou possess the whole | 516 | 2 |
| Only thy terrors, Lord, restrain | 279 | 8 |
| Only to believers shown | 207 | 1 |
| Only to Omniscience known | 768 | 2 |
| Only to thee, O God, is known | 240 | 3 |
| Only to thy glory live | 287 | 5 |
| Only to thy glory move | 661 | 3 |
| Only walking in thy might | 302 | 3 |
| Only wish for thee to die | 877 | 2 |
| Only wish to live for thee | 877 | 1 |
| Onward, Christians, onward go | 847 | 1 |
| †Onward, then, to glory move | 847 | 4 |
| †Open a door which earth and hell | 492 | 4 |
| Open are thy arms to embrace | 173 | 2 |
| Open, earth, and take it in | 86 | 6 |
| Open for thyself a way | 349 | 1 |
| Open it when shines the sun | 769 | 3 |
| *Open, Lord, my inward ear | 358 | 1 |
| Open mine eyes of faith! thy face | 133 | 3 |
| †Open mine eyes the Lamb to know | 129 | 6 |
| Open mine eyes that I may see | 113 | 3 |
| Open mine eyes to see thy face | 118 | 1 |
| †Open my faith's interior eye | 393 | 2 |
| Open, O Lord, my ear | 135 | 5 |
| Open our eyes and let us see | 88 | 2 |
| Open stands to mortal eyes | 715 | 6 |
| Open the book, and loose the seal | 90 | 1 |
| Open the door of faith and heaven | 82 | 8 |
| Open the door of faith and love | 118 | 5 |
| Open the door to preach thy word | 35 | 1 |
| Open the fountain from above | 492 | 2 |
| †Open the gates of righteousness | 616 | 6 |
| †Open the intercourse between | 169 | 5 |
| †Open their graves, and bring | 450 | 3 |
| †Open their mouth, and utterance give | 744 | 5 |
| Open there the ethereal scene | 730 | 2 |
| Open thine arms and take me in | 124 | 2 |
| Open thine arms and take me in | 132 | 1 |
| Open thine arms and take me in | 186 | 2 |
| †Open thou our minds, and lead us | 882 | 4 |
| †Open thou the crystal fountain | 839 | 2 |
| Open wide thine arms and breast | 191 | 2 |
| Opened is the gate of heaven | 722 | 2 |
| Opening sweets they all disclose | 348 | 1 |
| Openly to all displayed | 605 | 2 |
| Oppressed by sins, I lift my eye | 217 | 1 |
| Oppressed with various ills draw near | 969 | 2 |
| Opprest, insulted, and forlorn | 588 | 2 |

| | Hymn | Verse |
|---|---|---|
| Or all my woes relate | 112 | 1 |
| Or all thy Godhead know | 242 | 1 |
| Or altogether kill | 362 | 3 |
| Or angel-minds conceive | 384 | 8 |
| Or at thy feet I die | 146 | 2 |
| Or at thy table meet | 92 | 1 |
| Or basely fear his gifts to own | 30 | 3 |
| Or breathe the prayer divinely taught | 841 | 2 |
| Or broke by sickness in a day | 46 | 4 |
| Or, by sudden anguish torn | 672 | 7 |
| Or by thy cross ourselves o'erthrow | 670 | 1 |
| Or cast his words behind | 532 | 8 |
| Or cast us out who come to thee | 774 | 6 |
| Or caught the still small whisper, higher | 698 | 2 |
| Or cause our minds to rove | 966 | 2 |
| Or change, or interval, or end | 909 | 5 |
| Or contradict his will | 844 | 2 |
| Or count mine injurer my foe | 830 | 3 |
| Or count thee less than the most high | 254 | 3 |
| Or devils drag my soul away | 43 | 3 |
| Or do the thing I would not do | 849 | 2 |
| Or doubt thy truth, which cannot move | 408 | 4 |
| Or earth received her frame | 41 | 3 |
| Or e'er throw off my load | 138 | 4 |
| Or else—depart to hell | 43 | 4 |
| Or fall at my Deliverer's feet | 836 | 6 |
| Or feel at death dismay | 939 | 4 |
| Or feel the blood that flows for me | 861 | 2 |
| Or force him to depart | 208 | 2 |
| Or from thy paths depart | 436 | 2 |
| Or give my spirit ease | 781 | 2 |
| Or give to sin or Satan place | 306 | 2 |
| Or gladly wander to and fro | 68 | 5 |
| Or glorious, in our death | 21 | 2 |
| Or God appear to me | 128 | 1 |
| Or groan, to him who reads the heart | 268 | 2 |
| Or heart can e'er conceive | 941 | 1 |
| Or hold me back from home | 947 | 4 |
| Or how be justified | 625 | 2 |
| Or hurt whom they surround | 466 | 1 |
| †Or if on joyful wing | 848 | 5 |
| Or if the snare we enter | 818 | 2 |
| †Or, if thou grant a longer date | 467 | 6 |
| †Or if thou my soul require | 287 | 6 |
| Or if thou the means supply | 24 | 3 |
| Or immortality endures | 224 | 1 |
| Or immortality endures | 224 | 4 |
| Or impress of thy feet | 263 | 3 |
| Or in thy courts to wait | 543 | 4 |
| Or into friends convert | 465 | 6 |
| Or it had passed by me | 216 | 4 |
| Or lifted up my sinking head | 289 | 1 |
| Or like the morning flower | 610 | 10 |

| | Hymn | Verse |
|---|---|---|
| Or long for thy return to pine | 759 | 5 |
| Or lord of all my passions live | 126 | 2 |
| Or lost the virtue of thy name | 397 | 3 |
| Or man or angel's thought | 685 | 3 |
| Or mar him by familiar love | 470 | 6 |
| Or meet thy purer eyes | 184 | 10 |
| Or numbered with the blest | 43 | 4 |
| Or part whom God hath joined | 487 | 3 |
| Or pluck the sinner thence | 138 | 6 |
| Or quench the smallest spark of grace | 157 | 6 |
| Or quench this hell of wrath and pride | 830 | 2 |
| Or racked with care, he heaps up wealth | 565 | 3 |
| Or raised above themselves, aspire | 721 | 3 |
| Or raised the fruitful hills | 667 | 1 |
| Or rash, or idle, or unkind | 363 | 1 |
| Or rise to be hid in thy breast | 228 | 3 |
| Or said, or thought, on him was laid | 917 | 3 |
| Or secret thing to know | 842 | 3 |
| Or see the bloody cross appear | 315 | 2 |
| Or selfishness we meet | 485 | 2 |
| Or send them sorrowful away | 32 | 3 |
| Or send them to proclaim the word | 474 | 4 |
| Or serve his God aright | 487 | 1 |
| Or shake at death's alarms | 929 | 1 |
| Or shuns or meets the wandering thought | 240 | 3 |
| Or shuts me up in hell | 59 | 2 |
| Or sin against the majesty | 550 | 2 |
| Or sin against thy light and love | 170 | 1 |
| Or sin against thy love | 307 | 2 |
| Or sin, or righteousness, remove | 97 | 5 |
| Or sing my great Deliverer's praise | 30 | 1 |
| Or sink them to the sand | 226 | 9 |
| Or slaughtered hecatombs appease | 127 | 2 |
| Or smile, thy sceptre, or thy rod | 210 | 7 |
| Or spark of glimmering day | 699 | 1 |
| Or speak iniquity | 543 | 3 |
| †Or, stablished and confirmed by him | 721 | 3 |
| Or stay the almighty hand | 244 | 2 |
| Or stoop to find favour Through mercy alone | 212 | 2 |
| Or strong, I here disclaim | 217 | 3 |
| Or the besetting sin | 828 | 3 |
| Or the devouring fire | 432 | 4 |
| Or the world's pleasures, or its praise | 279 | 6 |
| Or thorns compose so rich a crown | 700 | 3 |
| Or those that brought them dare condemn | 891 | 4 |
| Or thousands are alike to thee | 396 | 5 |
| Or to beloved ones than self more dear | 850 | 3 |
| Or to defend his cause | 811 | 1 |
| Or tongues of various tone | 767 | 2 |
| Or turned aside the fatal hour | 289 | 1 |
| Or, undismayed, in deed and word | 279 | 1 |
| Or unimproved below | 222 | 2 |
| Or view thy unapproached light | 133 | 2 |

| | Hymn | Verse |
|---|---|---|
| Or virtue lies distressed | 637 | 7 |
| Or wake in darkness and unrest | 838 | 2 |
| Or wash away our stain | 703 | 1 |
| Or wearied give the sinner o'er | 157 | 8 |
| Or where earthquakes rock the place | 358 | 1 |
| Or who has grace so rich and free | 656 | Cho. |
| Or who, in Jesu's name baptized | 891 | 4 |
| Or wish my sufferings less | 301 | 4 |
| Or with the uttered name impart | 892 | 3 |
| Or with my Saviour dwell | 43 | 4 |
| †Or worn by slowly-rolling years | 46 | 4 |
| Or worthily sing thy unspeakable grace | 808 | 5 |
| Ordered by thy governance | 826 | — |
| †Order if some invert, confound | 470 | 7 |
| Other comforts I despise | 434 | 6 |
| *Other ground can no man lay | 516 | 1 |
| †Other knowledge I disdain | 809 | 2 |
| Other propriety disclaim | 332 | 4 |
| †Other refuge have I none | 143 | 2 |
| Other title I disclaim | 115 | 1 |
| Our Advocate above | 724 | 2 |
| †Our Advocate for ever lives | 827 | 8 |
| Our Advocate hath placed us there | 1001 | 8 |
| †Our Advocate there | 760 | 2 |
| Our Advocate with God | 277 | 2 |
| Our all in all, is he | 497 | 5 |
| Our all in all is love | 504 | 9 |
| Our all in earth and heaven | 411 | 2 |
| Our all let us delight to spend | 524 | 3 |
| Our all, no longer ours, but thine | 428 | 4 |
| †Our anchor sure and fast | 723 | 4 |
| Our balm in sorrow, and our stay in strife | 962 | 4 |
| Our beatified spirits he feeds | 499 | 7 |
| Our being receive | 491 | 3 |
| Our blighted works we know shall fail | 475 | 4 |
| Our bodies his glory display | 499 | 8 |
| Our bodies may far off remove | 534 | 1 |
| Our body rose, a breathing clod | 264 | 1 |
| Our bowels of compassion move | 237 | 1 |
| Our brethren shield in danger's hour | 1004 | 4 |
| †Our Brother, Saviour, Head | 497 | 5 |
| †Our brother the haven hath gained | 49 | 2 |
| Our business and strife Is thee to proclaim | 199 | 2 |
| Our Captain doth the fight maintain | 493 | 5 |
| †Our Captain leads us on | 315 | 4 |
| Our cares, and pains, and studies here | 473 | 2 |
| Our cautioned souls prepare | 55 | 1 |
| Our chastened souls have been | 602 | 1 |
| †Our claim admit, and from above | 456 | 2 |
| Our common Saviour praise | 208 | 1 |
| Our conflicts here shall soon be past | 333 | 4 |
| Our conquering King | 854 | 1 |
| †Our conquering Lord | 219 | 2 |

OUR CONSCIENCE                                              OUR FRIEND

|  | Hymn | Verse |
|---|---|---|
| Our conscience by thy word reprove | 89 | 3 |
| Our consecrated food | 1015 | — |
| Our Counsellor divine | 533 | 3 |
| Our cries thou seemest not to heed | 299 | 6 |
| Our curse and death to feel | 423 | 1 |
| Our curse and sufferings to remove | 774 | 1 |
| Our curse to remove | 808 | 2 |
| Our daily toil shall be | 966 | 4 |
| Our darkness chase, our sorrows cheer | 129 | 4 |
| Our day is spent in doing good | 222 | 1 |
| †Our days are as the grass | 610 | 10 |
| Our deep original wound to heal | 441 | 4 |
| †Our desperate state through sin declare | 84 | 7 |
| Our dreadful curse on Calvary | 731 | 2 |
| Our earnest suit for Abraham's seed | 451 | 1 |
| Our ear, our inmost soul, we bow | 90 | 3 |
| Our earthen vessels filled | 947 | 7 |
| *Our earth we now lament to see | 442 | 1 |
| Our election how to make | 480 | 2 |
| Our emptiness and woe | 771 | 2 |
| Our enemies and thine | 583 | 2 |
| Our endless work above | 652 | — |
| Our end, the glory of the Lord | 326 | 1 |
| Our everlasting Comforter | 533 | 3 |
| Our everlasting home above | 71 | 2 |
| Our everlasting Priest art thou | 708 | 1 |
| Our everlasting rest | 528 | 5 |
| Our every want and sorrow | 1026 | — |
| Our every want supplies | 898 | 2 |
| Our eyes and hearts to heaven we lift | 875 | 2 |
| †Our eyes and hearts to heaven we lift | 1016 | 2 |
| Our face like his shall shine | 537 | 9 |
| †Our fainting souls sustain | 704 | 4 |
| Our faith by our obedient love | 511 | 1 |
| Our faith by works to approve | 539 | 4 |
| Our faith shall never yield to fear | 569 | 2 |
| Our faith shall rest secure, and sing | 569 | 11 |
| Our faithful, unchangeable Friend | 660 | — |
| Our fallen nature's shame | 818 | 3 |
| †Our Father and Lord, Almighty art thou | 199 | 3 |
| Our Father and our love | 12 | 2 |
| Our Father, God, and King | 248 | 1 |
| Our Father governs all | 1003 | 3 |
| Our Father in heaven, With joy we partake | 1025 | 1 |
| Our feeble thought surpasses far | 655 | 5 |
| Our fellow-prisoner free | 52 | 3 |
| Our fellowship with thee | 531 | 3 |
| Our flesh, and fully dwell | 299 | 4 |
| Our flesh, soul, spirit, we resign | 655 | 4 |
| Our foolishness to mourn | 84 | 2 |
| †Our foreheads proclaim | 499 | 8 |
| †Our former years mis-spent | 983 | 5 |
| †Our friend is gone before | 52 | 2 |

| | Hymn | Verse |
|---|---|---|
| *Our friendship sanctify and guide | 524 | 1 |
| Our friends that went before | 482 | 3 |
| Our full consent, our whole desires | 91 | 5 |
| Our Gideon, and his Spirit's sword | 493 | 4 |
| Our gloomy guilt, and selfish guile | 528 | 1 |
| Our glorified Head | 760 | 2 |
| †Our glorious Leader claims our praise | 940 | 5 |
| Our glorious liberty | 623 | 3 |
| Our glorious mansion in the sky | 74 | 2 |
| Our God appeared a child of man | 648 | 2 |
| Our God contracted to a span | 685 | 1 |
| Our God from all eternity | 255 | 1 |
| †Our God in Christ! thine embassy | 11 | 3 |
| Our God is all in all | 435 | 6 |
| Our God is manifest below | 685 | 3 |
| Our good is all divine | 435 | 5 |
| Our gospel grace partake | 424 | 1 |
| Our gracious God inclines his ear | 981 | 3 |
| Our grateful sacrifice | 1022 | — |
| Our great High-priest in glory bears | 726 | 1 |
| Our guardian God | 854 | 2 |
| Our guilt and punishment remove | 298 | 4 |
| Our guilt and sufferings to remove | 441 | 4 |
| Our hands with work, our hearts with zeal | 858 | 3 |
| Our happy souls resounded | 276 | 4 |
| Our heart-felt poverty | 874 | 2 |
| Our hearts, and make us free indeed | 380 | 6 |
| Our hearts and our treasure already are there | 498 | 3 |
| Our hearts are known to thee | 831 | 14 |
| Our hearts are naked to thine eye | 666 | 3 |
| Our hearts away from thee | 204 | 5 |
| Our hearts can never quail | 1003 | 2 |
| Our hearts in solemn songs of praise | 647 | 1 |
| Our hearts shall beat for thee alone | 980 | 3 |
| Our hearts to embrace thy will | 654 | 4 |
| Our hearts to entertain our Lord | 507 | 1 |
| Our hearts to pay thee all thy praise | 980 | 3 |
| Our hearts we open wide | 411 | 2 |
| Our hearts with heavenly love inspire | 752 | 2 |
| Our hearts would now receive thee in | 616 | 9 |
| Our heathenish care, We cast it aside | 496 | 2 |
| †Our heathenish land | 219 | 7 |
| Our heavenly Friend | 495 | 3 |
| †Our heavenly guide | 760 | 3 |
| Our heavenly song shall be | 259 | 6 |
| Our heaven shall be still to sing of thy love | 808 | 7 |
| Our highest thoughts exceed | 610 | 8 |
| Our hope decline, our love grow cold | 677 | 3 |
| Our hope for years to come | 41 | 1 |
| Our hope for years to come | 41 | 7 |
| Our hope in time of ill | 546 | 1 |
| Our hosts have dared and passed the sea | 715 | 1 |
| Our humble prayers implore | 664 | 5 |

| | Hymn | Verse |
|---|---|---|
| Our humble, thankful hearts | 988 | 3 |
| †Our Husband, Brother, Friend | 533 | 3 |
| Our inbred enemies expel | 511 | 2 |
| Our inheritance above | 67 | 4 |
| Our inmost thoughts perceive | 83 | 1 |
| Our insufficiency | 874 | 3 |
| Our interest in his blood | 85 | 2 |
| Our Jesus, and him crucified | 505 | 4 |
| Our Jesus is gone up on high | 557 | 6 |
| *Our Jesus is gone up on high | 759 | 1 |
| Our Jesus receiving, our happiness prove | 19 | 5 |
| †Our Jesus shall be still our theme | 682 | 3 |
| Our Jesus shall from heaven descend | 483 | 5 |
| Our Jesus shall stir up his power | 280 | 3 |
| Our Jesus we discover | 854 | 1 |
| Our Jesu's conquering love | 719 | 2 |
| Our Jesu's praises The angels proclaim | 859 | 4 |
| Our journey pursue | 47 | 1 |
| Our journey pursue | 498 | 1 |
| Our joyful hearts and voices raise | 953 | 3 |
| Our joy is now to sing of thee | 652 | — |
| Our kindred spirits here | 510 | 4 |
| Our King's peculiar treasure prove | 464 | 2 |
| Our labour this, our only aim | 71 | 4 |
| Our leader pursue | 760 | 5 |
| Our lesson at thy feet | 801 | 2 |
| Our life in Christ concealed | 947 | 7 |
| †Our life is a dream | 47 | 3 |
| †Our life is hid with Christ in God | 537 | 6 |
| Our life, our health, our food | 988 | 3 |
| Our Life shall soon appear | 537 | 6 |
| †Our life, while thou preserv'st that life | 1002 | 6 |
| Our light and our defence | 591 | 4 |
| †Our lips and lives shall gladly show | 979 | 4 |
| Our little stock improve | 503 | 4 |
| Our lives shall make thy goodness known | 980 | 3 |
| Our living membership we show | 897 | 4 |
| *Our Lord is risen from the dead | 557 | 6 |
| Our Lord, our faith, our symbol, one | 891 | 2 |
| Our Lord, who made both earth and skies | 953 | 1 |
| Our Lord, who now his right obtains | 56 | 4 |
| Our loss is his infinite gain | 49 | 1 |
| Our loss of Eden to retrieve | 33 | 2 |
| Our lost, apostate race | 249 | 6 |
| Our love from earthly dross refine | 513 | 2 |
| Our love proceeds from thee | 533 | 2 |
| Our love so faint, so cold to thee | 763 | 3 |
| Our Maker and our King | 262 | 3 |
| Our Maker, Defender, Redeemer, and Friend | 611 | 5 |
| Our Master's honoured name | 897 | 3 |
| Our minds continue one | 537 | 3 |
| †Our misery doth for pity call | 249 | 6 |
| Our moments below | 495 | 4 |

| | Hymn | Verse |
|---|---|---|
| †Our mourning is all at an end | 73 | 2 |
| †Our mouth as in the dust we lay | 176 | 2 |
| Our multitude of sins forgive | 511 | 1 |
| Our mutual prayer accept and seal | 524 | 2 |
| †Our naked hearts to thee we raise | 528 | 2 |
| Our nation and our churches bless | 985 | 5 |
| Our nature shall no more | 387 | 3 |
| Our nature's turned, our mind | 96 | 5 |
| Our night in praise and prayer | 222 | 1 |
| †Our old companions in distress | 949 | 4 |
| Our old offending nature lies | 412 | 2 |
| †Our only help in danger's hour | 469 | 8 |
| Our only strength, thou art | 469 | 8 |
| Our own infirmity | 469 | 6 |
| Our own unfaithfulness | 531 | 2 |
| Our praise and lives we pay | 983 | 7 |
| Our prayer shall never cease | 619 | 6 |
| †Our Prophet, Priest, and King, to thee | 801 | 2 |
| Our purity of joy | 482 | 6 |
| Our ransomed souls adore thee | 276 | 2 |
| Our ransomed souls adore thee | 736 | 1 |
| Our ravished hearts o'erflow | 258 | 3 |
| Our real blessings prove | 624 | 2 |
| Our re-converted land | 464 | 2 |
| Our record, Lord, and thine | 459 | 4 |
| †Our residue of days or hours | 979 | 5 |
| Our righteousness divine | 21 | 6 |
| Our rising progeny | 468 | 3 |
| Our robes are robes of glorious light | 21 | 6 |
| Our sacrifice of praise | 345 | 7 |
| Our sacrifice of praise approve | 507 | 3 |
| Our sacrifice receive | 654 | 2 |
| Our safeguard and our tower | 482 | 1 |
| Our sanctifying God | 705 | 1 |
| Our Saviour and King | 219 | 4 |
| Our Saviour and our King | 814 | 1 |
| Our Saviour confess | 219 | 5 |
| Our Saviour from evil, For ever the same | 481 | 3 |
| Our Saviour in the sky | 757 | 1 |
| Our Saviour now prepares our home | 539 | 10 |
| Our Saviour thou | 276 | 2 |
| Our Saviour we adore | 673 | 3 |
| Our Saviour's swift approach declare | 62 | 3 |
| †Our scanty stock as soon as known | 874 | 3 |
| Our scanty thought surpasses far | 189 | 2 |
| Our seals set to | 276 | 1 |
| Our servants there and rising race | 997 | 3 |
| Our shelter from the stormy blast | 41 | 1 |
| Our shield and defender, The Ancient of days | 611 | 1 |
| Our sin and ignorance dispel | 686 | 2 |
| Our sin and wickedness we own | 176 | 2 |
| Our sin, how deep it stains | 786 | 1 |
| Our sin implores thy grace | 249 | 6 |

# OUR SINS — OUR WANT

| | Hymn | Verse |
|---|---|---|
| Our sins, ah! wherefore didst thou bear | 774 | 6 |
| Our sins its ready victims find | 412 | 5 |
| Our sins through faith removed | 806 | 1 |
| Our softer passions move | 226 | 12 |
| Our songs we make of Thee | 239 | 1 |
| †Our sons henceforth be wholly thine | 474 | 3 |
| Our souls and bodies place | 1000 | 1 |
| Our souls' and bodies' powers unite | 204 | 4 |
| Our souls and bodies shall be thine. | 980 | 3 |
| †Our souls and bodies we resign | 428 | 4 |
| †Our souls are in his mighty hand | 537 | 8 |
| Our souls arrive in peace | 664 | 4 |
| Our souls from every sinful stain | 254 | 2 |
| Our souls securely rest | 1000 | 2 |
| Our souls shall drink a fresh supply | 802 | 4 |
| Our souls sprang forth from thee | 264 | 1 |
| Our souls resemble thee | 256 | 6 |
| Our souls their change shall scarcely know | 504 | 7 |
| Our souls this day the living bread | 236 | 3 |
| Our souls this day the living bread | 1017 | 2 |
| Our souls to awaken and inspire | 89 | 2 |
| Our souls unto that day | 510 | 6 |
| Our souls upon thy truth we stay | 505 | 1 |
| Our souls with this intense desire | 526 | 2 |
| Our souls with vast amazement fill. | 226 | 11 |
| Our spirit, Lord, be one with thine. | 666 | 6 |
| Our spirit purged from nature's art | 528 | 3 |
| Our spirits by thine advent here | 690 | 3 |
| Our spirits sink in sore dismay | 698 | 5 |
| †Our spirits too shall quickly join | 949 | 5 |
| Our steps shall attend | 760 | 4 |
| Our strength, thy grace; our rule, thy word | 326 | 1 |
| Our subject is the same | 221 | 3 |
| Our suffering and our pain | 535 | 3 |
| Our supplicating cry | 459 | 1 |
| Our temple make thy throne | 989 | 4 |
| Our time as a stream | 47 | 3 |
| Our time of visitation | 736 | 1 |
| Our title clearly prove | 822 | 4 |
| Our title to heaven His merits we take | 5 | 5 |
| Our tongues to thine honour, And lives we employ | 199 | 3 |
| †Our trespasses forgive | 653 | 5 |
| Our troubles and tears | 760 | 1 |
| Our trusty loving Shepherd, he | 626 | 5 |
| Our undivided hearts | 91 | 5 |
| Our utmost, sorest need supply | 957 | 5 |
| Our utter impotence we see | 475 | 2 |
| Our voices we will raise | 991 | 2 |
| †Our vows, our prayers, we now present | 664 | 2 |
| Our wakening and uprising prove | 965 | 2 |
| Our wandering footsteps guide | 664 | 3 |
| Our want of faith supply | 464 | 1 |
| Our want received into thy hand | 874 | 3 |

| | Hymn | Verse |
|---|---|---|
| Our wants are in thy view | 745 | 2 |
| †Our wasting lives grow shorter still | 42 | 2 |
| Our weakness help, our darkness chase | 89 | 2 |
| Our weariness of life is gone | 222 | 2 |
| Our wild unruly passions bind | 505 | 3 |
| †Our willing feet shall stand | 619 | 2 |
| Our willing hearts adoring own | 955 | 1 |
| Our willing soul thy call obeys | 286 | 4 |
| Our words are lost; nor will we know | 26 | 6 |
| Our works can nothing win | 626 | 2 |
| Ours acknowledge for thine own | 890 | 1 |
| Ours the cross, the grave, the skies | 716 | 5 |
| Ours they are not, Lord, but thine | 411 | 1 |
| Ourselves, and all we have deny | 455 | 1 |
| Ourselves but newly found in thee | 82 | 1 |
| Ourselves, our house, our all | 892 | 6 |
| Ourselves to CHRIST the LORD | 532 | 1 |
| Ourselves we forsake | 495 | 4 |
| Outcast and despised of men | 195 | 3 |
| †Outcasts of men, to you I call | 30 | 5 |
| Out-flying the tempest and wind | 49 | 2 |
| †Out of great distress they came | 76 | 2 |
| Out of his holy place | 551 | 2 |
| Out of his own pierced side | 996 | 4 |
| Out of his plenitude receive | 673 | 3 |
| Out of my deadly sleep | 162 | 1 |
| Out of my sleep to awake | 83 | 7 |
| Out of my soul erase | 367 | 2 |
| Out of my stony griefs | 848 | 4 |
| †Out of myself for help I go | 772 | 2 |
| *Out of the deep I cry | 151 | 1 |
| Out of the deep on thee to call | 301 | 4 |
| †Out of the deep regard their cries | 462 | 4 |
| *Out of the depths I cry to thee | 626 | 1 |
| *Out of the depths of self-despair | 625 | 1 |
| Out of the house of bondage brought | 293 | 2 |
| Out of the narrow way | 188 | 2 |
| Out of their ashes rise | 536 | 6 |
| Out of their sins the nations shake | 443 | 1 |
| Out of thy grave the saint shall rise | 330 | 5 |
| Out of thy hand receive | 248 | 4 |
| Out of thy hands my cause | 436 | 4 |
| Out of thy richest grace supply | 473 | 1 |
| Out-soar the first-born cherub's flight | 377 | 4 |
| Overlooks the crowd below | 278 | 1 |
| Over me thy mantle spread | 109 | 4 |
| Over my evil heart | 311 | 4 |
| Over Salem's loved abode | 710 | 3 |
| Over, through, and in us all | 515 | 2 |
| Pain and shame alike they dare | 737 | 9 |
| †Pain and sickness, at thy word | 166 | 4 |
| Pain, and sin, and want, and care | 941 | 2 |

| | Hymn | Verse |
|---|---|---|
| Pain before thy face withdrew | 335 | 2 |
| †Pale death, with all his ghastly train | 614 | 3 |
| Palms in our hands we all shall bear | 537 | 10 |
| Palms of victory | 936 | 6 |
| Palms they carry in their hands | 75 | 1 |
| Pant for the cooling water-brook | 577 | 3 |
| Pant ye after second death | 6 | 4 |
| Pants for thee each mortal breast | 743 | 2 |
| Parched by the sun's directer ray | 46 | 2 |
| Pardon and accept me now | 168 | 5 |
| †Pardon, and grace, and heaven to buy | 330 | 3 |
| Pardon, and holiness, and heaven | 95 | 4 |
| Pardon, and holiness, and heaven | 209 | 2 |
| Pardon, and peace, and heavenly joys | 376 | 2 |
| Pardon and peace in Jesus find | 4 | 4 |
| Pardon for all flows from his side | 28 | 3 |
| Pardon for crimes of deepest dye | 656 | 3 |
| Pardon I accept unbought | 175 | 4 |
| Pardon in Christ for all mankind | 441 | 3 |
| Pardon in thy blood to gain | 876 | 3 |
| Pardon was written on my heart | 365 | 4 |
| Pardon ye all through him may have | 32 | 1 |
| †Pardoned for all that I have done | 369 | 6 |
| Pardoned, sanctified, and sealed | 479 | 3 |
| †Parent of good, thy bounteous hand | 241 | 3 |
| Parents, friends, 'twas God bestowed | 233 | 1 |
| Partake my victory | 315 | 4 |
| Partaker of my hope | 382 | 5 |
| Partaker of thy grace | 674 | 2 |
| Partakers of a nature pure | 380 | 8 |
| †Partakers of his triumph | 854 | 3 |
| Partakers of their joys | 735 | 4 |
| Partakers of the joys above | 490 | 3 |
| †Partakers of the Saviour's grace | 534 | 5 |
| Partakers of thy nature make | 894 | 2 |
| Partakers of thy Son | 894 | 2 |
| Partakers of your hope | 86 | 1 |
| Part from thee my ravished soul | 672 | 10 |
| †Part of his church below | 897 | 4 |
| Part of his host have crossed the flood | 949 | 2 |
| †Part of thy name divinely stands | 263 | 3 |
| Partner of an equal throne | 727 | 7 |
| Partner of thy weal or woe | 877 | 2 |
| Partners in his sufferings here | 936 | 1 |
| *Partners of a glorious hope | 522 | 1 |
| Partners of like precious faith | 519 | 2 |
| Partners of thine endless reign | 849 | 4 |
| Partners of thy endless reign | 718 | 10 |
| Partners with the saints in light | 520 | 4 |
| †Paschal Lamb, by God appointed | 722 | 2 |
| *Pass a few swiftly-fleeting years | 48 | 1 |
| Pass as a God of pardoning love | 124 | 4 |
| Pass away | 793 | 6 |

| | Hymn | Verse |
|---|---|---|
| Pass by me, and thy name declare | 283 | 4 |
| †Pass me not, O God, our Father | 790 | 2 |
| †Pass me not, O gracious Saviour | 790 | 3 |
| †Pass me not, O mighty Spirit | 790 | 4 |
| Pass secure the watery flood | 238 | 3 |
| Pass the former things away | 60 | 4 |
| Pass we thus our happy days | 529 | 4 |
| Passed the heavenly courts, and stood | 724 | 1 |
| Passed through the deep | 276 | 3 |
| Passing through the mortal vale | 101 | 5 |
| †Passion, and appetite, and pride | 293 | 7 |
| Pastors and people shout thy praise | 868 | 5 |
| Pastors from hence, and teachers rise | 868 | 2 |
| Past the reach of hell secure | 480 | 2 |
| †Patience to watch, and wait, and weep | 865 | 5 |
| Patience with thy rebel have | 173 | 3 |
| Patient, and pitiful, and kind | 865 | 7 |
| Patient inmate of my breast | 768 | 9 |
| Patient, pitiful, and kind | 520 | 3 |
| †Patient the appointed race to run | 71 | 4 |
| Patriarchs, first-born of men | 737 | 7 |
| Pavilioned in splendour, And girded with praise | 611 | 1 |
| Pay all their dues to thee | 788 | 5 |
| Pay on joy's returning morn | 580 | 3 |
| Pay we, gracious God, to thee | 50 | 1 |
| Peace, and joy, and righteousness | 348 | 3 |
| *Peace be on this house bestowed | 479 | 1 |
| *Peace, doubting heart! my God's I am | 272 | 1 |
| Peace is made 'twixt man and God | 722 | 2 |
| Peace, like a river, from his throne | 585 | 6 |
| Peace on all that here reside | 479 | 1 |
| Peace on earth, and mercy mild | 683 | 1 |
| Peace on earth to man forgiven | 257 | 1 |
| Peace, righteousness, and joy | 761 | 3 |
| Peace, righteousness, and joy, and love | 394 | 4 |
| Peace, righteousness, and joy impart | 131 | 4 |
| Peace, the seal of sin forgiven | 530 | 4 |
| Peace unspeakable, unknown | 20 | 2 |
| Peace upon earth, and unto men good-will | 691 | 3 |
| Pearl of price by Jesus bought | 921 | 1 |
| †People and realms of every tongue | 585 | 9 |
| Perennial verdure crowned its head | 589 | 2 |
| Perfect, and right, and pure, and good | 343 | 4 |
| Perfect in comeliness thou art | 568 | 2 |
| Perfect in power, in love, and purity | 646 | 3 |
| Perfect love shall cast out fear | 355 | 8 |
| Perfect love shall seal me his | 882 | 5 |
| Perfect me in holiness | 110 | 6 |
| Perfect me in love divine | 183 | 3 |
| Perfect me in love to-night | 287 | 6 |
| Perfect righteousness bring in | 110 | 5 |
| †Perfect then the work begun | 112 | 7 |
| Perfect through my Lord below | 13 | 4 |

| | Hymn | Verse |
|---|---|---|
| Perfected in holiness | 400 | 5 |
| Perfected in holiness | 623 | 6 |
| Perfecting the saints below | 518 | 1 |
| Perfectly resigned to thee | 381 | 1 |
| Perfectly restored in thee | 385 | 3 |
| Perfectly set free from all | 142 | 8 |
| Perfectly to him be joined | 355 | 10 |
| Perform my every work aright | 828 | 1 |
| Perform my oft-repeated vow | 80 | 5 |
| Perform thy awful will | 788 | 4 |
| Perform thy will below | 243 | 4 |
| Perish the grass, and fade the flower | 46 | 6 |
| †" Permit them to approach," he cries | 889 | 2 |
| †Persist to save my soul | 436 | 7 |
| Perverseness in my will | 382 | 2 |
| Physician of souls, unto me | 70 | 3 |
| Physician of the sin-sick mind | 114 | 1 |
| Pierced and nailed him to the tree | 66 | 2 |
| Pierced with grief for grieving thee | 768 | 1 |
| *Pierce, fill me with an humble fear | 313 | 1 |
| Pierce the gloom of sin and grief | 963 | 3 |
| Pierce to the bottom of my heart | 341 | 1 |
| †Pilgrims here on earth and strangers | 970 | 2 |
| Pilgrim through this barren land | 839 | 1 |
| Pining then for poisoned food | 768 | 4 |
| Pitched but a few frail days | 942 | 3 |
| †Pity, and heal my sin-sick soul | 132 | 2 |
| Pity a soul that fain would trust | 148 | 1 |
| Pity divine in Jesu's face | 226 | 12 |
| Pity drew him from above | 215 | 2 |
| †Pity from thine eye let fall | 168 | 6 |
| Pity is with thee the same | 112 | 3 |
| Pity my helpless unbelief | 117 | 3 |
| Pity my unsettled soul | 183 | 1 |
| †Pity the day of feeble things | 462 | 5 |
| Pity the souls that look to thee | 774 | 1 |
| Pity thy fallen creature's pain | 150 | 2 |
| †Pity to my dying cries | 112 | 5 |
| Placed according to thy will | 518 | 5 |
| Place him at the Saviour's feet | 51 | 4 |
| †Place no longer let us give | 295 | 2 |
| Plagued with an infirmity | 166 | 2 |
| Plague, earthquake, and famine, And tumult, and war | 273 | 4 |
| Plain as the sea and sky | 662 | 3 |
| Plant, Almighty Lord, in me | 243 | 4 |
| †Plant, and root, and fix in me | 355 | 5 |
| Plant in us thy humble mind | 520 | 3 |
| †Plant thy heavenly kingdom here | 937 | 5 |
| Plead for us on earth who dwell | 724 | 2 |
| Pleads the merit of his blood | 791 | 5 |
| Plead thy cause with sword and fire | 60 | 2 |
| †Plead we thus for faith alone | 521 | 3 |

| | Hymn | Verse |
|---|---|---|
| *Pleasant are thy courts above | 593 | 1 |
| Pleasant are thy courts below | 593 | 1 |
| Pleased a servant's form to wear | 194 | 2 |
| Pleased as man with men to appear | 683 | 3 |
| Pleased he ever is in thee | 194 | 5 |
| Pleased inmate of my peaceful breast | 770 | 5 |
| Pleasure, and wealth, and fame we give | 286 | 4 |
| †Pleasure, and wealth, and praise no more | 332 | 3 |
| Pledge of everlasting bliss | 631 | 7 |
| †Plenteous grace with thee is found | 143 | 4 |
| †Plenteous he is in truth and grace | 144 | 6 |
| †Plenteous of grace, descend from high | 752 | 3 |
| Plenteous redemption through his blood | 625 | 5 |
| *Plunged in a gulf of dark despair | 699 | 1 |
| Plunged in the Godhead's deepest sea | 374 | 3 |
| Plunge him, by a second birth | 477 | 1 |
| Plurality in One | 643 | 2 |
| Pointed the nail, and fixed the thorn | 23 | 3 |
| Point out the path before my face | 543 | 6 |
| Point out thy instruments, unknown | 871 | 1 |
| Point to the all-atoning blood | 744 | 4 |
| Points the word's unerring aim | 278 | 5 |
| Points to his side, and lifts his hands | 127 | 9 |
| Points us to the victor's crown | 728 | 6 |
| Poison our simplicity | 508 | 4 |
| †Poor, alas! thou know'st I am | 109 | 5 |
| †Poor am I, and in need; yet God | 566 | 10 |
| Poor and helpless here I lie | 166 | 2 |
| Poor and little though I be | 620 | 3 |
| Poor, and sad, and empty still | 623 | 5 |
| Poor, and vile, and abject here | 195 | 2 |
| †Poor and vile in my own eyes | 243 | 5 |
| Poor and vile in my own eyes | 381 | 1 |
| †Poor debtors, by our Lord's request | 11 | 4 |
| Poor, guilty, dying worms, in whom | 261 | 2 |
| Poor helpless souls the bounteous Lord | 638 | 5 |
| Poor idiots he teaches To show forth his praise | 211 | 2 |
| Poor ignorant wretches, We gladly embrace | 212 | 4 |
| Poor in spirit, meek in heart | 628 | 1 |
| Poor nothings! for his boundless grace | 492 | 1 |
| †Poor outcasts of men, Whose souls were despised | 211 | 5 |
| †Poor worms of earth, for help we cry | 467 | 2 |
| Portrayed it bears a bleeding Lamb | 269 | 2 |
| Possession of my heart | 152 | 2 |
| Possession of thine own | 216 | 8 |
| Possess it thou, who hast the right | 285 | 5 |
| Possess the promised rest | 940 | 4 |
| Possessor here of grace and love | 896 | 5 |
| Pour all its flames upon my head | 272 | 7 |
| Pour, mine eyes, a ceaseless flood | 27 | 2 |
| Pour out on sinners from above | 424 | 1 |
| †Pour out the promised gift on all | 749 | 3 |
| Pour out the Spirit of his grace | 111 | 3 |

| | Hymn | Verse |
|---|---|---|
| Pour out the supplicating grace | 294 | 1 |
| †Pour out your souls to God | 268 | 3 |
| Poured out his cries and tears | 725 | 3 |
| Pouring eye-sight on our eyes | 687 | 1 |
| Pour'st thy oil upon my head | 554 | 5 |
| Power, and endless adoration | 748 | 7 |
| Power complete to thee is given | 730 | 1 |
| Power he now to us imparts | 571 | 6 |
| Power his image to retrieve | 529 | 3 |
| Power into strengthless souls it speaks | 37 | 3 |
| †Power is all to Jesus given | 571 | 6 |
| †Power is all to Jesus given | 728 | 2 |
| Power, like thee, our Lord, to live | 529 | 3 |
| Power o'er hell, and earth, and heaven | 571 | 6 |
| †Power o'er the world, the fiend, and sin | 419 | 3 |
| Power supreme to thee is given | 737 | 5 |
| Power to believe, and go in peace | 416 | 1 |
| †Power to every messenger | 733 | 4 |
| Power to practise thy commands | 873 | 3 |
| Power to work for God again | 529 | 3 |
| †Powerful advocate with God | 257 | 6 |
| Powerful the wounded soul to heal | 337 | 3 |
| Praise, ardent, cordial, constant give | 983 | 7 |
| Praise be done to the Three in One | 663 | — |
| Praise by all to thee be given | 221 | 4 |
| Praise by all to thee be given | 350 | 8 |
| Praise by all to thee be given | 430 | 1 |
| Praise by all to thee be given | 430 | 6 |
| Praise by all to thee be given | 645 | 2 |
| Praise by day, day without night | 221 | 2 |
| Praise doth all to Christ belong | 727 | 4 |
| Praise Father, Son, and Holy Ghost | 964 | 8 |
| Praise Father, Son, and Holy Ghost | 974 | 10 |
| Praise from earth and heaven receive | 191 | 1 |
| †Praise God, from whom all blessings flow | 964 | 8 |
| †Praise God, from whom all blessings flow | 974 | 10 |
| Praise him above, ye heavenly host | 964 | 8 |
| Praise him above, ye heavenly host | 974 | 10 |
| Praise him, all creatures here below | 964 | 8 |
| Praise him, all creatures here below | 974 | 10 |
| Praise him, all ye stars and light | 640 | 1 |
| Praise him, angels in the height | 640 | 1 |
| Praise him every tuneful string | 641 | 3 |
| Praise him for his matchless power | 641 | 1 |
| Praise him for his noble deeds | 641 | 1 |
| †Praise him for our harvest-store | 631 | 6 |
| Praise him in the sacred dance | 641 | 2 |
| Praise him, praise him evermore | 75 | 4 |
| Praise him, praise him evermore | 605 | 5 |
| †Praise him that he gave the rain | 631 | 4 |
| †Praise him that he made the sun | 631 | 2 |
| Praise him till his glory fills | 605 | 6 |
| Praise him with believing hearts | 571 | 6 |

| | Hymn | Verse |
|---|---|---|
| Praise him with the host divine | 571 | 4 |
| †Praise him, ye saints, the God of love | 614 | 14 |
| Praise his name, whose praise rejoices | 580 | 1 |
| †Praise his name with one consent | 639 | 8 |
| Praise in songs the eternal King | 580 | 1 |
| Praise, laud, and bless his name always | 607 | 3 |
| Praise o'erflow our grateful soul | 737 | 1 |
| *Praise, O praise our God and King | 631 | 1 |
| Praise shall employ my nobler powers | 224 | 1 |
| Praise shall employ my nobler powers | 224 | 4 |
| Praise shall our glad tongue employ | 737 | 1 |
| Praise shall your glad tongues employ | 197 | 4 |
| Praise the attributes divine | 653 | 1 |
| Praise the God of our salvation | 640 | 2 |
| Praise the God on whom ye call | 571 | 1 |
| Praise the holy God of love | 641 | 1 |
| Praise the Lord! for he hath spoken | 640 | 1 |
| †Praise the Lord, for he is glorious | 640 | 2 |
| Praise the Lord in every breath | 641 | 4 |
| *Praise the Lord! who reigns above | 641 | 1 |
| Praise the Lord who stooped to die | 605 | 4 |
| Praise the Lord with all your powers | 639 | 1 |
| *Praise the Lord! ye heavens, adore him | 640 | 1 |
| Praise the mystic Three in One | 221 | 2 |
| Praise thy name with one accord | 733 | 1 |
| Praise to God alone be given | 243 | 5 |
| †Praise to God, whose mercy-token | 621 | 3 |
| Praise to thee, eternal Spirit | 990 | 6 |
| Praise to thee, in whom thy temple | 990 | 6 |
| †Praise to thee, O Master-Builder | 990 | 6 |
| Praises to our glorious King | 571 | 5 |
| Praises to our Jesus sing | 571 | 5 |
| Praise we all our lowly King | 400 | 2 |
| *Praise ye the Lord! 'tis good to raise | 225 | 1 |
| Pray always, and not faint | 299 | 1 |
| Pray always; pray, and never faint | 267 | 4 |
| Pray, and praise thee, without ceasing | 385 | 2 |
| †Pray for Jerusalem | 619 | 4 |
| Pray that help may be sent down | 829 | 6 |
| Pray we, every moment pray | 295 | Cho. |
| Pray we for our faith's increase | 480 | 2 |
| †Pray we on when all renewed | 295 | 5 |
| †Pray, without ceasing pray | 267 | 4 |
| Prayed to my God for grace | 551 | 2 |
| †Prayer is the burden of a sigh | 823 | 2 |
| †Prayer is the Christian's vital breath | 823 | 5 |
| †Prayer is the contrite sinner's voice | 823 | 4 |
| *Prayer is the soul's sincere desire | 823 | 1 |
| †Prayer is the simplest form of speech | 823 | 3 |
| Prayer the sublimest strains that reach | 823 | 3 |
| Preachers, who all the sinful race | 744 | 4 |
| Preach him to all, and cry in death | 37 | 6 |
| Preach his gospel to our heart | 899 | 1 |

| | HYMN | VERSE |
|---|---|---|
| Preach Jesus to them ere they die | 746 | 1 |
| Preach the reconciling Word | 733 | 4 |
| Preaching truth and doom to come | 720 | 3 |
| Precious, elect, and corner-stone | 670 | 1 |
| †Prepare, and then possess my heart | 155 | 8 |
| Prepare for thee the holiest place | 341 | 2 |
| Prepare, my soul, to meet him | 932 | 1 |
| Prepare the vessel of thy grace | 440 | 1 |
| Prepare your hearts to make him room | 380 | 1 |
| Prepared and mingled by thy skill | 337 | 3 |
| †Present alike in every place | 289 | 3 |
| Present before the throne of grace | 539 | 7 |
| Present, everlasting heaven | 530 | 4 |
| Present for past can ne'er atone | 127 | 5 |
| Present my heart and reins to try | 550 | 1 |
| Present my soul to heal | 188 | 3 |
| Present our living sacrifice | 616 | 11 |
| Present, though I mourn apart | 768 | 1 |
| Present to confirm the word | 873 | 1 |
| Present to heal, in me display | 135 | 1 |
| Present to Zion's King | 452 | 3 |
| Present us sanctified to God | 523 | 5 |
| †Present we know thou art | 485 | 3 |
| †Present we still in spirit are | 587 | 5 |
| Present with the celestial host | 532 | 5 |
| Present with thee the future are | 360 | 6 |
| Present with thy angel host | 910 | 7 |
| Present with thy heavenly host | 477 | 1 |
| Present with us thee we feel | 506 | 3 |
| Preserve by thine unceasing prayer | 893 | 2 |
| Preserve inseparably one | 489 | 2 |
| Preserve me every moment thine | 780 | 2 |
| Preserve me spotless here | 820 | 3 |
| Preserve my soul from sin | 813 | — |
| Preserve the creatures of thy love | 258 | 1 |
| Preserve them for thy glorious cause | 474 | 2 |
| Preserve us safe from sin and death | 814 | 2 |
| Preserved by his grace Throughout the dark hour | 481 | 2 |
| Preserved by power divine | 478 | 1 |
| Preserved by thy word, We worship thee now | 199 | 3 |
| Preserved every hour Through Jesus's name | 200 | 3 |
| Preserved from evil every hour | 366 | 2 |
| †Preserved through faith by power divine | 230 | 2 |
| Pressing on, and bearing up | 769 | 4 |
| Prevalent he intercedes | 718 | 6 |
| Prevent, accompany, and bless | 475 | 3 |
| Preventing what my lips would say | 99 | 2 |
| Prevents the morning ray | 625 | 4 |
| Previous to the general doom | 423 | 4 |
| Pride, and wrath, and every foe | 352 | 4 |
| Pride in its earliest motions find | 313 | 2 |
| Pride, my old, dreadful, tyrant-foe | 293 | 7 |
| Pride, when God is passing by | 768 | 5 |

|  | Hymn | Verse |
|---|---|---|
| †Primeval Beauty! in thy sight | 38 | 6 |
| †Prince of peace, thy peace bestow | 895 | 3 |
| Princes, Judges of the earth | 639 | 6 |
| Principalities and powers | 757 | 1 |
| †Principalities and powers | 829 | 2 |
| Print thine own resemblance there | 824 | 5 |
| †Prisoner of hope, I still attend | 123 | 3 |
| †Prisoner of hope, to thee I turn | 144 | 4 |
| *Prisoners of hope, arise | 387 | 1 |
| †Prisoners of hope, be strong, be bold | 380 | 5 |
| *Prisoners of hope, lift up your heads | 380 | 1 |
| Prized and loved by God alone | 508 | 6 |
| Proclaim, God sitteth on the throne | 831 | 11 |
| †Proclaim salvation from the Lord | 659 | 3 |
| Proclaim the angelic joys | 719 | 1 |
| Proclaims thy conquering arm | 671 | 3 |
| Promise in thy fear to live | 910 | 6 |
| Promise of our parting Lord | 758 | 1 |
| Promises so sweet and precious | 882 | 1 |
| Prone to leave the God I love | 866 | 3 |
| Prone to wander, Lord, I feel it | 866 | 3 |
| Pronounced the pardoning word | 623 | 1 |
| Pronounce me doubly blest | 304 | 7 |
| Pronounce the Tempter's doom | 299 | 8 |
| Pronounce the welcome word, "Well done!" | 443 | 2 |
| Prophet, and Priest, and King behold | 689 | 3 |
| †Prophet, and Priest, and King of peace | 107 | 2 |
| †Prophet, to me reveal | 193 | 6 |
| Prophets and kings desired long | 741 | 4 |
| Prosperity abound | 619 | 5 |
| Prostrate at thy feet we fall | 737 | 5 |
| Prostrate before thy awful throne | 913 | 1 |
| Prostrate before thy face we fall | 235 | 2 |
| Prostrate on their face before | 75 | 3 |
| Prostrate seraphim above | 260 | 2 |
| Protect and guide us in the way | 752 | 4 |
| Protect them wheresoe'er they go | 1004 | 4 |
| Protected by thy blood | 893 | 2 |
| †Protected by thy guardian grace | 543 | 8 |
| Proud and spurning all control | 621 | 2 |
| Provoke my hope or fear | 947 | 2 |
| Publishest the power of grace | 693 | 4 |
| Publish, spread his name abroad | 572 | 1 |
| †Publish, spread to all around | 641 | 2 |
| Publish we his praise below | 480 | 1 |
| Publish we the death divine | 701 | 2 |
| Purchased and redeemed of old | 735 | 3 |
| Purchased by that blood of thine | 757 | 3 |
| Purchased by the atoning blood | 890 | 2 |
| Purchased by the blood of God | 67 | 5 |
| Pure and spotless let us be | 385 | 3 |
| *Pure baptismal Fire divine | 766 | 1 |
| Pure eyes and Christian hearts | 662 | 1 |

| | Hymn | Verse |
|---|---|---|
| Pure in heart to see his face | 400 | 3 |
| Pure joy and everlasting peace | 447 | 4 |
| Pure love to every soul of man | 419 | 4 |
| †Pure love to God thy members find | 419 | 4 |
| Pure, unbounded love thou art | 385 | 1 |
| Pure, universal love thou art | 141 | 2 |
| Purest light his garment is | 601 | 1 |
| †Purged from the stains of sin | 735 | 3 |
| Purge every stain away | 943 | 13 |
| Purge in the refining flame | 512 | 2 |
| †Purge me from every sinful blot | 391 | 4 |
| Purge my iniquity | 184 | 2 |
| Purge the foul, inbred leprosy | 895 | 5 |
| Purge the love of sin away | 414 | 1 |
| Purify our faith like gold | 414 | 2 |
| Put away our sins to-night | 971 | 2 |
| Put forth thy hand, thy hand of grace | 114 | 3 |
| Put on me my glorious dress | 109 | 7 |
| Put their most dreadful forms | 675 | 10 |
| Puts all our foes to flight | 315 | 3 |
| | | |
| Quell your foes, and seal their doom | 348 | 5 |
| Quench all his fiery darts, and chase | 311 | 2 |
| Quenched corruption's earlier fires | 768 | 6 |
| Quenched the fiercest wrath of God | 748 | 5 |
| Quick as the apple of an eye | 308 | 2 |
| Quick as the apple of an eye | 313 | 3 |
| Quicken all my drooping powers | 156 | 1 |
| Quicken my mortal frame | 856 | 3 |
| Quicken my soul, instruct my heart | 169 | 2 |
| Quickened by thy imparted flame | 100 | 4 |
| *Quickened with our immortal Head | 419 | 1 |
| Quickened with our living Lord | 717 | 3 |
| Quickened your souls by faith divine | 4 | 9 |
| Quickly appeased and reconciled | 472 | 3 |
| Quiet now without my food | 628 | 3 |
| Quiet shalt thou never know | 299 | 1 |
| Quite from the virgin's womb | 750 | 4 |
| | | |
| Rage the waves and dash the sky | 601 | 3 |
| †Raised by the breath of love divine | 71 | 6 |
| Raised by the nurture of the Lord | 473 | 2 |
| Raised from the dust to stand restored | 670 | 2 |
| Raise for man the springing grain | 579 | 2 |
| Raise the fallen, cheer the faint | 143 | 3 |
| Raise the glorious harvest-home | 987 | 4 |
| Raise the new accordant song | 604 | 1 |
| *Raise the psalm: let earth adoring | 604 | 1 |
| Raise the song of harvest-home | 987 | 1 |
| Raise the song of harvest-home | 987 | 4 |
| Raise us to thy glorious throne | 688 | 2 |
| †Raise us up from earth to heaven | 720 | 8 |
| Raise your joys and triumphs high | 716 | 1 |

| | Hymn | Verse |
|---|---|---|
| Raise your songs of triumph high | 605 | 4 |
| Ransomed by thy dying love | 349 | 3 |
| Rapt, they search the written word | 817 | 4 |
| Raptures that shall never fail | 52 | 1 |
| Rashness midst remembered falls | 768 | 3 |
| Rather from the dread occasion | 819 | 3 |
| †Rather I would in darkness mourn | 307 | 3 |
| Rather I would in painful awe | 307 | 3 |
| †Rather this hour resume his breath | 467 | 5 |
| Ratify the nuptial vow | 995 | 1 |
| Ravished from our wishful eyes | 718 | 1 |
| Reaches out the crown of love | 922 | 2 |
| Reach forth: see, my whole heart I bow | 133 | 4 |
| Ready art thou now to save | 182 | 3 |
| Ready at thy demand to lay | 432 | 2 |
| Ready for all alarms | 267 | 3 |
| †Ready for all thy perfect will | 327 | 4 |
| †Ready for you the angels wait | 9 | 4 |
| Ready if thou always art | 149 | 1 |
| Ready its first approach to shun | 998 | 3 |
| Ready made for the mansions above | 488 | 8 |
| Ready now my Saviour stands | 383 | 1 |
| Ready prepared, and fitted here | 309 | 5 |
| †Ready the Father is to own | 9 | 2 |
| Ready the outcasts to receive | 163 | 4 |
| †Ready the Spirit of his love | 9 | 3 |
| †Ready thou art the blood to apply | 35 | 8 |
| Ready thy choice to approve | 510 | 1 |
| Ready to save I feel thee nigh | 775 | 1 |
| Ready your loving Saviour stands | 9 | 2 |
| Re-ascends his native heaven | 718 | 1 |
| Rebuilt by his command | 452 | 4 |
| Rebuke these storms, and set me safe on land | 596 | 2 |
| Recall me by that pitying look | 309 | 4 |
| Recall them by thy pitying eye | 461 | 1 |
| Received on Calvary | 202 | 3 |
| Receive it back unbought | 738 | 5 |
| Receive me into Christ my peace | 616 | 6 |
| Receive me up into thy Son | 283 | 3 |
| Receive me to thy breast | 68 | 8 |
| "Receive my soul," he cries | 22 | 3 |
| Receive the King of glory in | 557 | 8 |
| Receive the praise | 736 | 3 |
| Receive the son thou didst so long reprove | 596 | 3 |
| Receive thy ancient people home | 451 | 3 |
| Receive thy favoured son | 229 | 6 |
| Receive thy own peculiar care | 465 | 3 |
| Receive thy ready bride | 503 | 6 |
| Receiving its Lord from above | 220 | 2 |
| Recline my weary head upon | 147 | 6 |
| Reconciled by grace below | 51 | 2 |
| Recover his forfeited peace | 174 | 1 |
| Redeemed by thee, we plead | 450 | 1 |

| | HYMN | VERSE |
|---|---|---|
| Redeemed from all iniquity : | 17 | 5 |
| Redeemed from all iniquity . | 159 | 2 |
| Redeemed from death and guilty fears | 614 | 7 |
| Redeemed from sin, and free indeed | 419 | 1 |
| Redeemed from sin and wrath | 497 | 4 |
| Redeemed me from the mortal harm | 916 | 1 |
| Redeemed us by our conquering Lord | 493 | 4 |
| Redeemer, King, Creator | 747 | 4 |
| Redeemer of mankind | 701 | 1 |
| Redeem from all iniquity | 375 | 2 |
| Redeem me by thy grace alone | 106 | 4 |
| Redeem me from all sin | 406 | 6 |
| †Redeem my helpless soul | 654 | 4 |
| Redeem the time, be bold, be wise | 983 | 1 |
| †Redeem thy mis-spent moments past | 964 | 2 |
| Redeeming love has been my theme | 798 | 4 |
| Redemption in his blood | 387 | 1 |
| Redemption in his blood | 738 | 3 |
| Redemption through thy blood | 303 | 5 |
| Redemption through thy blood I have | 417 | 6 |
| Refine and purge our earthly parts | 752 | 3 |
| †Refining fire, go through my heart | 361 | 9 |
| Refresh my soul in death | 679 | 6 |
| Refuse his righteousness to impart | 30 | 3 |
| Regard a sinner's prayer | 150 | 1 |
| †Regard me with a gracious eye | 117 | 4 |
| Regard my fearful heart's desire | 181 | 3 |
| Regard my grief, regard thy own | 157 | 1 |
| †Regard our prayers for Zion's peace | 523 | 2 |
| †Regard thine own eternal prayer | 505 | 8 |
| *Regardless now of things below | 773 | 1 |
| Regardless of our own delight | 204 | 4 |
| Regardless of the pains I feel | 281 | 4 |
| Region of eternal day | 76 | 3 |
| Register the oath in heaven. | 910 | 8 |
| Reign in every heart alone | 676 | 3 |
| †Reign in me, Lord, thy foes control | 347 | 4 |
| Reign thou in my heart alone | 383 | 3 |
| Reign thou in righteousness and power | 546 | 3 |
| Reign through all eternity | 653 | 7 |
| Reign to all eternity | 937 | 6 |
| Reign triumphant | 748 | 7 |
| Reign triumphant at thy side | 885 | 2 |
| Reign triumphant with our Head | 723 | 6 |
| †Reign, true Messiah, reign | 731 | 9 |
| Reign, when death no more shall be | 937 | 6 |
| Reign, when sin shall be no more | 937 | 6 |
| Reign with Christ in endless day | 1008 | 3 |
| Reign with me triumphant now | 51 | 4 |
| Reinstate us in thy love | 683 | 7 |
| Reject it with disdain | 617 | 3 |
| Reject the inbred tyrant's yoke | 587 | 3 |
| Rejoice, again I say, rejoice | 729 | Cho. |

| | Hymn | Verse |
|---|---|---|
| *Rejoice evermore With angels above | 19 | 1 |
| *Rejoice for a brother deceased | 49 | 1 |
| Rejoice, give thanks, and shout thy praise | 543 | 8 |
| †Rejoice in glorious hope | 729 | 6 |
| Rejoice in God, rejoice in heaven | 761 | 6 |
| Rejoice in God sent down from heaven | 761 | Cho. |
| Rejoice in hope of that glad hour | 547 | 6 |
| Rejoice in hope, rejoice with me | 345 | Cho. |
| Rejoice in our redeeming love | 387 | 2 |
| Rejoice not over me | 274 | 1 |
| Rejoice! rejoice! Immanuel. | 690 | Cho. |
| Rejoice! rejoice! the Lord is king | 539 | 2 |
| *Rejoice, the Lord is King | 729 | 1 |
| Rejoice with all the sanctified | 65 | 4 |
| Rejoicing evermore | 21 | 4 |
| †Rejoicing in hope, And patient in grief | 273 | 2 |
| †Rejoicing in hope, We humbly go on | 484 | 2 |
| †Rejoicing now in earnest hope | 404 | 2 |
| Rejoicing this foundation lay | 992 | 2 |
| Relieve me again, and restore | 165 | 4 |
| Relieve my wants, assuage my woes | 114 | 1 |
| Relieve the thirsty soul, the faint | 379 | 3 |
| Relieves, and fills with plenteousness | 638 | 5 |
| Remains and stands for ever sure | 391 | 1 |
| Remembered songs of gladness | 587 | 2 |
| †Remember, Lord, my sins no more. | 369 | 3 |
| *Remember, Lord, the pious zeal | 629 | 1 |
| Remember, Lord, thy dying groans | 82 | 6 |
| Remember now thy faithful word | 635 | 1 |
| Remember us for good | 506 | 1 |
| Remind us of thy manger bed | 692 | 3 |
| Remissness and severity | 471 | 2 |
| Remove all my load | 160 | 3 |
| Remove from hence! to sin I say | 417 | 3 |
| Remove it, and I shall declare | 152 | 4 |
| †Remove this hardness from my heart | 403 | 4 |
| Remove this load of guilty woe | 181 | 3 |
| Remove thy judgments, lest I die | 565 | 5 |
| Removes me to that heavenly place | 59 | 2 |
| Removes the huge mountain Of indwelling sin | 3 | 6 |
| Rendered all distinctions void | 518 | 10 |
| Renderest every man his due | 242 | 3 |
| Render in thanks their lives to thee | 253 | 2 |
| Render we our God his right | 75 | 4 |
| Renewed thy mortal pain | 122 | 1 |
| Renew, enlarge, and fill our heart | 237 | 2 |
| Renew my broken vow | 697 | 9 |
| †Renew my will from day to day | 841 | 6 |
| Renew the glorious strife | 144 | 1 |
| †Renew thine image, Lord, in me | 353 | 5 |
| Repeats the story of her birth | 552 | 3 |
| Repelled his every fiery dart | 267 | 1 |
| Repentance be the last | 778 | 4 |

| | Hymn | Verse |
|---|---|---|
| Repentance, faith, and pardon give | 170 | 3 |
| †Repentance, permanent and deep | 778 | 3 |
| Repentance to impart | 106 | 2 |
| Repentance unto life bestow | 84 | 3 |
| Repent, believe, thou shalt be loosed from all | 794 | 3 |
| Replenished are thy lips with grace | 568 | 2 |
| Repose our faith on thee alone | 891 | 1 |
| Reprove my folly, but forgive | 770 | 3 |
| Request, and I will grant thy prayer | 541 | 3 |
| Require our ceaseless praise | 736 | 3 |
| Rescue me from fires undying | 933 | 14 |
| Resides in the eternal Son | 254 | 1 |
| Resigned to the burden we bear | 946 | 3 |
| Resigned, yet longing to depart | 919 | 2 |
| †Resolved at last, "To God," I cried | 561 | 4 |
| Resolved to seek my all in thee | 291 | 3 |
| Rest beneath the Almighty's shade | 597 | 1 |
| †Rest for my soul I long to find | 388 | 3 |
| Rest from toil, and weep no more | 878 | 5 |
| Rest in him, securely rest | 618 | 2 |
| Rest in thee I gasp to find | 116 | 1 |
| Rest of every troubled heart | 723 | 1 |
| Rest, on thee alone reclined | 999 | 2 |
| Rest upon us from above | 1006 | — |
| Rest with thee in heaven at last | 970 | 2 |
| †Resting in this glorious hope | 61 | 4 |
| Restlessly my God desire | 287 | 3 |
| Restless to be saved by thee | 173 | 3 |
| Restore, and make me meet for heaven | 375 | 2 |
| †Restore my sight! let thy free grace | 133 | 3 |
| Restore them, and remove thy road | 588 | 4 |
| Restore to thee thy own | 426 | 2 |
| †Restored by reconciling grace | 123 | 4 |
| Restored to life, and power, and thought | 965 | 2 |
| Restored to our unsinning state | 389 | 1 |
| Restorer of thine image lost | 261 | 1 |
| Restraining me from sin | 292 | 3 |
| †Rests secure the righteous man | 61 | 2 |
| Rests within his Shepherd's arms | 13 | 1 |
| Resume by the Chaldean bands | 432 | 4 |
| Retain our sense of sin forgiven | 483 | 1 |
| Retain the grace through thee bestowed | 525 | 1 |
| Retrieve them from the Tempter's power | 461 | 1 |
| Return, accept his proffered grace | 695 | 5 |
| Return, and visit this thy vine | 589 | 4 |
| Return and walk in Christ thy Way | 312 | 4 |
| †Return, O holy Dove, return | 787 | 4 |
| †Return, O Lord of hosts, return | 909 | 2 |
| *Return, O wanderer, to thy home | 792 | All. |
| Return to Christ our rest | 179 | 3 |
| Return to the Zion above | 946 | 1 |
| Return, ye ransomed sinners, home | 738 | Cho. |
| Return, ye weary wanderers, home | 4 | 2 |

| | Hymn | Verse |
|---|---|---|
| Returned with garments rolled in blood | 721 | 4 |
| Returning from his ways | 823 | 4 |
| Returning sinners to receive | 189 | 2 |
| Returning to thy glorious home | 72 | 5 |
| Re-united to our Lord | 98 | 2 |
| Revealed and ruled by thee | 863 | 2 |
| Reveal him now, if thou art he | 668 | 2 |
| Reveal the beauties of thy face | 146 | 1 |
| Reveal the charity divine | 122 | 3 |
| Reveal the things of God | 85 | 1 |
| Reveal thy glorious person thus | 770 | 7 |
| Reveal thy love, thy glorious name | 283 | 2 |
| †Reveal thyself before my closing eyes | 972 | 5 |
| Reveal thyself in me | 144 | 4 |
| Reveals thy justice and thy grace | 553 | 2 |
| Revere thy power, thy goodness bless | 235 | 3 |
| Revive at his first dawning light | 585 | 5 |
| Revive, illuminate the blind | 379 | 3 |
| Revive thy work amidst the years | 589 | 4 |
| Revive with ever-during bloom | 46 | 5 |
| Revived, and cheered, and blessed by thee | 252 | 4 |
| Revived my soul with grace | 657 | 7 |
| Revived on the third glorious day | 616 | 8 |
| Revives us with refreshing showers | 489 | 1 |
| Reward with an immortal crown | 69 | 1 |
| Riches, above what earth can grant | 880 | 2 |
| †Riches, as seemeth good to thee | 248 | 4 |
| Riches of Christ, on all bestowed | 14 | 4 |
| †Riches unsearchable | 21 | 4 |
| Rich in thy sevenfold energy | 752 | 3 |
| Rich with gems of heavenly grace | 990 | 4 |
| Ride on, and prosper in thy deed | 568 | 4 |
| Riding on the clouds his chariot | 720 | 1 |
| Rid me of my sin and grief | 116 | 2 |
| *Righteous God! whose vengeful phials | 60 | 1 |
| †Righteous I am in him, and strong | 616 | 3 |
| †Righteous Judge! for sin's pollution | 933 | 11 |
| Righteous judgment shall ordain | 604 | 4 |
| Righteous shall his sentence be | 605 | 7 |
| Righteousness from thee receive | 676 | 2 |
| Righteousness, ye skies, pour down | 86 | 6 |
| Right onward to thy rest | 837 | 1 |
| "Rise, and come to judgment!"—Lord | 54 | 5 |
| Rise eternal in my heart | 390 | 5 |
| Rise eternal in our heart | 515 | 3 |
| Rise every child a man of God | 474 | 3 |
| Rise, exalted by his fall | 20 | 2 |
| Rise from the altar of our heart | 490 | 5 |
| Rise glorious at the awful day | 974 | 3 |
| Rise, in his whole image rise | 487 | 4 |
| Rise into the life of God | 20 | 1 |
| Rise, our permanent abode | 67 | 5 |
| Rise, the woman's conquering Seed | 683 | 6 |

|   | Hymn | Verse |
|---|---|---|
| Rise to adore the mystery of love | 691 | 1 |
| Rise to all eternity | 143 | 4 |
| Rise to all thy life restored | 717 | 3 |
| Rise to realms where he is reigning | 720 | 9 |
| Rise, ye dead, to judgment come! | 51 | 5 |
| †Rise, ye men of Israel, rise | 278 | 6 |
| Risen with healing in his wings | 683 | 4 |
| Rising from the slaughtered Lamb | 350 | 6 |
| †Rising to sing my Saviour's praise | 328 | 4 |
| †Rites cannot change the heart | 892 | 3 |
| Rival of thy passion prove | 27 | 3 |
| Rivers of life divine I see | 948 | 4 |
| Rivers of milk and honey rise | 404 | 2 |
| Rivers of oil, and seas of blood | 127 | 3 |
| Rivers of salvation flow | 809 | 3 |
| Robbed of their false, pernicious peace | 461 | 4 |
| Robed in dreadful majesty | 66 | 2 |
| Robes her for her marriage morn | 990 | 4 |
| Rob us of thy heavenly love | 914 | 9 |
| *Rock of ages cleft for me | 709 | 1 |
| Rock of ages cleft for me | 709 | 3 |
| †Rock of my salvation, haste | 271 | 3 |
| Rocks and mountains, from his eye | 936 | 4 |
| Rocks and storms, and deaths defy | 1000 | 1 |
| Roll back, O God, from me | 296 | 1 |
| Roll down their golden sand | 747 | 1 |
| Roll round with the year | 47 | 1 |
| Rolling in fullest pride | 870 | 4 |
| Room to deny ourselves; a road | 965 | 6 |
| Rooted and fixed in God | 361 | 4 |
| Rooted and fixed in love | 27 | 5 |
| Rooted, grafted, built on thee | 904 | 2 |
| Rooted in humility | 243 | 4 |
| Rooted in humility | 628 | 1 |
| Rooting out the seeds of sin | 399 | 2 |
| Root out and kill the hellish seed | 299 | 7 |
| Root out every seed of ill | 522 | 3 |
| †Root out the wrath thou dost restrain | 830 | 3 |
| Roots of mountains heaving high | 570 | 1 |
| Rose into being at his word | 557 | 1 |
| Round thee and beneath are spread | 407 | 2 |
| Round thee and beneath are spread | 618 | 4 |
| Round the whole earth, and never stand | 553 | 3 |
| Round thy altars, O most high | 593 | 2 |
| Rule in all our hearts alone | 688 | 2 |
| Rule thou of right enthroned | 613 | 1 |
| Rulers, and governors, and powers | 985 | 1 |
| Rules his word the spacious globe | 601 | 1 |
| Rules the bright worlds, and moves their frame | 651 | 4 |
| Run the way of his commands | 487 | 1 |
| Run up with joy the shining way | 213 | 4 |
| Rushes on to our view, and eternity's here | 47 | 4 |

| | Hymn | Verse |
|---|---|---|
| Sabbath of celestial love | 952 | 3 |
| Sabbath of eternal rest | 952 | 3 |
| Sacred beyond heroic fame | 868 | 2 |
| Sacred precepts! quickly broken | 606 | 4 |
| Sad fruits of sin, my glorying be | 431 | 4 |
| Sad Rachel weeps her loss no more | 154 | 4 |
| Safe from all impending harm | 407 | 2 |
| Safe from diseases and decline | 46 | 5 |
| Safe from sin in thee they rest | 542 | 3 |
| Safe I laid me down and slept | 542 | 2 |
| Safe in his palace reigned | 93 | 5 |
| Safe in lowliness of heart | 349 | 2 |
| *Safe in the fiery furnace | 855 | 1 |
| Safe in the hollow of his hand | 228 | 1 |
| Safe in the hollow of thine hand | 289 | 3 |
| Safe in the love that ransomed me | 561 | 7 |
| Safe in thy arms I lay me down | 227 | 4 |
| Safe in thy breast my head I hide | 560 | 3 |
| Safe in thy decree we rest | 914 | 4 |
| Safe into the haven guide | 143 | 1 |
| Safe is the expanded wave | 921 | 4 |
| Safely on our heavenward way | 882 | 4 |
| Safely reach Immanuel's ground | 672 | 9 |
| Safely shall I pass the flood | 672 | 9 |
| *Safely through another week | 975 | 1 |
| Safely to arrive at home | 866 | 2 |
| Safety and strength in thee I have | 366 | 2 |
| Saints adore him, demons flee | 195 | 1 |
| Saints and angels joined in one | 75 | 1 |
| †Saints begin the endless song | 75 | 2 |
| Saints behold thine open face | 643 | 2 |
| Saints below with saints above | 653 | 3 |
| †Saints in glory perfect made | 921 | 5 |
| Saints shall their great King enjoy | 730 | 3 |
| Salvation find on this glad day | 782 | 3 |
| Salvation from sin, death, and hell | 269 | 4 |
| Salvation, happiness, and heaven | 314 | 3 |
| †Salvation in his name there is | 269 | 4 |
| †Salvation in that name is found | 138 | 9 |
| Salvation into glorious bliss | 269 | 4 |
| Salvation is in Jesu's name | 781 | 3 |
| Salvation is in Jesu's name | 803 | 4 |
| †Salvation! let the echo fly | 742 | 2 |
| Salvation! O salvation | 747 | 3 |
| *Salvation! O the joyful sound | 742 | 1 |
| †Salvation! O thou bleeding Lamb | 742 | 3 |
| Salvation, praise, ascribe to thee | 387 | 2 |
| Salvation shall be all my song | 574 | 13 |
| Salvation shall inspire our hearts | 742 | 3 |
| †Salvation to God Who sits on the throne | 859 | 4 |
| Salvation to the Lamb | 253 | 2 |
| Sanctifies, and makes us whole | 521 | 3 |
| Sanctify us all to-night | 971 | 3 |

| | Hymn | Verse |
|---|---|---|
| Sanctify us, Lord, and bless | 520 | 2 |
| Satan and sin are always near | 313 | 1 |
| †Satan, cease thy empty boast | 274 | 3 |
| Satan hath lost his mortal power | 706 | 5 |
| Satan, hear, and tremble now | 728 | 2 |
| †Satan his thousand arts essays | 458 | 4 |
| Satan shall be subdued | 267 | 1 |
| Satan, the world, and sin | 719 | 5 |
| Satan, the world, and sin, tread down | 277 | 4 |
| †Satan, with all his arts, no more | 815 | 4 |
| Satan's kingdom overthrow. | 299 | 5 |
| Satiate the hungry with good things | 901 | 3 |
| Save for the friends I held so dear | 924 | 3 |
| Save from every harm to-night | 971 | 1 |
| Save from wrath and make me pure | 709 | 1 |
| Save her for my Saviour's sake | 915 | 3 |
| Save in the death of Christ, my God | 700 | 2 |
| Save, Jesus, or I yield, I sink | 309 | 3 |
| Save, Lord, or I perish, I die | 174 | 3 |
| Save me by thy pardoning love | 151 | 2 |
| Save me by thy richest grace | 151 | 2 |
| Save me from death, from hell set free | 100 | 4 |
| Save me from the furious blast | 292 | 1 |
| Save me from the trying hour | 271 | 3 |
| Save me from this tyranny | 164 | 1 |
| Save me, gasping at thy feet | 151 | 5 |
| *Save me, O God; for thou alone | 549 | 1 |
| Save me quite from hell to heaven | 116 | 4 |
| Save me, save me, Lord, from sin | 185 | 2 |
| Save me, save me to the end | 116 | 4 |
| †Save me through faith in Jesu's blood | 148 | 5 |
| Save me with thine outstretched hand | 187 | 2 |
| Save, O save, thy ransomed one | 151 | 5 |
| Save our souls from inbred sin | 479 | 2 |
| Save their souls from endless death | 915 | 2 |
| Save the vilest of the race | 158 | 4 |
| †Save, till all these tempests end | 999 | 4 |
| Save us, a present Saviour thou | 95 | 3 |
| †Save us by grace, through faith alone | 774 | 3 |
| †Save us from the great and wise | 508 | 5 |
| †Save us, in the prosperous hour | 508 | 2 |
| †Save us in thy great compassion | 687 | 3 |
| Save us, to the utmost save | 852 | 2 |
| Saved again, to sinners tell | 335 | 3 |
| Saved by faith, which works by love | 521 | 4 |
| Saved by his love, incessant we shall sing | 691 | 6 |
| Saved from sin, by Jesus, now | 407 | 6 |
| †Saved from the fear of hell and death | 419 | 2 |
| Saved from the guilt and strength of sin | 732 | 3 |
| †Saved from the legal curse I am | 706 | 6 |
| Saved from the second death I feel | 246 | 1 |
| Saved them by thy grace alone | 53 | 3 |
| Saved through all eternity | 819 | 4 |

| | Hymn | Verse |
|---|---|---|
| Saved, to the utmost saved below | 502 | 5 |
| Saved, when possessed of thee, I am | 100 | 4 |
| Saved with them from future wrath | 519 | 2 |
| Saves, and to the utmost saves | 402 | 3 |
| Saves our fallen dying race | 693 | 4 |
| Saves you, not with sword and spear | 278 | 6 |
| Saving truth with joy to hear | 876 | 1 |
| Saviour, abide with us, and spread | 908 | 1 |
| Saviour, abide with us, and spread | 1024 | — |
| *Saviour, again to thy dear name we raise | 962 | 1 |
| Saviour, and be satisfied | 193 | 1 |
| Saviour and friend of all | 151 | 2 |
| †Saviour and Lord of all | 988 | 4 |
| †Saviour, and Prince of peace | 105 | 2 |
| Saviour, art thou pacified | 185 | 1 |
| *Saviour, cast a pitying eye | 116 | 1 |
| †Saviour, for this I thank thee now | 365 | 6 |
| *Saviour from sin, I wait to prove | 375 | 1 |
| †Saviour from sin, we thee receive | 389 | 2 |
| †Saviour, from thy wounded side | 175 | 5 |
| Saviour, I cast them both on thee | 836 | 1 |
| †Saviour, I long to testify | 363 | 3 |
| *Saviour, I now with shame confess | 180 | 1 |
| *Saviour, I still to thee apply | 887 | — |
| †Saviour, I thank thee for the grace | 415 | 2 |
| †Saviour, if in Zion's city | 594 | 3 |
| *Saviour, if thy precious love | 24 | 1 |
| Saviour in temptation thou | 142 | 4 |
| *Saviour, let thy sanction rest | 995 | 1 |
| †Saviour, lo, the isles are waiting | 743 | 3 |
| Saviour of all, if mine thou art | 388 | 3 |
| Saviour of *all*, I thee proclaim | 781 | 7 |
| *Saviour of all, to thee we bow | 507 | 1 |
| *Saviour of all, what hast thou done | 330 | 1 |
| †Saviour of men, thy searching eye | 279 | 6 |
| †Saviour of my soul, draw nigh | 112 | 4 |
| Saviour of offending man | 257 | 4 |
| *Saviour of sinful men | 482 | 1 |
| Saviour of sinners thee proclaim | 190 | 7 |
| Saviour of the favoured race | 75 | 4 |
| *Saviour of the sin-sick soul | 398 | 1 |
| *Saviour, on me the grace bestow | 72 | 1 |
| *Saviour, on me the want bestow | 304 | 1 |
| Saviour, our heaven on earth we gain | 419 | 4 |
| †Saviour, Prince, enthroned above | 106 | 2 |
| *Saviour, Prince of Israel's race | 101 | 1 |
| *Saviour, sprinkle many nations | 743 | 1 |
| Saviour, take the power and glory | 66 | 4 |
| *Saviour, the world's and mine | 27 | 1 |
| Saviour, thy love I wait to feel | 290 | 5 |
| Saviour, thy purchase own | 785 | 4 |
| Saviour, thy right assert | 275 | 5 |
| *Saviour, thy sacred day | 952 | 1 |

| | Hymn | Verse |
|---|---|---|
| †Saviour, to me in pity give | 104 | 2 |
| Saviour, to thee I still look up | 365 | 8 |
| †Saviour, to thee my soul looks up | 417 | 5 |
| *Saviour, to thee we humbly cry | 461 | 1 |
| *Saviour, we know thou art | 732 | 1 |
| *Saviour, we now rejoice in hope | 649 | 1 |
| *Saviour, when in dust to thee | 710 | 1 |
| †Saviour, where'er thy steps I see | 339 | 5 |
| *Saviour, whom our hearts adore | 730 | 1 |
| Saviour, who shall pluck me thence | 193 | 8 |
| Saw him weltering in his blood | 106 | 4 |
| †Saw ye not the cloud arise | 218 | 4 |
| †Say, are your hearts resolved as ours | 490 | 3 |
| Say, "Live for ever, wondrous King" | 712 | 3 |
| Say to me now, "Awake, awake" | 505 | 1 |
| Say to my soul, "Thou art my love" | 133 | 4 |
| Say to my soul, "Thy light is come" | 134 | 5 |
| Say to my trembling heart, "Be still!" | 337 | 5 |
| Say, thou Incarnate Deity | 772 | 3 |
| Says, Sinner, I am thine | 667 | 4 |
| Scarce believed the welcome sound | 623 | 1 |
| Scarce can my voice complain | 587 | 1 |
| Scarce we lift our weeping eyes | 710 | 1 |
| Scaring, wasting earth below | 570 | 5 |
| Scatter all my unbelief | 963 | 3 |
| Scatter all our guilty gloom | 399 | 1 |
| Scatter darkness, lest we stumble | 882 | 5 |
| Scatter it on the rock | 739 | 2 |
| Scatter o'er the desert ground | 579 | 3 |
| †Scatter the last remains of sin | 347 | 5 |
| Scatter thy foes, victorious King | 280 | 7 |
| Scatter thy life through every part | 361 | 9 |
| Scattered his gifts on men below | 868 | 1 |
| Scattered o'er all the earth abroad | 100 | 2 |
| †Scattered o'er all the earth they lie | 16 | 7 |
| Scattered through devious ways | 459 | 1 |
| Scattering all the night of nature | 687 | 1 |
| Scattering all the shades of night | 672 | 5 |
| Scatters my doubts, dispels my fears | 293 | 8 |
| Screened from his all-seeing eye | 633 | 1 |
| †Sealed with the baptismal seal | 890 | 2 |
| Seal it from thy courts above | 866 | 3 |
| Seal of my sins in Christ forgiven | 374 | 4 |
| Seal our souls for ever thine | 512 | 1 |
| Seal the promise on my heart | 915 | 4 |
| Seal thou my breast, and let me wear | 26 | 2 |
| Seal us heirs of full salvation | 530 | 2 |
| Seals are shattered | 715 | 4 |
| †Seals assuring | 715 | 4 |
| Searcher of hearts, in mine | 152 | 3 |
| Searching the inmost of the mind | 456 | 4 |
| Search, prove my heart; it pants for thee | 339 | 1 |
| †Seasons, and months, and weeks, and days | 978 | 4 |

| | Hymn | Verse |
|---|---|---|
| Seated at God's right hand again | 420 | 3 |
| †Seated at God's right hand again | 648 | 4 |
| Seated at thy Father's side | 722 | 3 |
| Second Adam from above | 683 | 7 |
| Secret intercourse with God | 529 | 2 |
| Secure against the threatening hour | 569 | 5 |
| Secure I am if thou art mine | 209 | 1 |
| Secure, insensible | 59 | 2 |
| Secure in that great day to rise | 917 | 4 |
| Secure in the city above | 70 | 3 |
| Secure in thee, my God and King | 437 | 6 |
| Secure of having thee in all | 560 | 4 |
| Secure that I can never die | 927 | 4 |
| Secure they keep their blest estate | 721 | 3 |
| †Secure us, of *his* royal race | 985 | 5 |
| Secure within the verge of hell | 306 | 4 |
| Secure within thine arms to lie | 289 | 5 |
| Secured by sovereign love | 632 | 5 |
| Securely to the grave | 584 | 5 |
| See all their brightest glories fade | 38 | 6 |
| See all the land below | 404 | 2 |
| †See all your sins on Jesus laid | 1 | 8 |
| See a sinful worm of earth | 477 | 1 |
| See a soul escaped to bliss | 52 | 1 |
| See at thy feet my spirit fail | 547 | 3 |
| See at thy feet of all the race | 159 | 1 |
| See for myself my smiling Lord | 927 | 3 |
| †See from his head, his hands, his feet | 700 | 3 |
| †See from his wounded side | 705 | 2 |
| †See from the Rock a fountain rise | 4 | 3 |
| See fulfilled the prophets warning | 933 | 1 |
| †See, he lifts his hands above | 718 | 5 |
| See, he shows the prints of love | 718 | 5 |
| †See him set forth before your eyes | 2 | 8 |
| See him stretched on yonder cross | 701 | 3 |
| See him to thy help come down | 407 | 1 |
| See him, who is ever pleading | 720 | 7 |
| †See him, who is gone before us | 720 | 7 |
| See him, who with sound of trumpet | 720 | 7 |
| *See how great a flame aspires | 218 | 1 |
| See how these Christians love | 822 | 4 |
| See I pant in thee to rest | 350 | 2 |
| *See Israel's gentle Shepherd stand | 889 | 1 |
| See it and his praise proclaim | 197 | 4 |
| *See, Jesu, thy disciples see | 486 | 1 |
| See, like ashes, my contrition | 933 | 17 |
| †See, Lord, the travail of thy soul | 408 | 2 |
| See, Lord, with tenderest pity see | 744 | 1 |
| See me from thy lofty throne | 101 | 1 |
| †See me, O Lord, athirst and faint | 378 | 4 |
| †See me, Saviour, from above | 106 | 3 |
| See me then, with pity see | 164 | 2 |
| See my nakedness and shame | 109 | 5 |

| | Hymn | Verse |
|---|---|---|
| See my soul, the breath of God | 368 | 1 |
| †See my utter helplessness | 188 | 5 |
| †See on the mountain-top | 314 | 2 |
| *See, sinners, in the gospel glass | 31 | 1 |
| See the almighty Jesus crowned | 56 | 2 |
| See the cause in Jesu's face | 168 | 2 |
| *See the Conqueror mounts in triumph | 720 | 1 |
| †See the eternal Son of God | 684 | 3 |
| See the flaming revelation | 936 | 2 |
| See the friend of sinners, see | 215 | 3 |
| See the Godhead face to face | 723 | 4 |
| †See the gospel church secure | 572 | 3 |
| See the King in royal state | 720 | 1 |
| See the long-expected day | 67 | 6 |
| See the Lord of earth and skies | 684 | 3 |
| †See the Lord, thy Keeper, stand | 618 | 4 |
| See the new creation rise | 60 | 3 |
| See the poor fainting sinner, see | 184 | 3 |
| See the prodigal is come | 191 | 2 |
| See the purchase of thy blood | 723 | 2 |
| †See the souls that hang on thee | 538 | 3 |
| †See the stars from heaven falling | 936 | 4 |
| †See, the streams of living waters | 594 | 2 |
| See! the suffering God appears | 8 | 4 |
| See the times of restitution | 60 | 3 |
| See the travail of thy soul | 193 | 1 |
| See the universal blaze | 936 | 2 |
| See the world beneath our feet | 723 | 5 |
| See there my Lord upon the tree | 34 | 5 |
| See there, the King of glory see | 23 | 1 |
| See there the meek, expiring Lamb | 706 | 6 |
| See there the starry crown | 277 | 4 |
| †See, these barren souls of ours | 348 | 3 |
| See, they throng the blissful shore | 921 | 5 |
| See, thou who dost in secret see | 119 | 3 |
| See thy faithful servants, see | 718 | 7 |
| See thy followers, O Lamb | 538 | 1 |
| †See us eager for salvation | 882 | 3 |
| †See where before the throne he stands | 127 | 9 |
| See where he bows his sacred head | 22 | 3 |
| †See where o'er desert wastes they err | 82 | 2 |
| †See where the God incarnate stands | 31 | 3 |
| †See where the lame, the halt, the blind | 32 | 2 |
| See with ineffable delight | 927 | 3 |
| See with joy each other's face | 480 | 1 |
| †See, ye sinners, see the flame | 350 | 6 |
| See your great redeeming God | 54 | 2 |
| See your lawful captive, see | 274 | 4 |
| Seek and join its source above | 766 | 2 |
| †" Seek ye my face;"—without delay | 558 | 3 |
| Seeking for some great thing to do | 842 | 3 |
| Seems fixed, yet wide my passions rove | 344 | 2 |
| Sees all thy children's wants, and knows | 831 | 5 |

| | Hymn | Verse |
|---|---|---|
| Sees my soul the King of kings | 325 | 4 |
| Sees the universe renewed | 61 | 3 |
| Seize as the purchase of thy blood | 444 | 3 |
| Seize on our sins, and burn up all | 412 | 5 |
| Seize the crown of righteousness | 521 | 2 |
| Seize them with faith divinely bold | 445 | 3 |
| Self-desperate, I believe | 360 | 7 |
| Self-inclined from thee to stray | 819 | 2 |
| †Selfish pursuits and nature's maze | 114 | 3 |
| Send deliverance from the skies | 299 | 6 |
| Send down thy likeness from above | 109 | 4 |
| †Send down thy likeness from above | 431 | 5 |
| Send down thy mild, pacific Dove | 505 | 5 |
| Send down thy Spirit from on high | 822 | 1 |
| Send down thy Spirit's sevenfold powers | 951 | 5 |
| †Send forth one ray of heavenly light | 130 | 2 |
| Send forth the prisoner from the pit | 150 | 4 |
| Send forth thy truth and light | 468 | 1 |
| Send him our souls to sanctify | 377 | 2 |
| Send him the sprinkled blood to apply | 377 | 2 |
| Send hope before to grasp it | 943 | 15 |
| Send me now the promised aid | 352 | 1 |
| Send me succour from above | 271 | 1 |
| Send that Intercessor down | 755 | 1 |
| Send that other Comforter | 755 | 1 |
| Send the answer from above | 900 | 1 |
| Send the Comforter to dwell | 755 | 3 |
| †Send then thy servants forth | 452 | 5 |
| Send thy blessings from above | 578 | 1 |
| †Send us the Spirit of thy Son | 377 | 2 |
| Sense shall point out the road | 108 | 8 |
| †Sent by my Lord, on you I call | 2 | 2 |
| †Sent down from above, Who governs the skies | 10 | 2 |
| Sent down from heaven to give us rest | 616 | 10 |
| †Sent down to make us meet | 761 | 5 |
| Sent from his throne above | 459 | 4 |
| Sent the gracious Comforter | 758 | 1 |
| Sent the mighty Conqueror | 717 | 2 |
| Sent to baptize into thy name | 476 | 2 |
| Sent to disciple all mankind | 476 | 2 |
| Separate from sin, I would | 769 | 5 |
| †Separate now from sinful men | 724 | 2 |
| Serene we wake, and calmly sleep | 1003 | 3 |
| †Serious, simple of intent | 817 | 4 |
| *Servant of all, to toil for man | 322 | 1 |
| Servant to thy servants here | 529 | 2 |
| Servants of one common Lord | 487 | 3 |
| Serve him with awe, with reverence love | 494 | 1 |
| Serve my Maker all my days | 243 | 1 |
| Serve thee as thy hosts above | 385 | 2 |
| Serve their Maker day and night | 76 | 2 |
| Serve with a single heart and eye | 429 | 4 |
| Serve with careful Martha's hands | 325 | 1 |

| | Hymn | Verse |
|---|---|---|
| Set free from present sorrow | 804 | 2 |
| Set me from the body free | 287 | 4 |
| Set me upon the rock, and hide | 283 | 3 |
| Set my conscience free from guilt | 824 | 3 |
| Set my heart at liberty | 116 | 2 |
| Set my imprisoned spirit free | 171 | 4 |
| Set the last great empire up | 730 | 1 |
| †Set upon thyself my feet | 271 | 4 |
| Set up the attracting sign | 452 | 1 |
| Set up thy kingdom in my heart | 134 | 1 |
| Sets the kingdoms on a blaze | 218 | 1 |
| Settle and fix my wavering soul | 137 | 10 |
| Settle, confirm, and stablish me | 436 | 9 |
| Settled comfort, perfect love | 86 | 4 |
| Settled peace I then shall find | 355 | 5 |
| Seven times hotter than before | 359 | 2 |
| Severed though in flesh we are | 538 | 3 |
| Shadowed by thy mighty hand | 193 | 8 |
| Shadows with his wings thy head | 618 | 4 |
| Shake off dull sloth, and joyful rise | 964 | 1 |
| †Shake off the chains of sin | 983 | 2 |
| Shake off thy guilty fears | 202 | 1 |
| Shake us till the curse remove | 60 | 2 |
| Shakes the trembling gates of hell | 218 | 2 |
| Shall a house be builded here | 990 | 1 |
| Shall all its love display | 943 | 13 |
| Shall all our sins destroy | 729 | 5 |
| Shall all stretch out their hands to thee | 492 | 3 |
| Shall all the world command | 740 | 3 |
| Shall all thy law perform | 357 | 7 |
| Shall all with open face behold | 284 | 5 |
| Shall always pray, give thanks, rejoice | 866 | 1 |
| Shall as his patient Master be | 330 | 5 |
| Shall bear the image of its Lord | 443 | 3 |
| Shall bear triumphant home | 54 | 5 |
| Shall be brought forth in me | 382 | 4 |
| Shall be caught up to the skies | 58 | 2 |
| Shall be scattered by thy might | 598 | 3 |
| Shall bethink him, in its beauty | 990 | 3 |
| Shall bid his faithful ones rejoice | 602 | 2 |
| Shall bid the greedy grave restore | 927 | 2 |
| Shall bless the conduct of his grace | 814 | 4 |
| Shall bless the day that I was born | 230 | 4 |
| Shall bless thy coming in | 618 | 5 |
| Shall both in ruin end | 540 | 6 |
| Shall break our eternal repose | 220 | 5 |
| Shall bring me into The plentiful place | 273 | 7 |
| Shall but refine this flesh | 930 | 2 |
| Shall cast the dire accuser down | 280 | 5 |
| Shall check the murmur and the sigh | 658 | 2 |
| Shall cheer us on our way | 984 | 6 |
| Shall come, and make us priests and kings | 380 | 7 |
| Shall come to our rescue, and hasten us home | 498 | 4 |

| | Hymn | Verse |
|---|---|---|
| Shall come to thee, O Israel | 690 | Cho. |
| Shall comprehend and feel | 413 | 3 |
| Shall conquer in the battle | 856 | 2 |
| †Shall creatures of a meaner frame | 788 | 5 |
| Shall crowds of slain deplore | 740 | 6 |
| Shall damp whom Jesu's presence cheers | 919 | 3 |
| Shall dawn on every cross and care | 965 | 5 |
| Shall die, a sinner at thy feet | 816 | 2 |
| Shall evermore abide | 64 | 2 |
| Shall evermore endure | 74 | 2 |
| Shall every stumbling-block remove | 288 | 5 |
| Shall feel thee a consuming fire | 241 | 4 |
| Shall feel your sins forgiven | 1 | 10 |
| Shall fill heaven's sounding courts with praise | 333 | 5 |
| Shall fill thy courts with sounding praise | 608 | 3 |
| Shall find redemption nigh | 731 | 4 |
| Shall find the pearl which others spurn | 401 | 5 |
| Shall find thy succours ever near | 636 | 4 |
| Shall flow to nations yet unknown | 585 | 6 |
| Shall flow with a current of love | 777 | 2 |
| Shall foster and mature the grain | 739 | 5 |
| Shall gloriously hurry our souls to the skies | 498 | 4 |
| Shall guard me in that dangerous hour | 849 | 2 |
| Shall guide me all my happy days | 800 | 3 |
| Shall have him for their own | 943 | 3 |
| Shall have in her their dwelling place | 595 | 1 |
| †Shall I—amidst a ghastly band | 80 | 3 |
| Shall I be found at thy right hand | 338 | 6 |
| Shall I be with the damned cast out | 43 | 4 |
| Shall I ever see thy face | 943 | 14 |
| Shall I ever win the prize itself | 943 | 14 |
| Shall I ever win thy grace | 943 | 14 |
| *Shall I, for fear of feeble man | 279 | 1 |
| Shall I my everlasting days | 44 | 4 |
| Shall I never, never know | 354 | 2 |
| Shall I presume to share | 587 | 3 |
| Shall I regret my parted friends | 947 | 4 |
| Shall I, the hallowed cross to shun | 30 | 3 |
| †Shall I, through indolence supine | 471 | 3 |
| †Shall I, to soothe the unholy throng | 279 | 3 |
| Shall in the believer Spring up to the skies | 3 | 3 |
| Shall its thousand voices raise | 604 | 3 |
| Shall Jesu's sufferers know | 482 | 4 |
| Shall join our souls to thee | 1002 | 6 |
| Shall join the disembodied saints | 948 | 1 |
| Shall keep us thine for ever | 853 | 2 |
| Shall know the greatness of thy power | 492 | 6 |
| Shall laugh, and their attempts deride | 541 | 2 |
| Shall lead my captive soul astray | 332 | 3 |
| Shall leave the blest effect behind | 331 | 2 |
| Shall life and power impart | 406 | 2 |
| Shall lift us to the skies | 898 | 4 |
| Shall lighten every land | 740 | 3 |

| | Hymn | Verse |
|---|---|---|
| Shall live, a saint in love complete. | 816 | 2 |
| Shall live to God at last | 282 | 2 |
| Shall magnify my Maker's name | 229 | 3 |
| †Shall magnify the sovereign grace | 280 | 8 |
| Shall make the contrite sinner's heart | 759 | 3 |
| Shall make us all entire | 329 | 2 |
| Shall make us throughly clean | 389 | 2 |
| Shall mark its bounds from east to west | 589 | 6 |
| Shall meet around the throne | 814 | 4 |
| Shall meet thee in the skies | 15 | 4 |
| Shall melt away, and droop, and die | 802 | 4 |
| Shall me with spirit and life inspire | 881 | 2 |
| Shall mightily prevail | 453 | 1 |
| Shall multiply and grow | 732 | 2 |
| Shall my protection prove | 813 | — |
| Shall never feel it more | 416 | 6 |
| Shall never lose its power | 798 | 3 |
| Shall never more depart | 809 | 4 |
| Shall never part again | 535 | 3 |
| Shall pass, but such as serve my Lord | 828 | 4 |
| Shall peace the herald go | 586 | 3 |
| Shall perfect holiness below | 815 | 5 |
| Shall perish by thy fire | 642 | 5 |
| Shall pluck you from his hand | 267 | 2 |
| Shall pompously attend | 58 | 1 |
| Shall pray, and pray aright | 865 | 6 |
| Shall praise thy name for ever | 276 | 4 |
| Shall put on their choice array | 604 | 4 |
| Shall quit, like me, the vale of tears | 48 | 1 |
| Shall re-echo through the sky Alleluia | 663 | — |
| Shall rend the veil in twain | 944 | 7 |
| Shall rich abundance prove | 874 | 3 |
| Shall rise and break through all | 139 | 6 |
| Shall rise and flourish large and fair | 868 | 4 |
| Shall rise in the depth of the vale | 777 | 2 |
| Shall save me till my latest hour | 69 | 1 |
| Shall see, and put the Godhead on | 284 | 5 |
| Shall see him in the latter day | 928 | 2 |
| Shall see him with our glorious friends | 497 | 5 |
| Shall see that self-same Saviour nigh | 927 | 3 |
| Shall see thee stand | 853 | 4 |
| Shall serve thee without fear | 357 | 4 |
| Shall silence keep before the Lord | 815 | 6 |
| Shall sing like those in glory | 853 | 1 |
| Shall sink and die away | 719 | 4 |
| Shall sink me into nothing here | 669 | 2 |
| †Shall soon his fallen Zion raise | 111 | 3 |
| Shall soon in your behalf appear | 380 | 1 |
| Shall soon resign this fleeting breath | 45 | 1 |
| Shall soon the saints receive | 65 | 5 |
| Shall speak me up to thee | 292 | 5 |
| Shall speak thy co-extended praise | 155 | 2 |
| Shall stand for ever good | 903 | 1 |

| | Hymn | Verse |
|---|---|---|
| Shall stand in Jesu's righteousness | 57 | 3 |
| Shall stand unmoved amidst them all | 57 | 4 |
| Shall stand where my Forerunner stands | 726 | 3 |
| Shall still remove | 1026 | — |
| †Shall still the proud Philistine's noise | 280 | 6 |
| Shall strangely be brought out of me | 159 | 2 |
| Shall such grace be vainly brought me | 933 | 10 |
| Shall surely come from thee | 301 | 6 |
| Shall surely follow me | 556 | 5 |
| Shall then be seen and known | 943 | 3 |
| Shall then no longer move | 361 | 11 |
| Shall the ransomed people sing Alleluia | 663 | — |
| Shall the saints his banner see | 936 | 5 |
| Shall the true Messiah see | 66 | 2 |
| Shall the woods keep holyday | 604 | 4 |
| Shall there our spirits wound | 482 | 4 |
| Shall these vile bodies shine | 930 | 4 |
| Shall they no more thy favour share | 588 | 2 |
| Shall throng the sacred floor | 619 | 2 |
| Shall thy consummate joy receive | 254 | 3 |
| Shall turn our earth to heaven | 447 | 3 |
| Shall utter forth thy praise | 587 | 4 |
| Shall wash us white as snow | 705 | 2 |
| Shall we not gladly raise the cry | 695 | 4 |
| Shall willingly confess thee | 613 | 2 |
| Shall with a shout descend | 58 | 1 |
| Shalt chase all our sorrows away | 946 | 4 |
| Shalt from every ill deliver | 819 | 4 |
| Shalt govern all the earth | 581 | 4 |
| Shalt keep me faithful to the end | 69 | 1 |
| Shalt lead me to the promised land | 293 | 1 |
| Shalt sink into a plain | 382 | 3 |
| Shalt thither bring Our willing feet | 591 | 3 |
| Share thine everlasting crown | 877 | 4 |
| Sharon's fertile excellence | 348 | 2 |
| Shed forth the virtue of thy name | 139 | 2 |
| Shed in my heart abroad | 117 | 5 |
| Shed in my heart abroad | 361 | 4 |
| Shed in our hearts abroad | 654 | 5 |
| Shed in our hearts thy love abroad | 523 | 2 |
| Shed in their hearts thy love abroad | 255 | 1 |
| Shed thy beams upon our eyes | 720 | 6 |
| Shed thy gracious radiance here | 753 | 1 |
| Shed thy love, thy Spirit shed | 506 | 2 |
| Shed thy love, thy tenderness | 110 | 4 |
| Shed thy over-shadowing love | 514 | 3 |
| Sheds not its glorious ray | 870 | 1 |
| †She had no friend or patron kind | 827 | 7 |
| †She had no promise to succeed | 827 | 5 |
| She stands as she ever hath stood | 73 | 3 |
| Shelter from the noon-day heat | 753 | 4 |
| Shelter me from Satan's power | 271 | 3 |
| Shelter me with preserving grace | 998 | 2 |

| | Hymn | Verse |
|---|---|---|
| *Shepherd Divine, our wants relieve | 297 | 1 |
| *Shepherd of Israel, hear | 459 | 1 |
| *Shepherd of souls, with pitying eye | 82 | 1 |
| Shepherd, to thy sheep-fold take *him* | 895 | 3 |
| Shine away our sin and shame | 975 | 3 |
| Shine forth with all the Deity | 258 | 2 |
| Shine in every drooping heart | 399 | 1 |
| †Shine on thy work, disperse the gloom | 134 | 5 |
| Shine through the gloom, and point me to the skies | 972 | 5 |
| Shine through thy works abroad | 226 | 11 |
| Shine to the perfect day | 347 | 4 |
| Shine upon us, Saviour, shine | 582 | 1 |
| Shining to the perfect day | 963 | 3 |
| Shining unto the perfect day | 281 | 2 |
| Shining with her gentle light | 631 | 3 |
| Shines clearly as the morning light | 240 | 4 |
| Shines, the everlasting Light | 936 | 3 |
| Ships from the isles shall meet | 586 | 4 |
| Short as the watch that ends the night | 41 | 4 |
| †Short of thy love I would not stop | 97 | 3 |
| Short toil, eternal rest | 943 | 1 |
| Shorten these vindictive days | 937 | 3 |
| †Should all the forms that men devise | 879 | 4 |
| †Should all the hosts of death | 675 | 10 |
| Should any of thy grace despair | 39 | 5 |
| Should bruise this wretched soul of mine | 181 | 4 |
| Should constant joys create | 12 | 3 |
| Should fright us from the shore | 938 | 6 |
| †Should I from thee, my God, remove | 577 | 4 |
| Should I hope to lurk unknown | 633 | 4 |
| Should I not to thee appear | 633 | 4 |
| Should know, should feel my sins forgiven | 30 | 2 |
| Should let my sin this moment go | 105 | 4 |
| Should live and sin no more | 342 | 5 |
| Should not the servant tread it still | 857 | 1 |
| †Should pining sickness waste away | 841 | 4 |
| Should turn, repent, and live | 144 | 6 |
| Should within the arms divine | 18 | 2 |
| Should with the sacred hours abide | 957 | 4 |
| †Shout, all the people of the sky | 56 | 4 |
| Shout for gladness, shout and sing | 579 | 3 |
| Shout his praises to the skies | 278 | 6 |
| †Shout in the midst of us, O King | 977 | 4 |
| Shout in the refiner's fire | 238 | 3 |
| Shout, or silently adore | 260 | 3 |
| Shout the angel-choirs aloud | 571 | 3 |
| †Shout the God enthroned above | 571 | 5 |
| Shout the Lamb that died for all | 75 | 3 |
| Shout the loved Immanuel's name | 194 | 3 |
| Shout, while we on earth reply | 53 | 1 |
| Shout, ye first-born sons of fire | 727 | 4 |
| Shouting their heavenly Zion gain | 386 | 4 |
| Shouts, with all the sons of God | 61 | 3 |

| | Hymn | Verse |
|---|---|---|
| Show charity in all . | 822 | 4 |
| Show forth all thy power in me | 116 | 2 |
| Show forth all thy power in me | 151 | 1 |
| Show forth in me thy saving power | 272 | 4 |
| *Show forth thy mercy, gracious Lord | 566 | 6 |
| Show his truth, and power, and grace | 506 | 1 |
| Show how true believers die | 509 | 6 |
| Show how true believers live | 509 | 4 |
| †Show me, as my soul can bear | 358 | 4 |
| Show me in Christ thy smiling face | 148 | 2 |
| Show me, Lord, the dazzling prize . | 877 | 1 |
| Show me the atoning blood | 101 | 5 |
| Show me the blood that bought my peace. | 150 | 4 |
| †Show me the naked sword . | 103 | 2 |
| Show me the way to shun . | 43 | 5 |
| †Show my forgetful feet the way | 789 | 4 |
| *Show pity, Lord; O Lord, forgive. | 574 | 1 |
| Show the brightness of thy face | 582 | 1 |
| Show the same path to heaven | 940 | 5 |
| Show the world thy heavenly name | 748 | 6 |
| †Show them the blood that bought their peace | 462 | 3 |
| Show them the tokens of thy love . | 35 | 5 |
| Show thine everlasting love | 852 | 2 |
| Show this token upon me | 164 | 6 |
| Show thy reconciled face | 975 | 3 |
| Show thyself the Prince of peace . | 509 | 1 |
| Show us rooted in thy love . | 531 | 2 |
| Show us thy bleeding hands and feet | 486 | 5 |
| Show we not in vain believed | 522 | 1 |
| Showed in all the heathen's sight . | 605 | 2 |
| Shower, O shower them, Lord, on me | 593 | 3 |
| Showers his blessings from the skies | 238 | 1 |
| Showers his blessings from the skies | 1019 | 2 |
| Showers, the thirsty land refreshing | 790 | 1 |
| Shows his wounds, and spreads his hands. | 168 | 4 |
| Shows the purchase of his merit | 922 | 2 |
| Shows us his eternal love . | 207 | 2 |
| *Shrinking from the cold hand of death | 45 | 1 |
| †Shudder not to pass the stream | 921 | 4 |
| Shunned the wounded Comforter . | 768 | 7 |
| Shut my heart up like a flower | 769 | 3 |
| Shut up in endless wrath . | 587 | 3 |
| Shut up in sin and unbelief . | 129 | 5 |
| †Shut up in unbelief I groan | 118 | 2 |
| Sighs the unutterable prayer | 758 | 5 |
| Sight, riches, healing of the mind . | 796 | 4 |
| Sight to the inly blind | 870 | 2 |
| Signal of peace to earth displayed . | 951 | 1 |
| Signify thy Father's will | 676 | 1 |
| Signify thy kingdom near . | 748 | 1 |
| Sign our uncontested pardon | 530 | 1 |
| †Silence—for the Almighty know me | 570 | 6 |
| †Silent, (alas! thou know'st how long) | 135 | 6 |

|  | HYMN | VERSE |
|---|---|---|
| Silent am I now and still | 358 | 2 |
| Silent I stand before thy face | 92 | 2 |
| Silent joy my heart o'erflows | 554 | 2 |
| †Simple, teachable, and mild | 628 | 3 |
| Simply do I now draw near | 175 | 1 |
| Simply to thy cross I cling | 709 | 2 |
| Sin and death shall not prevail | 640 | 2 |
| Sin and night before him flee | 714 | 5 |
| Sin and Satan I defy | 359 | 3 |
| Sin be more than hell abhorred | 187 | 3 |
| Sin, earth, and hell I now defy | 227 | 5 |
| Sin for ever shall depart | 383 | 2 |
| Sin in all its strength returns | 359 | 2 |
| Sin increases more and more | 359 | 2 |
| Sin is sure to overtake me | 819 | 1 |
| Sin must remain; howe'er expelled | 816 | 2 |
| Sin never can advance thy praise | 177 | 5 |
| †Sin only let me not commit | 177 | 5 |
| Sin shall have in him no part | 407 | 4 |
| Sin, the world, and hell defy | 274 | 4 |
| Sin, the world, and Satan's snare | 819 | 3 |
| Sin to condemn, and man to save | 375 | 3 |
| *Since all the downward tracks of time | 846 | 1 |
| †Since by thy light myself I see | 99 | 2 |
| Since faith alone confirms me his | 154 | 1 |
| Since first with me he strove | 182 | 2 |
| Since he is ours, and we are his | 1001 | 9 |
| Since I am called by thy great name | 431 | 6 |
| Since I, even I, have mercy found | 33 | 4 |
| Since I have found favour, He all things will do | 198 | 5 |
| Since in all pain thy tender love | 279 | 5 |
| Since sealed with Jesu's blood it is | 909 | 4 |
| Since such the will of the most High | 913 | 2 |
| *Since the Son hath made me free | 390 | 1 |
| †Since thou a pitying ear didst give | 614 | 2 |
| Since thou didst in the flesh appear | 397 | 5 |
| †Since thou hast bid me come to thee | 272 | 5 |
| †Since thou hast risen from the grave | 923 | 4 |
| Since thou wouldst have the sinner blest | 171 | 3 |
| †Since thou wouldst have us free from sin | 389 | 3 |
| Since we assembled last | 478 | 2 |
| †Since, with pure and firm affection | 597 | 3 |
| Sinful souls shall bring their burden | 990 | 3 |
| Sinful though my heart may be | 790 | 2 |
| Sing all day long | 736 | 2 |
| Sing all heaven, and fall at his feet | 491 | 7 |
| Sing all the saints thy love hath made | 253 | 4 |
| Sing, and stop, and gaze, and fall | 221 | 2 |
| Sing as in the ancient days | 519 | 1 |
| Sing his praise, his truth display | 604 | 1 |
| Sing Holy, Holy, Holy | 958 | 1 |
| Sing how he spoiled the hosts of hell | 712 | 3 |
| Sing, rejoice, before the Lord | 605 | 5 |

| | Hymn | Verse |
|---|---|---|
| Sing the sweet promise of his grace | 659 | 2 |
| Sing the wonders he hath done | 53 | 1 |
| Sing thy praise and bless thy name | 580 | 1 |
| *Sing to the great Jehovah's praise | 979 | 1 |
| †Sing to the Lord; exalt him high | 225 | 3 |
| Sing to the Lord with cheerful voice | 607 | 1 |
| Sing unto the Lord your songs | 197 | 5 |
| †Sing we then in Jesu's name | 519 | 3 |
| *Sing we to our conquering Lord | 605 | 1 |
| Sing, ye heavens; thou earth reply | 716 | 1 |
| Sing ye in triumphant strains | 728 | 1 |
| Singing loud with cheerful voice | 714 | 1 |
| Singing to thy crown remove | 921 | 3 |
| Single, against hell, earth, and sin | 269 | 1 |
| Single, yet undismayed, I am | 269 | 1 |
| Sink as low, and mount as high | 260 | 3 |
| Sink heart and voice oppressed | 943 | 8 |
| Sink into a sea of light | 643 | 2 |
| Sink into the purple flood | 20 | 1 |
| Sink the mountain to a plain | 463 | 4 |
| Sink with Christ among the dead | 192 | 2 |
| Sinking at his awful will | 601 | 4 |
| Sinking into endless woe | 215 | 2 |
| Sinking to the grave I lie | 672 | 7 |
| Sinks and expires the Son of God | 23 | 1 |
| Sinner, receive thy sight | 135 | 10 |
| Sinners alone his grace receives | 30 | 5 |
| Sinners, and be saved from sin | 86 | 6 |
| Sinners, a vile and thankless race | 655 | 2 |
| *Sinners, believe the gospel word | 32 | 1 |
| Sinners, call upon his name | 197 | 4 |
| †Sinners, expect those heaviest showers | 63 | 2 |
| Sinners from their sins to bless | 717 | 2 |
| Sinners, he prays for you and me | 33 | 1 |
| Sinners Jesus came to call | 791 | 4 |
| *Sinners, lift up your hearts | 761 | 1 |
| *Sinners, obey the gospel-word | 9 | 1 |
| †Sinners, obey the heavenly call | 107 | 3 |
| Sinners, obey your Maker's call | 4 | 2 |
| †Sinners of old thou didst receive | 397 | 2 |
| Sinners, of whom the chief I am | 190 | 7 |
| *Sinners, rejoice; your peace is made | 721 | 1 |
| Sinners shall learn thy sovereign grace | 574 | 12 |
| Sinners shall lift their guilty head | 57 | 2 |
| †Sinners, turn, while God is near | 8 | 3 |
| *Sinners, turn, why will ye die | 6 | 1 |
| †Sinners, turn, why will ye die | 6 | 2 |
| †Sinners, turn, why will ye die | 6 | 3 |
| Sinners, your heads lift up | 845 | 4 |
| *Sinners, your hearts lift up | 86 | 1 |
| Sins against thy light and love | 101 | 2 |
| Sins against thy Spirit done | 768 | 10 |
| Sins against thyself alone | 768 | 2 |

| | Hymn | Verse |
|---|---|---|
| Sins like these my heart deceive | 768 | 6 |
| Sins that crucified my God | 101 | 2 |
| Sins too great for us to bear | 579 | 1 |
| †Sins unnumbered I confess | 768 | 2 |
| †Sin's deceitfulness hath spread | 110 | 4 |
| Sin's strong-holds it now o'erthrows | 218 | 2 |
| †Sion, shout thy Lord and King | 197 | 6 |
| Sit, great Master, at thy feet | 882 | 3 |
| Sit in heavenly places down | 423 | 2 |
| Sit loose to all below | 533 | 4 |
| Sit thou, in glory sit | 275 | 1 |
| Sits at God's right hand above | 519 | 4 |
| Sitteth he in royal state | 606 | 1 |
| Skilful deed or wisest thought | 753 | 6 |
| Slay him with thy Spirit, Lord | 383 | 3 |
| †Slay me, and I in thee shall trust | 362 | 6 |
| Slay, raise me, by thy power | 362 | 5 |
| †Slay the dire root and seed of sin | 341 | 2 |
| Slay the old Adam with thy breath | 362 | 2 |
| Sleep that may me more vigorous make | 974 | 4 |
| Slept within his arms, and rose | 542 | 2 |
| Slings the sin-destroying stone | 278 | 5 |
| Sloth, when souls in darkness die | 768 | 5 |
| †Slower of heart than Thomas, I | 861 | 2 |
| Small and feeble was his day | 218 | 2 |
| Small, and still, and inward thine | 193 | 6 |
| Small as it is, 'tis all my store | 481 | 1 |
| †Smell the sweet odour of our prayers | 507 | 3 |
| Smile at the destroyer nigh | 13 | 2 |
| Smile to see them idly rage | 359 | 3 |
| Smite on my unworthy breast | 101 | 4 |
| Smooth let it be or rough | 837 | 1 |
| Snatches from hell and lifts to heaven | 448 | 1 |
| So arm me with thy power | 416 | 6 |
| †So as our Sabbaths hasten past | 961 | 5 |
| †So at last when he appeareth | 720 | 9 |
| †So be it! let this system end | 64 | 7 |
| †So blooms the human face divine | 46 | 3 |
| So by my woes to be | 848 | 4 |
| †So cleanse our offering | 892 | 6 |
| So evermore shall we rejoice | 666 | 2 |
| So faithful and true, So plenteous in grace | 198 | 1 |
| So far the riches of his grace | 610 | 8 |
| So fearless shall we urge our way | 655 | 6 |
| So follow those who followed thee | 945 | 2 |
| So foolish, impotent, and poor | 21 | 3 |
| So freely spilt for me | 343 | 1 |
| So free, so infinite his grace! | 201 | 3 |
| So God protects and covers them | 622 | 2 |
| So great, so strong, so high | 407 | 1 |
| So hold me fast, and drag me down | 566 | 7 |
| †So I ask thee for the daily strength | 842 | 5 |
| So I may thee regain | 358 | 3 |

| | Hymn | Verse |
|---|---|---|
| †So I may thy Spirit know | 381 | 3 |
| So I may with thee be one | 381 | 3 |
| So I watch and wait on thee | 620 | 2 |
| So in thy strength shall I go on | 196 | 3 |
| So in thy ways to run | 821 | — |
| †So let thy grace surround me still | 632 | 5 |
| So longs my soul, O God, for thee | 567 | 1 |
| So many years on sin bestowed | 977 | 2 |
| †So may each future age proclaim | 997 | 4 |
| So may our works, in thee begun | 966 | 4 |
| So may thy influence us inspire | 494 | 6 |
| So may we catch thy every ray | 494 | 6 |
| So mightily wrought in the primitive days | 219 | 5 |
| So not heaven's host shall swifter move | 236 | 2 |
| So oft have I, alas! drawn near | 93 | 2 |
| So plenteous is the store | 250 | 4 |
| So purer light shall mark the road | 787 | 6 |
| So ready to abate | 610 | 6 |
| So safe shalt thou go on | 831 | 3 |
| So shall assembled saints with me | 634 | 4 |
| So shall each murmuring thought be gone | 337 | 4 |
| So shall he lift me up at last | 307 | 5 |
| So shall he send his influence down | 585 | 4 |
| So shall I all my strength exert | 433 | 5 |
| So shall I all thy doctrines know | 887 | — |
| †So shall I bless thy pleasing sway | 275 | 6 |
| †So shall I do thy will below | 275 | 7 |
| So shall I live; and yet not I | 362 | 7 |
| So shall I love my God | 43 | 6 |
| So shall I see; yet seeing live | 133 | 1 |
| So shall I spend my life's short day | 43 | 6 |
| So shall I still the blessing gain | 304 | 4 |
| So shall I walk aright | 337 | 2 |
| So shall my heart his presence prove | 328 | 2 |
| So shall my walk be close with God | 787 | 6 |
| †So shall our lives thy power proclaim | 492 | 3 |
| †So shall the bright succession run | 868 | 4 |
| So shall the fervour of my zeal | 300 | 2 |
| †So shall the world believe | 459 | 4 |
| †So shall the world believe and know | 505 | 9 |
| †So shall thine enemies be dumb | 589 | 7 |
| So shall thy vine its leaf renew | 589 | 5 |
| So shall thy work be done | 831 | 3 |
| So shall we all thy love receive | 527 | 5 |
| So shall we ever live, and move | 654 | 5 |
| †So shall we pray, and never cease | 377 | 3 |
| So shall we thankfully confess | 377 | 3 |
| So shalt thou wondering own his way | 831 | 12 |
| So soon unfaithful prove | 184 | 6 |
| So strong the principle divine | 374 | 3 |
| So strong to deliver, So good to redeem | 198 | 1 |
| So sweetly o'erflowing, So plenteous the store | 199 | 1 |
| So terribly glorious His coming shall be | 273 | 6 |

| | Hymn | Verse |
|---|---|---|
| So the righteous shall be seen | 598 | 3 |
| So thou wilt grant but this | 696 | 5 |
| So to the Jews old Canaan stood | 938 | 3 |
| So true to thy word, So loving and kind | 5 | 1 |
| So united in heart | 491 | 5 |
| †So vile I am, how dare I hope to stand | 794 | 2 |
| So we may Jesus gain | 478 | 3 |
| †So, whene'er the signal's given | 1008 | 3 |
| †So when my latest breath | 944 | 7 |
| †So when on Zion thou shalt stand | 838 | 6 |
| So when thy truth began its race | 553 | 3 |
| So wide, it never passed by one | 216 | 4 |
| So will the Lord his follower join | 328 | 2 |
| †So wretched and obscure | 21 | 3 |
| Soar, thou native of the skies | 921 | 1 |
| †Soar we now where Christ hath led | 716 | 5 |
| Soften, and melt, and pierce, and break | 361 | 6 |
| Soften the obdurate crowd | 463 | 4 |
| Soften this hard heart, or lament | 153 | 1 |
| Soften this obdurate stone | 101 | 1 |
| Soften thy truths, and smooth my tongue | 279 | 3 |
| Sojourned from age to age | 565 | 8 |
| Sojourns in this vale of tears | 684 | 1 |
| *Soldiers of Christ, arise | 266 | 1 |
| Sole Comforter of souls forlorn | 779 | 2 |
| Sole disposer of thine own | 914 | 1 |
| †Sole, self-existing God and Lord | 247 | 3 |
| Solemnize our nuptials there | 516 | 3 |
| Solid comfort, settled hope | 480 | 2 |
| Solid joys and lasting treasure | 594 | 3 |
| Some better thing than this for me | 284 | 3 |
| Some cursed thing unknown | 152 | 2 |
| Some idol, which I will not own | 152 | 2 |
| Some mansion for my soul prepare | 974 | 6 |
| Some secret bosom-sin | 152 | 2 |
| Some softening gleam of love and prayer | 965 | 5 |
| Some solid ground to rest upon | 879 | 2 |
| Some sure support against despair | 574 | 5 |
| *Sometimes a light surprises | 804 | 1 |
| Songs in the night season give | 287 | 2 |
| Songs of praises | 839 | 3 |
| Son of God, appear, appear | 399 | 1 |
| †Son of God, arise, arise | 383 | 3 |
| *Son of God, if thy free grace | 187 | 1 |
| Son of God, thyself reveal | 354 | 6 |
| Son of his age, his only son | 286 | 2 |
| Son of peace, receive thy crown | 479 | 1 |
| Son of the Living God appear | 486 | 3 |
| *Son of thy Sire's eternal love | 236 | 1 |
| Sons of earth, and hosts of heaven | 850 | 8 |
| Sons of earth and hosts of heaven | 737 | 5 |
| †Sons of earth, the triumph join | 571 | 4 |
| †Sons of God, your Saviour praise | 218 | 3 |

| | Hymn | Verse |
|---|---|---|
| Sons of men and angels, praise | 727 | 2 |
| Sons of men and angels say | 716 | 1 |
| Sons of men, his praises sing | 728 | 1 |
| †Soon as from earth I go | 43 | 2 |
| †Soon as in thee we gain a part | 528 | 3 |
| †Soon as our pardoned hearts believe | 261 | 3 |
| †Soon as the breath of man expires | 638 | 3 |
| †Soon as the evening shades prevail | 552 | 3 |
| Soon as this nature dies | 362 | 6 |
| Soon as thy saving grace appears | 396 | 5 |
| Soon end in joyous day | 831 | 9 |
| †Soon finds each fevered day | 388 | 3 |
| Soon he takes us up to heaven | 480 | 3 |
| Soon I shall lie in death's deep ocean drowned | 596 | 2 |
| Soon our soul and dust shall join | 61 | 4 |
| †Soon shall I learn the exalted strains | 658 | 5 |
| Soon shall every tear be dry | 847 | 3 |
| Soon shall victory tune your song | 847 | 2 |
| Soon shalt thou hear the Bridegroom's voice | 857 | 6 |
| Soon the Lamb of God shall take | 383 | 2 |
| Soon will he sadly from you turn | 695 | 6 |
| Soothes our dread, exceeding nigh | 570 | 1 |
| †Sorely tempted and distressed | 914 | 7 |
| Sore troubled that we In Jesus rejoice | 859 | 2 |
| Sorrow and love flow mingled down | 700 | 3 |
| †Sorrow, and sin, and death are o'er | 154 | 4 |
| Sorrow then shall yield to joy | 349 | 4 |
| Sorrow vanquished, labour ended | 793 | 5 |
| Sorrowed, suffered, to redeem | 989 | 3 |
| Sorrows, and sins, and doubts, and fears | 404 | 4 |
| Sought thy chidings to defer | 768 | 7 |
| Soul of each believing soul | 197 | 6 |
| Soul of my soul remain | 340 | 3 |
| Sound his praise through every land | 580 | 3 |
| Sound the depths of Deity | 260 | 3 |
| Sound throughout its courts his praise | 989 | 3 |
| Sounds from the sacred word | 786 | 2 |
| Source of power, he rules alone | 727 | 3 |
| Source of the old prophetic fire | 87 | 1 |
| Sovereign both of earth and sky | 737 | 6 |
| †Sovereign Father, heavenly King | 257 | 2 |
| *Sovereign of all the worlds on high | 764 | 1 |
| *Sovereign of all! whose will ordains | 465 | 1 |
| Sovereign of earth, hell, air, and sky | 38 | 7 |
| †Sovereign, universal King | 676 | 3 |
| Sow in tears, in joy to reap | 623 | 5 |
| *Sow in the morn thy seed | 739 | 1 |
| †Spare me till I my strength of soul | 356 | 5 |
| †Spare, O God, in mercy spare him | 933 | 19 |
| Spare, O God, thy suppliant groaning | 933 | 12 |
| Spare, or take what thou hast given | 914 | 1 |
| Spark of thy celestial flame | 766 | 2 |
| †Speak, and a holy thing and clean | 159 | 2 |

# SPEAK, AND — SPIRIT DIVINE

| | HYMN | VERSE |
|---|---|---|
| Speak, and all this war shall cease | 110 | 5 |
| Speak, and bid the sun stand still | 158 | 3 |
| Speak, and it shall be done | 303 | 6 |
| Speak, and let the dying live | 151 | 4 |
| Speak, and let the lost be found | 151 | 4 |
| †Speak, and the deaf shall hear thy voice | 139 | 7 |
| Speak, and the tokens show | 486 | 6 |
| Speak, and thy word the dead shall raise | 881 | 2 |
| †Speak but the reconciling word | 505 | 4 |
| Speak but the word, our souls shall wake | 977 | 3 |
| †Speak, gracious Lord, my sickness cure | 131 | 4 |
| Speak, if still thou canst forgive | 151 | 4 |
| Speak into my soul thy name | 355 | 3 |
| Speak it to my soul, that I | 182 | 1 |
| Speak, Jesu, speak into my heart | 150 | 5 |
| Speak, Lord, thy servant heareth now | 353 | 4 |
| Speak, Lord, thy servants hearken now | 90 | 3 |
| Speak my Lord's sincerity | 769 | 2 |
| Speak my paradise restored | 106 | 4 |
| Speak on, and fill my soul with grace | 881 | 2 |
| Speak, or thou never hence shalt move | 141 | 1 |
| Speak, O speak, the kind release | 110 | 1 |
| Speak peace into our hearts and say | 486 | 4 |
| Speak some word of power to me | 790 | 4 |
| Speak the mystery revealed | 937 | 5 |
| Speak the reconciling word | 106 | 3 |
| Speak the sacred number sealed | 937 | 5 |
| Speak the sanctifying word | 383 | 3 |
| †Speak the second time, Be clean | 398 | 2 |
| Speak the soul-redeeming word | 106 | 5 |
| †Speak the word, and we shall be | 299 | 3 |
| Speak the word of full release | 971 | 2 |
| Speak thy own words into my heart | 881 | 1 |
| Speak to me, Almighty Lord | 166 | 4 |
| Speak to my heart, in blessings speak | 141 | 1 |
| Speak to my inmost soul, and say | 344 | 8 |
| †Speak to my warring passions, "Peace!" | 337 | 5 |
| Speak to our hearts, and let us feel | 214 | 1 |
| Speak to our hearts, and tell us now | 774 | 7 |
| Speak us freely justified | 900 | 3 |
| Speak we by our lives his praise | 522 | 1 |
| †Speak with that voice which wakes the dead | 83 | 5 |
| Speaks all the promises | 659 | 5 |
| Speed forth thy flight | 870 | 3 |
| Speed, speed thy work, cast sloth away | 857 | 3 |
| Speed the foot, and touch the tongue | 743 | 3 |
| †Speed them through the mighty ocean | 878 | 3 |
| *Speed thy servants, Saviour, speed them | 878 | 1 |
| Spilt again thy precious blood | 101 | 2 |
| Spirit and life thy words impart | 801 | 2 |
| Spirit, Comforter divine | 221 | 4 |
| *Spirit divine! attend our prayers | 771 | 1 |
| †Spirit divine! attend our prayers | 771 | 7 |

| | Hymn | Verse |
|---|---|---|
| Spirit in them and life is found | 881 | 1 |
| Spirit of burning, come | 361 | 8 |
| Spirit of eternity | 757 | 3 |
| Spirit of faith and holiness | 733 | 3 |
| *Spirit of faith, come down | 85 | 1 |
| Spirit of faith, descend and show | 85 | 3 |
| †Spirit of faith, inspire | 323 | 3 |
| Spirit of faith my heart to raise | 960 | — |
| Spirit of finished holiness | 367 | 1 |
| Spirit of grace and glory too | 653 | 7 |
| †Spirit of grace, and health, and power | 236 | 2 |
| Spirit of health, and life, and power | 361 | 3 |
| Spirit of health, remove | 367 | 1 |
| †Spirit of Holiness | 253 | 3 |
| Spirit of humble fear divine | 960 | — |
| Spirit of perfect love | 367 | 1 |
| Spirit of power, and health, and love | 107 | 1 |
| Spirit of power within | 367 | 1 |
| Spirit of sacrifice and praise | 960 | — |
| †Spirit of truth and love | 870 | 3 |
| Spirit of truth and righteousness | 302 | 4 |
| *Spirit of truth, essential God | 255 | 1 |
| *Spirit of truth! on this thy day | 767 | 1 |
| Spirit of victory and power | 171 | 2 |
| Spiritually dead in sin | 6 | 4 |
| Spoke into order all that is | 750 | 2 |
| Spoken by thee while present here | 754 | 1 |
| Spotless, and peaceable, and kind | 478 | 3 |
| †Spotless, sincere, without offence | 254 | 2 |
| Spouse of Christ, arrayed and waiting | 990 | 4 |
| Spreading the beams of grace | 870 | 3 |
| Spreads heavenly peace around | 880 | 4 |
| Spread thy love to all around | 538 | 3 |
| Spread thy miracles of grace | 335 | 4 |
| Spread thy warmth throughout my heart | 766 | 1 |
| Springing from eternal love | 594 | 2 |
| Spring in his path to birth | 586 | 3 |
| Spring of life, thyself impart | 390 | 5 |
| Spring thou up within my heart | 143 | 4 |
| Spring up into eternal life | 513 | 3 |
| Spring up, O well, I ever cry | 405 | 7 |
| Spring up, O well, in heavenly power | 364 | 2 |
| Spring up within my soul | 405 | 7 |
| Springs forth obedient to thy call | 353 | 6 |
| Springs from the presence of the Lord | 563 | 5 |
| †Springs the watered wilderness | 578 | 3 |
| Sprinkled with the atoning blood | 851 | 1 |
| Sprinkled with the atoning blood | 851 | 8 |
| Sprinkled with water and with blood | 452 | 6 |
| Sprinkle me ever with thy blood | 346 | 2 |
| Sprinkle the sinner with thy blood | 861 | 1 |
| Sprinkle thy blood upon my heart | 186 | 4 |
| Sprinkle us ever with thy blood | 237 | 1 |

| | Hymn | Verse |
|---|---|---|
| Sprung from the Father and the Word | 750 | 1 |
| Sprung from the Father and the Word | 750 | 6 |
| Sprung from the man whose guilty fall | 574 | 3 |
| Stablish and keep my settled heart | 114 | 4 |
| Stablish *his* throne in glorious peace | 465 | 10 |
| Stablish our posterity | 464 | 1 |
| Stablish thy dominion here | 748 | 1 |
| Stablish with me the covenant new | 869 | 1 |
| Stablish with thy grace my heart | 183 | 2 |
| Stablished it in floating seas | 601 | 1 |
| Stablished with abiding grace | 355 | 4 |
| Stablishes in righteousness | 554 | 3 |
| †Stamped with an infinite desert | 321 | 4 |
| Stamped with real holiness | 368 | 4 |
| Stamped with the humble character | 473 | 2 |
| Stamped with the Triune character | 261 | 4 |
| Stamp it on our face and heart | 522 | 4 |
| Stamp thine image in its place | 683 | 7 |
| Stamp thine image on our heart | 512 | 1 |
| Stand all engaged to make me blessed | 577 | 1 |
| Stand amazed, ye heavens, at this | 684 | 3 |
| Stand, as the Rock of ages, sure | 57 | 3 |
| Stand before yon dazzling throne | 75 | 1 |
| Stand by my feeble soul | 105 | 3 |
| †Stand by them in the fiery hour | 462 | 6 |
| Stand dressed in living green | 938 | 3 |
| Stand fast in glorious liberty | 533 | 4 |
| Stand forth a slaughtered Lamb | 128 | 6 |
| Stand forth his faithful witnesses | 897 | 3 |
| Stand forth thy chosen witnesses | 17 | 3 |
| Stand in that dreadful day unknown | 927 | 1 |
| Stand in the temple of our God | 492 | 6 |
| Stand, not daring to draw near | 101 | 4 |
| Stand, O Son of man, confest | 359 | 1 |
| †Stand then against your foes | 266 | 3 |
| †Stand then in his great might | 266 | 2 |
| *Stand the omnipotent decree | 61 | 1 |
| Stand to your arms, the foe is nigh | 314 | 1 |
| Stand we in the ancient way | 295 | 2 |
| Standing is at God's right hand | 72 | 6 |
| †Standing now as newly slain | 175 | 2 |
| Stands fast the city of the Lord | 595 | 1 |
| Stands our adamantine tower | 238 | 4 |
| Stands our city on a rock | 67 | 2 |
| Stands our never-failing hope | 723 | 4 |
| Stands to all eternity | 601 | 2 |
| Starting from the wilderness | 348 | 6 |
| Startled nature dreads to die | 672 | 7 |
| *Stay, thou insulted Spirit, stay | 161 | 1 |
| Stay us on thy only love | 508 | 3 |
| Steadfast, and fixed, and sure | 622 | 1 |
| Steadfast in the faith to be | 753 | 9 |
| †Steadfast let us cleave to thee | 516 | 3 |

| | Hymn | Verse |
|---|---|---|
| Steadfastly behold thy face | 355 | 4 |
| Steadfastly set your face | 267 | 3 |
| Steadfastly to Jesus cleave | 13 | 2 |
| Steadily to Christ look up | 400 | 6 |
| Steal our hearts from God away | 914 | 9 |
| Stem the torrent of my pride | 158 | 3 |
| Steps unto heaven | 848 | 3 |
| Still all my song shall be | 848 | 1 |
| Still all my song shall be | 848 | 5 |
| Still and quiet may I lie | 188 | 3 |
| Still and silent is the sound | 358 | 1 |
| Still beneath thy weight I groan | 382 | 1 |
| Still be the cheerful homage paid | 978 | 4 |
| Still be thy arms my sure defence | 272 | 4 |
| Still be written on our heart | 427 | 2 |
| Still, by the power of his great name | 993 | 3 |
| Still echoing in my ear | 799 | 1 |
| Still forget the things behind | 521 | 2 |
| Still for more on thee we call | 518 | 2 |
| Still for thee my powers employ | 672 | 1 |
| *Still for thy loving-kindness, Lord | 92 | 1 |
| †Still for us his death he pleads | 718 | 6 |
| Still hear and do thy sovereign will | 494 | 4 |
| †Still heavy is thy heart | 831 | 10 |
| Still he calls mankind his own | 718 | 4 |
| Still he loves the earth he leaves | 718 | 4 |
| Still he, who felt temptation's power | 849 | 2 |
| †Still hide me in thy secret place | 998 | 2 |
| Still his dazzling body bears | 66 | 3 |
| Still his outstretched arm we see | 605 | 1 |
| †Still I cannot part with thee | 164 | 3 |
| Still I trust the same to prove | 278 | 3 |
| Still I would myself despise | 243* | 5 |
| Still impotently near | 359 | 3 |
| Still in every state resigned | 243 | 4 |
| Still in thee may I be found | 672 | 1 |
| †Still in the pure espousal | 996 | 2 |
| Still in the vale confined | 947 | 4 |
| Still keeping at thy side | 842 | 5 |
| Still keep me near thy side | 675 | 5 |
| Still lead me, lest I go astray | 373 | 8 |
| †Still let him with my weakness stay | 312 | 3 |
| Still let it to its source aspire | 513 | 4 |
| Still let me guard the holy fire | 327 | 3 |
| †Still let me live thy blood to show | 356 | 4 |
| Still let me pray, and watch, and weep | 172 | 3 |
| Still let me seek to thee for aid | 311 | 3 |
| Still let me, till my days are past | 307 | 5 |
| †Still let them counsel take | 832 | 4 |
| †Still let the publicans draw near | 82 | 8 |
| Still let the Spirit cry | 268 | 4 |
| †Still let thy love point out my way | 373 | 8 |
| †Still let thy tears, thy groans, thy sighs | 23 | 9 |

|  | Hymn | Verse |
|---|---|---|
| †Still let thy wisdom be my guide | 196 | 2 |
| †Still let us, gracious Lord | 533 | 4 |
| Still let us in thy footsteps go | 524 | 1 |
| Still let us in thy Spirit live | 489 | 2 |
| Still let us keep our end in view | 204 | 2 |
| †Still let us, Lord, by thee be blest | 649 | 3 |
| †Still let us on our guard be found | 204 | 5 |
| Still let us on thyself rely | 524 | 1 |
| †Still let us own our common Lord | 504 | 2 |
| †Still let us pray, and never cease | 465 | 10 |
| Still let us to each other cleave | 489 | 2 |
| Still live, united to their Head | 945 | 1 |
| *Still, Lord, I languish for thy grace | 146 | 1 |
| †Still, Lord, thy saving health display | 655 | 6 |
| Still, Lord, with joy we bless thee | 1026 | — |
| Still may I cleave to thee | 311 | 4 |
| Still may I strive, and watch, and pray | 313 | 4 |
| †Still may I walk as in thy sight | 307 | 5 |
| Still may we dwell secure | 41 | 2 |
| Still may we stand before thy face | 494 | 4 |
| †Still may we to our centre tend | 527 | 3 |
| Still my helpless soul I cast | 278 | 8 |
| Still my soul's sure anchor be | 183 | 8 |
| †Still nigh me, O my Saviour, stand | 272 | 4 |
| †Still, O Lord, (for thine we are) | 517 | 3 |
| †Still, O Lord, our faith increase | 522 | 3 |
| †Still, O thou patient God of love | 916 | 3 |
| Still on heavenly manna feeding | 1007 | — |
| Still on the waves thou treadest | 587 | 6 |
| Still our choicest strains we bring | 701 | 1 |
| Still our fellowship increase | 515 | 1 |
| Still our souls shall cry to thee | 900 | 4 |
| Still present with thy people, thou | 386 | 3 |
| Still preserve me safe from harms | 112 | 7 |
| Still preserves, and still provides | 245 | 2 |
| Still protect me with thy love | 292 | 3 |
| †Still prove thyself through all the way | 1003 | 4 |
| †Still restless nature dies and grows | 651 | 3 |
| †Still shall thy grace to me abound | 561 | 8 |
| Still sink thy spirits down | 831 | 10 |
| Still stand it to our eyes alone | 951 | 2 |
| Still, still unchanging, watch beside | 849 | 5 |
| †Still stir me up to strive | 436 | 6 |
| Still support and comfort me | 143 | 2 |
| Still sustain us by thy love | 905 | 2 |
| Still the joyful theme pursue | 701 | 1 |
| Still the Lamb as slain appears | 193 | 7 |
| Still they mark each warrior's way | 829 | 4 |
| Still thine arms are open wide | 182 | 4 |
| Still thou dost the kingdom preach | 693 | 4 |
| Still thou giv'st me all in love | 434 | 7 |
| †Still thou go'st about to teach | 693 | 4 |
| †Still thou journeyest where I am | 112 | 3 |

| | Hymn | Verse |
|---|---|---|
| Still thou seest I am not lost | 275 | 3 |
| Still thou stand'st before the throne | 193 | 7 |
| Still thou wilt not leave thine own | 182 | 3 |
| †Still thy comforts do not fail | 768 | 9 |
| Still thy compassions move | 112 | 3 |
| Still thy gracious words I hear | 191 | 4 |
| Still thy healing aids avail | 768 | 9 |
| Still thy servants' strength repair | 905 | 2 |
| Still thy timely help afford | 187 | 1 |
| Still to my heart thyself reveal | 374 | 2 |
| Still to my soul thyself reveal | 351 | 8 |
| Still to preserve thy servant pure | 820 | 2 |
| Still to press forward in thy way | 210 | 5 |
| Still to us his name declare | 517 | 3 |
| Still tossed on a sea of distress | 47 | 2 |
| Still undisturbed remained | 93 | 5 |
| Still walking in your Captain's sight | 267 | 3 |
| Still watch and weep in vain | 587 | 1 |
| †Still we believe, almighty Lord | 255 | 2 |
| Still we gasp thy grace to know | 348 | 6 |
| †Still we wait for thine appearing | 687 | 2 |
| †Still will I strive, and labour still | 281 | 5 |
| Still will we make thy mercies known | 978 | 5 |
| †Still with and in thy people dwell | 525 | 3 |
| Still with me let thy grace abide | 196 | 2 |
| Still with thy rebel strive | 347 | 2 |
| Still worse and worse my case I find | 781 | 2 |
| Stilled its tossing, hushed its roar | 921 | 4 |
| Stills the proud Philistine's boast | 278 | 7 |
| Stir up thy strength, almighty Lord | 568 | 3 |
| †Stir up thy power, appear, appear | 465 | 2 |
| Stone on stone the workmen place | 990 | 2 |
| Stone to flesh again convert | 173 | 1 |
| Stone to flesh, O God, convert | 101 | 1 |
| Stood a leper in thy light | 768 | 8 |
| Stood thine everlasting throne | 601 | 2 |
| Stoop, in condescending grace | 762 | 1 |
| Stoop to a poor sinner, stoop | 112 | 3 |
| Stoop to creature-happiness | 434 | 3 |
| Stoop to the poor heart of man | 762 | 1 |
| Stop, and gaze, and fall, and own | 701 | 2 |
| Stop me at the first beginning | 819 | 2 |
| Stop the whirlwind of my will | 158 | 3 |
| Stormed by a host of foes within | 269 | 1 |
| Storms and earthquakes it defies | 67 | 3 |
| Storms which, when he bids you, blow | 639 | 4 |
| Straight we found his glad salvation | 580 | 4 |
| Strange flames far from my heart remove | 373 | 2 |
| Strangely upheld by thy right hand | 366 | 3 |
| Stranger long to thee, and rest | 191 | 2 |
| †Strangers and pilgrims here below | 71 | 2 |
| Strangers to the life divine | 7 | 1 |
| Strangers, yea, enemies to God | 82 | 3 |

| | Hymn | Verse |
|---|---|---|
| Streaming from thy throne above | 757 | 2 |
| Streaming thence in fresh supplies | 618 | 1 |
| Streams of grace our thirst repress | 348 | 6 |
| Streams of mercy, never ceasing | 866 | 1 |
| Streams through airy channels flow | 578 | 1 |
| Strength and comfort from thy word | 156 | 3 |
| Strength in thee thy people have | 542 | 3 |
| Strength of my failing flesh and heart | 918 | — |
| Strength when my footsteps slide | 602 | 3 |
| Strengthened by thy Spirit's might | 27 | 5 |
| Strengthened with the bread of life | 847 | 1 |
| Strengthen my feet with steady pace | 210 | 5 |
| Stretched the hand, and strained the sight | 743 | 3 |
| Stretched forth thy everlasting arms | 924 | 4 |
| Stretch my faith's capacity | 372 | — |
| Stretch out the arms of faith and prayer | 539 | 6 |
| Stretch out thine arm omnipotent | 138 | 1 |
| Strike all your harps of gold | 699 | 5 |
| Strike notes of deeper sadness | 587 | 2 |
| Strike this hard rocky heart of mine | 778 | 2 |
| Strike with the hammer of thy word | 84 | 1 |
| Strike with the hammer of thy word | 105 | 1 |
| Strike with thy love's resistless stroke | 102 | 2 |
| Stripped of our former peace and power | 806 | 1 |
| Stripped of their fancied righteousness | 461 | 4 |
| †Strive man to win that glory | 943 | 15 |
| †Strive we, in affection strive | 519 | 2 |
| Striving till he casts out sin | 758 | 4 |
| Strong and living stones, are bound | 990 | 2 |
| Strong and mighty, thee to bless | 727 | 5 |
| Strong, and permanent, and clear | 390 | 5 |
| Strong deliverer | 839 | 2 |
| †Strong I am, for he is strong | 197 | 3 |
| Strong in the grace to-day bestowed | 835 | 2 |
| Strong in the Lord, and thy great might | 439 | 1 |
| Strong in the Lord of hosts | 266 | 1 |
| Strong in the strength which God supplies | 266 | 1 |
| Strong in thine omnipotence | 542 | 1 |
| Strong in thy omnipotence | 193 | 8 |
| Strong is his arm, and shall fulfil | 650 | 3 |
| Strong mail of craft and power | 856 | 1 |
| †Stronger his love than death or hell | 147 | 2 |
| Stronger than all the powers of hell | 138 | 7 |
| Stronger than death and hell | 96 | 3 |
| Stronger than love, I fondly thought | 288 | 3 |
| Stronger than sin, thy grace exert | 775 | 3 |
| †Stronger than the strong man, thou | 299 | 5 |
| †Struggle through thy latest passion | 922 | 3 |
| Struggle to utter my request | 153 | 2 |
| Struggling in a mother's heart | 914 | 6 |
| †Stung by the scorpion sin | 34 | 5 |
| *Stupendous height of heavenly love | 686 | 1 |
| *Stupendous love of God most high | 25 | 1 |

| | Hymn | Verse |
|---|---|---|
| Subdue the rebel in our soul | 752 | 4 |
| Subdue the yielding soul | 966 | 5 |
| Subject all nations to thy throne | 541 | 3 |
| Subject of all my converse be | 328 | 2 |
| Subject of all our songs | 536 | 1 |
| Subject then to no decay | 941 | 2 |
| Subject to none but thee | 465 | 1 |
| Sublimer sweets than nature knows | 880 | 3 |
| †Sublime upon his azure throne | 64 | 6 |
| †Submissive to thy just decree | 913 | 3 |
| ‡Subservient to thy daily praise | 966 | 4 |
| †Subsists as in us all one soul | 537 | 4 |
| Succouring his faithful band | 720 | 6 |
| Succour still I find in thee | 542 | 1 |
| Succour there is for me laid up | 781 | 3 |
| Such as in the martyrs glowed | 519 | 2 |
| Such as may every conscience reach | 456 | 3 |
| ‡Such blessings from thy gracious hand | 664 | 5 |
| Such ever bring thee where they come | 864 | 2 |
| Such guilty, daring worms to spare | 656 | 2 |
| †Such happiness, O Lord, have we | 62 | 2 |
| Such may all our Sabbaths prove | 975 | 5 |
| Such our whole employment be | 529 | 2 |
| Such plenteous redemption in thee | 174 | 1 |
| Such power belongs to thee alone | 145 | 1 |
| Such wonders love can do | 713 | 2 |
| Sudden, I found thee near to save | 289 | 4 |
| Suddenly from earth released | 52 | 5 |
| Suddenly return, and never | 385 | 2 |
| Suffered no more to rove | 296 | 3 |
| Suffered once for man below | 710 | 1 |
| Sufferers in his righteous cause | 76 | 1 |
| Suffer me to kiss thy feet | 168 | 5 |
| Suffer the sinners to draw near | 396 | 1 |
| Suffer, with thy Lord to reign | 922 | 4 |
| Suffice for us that God, we know | 685 | 3 |
| †Suffice that for the season past | 203 | 7 |
| Sufficient is thine arm alone | 41 | 2 |
| Sufficient, sovereign, saving grace | 39 | 3 |
| Suggest, and hearken to my prayer | 99 | 1 |
| *Summoned my labour to renew | 321 | 1 |
| Summoning the world to judgment | 720 | 7 |
| †Sun and moon are both confounded | 936 | 3 |
| Sun and moon, rejoice before him | 640 | 1 |
| Sun, and moon with borrowed light | 639 | 2 |
| Sun and shield alike thou art | 593 | 3 |
| †Sun, moon, and stars convey thy praise | 553 | 3 |
| Sun, moon, and stars forgot | 848 | 5 |
| *Sun of my soul! thou Saviour dear | 973 | 1 |
| Sun of righteousness, arise | 963 | 1 |
| Sung by ransomed hosts above | 866 | 1 |
| Superior power, and guardian grace | 675 | 10 |
| Superior sense may I display | 320 | 1 |

| | Hymn | Verse |
|---|---|---|
| †Superior to their smile or frown | 439 | 2 |
| Superior to the joys below | 420 | 1 |
| Supplies the city of our God | 569 | 4 |
| Supplies their every need | 874 | 1 |
| Supply all their wants | 495 | 3 |
| †Supply what every member wants | 527 | 5 |
| Supplying all their need | 888 | 1 |
| Supported by his smile | 325 | 2 |
| Supported by the great I AM | 223 | 1 |
| Supported by thy care | 1002 | 2 |
| Supporters of the heavenly dome | 72 | 2 |
| Support my feebleness of mind | 379 | 3 |
| Support my feebleness of mind | 916 | 5 |
| Support my weakness with thy might | 196 | 3 |
| Support thy great vicegerent here | 465 | 2 |
| †Supreme and all-sufficient God | 642 | 5 |
| Supreme, essential One, adored | 259 | 6 |
| Supreme in mercy as in power | 638 | 6 |
| Supreme in power and grace | 1000 | 1 |
| Supreme, till all his foes are slain | 629 | 9 |
| Supremely great and good | 307 | 1 |
| Sure as now the grief I feel | 335 | 3 |
| Sure, as the saints around thy throne | 261 | 3 |
| Sure confidence in thee I have | 548 | 5 |
| Sure earnest of that happiness | 258 | 3 |
| Sure evidence of things unseen | 708 | 3 |
| †Sure I am it is thy will | 910 | 5 |
| Sure, if with God on earth I live | 80 | 6 |
| Sure my soul's anchor may remain | 189 | 1 |
| Sure salvation is its end | 521 | 4 |
| Sure to emerge, and rise again | 61 | 2 |
| Sure to win the victory | 278 | 4 |
| Sure whatever is, is best | 914 | 4 |
| Surely all my happy days | 554 | 6 |
| "Surely," he saith, "I quickly come" | 405 | 2 |
| †Surely he will lift me up | 115 | 4 |
| †Surely he will not long delay | 948 | 3 |
| †Surely his healing power is nigh | 781 | 5 |
| †Surely in us the hope | 345 | 4 |
| Surely I shall find him there | 192 | 1 |
| Surely I shall rise again | 274 | 3 |
| Surely I shall soon be made | 382 | 5 |
| †Surely I shall, the sinner I | 357 | 4 |
| Surely it shall on me take place | 406 | 3 |
| Surely it shall speak at last | 142 | 2 |
| †Surely now the bitterness | 112 | 6 |
| Surely now the Holy Ghost | 86 | 1 |
| Surely on me my Father smiled | 365 | 3 |
| †Surely thou canst, I do not doubt | 356 | 7 |
| Surely thou canst make me stand | 142 | 4 |
| †Surely thou canst not let me die | 784 | 5 |
| †Surely thou didst unite | 510 | 4 |
| Surely thou shalt bring me through | 819 | 4 |

| | Hymn | Verse |
|---|---|---|
| Surely thy death shall raise me up | 815 | 3 |
| †Surely we now your souls embrace | 539 | 7 |
| Surely we shall thy mercy find | 380 | 3 |
| Surely, with that dying word | 106 | 7 |
| Surety, who all my debt hast paid | 145 | 5 |
| Surrounded and upheld by thee | 329 | 3 |
| *Surrounded by a host of foes | 269 | 1 |
| Surround, sustain, and strengthen me | 309 | 2 |
| Sustain and bless us by thy sway | 648 | 6 |
| Sustain the life thyself hast given | 392 | 1 |
| Survey by the light of my Lord | 70 | 2 |
| Swallowed up in endless day | 349 | 4 |
| Swallow up my soul in love | 350 | 3 |
| Swearers, for you he spilt his blood | 36 | 1 |
| Sweetest symphony of praise | 538 | 3 |
| Sweet fellowship they find | 823 | 6 |
| †Sweet fields beyond the swelling flood | 938 | 3 |
| †Sweet is the day of sacred rest | 599 | 2 |
| †Sweet is the memory of his name | 903 | 5 |
| *Sweet is the memory of thy grace | 637 | 1 |
| *Sweet is the sunlight after rain | 957 | 1 |
| *Sweet is the work, my God, my King | 599 | 1 |
| Sweet it is to trust in thee | 970 | 1 |
| Sweet messenger of rest | 787 | 4 |
| *Sweet place; sweet place alone | 942 | 1 |
| Sweet truth to me! I shall arise | 931 | Cho. |
| Sweetly breathe thyself away | 921 | 3 |
| Sweetly cheer the night of woe | 672 | 3 |
| Sweetly compose my weary breast | 328 | 3 |
| Sweetly each, with each combined | 522 | 2 |
| Sweetly in thy bosom bear | 193 | 4 |
| Sweetly let my spirit prove | 381 | 4 |
| †Sweetly may we all agree | 518 | 7 |
| Sweetly of one heart and mind | 487 | 3 |
| Sweetly on our spirits move | 538 | 2 |
| Sweetly waiting at thy feet | 325 | 3 |
| Swells my soul to compass thee | 27 | 6 |
| Swells the high trump that wakes the dead | 934 | 2 |
| Swell the loud anthem of thy praise | 559 | 4 |
| Swell the raptured songs above | 672 | 4 |
| Swell the triumph of his train | 66 | 1 |
| †Swept from the face of earth | 883 | 3 |
| †Swift as the eagle cuts the air | 802 | 5 |
| †Swift to its close ebbs out life's little day | 972 | 2 |
| †Swift to my rescue come | 296 | 3 |
| Swift to our heavenly country move | 71 | 2 |
| Swift to succour sinking man | 215 | 2 |
| Swifter than the lightning's ray | 941 | 2 |
| Swiftly acquire, and ne'er forego | 473 | 4 |
| Swiftly to their wish be given | 921 | 5 |
| †Sworn to destroy, let earth assail | 138 | 7 |

| TAKE ALL | TAKEN FROM |
|---|---|

|  | Hymn | Verse |
|---|---|---|
| Take all our sins away | 900 | 2 |
| Take all, take all my sins away | 33 | 8 |
| †Take away my darling sin | 158 | 2 |
| Take away my inbred sin | 398 | 2 |
| Take away the heart of stone | 158 | 1 |
| Take, empty it, O Lord, and fill | 410 | 2 |
| Take every virtue, every grace | 266 | 4 |
| Take (for thou didst their ransom find) | 445 | 2 |
| Take it as through Jesus given | 1012 | — |
| Take life or friends away | 948 | 7 |
| Take me into thee, my Lord | 354 | 4 |
| Take me, Jesus, to thine arms | 112 | 7 |
| Take me now, possess me whole | 193 | 1 |
| Take me, whom thyself hast bought | 358 | 4 |
| Take my body, spirit, soul | 434 | 1 |
| Take my cancelled sin away | 676 | 2 |
| Take my heart;—but make it new | 430 | 4 |
| Take my heart, O take and seal it | 866 | 3 |
| Take my memory, mind, and will | 430 | 4 |
| †Take my poor heart, and let it be | 26 | 2 |
| †Take my soul and body's powers | 430 | 4 |
| Take on thee my every care | 13 | 3 |
| Take, O take my sins away | 151 | 6 |
| Take, O take our sins away | 257 | 5 |
| Take our body, spirit, soul | 516 | 2 |
| Take our load of guilt away | 29 | 2 |
| Take possession of my breast | 824 | 4 |
| Take possession of my heart | 149 | 1 |
| Take possession of thine own | 423 | 4 |
| Take the crown so freely given | 13 | 4 |
| †Take the dear purchase of thy blood | 145 | 5 |
| Take the dear purchase of thy blood | 375 | 4 |
| †Take the dear purchase of thy blood | 523 | 5 |
| Take the everlasting praise | 233 | 3 |
| Take the everlasting praise | 1021 | 2 |
| Take the kingdom | 748 | 5 |
| Take the King of glory in | 718 | 2 |
| Take the King of glory in | 718 | 3 |
| †Take the pledge we offer now | 895 | 2 |
| Take the power of sin away | 110 | 6 |
| Take the purchase of thy blood | 350 | 4 |
| Take the weary wanderer home | 191 | 2 |
| †Take this heart of stone away | 173 | 5 |
| Take this poor fluttering soul to rest | 114 | 3 |
| †Take thou my cup, and it | 887 | 3 |
| Take thou, O take this guilty heart | 773 | 4 |
| Take, thou universal Good | 1022 | — |
| †Take to thee thy royal power | 937 | 6 |
| Take to thyself my ransomed heart | 146 | 4 |
| Take to thyself thy mighty power | 236 | 1 |
| Take up the torch, and wave it wide | 857 | 4 |
| †Take when thou wilt into thy hands | 432 | 4 |
| Taken from our head to-day | 718 | 7 |

| | HYMN | VERSE |
|---|---|---|
| Taken to an early rest | 52 | 5 |
| Takes all our sins away | 703 | 2 |
| Takes his seat above the sky | 571 | 3 |
| Takes into his school, And gives him to see | 211 | 3 |
| Takes us to his throne above | 53 | 1 |
| Talk o'er the records of thy will | 328 | 1 |
| *Talk with us, Lord, thyself reveal | 214 | 1 |
| †Tallest of the earth-born race | 278 | 2 |
| Tamely to thy yoke submit | 508 | 5 |
| Tame the old Adam in our soul | 505 | 3 |
| Tarry till the Lord appears | 142 | 1 |
| Taste our glorious liberty | 508 | 8 |
| Taste we in the gifts the grace | 1012 | — |
| †Tasting that the Lord is good | 768 | 4 |
| Taught by the art of God | 578 | 2 |
| †Taught in thee is a salvation | 595 | 3 |
| Teachably intelligent | 817 | 4 |
| *Teacher of hearts, 'tis thine alone | 871 | 1 |
| Teach me some celestial measure | 866 | 1 |
| †Teach me the happy art | 436 | 5 |
| Teach me the measure of my days | 564 | 1 |
| Teach me the new, the joyful song | 366 | 4 |
| Teach me to die, that so I may | 974 | 3 |
| Teach me to know how frail I am | 564 | 1 |
| †Teach me to live, that I may dread | 974 | 3 |
| Teach me to love thy sacred word | 880 | 5 |
| Teach my heart that God is love | 676 | 1 |
| Teach the lesson of thy cross | 358 | 3 |
| Teach to judge and act aright | 756 | 2 |
| †Teach us to know the Father, Son | 751 | 3 |
| Tears of joy mine eyes o'erflow | 188 | 6 |
| Tear their vain confidence away | 443 | 1 |
| Tear these idols from my heart | 158 | 2 |
| Tear up the graves, and cleave the ground | 57 | 1 |
| Tell anew his high salvation | 604 | 1 |
| Tell him, "We will not let thee go" | 380 | 5 |
| Tell him ye wait his grace to prove | 380 | 4 |
| †Tell it out beneath the heaven | 604 | 2 |
| Tell it out from morn till even | 604 | 2 |
| †Tell me again my peace is made | 184 | 4 |
| Tell me, I still beseech thee, tell | 140 | 4 |
| Tell me, Lord, that thou art mine | 620 | 8 |
| Tell me now, in love divine | 245 | 4 |
| Tell me, O tell me, who thou art | 113 | 2 |
| Tell me thy love, thy secret tell | 144 | 4 |
| Tell me Thy name, and tell me now | 140 | 2 |
| Tell me thy name, thy nature tell | 113 | 1 |
| Tell me we shall meet above | 915 | 4 |
| †Tell of his wondrous faithfulness | 659 | 2 |
| Tell that God for ever reigneth | 604 | 2 |
| Tell them, "I have died for you!" | 463 | 3 |
| †Tell them that the day is coming | 604 | 3 |
| Tell, to after-ages tell | 572 | 3 |

| | Hymn | Verse |
|---|---|---|
| Temperance and gentleness | 520 | 3 |
| Tempered by the art of God | 518 | 6 |
| Temper, not conceal his rays | 817 | 6 |
| Temples divine of living stones | 68 | 4 |
| Temples of the living God | 479 | 3 |
| Tempt as ye will, my soul repels | 285 | 6 |
| Tempted in every point like me | 157 | 1 |
| Tempted more than I can bear | 819 | 3 |
| Tenderly did he restore | 606 | 5 |
| †Tender Spirit, dwell with me | 769 | 3 |
| Ten thousand deaths deserve to die | 365 | 8 |
| Ten thousand more with grace supply | 873 | 3 |
| †Ten thousand snares my path beset | 281 | 4 |
| Ten thousand thousand are their tongues | 678 | 1 |
| Ten thousand thousand more | 732 | 3 |
| †Ten thousand thousand precious gifts | 657 | 8 |
| Ten thousand times preserved from sin | 178 | 2 |
| Ten thousand times thy goodness grieved | 161 | 3 |
| Ten thousand times thy goodness seen | 161 | 3 |
| †Ten thousand to their endless home | 949 | 3 |
| Ten thousand wants have I | 93 | 1 |
| Terrible in majesty | 571 | 2 |
| Terrible majesty is thine | 38 | 3 |
| *Terrible thought! shall I alone | 80 | 1 |
| Testify his faithfulness | 735 | 1 |
| Testify that thou art true | 348 | 1 |
| Than all earth's treasures can afford | 437 | 3 |
| Than basely in our lives disown | 454 | 6 |
| Than e'er by light irreverence turn | 307 | 3 |
| Than gold and pearls more precious far | 431 | 5 |
| Than heart can e'er conceive | 244 | 2 |
| Than it ever seemed before | 878 | 5 |
| Than I to ask, or to receive | 782 | 1 |
| Than nothing am, till thou art mine | 38 | 3 |
| Than sands upon the ocean shore | 190 | 5 |
| Than seem to serve thee without zeal | 454 | 7 |
| Than sin against the gospel law | 307 | 3 |
| Than storm, than earthquake, or than fire | 698 | 2 |
| Than the earth profounder far | 639 | 8 |
| Than the evil of my heart | 819 | 2 |
| Than thousands in the tents of sin | 590 | 4 |
| Than to please thee perfectly | 842 | 6 |
| Than us, who cast our faith away | 454 | 8 |
| Than we on earth, to do thy will | 236 | 2 |
| Than what the world may claim | 162 | 2 |
| Than when thy sheep | 276 | 3 |
| Thankful for their answered prayer | 735 | 1 |
| †Thankful I take the cup from thee | 337 | 3 |
| †Thanks be all ascribed to thee | 53 | 3 |
| Thanks for all that we receive | 233 | 3 |
| Thanks for all that we receive | 1021 | 1 |
| †Thanks we give, and adoration | 1008 | 2 |
| Thanksgiving and the voice of praise | 111 | 5 |

| | HYMN | VERSE |
|---|---|---|
| That all around our works may see | 526 | 6 |
| †That all-comprising peace bestow | 252 | 6 |
| That all hereafter might | 510 | 4 |
| That all I do is right | 367 | 3 |
| That all mankind thy truth may see | 391 | 2 |
| That all mankind with me may prove | 33 | 5 |
| That all may hear the quickening sound | 33 | 4 |
| That all may know their gracious hour | 162 | 4 |
| That all may see his love displayed | 953 | 2 |
| That all may turn and live | 162 | 3 |
| That all may turn and live | 182 | 4 |
| That all might come to God | 162 | 4 |
| That all my powers, with all their might | 210 | 6 |
| That all my powers, with all their might | 964 | 7 |
| That all of woman born may see | 771 | 6 |
| That all our works are nothing worth | 822 | 1 |
| That all the earth surveys | 12 | 2 |
| That all the earth thy hand may see | 588 | 4 |
| That all the God unknown | 452 | 2 |
| That all who to thy wounds will flee | 190 | 9 |
| That all who trust in thee alone | 648 | 3 |
| That always cleaves to ill | 382 | 2 |
| That angels ever bore | 675 | 1 |
| That antepast of heaven | 97 | 3 |
| That arm shall quell | 855 | 2 |
| That ascertains the kingdom mine | 376 | 5 |
| That awful hour unknown | 55 | 2 |
| That bids our sorrows cease | 1 | 3 |
| That bids us turn and live | 983 | 4 |
| †That blessed law of thine | 340 | 2 |
| That blessed portion shall receive | 557 | 4 |
| †That blessed sense of guilt impart | 84 | 6 |
| That blood I trust, that blood alone | 909 | 4 |
| †That blood which cleanses from all sin | 523 | 6 |
| That blood which doth for sinners speak | 774 | 5 |
| That blood which he for all did shed | 148 | 5 |
| †That bloody banner see | 277 | 3 |
| That burst our bonds in sunder | 854 | 1 |
| That, by thy glorious Spirit fired | 330 | 3 |
| That, by thy grace our souls are fed | 906 | 2 |
| That call for patient care | 842 | 7 |
| That calls thy exiles home | 536 | 5 |
| That calms my troubled breast | 832 | 2 |
| That can for sin atone | 865 | 4 |
| That can in Jesu's name believe | 401 | 1 |
| That cannot see his path | 587 | 3 |
| That caused thy needless fear | 831 | 13 |
| That Christ is God indeed | 673 | 2 |
| That city of God the great King | 946 | 1 |
| That comes a sinner unto me | 31 | 4 |
| †That comfort was mine | 807 | 2 |
| That consciousness of guilt which fears | 104 | 1 |
| That crowds were born to glory here | 994 | 3 |

|  | Hymn | Verse |
|---|---|---|
| That dear disfigured face | 128 | 5 |
| That drove thee from my breast | 787 | 4 |
| That eager hearts expect | 943 | 6 |
| That earliest wedding-day | 996 | 1 |
| That efficacious blood apply | 528 | 6 |
| That endless banishment from thee | 181 | 6 |
| That endless misery | 83 | 6 |
| That endless song above | 204 | 8 |
| That ever mortals knew | 675 | 1 |
| That every fallen soul of man | 33 | 5 |
| That every grace and every gift | 875 | 2 |
| That every grace, and every gift | 1016 | 2 |
| That every knee shall bow | 727 | 5 |
| That every soul shall bow at last | 448 | 2 |
| That faith and love may make all one | 457 | 2 |
| That falls on Hermon's hill | 630 | 5 |
| That famous Plant thou art | 531 | 1 |
| That Father, Word, and Spirit, are One | 261 | 3 |
| That favourite name of Love | 249 | 4 |
| That feeds the strength of every saint | 802 | 2 |
| That feed the running rills | 667 | 1 |
| That flow from his heavenly throne | 79 | 1 |
| That flows replenished from above | 590 | 3 |
| That fountain in his day | 798 | 2 |
| That from their brethren fly | 459 | 1 |
| That from the master's table fall | 164 | 4 |
| That full divine conformity | 408 | 1 |
| That fulness of the Deity | 262 | 4 |
| That glitters through the skies | 277 | 4 |
| That glorious bliss to share | 52 | 6 |
| That God hath sent thee from above | 505 | 9 |
| That God I face to face shall see | 928 | 3 |
| That God is only love | 152 | 4 |
| That God is true | 276 | 1 |
| That God, my God, inhabits there | 851 | 2 |
| That grace may let me go | 150 | 8 |
| †That great decree I shall declare | 541 | 3 |
| †That great mysterious Deity | 833 | 5 |
| That great name by which we live | 989 | 4 |
| That Guide infallible impart | 754 | 3 |
| That happy station to secure | 600 | 4 |
| That has deigned to approve | 231 | 8 |
| That hath the Saviour brought | 685 | 3 |
| That hath us now o'ertaken | 856 | 1 |
| That haven of repose to find | 535 | 3 |
| That have obtained the prize | 949 | 1 |
| That, having all things done | 266 | 2 |
| That he alone delivereth | 595 | 6 |
| That he for us hath died | 96 | 2 |
| That *he* here may love and fear thee | 895 | 2 |
| That he is ours, and we are his | 897 | 2 |
| That he may serve his God | 544 | 4 |
| *That health of soul I gasp to know | 816 | 1 |

| | Hymn | Verse |
|---|---|---|
| That hear this joyful sound. | 741 | 3 |
| That heavenly fabric stands. | 74 | 1 |
| †That heavenly Teacher of mankind | 754 | 3 |
| That heightened all their highest joys | 721 | 5 |
| That hidden life to share | 947 | 6 |
| That hides my life above | 282 | 3 |
| That his brow adorns | 793 | 3 |
| That his eternal light may guide | 966 | 1 |
| That holiness I long to feel | 408 | 1 |
| That hurries to and fro | 842 | 3 |
| †That hurrying strife far off remove | 204 | 6 |
| That I, a child of wrath and hell | 30 | 2 |
| That I am born of God | 765 | 3 |
| That I am sin, and thou art love | 177 | 4 |
| That I, even I may learn | 877 | 1 |
| That I from thee may never stray | 196 | 2 |
| †That I from thee no more may part | 308 | 2 |
| That I have any hope of heaven | 188 | 6 |
| That I have trampled on thy blood. | 162 | 1 |
| That I his praises may record | 616 | 6 |
| That I in the new earth may claim | 304 | 2 |
| That I may be always thine. | 183 | 3 |
| That I may do thy will | 357 | 3 |
| That I may dread thy gracious power | 186 | 6 |
| That I may ever live with thee | 923 | 4 |
| That I may from evil near | 187 | 3 |
| That I may long obey | 920 | 2 |
| That I may never grieve thee more. | 171 | 2 |
| That I may now enlightened be | 436 | 3 |
| That I may now perceive thee near. | 128 | 4 |
| That I may obedient prove | 243 | 1 |
| That I may praise thy name | 634 | 4 |
| That I may thank thee all my days. | 559 | 4 |
| That I may thy glory see | 819 | 4 |
| That I may timely comprehend | 565 | 1 |
| That I may understand thy word | 113 | 3 |
| That I may with zealous care | 243 | 4 |
| That I might in thee be blest | 215 | 4 |
| That I might in thy footsteps tread | 330 | 4 |
| That I might live to thee | 360 | 2 |
| That I might share it with my Lord | 72 | 5 |
| That I my heavenly Master know | 472 | 1 |
| That I never, never more | 188 | 4 |
| That I no more may do | 340 | 1 |
| That I shall find my all in thee | 163 | 1 |
| That I shall serve thee without fear | 401 | 5 |
| That I should fit myself for thee | 132 | 5 |
| That I should holy be | 105 | 4 |
| That I should in thee be blest | 18 | 2 |
| That I so late to thee did turn | 210 | 2 |
| That I the joyful choir may join | 612 | 4 |
| That I thy life may have | 182 | 3 |
| That I thy mercy may declare | 288 | 2 |

| | Hymn | Verse |
|---|---|---|
| †That I thy mercy may proclaim | 391 | 2 |
| That I thy mercy's praise may spread | 171 | 1 |
| That I thy mind in me might have | 375 | 3 |
| That I to all mankind may prove | 365 | 6 |
| That I to sin shall never cleave | 416 | 6 |
| That I with thee may rise | 347 | 3 |
| That I would die to be thy guest | 167 | 4 |
| That infant lips can try | 823 | 3 |
| That in our Saviour was | 96 | 5 |
| That in the Father's courts my glorious dress | 794 | 6 |
| That in this house have called upon thy name | 962 | 2 |
| That in us its silent leaven | 882 | 6 |
| That Jesus died for me | 781 | 5 |
| That Jesus is the Lord | 85 | 2 |
| That Jesus is thy healing name | 375 | 1 |
| That keeps us still apart | 459 | 2 |
| That, kept by mercy's power | 125 | 3 |
| That kind, upbraiding glance, which broke | 309 | 4 |
| That knows and cleaves to thee | 179 | 2 |
| That leads me to the Lamb | 787 | 1 |
| That leads me to the Lamb | 787 | 6 |
| That leads to it be thine | 837 | 2 |
| That leads to joys on high | 789 | 4 |
| That leads us to the courts above | 380 | 6 |
| That life and all things casts behind | 853 | 6 |
| That lifted up by pardoning grace | 670 | 2 |
| That light shall enkindle in me | 911 | 3 |
| That living bread, that heavenly wine | 908 | 2 |
| That living temple of thy Son | 121 | 3 |
| That living water now bestow | 864 | 1 |
| That lonely unfrequented way | 21 | 1 |
| That look'st from heaven below | 943 | 7 |
| That looks to thee when sin is near | 301 | 3 |
| That lovely Jerusalem here | 73 | 3 |
| That love the dear abode | 619 | 4 |
| That made both earth and heaven | 618 | 1 |
| That made thy soul a sacrifice | 122 | 3 |
| That makes me free indeed | 402 | 3 |
| That makes me meet for home | 172 | 2 |
| That makes thy children free | 842 | 8 |
| That makes us meet for heaven | 705 | 4 |
| That man with God might reign | 413 | 3 |
| That may our souls o'erpower | 818 | 1 |
| That mercy they may taste and live | 189 | 2 |
| †That mighty faith on me bestow | 342 | 3 |
| That mindful of thy word | 828 | 1 |
| That moment, Lord, reprove | 308 | 3 |
| That mourns in lonely exile here | 690 | 1 |
| That moves in earth, or air, or sky | 235 | 3 |
| That name in-spoken to my heart | 249 | 4 |
| That ne'er were loved like me | 788 | 5 |
| That, now beholding thee | 304 | 5 |
| That never, never dies | 44 | 5 |

| | Hymn | Verse |
|---|---|---|
| That noisy burst of selfish love | 204 | 6 |
| That none should boast himself of aught | 626 | 2 |
| That ocean of love without bottom or shore | 808 | 11 |
| That only bliss for which it pants | 948 | 1 |
| That only ground of all our hope | 394 | 2 |
| That only name to sinners given | 206 | 3 |
| That our souls may remain | 491 | 4 |
| That palace of our glorious King | 71 | 5 |
| That pants to sing thy praise | 242 | 1 |
| †That path with humble speed I'll seek | 285 | 4 |
| †That peace of God, that peace of thine | 754 | 5 |
| That perfect love might cast out fear | 375 | 3 |
| That plants my God in me | 361 | 3 |
| That pledge of love for ever there | 26 | 2 |
| That precious, bleeding sacrifice | 2 | 8 |
| That precious, bleeding sacrifice | 394 | 2 |
| That precious gift of charity | 822 | 1 |
| That proceeds from the Father and Son | 488 | 3 |
| †That promise made to Adam's race | 754 | 2 |
| That proudly stalks along | 278 | 1 |
| That, quickened by thy dying love | 451 | 3 |
| That raiseth me | 848 | 1 |
| That rides upon the stormy sky | 12 | 2 |
| That sacred, infinite desire | 304 | 3 |
| That, saved, we may thy goodness feel | 250 | 2 |
| That saw the Lord arise | 956 | 1 |
| That see the light or feel the sun | 553 | 4 |
| That see this heavenly light | 741 | 4 |
| That shall adorn thy dwelling-place | 992 | 3 |
| That shall our souls release | 536 | 8 |
| That shin'st in deepest night | 737 | 2 |
| That, silenced by thy mercy's power | 126 | 6 |
| That sing Jehovah's praise | 920 | 5 |
| That sink into the grave | 635 | 2 |
| That sinner am I | 707 | 5 |
| That sinners may adore | 625 | 3 |
| That sinners may with angels join | 262 | 1 |
| That smote the sea | 854 | 1 |
| That so I might be free | 551 | 5 |
| †That so thy wondrous way | 581 | 2 |
| That spake at first the world from nought | 203 | 4 |
| That spread the earth and heaven abroad | 638 | 4 |
| That strives with thee my heart to share | 344 | 4 |
| That still on earth we live | 482 | 2 |
| That still the universe sustains | 638 | 4 |
| That still thine inmost bowels cry | 773 | 2 |
| That still thou seekest those who flee | 773 | 2 |
| That still thy precious name we know | 483 | 1 |
| That suffered in my stead | 122 | 3 |
| That takes those gifts with joy | 657 | 8 |
| †That, taught according to thy will | 470 | 2 |
| That, taught by thy good Spirit and led | 471 | 4 |
| That tears my anxious breast | 43 | 4 |

| | Hymn | Verse |
|---|---|---|
| That, that is the fulness; but this is the taste | 205 | 5 |
| That the kingdom thou preparest | 895 | 1 |
| That them I may no more forget | 369 | 3 |
| That they may set forth thy pure word | 822 | 3 |
| That this changeful world's affairs | 826 | — |
| That thou art all in all | 1014 | — |
| That thou art God, and God is love | 782 | 3 |
| That thou are pure, essential love | 261 | 3 |
| That thou at last wilt take us up | 649 | 1 |
| That thou hast died for all | 118 | 3 |
| That thou hast pardoned me | 245 | 4 |
| That thou, my God, shouldst die for me | 201 | 1 |
| That thou shouldst us to glory bring | 26 | 5 |
| That thou such mercies hast bestowed | 206 | 1 |
| That thou, the everlasting Lord | 157 | 5 |
| That thou wilt enter in | 208 | 3 |
| That thou wilt raise me up | 548 | 5 |
| That, though thou cause thy servant grief | 838 | 8 |
| That through the ages all along | 751 | ·3 |
| That thy bright beams on me have shined | 210 | 4 |
| That thy Church with ardour due | 826 | — |
| †That token of thine utmost good | 397 | ·8 |
| That to thy name belongs | 536 | 1 |
| That touch of love, that pledge of heaven | 365 | 3 |
| That tramples down and casts behind | 301 | 2 |
| That trembles at the approach of sin | 186 | 6 |
| That trembles at thy frown | 94 | ·3 |
| That trembles at thy word | 960 | — |
| That trembles in the breast | 823 | 1 |
| That true immortal bread | 1011 | — |
| That Truth to keep, that Life to win | 671 | 4 |
| That turn aside to lies | 566 | 4 |
| That veils and darkens thy designs | 563 | 1 |
| †That vine is desolate and torn | 589 | 3 |
| That vow renewed shall daily hear | 912 | ·5 |
| That was for sinners shed | 907 | 2 |
| That was in Christ, your Head | 266 | 4 |
| That was in thee receive | 504 | ·5 |
| That we all might pardon find | 717 | 1 |
| That we boldly may declare | 733 | 4 |
| That we may meet in heaven | 485 | 2 |
| That we may not hear in vain | 882 | 2 |
| That we may not go astray | 882 | 4 |
| That we may win the heavenly prize | 821 | — |
| That we may with thanks receive | 1012 | — |
| That we might now receive | 506 | 2 |
| That we might one remain | 510 | 3 |
| That we never can part | 491 | 5 |
| That we our Eden might regain | 380 | 6 |
| That we should be wholly thine | 427 | 2 |
| †That we should look, poor wanderers | 943 | 2 |
| That we, the abjects we, might hope | 774 | ·8 |
| That we who these foundations lay | 992 | ·5 |

| | Hymn | Verse |
|---|---|---|
| That were a present far too small | 700 | 4 |
| That what is suitable and just | 470 | 3 |
| That what I still to him commend | 810 | — |
| That when thou comest on thy throne | 43 | 5 |
| That who to us, to thee belongs | 891 | 6 |
| That will not let us part | 534 | 1 |
| That will not yield to love | 103 | 1 |
| †That wisdom, Lord, on us bestow | 319 | 2 |
| That, with hearts and minds uplifted | 720 | 8 |
| That, with his tears, for thee hath flowed | 32 | 4 |
| That, with loving wonder smitten | 748 | 6 |
| That with thee above the skies | 737 | 12 |
| That with the world, myself, and thee | 974 | 2 |
| That worms should seek for dwellings | 943 | 2 |
| That would not stoop to thee | 358 | 4 |
| That you might come to heaven | 36 | 3 |
| That you might sin no more | 36 | 2 |
| The absence of thy peace | 307 | 3 |
| The abundance of a loving heart | 363 | 2 |
| The abyss of Deity | 750 | 3 |
| The acceptable year | 983 | 2 |
| †The Æthiop then shall change his skin | 139 | 8 |
| The age that in heaven they spend | 49 | 3 |
| The all-atoning Lamb | 85 | 3 |
| The all-atoning Lamb | 738 | 3 |
| The all-obtaining grace | 805 | 1 |
| The almighty God of love | 239 | 5 |
| The almighty Three, the eternal One | 651 | 1 |
| The Almighty's Fellow thou | 194 | 5 |
| The anchor of their steadfast hope | 462 | 3 |
| The ancient prince of hell | 856 | 1 |
| The ancient seers record thy praise | 647 | 3 |
| The ancient seers thou didst inspire | 457 | 4 |
| The Angel of the Covenant proves | 888 | 2 |
| The angel-reapers shall descend | 739 | 6 |
| The anguish and distracting care | 386 | 5 |
| The answer of his powerful prayer | 726 | 3 |
| The answer of thy promise give | 780 | 1 |
| The apostles of my Lord | 421 | 2 |
| The apostolic promise given | 759 | 4 |
| The appearing of my Lord | 123 | 3 |
| The arm of my Redeemer | 855 | 2 |
| The arms of love that compass me | 37 | 4 |
| The arms of thy pursuing love | 773 | 2 |
| †The arrow is flown | 47 | 4 |
| The art of governing like thee | 471 | 5 |
| †The atonement of thy blood apply | 846 | 4 |
| The awful midnight cry | 54 | 1 |
| †The badge and token this | 897 | 2 |
| The baits of pleasing ill | 301 | 2 |
| The balm of Gilead I receive | 112 | 5 |
| The balm of pardoning love | 105 | 2 |
| The balm of thy mercy apply | 174 | 3 |

| | Hymn | Verse |
|---|---|---|
| The balmy sound drinks in | 84 | 5 |
| The banners of thy host | 226 | 6 |
| The bar of unbelief remove | 118 | 5 |
| †The barren souls shall be restored | 111 | 4 |
| The battle is the Lord's | 278 | 6 |
| †The beam that shines from Zion's hill | 740 | 3 |
| The beast and devil in my soul | 132 | 3 |
| The beasts with food his hands supply | 225 | 4 |
| The beatific sight | 253 | 3 |
| The beatific sight | 333 | 5 |
| The beauty of the oak and pine | 992 | 3 |
| The benefit divine | 465 | 8 |
| The best and dearest Father | 943 | 12 |
| The best concerted schemes are vain | 526 | 1 |
| †The bleeding martyrs, they | 942 | 12 |
| The bleeding Prince of life and peace | 28 | 2 |
| The bleeding sacrifice | 202 | 1 |
| The bleeding Saviour's name | 898 | 1 |
| The blessed end in view | 510 | 5 |
| The blessed gospel of thy Son | 993 | 3 |
| The blessed hope I feel | 172 | 3 |
| The blessed ones, with joy the chorus swell | 663 | — |
| The blessing from above | 630 | 6 |
| The blessing is given Wherever thou art | 10 | 3 |
| The blessing of God's chosen race | 14 | 1 |
| †The blessing of thy love bestow | 155 | 5 |
| The blessing seek and find | 118 | 4 |
| The blessing unimproved | 806 | 1 |
| The blessing which we crave | 797 | 3 |
| †The blessings all on you be shed | 539 | 8 |
| The blessings of thy brotherhood | 891 | 3 |
| The blessings of thy righteous reign | 442 | 4 |
| The blessings of thy grace impart | 843 | 2 |
| †The blest no sun save Jesus see | 951 | 4 |
| †The blind are restored Through Jesus's name | 40 | 3 |
| The blind his sight receive | 139 | 7 |
| The blind rejoiced to hear the cry | 695 | 3 |
| The bliss for Adam's race designed | 444 | 1 |
| †The bliss of those that fully dwell | 384 | 8 |
| The bliss unmixed, the glorious prize | 926 | 2 |
| The bliss we lost in one | 98 | 1 |
| The bliss wherein through Christ they live | 721 | 6 |
| †The blood of goats and bullocks slain | 702 | 2 |
| The blood of sprinkling speaks, and prays | 902 | 2 |
| The blood that did for us atone | 721 | 2 |
| The blood that ransomed sinners lost | 778 | 4 |
| The blood thou hast shed | 160 | 1 |
| The boasting soul that knows his God | 422 | 2 |
| The bodies in need | 495 | 2 |
| †The bondage of corruption break | 108 | 6 |
| The bond of sure and promised peace | 909 | 4 |
| The bond-woman's base son cast out | 356 | 7 |
| †The boundless love that found out me | 365 | 7 |

| | Hymn | Verse |
|---|---|---|
| The bounds of the eternal hills | 992 | 1 |
| The bounteous God of love | 578 | 3 |
| The bountiful donor Of all we enjoy | 199 | 3 |
| The brand to pluck out of the fire | 174 | 2 |
| The breadth, length, depth, and height to prove | 796 | 7 |
| The breadth of Immanuel's land | 70 | 2 |
| The bread thy mystic body be | 901 | 3 |
| The breath of our new life | 822 | 2 |
| The breath that first it gave. | 42 | 3 |
| The breath thou giv'st, for thee employ | 230 | 1 |
| The breezes, and the sunshine | 988 | 1 |
| The brethren we have lost restore | 461 | 1 |
| The brightest of the seven | 954 | 2 |
| The bright example may pursue | 286 | 3 |
| The bright inheritance of saints | 944 | 4 |
| The brightness of eternal day | 283 | 1 |
| The brightness of thy face | 258 | 2 |
| The bruised reed he never breaks | 725 | 4 |
| The bud may have a bitter taste | 845 | 3 |
| †The burden, for me to sustain | 23 | 4 |
| The burden of our bleeding heart | 461 | 2 |
| The burden thou didst bear | 703 | 4 |
| The business pursue. | 231 | 10 |
| †The busy tribes of flesh and blood | 41 | 5 |
| The busy world exclude | 119 | 2 |
| The calm of evening settles on my breast | 967 | 4 |
| The Canaan of thy perfect love | 391 | 7 |
| †The captive exiles make their moans | 462 | 2 |
| The carnal mind, remove | 404 | 5 |
| The cause of grief destroy | 124 | 3 |
| †The cause of my misgiving fear | 833 | 5 |
| The centre of my bliss | 942 | 6 |
| †The chaff of sin, the accursed thing | 502 | 2 |
| The character divine. | 477 | 2 |
| †The cheerful tribute will I give | 658 | 6 |
| The chief of sinners, me | 406 | 3 |
| The chief, the vilest sinner see | 159 | 1 |
| †The Christ, by raptured seers foretold | 689 | 3 |
| The Christ, the promised seed | 360 | 4 |
| The Christian, he alone is great | 439 | 2 |
| The Christian, he alone is wise | 439 | 2 |
| The Christian lives to Christ alone | 428 | 2 |
| The Christian savages remain | 82 | 3 |
| The Christian while he sings | 804 | 1 |
| The Christian's native air | 823 | 5 |
| The church can never fail | 572 | 3 |
| The Church her voice upraises | 958 | 5 |
| *The Church in her militant state | 77 | 1 |
| The church of pardoned sinners | 736 | 2 |
| The church of the first-born | 535 | 4 |
| The church of the first-born to join | 71 | 6 |
| The church on earth can never fail | 16 | 6 |
| †The church through all her bounds | 737 | 8 |

| | Hymn | Verse |
|---|---|---|
| The church, to earth's remotest bounds | 647 | 4 |
| †The church, triumphant in thy love | 15 | 2 |
| The circle of the day | 788 | 2 |
| The citizens of heaven | 630 | 8 |
| The city move so mightily | 695 | 2 |
| The city of God remaineth | 856 | 4 |
| The city of our God | 619 | 4 |
| The city of saints shall appear | 73 | 1 |
| The city on the hill | 526 | 5 |
| The city so holy and clean | 73 | 2 |
| The clarions of the sky | 719 | 1 |
| †The cleansing blood to apply | 761 | 4 |
| The cloud of thy protecting love | 326 | 1 |
| The clouds and darkness chase | 502 | 3 |
| The clouds disperse, the shadows fly | 95 | 6 |
| The clouds shot hail, they lightened | 587 | 5 |
| The clouds ye so much dread | 845 | 2 |
| The co-eternal Son of God | 665 | 3 |
| The Comforter shall surely come | 759 | 3 |
| The comfort is unspeakable | 630 | 2 |
| The coming of our Lord | 460 | 2 |
| The coming of thy kingdom be | 444 | 4 |
| The common peace we feel | 500 | 5 |
| The common Saviour's name | 356 | 3 |
| The confines of eternal night | 493 | — |
| The Conqueror could detain | 713 | 3 |
| The consecrated cross | 301 | 2 |
| The consecrating flame | 989 | 4 |
| The conscious awe impart | 103 | 3 |
| The conscious creature feels thy nod | 241 | 1 |
| The conscious sinner see | 781 | 6 |
| The contrite sense, the grief divine | 778 | 2 |
| The contrite soul he formed anew | 867 | 3 |
| The Counsellor and Prince of peace | 548 | 3 |
| The counsel of his grace in me | 384 | 3 |
| The counsel of thy grace fulfil | 171 | 4 |
| The counsel of thy grace fulfil | 366 | 5 |
| †The counsel of thy love fulfil | 389 | 4 |
| The countless myriads of her sons | 557 | 1 |
| The countless wonders of thy grace | 561 | 8 |
| The court of God most high | 942 | 1 |
| The courts of heaven are filled | 991 | 1 |
| The Covenant-Angel stands | 675 | 3 |
| The covenant blood apply | 150 | 4 |
| The covenant God in thee hath made | 162 | 2 |
| The covenant is sure | 162 | 5 |
| †The covenant of forgiveness seal | 511 | 2 |
| The covenant of redeeming love | 129 | 1 |
| The covenant of redemption seal | 438 | 1 |
| The covenant of thy general grace | 162 | 5 |
| The covenant thou hast ratified | 162 | 4 |
| †The covenant we this moment make | 532 | 3 |
| The creature is their sole delight | 977 | 1 |

| | Hymn | Verse |
|---|---|---|
| The creatures all agree | 832 | 6 |
| The creatures all obey their Lord | 836 | 5 |
| The creatures all shall lead to thee | 108 | 8 |
| The creatures of thy grace | 256 | 3 |
| The crooked Serpent slay | 299 | 7 |
| The crooked then shall straight become | 289 | 8 |
| †The crooked things shall at thy word | 836 | 5 |
| The cross, all stained with hallowed blood | 388 | 5 |
| The cross despise | 858 | 4 |
| The cross, endured, my God, by thee | 279 | 3 |
| The cross is all thy splendour | 943 | 5 |
| The cross on which he bows his head | 898 | 4 |
| The cross, shall wear the crown | 333 | 3 |
| The crowned Lord of all | 681 | 7 |
| The crown of all—a thankful heart | 1023 | — |
| The crown of righteousness divine | 440 | 2 |
| The Crucified thy praise | 943 | 5 |
| The crumbs that from thy table fall | 696 | 4 |
| The crumbs that from thy table fall | 696 | 5 |
| The cup in token of his blood | 907 | 2 |
| †The cup of blessings, blessed by thee | 901 | 3 |
| The current of thy grace | 778 | 2 |
| The cursed thing remove | 105 | 3 |
| The darkness deepens; Lord, with me abide | 972 | 1 |
| The darkness from my soul remove | 354 | 2 |
| The darkness of my carnal mind | 100 | 2 |
| The darkness of the sky | 551 | 3 |
| The darkness shall be lost in day | 289 | 8 |
| The darkness shall be turned to light | 836 | 4 |
| The darkness shineth as the light | 339 | 1 |
| The darkness which through thee I feel | 150 | 2 |
| The day for sinners to be glad | 616 | 8 |
| *The day is past and over | 968 | 1 |
| The day obeys the sun | 226 | 3 |
| The day of battle is at hand | 314 | 1 |
| *The day of Christ, the day of God | 254 | 1 |
| The day of eternity come | 73 | 1 |
| The day of feeble things | 383 | 1 |
| The day of God is come | 739 | 6 |
| The day of grace is past and gone | 932 | 3 |
| The day of liberty draws near | 380 | 1 |
| The day of salvation, That lifts up my head | 198 | 4 |
| †The day of small and feeble things | 157 | 7 |
| The day of small and feeble things | 365 | 2 |
| *The day of wrath, that dreadful day | 934 | 1 |
| The day shall break | 595 | 5 |
| The daylight is serene | 943 | 9 |
| †The days of old, in vision | 587 | 2 |
| The dead by his call Are raised from their sin | 40 | 5 |
| †The dead in Christ shall first arise | 932 | 2 |
| The dead-reviving news | 452 | 1 |
| The dead shall feel thy power | 139 | 8 |
| The dead to sin shall find the grace | 284 | 4 |

| | Hymn | Verse |
|---|---|---|
| The dead which they contained before | 932 | 1 |
| The dead who ever live to God | 917 | 4 |
| The dead's alive! the lost is found | 9 | 5 |
| †The deaf hear his voice And comforting word | 40 | 4 |
| The deaf, the dumb, the sick, the poor | 32 | 2 |
| †The dearest idol I have known | 787 | 5 |
| †The dear tokens of his passion | 66 | 3 |
| The death of sin remove | 485 | 3 |
| The death that never dies | 83 | 5 |
| The debt's discharged, the ransom's paid | 184 | 4 |
| The debt we to thy Father owed | 129 | 2 |
| The deed, the time, the manner choose | 429 | 2 |
| The deepest stains of sin efface | 395 | 7 |
| †The depth of all-redeeming love | 216 | 6 |
| The depth of humble love | 216 | 9 |
| The depth of inbred sin | 358 | 4 |
| The depth of love, of God, reveal | 438 | 1 |
| The depths of love divine | 87 | 4 |
| The desert all renewed shall rise | 111 | 4 |
| The design of thy love | 491 | 5 |
| †The dictates of thy sovereign will | 655 | 3 |
| The dignity of love | 472 | 2 |
| The double grace bestow | 105 | 2 |
| The double power of quickening grace | 461 | 3 |
| The dreary regions of the dead | 43 | 1 |
| The drops of dew, shall bless thee | 613 | 2 |
| The drop which sweetens every toil | 822 | 2 |
| The dulness of our blinded sight | 751 | 2 |
| The dumb in songs of praise rejoice | 139 | 7 |
| The dumb shall sing thy praise | 135 | 6 |
| The dumb they are talking Of Jesus's grace | 40 | 3 |
| The dwellings of the just | 562 | 4 |
| The dwellings of thy love | 591 | 1 |
| †The dying thief rejoiced to see | 798 | 2 |
| The earnest of heaven Is love in the heart | 10 | 3 |
| †The earth, and all the works therein | 57 | 5 |
| The earth and heaven for ever | 613 | 3 |
| The earth in cheerful green | 226 | 8 |
| The earth in righteousness renew | 457 | 1 |
| *The earth is the Lord's, And all it contains | 496 | 1 |
| The earth no more her slain conceal | 57 | 2 |
| The earth receive its doom | 536 | 5 |
| The earth reeled to and fro | 587 | 5 |
| *The earth with all her fulness owns | 557 | 1 |
| †The earth with its store Of wonders untold | 611 | 3 |
| The earthquake speaks thy power | 62 | 4 |
| The effectual grace supply | 25 | 5 |
| The empty stall no herd afford | 803 | 2 |
| The endless theme of heavenly strains | 638 | 6 |
| The end of all thy griefs below | 330 | 1 |
| The end of Jesu's coming show | 443 | 2 |
| The end of our meeting On earth let us see | 484 | 3 |
| The end of things created | 932 | 1 |

| | Hymn | Verse |
|---|---|---|
| The end of things created | 932 | 4 |
| †The enemy his tares hath sown | 280 | 5 |
| The enemy within | 310 | 3 |
| The enemy within | 407 | 3 |
| The eternal laws of truth and right | 698 | 2 |
| The eternal Sabbath-day | 984 | 6 |
| The eternal Spirit lives in me | 928 | 3 |
| The eternal Spirit of your Lord | 111 | 6 |
| The eternal states of all the dead | 42 | 5 |
| The Ethiopian stranger | 586 | 4 |
| The evening leaves me, and my heart how dead | 967 | 3 |
| The ever-blessed name | 323 | 2 |
| The everlasting arms | 407 | 2 |
| The everlasting arms | 618 | 4 |
| The everlasting day | 423 | 4 |
| †The everlasting doors | 65 | 5 |
| The everlasting Father own | 647 | 1 |
| The everlasting hills | 618 | 1 |
| The everlasting love | 172 | 2 |
| The evil heart, the carnal mind | 310 | 3 |
| The evil of to-day I bear | 835 | 2 |
| The excellence divine | 356 | 8 |
| The excellence divine | 407 | 1 |
| The eye of faith is dim | 920 | 6 |
| The fabric still sustain | 624 | 1 |
| The fading glory disappears | 46 | 4 |
| The faithful God of love | 282 | 3 |
| The faithful saying I receive | 815 | 3 |
| The faithful shall my presence feel | 629 | 5 |
| The faith in thine all-cleansing blood | 774 | 5 |
| The faith shall bring the power | 342 | 5 |
| The faith that always works by love | 455 | 2 |
| The faith that bids our terrors cease | 686 | 3 |
| The faith that conquers all | 85 | 4 |
| The faith that purges every stain | 455 | 2 |
| The faith that sweetly works by love | 14 | 1 |
| The faith thou never wilt reprove | 455 | 2 |
| The faith unfeigned and unreproved | 805 | 1 |
| The fallen raise, the mourners cheer | 462 | 4 |
| The falling of a tear | 823 | 2 |
| The famine all thy fulness brings | 62 | 4 |
| The Father hath on Christ bestowed | 107 | 1 |
| The Father hath punished for you his dear Son | 707 | 2 |
| †The Father hears him pray | 202 | 4 |
| The Father in my name shall send | 754 | 1 |
| The Father of celestial powers | 262 | 3 |
| The Father of our dying Lord | 380 | 2 |
| The father of the faithful race | 111 | 1 |
| †The Father shining on his throne | 333 | 6 |
| †The Father, Son, and Holy Ghost | 9 | 5 |
| The Father's co-eternal Son | 28 | 1 |
| The Father's everlasting Son | 648 | 1 |
| The Father's promised Paraclete | 752 | 2 |

# THE FATHER'S          THE FRIEND

| | HYMN | VERSE |
|---|---|---|
| The Father's wrath and me | 92 | 8 |
| The favour and the peace of God | 9 | 7 |
| The favour and the power of God | 525 | 1 |
| The feast itself thou art | 905 | 1 |
| †The fell disease on every side | 986 | 2 |
| The fellowship divine | 169 | 4 |
| The fellowship divine | 630 | 7 |
| The fellowship of saints | 487 | 4 |
| The fellowship of saints make known | 17 | 5 |
| The fever owned thy touch and fled | 289 | 4 |
| †The few that truly call thee Lord | 17 | 2 |
| The field illude the tiller's toil | 803 | 2 |
| †The fields wherein my lot is cast | 549 | 3 |
| The fiend to his own hell | 311 | 2 |
| The fiend who strives to take my crown | 916 | 3 |
| The fiercer the blast | 498 | 4 |
| The fiery furnace burns | 359 | 2 |
| The fiery test abide | 329 | 3 |
| The filial awe, the fleshly heart | 308 | 2 |
| The fire forgets its power to burn | 272 | 3 |
| The fire of thy presence Their spirits doth fill | 869 | 3 |
| The fire of tribulation | 853 | 3 |
| †The fire our graces shall refine | 329 | 4 |
| The first abhorred approach of ill | 313 | 3 |
| The first apostate man | 106 | 4 |
| The first apostles of his infant fame | 691 | 4 |
| The first approach of sin to find | 311 | 4 |
| The first-born, fairest sons of light | 38 | 6 |
| The first-born sons of light | 147 | 2 |
| The first I prove below | 674 | 2 |
| The flame of angelical love | 73 | 5 |
| The flaming heavens together roll | 934 | 2 |
| The flesh that weighs my spirit down | 916 | 3 |
| The flocks be cut off from their place | 803 | 2 |
| †The floods, O Lord, lift up their voice | 600 | 3 |
| The floods they are roaring, But Jesus is here | 859 | 2 |
| †The floods, with angry noise | 601 | 3 |
| †The flowery spring at thy command | 978 | 2 |
| *The foe behind, the deep before | 715 | 1 |
| The foes that gather round thee | 613 | 1 |
| The followers of their faith and prayer | 535 | 5 |
| The folly of our darkened heart | 90 | 3 |
| †The foolish builders, scribe and priest | 617 | 3 |
| †The formalists confound, convert | 94 | 5 |
| The former and the latter rain | 630 | 6 |
| The foundation we own | 495 | 4 |
| The fountain I own | 231 | 2 |
| The fountain is undried | 781 | 1 |
| The fountain of eternal love | 612 | 1 |
| The Fountain of life from above | 777 | 2 |
| The fountain of the Godhead owned | 642 | 2 |
| The frequent hymn be duly paid: Alleluia | 663 | — |
| The friend and Saviour of mankind | 31 | 1 |

| | Hymn | Verse |
|---|---|---|
| The friend of earth-born man | 262 | 3 |
| The friends of Jesus are | 535 | 1 |
| The fruit of his eternal love. | 867 | 2 |
| The fruit of thy passion, Thy holiness give | 481 | 5 |
| The fruits of righteousness | 424 | 2 |
| The fugitives remain. | 452 | 5 |
| The full accomplishment attend | 460 | 2 |
| The full reward of heavenly bliss | 945 | 2 |
| The fulness of his blessing pours | 489 | 1 |
| †The fulness of my vast reward | 284 | 3 |
| The fulness of the Deity | 525 | 2 |
| The fulness of the Gentiles call | 39 | 6 |
| The fulness of the Gentiles call | 749 | 3 |
| The fulness of the Gentiles come | 589 | 7 |
| The fulness of thy joy, and peace | 549 | 7 |
| The fulness of thy promise prove | 163 | 1 |
| The fulness of thy saving grace | 363 | 3 |
| The future, who shall live to see | 835 | 1 |
| The garments he assumes | 650 | 1 |
| The gate of heaven is Christ my Lord | 616 | 6 |
| †The gates of hell cannot prevail | 16 | 6 |
| †The gay who rest nor worship prize | 951 | 2 |
| The general Saviour of mankind | 39 | 2 |
| The genuine, meek humility | 9 | 9 |
| The gift divine I ask of thee | 364 | 1 |
| The gift hath obtained | 760 | 2 |
| The gift in Jesu's name | 86 | 7 |
| The gift of faith is all divine | 118 | 3 |
| The gift of Jesus, come | 506 | 3 |
| The gift of Jesu's love | 738 | 5 |
| The gift unspeakable | 216 | 6 |
| The gift unspeakable | 415 | 2 |
| The gift unspeakable | 717 | 3 |
| †The gift unspeakable | 757 | 3 |
| The gift unspeakable impart | 118 | 2 |
| †The gift unspeakable impart | 148 | 3 |
| The gift unspeakable impart | 476 | 4 |
| The gift unspeakable obtains | 14 | 2 |
| The gift unspeakable sent down | 377 | 1 |
| †The gift which he on one bestows | 500 | 3 |
| The gifts of God are strewn | 747 | 2 |
| The gifts thou hast given, For Jesus's sake | 1025 | 1 |
| The giver of concord and love | 220 | 2 |
| The glad day of gospel grace | 197 | 1 |
| The glad morning appears | 231 | 1 |
| The gladly solemn sound | 738 | 1 |
| †The gladness of that happy day | 677 | 3 |
| The gloom of hellish night | 446 | 5 |
| The glories of eternal day | 129 | 6 |
| The glories of my God and King | 1 | 1 |
| The glories of my heavenly King | 568 | 1 |
| The glories of the Almighty Sire | 636 | 2 |
| The glories of thy face | 543 | 1 |

| | Hymn | Verse |
|---|---|---|
| The glories of thy name | 249 | 2 |
| The glories promised in thy word | 563 | 5 |
| The glories that compose thy name | 577 | 1 |
| The glorious beams of heavenly light | 493 | 1 |
| The glorious co-eternal Son | 333 | 6 |
| †The glorious crown of righteousness | 405 | 3 |
| The glorious joy unspeakable | 253 | 3 |
| The glory, Lord, be thine | 465 | 8 |
| The glory of his cross | 811 | 1 |
| The glory of his grace | 208 | 1 |
| The glory of my brightest days | 213 | 1 |
| The glory of the Lamb of God | 694 | 2 |
| The glory of thy face | 771 | 6 |
| The glory of thy grace | 537 | 1 |
| The glory of thy perfect day | 694 | 1 |
| The glory, power, and praise receive | 253 | 1 |
| The glowing seraphs round the throne | 658 | 5 |
| The Godhead reconciled | 252 | 5 |
| The God incarnate, Man divine | 681 | 5 |
| *The God of Abraham praise | 800 | 1 |
| †The God of Abraham praise | 800 | 2 |
| †The God of Abraham praise | 800 | 3 |
| The God of ages, praise | 981 | 1 |
| †The God of all-redeeming grace | 614 | 13 |
| The God of all that breathe | 137 | 6 |
| The God of grace, who all invites | 489 | 1 |
| The God of grace will ne'er despise | 574 | 6 |
| The God of his salvation love | 557 | 5 |
| The God of his salvation own | 557 | 5 |
| The God of love | 1026 | -- |
| †The God of love, to earth he came | 36 | 3 |
| The God of my life to proclaim | 231 | 11 |
| The God of my salvation | 855 | 1 |
| The God of my salvation praise | 803 | 2 |
| The God of my salvation see | 388 | 2 |
| The God of our salvation | 276 | 2 |
| The God of our salvation | 736 | 1 |
| The God of pardoning love | 252 | 4 |
| The God of truth and grace | 221 | 1 |
| The God of truth and love | 729 | 2 |
| †The God that rules on high | 12 | 2 |
| The God who always bears in mind | 144 | 5 |
| †The God who reigns on high | 800 | 10 |
| †The godly grief, the pleasing smart | 9 | 8 |
| The gold and silver, make them thine | 992 | 3 |
| The good desired and wanted most | 473 | 1 |
| The good seed on the land | 988 | 1 |
| †The good, the fruitful ground | 739 | 3 |
| The good, the kind physician, thou | 397 | 4 |
| The good wherewith I would be blest | 167 | 3 |
| The goodly apostolic band | 647 | 3 |
| †The goodly land I see | 800 | 6 |

| | Hymn | Verse |
|---|---|---|
| The goodness I experience now | 547 | 7 |
| The goodness must endure | 250 | 6 |
| †The gospel by our Saviour blessed | 875 | 3 |
| The Gospel doth thy fulness show | 284 | 4 |
| The gospel-faith divine impart | 780 | 1 |
| The gospel of thy general grace | 866 | 4 |
| The gospel song | 736 | 2 |
| †The gospel trumpet hear | 738 | 6 |
| The grace already given | 265 | 2 |
| The grace be now on me bestowed | 103 | 3 |
| The grace for Jesu's sake | 86 | 2 |
| The grace infused, the love revealed | 416 | 2 |
| The grace is far above | 685 | 3 |
| *The grace of Jesus Christ the Son | 1005 | 1 |
| The grace of one descends on all | 630 | 5 |
| The grace that sure salvation brings | 312 | 2 |
| The grace thou dost this moment give | 812 | — |
| The grace through every vessel flows | 500 | 3 |
| The grace through Jesus given | 80 | 6 |
| The grace to declare And goodness of God | 1025 | 1 |
| The grace to sinners showed | 253 | 2 |
| The grace which all may find | 85 | 3 |
| The grace which calls us to thy throne | 955 | 1 |
| The grace which calls us to thy throne | 955 | 4 |
| The grace which sure salvation brings | 901 | 3 |
| The grace which we implore | 991 | 4 |
| †The graces of my second birth | 357 | 8 |
| †The gracious fruits of righteousness | 392 | 2 |
| The gracious joy and peace | 834 | 1 |
| The gracious Spirit divine | 307 | 1 |
| The gracious theme, for ever new | 638 | 2 |
| The gracious wonder show | 402 | 2 |
| The grand and full atonement made | 706 | 2 |
| The grand millennial reign begun | 61 | 3 |
| The grave as little as my bed | 974 | 3 |
| The grave cannot detain me | 923 | 4 |
| †The graves of all his saints he blessed | 929 | 2 |
| The great archangels sing | 800 | 10 |
| *The great archangel's trump shall sound | 57 | 1 |
| The great congregation His triumph shall sing | 859 | 3 |
| The great effectual door | 35 | 1 |
| The great Jehovah's name | 641 | 2 |
| The great old saints of other days | 698 | 2 |
| The great Redeemer's breast | 147 | 6 |
| *The great redeeming Angel, thee | 894 | 1 |
| The great redeeming work is done | 706 | 1 |
| The great salvation now explain | 384 | 9 |
| The Great, the Holy, and the High | 316 | 3 |
| The greatness of redeeming love | 147 | 1 |
| The greedy grave my reins consume | 927 | 4 |
| †The greedy sea shall yield her dead | 57 | 2 |
| The ground of nature's feuds remove | 449 | 2 |
| The growing empire of their King | 867 | 3 |

|  | Hymn | Verse |
|---|---|---|
| The guardian and the friend | 1003 | 4 |
| The guard of all thy mercies give | 307 | 1 |
| The guide of all my days | 584 | 1 |
| †The guiltless shame, the sweet distress | 9 | 9 |
| The gulf of gloom below | 587 | 5 |
| The hallowed house of God | 93 | 4 |
| The hallowed path they trace | 996 | 7 |
| The halt they are walking, And running their race | 40 | 3 |
| The hands that work preserve from ill | 992 | 5 |
| The hand that made us is divine | 552 | 6 |
| The happiness of heaven | 304 | 1 |
| The happiness of heaven | 360 | 3 |
| The hardness from my heart remove | 146 | 2 |
| †The hardness from their hearts remove | 35 | 5 |
| The harlot in distress | 106 | 6 |
| The harpers I might hear | 942 | 11 |
| *The harvest of my joys is passed | 776 | 1 |
| The harvest truly, Lord, is great | 745 | 2 |
| The hasty flights I took | 575 | 2 |
| †The heads that guide endue with skill | 992 | 5 |
| †The healing balm, the holy oil | 822 | 2 |
| The heart of stone believe | 139 | 7 |
| The heart-renewing love | 734 | 2 |
| The heart-taught truth have well confessed | 891 | 6 |
| The heart that believes | 760 | 3 |
| The heart that was in thee | 527 | 4 |
| The heart thou waitest to receive | 775 | 2 |
| The heart unkind, the heart untrue | 543 | 3 |
| The hearts of all mankind | 239 | 8 |
| The heat and burden of the toilsome day | 967 | 1 |
| The heathen in his blindness | 747 | 2 |
| †The heathen lands that lie beneath | 585 | 5 |
| *The heathen perish; day by day | 746 | 1 |
| †The heathen too could see | 623 | 3 |
| †The heavenly choir | 808 | 9 |
| The heavenly feast above | 907 | 3 |
| The heavenly gift, the dew of grace | 409 | 5 |
| The heavenly kingdom suffers force | 277 | 4 |
| The heavenly life display | 761 | 4 |
| The heavenly light divine | 526 | 6 |
| †The heavenly manna faith imparts | 507 | 6 |
| The heavenly manna falls | 958 | 4 |
| The heavenly new Jerusalem | 72 | 4 |
| The heavenly offspring to destroy | 458 | 4 |
| The heavenly spouse dost seal | 996 | 6 |
| †The heavenly treasure now we have | 537 | 7 |
| The heaven of heavens, the throne | 942 | 1 |
| The heaven of loving thee alone | 289 | 7 |
| The heaven prepared for me | 947 | 1 |
| *The heavens declare thy glory, Lord | 553 | 1 |
| The heavens shall pass away | 536 | 5 |
| The height and depth of Deity | 754 | 6 |
| The heightened fear of death I find | 181 | 5 |

# THE HEIGHTS　　　　　　　　　　THE IDOL

|  | HYMN | VERSE |
|---|---|---|
| The heights and depths of grace | 128 | 5 |
| The heights and depths of love divine | 378 | 2 |
| The heights and depths of love divine | 666 | 1 |
| The heirs of all-redeeming grace | 891 | 5 |
| The hellish art no more | 447 | 3 |
| The help as from thy hand receive | 524 | 1 |
| The help for which on thee I call | 813 | — |
| The help of thy Spirit restore | 174 | 2 |
| The help which upon earth is wrought | 270 | 3 |
| The helpless all for succour came | 395 | 1 |
| The helpless sons of men | 307 | 4 |
| The helpless thou delight'st to raise | 614 | 5 |
| The heritage of love | 404 | 5 |
| The heritage that once was thine | 588 | 1 |
| The hidden manna, and the tree | 343 | 7 |
| The hidden manna, and the tree | 539 | 9 |
| The hidden manna give | 901 | 3 |
| The hidden mystery make known | 476 | 3 |
| The highest name in earth or heaven | 576 | 3 |
| The highway furrows stock | 739 | 2 |
| The hills leaped after them as lambs | 223 | 2 |
| The hilly bulwarks rise | 622 | 2 |
| The hindering thing remove | 982 | 2 |
| The hindrance must be all in me | 146 | 3 |
| The hindrances out of the way | 145 | 2 |
| †The Holy Ghost, if I depart | 759 | 3 |
| The Holy Ghost receive | 486 | 4 |
| The Holy Ghost sent down from heaven | 759 | 4 |
| The Holy Ghost, the Comforter | 754 | 1 |
| The Holy Ghost to man is given | 761 | Cho. |
| The holy joy prolong | 976 | 1 |
| †The holy, meek, unspotted Lamb | 190 | 3 |
| The Holy Spirit pleads | 823 | 7 |
| The Holy Three are with us | 996 | 2 |
| †The holy to the holiest leads | 15 | 4 |
| *The holy unconcern | 877 | 1 |
| The homage due, great Lord, to thee | 770 | 3 |
| The honours of our native place | 573 | 2 |
| The honours of their God | 637 | 11 |
| The honours of thy glorious name | 997 | 4 |
| The honours of thy name | 1 | 2 |
| †The hosts of God encamp around | 562 | 4 |
| *The hour of my departure's come | 924 | 1 |
| †The hour of my departure's come | 924 | 5 |
| The hours of dark may be | 968 | Cho. |
| The house of our Father above | 73 | 1 |
| †The huge celestial bodies roll | 64 | 4 |
| The human lineaments which shine | 698 | 4 |
| The humble, contrite heart | 106 | 2 |
| The humble poor believe | 1 | 5 |
| The humbler creation, Though feeble their lays | 611 | 6 |
| The hungry, dying spirit's food | 379 | 2 |
| The idol from my breast I'd tear | 291 | 3 |

| | Hymn | Verse |
|---|---|---|
| The idol from our bleeding heart | 286 | 5 |
| The ill that I this day have done | 974 | 2 |
| The immortal armies of the sky | 241 | 1 |
| The immortal God for me hath died | 28 | 1 |
| The immortal God hath died for me | 28 | 1 |
| The immortal Son of man | 55 | 2 |
| The incarnate Deity | 685 | 1 |
| †The incommunicable right | 259 | 4 |
| The indwelling Comforter | 873 | 2 |
| The inexorable throne | 44 | 3 |
| The inheritance of heaven | 854 | 3 |
| The Intercessor prays | 423 | 3 |
| The Invisible appears in sight | 95 | 6 |
| The Invisible appears on earth | 689 | 1 |
| The invitation is to ALL | 2 | 2 |
| The inward, pure, baptizing grace | 476 | 8 |
| The iron sinew in my neck | 186 | 5 |
| The iron sinew in our neck | 176 | 4 |
| The irrevocable word we hear | 913 | 1 |
| The joy and desire of my heart | 228 | 1 |
| The joy from out our hearts arise | 204 | 6 |
| The joy of believing, The heaven of love | 19 | 5 |
| The joy of earth and heaven | 34 | 2 |
| The joy of perfect love | 446 | 2 |
| The joy that human thought transcends | 251 | 4 |
| The joyful news of sins forgiven | 675 | 4 |
| The joyful sound proclaim | 747 | 3 |
| †The joys of day are over | 968 | 2 |
| The joys of heaven we prove | 630 | 3 |
| The joys of holiness below | 252 | 6 |
| The joys of that holiest place | 946 | 2 |
| The joys of unity to prove | 442 | 4 |
| The jubilee of heaven | 979 | 6 |
| The Judge of mankind doth appear | 932 | 1 |
| The Judge of mankind doth appear | 932 | 4 |
| The Judge shall call me from the tomb | 927 | 2 |
| The justice or the grace | 263 | 5 |
| The keen conviction dart | 309 | 4 |
| The keys of death and hell | 729 | 3 |
| The kindling of thy love | 214 | 1 |
| The kindness thou to me hast shown | 378 | 2 |
| The kingdom fixed within | 416 | 2 |
| The kingdom from above | 172 | 2 |
| †The kingdom, Lord, is thine alone | 248 | 3 |
| The kingdom of an inward heaven | 134 | 1 |
| †The kingdom of established peace | 251 | 5 |
| The kingdom of our God | 872 | 1 |
| The kingdom of thy Christ prepare | 457 | 8 |
| The kingdom of thy peace restored | 525 | 1 |
| The kingdom that I seek | 837 | 2 |
| The kingdom who seek Of Jesus's grace | 496 | 3 |
| The kingdoms all obey his word | 56 | 3 |
| The kingdoms are but one | 15 | 3 |

| | Hymn | Verse |
|---|---|---|
| The kingdoms of the earth shall be | 448 | 2 |
| †The King himself comes near | 956 | 2 |
| The King in his beauty displayed | 70 | 1 |
| The King is now our friend | 539 | 2 |
| The King Messiah reigns | 665 | 5 |
| The King Messiah reigns | 727 | 2 |
| The King of saints, and angels too | 557 | 11 |
| The King shall in his beauty view | 928 | 4 |
| The King who reigns in Salem's towers | 740 | 3 |
| The King, whose glorious face ye see | 262 | 4 |
| The knowledge fit for man to know | 473 | 4 |
| The knowledge of myself bestow | 100 | 3 |
| The knowledge of our cure | 84 | 5 |
| The knowledge of our sickness give | 84 | 5 |
| The knowledge of thyself bestow | 261 | 2 |
| The knowledge of thyself impart | 90 | 3 |
| The known and unknown worlds obey | 585 | 1 |
| The labour of thy dying love | 388 | 5 |
| The labourers are few | 745 | 2 |
| The lambent flames around me play | 272 | 3 |
| The Lamb ere earth's foundation slain | 773 | 4 |
| The Lamb for sinners slain | 747 | 4 |
| The Lamb is their light and their sun | 73 | 4 |
| The Lamb of God was slain | 1 | 8 |
| †The Lamb on the throne | 499 | 7 |
| The Lamb shall take my sins away | 401 | 3 |
| †The Lamb's apostles there | 942 | 11 |
| The Lamb's the city's light | 942 | 8 |
| The lame shall leap for joy | 135 | 7 |
| The lamp of life deny | 747 | 3 |
| The land of perfect holiness | 408 | 6 |
| The land of rest from inbred sin | 408 | 6 |
| The land of rest, the saints' delight | 947 | 1 |
| The last I die to know | 674 | 2 |
| The last offers of thy grace | 463 | 1 |
| The latent Godhead lay | 685 | 2 |
| The latest lightning glare | 64 | 3 |
| The latest trumpet of the seven | 61 | 4 |
| The law of liberty from sin | 340 | 2 |
| The law of life which is in thee | 448 | 3 |
| The law of perfect liberty | 448 | 3 |
| The law of sin and death to end | 448 | 3 |
| The least of Jesu's witnesses | 17 | 6 |
| The legal offerings all foreshowed | 702 | 1 |
| The length, and breadth, and depth, and height | 440 | 1 |
| The length, and breadth, and height | 147 | 2 |
| The length, and breadth, and height to prove | 216 | 2 |
| The length and breadth I never saw | 91 | 3 |
| †The length and breadth of love reveal | 754 | 6 |
| The lepers cleanse, and raise the dead | 32 | 3 |
| †The lepers from all Their spots are made clean | 40 | 5 |
| The leprosy lies deep within | 574 | 4 |
| The liberty from sin | 416 | 2 |

| | Hymn | Verse |
|---|---|---|
| The Life, and heaven of heaven | 886 | — |
| The Life divine, the little leaven | 379 | 5 |
| The life eternal give | 118 | 1 |
| The life I lose for thee, my Lord | 362 | 8 |
| The life of angels live | 342 | 2 |
| The life of eternity know | 79 | 2 |
| The life of my delights | 213 | 1 |
| The life of nature from this hour | 409 | 3 |
| The life that knows no ending | 943 | 1 |
| The Life, the Truth, the Way | 169 | 2 |
| The Life, the Truth, the Way | 823 | 8 |
| The light first had its birth | 958 | 2 |
| The light of his heavenly face | 946 | 2 |
| The light that gilds thy blest abode | 694 | 2 |
| The light that shines so clear | 88 | 3 |
| The light, the life, the heaven of love | 154 | 4 |
| The lights thou hast kindled In darkness around | 869 | 5 |
| †The lion roaring for his prey | 458 | 3 |
| The lion seeks my soul to slay | 310 | 2 |
| The listening spheres attend | 800 | 9 |
| The little flock, the saints elect | 801 | 1 |
| The living and the dead | 986 | 3 |
| †The living bread, sent down from heaven | 901 | 4 |
| The living God through sin forsake | 89 | 3 |
| The living law of holiest love | 438 | 2 |
| The living law of perfect love | 511 | 3 |
| The living, the living Shall show forth thy praise | 199 | 2 |
| The living way to heaven is seen | 706 | 3 |
| The loathsome leper shall be clean | 139 | 8 |
| The loaves a thousand-fold increased | 875 | 3 |
| The long-sought blessing give | 117 | 4 |
| The long-suspended blow | 104 | 1 |
| †The Lord alone shall be my cup | 549 | 2 |
| The Lord be magnified | 566 | 9 |
| †The Lord descended from above | 551 | 3 |
| The Lord eternally the same | 223 | 5 |
| The Lord for evermore | 627 | 3 |
| The Lord from heaven be kind to them | 619 | 4 |
| The Lord from Zion forth shall send | 613 | 1 |
| The Lord hath called me by my name | 272 | 1 |
| The Lord hath judgments for the proud | 610 | 4 |
| The Lord hath triumphed gloriously | 715 | 2 |
| The Lord, He is the God, confess | 412 | 6 |
| †The Lord himself my portion is | 548 | 2 |
| †The Lord his people loves | 591 | 5 |
| †The Lord in his great wrath shall bring | 613 | 3 |
| The Lord in Israel reigned alone | 223 | 1 |
| The Lord, in the day | 707 | 2 |
| †The Lord I now can say is mine | 616 | 2 |
| †The Lord I will for ever bless | 548 | 3 |
| †The Lord is by his judgments known | 545 | 3 |
| *The Lord is King, and earth submits | 280 | 1 |
| The Lord is praised and magnified | 595 | 4 |

| | Hymn | Verse |
|---|---|---|
| *The Lord Jehovah reigns | 650 | 1 |
| †The Lord makes bare his arm | 741 | 6 |
| The Lord my Righteousness | 145 | 5 |
| The Lord my Righteousness I praise | 422 | 2 |
| The Lord my strength and righteousness | 574 | 13 |
| The Lord of angels came | 889 | 2 |
| The Lord of earth and heaven | 673 | 1 |
| The Lord of earth and sky | 232 | 1 |
| *The Lord of earth and sky | 981 | 1 |
| The Lord of every motion there | 344 | 4 |
| The Lord, of glorious power possessed | 557 | 11 |
| The Lord of glory dies for man | 712 | 2 |
| The Lord of hosts proclaim | 641 | 2 |
| †The Lord of hosts, the God most high | 689 | 4 |
| The Lord of hosts, the King of kings | 647 | 2 |
| †The Lord of old for Jacob fought | 569 | 7 |
| *The Lord of Sabbath let us praise | 950 | 1 |
| The Lord our righteousness | 800 | 7 |
| The Lord Our Righteousness is near | 625 | 6 |
| †The Lord pours eye-sight on the blind | 224 | 3 |
| †The Lord protects and cheers his own | 590 | 5 |
| The Lord protects, for ever near | 272 | 1 |
| The Lord Sabaoth's Son | 856 | 2 |
| The Lord shall be thy part | 943 | 15 |
| The Lord shall comfort all that mourn | 120 | 2 |
| The Lord shall give them gospel peace | 111 | 2 |
| The Lord shall show when he sees fitting | 595 | 4 |
| The Lord shall reign victoriously | 715 | 2 |
| †The Lord supports our infant days | 637 | 8 |
| The Lord supports the fainting mind | 224 | 3 |
| The Lord that all our foes o'ercame | 557 | 9 |
| The Lord, that o'er all nature reigns | 600 | 1 |
| †The Lord the amazing work hath wrought | 616 | 8 |
| The Lord, the gracious Lord | 144 | 5 |
| †The Lord, the mighty God, thou art | 249 | 4 |
| The Lord thy God delight to praise | 638 | 1 |
| †The Lord thy God, O Zion, reigns | 638 | 6 |
| *The Lord unto my Lord hath said | 275 | 1 |
| *The Lord unto my Lord thus said | 613 | 1 |
| The Lord who reigns above | 601 | 4 |
| †The Lord will not forsake | 602 | 2 |
| †The Lord will save his people here | 545 | 2 |
| The Lord will to his temple come | 380 | 1 |
| †The Lord, ye know, is God indeed | 607 | 2 |
| The Lord's anointed one | 465 | 3 |
| *The Lord's my Shepherd, I'll not want | 556 | 1 |
| The Lord's redeemed their heads shall raise | 386 | 6 |
| The Lord's right hand exalted is | 616 | 5 |
| †The Lord's right hand hath wonders wrought | 616 | 5 |
| The loud waters | 621 | 2 |
| The love and joy unknown | 123 | 5 |
| The love diffused abroad | 389 | 6 |
| The love divine | 853 | 2 |

| | Hymn | Verse |
|---|---|---|
| The love of all beneath | 96 | 8 |
| †The love of Christ doth me constrain | 279 | 7 |
| The love of Christ to me | 147 | 1 |
| The love of God and love of man | 630 | 6 |
| The love of God I cannot see | 135 | 8 |
| The love of himself in my heart | 911 | 2 |
| The love of Jesus, what it is | 680 | 4 |
| The love of our Friend | 808 | 10 |
| The love that all heaven's host inspires | 210 | 6 |
| The love, the perfect love of God | 145 | 3 |
| The loving firm fidelity | 828 | 1 |
| The lowliest garb of penitence and prayer | 794 | 6 |
| †The madman in a tomb had made | 697 | 2 |
| The majesty divine | 248 | 2 |
| The Majesty on high | 823 | 3 |
| The manna of thy love | 704 | 4 |
| The manna of thy love | 801 | 2 |
| The manna of thy love | 1011 | — |
| The manna that comes down from heaven | 392 | 1 |
| The manner of my final rest | 919 | 1 |
| The man of sin consume | 362 | 2 |
| The man of sin consume | 383 | 3 |
| The man of thy right hand | 465 | 7 |
| The man that dares their god despise | 439 | 2 |
| The man thou dost approve | 828 | 5 |
| The Man transfixed on Calvary | 122 | 2 |
| The man who on thy love depends | 245 | 2 |
| †The man whose hands and heart are clean | 557 | 4 |
| †The mansion for thyself prepare | 132 | 4 |
| The marriage of the Lamb | 947 | 6 |
| The Master of all | 495 | 1 |
| The Master praises; what are men | 857 | 2 |
| The Master's blessed will | 325 | 1 |
| The meanest instruments to o'erthrow | 475 | 1 |
| The meaning of the written word | 255 | 2 |
| The measured waters sink and rise | 1001 | 6 |
| †The Mediator's God-like sway | 665 | 5 |
| The medicine of my broken heart | 209 | 1 |
| The meed of all thy sufferings these | 82 | 6 |
| †The meek and lowly heart | 96 | 5 |
| †The meek, the still, the lowly mind | 23 | 8 |
| The meltings of a broken heart | 9 | 8 |
| The members and their Head | 862 | 1 |
| The men designed by thee | 871 | 1 |
| †The men of careless lives, who deem | 461 | 5 |
| †The men of grace have found | 12 | 4 |
| The men of heart sincere | 622 | 3 |
| †The men whom thou hast inly moved | 871 | 2 |
| The men whom ye despise | 21 | 3 |
| *The men who slight thy faithful word | 94 | 1 |
| The mention of thy glory | 943 | 4 |
| The mercies of thy faithful word | 559 | 4 |
| †The mercy I feel To others I show | 5 | 2 |

| | Hymn | Verse |
|---|---|---|
| The mercy for Jesus's sake | 79 | 2 |
| The mercy of my God | 304 | 4 |
| The mercy of our pardoning Lord | 1005 | 1 |
| The mercy that hath loosed my bands | 614 | 12 |
| The merit of thy death | 292 | 4 |
| The merits of thy righteousness | 702 | 3 |
| The Messenger divine | 459 | 4 |
| The middle wall is broken down | 706 | 8 |
| The middle wall of sin remove | 117 | 5 |
| The middle wall remove | 146 | 1 |
| The midnight peal, Behold I come | 857 | 6 |
| The mighty comfort feel | 485 | 3 |
| The mighty glory in his might | 422 | 1 |
| The mighty promise shines | 659 | 4 |
| The mighty Spirit send | 299 | 6 |
| The mighty works, or mightier name | 659 | 1 |
| The millennial year | 47 | 4 |
| The mind that was in thee | 504 | 6 |
| The mind which was in Christ impart | 391 | 5 |
| The mingled current flow | 705 | 2 |
| The miracle repeat | 733 | 3 |
| The miracle thy grace hath done | 781 | 6 |
| †The modest and meek The earth shall possess | 496 | 3 |
| The momentary glories waste | 46 | 2 |
| The moment is gone | 47 | 4 |
| The moon takes up the wondrous tale | 552 | 3 |
| The more shall he receive | 696 | 3 |
| The more we serve, the more we love | 858 | 3 |
| The morning and the evening star | 589 | 6 |
| The morning breaks, the shadows flee | 141 | 2 |
| *The morning flowers display their sweets | 46 | 1 |
| The morning star appears at last | 365 | 9 |
| The mortal affliction is past | 49 | 3 |
| The mortal Son of man | 665 | 3 |
| The mortal wound receive | 362 | 7 |
| The most gigantic strength of man | 422 | 1 |
| †The most impossible of all | 401 | 2 |
| The most inveterate plague can cure | 896 | 3 |
| The mother of spirits distrest | 946 | 1 |
| The motion of a hidden fire | 823 | 1 |
| The mountain-obstacles remove | 475 | 5 |
| The mountain sin remove | 150 | 5 |
| The mountains are not found | 63 | 3 |
| The mountains at thy presence flow | 836 | 4 |
| The mountains melt, the solid ground | 64 | 3 |
| The mountains shall give place | 162 | 5 |
| The mountains skipped like frighted rams | 223 | 2 |
| The mourner shall not always weep | 545 | 8 |
| The mournful, broken hearts rejoice | 1 | 5 |
| The mournful cheer, the drooping lead | 379 | 3 |
| The music of the heart | 641 | 8 |
| The mystery of thy passion show | 330 | 1 |
| The mystery so long unknown | 379 | 5 |

| | Hymn | Verse |
|---|---|---|
| The mystery unknown | 870 | 3 |
| The mystic charity | 459 | 3 |
| The mystic heaven and earth within | 662 | 3 |
| The mystic joys of penitence | 9 | 7 |
| The mystic power we prove | 96 | 3 |
| The name all-victorious Of Jesus extol | 859 | 1 |
| The name inscribed in the white stone | 379 | 5 |
| The name of Christ your Lord | 897 | 1 |
| The name of Jesus is a tower | 282 | 3 |
| The name, or mode, or form, I take | 304 | 6 |
| The name through which we live | 733 | 4 |
| The name to sinners given | 37 | 2 |
| *The name we still acknowledge | 854 | 1 |
| The narrow stream of death | 949 | 2 |
| The nations melt, the tumult dies | 569 | 6 |
| The nations of the earth constrain | 442 | 4 |
| The nations to his bar | 65 | 2 |
| The nature of our Head above | 438 | 2 |
| The nature of thy sinless Son | 284 | 5 |
| The nature of thy Son | 892 | 3 |
| The nature pure, the life divine | 782 | 4 |
| The needful thing, the better part | 548 | 2 |
| The never-ceasing prayer | 311 | 3 |
| The new apostles choose | 452 | 1 |
| The new-born Son of man | 772 | 4 |
| The new creation rise | 64 | 7 |
| The new, eternal song | 222 | 4 |
| The new eternal song of love | 648 | 6 |
| The new heaven and earth's Creator | 687 | 1 |
| The new Jerusalem above | 497 | 2 |
| The new Jerusalem descend | 64 | 7 |
| The new Jerusalem to find | 71 | 4 |
| The news of heavenly grace | 738 | 6 |
| †The news of his coming I hear | 77 | 2 |
| †The next, and every moment, Lord | 409 | 6 |
| The night of death has past | 595 | 5 |
| The night of doubts and fears is past | 365 | 9 |
| The night that hangs upon my soul | 100 | 2 |
| The nobleness of Lydia's heart | 884 | — |
| The noblest joys of heavenly love | 513 | 1 |
| †The noisy winds stand ready there | 226 | 5 |
| The notice of thine eye | 632 | 1 |
| The object of my love and fear | 669 | 2 |
| The occasion of his stumbling prove | 470 | 6 |
| †The o'erwhelming power of saving grace | 9 | 10 |
| The offering smokes through earth and skies | 902 | 4 |
| The offerings of a thankful mind | 616 | 11 |
| The oil of gladness on our heads | 825 | 2 |
| The oil of joy for abject grief | 107 | 5 |
| The old leaven is put away | 714 | 6 |
| The omnipotence divine | 583 | 2 |
| The omnipotence of love | 251 | 5 |
| The omnipotence of love | 342 | 6 |

| | Hymn | Verse |
|---|---|---|
| The omnipotent Jehovah knows | 223 | 5 |
| The one eternal God | 583 | 2 |
| The one eternal God and true | 122 | 2 |
| The only church and true | 94 | 2 |
| †The opening heavens around me shine | 213 | 3 |
| †The opposite extremes I see | 471 | 2 |
| The ordinance divine | 295 | 1 |
| The original grace | 491 | 3 |
| The original infirmity | 816 | 1 |
| The original offence | 367 | 2 |
| The outcasts forth, to own | 450 | 3 |
| †The painful thirst, the fond desire | 392 | 4 |
| †The pain of life shall there be o'er | 386 | 5 |
| The palace of angels and God | 73 | 1 |
| The panoply of God | 266 | 2 |
| The paradise of perfect love | 442 | 4 |
| The pardoning God of boundless grace | 548 | 4 |
| The pardoning love of God | 605 | 3 |
| The pardon of our sin | 626 | 2 |
| *The past no longer in my power | 835 | 1 |
| The pastors of thy church apprize | 871 | 1 |
| The pasture I languish to find | 228 | 1 |
| The pastures of the blessed | 943 | 9 |
| †The path of life thou wilt display | 549 | 7 |
| The path of prayer thyself hast trod | 823 | 8 |
| The patient, speechless Man of woe | 883 | 2 |
| The patriarchs and prophets old | 535 | 5 |
| †The patriarchs of old | 942 | 10 |
| The pattern trace which thou hast given | 886 | — |
| The peace, and joy, and righteousness | 872 | 1 |
| †The peace and joy of faith | 497 | 4 |
| The peace he did leave | 707 | 4 |
| †The peace which man can ne'er conceive | 123 | 5 |
| The peaceful answer give | 532 | 5 |
| The penitent by thee believe | 770 | 1 |
| The penitent desire | 102 | 2 |
| The people bought, O Lord, by thee | 81 | 4 |
| The people hungry, scattered, faint | 32 | 4 |
| The people that can Be joyful in thee | 198 | 2 |
| †The people that in darkness lay | 203 | 2 |
| *The people that in darkness lay | 493 | 1 |
| The perfect bliss to prove | 415 | 3 |
| The perfect law of love | 340 | 2 |
| The perfect love unknown | 342 | 4 |
| The perfect power of godliness | 251 | 5 |
| The perfect righteousness | 756 | 3 |
| The Pharisee within | 93 | 5 |
| The piercing wit, the active limb | 225 | 5 |
| The pillar of light | 760 | 4 |
| †The pit its mouth hath opened wide | 82 | 5 |
| The pity of our Lord | 981 | 3 |
| The pity of the bleeding Lamb | 527 | 4 |
| †The pity of the Lord | 610 | 9 |

| | Hymn | Verse |
|---|---|---|
| The place, at least, where we are met | 799 | 3 |
| The place for us designed | 67 | 6 |
| The place of thy people's abode | 228 | 2 |
| The place where Jesus lay | 713 | 1 |
| †The plague, and dearth, and din of war | 62 | 3 |
| The plague is still incurable | 781 | 1 |
| The plague presents thy healing wings | 62 | 4 |
| The planets beaming on their heavenly way | 663 | — |
| The planting of the Lord below | 107 | 6 |
| The pleasing theme renew | 657 | 9 |
| The pleasures to taste For which they were born | 19 | 5 |
| The pledge of our Lord | 760 | 1 |
| The pledge, the witness, and the seal | 1005 | 3 |
| The pledge thou wilt at last receive | 104 | 2 |
| The plenitude of God | 303 | 5 |
| The plenitude of gospel grace | 9 | 6 |
| The plenitude of gospel grace | 445 | 2 |
| †The plenteous and continual dew | 589 | 5 |
| The pointless darts of death | 96 | 3 |
| The pomp of that tremendous day | 59 | 4 |
| The poor and helpless to relieve | 364 | 4 |
| The poor and rich, the low and high | 439 | 3 |
| The poor man's birthright, and his balm | 957 | 2 |
| The portal of eternal day | 616 | 6 |
| The powerful stamp I long to feel | 376 | 5 |
| The power I never knew | 91 | 2 |
| The power into our hearts inspire | 294 | 2 |
| The power of faith and love | 25 | 6 |
| The power of God in Christ we have | 616 | 5 |
| The power of God in man thou art | 881 | 1 |
| The power of godliness is lost | 454 | 4 |
| The power of godliness to show | 439 | 3 |
| The power of his Spirit Shall joyfully own | 496 | 3 |
| The power of Jesus's name | 278 | 7 |
| The power of outward sin | 368 | 2 |
| The power of thy passion below | 174 | 4 |
| The power of thy Spirit Hath set our hearts free | 19 | 2 |
| The power of thy Spirit make known | 911 | 1 |
| The power of thy victorious blood | 872 | 1 |
| The power omnipotent is thine | 237 | 3 |
| The power omnipotent is thine | 241 | 4 |
| The power on thee to call | 435 | 6 |
| The power that sets me free | 288 | 2 |
| The power to watch and pray | 297 | 1 |
| The powers of hell | 855 | 2 |
| The powers of hell are captive led | 557 | 6 |
| The powers of hell surround | 314 | 1 |
| The powers on earth that be | 465 | 1 |
| The praise let him have | 219 | 1 |
| The praise of every virtuous thought | 435 | 5 |
| The praise of him who is thy God | 567 | 4 |
| The praise of our salvation | 853 | 1 |
| The praise that to thy name belongs | 437 | 5 |

| | HYMN | VERSE |
|---|---|---|
| The praises of my God shall still | 562 | 1 |
| The praises of redeeming love they sang | 691 | 8 |
| The prayer is accepted, the sinner is free | 707 | 5 |
| The prayer oft mixed with tears before | 841 | 7 |
| The prayers of saints to heaven ascend | 528 | 1 |
| †The praying Spirit breathe | 296 | 2 |
| The precious promises are sealed | 706 | 4 |
| The precipice on either hand | 471 | 2 |
| †The presence divine | 760 | 4 |
| The presence of his Son | 202 | 4 |
| The presence of their Lord | 862 | 1 |
| The pride that lurks within | 858 | 4 |
| The primal marriage blessing | 996 | 1 |
| The Prince and the author of peace | 220 | 2 |
| The Prince is ever in them | 943 | 9 |
| The Prince of peace | 800 | 7 |
| The Prince of peace proclaim | 684 | 4 |
| The prisoner leaps to lose his chain | 585 | 10 |
| The prisoner of the Lord | 150 | 8 |
| The prisoner of thy love | 105 | 3 |
| The prisoner relieve | 495 | 3 |
| The prisoners of the Lord | 345 | 1 |
| The prodigal thou wilt not spurn | 178 | 4 |
| The promise, by thy mercy made | 408 | 3 |
| The promise I know is for me | 78 | 1 |
| The promise is for me | 301 | 6 |
| The promise is securely made | 759 | 2 |
| The promise made to Abraham's race | 450 | 1 |
| *The promise of my Father's love | 903 | 1 |
| The promise of that faithful word | 944 | 5 |
| The promise ratified by thee | 380 | 9 |
| †The promise stands for ever sure | 380 | 8 |
| The promise to our children came | 891 | 3 |
| The promise to receive | 761 | 1 |
| The promised blessing give | 486 | 1 |
| The promised blessing's come | 194 | 4 |
| The promised Deity | 756 | 1 |
| The promised Intercessor give | 294 | 4 |
| The promised joy I soon shall have | 835 | 3 |
| †The promised land, from Pisgah's top | 405 | 4 |
| The proofs of godly fear we give | 319 | 2 |
| The proof we in ourselves receive | 261 | 3 |
| †The prophet of the cross no more | 799 | 4 |
| The prophet spake of thee | 883 | 4 |
| The prophets there behold | 942 | 10 |
| The prophets wrote and spoke | 87 | 2 |
| The publican's friend And Advocate too | 5 | 4 |
| The purchased Comforter impart | 254 | 2 |
| The purchased rest | 854 | 3 |
| The purchased souls of all mankind | 445 | 2 |
| The purchase of his agonies | 867 | 2 |
| The purchase of his blood | 897 | 2 |
| The purchase of our dying Lord | 759 | 6 |

| | Hymn | Verse |
|---|---|---|
| The purchase of thy death divide . | 404 | 5 |
| The purchase of thy passion claim . | 749 | 5 |
| The pure and perfect love shall yield | 331 | 3 |
| The pure, benevolent desire | 81 | 2 |
| The pure celestial fire to impart . | 327 | 1 |
| The pure in heart shall see thy face | 284 | 4 |
| The quiet waters by. | 556 | 1 |
| †The race we all are running now | 947 | 5 |
| †The raging fire and stormy sea | 788 | 4 |
| The ransomed nations bow . | 800 | 11 |
| †The ransomed sons of God . | 497 | 3 |
| The ransom of his life was paid . | 39 | 4 |
| The ravens that call On thee for their food | 1013 | 1 |
| †The reconciling word | 387 | 2 |
| The redeemed of the Lord . | 491 | 2 |
| †The reign of sin and death is o'er . | 706 | 5 |
| The rest of saints above | 25 | 6 |
| The riches of his grace | 37 | 4 |
| †The riches of his grace | 630 | 8 |
| The riches of thy grace | 184 | 8 |
| The rich in flattering riches trust . | 422 | 1 |
| The righteous Judge is at the gate . | 558 | 6 |
| The righteousness divine . | 402 | 1 |
| †The righteousness that never ends . | 251 | 4 |
| The rigid satisfaction | 818 | 4 |
| The ripened fruit of righteousness . | 331 | 2 |
| The rising God forsakes the tomb . | 712 | 2 |
| The rock in sunder cleave . | 105 | 1 |
| The rock into a fountain flows | 223 | 5 |
| The rock of pure, almighty love | 247 | 4 |
| The rock that never shall remove . | 247 | 4 |
| The Rock that rent in twain | 64 | 1 |
| The rocks on either hand . | 468 | 2 |
| †The rolling sun, the changing light. | 553 | 2 |
| †The rougher our way | 498 | 4 |
| The ruined earth and heaven | 536 | 7 |
| The ruins of my soul repair . | 186 | 3 |
| The rush of numerous years bears down . | 422 | 1 |
| The sabbath of thy love | 403 | 4 |
| The sacramental seal apply . | 476 | 5 |
| The sacred annals speak thy fame . | 386 | 2 |
| †The sacred cup of saving grace | 614 | 9 |
| The sacred discipline be given | 473 | 1 |
| †The sacred lessons of thy grace . | 89 | 4 |
| The sacred sons of grace . | 21 | 5 |
| The sacred watchfulness impart . | 309 | 1 |
| The saints above, how great their joys | 940 | 1 |
| The saints enjoy in heaven . | 954 | 2 |
| The saints' eternal Comforter | 647 | 5 |
| The saints have a mountain Of blessings in him . | 496 | 1 |
| The saints in an agony wait | 77 | 1 |
| †The saints in his presence receive . | 73 | 5 |
| †The saints in prayer appear as one . | 823 | 6 |

| | Hymn | Verse |
|---|---|---|
| The saints in thee their all possess | 629 | 3 |
| The saints' secure abode | 333 | 2 |
| †The saints shall flourish in his days | 585 | 6 |
| The saints thy sanctity receive | 770 | 1 |
| *The saints who die of Christ possest | 926 | 1 |
| The salt may lose its seasoning power | 317 | 1 |
| The same delight we prove | 504 | 9 |
| The same from age to age endure | 396 | 3 |
| The same in dignity and power | 647 | 5 |
| The same in heart and mind | 630 | 2 |
| The same in mind and heart | 534 | 5 |
| The same that was in thee | 459 | 2 |
| The same through all succeeding years | 89 | 1 |
| The same through one eternal day | 294 | 1 |
| The same thy truth and grace endure | 408 | 7 |
| The sanctifying grace | 172 | 2 |
| The sanctifying Spirit speak | 303 | 5 |
| The saving power impart | 85 | 3 |
| The saving power of Jesu's name | 306 | 1 |
| The Saviour I adore | 809 | 3 |
| The Saviour lives again | 713 | 3 |
| The Saviour of mankind | 34 | 1 |
| The Saviour of mankind | 151 | 3 |
| The Saviour of mankind | 717 | 1 |
| The Saviour of men | 488 | 5 |
| The Saviour of our race | 745 | 4 |
| The Saviour Son be glorified | 752 | 5 |
| The Saviour wakened from his sleep | 697 | 1 |
| *The Saviour, when to heaven he rose | 868 | 1 |
| The Saviour's grace for all is free | 115 | 3 |
| The Saviour's praises speak | 699 | 4 |
| †The sceptre well becomes his hands | 585 | 2 |
| The scriptures to our hearts apply | 255 | 3 |
| †The sea beheld his power, and fled | 223 | 2 |
| The sea is turned to solid land | 223 | 5 |
| The sea, that roars at thy command | 1002 | 4 |
| The seal of thine eternal love | 163 | 1 |
| The seat of everlasting love | 497 | 2 |
| The second gift impart | 354 | 3 |
| The secret mind of God to man | 255 | 2 |
| †The secret of the Lord thou art | 379 | 5 |
| The secret of thy love | 358 | 2 |
| The secret of thy love reveal | 97 | 6 |
| The secret of thy love unfold | 140 | 3 |
| The secret place of thunder | 587 | 4 |
| †The secret pride, the subtle sin | 204 | 3 |
| The secrets of my breast | 632 | 2 |
| The seed of sin's disease | 367 | 1 |
| The seed shall surely grow | 734 | 1 |
| The seed-time and the harvest | 988 | 3 |
| The seeing eye, the feeling sense | 9 | 7 |
| †The self-existing God supreme | 673 | 3 |
| The sense of acceptance to give | 165 | 1 |

| | Hymn | Verse |
|---|---|---|
| The sense of his goodness impart | 911 | 2 |
| The sense of pardoning love | 188 | 1 |
| The sense of sin forgiven | 97 | 3 |
| The sense of thy favour inspire | 165 | 3 |
| The sensible distress | 104 | 2 |
| The servant as his Lord shall be | 401 | 5 |
| †The servant faithfully discreet | 470 | 5 |
| The servant is above his Lord | 227 | 1 |
| The servant of thy church to live | 17 | 7 |
| The servant shall be as his Lord | 366 | 1 |
| The servant shall be as his Lord | 375 | 1 |
| The servant shall be as his Lord | 380 | 7 |
| The servant shall be as his Lord | 380 | 9 |
| The servant to my bosom take | 470 | 6 |
| The servants I employ | 609 | 3 |
| The servants of his will | 897 | 2 |
| The servants of mankind | 526 | 4 |
| †The servile progeny of Ham | 444 | 3 |
| The settled peace, the constant mind | 172 | 2 |
| The seventh trumpet speaks him near | 56 | 1 |
| The shades of overspreading death | 585 | 5 |
| †The sharpness of thy two-edged sword | 870 | 2 |
| The Shechina shall rest | 760 | 4 |
| The sheep for whom their Shepherd bled | 81 | 4 |
| The sheep for whom their Shepherd died | 433 | 5 |
| The sheep he never can devour | 501 | 4 |
| The sheep of Israel's fold | 897 | 4 |
| The sheep that cannot find the fold | 744 | 1 |
| †The Shepherd who died His sheep to redeem | 40 | 2 |
| The shining constellations join, and say Alleluia | 663 | — |
| The shorter our stay | 498 | 4 |
| The short-lived beauties die away | 46 | 2 |
| The short-lived beauties die away | 46 | 4 |
| The shout of them that feast | 948 | 10 |
| The sick, and spiritless, and faint | 744 | 2 |
| The sick, O Lord, around thee lay | 969 | 1 |
| The sick to be relieved and healed | 395 | 1 |
| The sighs that waft your souls to heaven | 9 | 8 |
| The sight beatific they prove | 946 | 2 |
| The sight that veils the seraph's face | 9 | 10 |
| The signature of love divine | 376 | 5 |
| †The sign of faith ordained by thee | 891 | 2 |
| The signs infallible | 96 | 1 |
| The silver trumpet calls | 958 | 4 |
| The simplest believer His promise may prove | 211 | 4 |
| The sin-atoning Victim died | 809 | 2 |
| The sin-convincing Spirit blew | 93 | 7 |
| The sin-sick soul thou lov'st much more | 397 | 6 |
| The sin-subduing power | 416 | 1 |
| The sinfulness of sin | 135 | 8 |
| The sinner a sinner no more | 174 | 4 |
| The sinner who for thee doth grieve | 545 | 4 |
| The sinner's Advocate shall reign | 629 | 9 |

| | Hymn | Verse |
|---|---|---|
| The sinner's pardon seal | 900 | 3 |
| †The sinners suddenly convince | 81 | 8 |
| The sinners that stray | 219 | 6 |
| The sins of all the world away | 81 | 2 |
| The sins with which I cannot part | 778 | 1 |
| The slaughtered Lamb | 800 | 11 |
| The slightest touch of sin to feel | 313 | 3 |
| The slumber from my spirit shake | 303 | 1 |
| †The smoke of thy atonement here | 902 | 3 |
| The sober Christian feast | 1014 | — |
| The softening power of love impart | 176 | 4 |
| The soft, refreshing dew | 630 | 5 |
| The solemn midnight cry | 55 | 3 |
| The sole return thy love requires | 654 | 8 |
| The solid marbles rend | 22 | 2 |
| The Son and Spirit we adore | 663 | — |
| The Son of God is come | 678 | 1 |
| The Son of God, the Son of man | 227 | 2 |
| The Son of man, the God of heaven | 689 | 1 |
| The Son, thine offspring, flowed | 642 | 3 |
| The Son with joy looks down, and sees | 867 | 2 |
| The song of them that triumph | 943 | 10 |
| The songs which from thy servants rise | 959 | 1 |
| The sons of Adam in distress | 563 | 4 |
| The sooner 'tis past | 498 | 4 |
| The soul-composing power | 466 | 2 |
| The soul-distracting sin | 296 | 1 |
| The soul that on thy love is cast | 590 | 6 |
| The soul that trusts in thee | 614 | 4 |
| †The soul-transforming word | 459 | 3 |
| The souls I from my Lord receive | 471 | 3 |
| The souls redeemed by thee | 447 | 2 |
| The souls that here agree | 501 | 5 |
| The souls that would be one in thee | 513 | 1 |
| The souls to relieve | 495 | 2 |
| The souls we here present to thee | 474 | 1 |
| The souls whom Jesus died to save | 470 | 10 |
| The souls whom once in thee we loved | 461 | 2 |
| The sound and glory of his name | 569 | 9 |
| The sovereign righteousness we own | 913 | 1 |
| The spacious earth around | 742 | 2 |
| *The spacious firmament on high | 552 | 1 |
| The speechless awe that dares not move | 9 | 10 |
| The Spirit and the Bride say, "Come" | 792 | 2 |
| †The Spirit breathe of inward life | 456 | 6 |
| The Spirit comes, and sinners live | 759 | 1 |
| The spirit in the letter lost | 91 | 6 |
| The Spirit invites, in the bride | 77 | 1 |
| The Spirit is come | 760 | 1 |
| The Spirit of burning now impart | 490 | 5 |
| The spirit of ceaseless prayer impart | 294 | 3 |
| †The Spirit of convincing speech | 456 | 3 |
| †The Spirit of faith, in this thy day | 456 | 5 |

| | HYMN | VERSE |
|---|---|---|
| †The Spirit of faith, Of faith in thy blood | 3 | 6 |
| The Spirit of God with ours | 96 | 5 |
| The Spirit of grace impart | 465 | 9 |
| †The Spirit of interceding grace | 297 | 3 |
| The Spirit of life, and power, and love | 377 | 1 |
| The Spirit of love, and health, and power | 380 | 7 |
| The Spirit of love and power | 119 | 4 |
| The Spirit of power, Of health, and of love | 3 | 5 |
| The spirit of rapture unknown | 371 | 2 |
| †The Spirit of refining fire | 456 | 4 |
| *The Spirit of the Lord our God | 107 | 1 |
| The spirit of thy word impart | 89 | 1 |
| The Spirit on all believers shed | 630 | 3 |
| The Spirit, one and seven | 333 | 6 |
| The Spirit sent from heaven | 958 | 2 |
| †The Spirit takes delight to view | 867 | 3 |
| The Spirit we receive | 21 | 4 |
| The Spirit's course in me restrain | 279 | 1 |
| The Spirit's law of life divine | 340 | 2 |
| The spotless Lamb of God is slain | 706 | 4 |
| The spotless purity | 410 | 3 |
| The sprightly man, or warlike horse | 225 | 5 |
| The spring whence all these blessings flow | 868 | 5 |
| The staff from off my shoulder broke | 293 | 2 |
| The stamp of perfect love | 329 | 4 |
| The standard of your God | 314 | 2 |
| The starry crown to victors due | 928 | 4 |
| The steward of the Lord | 432 | 1 |
| The still small voice I long to hear | 425 | 1 |
| †The stone to flesh again convert | 186 | 4 |
| The stone to flesh convert | 361 | 6 |
| The stony heart remove | 103 | 3 |
| †The storm is laid, the winds retire | 1002 | 4 |
| The storm of sin I see | 292 | 1 |
| The storms of affliction beneath | 499 | 2 |
| The story of thy love repeat | 33 | 4 |
| *The strain upraise of joy and praise, Alleluia | 663 | — |
| †The stranger homeward bends | 942 | 2 |
| The stranger receive | 495 | 3 |
| The streaming blood divine | 128 | 3 |
| The streams of immortal delight | 79 | 1 |
| The strength of sin subdue | 361 | 5 |
| The strength of sin, the tempter's power | 916 | 5 |
| The strictest life is but in vain | 626 | 2 |
| The stroke I patiently sustain | 331 | 1 |
| The strong man, armed with guilt of sin | 93 | 5 |
| The stubble of thy foe | 138 | 2 |
| The stumbling-block remove | 472 | 2 |
| The substance in the shade | 91 | 6 |
| The substance of those rites revealed | 702 | 5 |
| The sufferer, bruised beneath your load | 712 | 1 |
| †The suffering scarce, alas! can know | 951 | 3 |
| The suffering Son of God | 35 | 4 |

| | Hymn | Verse |
|---|---|---|
| The summer of my comforts fled | 776 | 1 |
| The summer rays with vigour shine | 978 | 2 |
| The summons obey | 495 | 1 |
| The sun gone down | 848 | 2 |
| †The sun in its meridian height | 974 | 9 |
| The sun may set on weeping eyes | 559 | 2 |
| †The Sun of righteousness on me | 141 | 5 |
| The Sun of righteousness shall rise | 157 | 7 |
| The Sun of righteousness to appear | 686 | 1 |
| The sure confirming seal | 897 | 2 |
| The sure, inviolable peace | 331 | 2 |
| The sure irrevocable word | 448 | 2 |
| †The sure provisions of my God | 555 | 5 |
| The sweet anointing grace | 630 | 4 |
| The sweet comfort and peace | 807 | 1 |
| The sweetness of my mercy share | 4 | 7 |
| The sweetness of thy pardoning grace | 1011 | — |
| The sweetness of thy saving name | 864 | 3 |
| The sweetness of thy yoke to prove | 344 | 2 |
| †The task thy wisdom hath assigned | 324 | 2 |
| The tearless life, is there | 943 | 1 |
| The tears shall be wiped from our eyes | 946 | 4 |
| The tears that tell your sins forgiven | 9 | 8 |
| The tempests that rise | 498 | 4 |
| The temple filled with light divine | 121 | 4 |
| The temple of indwelling God | 376 | 3 |
| The temple of my soul prepare | 374 | 1 |
| †The temple of the Lord are these | 94 | 2 |
| †The temple of the Lord—they pull | 94 | 3 |
| The temple of thine own elect | 992 | 6 |
| The temple's veil in sunder breaks | 22 | 2 |
| The tender blade, the stalk, the ear | 739 | 4 |
| The tender conscience, give | 308 | 2 |
| The tender, fleshly heart | 103 | 3 |
| The terrors of the Lord display | 443 | 1 |
| The theme of God's salvation | 804 | 2 |
| The thing impossible perform | 459 | 2 |
| The thing impossible shall be | 401 | 3 |
| *The thing my God doth hate | 340 | 1 |
| The thing prepared for me | 805 | 2 |
| The thing that we would have | 797 | 3 |
| †The thing surpasses all my thought | 360 | 8 |
| The things belonging to our peace | 455 | 3 |
| The things concerning thee | 872 | 2 |
| †The things eternal I pursue | 68 | 3 |
| The things impossible to men | 138 | 4 |
| †The things impossible to men | 475 | 3 |
| The things of earth, for thee I leave | 114 | 3 |
| †The things that were not, His mercy bids live | 212 | 5 |
| †The things unknown to feeble sense | 95 | 5 |
| The things which freely of his love | 96 | 4 |
| *The thirsty are called to their Lord | 78 | 1 |
| The thoughts of such amazing bliss | 12 | 3 |

| | Hymn | Verse |
|---|---|---|
| The thought that breathes, the word that burns | 698 | 3 |
| The thousands of his sheep | 675 | 6 |
| The thousands of our Israel see | 82 | 1 |
| The threatening Gittite slays | 278 | 7 |
| The threefold grace is said | 996 | 2 |
| The Three in One to sing | 991 | 2 |
| The thunder of thy power | 305 | 1 |
| †The thunders of his hand | 650 | 2 |
| The tide of time shall never | 586 | 6 |
| The time by God designed | 805 | 2 |
| †The toils of day are over | 968 | 3 |
| The tokens of his dying love | 726 | 1 |
| The tokens of thy dying love | 901 | 2 |
| The tokens of thy grace | 765 | 1 |
| The tomb in vain forbids his rise | 712 | 2 |
| The torch that lights time's thickest gloom | 857 | 4 |
| The tower to which I flee | 602 | 4 |
| The transports of a grateful heart | 636 | 1 |
| The treasures of the earth and sea | 992 | 4 |
| The triumph of our Lord | 74 | 2 |
| The triumphs of his grace | 1 | 1 |
| The triumphs of thy love | 275 | 7 |
| The triumphs of thy love display | 236 | 1 |
| The Triune God of holiness | 262 | 2 |
| †The trivial round, the common task | 965 | 6 |
| The troubles for thy sake they feel | 629 | 1 |
| The troubles, griefs, and burdens feel | 470 | 9 |
| The troubles that come | 498 | 4 |
| †The true and faithful Witness, we | 673 | 2 |
| The true foundation-stone | 989 | 1 |
| The true immortal seed | 453 | 1 |
| The true Messiah to proclaim | 452 | 2 |
| The true simplicity impart | 528 | 1 |
| The true simplicity impart | 884 | — |
| The trumpet sounds! the graves restore | 932 | 1 |
| The trumpet's welcome sound | 65 | 6 |
| The trump of God shall sound, Rejoice | 729 | 6 |
| The trust I have to see thy face | 365 | 9 |
| The truth in sinners' hearts reveal | 873 | 1 |
| The truth of his words For ever remains | 496 | 1 |
| The truth of Jesu's love | 735 | 2 |
| The truth of my religion prove | 364 | 5 |
| The truth that makes you free indeed | 111 | 6 |
| The truth thus symboled on the brow | 891 | 5 |
| †The types and figures are fulfilled | 706 | 4 |
| The tyrant, brandishing his sting | 181 | 5 |
| The uncontrolled, almighty Lord | 275 | 3 |
| The unction from above | 65 | 4 |
| The unction from above | 630 | 3 |
| The understanding heart bestow | 887 | — |
| The undivided Three | 644 | 4 |
| †The ungodly, filled with guilty fears | 932 | 3 |
| The united choirs of angels sing | 494 | 2 |

| | Hymn | Verse |
|---|---|---|
| The universal friend. | 452 | 2 |
| †The universal King. | 282 | 2 |
| The universal King. | 603 | 1 |
| The universal Lord. | 731 | 1 |
| The universal praise | 1022 | — |
| The universe his word obeyed | 284 | 2 |
| †The unspeakable grace | 488 | 4 |
| The unutterable happiness. | 721 | 6 |
| The unutterable name | 948 | 5 |
| The unutterable prayer | 268 | 2 |
| The unutterable tenderness. | 9 | 9 |
| †The unwearied sun, from day to day | 552 | 2 |
| The upward glancing of an eye | 823 | 2 |
| The various forms of human woe. | 441 | 2 |
| The veil from Jacob's heart remove | 451 | 3 |
| The veil is on my heart | 117 | 2 |
| †The veil is rent in Christ alone | 706 | 8 |
| The veil of outward things pass through. | 92 | 4 |
| The veil of sin again remove | 186 | 4 |
| †The veil of unbelief remove | 122 | 4 |
| The very wounds that shame would hide. | 969 | 6 |
| The victory by my Saviour got | 421 | 1 |
| The victory of his cross | 277 | 2 |
| The vilest and worst May come unto me. | 8 | 2 |
| The vilest offender May turn and find grace | 5 | 1 |
| The vineyard of their Lord. | 535 | 2 |
| The virtue of his name | 85 | 3 |
| The virtue of Jesus's love | 911 | 1 |
| The virtue of thy grace | 734 | 1 |
| The virtue of thy love | 417 | 1 |
| The virtue of thy name | 135 | 1 |
| The virtue of thy name | 732 | 1 |
| The virtue of thy passion show | 275 | 7 |
| The virtues of thy wondrous name | 527 | 4 |
| The vocal universe. | 605 | 6 |
| The voice of interceding prayer | 799 | 4 |
| †The voice of joy, and love, and praise | 616 | 4 |
| The voice of melody shall sound | 111 | 4 |
| *The voice that breathed o'er Eden. | 996 | 1 |
| The voice that rolls the stars along | 659 | 5 |
| The voice that speaks in thunder | 667 | 4 |
| *The voice that speaks Jehovah near | 425 | 1 |
| The vows he hath vowed to the Lord | 911 | 1 |
| The voyage of life's at an end | 49 | 3 |
| The warmest charity | 527 | 4 |
| The warmth to swell the grain | 988 | 1 |
| The war proclaims the Prince of peace | 62 | 4 |
| The warrior's delight Is slaughter and blood | 273 | 5 |
| The watchful power bestow | 828 | 2 |
| The watching power impart | 296 | 2 |
| The watchman wakes in vain | 624 | 1 |
| †The watchmen join their voice | 741 | 5 |
| The water and the blood applied | 705 | 2 |

| | Hymn | Verse |
|---|---|---|
| †The water cannot cleanse | 705 | 3 |
| The watery deep I pass | 800 | 5 |
| The watery worlds are all his own | 603 | 2 |
| The waves an awful distance keep | 272 | 2 |
| †The waves of the sea Have lift up their voice | 859 | 2 |
| †The wayfaring men Though fools, shall not stray | 211 | 4 |
| The Way, the Truth, the Life of grace | 590 | 2 |
| The way to heaven through saving grace | 454 | 6 |
| The weakest believers Acknowledge for thine | 10 | 4 |
| The weakest believer That hangs upon him | 198 | 1 |
| The weakest soul that trusts in thee | 649 | 3 |
| The wealth of land and sea | 863 | 2 |
| The weary and burdened, The reprobate race | 40 | 2 |
| The weary find eternal rest | 585 | 10 |
| The weary pilgrim's home | 497 | 2 |
| The weary sinner's friend | 139 | 1 |
| The weary, wandering pilgrim's home | 379 | 2 |
| The welcome burden of thy cross | 474 | 2 |
| The wheat into thy garner bring | 502 | 2 |
| †The while I fain would tread the heavenly way | 794 | 3 |
| The whisper of thy grace | 358 | 1 |
| The whole creation is thy charge | 563 | 3 |
| †The whole creation join in one | 678 | 4 |
| The whole heavenly company sing | 499 | 4 |
| †The whole triumphant host | 800 | 12 |
| The whole wide world rejoices now | 715 | 2 |
| The widow and the fatherless | 224 | 3 |
| †The widow's and the orphan's Friend | 827 | 4 |
| The widow's and the orphan's groan | 364 | 4 |
| The wild boar revels in its shade | 589 | 3 |
| The winds and waves obey him | 988 | 2 |
| The winds and waves submissive heard | 1004 | 2 |
| The winds shall cease, the waves subside | 505 | 4 |
| *The winds were howling o'er the deep | 697 | 1 |
| The wine and oil of grace pour in | 112 | 4 |
| The wings of faith and love | 221 | 3 |
| The wings of love, and arms of faith | 213 | 5 |
| The wings of peaceful love | 771 | 5 |
| †The winter's night and summer's day | 222 | 3 |
| The wisdom and the power of God | 629 | 8 |
| The wisdom coming from above | 14 | 1 |
| The wisdom from above | 468 | 7 |
| The wisdom from above | 887 | — |
| The wisdom of the Deity | 475 | 4 |
| The wisdom, wealth, and strength of grace | 422 | 2 |
| The wish which doth from thee proceed | 513 | 2 |
| The withering fig-tree droop and die | 803 | 2 |
| The witness in himself he hath | 85 | 4 |
| The witness in ourselves we have | 96 | 4 |
| The witness of Jesus returned to his home | 760 | 1 |
| The witness, pledge, and seal | 757 | 3 |
| The wolf can never harm | 501 | 3 |
| The wonderful coming Of Jesus declare | 273 | 4 |

|  | Hymn | Verse |
|---|---|---|
| The wonderful I AM | 667 | 1 |
| The wonders of his love | 907 | 3 |
| The wonders of redeeming grace | 9 | 4 |
| The wonders of thy name | 472 | 5 |
| The wonders of thy law | 88 | 2 |
| The wonders of thy love | 979 | 4 |
| The wonders wrought by Jesu's name | 159 | 2 |
| The wonders wrought by Jesu's name | 439 | 3 |
| The wonder, "Why such love to me." | 9 | 9 |
| The wondrous name. | 800 | 9 |
| The word is ever nigh | 192 | 3 |
| The word of general grace | 745 | 4 |
| The word of God can never fail | 401 | 3 |
| †The word of God is sure | 345 | 6 |
| The word of healing to my soul | 164 | 6 |
| †The word of life, dispensed to-day | 955 | 3 |
| The word of life we sow | 734 | 1 |
| The word of peace is now restored | 714 | 6 |
| †The word thy sacred lips has past | 448 | 2 |
| †The words of his unbounded love | 888 | 2 |
| The work and praise are all his own | 331 | 3 |
| The work is but begun | 674 | 2 |
| The work of an almighty hand | 552 | 2 |
| The work of faith in us fulfil | 523 | 3 |
| The work of faith with power | 229 | 6 |
| The work of thine almighty hand | 733 | 1 |
| The work of thy mercy revive | 165 | 2 |
| The work our feeble strength defies | 475 | 2 |
| The work thou hast begun | 292 | 4 |
| †The works of God, above, below | 662 | 2 |
| The world, and founded all that is | 557 | 2 |
| †The world, and Satan's malice | 276 | 4 |
| The world and the devil Fall under my feet | 200 | 6 |
| The world and the devil Through him we o'ercame | 481 | 3 |
| The world can never fill | 787 | 3 |
| †The world cannot withstand | 277 | 6 |
| †The world he suffered to redeem | 39 | 4 |
| The world may know thy saving name | 781 | 7 |
| The world may their reception find | 451 | 3 |
| The world must sink beneath the hand | 277 | 6 |
| The world of ill, the vale of pain | 916 | 3 |
| The world, sin, death, and hell o'erthrew | 557 | 9 |
| †The world, sin, death, oppose in vain | 353 | 3 |
| The world, the Christian world, convince | 94 | 4 |
| The world was united to bless | 220 | 2 |
| †The world with feeble saints agree | 816 | 2 |
| The world with sin and Satan | 853 | 3 |
| The world's dark night is hastening on | 857 | 3 |
| The world's foundations first were laid | 752 | 1 |
| The world's foundations strongly laid | 600 | 1 |
| The worlds of science and of art | 863 | 2 |
| The wormwood and the gall | 681 | 6 |
| The worship he approves | 93 | 4 |

| | Hymn | Verse |
|---|---|---|
| †The Spirit of faith, Of faith in thy blood | 3 | 6 |
| The Spirit of God with ours | 96 | 5 |
| The Spirit of grace impart | 465 | 9 |
| †The Spirit of interceding grace | 297 | 3 |
| The Spirit of life, and power, and love | 377 | 1 |
| The Spirit of love, and health, and power | 380 | 7 |
| The Spirit of love and power | 119 | 4 |
| The Spirit of power, Of health, and of love | 3 | 5 |
| The spirit of rapture unknown | 371 | 2 |
| †The Spirit of refining fire | 456 | 4 |
| *The Spirit of the Lord our God | 107 | 1 |
| The spirit of thy word impart | 89 | 1 |
| The Spirit on all believers shed | 630 | 3 |
| The Spirit, one and seven | 333 | 6 |
| The Spirit sent from heaven | 958 | 2 |
| †The Spirit takes delight to view | 867 | 3 |
| The Spirit we receive | 21 | 4 |
| The Spirit's course in me restrain | 279 | 1 |
| The Spirit's law of life divine | 340 | 2 |
| The spotless Lamb of God is slain | 706 | 4 |
| The spotless purity | 410 | 8 |
| The sprightly man, or warlike horse | 225 | 5 |
| The spring whence all these blessings flow | 868 | 5 |
| The staff from off my shoulder broke | 293 | 2 |
| The stamp of perfect love | 329 | 4 |
| The standard of your God | 314 | 2 |
| The starry crown to victors due | 928 | 4 |
| The steward of the Lord | 432 | 1 |
| The still small voice I long to hear | 425 | 1 |
| †The stone to flesh again convert | 186 | 4 |
| The stone to flesh convert | 861 | 6 |
| The stony heart remove | 103 | 3 |
| †The storm is laid, the winds retire | 1002 | 4 |
| The storm of sin I see | 292 | 1 |
| The storms of affliction beneath | 499 | 2 |
| The story of thy love repeat | 33 | 4 |
| *The strain upraise of joy and praise, Alleluia | 663 | — |
| †The stranger homeward bends | 942 | 2 |
| The stranger receive | 495 | 3 |
| The streaming blood divine | 128 | 3 |
| The streams of immortal delight | 79 | 1 |
| The strength of sin subdue | 361 | 5 |
| The strength of sin, the tempter's power | 916 | 5 |
| The strictest life is but in vain | 626 | 2 |
| The stroke I patiently sustain | 331 | 1 |
| The strong man, armed with guilt of sin | 93 | 5 |
| The stubble of thy foe | 138 | 2 |
| The stumbling-block remove | 472 | 2 |
| The substance in the shade | 91 | 6 |
| The substance of those rites revealed | 702 | 5 |
| The sufferer, bruised beneath your load | 712 | 1 |
| †The suffering scarce, alas! can know | 951 | 3 |
| The suffering Son of God | 35 | 4 |

| | Hymn | Verse |
|---|---|---|
| The summer of my comforts fled | 776 | 1 |
| The summer rays with vigour shine | 978 | 2 |
| The summons obey | 495 | 1 |
| The sun gone down | 848 | 2 |
| †The sun in its meridian height | 974 | 9 |
| The sun may set on weeping eyes | 559 | 2 |
| †The Sun of righteousness on me | 141 | 5 |
| The Sun of righteousness shall rise | 157 | 7 |
| The Sun of righteousness to appear | 686 | 1 |
| The sure confirming seal | 897 | 2 |
| The sure, inviolable peace | 331 | 2 |
| The sure irrevocable word | 448 | 2 |
| †The sure provisions of my God | 555 | 5 |
| The sweet anointing grace | 630 | 4 |
| The sweet comfort and peace | 807 | 1 |
| The sweetness of my mercy share | 4 | 7 |
| The sweetness of thy pardoning grace | 1011 | — |
| The sweetness of thy saving name | 864 | 3 |
| The sweetness of thy yoke to prove | 344 | 2 |
| †The task thy wisdom hath assigned | 324 | 2 |
| The tearless life, is there | 943 | 1 |
| The tears shall be wiped from our eyes | 946 | 4 |
| The tears that tell your sins forgiven | 9 | 8 |
| The tempests that rise | 498 | 4 |
| The temple filled with light divine | 121 | 4 |
| The temple of indwelling God | 376 | 3 |
| The temple of my soul prepare | 374 | 1 |
| †The temple of the Lord are these | 94 | 2 |
| †The temple of the Lord—they pull | 94 | 3 |
| The temple of thine own elect | 992 | 6 |
| The temple's veil in sunder breaks | 22 | 2 |
| The tender blade, the stalk, the ear | 739 | 4 |
| The tender conscience, give | 308 | 2 |
| The tender, fleshly heart | 103 | 3 |
| The terrors of the Lord display | 443 | 1 |
| The theme of God's salvation | 804 | 2 |
| The thing impossible perform | 459 | 2 |
| The thing impossible shall be | 401 | 3 |
| *The thing my God doth hate | 340 | 1 |
| The thing prepared for me | 805 | 2 |
| The thing that we would have | 797 | 3 |
| †The thing surpasses all my thought | 360 | 8 |
| The things belonging to our peace | 455 | 3 |
| The things concerning thee | 872 | 2 |
| †The things eternal I pursue | 68 | 3 |
| The things impossible to men | 138 | 4 |
| †The things impossible to men | 475 | 3 |
| The things of earth, for thee I leave | 114 | 3 |
| †The things that were not, His mercy bids live | 212 | 5 |
| †The things unknown to feeble sense | 95 | 5 |
| The things which freely of his love | 96 | 4 |
| *The thirsty are called to their Lord | 78 | 1 |
| The thoughts of such amazing bliss | 12 | 3 |

| | Hymn | Verse |
|---|---|---|
| The thought that breathes, the word that burns | 698 | 8 |
| The thousands of his sheep | 675 | 6 |
| The thousands of our Israel see | 82 | 1 |
| The threatening Gittite slays | 278 | 7 |
| The threefold grace is said | 996 | 2 |
| The Three in One to sing | 991 | 2 |
| The thunder of thy power | 805 | 1 |
| †The thunders of his hand | 650 | 2 |
| The tide of time shall never | 586 | 6 |
| The time by God designed | 805 | 2 |
| †The toils of day are over | 968 | 8 |
| The tokens of his dying love | 726 | 1 |
| The tokens of thy dying love | 901 | 2 |
| The tokens of thy grace | 765 | 1 |
| The tomb in vain forbids his rise | 712 | 2 |
| The torch that lights time's thickest gloom | 857 | 4 |
| The tower to which I flee | 602 | 4 |
| The transports of a grateful heart | 636 | 1 |
| The treasures of the earth and sea | 992 | 4 |
| The triumph of our Lord | 74 | 2 |
| The triumphs of his grace | 1 | 1 |
| The triumphs of thy love | 275 | 7 |
| The triumphs of thy love display | 236 | 1 |
| The Triune God of holiness | 262 | 2 |
| †The trivial round, the common task | 965 | 6 |
| The troubles for thy sake they feel | 629 | 1 |
| The troubles, griefs, and burdens feel | 470 | 9 |
| The troubles that come | 498 | 4 |
| †The true and faithful Witness, we | 673 | 2 |
| The true foundation-stone | 989 | 1 |
| The true immortal seed | 453 | 1 |
| The true Messiah to proclaim | 452 | 2 |
| The true simplicity impart | 528 | 1 |
| The true simplicity impart | 884 | — |
| The trumpet sounds! the graves restore | 932 | 1 |
| The trumpet's welcome sound | 65 | 6 |
| The trump of God shall sound, Rejoice | 729 | 6 |
| The trust I have to see thy face | 865 | 9 |
| The truth in sinners' hearts reveal | 873 | 1 |
| The truth of his words For ever remains | 496 | 1 |
| The truth of Jesu's love | 735 | 2 |
| The truth of my religion prove | 864 | 5 |
| The truth that makes you free indeed | 111 | 6 |
| The truth thus symboled on the brow | 891 | 5 |
| †The types and figures are fulfilled | 706 | 4 |
| The tyrant, brandishing his sting | 181 | 5 |
| The uncontrolled, almighty Lord | 275 | 3 |
| The unction from above | 65 | 4 |
| The unction from above | 630 | 3 |
| The understanding heart bestow | 887 | — |
| The undivided Three | 644 | 4 |
| †The ungodly, filled with guilty fears | 932 | 3 |
| The united choirs of angels sing | 494 | 2 |

| | Hymn | Verse |
|---|---|---|
| The universal friend. | 452 | 2 |
| †The universal King. | 282 | 2 |
| The universal King. | 603 | 1 |
| The universal Lord. | 731 | 1 |
| The universal praise | 1022 | — |
| The universe his word obeyed | 234 | 2 |
| †The unspeakable grace | 488 | 4 |
| The unutterable happiness. | 721 | 6 |
| The unutterable name | 948 | 5 |
| The unutterable prayer | 268 | 2 |
| The unutterable tenderness. | 9 | 9 |
| †The unwearied sun, from day to day | 552 | 2 |
| The upward glancing of an eye | 823 | 2 |
| The various forms of human woe. | 441 | 2 |
| The veil from Jacob's heart remove | 451 | 3 |
| The veil is on my heart | 117 | 2 |
| †The veil is rent in Christ alone | 706 | 8 |
| The veil of outward things pass through. | 92 | 4 |
| The veil of sin again remove | 186 | 4 |
| †The veil of unbelief remove | 122 | 4 |
| The very wounds that shame would hide. | 969 | 6 |
| The victory by my Saviour got | 421 | 1 |
| The victory of his cross | 277 | 2 |
| The vilest and worst May come unto me. | 8 | 2 |
| The vilest offender May turn and find grace | 5 | 1 |
| The vineyard of their Lord. | 535 | 2 |
| The virtue of his name | 85 | 3 |
| The virtue of Jesus's love | 911 | 1 |
| The virtue of thy grace | 734 | 1 |
| The virtue of thy love | 417 | 1 |
| The virtue of thy name | 135 | 1 |
| The virtue of thy name | 732 | 1 |
| The virtue of thy passion show | 275 | 7 |
| The virtues of thy wondrous name | 527 | 4 |
| The vocal universe. | 605 | 6 |
| The voice of interceding prayer | 799 | 4 |
| †The voice of joy, and love, and praise | 616 | 4 |
| The voice of melody shall sound | 111 | 4 |
| *The voice that breathed o'er Eden. | 996 | 1 |
| The voice that rolls the stars along | 659 | 5 |
| The voice that speaks in thunder | 667 | 4 |
| *The voice that speaks Jehovah near | 425 | 1 |
| The vows he hath vowed to the Lord | 911 | 1 |
| The voyage of life's at an end | 49 | 3 |
| The warmest charity | 527 | 4 |
| The warmth to swell the grain | 988 | 1 |
| The war proclaims the Prince of peace | 62 | 4 |
| The warrior's delight Is slaughter and blood | 273 | 5 |
| The watchful power bestow | 828 | 2 |
| The watching power impart | 296 | 2 |
| The watchman wakes in vain | 624 | 1 |
| †The watchmen join their voice | 741 | 5 |
| The water and the blood applied | 705 | 2 |

| | Hymn | Verse |
|---|---|---|
| †The water cannot cleanse | 705 | 3 |
| The watery deep I pass | 800 | 5 |
| The watery worlds are all his own | 603 | 2 |
| The waves an awful distance keep | 272 | 2 |
| †The waves of the sea Have lift up their voice | 859 | 2 |
| †The wayfaring men Though fools, shall not stray | 211 | 4 |
| The Way, the Truth, the Life of grace | 590 | 2 |
| The way to heaven through saving grace | 454 | 6 |
| The weakest believers Acknowledge for thine | 10 | 4 |
| The weakest believer That hangs upon him | 198 | 1 |
| The weakest soul that trusts in thee | 649 | 3 |
| The wealth of land and sea | 863 | 2 |
| The weary and burdened, The reprobate race | 40 | 2 |
| The weary find eternal rest | 585 | 10 |
| The weary pilgrim's home | 497 | 2 |
| The weary sinner's friend | 139 | 1 |
| The weary, wandering pilgrim's home | 379 | 2 |
| The welcome burden of thy cross | 474 | 2 |
| The wheat into thy garner bring | 502 | 2 |
| †The while I fain would tread the heavenly way | 794 | 3 |
| The whisper of thy grace | 358 | 1 |
| The whole creation is thy charge | 563 | 3 |
| †The whole creation join in one | 678 | 4 |
| The whole heavenly company sing | 499 | 4 |
| †The whole triumphant host | 800 | 12 |
| The whole wide world rejoices now | 715 | 2 |
| The widow and the fatherless | 224 | 3 |
| †The widow's and the orphan's Friend | 827 | 4 |
| The widow's and the orphan's groan | 364 | 4 |
| The wild boar revels in its shade | 589 | 3 |
| The winds and waves obey him | 988 | 2 |
| The winds and waves submissive heard | 1004 | 2 |
| The winds shall cease, the waves subside | 505 | 4 |
| *The winds were howling o'er the deep | 697 | 1 |
| The wine and oil of grace pour in | 112 | 4 |
| The wings of faith and love | 221 | 3 |
| The wings of love, and arms of faith | 213 | 5 |
| The wings of peaceful love | 771 | 5 |
| †The winter's night and summer's day | 222 | 3 |
| The wisdom and the power of God | 629 | 8 |
| The wisdom coming from above | 14 | 1 |
| The wisdom from above | 468 | 7 |
| The wisdom from above | 887 | — |
| The wisdom of the Deity | 475 | 4 |
| The wisdom, wealth, and strength of grace | 422 | 2 |
| The wish which doth from thee proceed | 513 | 2 |
| The withering fig-tree droop and die | 803 | 2 |
| The witness in himself he hath | 85 | 4 |
| The witness in ourselves we have | 96 | 4 |
| The witness of Jesus returned to his home | 760 | 1 |
| The witness, pledge, and seal | 757 | 3 |
| The wolf can never harm | 501 | 3 |
| The wonderful coming Of Jesus declare | 273 | 4 |

|  | Hymn | Verse |
|---|---|---|
| The wonderful I AM | 667 | 1 |
| The wonders of his love | 907 | 3 |
| The wonders of redeeming grace | 9 | 4 |
| The wonders of thy name | 472 | 5 |
| The wonders of thy law | 88 | 2 |
| The wonders of thy love | 979 | 4 |
| The wonders wrought by Jesu's name | 159 | 2 |
| The wonders wrought by Jesu's name | 439 | 3 |
| The wonder, "Why such love to me." | 9 | 9 |
| The wondrous name. | 800 | 9 |
| The word is ever nigh | 192 | 3 |
| The word of general grace | 745 | 4 |
| The word of God can never fail | 401 | 3 |
| †The word of God is sure | 345 | 6 |
| The word of healing to my soul | 164 | 6 |
| †The word of life, dispensed to-day | 955 | 3 |
| The word of life we sow | 734 | 1 |
| The word of peace is now restored | 714 | 6 |
| The word thy sacred lips has past | 448 | 2 |
| †The words of his unbounded love | 888 | 2 |
| The work and praise are all his own | 331 | 3 |
| The work is but begun | 674 | 2 |
| The work of an almighty hand | 552 | 2 |
| The work of faith in us fulfil | 523 | 3 |
| The work of faith with power | 229 | 6 |
| The work of thine almighty hand | 733 | 1 |
| The work of thy mercy revive | 165 | 2 |
| The work our feeble strength defies | 475 | 2 |
| The work thou hast begun | 292 | 4 |
| †The works of God, above, below | 662 | 2 |
| The world, and founded all that is | 557 | 2 |
| †The world, and Satan's malice | 276 | 4 |
| The world and the devil Fall under my feet | 200 | 6 |
| The world and the devil Through him we o'ercame | 481 | 3 |
| The world can never fill | 787 | 3 |
| †The world cannot withstand. | 277 | 6 |
| †The world he suffered to redeem | 39 | 4 |
| The world may know thy saving name | 781 | 7 |
| The world may their reception find. | 451 | 3 |
| The world must sink beneath the hand | 277 | 6 |
| The world of ill, the vale of pain | 916 | 3 |
| The world, sin, death, and hell o'erthrew | 557 | 9 |
| †The world, sin, death, oppose in vain | 353 | 3 |
| The world, the Christian world, convince | 94 | 4 |
| The world was united to bless | 220 | 2 |
| †The world with feeble saints agree | 816 | 2 |
| The world with sin and Satan | 853 | 3 |
| The world's dark night is hastening on | 857 | 3 |
| The world's foundations first were laid | 752 | 1 |
| The world's foundations strongly laid | 600 | 1 |
| The worlds of science and of art | 863 | 2 |
| The wormwood and the gall | 681 | 6 |
| The worship he approves | 93 | 4 |

| | Hymn | Verse |
|---|---|---|
| The worst need keep him out no more | 208 | 2 |
| The wounds of Jesus, for my sin | 189 | 1 |
| The wounds, the blood! they heard its voice | 721 | 5 |
| The wounds which all my sorrows heal | 128 | 5 |
| The wrath of an almighty God | 181 | 2 |
| †The year of gospel-grace | 988 | 8 |
| The year of Jubilee is come. | 788 | Cho. |
| †The year rolls round, and steals away | 42 | 8 |
| The years of his right hand. | 587 | 4 |
| The years of lost fruition | 587 | 2 |
| Thee, alas, I long have known | 882 | 1 |
| †Thee, all the choir of angels sing | 647 | 2 |
| Thee, and only thee, I know | 434 | 4 |
| Thee, and only thee request. | 411 | 2 |
| Thee, and only thee, to feel. | 27 | 4 |
| Thee, as man for sinners slain | 743 | 2 |
| Thee behold with open face. | 890 | 1 |
| Thee behold with open face. | 852 | 1 |
| Thee, by thy painful agony. | 33 | 8 |
| Thee, by whose almighty name | 53 | 3 |
| Thee, descending on a cloud | 18 | 3 |
| Thee, every soul of man may find | 865 | 7 |
| †Thee, Father, Son, and Holy Ghost | 532 | 5 |
| †Thee, Holy Father, we confess | 259 | 3 |
| Thee, Holy Son, adore | 259 | 3 |
| Thee hosts of martyrs own. | 737 | 9 |
| †Thee I can love, and thee alone | 285 | 7 |
| Thee I restlessly require | 854 | 1 |
| Thee I shall soon in heaven adore | 234 | 4 |
| †Thee I shall then for ever praise | 159 | 3 |
| Thee in affliction's furnace praise | 829 | 1 |
| Thee in mercy rich we prove | 727 | 6 |
| Thee in the midst to find | 486 | 2 |
| Thee in the midst we wait to feel | 490 | 4 |
| Thee in thy bloody vesture see | 774 | 9 |
| †Thee in thy glorious realm they praise | 15 | 8 |
| Thee it delights thy church to own | 648 | 1 |
| Thee its great Author let it show | 513 | 2 |
| †Thee, Jesus, alone | 231 | 2 |
| *Thee, Jesus, full of truth and grace | 329 | 1 |
| Thee, Jesus, let our hearts adore | 629 | 2 |
| *Thee, Jesu, thee, the sinner's friend | 144 | 1 |
| Thee let all in earth and skies | 243 | 1 |
| †Thee let all mankind admire | 748 | 3 |
| Thee let all my powers confess | 194 | 3 |
| Thee let every creature bless | 243 | 5 |
| †Thee let me drink, and thirst no more | 364 | 2 |
| Thee let them preach, the common Lord | 745 | 4 |
| †Thee let us praise, our common Lord | 204 | 7 |
| Thee, Lord, let heaven and earth adore | 332 | 5 |
| †Thee, Lord, with joyful lips we praise | 616 | 9 |
| Thee, lovelier than the sons of men | 210 | 2 |
| Thee may I always nearer feel | 318 | 1 |

| | Hymn | Verse |
|---|---|---|
| Thee may I feel, for God is love | 155 | 8 |
| Thee may I love, for God thou art | 155 | 8 |
| Thee may I publish all day long | 328 | 4 |
| †Thee may I set at my right hand | 824 | 3 |
| Thee merciful and true | 410 | 1 |
| Thee my eternal life | 144 | 1 |
| Thee my latest breath proclaim | 194 | 3 |
| Thee my Life in death I know | 554 | 4 |
| Thee, my Lord (thou then wilt say) | 197 | 1 |
| Thee, my most indulgent God | 243 | 2 |
| Thee, my most indulgent God | 1018 | — |
| Thee, my soul, his own to make | 194 | 1 |
| Thee, my spirit gasps to meet | 352 | 3 |
| Thee, O my all-sufficient good | 403 | 5 |
| *Thee, O my God and King | 191 | 1 |
| †Thee, only thee, I fain would find | 163 | 3 |
| Thee, only thee, resolved to know | 824 | 1 |
| Thee, only thee, resolved to obey | 832 | 3 |
| Thee only would I know | 184 | 1 |
| Thee only would I know | 354 | 5 |
| Thee, Saviour, we adore | 329 | 1 |
| Thee set forth before our eyes | 876 | 2 |
| Thee shall I love in endless day | 210 | 7 |
| †Thee, Son of man, by faith we see | 329 | 3 |
| †Thee, sovereign Lord, let all confess | 235 | 3 |
| Thee, Spirit of truth and holiness | 259 | 3 |
| Thee the creation sings | 226 | 1 |
| Thee the eternal God sustains | 407 | 2 |
| †Thee the first-born sons of light | 221 | 2 |
| Thee the friend of sinners sing | 701 | 1 |
| †Thee the great Jehovah deigns | 407 | 2 |
| Thee the great Lord of earth and skies | 652 | — |
| †Thee, the paternal grace divine | 129 | 3 |
| Thee, the righteous Judge of all | 737 | 5 |
| Thee the unholy cannot see | 522 | 3 |
| Thee they ever keep in view | 529 | 1 |
| Thee they seek, as God of heaven | 748 | 2 |
| Thee they sing with glory crowned | 221 | 3 |
| Thee, thy Israel's Strength and Hope | 508 | 7 |
| Thee to gain, himself was sold | 24 | 2 |
| Thee to know and love alone | 18 | 3 |
| Thee to know, thy power to prove | 716 | 6 |
| Thee to perfection who can know | 240 | 1 |
| †Thee to perfection who can tell | 1001 | 7 |
| Thee to praise and glorify | 653 | 3 |
| Thee to serve with perfect love | 653 | 3 |
| *Thee we adore, eternal name | 42 | 1 |
| Thee we call the Word of God | 748 | 4 |
| †Thee we expect, our faithful Lord | 486 | 2 |
| Thee we now presume to sing | 257 | 2 |
| †Thee we preach to sinful men | 876 | 3 |
| Thee we shall in glory view | 885 | 2 |
| Thee we worship evermore | 645 | 2 |

| | Hymn | Verse |
|---|---|---|
| Thee we would be always blessing | 385 | 2 |
| Thee while man, the earth-born, sings | 260 | 2 |
| †Thee while the first archangel sings | 316 | 2 |
| Thee, who only know'st them, grieve | 768 | 6 |
| Thee will I for ever praise | 197 | 1 |
| Thee will I hold when all things else I miss | 851 | 2 |
| Thee will I love, beneath thy frown | 210 | 7 |
| Thee will I love, my joy, my crown | 210 | 1 |
| †Thee will I love, my joy, my crown | 210 | 7 |
| Thee will I love, my Lord, my God | 210 | 7 |
| *Thee will I love, my strength, my tower | 210 | 1 |
| Thee will I love, till the pure fire | 210 | 1 |
| Thee will I love with all my power | 210 | 1 |
| †Thee will I praise among thine own | 576 | 2 |
| *Thee will I praise with all my heart | 545 | 1 |
| Thee will I to the world extol | 576 | 2 |
| Thee with all our being love | 661 | 3 |
| Thee with all our powers we praise | 661 | 3 |
| Thee with my heart I never knew | 93 | 3 |
| Thee with thankful hearts we prove | 257 | 3 |
| †Thee, with the tribes assembled | 587 | 5 |
| †Thee without faith I cannot please | 148 | 4 |
| Their babes who pamper and admire | 467 | 4 |
| Their baffled hopes destroy | 985 | 3 |
| Their beauty this, their glorious dress | 190 | 11 |
| Their blinded votaries convert | 444 | 3 |
| Their blindness both of heart and mind | 473 | 3 |
| †Their bones, as quite dried up | 450 | 2 |
| Their bread, proportioned to the day | 636 | 3 |
| Their brother to the bar | 43 | 3 |
| Their ceaseless sacrifice of praise | 16 | 2 |
| Their charge to undertake | 871 | 2 |
| Their children's souls we know they wrong | 469 | 5 |
| Their common beams unite | 262 | 1 |
| Their constant service there | 591 | 2 |
| Their cruel fondness blame | 469 | 5 |
| †Their daily delight Shall be in thy name | 198 | 3 |
| Their darkness turn to light | 586 | 2 |
| Their dire captivity to own | 81 | 3 |
| Their duty by my life explain | 472 | 2 |
| Their eager hopes thy house to see | 629 | 1 |
| *Their earthly task who fail to do | 858 | 1 |
| Their endless circles run | 226 | 3 |
| Their everlasting circles run | 802 | 3 |
| Their exceeding great reward | 817 | 2 |
| Their faithful hearts with us prepare | 898 | 1 |
| Their Father's kingdom then shall see | 935 | 4 |
| Their fatness on the ground | 226 | 7 |
| Their feebleness of mind defend | 462 | 6 |
| †Their fury cannot move | 601 | 4 |
| Their glorious circuit run | 446 | 3 |
| Their golden trumpets sound | 931 | 3 |
| Their great and eternal reward | 73 | 5 |

| | Hymn | Verse |
|---|---|---|
| Their great Original proclaim | 552 | 1 |
| Their great Redeemer's name | 543 | 7 |
| †Their guilt shall strike the wicked dumb | 540 | 5 |
| Their happiness the things of earth | 977 | 1 |
| Their healing wings display | 446 | 6 |
| Their heavenly ecstasies | 643 | 3 |
| Their heavenly origin display | 95 | 5 |
| Their heaven on earth begun | 15 | 1 |
| Their hellish arts they try | 315 | 1 |
| Their help Omnipotence | 1002 | 1 |
| Their highest joy, shall be | 941 | 3 |
| Their honours, wealth, and pleasures mean | 68 | 3 |
| Their hopes to God shall raise | 566 | 3 |
| Their House of Mercy, come | 166 | 1 |
| Their humble praises bring | 814 | 1 |
| Their humble wailings pierce the skies | 462 | 1 |
| Their joy is all sadness, Their mirth is all vain | 19 | 4 |
| Their joy is to walk in The light of thy face | 198 | 2 |
| Their joy through Jesu's pains abounds | 721 | 2 |
| Their joys, in pangs renew | 587 | 2 |
| Their King and Priest for ever | 613 | 2 |
| Their land from error's chain | 747 | 1 |
| Their lasting silence break | 699 | 4 |
| Their late, but permanent repose | 114 | 1 |
| Their laughter is madness, Their pleasure is pain | 19 | 4 |
| Their light and strength, their shield and sun | 590 | 5 |
| Their light where'er they go | 446 | 4 |
| Their longed-for Prince of peace | 942 | 10 |
| Their Lord and ours the same | 945 | 1 |
| Their Lord's authority betray | 470 | 7 |
| Their Maker and their King | 684 | 2 |
| Their Master's purchased joy to know | 926 | 3 |
| Their mighty joys we know | 15 | 2 |
| Their mission fully prove | 745 | 5 |
| Their motions speak thy skill | 263 | 2 |
| Their mourning days are o'er | 941 | 2 |
| Their pleasures, wealth, and power, and state | 439 | 2 |
| Their refuge and their stay | 602 | 2 |
| Their righteous sentence to receive | 48 | 1 |
| Their Saviour and their God | 741 | 6 |
| Their scars with glory crowned | 942 | 12 |
| †Their selfish will in time subdue | 468 | 4 |
| Their services could never please | 702 | 3 |
| Their sins on earth forgiven | 304 | 1 |
| Their sorrows cheer, their wants relieve | 397 | 2 |
| Their souls for ever bears | 622 | 2 |
| Their souls for lack of knowledge die | 82 | 4 |
| †Their souls with faith supply | 872 | 2 |
| †Their sound goeth forth, "Christ Jesus is Lord" | 869 | 4 |
| Their Tempter, with his angel-face | 461 | 3 |
| Their triumphant Lord, and ours | 718 | 3 |
| Their triumph to his death | 940 | 3 |
| Their true Anointed One | 450 | 3 |

| | Hymn | Verse |
|---|---|---|
| Their victorious Lord is ours | 571 | 4 |
| Their wonted fruit should bear | 804 | 4 |
| Their works enhance the bliss prepared | 926 | 3 |
| Their works of righteousness | 115 | 1 |
| Their young Hosannas to his name | 585 | 9 |
| Theirs is the water and the blood | 891 | 3 |
| Them and their god alike I dare | 30 | 4 |
| Them down I always am | 432 | 2 |
| Them in its misery detain | 461 | 6 |
| Them one, and sanctifies the whole | 749 | 1 |
| Them ready to perish Thou lov'st to sustain | 1018 | 1 |
| †Them, snatched out of the flame | 452 | 2 |
| Them the Lamb shall always feed | 76 | 4 |
| Them the Spirit hath declared | 51 | 1 |
| †Themselves the slaves of sense and praise | 467 | 4 |
| †Then all the chosen seed | 814 | 4 |
| Then ask the monster, "Where's thy sting?" | 712 | 3 |
| Then blessed only are the just | 541 | 5 |
| Then brightly appeareth The arm of thy might | 869 | 2 |
| †Then by faith we know and feel | 755 | 2 |
| Then can I never fail | 944 | 6 |
| Then children, relatives, and friends | 624 | 2 |
| †Then dig about our root | 981 | 5 |
| †Then every murmuring thought and vain | 369 | 5 |
| Then every soul, in Jesus blest | 443 | 3 |
| Then feel thy halcyon rest within | 770 | 6 |
| Then for that harvest O prepare | 935 | 2 |
| Then grief expires, and pain, and strife | 456 | 6 |
| Then hear thyself within me pray | 134 | 4 |
| Then he finds the scripture key | 876 | 1 |
| Then he speaks, and preaches thee | 876 | 1 |
| Then he went through before | 920 | 3 |
| Then high incensed just check their pride | 541 | 2 |
| Then I into nothing fall | 414 | 1 |
| Then I see the perfect day | 414 | 1 |
| Then I shall be filled with God | 18 | 3 |
| Then I shall in thee believe | 243 | 3 |
| Then I shall my life despise | 877 | 1 |
| Then I shall the secret know | 413 | 3 |
| †Then in a nobler, sweeter song | 798 | 5 |
| Then in hymns of praise adore | 75 | 3 |
| Then in mercy, Lord, draw near them | 878 | 6 |
| †Then infuse the teaching grace | 302 | 4 |
| †Then leave me not when griefs assail | 558 | 4 |
| Then lend *him* to our love | 892 | 2 |
| †Then let me hang upon his word | 833 | 2 |
| †Then let me on the mountain-top | 297 | 6 |
| Then let me see thy face, and die | 284 | 2 |
| †Then let me suddenly remove | 947 | 6 |
| Then let or earth or hell assail | 437 | 9 |
| †Then let our humble faith address | 725 | 5 |
| Then let our songs abound | 12 | 4 |
| Then let the beasts of earth, with varying strain | 663 | — |

|  | Hymn | Verse |
|---|---|---|
| †Then let the last loud trumpet sound | 929 | 4 |
| †Then let the thundering trumpet sound | 64 | 3 |
| †Then let the worms demand their prey | 927 | 4 |
| Then let them burn with sacred love | 490 | 3 |
| Then let them taste the heavenly powers | 490 | 3 |
| †Then let us adore, And give him his right | 859 | 5 |
| †Then let us all thy fulness know | 502 | 5 |
| †Then let us attend | 495 | 3 |
| †Then let us ever bear | 510 | 5 |
| †Then let us gladly bring | 345 | 7 |
| †Then let us hasten to the day | 537 | 12 |
| †Then let us in his name sing on | 954 | 3 |
| †Then let us lawfully contend | 537 | 11 |
| †Then let us make our boast | 478 | 3 |
| Then let us proclaim Our life-giving Lord | 40 | 6 |
| †Then let us prove our heavenly birth | 863 | 3 |
| †Then let us rejoice | 760 | 5 |
| †Then let us render him his own | 953 | 3 |
| Then let us render him his right | 616 | 11 |
| †Then let us see that day supreme | 254 | 3 |
| †Then let us sit beneath his cross | 28 | 4 |
| †Then let us still profess | 897 | 3 |
| †Then let us submit His grace to receive | 5 | 5 |
| †Then let us wait the sound | 536 | 8 |
| †Then let us wait to hear | 65 | 6 |
| Then let winds blow, or thunders roar | 279 | 10 |
| †Then loud be their trump, And stirring their sound | 869 | 5 |
| Then, lowly kneeling, wait thy word of peace | 962 | 1 |
| †Then may we hope, the angelic hosts among | 691 | 6 |
| Then my soul shall upward move | 766 | 2 |
| †Then my soul with strange delight | 413 | 3 |
| Then, O essential Love, come in | 341 | 2 |
| †Then, O my Lord, prepare | 984 | 2 |
| †Then, O my soul, be never more | 614 | 6 |
| Then, only then, we feel | 85 | 2 |
| Then our earthly trials end | 937 | 2 |
| Then our souls in thee attain | 756 | 3 |
| Then point to realms of cloudless day | 849 | 5 |
| Then receive us to thy breast | 643 | 4 |
| Then rise with his ascending Lord | 713 | 5 |
| Then, rising and refreshed, we leave thy throne | 850 | 6 |
| Then Satan doth fear, His citadels fall | 869 | 4 |
| †Then, Saviour, then my soul receive | 59 | 6 |
| Then, Saviour, then to thee I come | 25 | 6 |
| Then shall heaven new joys illumine | 604 | 3 |
| Then shall his love be fully showed | 685 | 5 |
| †Then shall I answer thy design | 775 | 4 |
| †Then shall I end my sad complaints | 920 | 5 |
| †Then shall I see, and hear, and know | 599 | 6 |
| †Then shall it flourish wide and fair | 589 | 6 |
| Then shall my feet no longer rove | 361 | 4 |
| †Then shall my feet no more depart | 788 | 7 |
| Then shall my heart from earth be free | 344 | 4 |

| | Hymn | Verse |
|---|---|---|
| Then shall my labours have an end | 939 | 6 |
| †Then shall our prostrate souls adore | 412 | 6 |
| Then shall we do, with pure delight | 438 | 2 |
| †Then shall we exercise | 447 | 3 |
| Then speak the killing, quickening word | 362 | 5 |
| Then thank the Lord, O thank the Lord | 988 | Cho. |
| Then the full corn shall appear | 987 | 2 |
| †Then the last judgment-day shall come | 927 | 2 |
| †Then the tide of vengeful slaughters | 621 | 2 |
| †Then the whole earth again shall rest | 443 | 3 |
| Then their sinking hopes sustain | 878 | 6 |
| †Then, then acknowledge, and set free | 81 | 4 |
| Then, then let it spread | 219 | 7 |
| †Then, then, my utmost Saviour, raise | 409 | 4 |
| Then, then we conceive | 488 | 4 |
| Then, then, when all our joys are given | 761 | 6 |
| †Then, thou church triumphant come | 987 | 4 |
| Then to mine inmost soul made known | 883 | 4 |
| Then to their flocks, still praising God, return | 691 | 4 |
| †Then to the watchful shepherds it was told | 691 | 2 |
| Then to win and close my race | 877 | 3 |
| Then was joy to Israel's daughters | 580 | 2 |
| †Then welcome, harmless grave | 931 | 6 |
| Then we'll give thee nobler praise | 1007 | — |
| Then we that yet remain | 58 | 2 |
| †Then when on earth I breathe no more | 841 | 7 |
| †Then, when the mighty work is wrought | 503 | 6 |
| †Then, when the work is done | 229 | 6 |
| Then, when thy voice shall bid our conflict cease | 962 | 4 |
| †Then will he own my worthless name | 811 | 4 |
| †Then will I teach the world thy ways | 574 | 12 |
| Then will we, at thy call | 892 | 6 |
| Then we will sing more sweet, more loud | 682 | 4 |
| Then with all that is in thee | 372 | — |
| Then with all thy saints descend | 937 | 2 |
| †Then, with my waking thoughts | 848 | 4 |
| †Thence he arose, ascending high | 929 | 3 |
| Thence shall judgment be awarded | 933 | 5 |
| †Thence, when the glorious end | 739 | 6 |
| There afford us, Lord, a taste | 975 | 4 |
| †There all our griefs are spent | 482 | 5 |
| There all our sorrows end | 482 | 5 |
| †There all the ship's company meet | 49 | 3 |
| There almighty vengeance reigns | 633 | 2 |
| There angels at thy footstool bow | 544 | 1 |
| There angels at thy footstool bow | 544 | 5 |
| There angels to him sing | 942 | 9 |
| †There are briers besetting every path | 842 | 7 |
| There are no bonds for me | 842 | 8 |
| There are no pardons in the tomb | 792 | 3 |
| There are who suffer for thy sake | 483 | 4 |
| There arrest, the fugitive | 633 | 3 |
| There breathing peace around | 595 | 3 |

| | Hymn | Verse |
|---|---|---|
| There by faith for ever dwell | 27 | 4 |
| There by wrestling faith obtain | 529 | 3 |
| There crowns with everlasting bliss | 595 | 3 |
| †There dwells my Lord, my King | 942 | 9 |
| †There dwells the Lord our King | 800 | 7 |
| There dwells the Lord our Righteousness | 404 | 3 |
| †There everlasting spring abides | 938 | 2 |
| There faith prevails, and love adores | 644 | 4 |
| There for ever purified | 987 | 4 |
| There for ever to abide | 722 | 3 |
| There for me the Saviour stands | 168 | 4 |
| There for sinners thou art pleading | 722 | 3 |
| There for thee alone we look | 876 | 2 |
| There from their travels cease | 942 | 10 |
| There, from the rivers of his grace | 12 | 3 |
| There great and holy things are heard | 595 | 3 |
| There gushed a crimson flood | 892 | 4 |
| †There happier bowers than Eden's bloom | 939 | 3 |
| †There he helps our feeble moans | 758 | 5 |
| There he prepares the fruitful rain | 225 | 3 |
| †There his triumphal chariot waits | 557 | 7 |
| There I have set the lamp divine | 629 | 8 |
| †There, in the place beside thy throne | 283 | 3 |
| *There is a book who runs may read | 662 | 1 |
| There is a calm, a sure retreat | 825 | 1 |
| There is a cross in every lot | 842 | 7 |
| *There is a fountain filled with blood | 798 | 1 |
| There is a hand, unseen, that saves | 1003 | 1 |
| *There is a land of pure delight | 938 | 1 |
| †There is a place where Jesus sheds | 825 | 2 |
| †There is a spot where spirits blend | 825 | 3 |
| †There is a stream, whose gentle flow | 569 | 4 |
| †There is my house and portion fair | 68 | 7 |
| There is neither bond nor free | 518 | 9 |
| There is no other God but one | 254 | 1 |
| There is the consuming fire | 633 | 2 |
| †There is the throne of David | 943 | 10 |
| There let holy tempers rise | 349 | 1 |
| †There let it for thy glory burn | 327 | 2 |
| There let them all be seen | 452 | 6 |
| There let the valleys sing in gentler chorus Alleluia | 663 | — |
| †There let the way appear | 848 | 3 |
| †There, like a trumpet loud and strong | 226 | 6 |
| There milk and honey flow | 800 | 6 |
| There my exalted Saviour stands | 947 | 3 |
| There none obtain thy aid, none sing thy praise | 596 | 2 |
| There no tumult can alarm thee | 597 | 1 |
| There only, I covet to rest | 228 | 3 |
| There on the golden altar laid | 860 | 2 |
| †There saints and angels join | 731 | 7 |
| †There shall the horn of David bud | 629 | 8 |
| There should I rest in peace | 942 | 5 |
| †There should temptations cease | 942 | 5 |

| | Hymn | Verse |
|---|---|---|
| There sighing grief shall weep no more | 386 | 5 |
| †There sup with us in love divine | 948 | 2 |
| There the endless reign begin | 730 | 2 |
| There the humble walk secure | 349 | 2 |
| There the pale planet rules the night | 226 | 8 |
| †There the pompous triumph waits | 718 | 2 |
| †There, the rough mountains of the deep | 226 | 9 |
| †There the simple cannot stray | 849 | 2 |
| †There, there at his feet | 491 | 6 |
| †There, there before the throne thou art | 773 | 4 |
| †There, there on eagle-wing we soar | 825 | 4 |
| There they behold thy mercy-seat | 864 | 1 |
| There they shall in raptures live | 941 | 1 |
| There thou dost our place prepare | 722 | 8 |
| †There thou hast bid the globes of light | 226 | 8 |
| There thou sittest on thy throne | 683 | 2 |
| There thy blood-bought right maintain | 824 | 4 |
| There thy face unclouded see | 718 | 10 |
| There thy quicker hand would find | 633 | 8 |
| There to be with him who never | 878 | 8 |
| †There to reap in joy for ever | 878 | 8 |
| There to reign enthroned with thee | 601 | 5 |
| There we in Jesu's praise shall join | 947 | 6 |
| †There we shall meet again | 536 | 4 |
| There we shall see each other's face | 535 | 4 |
| †There we shall see his face | 12 | 8 |
| †There we shall with thee remain | 718 | 10 |
| There we sit in heavenly places | 720 | 5 |
| There with him in glory stand | 720 | 5 |
| There with him we reign in love | 519 | 4 |
| †There your exalted Saviour see | 420 | 8 |
| Therefore are they next the throne | 76 | 2 |
| †Therefore my heart is very glad | 549 | 6 |
| †Therefore shall ye draw with joy | 197 | 4 |
| Therefore thy greatness will I sing | 487 | 8 |
| †Therefore we come, thy gentle call obeying | 850 | 6 |
| Therefore will not say thee nay | 824 | 1 |
| These are the temple of the Lord | 94 | 1 |
| These are they that bore the cross | 76 | 1 |
| †These clouds of pride and sin dispel | 785 | 2 |
| These endless doubts and fears to end | 128 | 8 |
| These eyes shall see them all | 536 | 6 |
| †These eyes shall see them fall | 536 | 6 |
| These for sin could not atone | 709 | 2 |
| These freshest tokens of thy love | 875 | 2 |
| These freshest tokens of thy love | 1016 | 1 |
| These gushing tears are wiped away | 482 | 6 |
| These hallowed courts shall ring | 991 | 2 |
| These heavens, and meted out the skies | 1001 | 6 |
| These heirs of immortality | 474 | 1 |
| These horrid clouds that press my frighted soul | 596 | 1 |
| These hours to hallow; bless them still | 951 | 5 |
| These like clouds o'er noontide blaze | 817 | 6 |

| | Hymn | Verse |
|---|---|---|
| These lips his praises shall rehearse | 536 | 6 |
| †These lively hopes we owe | 930 | 5 |
| These presenting with thine own | 198 | 7 |
| These solemn, these devoted hours | 955 | 1 |
| †These temples of his grace | 578 | 2 |
| These things shall vanish all | 856 | 4 |
| †These walls we to thy honour raise | 994 | 2 |
| These withering limbs with thee I trust | 584 | 6 |
| These wondrous gatherings day by day | 695 | 1 |
| These words shall still sustain me | 923 | 4 |
| These wretched souls of ours | 411 | 1 |
| They all are robed in purest white | 948 | 5 |
| They all at once thy glory see | 460 | 3 |
| They all exulting stand | 800 | 9 |
| They all our steps attend | 21 | 5 |
| They all shall soon escape to land | 947 | 5 |
| They all were of one heart and soul | 16 | 3 |
| They and we are in thine hand | 738 | 2 |
| They are, and shall be still sustained | 997 | 1 |
| They are born from the skies | 231 | 9 |
| They are restrained to none | 216 | 1 |
| They call us to deliver | 747 | 1 |
| They cannot break the firm decree | 401 | 4 |
| They cannot change a sinful heart | 92 | 6 |
| They cannot harm, for God is there | 272 | 2 |
| They cannot keep a blessing back | 832 | 4 |
| They cannot purchase love | 92 | 6 |
| They cannot reach the mystery | 147 | 2 |
| They cast their crowns before the throne | 926 | 4 |
| †They chant the splendours of thy name | 636 | 2 |
| They close pursue the Lamb | 948 | 5 |
| They could not speak a greater word | 421 | 2 |
| †They drink the vivifying stream | 948 | 6 |
| They ever cry | 800 | 12 |
| They evermore proclaim | 34 | 8 |
| They felt it sprinkled through the skies | 721 | 5 |
| They find with Christ in paradise | 926 | 2 |
| They flourish in perpetual bloom | 948 | 4 |
| They fly forgotten, as a dream | 41 | 6 |
| They from all their toils are freed | 51 | 1 |
| †They go from strength to strength | 591 | 3 |
| They hang the trumpet in the hall | 740 | 6 |
| They have all their sufferings past | 76 | 3 |
| They have heard the glad sound | 219 | 3 |
| They have learned the angel-art | 817 | 1 |
| They have liberty found | 219 | 3 |
| They hear the word thy lips have said | 875 | 1 |
| They in the rest of Paradise who dwell | 663 | — |
| They joyfully conspired to raise | 16 | 2 |
| They kindle to a flame | 800 | 11 |
| They know not that by me they live | 88 | 1 |
| They know thou art not slow to hear | 1002 | 3 |
| They lean upon their helper God | 592 | 4 |

| | Hymn | Verse |
|---|---|---|
| They listen, and heaven Springs up in their heart. | 40 | 4 |
| They lived, and spake, and thought the same | 16 | 2 |
| They lodge in Jesu's breast. | 62 | 1 |
| They make thee spill thy blood in vain | 82 | 3 |
| They mangle their own flesh, and slay | 442 | 2 |
| †They marked the footsteps that he trod | 940 | 4 |
| They mount above the sky. | 941 | 1 |
| They never can be freed | 345 | 2 |
| They never could prevail | 271 | 2 |
| They never shall confound me | 923 | 2 |
| They now engross him whole | 108 | 3 |
| They now to mortals bring. | 684 | 2 |
| They, numerous as at morning light | 613 | 2 |
| They our happy brother greet | 51 | 4 |
| They perish, whom thyself hast bought | 82 | 4 |
| They pluck the ambrosial fruit | 948 | 6 |
| They pour effectual prayers | 202 | 3 |
| They praise thee still, And happy they | 591 | 2 |
| They reign in the smile of their Lord | 78 | 5 |
| They saw, and kindled at the sight. | 721 | 4 |
| †They saw him in the courts above | 721 | 5 |
| They saw thee, and they trembled. | 587 | 5 |
| They see their dear Lord, And follow the Lamb | 40 | 3 |
| They shall as their right Thy righteousness claim | 198 | 3 |
| They shall be blest indeed | 526 | 1 |
| They shall extol thy power | 543 | 8 |
| They shall thy appearing feel | 623 | 5 |
| They show the labour of thy hands | 263 | 3 |
| They sing the Lamb in hymns above | 15 | 2 |
| †They stand, those halls of Zion | 943 | 9 |
| They strongly speak for me | 202 | 3 |
| They tell us of the dread "decease" | 698 | 5 |
| †They that be whole, thyself hast said | 396 | 2 |
| They the heights of glory see | 260 | 3 |
| They their latest foe o'ercame | 53 | 3 |
| They their silent homage pay | 75 | 8 |
| They throng the air, and darken heaven | 314 | 4 |
| They thunder, they lighten, The waters o'erflow | 869 | 3 |
| They too their willing head should bow | 947 | 5 |
| They too the prize shall gain | 947 | 5 |
| They tremble at his power. | 278 | 2 |
| They triumph by his glorious wounds | 721 | 2 |
| They tyrannize their hour. | 815 | 2 |
| They were bound, but thou hast freed them | 878 | 1 |
| They will not stay behind | 947 | 4 |
| They, with united breath | 940 | 3 |
| They wrestled hard, as we do now. | 940 | 2 |
| Thine all the merits, mine the great reward | 794 | 7 |
| Thine, and only thine, I am | 434 | 1 |
| †Thine anger casts the sinner down. | 670 | 2 |
| †Thine arm hath safely brought us. | 276 | 3 |
| Thine arm, unseen, conveyed me safe | 657 | 5 |
| Thine arms are my defence. | 820 | 6 |

| | Hymn | Verse |
|---|---|---|
| Thine attributes proclaim | 249 | 2 |
| Thine awful judgments are abroad | 986 | 1 |
| †Thine earthly Sabbaths, Lord, we love | 959 | 2 |
| Thine eternal house above | 601 | 5 |
| Thine everlasting praise | 253 | 4 |
| Thine everlasting reign | 727 | 7 |
| Thine everlasting throne | 216 | 8 |
| Thine everlasting truth we prove | 1001 | 5 |
| Thine eye diffused a quickening ray | 201 | 4 |
| Thine eye doth all things see | 239 | 4 |
| †Thine eye observed from far | 191 | 3 |
| Thine hand confess | 736 | 1 |
| Thine hand our lives did cover | 276 | 3 |
| Thine heart-renewing power | 253 | 3 |
| Thine heritage the Gentiles take | 749 | 5 |
| Thine I live, thrice happy I | 430 | 5 |
| Thine image in my soul to see | 155 | 3 |
| Thine image in thy Son I claim | 284 | 6 |
| Thine image to my soul restore | 110 | 6 |
| Thine image to regain | 311 | 5 |
| Thine image to regain | 834 | 1 |
| Thine image to retrieve | 92 | 4 |
| Thine in whom I live and move | 358 | 5 |
| Thine is the loom, the forge, the mart | 863 | 2 |
| Thine is the power: behold, I sit | 675 | 8 |
| Thine is the work, and only thine | 132 | 5 |
| †Thine it is, O Lord, to save | 542 | 3 |
| Thine let our offspring be | 889 | 3 |
| †Thine, Lord, is wisdom, thine alone | 241 | 2 |
| Thine, Lord, we are, and ours thou art | 237 | 2 |
| Thine may we die, thine may we live | 26 | 8 |
| Thine officers to ordain | 871 | 1 |
| Thine oil anoints my head | 555 | 4 |
| Thine only love request | 179 | 3 |
| Thine only may I live and die | 375 | 5 |
| †Thine, only thine, we pant to be | 654 | 2 |
| Thine open hand supplies | 1022 | — |
| Thine ordinance to crown | 477 | 1 |
| †Thine own a moment claim | 892 | 2 |
| Thine own from Satan's tyranny | 690 | 2 |
| Thine own immortal strength put on | 386 | 1 |
| Thine own in a strange land | 106 | 5 |
| †Thine the kingdom, power, and glory | 748 | 2 |
| Thine the merit of his blood | 921 | 2 |
| Thine the ransomed nations are | 748 | 2 |
| Thine the righteousness of God | 921 | 2 |
| Thine the sharp thorns, and mine the golden crown | 794 | 7 |
| Thine the work, the praise is thine | 358 | 5 |
| Thine through all eternity | 517 | 4 |
| Thine utmost counsel to fulfil | 59 | 5 |
| Thine utmost miracle of love | 159 | 1 |
| Thine was the work, and thine alone | 702 | 2 |
| Thine we are, a heaven-born race | 661 | 3 |

| | HYMN | VERSE |
|---|---|---|
| Thine we are, thou Son of God | 350 | 4 |
| Thine wholly, thine alone, I am | 344 | 7 |
| Thine wholly, thine alone, I am | 373 | 1 |
| Thine, wholly thine, I long to be | 332 | 1 |
| Thine, wholly thine, shall be | 229 | 4 |
| Thine, wholly thine, shall be | 979 | 5 |
| Thine, wholly thine, to die and live | 473 | 5 |
| Thine, wholly thine, to live and die | 332 | 1 |
| Thine, whose eyes in darkness see | 244 | 3 |
| Things in heaven, and earth, and hell | 195 | 1 |
| †Things that are not, as though they were | 360 | 6 |
| †Think, good Jesu, my salvation | 933 | 9 |
| Think of that tremendous bar | 605 | 7 |
| Think on us, who think on thee | 900 | 1 |
| Think their houses shall endure | 67 | 1 |
| Thirsting, as for dews of even | 743 | 2 |
| This all my hope, and all my plea | 346 | 1 |
| This anchor shall my soul sustain | 189 | 6 |
| This awful God is ours | 12 | 2 |
| †This blessed word be mine | 421 | 2 |
| This blessing, above all | 301 | 4 |
| This blest cup of sacrifice | 904 | 2 |
| This choicest fruit of faith bestow | 307 | 2 |
| This consecrated hour | 771 | 4 |
| This day hath God fulfilled his promised word | 691 | 2 |
| This day is born a Saviour, Christ the Lord | 691 | 2 |
| †This day the covenant I sign | 909 | 4 |
| †This day with this day's bread | 653 | 4 |
| *This day with this day's bread | 1010 | — |
| †This delight I fain would prove | 167 | 4 |
| This dungeon of despairing grief | 129 | 5 |
| This earth, he cries, is not my place | 947 | 1 |
| This earth, we know, is not our place | 71 | 2 |
| This earth without my God | 117 | 1 |
| †This eucharistic feast | 898 | 2 |
| This fainting soul of mine | 436 | 6 |
| This from the other days of woe | 951 | 3 |
| This fruit of righteousness | 630 | 1 |
| This glorious hope affords | 58 | 3 |
| This God-like miracle of love | 656 | 4 |
| †This happiness in part is mine | 68 | 2 |
| This hardness shall depart | 110 | 4 |
| This havoc of his creatures see | 442 | 3 |
| †This heart shall be his constant home | 405 | 2 |
| This heavenly land from ours | 938 | 2 |
| This he gives you | 791 | 3 |
| This holy flame, this heavenly fire | 878 | 4 |
| This horror of offending God | 172 | 4 |
| This house still let thy presence fill | 431 | 3 |
| This I always will require | 27 | 4 |
| This instant now by him I live | 726 | 3 |
| †This instant now I may receive | 726 | 3 |
| This is my confidence of hope | 928 | 3 |

|  | Hymn | Verse |
|---|---|---|
| This is my joy in dying | 923 | 4 |
| This is my only plea | 162 | 2 |
| This is my Son: O hear ye him | 698 | 6 |
| This is not our place | 498 | 1 |
| This is the acceptable day | 2 | 9 |
| †This is the bond of perfectness | 504 | 6 |
| This is the day our God hath made | 616 | 8 |
| This is the day our rising Lord | 954 | 1 |
| †This is the day the Lord hath made | 953 | 2 |
| †This is the day which God hath blessed | 954 | 2 |
| †This is the dear redeeming grace | 406 | 3 |
| †This is the faith we humbly seek | 774 | 5 |
| *This is the field, the world below | 935 | 1 |
| This is the gospel grace | 630 | 3 |
| This is the song, the heavenly song, that Christ the King approves: Alleluia | 663 | — |
| This is the strain, the eternal strain, the Lord Almighty loves: Alleluia | 663 | — |
| †This is the strait and royal way | 330 | 6 |
| †This is the time: I surely may | 782 | 3 |
| †This is the time; no more delay | 2 | 9 |
| This is the total sum | 797 | 3 |
| This is the victory | 277 | 6 |
| This is their supreme delight | 941 | 3 |
| This is thy grand prerogative | 656 | 2 |
| This is thy will and faithful word | 366 | 1 |
| †This is thy will, I know | 105 | 4 |
| This lesson from above | 822 | 1 |
| This man receiveth sinners still | 32 | 1 |
| This mark of true perfection find | 363 | 1 |
| This moment be subdued | 417 | 4 |
| This moment cleanse me from my sin | 780 | 2 |
| This moment end my legal years | 404 | 4 |
| This moment I receive | 409 | 5 |
| †This moment I thy truth confess | 409 | 5 |
| This moment let it be | 362 | 1 |
| This moment let it be | 362 | 8 |
| †This moment, Lord, thou ready art | 782 | 2 |
| This moment turn to thee | 105 | 4 |
| This mountain, sin, remove | 417 | 1 |
| This my one, my ceaseless prayer | 352 | 3 |
| This only plague I pray remove | 161 | 5 |
| This only portion, Lord, be mine | 147 | 3 |
| This only shall be all my plea | 175 | 5 |
| †This only thing do I require | 17 | 7 |
| This, only this be given | 403 | 6 |
| This, only this, dost thou require | 38 | 5 |
| This, only this, is all my plea | 115 | 1 |
| This, only this, will I require | 285 | 8 |
| †This only woe I deprecate | 161 | 5 |
| †This pain, this consecrated pain | 331 | 3 |
| This pledge accepted, daily bring | 892 | 6 |
| This rebel heart by love subdue | 186 | 4 |

| | Hymn | Verse |
|---|---|---|
| This ruinous earth and skies | 64 | 7 |
| This shall stand, and only this | 516 | 1 |
| This short-enduring world can give | 285 | 6 |
| This slumber from my soul | 305 | 1 |
| †This slumber from my soul O shake | 306 | 2 |
| This solemn moment fly | 949 | 3 |
| This spark of heavenly fire | 368 | 1 |
| *This stone to thee in faith we lay | 993 | 1 |
| This stubborn soul of mine | 270 | 3 |
| This sudden tide of care | 296 | 1 |
| This tabernacle, sink below | 74 | 1 |
| This the crown I fain would seize | 167 | 3 |
| This, the day of Pentecost | 86 | 1 |
| This the new, the gospel song | 623 | 2 |
| †This the universal bliss | 20 | 4 |
| This the word; I claim it now | 352 | 1 |
| *This, this is he that came | 705 | 1 |
| †This, this is our high calling's prize | 284 | 6 |
| *This, this is the God we adore | 660 | — |
| This, this may be our endless song | 751 | 3 |
| This thy primitive design | 18 | 2 |
| This to all mankind is known | 197 | 5 |
| This travail and pain, This trembling and strife | 273 | 4 |
| This unbelief remove | 403 | 4 |
| This universe was made | 950 | 2 |
| This veil of unbelief remove | 113 | 1 |
| This weary world we cast behind | 71 | 4 |
| This well-wrought frame decay | 930 | 1 |
| This work shall make my heart rejoice | 577 | 5 |
| Thither all our wishes fly | 519 | 4 |
| Thither he bids us rise | 976 | 3 |
| Thither, Lord! guide my way | 942 | 13 |
| †Thither may we repair | 52 | 6 |
| †Thither our faithful souls he leads | 976 | 3 |
| Thither our steady course we steer | 71 | 3 |
| †Thither the tribes repair | 619 | 3 |
| †Those amaranthine bowers | 67 | 5 |
| Those everlasting lines | 659 | 4 |
| †Those feeble types, and shadows old | 702 | 5 |
| Those gloomy thoughts that rise | 938 | 5 |
| †Those mighty orbs proclaim thy power | 263 | 2 |
| Those under-regions of the skies | 226 | 4 |
| †Those vessels soon fail, Though full of thy light | 869 | 2 |
| Those who disregard thy frown | 463 | 4 |
| Those who dwell in her he blesses | 595 | 2 |
| Those who now are one in thee | 514 | 1 |
| Those who set at nought and sold him | 66 | 2 |
| †Thou all our works in us hast wrought | 435 | 5 |
| Thou all-sufficient art | 137 | 12 |
| Thou all-sufficient Love Divine | 209 | 1 |
| Thou all the debt hast paid | 162 | 2 |
| Thou alone the way canst show | 158 | 1 |
| Thou, and only thou, art great | 727 | 1 |

| | Hymn | Verse |
|---|---|---|
| Thou, and thy ark of perfect power | 629 | 2 |
| †Thou art a cooling fountain | 958 | 3 |
| Thou art a Spirit pure | 239 | 2 |
| Thou art all in all to me | 434 | 4 |
| Thou art, and hast for me | 806 | 2 |
| Thou art, and still shalt be | 407 | 6 |
| Thou art, and wilt for ever be | 175 | 2 |
| Thou art bidden to the feast | 520 | 1 |
| Thou art by thy great Father known | 668 | 1 |
| †Thou art coming to a King | 824 | 2 |
| Thou art crowned with life and love | 52 | 4 |
| †Thou art darkness in my mind | 382 | 2 |
| Thou art entered into joy | 50 | 5 |
| Thou art everywhere concealed | 876 | 2 |
| Thou art full of truth and grace | 143 | 3 |
| Thou art God in every place | 633 | 1 |
| Thou art God unchangeable | 355 | 3 |
| Thou art gone up on high | 583 | 1 |
| *Thou art gone up on high | 757 | 1 |
| Thou art grieved, yet I am blest | 768 | 9 |
| Thou art Indwelling Sin | 382 | 1 |
| Thou art in me; thy supplies | 193 | 3 |
| Thou art in the midst of foes | 829 | 1 |
| Thou art Lord of winds and waves | 878 | 1 |
| †Thou art merciful to all | 242 | 4 |
| Thou art my castle and defence | 551 | 1 |
| †Thou art my daily Bread | 193 | 5 |
| Thou art my Father and my God | 577 | 2 |
| †Thou art my God, and thee I praise | 616 | 12 |
| Thou art my God, I sing thy grace | 616 | 12 |
| Thou art my health, my sun, my song | 838 | 4 |
| Thou art my help; my Saviour thou | 566 | 10 |
| *Thou art my hiding-place: in thee | 561 | 7 |
| Thou art my Lord, my God | 85 | 2 |
| Thou art my Lord, my only good | 549 | 1 |
| Thou art my pardoning Lord | 179 | 2 |
| Thou art my Son, begot this day | 541 | 3 |
| Thou art my soul's bright morning star | 213 | 2 |
| Thou art my support and rest | 187 | 4 |
| Thou art my Way, my leader be | 312 | 6 |
| Thou art now, as yesterday | 166 | 1 |
| Thou art, O Christ, our all in all | 533 | 2 |
| †Thou art our flesh and bone | 723 | 6 |
| Thou art ours, and we are thine | 179 | 3 |
| Thou art scattering, full and free | 790 | 1 |
| Thou art sin and sinfulness | 382 | 2 |
| Thou art still our rock on high | 570 | 6 |
| †Thou art the anchor of my hope | 815 | 3 |
| †Thou art the Eternal Light | 737 | 2 |
| Thou art the God of light | 596 | 1 |
| Thou art the God of love | 596 | 3 |
| Thou art the God of power | 596 | 2 |
| Thou art the God, thou art the Lord | 494 | 3 |

|  | HYMN | VERSE |
|---|---|---|
| Thou art the good I seek below | 290 | 8 |
| †Thou art the Life; the rending tomb | 671 | 3 |
| †Thou art the Truth; thy word alone | 671 | 2 |
| *Thou art the Way; by thee alone | 671 | 1 |
| †Thou art the Way, the Truth, the Life | 671 | 4 |
| Thou art their Lord, their God and King | 450 | 3 |
| †Thou art thyself the Way | 48 | 6 |
| Thou art to all already given | 902 | 5 |
| Thou art to heaven gone | 728 | 6 |
| Thou art wisdom, power, and love | 358 | 5 |
| Thou art worthy to receive | 722 | 4 |
| Thou art worthy to receive | 748 | 7 |
| Thou, a Spirit invisible | 242 | 1 |
| Thou beam of the eternal beam | 494 | 6 |
| Thou before my foes dost feed | 554 | 5 |
| Thou bidd'st descend the fruitful shower | 241 | 3 |
| *Thou bidd'st me ask, and with the word | 778 | 1 |
| Thou bidd'st me now the land possess | 293 | 3 |
| Thou bidd'st us ask thy grace, and have | 118 | 4 |
| †Thou bidd'st us knock and enter in | 118 | 4 |
| Thou Bread of life, and Well | 1014 | — |
| Thou break'st my heart of stone | 106 | 7 |
| Thou by the earth art owned | 613 | 1 |
| Thou, by thy dying, death hast slain | 353 | 3 |
| Thou by thy threatenings move | 103 | 1 |
| Thou, by thy two-edged sword | 105 | 1 |
| Thou by thy voice the marble rent | 105 | 1 |
| Thou by thy word upholdest all | 235 | 1 |
| Thou callest by their name | 860 | 6 |
| †Thou callest me to seek thy face | 214 | 4 |
| Thou canst for thine own people do | 475 | 3 |
| †Thou canst from every sin secure | 820 | 2 |
| Thou canst make me understand | 358 | 5 |
| Thou canst make the blind to see | 790 | 4 |
| Thou canst not find the gate of heaven | 439 | 3 |
| Thou canst not in a moment save | 776 | 1 |
| Thou canst not let me sin | 282 | 4 |
| Thou canst not then deny the rest | 294 | 5 |
| †Thou canst not toil in vain | 739 | 5 |
| †Thou canst o'ercome this heart of mine | 139 | 4 |
| Thou canst save, and only thou | 620 | 1 |
| Thou canst save me in this hour | 158 | 1 |
| Thou canst the saving grace impart | 395 | 6 |
| Thou canst this instant now forgive | 395 | 6 |
| †Thou canst, thou wilt for one short day | 820 | 3 |
| †Thou canst, thou wilt, I dare believe | 416 | 6 |
| Thou canst, thou wilt, in me fulfil | 408 | 3 |
| Thou canst, thou wilt my helper be | 282 | 8 |
| Thou canst, thou wilt the sinner save | 189 | 3 |
| Thou canst, thou wouldst, this moment save | 118 | 4 |
| Thou cloth'st the lilies of the field | 236 | 3 |
| Thou cloth'st the lilies of the field | 1017 | 1 |
| Thou continuest still the same | 182 | 4 |

| | Hymn | Verse |
|---|---|---|
| Thou deathless Conqueror | 737 | 12 |
| Thou didst for all mankind atone | 902 | 1 |
| Thou didst free salvation bring | 722 | 1 |
| Thou didst from earth triumphant rise | 648 | 3 |
| Thou didst in our behalf appear | 981 | 4 |
| Thou didst not, Lord, refuse | 322 | 1 |
| Thou didst receive the full reward | 72 | 5 |
| Thou didst suffer to release us | 722 | 1 |
| †Thou didst the meek example leave | 330 | 4 |
| Thou didst, thou didst, thy peace impart | 865 | 4 |
| Thou didst thy work begin | 674 | 1 |
| †Thou didst undertake for me | 358 | 3 |
| Thou didst with all things part | 137 | 5 |
| Thou diedst, and couldst not die in vain | 380 | 6 |
| Thou diedst for love to me | 851 | 3 |
| *Thou doest all things well | 838 | 1 |
| Thou doest all things well | 838 | 8 |
| Thou dost all our fears control | 723 | 1 |
| Thou dost, and honour, give | 248 | 4 |
| Thou dost approve what I desire | 909 | 3 |
| Thou dost comfort me again | 197 | 1 |
| †Thou dost conduct thy people | 853 | 3 |
| Thou dost desire my worthless heart | 38 | 5 |
| Thou dost eternal life reveal | 261 | 2 |
| Thou dost even now thy banquet crown | 902 | 5 |
| Thou dost in all his glory reign | 648 | 4 |
| Thou dost, in heaven above | 239 | 5 |
| Thou dost it all alone | 270 | 3 |
| Thou dost not take delight to grieve | 307 | 4 |
| Thou dost our upright hearts unite | 513 | 1 |
| Thou dost, thy Father's image, shine | 648 | 4 |
| Thou dost thy sons sustain | 578 | 1 |
| Thou dost to thy poor servants bear | 470 | 9 |
| Thou dost to us make known | 248 | 6 |
| Thou dost with sinners bear | 250 | 2 |
| †Thou dost with sweet complacence see | 121 | 4 |
| Thou dwell'st for evermore | 239 | 3 |
| Thou enrol my humble name | 594 | 3 |
| Thou everlasting lover | 667 | 3 |
| †Thou everywhere hast sway | 831 | 6 |
| Thou fillest all, and thou alone | 90 | 2 |
| Thou for me a curse wast made | 215 | 4 |
| †Thou for our pain didst mourn | 737 | 3 |
| Thou from 'eternity hast been | 239 | 2 |
| Thou from sin dost save me now | 142 | 4 |
| †Thou gav'st the word, and must apply | 770 | 4 |
| Thou gentle, bleeding Lamb | 215 | 4 |
| Thou giv'st the mourner rest | 637 | 7 |
| Thou giv'st the power thy grace to move | 26 | 4 |
| *Thou God of glorious majesty | 59 | 1 |
| †Thou God of power, thou God of love | 190 | 10 |
| *Thou God of truth and love | 510 | 1 |
| *Thou God that answerest by fire | 412 | 1 |

| | Hymn | Verse |
|---|---|---|
| †Thou God that answerest by fire | 490 | 5 |
| *Thou God unsearchable, unknown | 130 | 1 |
| Thou gracious, bleeding Lamb | 436 | 3 |
| †Thou great and good, thou just and wise | 577 | 2 |
| Thou great Interpreter divine | 90 | 1 |
| Thou great Melchizedek | 682 | 2 |
| *Thou great mysterious God unknown | 97 | 1 |
| *Thou great Redeemer, dying Lamb | 682 | 1 |
| †Thou great tremendous God | 103 | 3 |
| †Thou hast a great deliverance wrought | 293 | 2 |
| Thou hast a table spread | 905 | 2 |
| Thou hast all thy blessings shed | 53 | 2 |
| Thou hast atonement made | 818 | 4 |
| Thou hast been troubled, tempted, tried | 969 | 6 |
| Thou hast blotted out my sin | 197 | 1 |
| Thou hast borne their spirits hence | 53 | 2 |
| †Thou hast bowed the dying head | 711 | 4 |
| Thou hast brought back to life again | 438 | 1 |
| Thou hast brought me to thine inn | 112 | 6 |
| Thou hast brought to life again | 717 | 1 |
| Thou hast displayed thy power | 732 | 3 |
| †Thou hast employed thy servants | 736 | 2 |
| Thou hast exalted him | 717 | 2 |
| Thou hast filled a mortal bier | 711 | 4 |
| Thou hast for all a ransom paid | 190 | 5 |
| Thou hast for all a ransom paid | 774 | 8 |
| Thou hast for Jesu's sake forgiven | 245 | 3 |
| Thou hast for me a ransom paid | 330 | 2 |
| Thou hast for sinners died | 162 | 4 |
| Thou hast full atonement made | 215 | 1 |
| Thou hast full atonement made | 722 | 2 |
| Thou hast glorified thy Son | 50 | 1 |
| Thou hast, in honour of thy Son | 377 | 1 |
| Thou hast in Jesus given | 360 | 3 |
| Thou hast in part fulfilled | 460 | 1 |
| †Thou hast in triumph led | 583 | 2 |
| †Thou hast in unbelief shut up | 150 | 3 |
| Thou hast in us thy arm revealed | 493 | 2 |
| Thou hast made the sinner whole | 215 | 1 |
| Thou hast more than conquered death | 52 | 4 |
| †Thou hast my flesh, thy hallowed shrine | 431 | 3 |
| Thou hast my full ransom paid | 215 | 4 |
| Thou hast my spirit, there display | 431 | 2 |
| Thou hast my succour been | 292 | 3 |
| †Thou hast obtained the grace | 162 | 3 |
| †Thou hast o'erthrown the foe | 737 | 4 |
| Thou hast once for sinners died | 182 | 4 |
| †Thou hast on us the grace bestowed | 248 | 5 |
| †Thou hast our bonds in sunder broke | 493 | 4 |
| Thou hast our sickness borne | 737 | 3 |
| †Thou hast pronounced the mourners blest | 134 | 2 |
| Thou hast raised me from my fall | 215 | .1 |
| Thou hast received for men | 757 | 2 |

| | Hymn | Verse |
|---|---|---|
| Thou hast saved me by thy grace | 112 | 5 |
| Thou hast saved me heretofore | 142 | 4 |
| Thou hast shed the human tear | 711 | 3 |
| Thou hast spoiled, and captive led | 757 | 1 |
| Thou hast the Spirit, and the Word | 595 | 3 |
| Thou hast the words of endless life | 137 | 2 |
| Thou hast to each assigned | 536 | 2 |
| Thou hast vouchsafed a longer space | 982 | 1 |
| Thou hast withdrawn thy grace | 110 | 2 |
| Thou hatest all iniquity | 270 | 4 |
| †Thou hatest all that evil do | 543 | 3 |
| †Thou hear'st me for salvation pray | 416 | 3 |
| Thou hear'st thy children cry | 637 | 9 |
| Thou hear'st thy every creature's call | 235 | 1 |
| Thou heaven's gates hast opened wide | 737 | 4 |
| *Thou hidden God, for whom I groan | 150 | 1 |
| *Thou hidden love of God, whose height | 344 | 1 |
| *Thou hidden source of calm repose | 209 | 1 |
| †Thou holdest my soul In spiritual life | 200 | 5 |
| †Thou in Cana didst appear | 995 | 2 |
| Thou in the midst of us shalt be | 485 | 1 |
| Thou in thine abundant grace | 50 | 1 |
| Thou in thy flesh wast sent | 164 | 2 |
| †Thou, in thy youthful prime | 52 | 5 |
| Thou in whom we live and move | 598 | 1 |
| Thou jealous God, stir up thy power | 461 | 5 |
| *Thou, Jesu, art our King | 737 | 1 |
| *Thou, Jesu, thou my breast inspire | 440 | 1 |
| Thou, Jesus, hast blessed | 219 | 4 |
| Thou, Jesus, hast confounded | 276 | 4 |
| Thou, Jesus, love me as thy own | 305 | 5 |
| Thou, Jesus, thou alone, canst heal | 395 | 4 |
| Thou jubilant abyss of ocean, cry Alleluia | 663 | — |
| *Thou Judge of quick and dead | 55 | 1 |
| †Thou knowest all the future; gleams of gladness | 850 | 4 |
| †Thou knowest all the past; how long and blindly | 850 | 2 |
| †Thou knowest all the present, each temptation | 850 | 3 |
| *Thou knowest, Lord, the weariness and sorrow | 850 | 1 |
| †Thou knowest, not alone as God, all knowing | 850 | 5 |
| Thou knowest 'tis all my heart's desire | 17 | 7 |
| Thou knowest very well | 797 | 2 |
| Thou know'st (for all to thee is known) | 147 | 5 |
| †Thou know'st for my offence he died | 360 | 2 |
| Thou know'st how unsubdued my will | 99 | 3 |
| Thou know'st how wide my passions rove | 99 | 3 |
| Thou know'st I hunger, Lord, and thirst | 834 | 1 |
| Thou know'st, I never can forgive | 830 | 2 |
| †Thou know'st, in the spirit of prayer | 946 | 3 |
| Thou know'st, O Lord, and thou alone | 147 | 5 |
| Thou know'st that thee I love | 147 | 5 |
| †Thou know'st the baseness of my mind | 99 | 3 |
| Thou know'st the sense I mean | 632 | 3 |
| Thou know'st the Son, and must make known | 770 | 4 |

| | Hymn | Verse |
|---|---|---|
| Thou know'st the Spirit's will | 144 | 3 |
| †Thou know'st the pains thy servants feel | 637 | 9 |
| Thou know'st the trials yet behind | 916 | 5 |
| †Thou know'st the way to bring me back | 186 | 3 |
| Thou know'st who only bows the knee | 81 | 1 |
| *Thou Lamb of God, thou Prince of Peace | 338 | 1 |
| Thou laugh'st to scorn the gods of earth | 241 | 1 |
| Thou long hast known my desperate case | 166 | 2 |
| *Thou, Lord, art a shield for me | 542 | 1 |
| *Thou, Lord, hast blest my going out | 998 | 1 |
| Thou, Lord, hast lifted up my head | 289 | 4 |
| Thou, Lord, my refuge art | 634 | 3 |
| *Thou, Lord, my witness art | 627 | 1 |
| Thou, Lord, of life the fountain art | 364 | 1 |
| *Thou, Lord, on whom I still depend | 69 | 1 |
| Thou, Lord, on whom my soul is stayed | 227 | 6 |
| †Thou, Lord, our relief In trouble hast been | 19 | 2 |
| †Thou, Lord, the dreadful fight hast won | 338 | 5 |
| Thou, Lord, whose blood so freely flowed | 133 | 6 |
| Thou, Lord, with unexampled grace | 648 | 2 |
| †Thou loving, all-atoning Lamb | 33 | 3 |
| Thou lov'st to prop the feeble knee | 290 | 2 |
| †Thou lov'st whate'er thy hands have made | 239 | 6 |
| Thou majesty divine | 567 | 2 |
| *Thou Man of griefs, remember me | 181 | 1 |
| Thou Man of sorrows, say | 772 | 3 |
| Thou may'st smile at all my foes | 594 | 1 |
| Thou might'st leave me, but the rather | 790 | 2 |
| Thou must save and thou alone | 709 | 2 |
| Thou my curse and sin remove | 151 | 2 |
| Thou my debt of death hast paid | 215 | 1 |
| *Thou, my God, art good and wise | 243 | 1 |
| †Thou my impetuous spirit guide | 138 | 3 |
| Thou my keeper and my guide | 193 | 4 |
| †Thou my Life, my treasure be | 354 | 5 |
| Thou my life! O let me be | 904 | 2 |
| †Thou my one thing needful be | 434 | 2 |
| Thou my pain, my curse hast took | 27 | 1 |
| Thou my sure protection be | 271 | 3 |
| Thou my true Bethesda be | 166 | 1 |
| †Thou neither canst be felt nor seen | 239 | 2 |
| Thou never canst delight | 543 | 2 |
| Thou never canst unfaithful prove | 380 | 3 |
| Thou never, never wilt forsake | 227 | 7 |
| Thou never, never wilt forsake | 545 | 4 |
| Thou never wilt reprove | 360 | 11 |
| Thou now dost into some inspire | 81 | 2 |
| Thou, O Christ, art all in all | 518 | 10 |
| †Thou, O Christ, art all I want | 143 | 3 |
| †Thou, O God, art wise alone | 244 | 3 |
| Thou, O Lord, and thou alone | 601 | 2 |
| †Thou, O Lord, in tender love | 325 | 3 |
| †Thou, O Lord, my portion art | 325 | 4 |

| | Hymn | Verse |
|---|---|---|
| †Thou, O love, my portion art | 434 | 6 |
| †Thou, O my God, thou only art | 169 | 2 |
| Thou of comforters the best | 753 | 3 |
| Thou of life the fountain art | 143 | 4 |
| Thou omnipresent God of love | 861 | 3 |
| Thou on God hast set thy love | 597 | 3 |
| †Thou on my neck didst fall | 191 | 4 |
| †Thou on the Lord rely | 831 | 3 |
| Thou only art able to bless | 220 | 3 |
| Thou only art the great I AM | 332 | 4 |
| Thou only canst bestow | 778 | 2 |
| Thou only canst drive back the tide | 138 | 8 |
| Thou only canst inform the mind | 671 | 2 |
| Thou only canst my spirit fill | 405 | 8 |
| †Thou only canst our wills control | 505 | 3 |
| Thou only canst remove | 145 | 2 |
| Thou only canst remove | 150 | 2 |
| Thou only canst thyself reveal | 90 | 1 |
| †Thou only didst the blessing give | 465 | 8 |
| †Thou only dost the Father know | 668 | 2 |
| Thou only dost thyself explain | 255 | 2 |
| Thou only hast done all things right | 429 | 3 |
| Thou only hast power to relieve | 165 | 1 |
| †Thou only know'st, who didst obtain | 384 | 9 |
| †Thou only, Lord, the work hast done | 203 | 3 |
| †Thou, only thou, the kind and good | 744 | 3 |
| Thou, only thou, to me be given | 163 | 3 |
| Thou our life of grace maintain | 653 | 5 |
| Thou our long-sought Eden art | 515 | 3 |
| Thou our mortal griefs hast borne | 711 | 3 |
| Thou our only refuge art | 723 | 1 |
| Thou our sacrifice receive | 427 | 1 |
| †Thou our throbbing flesh hast worn | 711 | 3 |
| Thou pardoning God descend | 125 | 5 |
| Thou poor, despised, afflicted Man | 883 | 1 |
| Thou pouredst forth thy guiltless blood | 373 | 5 |
| Thou purging fire, thou quickening flame | 494 | 6 |
| †Thou rather wouldst that we were cold | 454 | 7 |
| Thou reachest out my cup of bliss | 548 | 2 |
| Thou reign'st with God most high | 737 | 5 |
| Thou rulest my passion, My pride and self-will | 200 | 5 |
| †Thou Saviour of all | 219 | 6 |
| Thou sav'st me from sickness, From sin dost retrieve | 200 | 4 |
| Thou sav'st the souls whose humble love | 637 | 10 |
| Thou seest, at last, I willing am | 332 | 1 |
| †Thou seest I know not what to do | 836 | 3 |
| †Thou seest me deaf to thy command | 135 | 5 |
| †Thou seest me helpless and distrest | 395 | 3 |
| †Thou seest my feebleness | 305 | 4 |
| Thou seest my heart's desire | 416 | 3 |
| Thou seest my wants, for help they call | 99 | 2 |
| †Thou seest our weakness, Lord | 831 | 14 |

| | Hymn | Verse |
|---|---|---|
| †Thou seest their wants, thou know'st their names | 458 | 2 |
| Thou seest the sore anguish I feel | 174 | 3 |
| †Thou shalt an iron sceptre sway | 541 | 4 |
| Thou shalt be, and thou art | 943 | 15 |
| Thou shalt call on him in trouble | 597 | 3 |
| Thou shalt cleanse me from all sin | 112 | 6 |
| Thou shalt dread no hidden snare | 597 | 1 |
| Thou shalt from heaven come down | 55 | 2 |
| Thou shalt save me evermore | 142 | 4 |
| Thou shalt the work of faith fulfil | 303 | 6 |
| Thou shalt thy Spirit give | 360 | 7 |
| *Thou Shepherd of Israel, and mine | 228 | 1 |
| †Thou shin'st with everlasting rays | 38 | 2 |
| †Thou sittest on the throne | 643 | 2 |
| Thou Son of David, have | 164 | 1 |
| Thou Son of David, have | 164 | 3 |
| Thou Son of David, hear | 135 | 9 |
| Thou Son of David, show | 164 | 3 |
| *Thou Son of God, whose flaming eyes | 83 | 1 |
| Thou source of unexhausted love | 779 | 2 |
| Thou sovereign Lord of all | 637 | 6 |
| †Thou Spirit of the Lord, go forth | 746 | 3 |
| Thou sprang'st into the jaws of death | 23 | 5 |
| †Thou standest in the holy place | 902 | 2 |
| Thou stand'st the ever-slaughtered Lamb | 708 | 2 |
| Thou still art bestowing, And giving us more | 199 | 1 |
| Thou still art ready to receive | 303 | 2 |
| Thou strength of his almighty hand | 752 | 3 |
| Thou surely wilt preserve thy own | 469 | 10 |
| Thou sweetly orderest all that is | 38 | 4 |
| Thou tell thy name to me | 297 | 5 |
| †Thou that a will in me hast wrought | 799 | 6 |
| Thou that dwellest in the skies | 620 | 1 |
| Thou that hast borne my sins away | 894 | 1 |
| Thou the acceptable year | 578 | 2 |
| Thou the anointing Spirit art | 751 | 1 |
| Thou the blood of life hast shed | 711 | 4 |
| Thou the dying thief forgavest | 933 | 13 |
| Thou, the Father's only Son | 194 | 5 |
| Thou the Gift, and Giver too | 758 | 6 |
| †Thou the good Shepherd art | 193 | 4 |
| Thou, the great eternal God | 423 | 1 |
| *Thou, the great, eternal Lord | 244 | 1 |
| †Thou the heart's most precious guest | 753 | 3 |
| Thou the living way hast showed | 723 | 2 |
| †Thou the sinful woman savedst | 933 | 13 |
| Thou, the Son of man, alone | 952 | 1 |
| Thou the sovereign Potentate | 727 | 1 |
| Thou the true, the heavenly Vine | 193 | 2 |
| Thou the victory hast won | 53 | 3 |
| Thou thine own dost lead secure | 737 | 4 |
| Thou, thou the King of Glory art | 648 | 1 |
| Thou thunderest, and amazed they fly | 241 | 1 |

| | Hymn | Verse |
|---|---|---|
| Thou thy confessors confess | 873 | 1 |
| Thou thy goodness hast displayed | 242 | 2 |
| †Thou thy messengers hast sent | 463 | 2 |
| Thou thyself my teacher be | 877 | 1 |
| Thou thyself within us move | 520 | 2 |
| Thou to thy chosen dost afford | 612 | 3 |
| Thou to us hast opened heaven | 723 | 2 |
| Thou to whom my every passion | 819 | 1 |
| Thou treasurest up my counted tears | 575 | 2 |
| *Thou, true and only God, lead'st forth | 241 | 1 |
| Thou vast, unfathomable sea | 184 | 9 |
| Thou vast unfathomable sea | 494 | 5 |
| *Thou very Paschal Lamb | 704 | 1 |
| †Thou waitest to be gracious still | 259 | 2 |
| Thou wast ere time began his race | 240 | 2 |
| Thou wast here their sure defence | 53 | 2 |
| Thou when Jesus doth appear | 382 | 3 |
| Thou, when the appointed hour was come | 353 | 2 |
| *Thou who art enthroned above | 598 | 1 |
| †Thou, who didst come to bring | 870 | 2 |
| †Thou who didst for all atone | 676 | 2 |
| †Thou who didst so greatly stoop | 413 | 2 |
| Thou, who dost the evil see | 733 | 2 |
| Thou who fillest all in all | 518 | 2 |
| Thou who for all hast died | 35 | 5 |
| Thou who for us hast died | 486 | 5 |
| †Thou who hast given me eyes to see | 662 | 4 |
| *Thou, who hast in Zion laid | 989 | 1 |
| †Thou who hast kept us to this hour | 483 | 5 |
| Thou who hast purchased life for all | 448 | 1 |
| †Thou, who hast our place prepared | 937 | 2 |
| Thou, who hast seen my evil ways | 180 | 4 |
| Thou who hast tasted death for me | 919 | 1 |
| Thou who hast the wine-press trod | 748 | 5 |
| †Thou who once didst shake the place | 733 | 3 |
| *Thou whose Almighty word | 870 | 1 |
| Thou wilt in me reveal thy name | 150 | 3 |
| Thou wilt in no wise cast me out | 163 | 5 |
| Thou wilt my guilty soul forgive | 410 | 1 |
| Thou wilt my offspring bless | 894 | 1 |
| †Thou wilt not break a bruised reed | 157 | 6 |
| Thou wilt not leave me in despair | 560 | 1 |
| Thou wilt not leave me in the grave | 548 | 5 |
| Thou wilt not suffer me to fall | 282 | 4 |
| Thou wilt not yet depart | 182 | 3 |
| Thou wilt perform thy faithful word | 380 | 7 |
| Thou wilt pity and forgive | 579 | 1 |
| Thou wilt redeem my soul | 136 | 9 |
| Thou wilt repeat thy sovereign word | 693 | 2 |
| Thou wilt return and claim me, Lord | 384 | 4 |
| Thou wilt the benefit bestow | 118 | 3 |
| Thou wilt the next bestow | 812 | — |
| †Thou wilt the path of life display | 548 | 6 |

|  | Hymn | Verse |
|---|---|---|
| Thou wilt the root remove | 674 | 1 |
| Thou wilt thy brethren make | 724 | 3 |
| Thou wilt thy light afford | 150 | 3 |
| Thou wilt, thyself impart | 356 | 7 |
| Thou wilt victorious prove | 139 | 4 |
| Thou without beginning art | 242 | 1 |
| Thou with perfect righteousness | 242 | 3 |
| Thou, with the Father, and the Son | 851 | 2 |
| Thou with thy promised Father come | 155 | 7 |
| Thou with unexampled grace | 737 | 3 |
| Though all my crimes before thee lie | 574 | 7 |
| Though all my simpleness I own | 163 | 4 |
| Though all the field should wither | 804 | 4 |
| Though bitter to the taste it be | 337 | 3 |
| Though dark and sad the night | 851 | 2 |
| †Though dark my path, and sad my lot | 841 | 2 |
| Though dear as life the idol be | 291 | 3 |
| Though death and hell obstruct the way | 675 | 9 |
| Though dust and ashes in thy sight | 865 | 1 |
| Though duteous to thy high command | 133 | 1 |
| †Though earth and hell the word gainsay | 401 | 3 |
| Though earth's self-righteous sons engage | 30 | 4 |
| †Though eighteen hundred years are past | 397 | 5 |
| Though every comfort be withdrawn | 189 | 5 |
| Though every prospect pleases | 747 | 2 |
| *Though God in Christ reveal | 806 | 1 |
| †Though great our sins and sore our wounds | 626 | 5 |
| Though heaven and earth shall pass away | 934 | 3 |
| Though I am cold and dead | 115 | 4 |
| Though I am slow of heart | 358 | 5 |
| Though I have done thee such despite | 161 | 1 |
| †Though I have grieved thy Spirit, Lord | 574 | 10 |
| †Though I have most unfaithful been | 161 | 3 |
| †Though I have steeled my stubborn heart | 161 | 2 |
| Though I resign my breath | 931 | 5 |
| Though I to thee the whole resign | 127 | 5 |
| †Though in affliction's furnace tried | 272 | 7 |
| Though in my flesh I feel the thorn | 230 | 2 |
| Though it seem to tarry long | 142 | 2 |
| Though joys be withered all and dead | 189 | 5 |
| †Though late, I all forsake | 137 | 9 |
| Though late, we deeply mourn | 983 | 5 |
| †Though like the wanderer | 848 | 2 |
| Though love wax cold, and faith grow dim | 698 | 6 |
| Though mercy long delay | 865 | 5 |
| Though most unworthy to draw near | 543 | 4 |
| Though my heart fail, and flesh decay | 189 | 6 |
| †Though my sins as mountains rise | 110 | 3 |
| †Though nature gives my God the lie | 815 | 5 |
| *Though nature's strength decay | 800 | 5 |
| Though now divided by the stream | 949 | 2 |
| Though now the Serpent bruise his heel | 280 | 4 |
| Though opposed by many a foe | 847 | 4 |

| | Hymn | Verse |
|---|---|---|
| Though our bodies continue below | 491 | 2 |
| Though returning to his throne | 718 | 4 |
| Though Satan rage, and kingdoms rise | 569 | 6 |
| Though sin and Satan still are near | 281 | 1 |
| Though sin assail, and hell, thrown wide | 272 | 7 |
| Though strength, and health, and friends be gone | 189 | 5 |
| Though sundered far, by faith they meet | 825 | 3 |
| †Though tempests shake the angry deep | 1003 | 3 |
| Though ten thousand be laid low | 597 | 2 |
| Though the eye of sinful man thy glory may not see | 646 | 3 |
| Though the gates of hell assail | 271 | 2 |
| Though the shattered earth remove | 67 | 2 |
| †Though the sons of night blaspheme | 728 | 4 |
| Though through thy deceit I fall | 274 | 3 |
| Though thy wrath against me burned | 197 | 1 |
| Though to man thou seemest slow | 299 | 6 |
| Though ungrateful we have been | 975 | 2 |
| †Though vine nor fig-tree neither | 804 | 4 |
| Though wandering on earth | 498 | 1 |
| †Though waves and storms go o'er my head | 189 | 5 |
| Thousands of rams his favour buy | 127 | 2 |
| Thousands on thousands pass away | 746 | 1 |
| Thousand thousand saints attending | 66 | 1 |
| †Three in person, one in power | 645 | 2 |
| Three, in simplest Unity | 260 | 2 |
| †Three Persons equally divine | 259 | 5 |
| †Thrice blessed, bliss-inspiring hope | 333 | 4 |
| †Thrice comfortable hope | 832 | 2 |
| †Thrice happy employ | 808 | 8 |
| Thrice happy he, O Lord of hosts | 591 | 5 |
| Thrice happy he who views with scorn | 344 | 7 |
| Thrice happy I am | 205 | 2 |
| Thrice happy who his guest retains | 14 | 6 |
| Thrice holy Fount, thrice holy Fire | 752 | 2 |
| Thrice Holy! thine the kingdom is | 237 | 3 |
| Thrice Holy! thine the kingdom is | 241 | 4 |
| Throned where earth must crouch below me | 570 | 6 |
| Throned with thy Father, through the round | 665 | 6 |
| Throned with thy Sire, through half the round | 665 | 1 |
| Through all eternity | 128 | 8 |
| Through all eternity | 179 | 3 |
| Through all eternity | 251 | 2 |
| Through all eternity | 572 | 4 |
| Through all eternity | 947 | 8 |
| Through all eternity pursue | 638 | 2 |
| Through all eternity the same | 616 | 12 |
| Through all eternity to prove | 141 | 7 |
| †Through all eternity, to thee | 657 | 10 |
| Through all her palaces | 573 | 3 |
| †Through all his mighty works | 650 | 3 |
| Through all its latent mazes there | 344 | 6 |
| Through all our coasts redundant stores | 978 | 3 |
| *Through all the changing scenes of life | 562 | 1 |

| | Hymn | Verse |
|---|---|---|
| Through all the courts of Paradise | 867 | 1 |
| Through all the earth abroad | 741 | 6 |
| Through all the paths of duty move | 306 | 5 |
| Through all the powers of earth and hell | 655 | 6 |
| Through all their land | 800 | 9 |
| Through all these spacious works of thine | 651 | 2 |
| Through all yon radiant circles move | 977 | 5 |
| Through a wilderness of cares | 238 | 2 |
| Through a world of dangers led | 238 | 2 |
| Through a world of dangers led | 1019 | 3 |
| Through blood, ye must the entrance gain | 277 | 5 |
| Through burning climes they pass unhurt | 1002 | 2 |
| Through Christ, the living Head | 822 | 2 |
| Through cloud and sunshine, O abide with me | 972 | 8 |
| Through constant watching wise | 842 | 2 |
| Through each kindred, tribe, and tongue | 604 | 1 |
| †Through each perplexing path of life | 664 | 8 |
| Through earth beneath, and heaven above | 337 | 1 |
| Through earth extended wide | 453 | 1 |
| Through earth triumphantly ride on | 568 | 4 |
| Through earth's sepulchres it ringeth | 933 | 8 |
| Through endless ages love | 262 | 1 |
| Through endless ages still the same | 235 | 1 |
| Through every conflict but the last | 849 | 5 |
| Through every fiery hour | 818 | 1 |
| Through every hallowed breast | 528 | 5 |
| Through every instrument of ill | 834 | — |
| Through every land, by every tongue | 615 | 1 |
| Through every nation send | 452 | 2 |
| †Through every period of my life | 657 | 9 |
| Through faith begotten from above | 368 | 4 |
| Through faith in him who died for all | 744 | 5 |
| Through faith in Jesu's name | 162 | 2 |
| Through faith in that all-saving blood | 860 | 2 |
| Through faith I see thee face to face | 141 | 3 |
| †Through fire and water bring | 436 | 8 |
| Through floods of temptation, And flames of desire | 273 | 7 |
| *Through God I will his word proclaim | 575 | 1 |
| †Through grace we hearken to thy voice | 208 | 8 |
| †Through hidden dangers, toils, and deaths | 657 | 6 |
| Through him who died our souls to save | 394 | 3 |
| Through his eternal Son | 266 | 1 |
| Through his preserving care | 661 | 2 |
| Through Jesu's blood | 800 | 8 |
| Through Jesus Christ the Just | 323 | 1 |
| Through Jesus Christ, thy Son | 821 | — |
| Through Jesus for acceptance cry | 121 | 4 |
| Through Jesus I can all things do | 293 | 5 |
| Through Jesus strengthening me | 356 | 9 |
| Through Jesus strengthening me | 432 | 3 |
| Through Jesus to thy throne apply | 121 | 4 |
| Through many a conflict here | 277 | 5 |
| †Through much distress and pain | 277 | 5 |

| | HYMN | VERSE |
|---|---|---|
| Through much tribulation, Through water and fire | 273 | 7 |
| Through night's lone silence brought | 587 | 2 |
| Through our ministerial hands | 873 | 3 |
| †Through pride and desire Unhurt we have gone | 481 | 3 |
| Through sin for ever die | 80 | 1 |
| Through skies, and seas, and solid ground | 226 | 10 |
| Through sleep and darkness safely brought | 965 | 2 |
| Through ten thousand thousand snares | 238 | 2 |
| Through the atoning blood | 307 | 1 |
| Through the blood of the Lamb | 219 | 3 |
| *Through the day thy love hath spared us | 970 | 1 |
| Through the last courses of the sun | 868 | 4 |
| Through the life of him who died | 904 | 1 |
| Through the long round of endless days | 868 | 5 |
| Through the low vale of humble love | 317 | 2 |
| Through the mortal vale I go | 554 | 4 |
| Through the name we ever bless | 826 | — |
| Through the silent watches guard us | 970 | 1 |
| Through the Spirit, ever one | 817 | 8 |
| Through the virtue of thy blood | 722 | 2 |
| Through the week our praise demand | 975 | 2 |
| Through the whole earth his goodness shines | 637 | 2 |
| Through the wild sea thou leddest | 587 | 6 |
| Through the world far and wide | 870 | 4 |
| Through thee I will thy word proclaim | 575 | 3 |
| Through thee we now together came | 536 | 1 |
| †Through thee we now together came | 537 | 2 |
| Through thee we shall | 853 | 3 |
| †Through thee, who all our sins hast borne | 71 | 5 |
| Through thee, who know'st our every need | 236 | 3 |
| Through thee, who know'st our every need | 1017 | 2 |
| Through this dark vale of tears | 591 | 3 |
| †Through this life's ever-varying scene | 692 | 5 |
| Through thy incarnate Son | 248 | 6 |
| Through thy intercession, live | 676 | 1 |
| Through thy meritorious pain | 676 | 2 |
| Through thy well-beloved Son | 890 | 1 |
| Through torrents of temptation | 853 | 3 |
| Through unbelief I stagger not | 360 | 8 |
| Through varied deaths my soul hath led | 289 | 1 |
| Through water and fire In him we went on | 481 | 3 |
| †Through waves, and clouds, and storms | 831 | 9 |
| Through which we endless life possess | 754 | 4 |
| Through whom we out of Egypt came | 704 | 1 |
| Throughout every place | 219 | 1 |
| Throughout his consecrated day | 953 | 4 |
| Throughout my fallen soul I feel | 830 | 1 |
| Throughout my soul shall shine | 356 | 8 |
| Throughout our universe | 239 | 6 |
| †Throughout the day, O Christ, in thee | 966 | 3 |
| ‡Throughout the deep thy footsteps shine | 1001 | 4 |
| †Throughout the desert way | 704 | 3 |
| Throughout the evil day | 266 | 3 |

| | Hymn | Verse |
|---|---|---|
| Throughout the evil day | 309 | 1 |
| Throughout the fiery hour | 436 | 7 |
| Throughout the flaming void | 64 | 5 |
| †Throughout the universe it reigns | 250 | 6 |
| Throughout the vale appear | 450 | 2 |
| †Throughout the world its breadth is known | 216 | 4 |
| Throughout the world proclaim | 738 | 3 |
| Throughout the world thy gospel spread | 448 | 4 |
| Throughout the world thy gospel spread | 492 | 5 |
| Throughout this evil day | 153 | 2 |
| Throw this universe aside | 60 | 4 |
| †Thus Abraham, the friend of God | 190 | 7 |
| Thus all heaven's armies bought with blood | 190 | 7 |
| Thus cold in death that bosom lay | 713 | 2 |
| Thus employed in heaven they are | 941 | 4 |
| Thus let thousands turn and live | 873 | 3 |
| Thus, Lord, while we remember thee | 950 | 1 |
| †Thus low the Lord of life was brought | 713 | 2 |
| †Thus may I pass my days | 311 | 5 |
| †Thus may I show the Spirit within | 864 | 5 |
| Thus may our souls adoring own | 955 | 4 |
| Thus may we abide in union | 1006 | — |
| †Thus, O thus, an entrance give | 672 | 11 |
| *Thus saith the Lord! Who seek the Lamb | 111 | 1 |
| †Thus searching the deep things of God | 770 | 7 |
| Thus shall we to our sacred name | 822 | 4 |
| Thus strengthened with all might | 865 | 6 |
| Thus supported | 878 | 6 |
| Thus thy blest command fulfilling | 895 | 1 |
| †Thus thy testimony give | 873 | 3 |
| Thus to sing, and thus to love | 716 | 6 |
| Thus unto my heart appear | 824 | 5 |
| Thus, we pray, unseen but surely | 990 | 2 |
| †Thus while we bestow | 495 | 4 |
| †Thus Wisdom's words discover | 667 | 3 |
| Thy absence I refused to feel | 180 | 2 |
| Thy absence I this moment feel | 130 | 8 |
| Thy agony, and sweat of blood | 157 | 2 |
| Thy aid I every moment need | 916 | 2 |
| Thy all-enlivening power display | 437 | 1 |
| Thy all-redeeming love | 162 | 5 |
| Thy all-redeeming love | 745 | 5 |
| Thy all-sufficiency confess | 770 | 2 |
| Thy all-sufficient grace bestow | 187 | 2 |
| Thy all-sufficient power | 105 | 4 |
| †Thy all-surrounding sight surveys | 632 | 2 |
| Thy all-sustaining power we prove | 654 | 1 |
| Thy all-sustaining power we prove | 1020 | — |
| Thy all-victorious righteousness | 157 | 6 |
| †Thy arm, Lord, is not shortened now | 386 | 3 |
| Thy arms of love still open are | 189 | 2 |
| Thy banished ones no more enslaved | 589 | 7 |
| Thy beams, unslumbering Love | 838 | 6 |

| | Hymn | Verse |
|---|---|---|
| Thy beatific face display | 283 | 1 |
| Thy being no succession knows | 651 | 3 |
| Thy benefits of old | 558 | 5 |
| Thy bleeding cross subdued | 583 | 2 |
| Thy blessed face to see | 920 | 4 |
| Thy blessed unction from above | 751 | 1 |
| Thy blessing is endued with soothing power | 967 | 2 |
| Thy blessing to receive | 175 | 1 |
| Thy blessing we implore | 35 | 1 |
| Thy blessings I restore | 432 | 5 |
| Thy blessings' unexhausted store | 392 | 2 |
| Thy blood applied shall make me whole | 779 | 3 |
| Thy blood atoned for all | 193 | 7 |
| Thy blood-besprinkled witnesses | 732 | 1 |
| Thy blood be upon me, and always abide | 160 | 5 |
| Thy blood is still our ransom found | 902 | 2 |
| Thy blood shall wash us white as snow | 523 | 5 |
| Thy blood wash all these stains away | 373 | 6 |
| Thy blood was shed for me | 175 | Cho. |
| Thy blood we steadfastly believe | 389 | 2 |
| Thy blood will wash out every stain | 773 | 4 |
| Thy bloody sweat, thy grief and shame | 33 | 3 |
| Thy boasted victory, O grave | 337 | 6 |
| Thy body and thy blood | 908 | 2 |
| Thy book be my companion still | 328 | 1 |
| Thy bounteous love to all is showed | 235 | 1 |
| †Thy bountiful care What tongue can recite | 611 | 4 |
| Thy bowels yearned, and sounded "Live!" | 206 | 2 |
| Thy breath can raise the billows steep | 226 | 9 |
| Thy bride, who bids thee come | 299 | 8 |
| Thy brightest glories shine above | 592 | 2 |
| Thy brightest majesty | 64 | 8 |
| †Thy bright example I pursue | 322 | 2 |
| Thy bright, unclouded face | 74 | 5 |
| Thy bulwarks with salvation strong | 939 | 2 |
| Thy burning charity | 300 | 1 |
| †Thy call I exult to obey | 78 | 2 |
| †Thy call if I ever have known | 165 | 3 |
| Thy call now let me hear | 164 | 6 |
| Thy ceaseless praise we sing | 737 | 1 |
| *Thy ceaseless, unexhausted love | 250 | 1 |
| Thy chariots through the sky | 583 | 1 |
| Thy children's wants a fresh supply | 236 | 3 |
| Thy children's wants a fresh supply | 1017 | 1 |
| Thy children to defend | 1005 | 2 |
| Thy chosen flock of yore | 587 | 6 |
| Thy chosen ministers reveal | 871 | 2 |
| Thy chosen ones depend | 533 | 3 |
| Thy co-eternal Son display | 148 | 2 |
| Thy comfortable voice | 358 | 1 |
| Thy condescending counsel take | 455 | 1 |
| Thy condescending goodness praise | 11 | 3 |
| †Thy condescending grace | 137 | 3 |

| | Hymn | Verse |
|---|---|---|
| Thy confessors to approve | 62 | 6 |
| Thy conscience as the noon-day clear | 964 | 3 |
| Thy constancy of love | 250 | 5 |
| Thy constant comfort place | 627 | 4 |
| Thy counsel doth excel | 244 | 3 |
| Thy counsel we approve | 387 | 2 |
| Thy countless attributes to show | 240 | 1 |
| Thy courts with grateful fragrance fill | 494 | 4 |
| Thy covenant cannot move | 162 | 5 |
| Thy creature, Lord, again create | 840 | 1 |
| Thy creatures more than thee I loved | 210 | 3 |
| Thy cross and passion on the tree | 33 | 3 |
| Thy cross can abide | 160 | 3 |
| Thy daily stage of duty run | 964 | 1 |
| Thy dainties, and be satisfied | 507 | 4 |
| Thy dearest children are | 818 | 1 |
| †Thy death hath bought the power | 162 | 4 |
| Thy debt is paid, thy soul is free | 36 | 4 |
| Thy deeds, O Lord, are wonder | 587 | 4 |
| Thy Deity of love | 150 | 2 |
| †Thy Deity the saints adore | 770 | 2 |
| Thy delegate and thee | 465 | 5 |
| Thy depth of mercy prove | 184 | 9 |
| Thy drawings from above | 97 | 2 |
| Thy dreadful wrath severe | 43 | 5 |
| Thy dwelling in the sky | 464 | 1 |
| Thy dying in my body bear | 330 | 4 |
| Thy earthly loss is heavenly gain | 857 | 2 |
| Thy earthly temples, are | 591 | 1 |
| Thy easy service prove | 471 | 5 |
| Thy eternal house above | 554 | 6 |
| Thy everlasting arms of love | 227 | 4 |
| Thy everlasting love to man | 377 | 4 |
| Thy everlasting righteousness | 303 | 5 |
| †Thy everlasting truth | 831 | 5 |
| Thy everlasting truth declare | 492 | 5 |
| Thy every act pure blessing is | 831 | 6 |
| †Thy every perfect servant, Lord | 330 | 5 |
| Thy every promise, true | 356 | 1 |
| Thy eyes must all my thoughts survey | 99 | 2 |
| Thy face I am strengthened to see | 70 | 2 |
| Thy face, Lord, will I seek | 558 | 3 |
| Thy fainting pangs, and bloody sweat | 181 | 1 |
| Thy fair, unspotted bride | 531 | 3 |
| Thy faithful followers to cheer | 861 | 4 |
| Thy faithful mercies never end | 576 | 2 |
| Thy faithful mercies own | 335 | 4 |
| Thy faithful promise seal | 342 | 1 |
| †Thy faithful, wise, and mighty love | 288 | 5 |
| Thy faithful witness will I be | 279 | 10 |
| *Thy faithfulness, Lord, Each moment we find | 5 | 1 |
| Thy faith hath made thee whole | 164 | 6 |
| Thy family complete | 452 | 6 |

| | Hymn | Verse |
|---|---|---|
| Thy Father calls for thee | 792 | 1 |
| †Thy fatherly chastisements own | 455 | 4 |
| Thy Father's perfect will | 193 | 6 |
| †Thy favour, and thy nature too | 252 | 2 |
| Thy favourite creature, man | 239 | 7 |
| Thy favourite Jesu's name | 138 | 8 |
| Thy feeble flesh abhorred to bear | 181 | 2 |
| Thy feeble, tempted followers here | 483 | 2 |
| Thy feet, alas, I cannot see | 861 | 2 |
| Thy feet, thy hands, thy side | 35 | 5 |
| †Thy feet were nailed to yonder tree | 85 | 6 |
| Thy fertilizing power | 771 | 4 |
| Thy fiery pillar brightened | 587 | 5 |
| Thy finger on my Bible trace | 770 | 5 |
| Thy flesh for all the world is given | 901 | 4 |
| Thy flowing wounds supply | 798 | 4 |
| Thy foot sinks deep as hell | 382 | 1 |
| Thy footsteps are not known | 587 | 6 |
| Thy footsteps in my closet hear | 770 | 5 |
| Thy former mercies here renew | 864 | 3 |
| Thy free, thine everlasting love | 365 | 6 |
| Thy free, unbounded grace | 983 | 6 |
| Thy full channels gushing o'er | 579 | 2 |
| Thy fulness I require | 416 | 3 |
| Thy gates with praises shine | 942 | 7 |
| Thy gifts abundantly increase | 523 | 2 |
| †Thy gifts, alas, cannot suffice | 415 | 5 |
| Thy gifts I only can receive | 131 | 2 |
| Thy gifts to thee we render back | 587 | 1 |
| †Thy glories blaze all nature round | 226 | 10 |
| Thy glorious arm display | 450 | 4 |
| †Thy glorious face in Christ display | 126 | 6 |
| †Thy glorious name and nature's powers | 248 | 6 |
| Thy glorious name to bless | 652 | — |
| Thy glorious power we sing | 248 | 1 |
| Thy glorious Son reveal | 717 | 3 |
| Thy glory and thy grace | 667 | 3 |
| Thy glory be my aim | 323 | 2 |
| Thy glory be our single aim | 524 | 1 |
| Thy glory be our whole design | 204 | 2 |
| Thy glory be the end | 108 | 7 |
| Thy glory fills both earth and sky | 244 | 1 |
| Thy glory fills both earth and sky | 647 | 2 |
| Thy glory if we now intend | 526 | 2 |
| Thy glory let all flesh behold | 444 | 4 |
| †Thy glory never hence depart | 993 | 6 |
| Thy glory not our own | 204 | 2 |
| Thy glory to display | 97 | 5 |
| Thy glory to the perfect day | 431 | 2 |
| Thy glory was our rear-ward | 276 | 3 |
| Thy glory why didst thou enshrine | 772 | 3 |
| †Thy Godhead brooding o'er the abyss | 750 | 2 |
| Thy Godhead we adore | 239 | 3 |

|  | Hymn | Verse |
|---|---|---|
| Thy golden gates appear | 944 | 3 |
| †Thy golden sceptre from above | 133 | 4 |
| †Thy good and holy will | 653 | 3 |
| †Thy goodness and thy truth to me | 250 | 3 |
| Thy goodness and thy truth we praise | 377 | 1 |
| Thy goodness and thy truth we prove | 377 | 1 |
| Thy goodness bade me be | 229 | 1 |
| Thy goodness I'll pursue | 657 | 9 |
| Thy goodness in full glory shines | 563 | 1 |
| Thy goodness is the sight I prize | 283 | 2 |
| Thy goodness is unchangeable | 708 | 2 |
| Thy goodness, Lord, is over all | 576 | 2 |
| Thy goodness, Lord, shall still defend | 602 | 4 |
| Thy goodness thankfully adores | 384 | 5 |
| Thy goodness to proclaim | 204 | 7 |
| Thy goodness to proclaim | 526 | 2 |
| Thy goodness we'll adore | 1002 | 5 |
| Thy goodness we praise | 808 | 1 |
| Thy goodness we proclaim | 482 | 1 |
| Thy goodness we rehearse | 239 | 6 |
| Thy gospel makes the simple wise | 553 | 5 |
| †Thy gospel-minister | 877 | 3 |
| Thy gospel then shall greatly grow | 453 | 1 |
| Thy gospel through the world to spread | 474 | 4 |
| Thy grace and mercy prove | 252 | 4 |
| Thy grace be to our spirits given | 1011 | — |
| Thy grace for every sinner free | 492 | 3 |
| †Thy grace I languish to receive | 119 | 4 |
| Thy grace is always nigh | 175 | 2 |
| Thy grace is ever nigh | 637 | 9 |
| Thy grace is free for all | 164 | 3 |
| Thy grace is free for all | 164 | 4 |
| Thy grace is life for evermore | 559 | 2 |
| Thy grace let every sinner know | 206 | 4 |
| Thy grace restores below | 750 | 5 |
| Thy grace to minister | 872 | 2 |
| Thy grace to wantonness | 307 | 3 |
| Thy grace was my relief | 584 | 4 |
| Thy grace will here be free indeed | 774 | 2 |
| Thy grace with glory crown | 74 | 5 |
| Thy gracious eye surveyed us | 667 | 3 |
| Thy gracious Father's sovereign will | 353 | 4 |
| Thy gracious Father to proclaim | 616 | 10 |
| Thy gracious plenitude reveal | 525 | 3 |
| Thy great confirming grace bestow | 649 | 2 |
| Thy great design fulfil | 788 | 4 |
| Thy great mysterious majesty | 121 | 2 |
| Thy great will delight to prove | 390 | 1 |
| Thy greatness to proclaim | 248 | 5 |
| Thy hallowed courts I trod | 93 | 2 |
| Thy hand hath conducted me through | 231 | 5 |
| †Thy hand, how wide it spreads the sky | 226 | 2 |
| †Thy hand in autumn richly pours | 978 | 3 |

| | HYMN | VERSE |
|---|---|---|
| †Thy hand, in sight of all my foes | 555 | 4 |
| Thy hand shall save me from my fall | 130 | 4 |
| †Thy hands created me, thy hands | 614 | 12 |
| Thy hands have brought salvation down | 879 | 1 |
| Thy hands stretched out they all may see | 35 | 6 |
| Thy happy name, they weep | 943 | 4 |
| Thy harmonizing name | 204 | 7 |
| Thy head, my Saviour and my Lord | 879 | 1 |
| Thy healing influence give | 108 | 5 |
| Thy healing influence give | 1009 | — |
| Thy health's eternal spring | 567 | 4 |
| †Thy heart, I know, thy tender heart | 144 | 2 |
| Thy heart still melts with tenderness | 189 | 2 |
| Thy heavenly Father's will | 340 | 3 |
| Thy heavenly Father's will | 756 | 3 |
| Thy heavenly succour give | 696 | 1 |
| Thy help in utmost need implore | 770 | 2 |
| Thy help is always nigh | 146 | 2 |
| Thy help is ever near | 546 | 4 |
| Thy holiness is all thy own | 247 | 1 |
| Thy holy arm display | 271 | 1 |
| Thy holy mount to gain | 452 | 5 |
| Thy Holy Spirit breathe | 347 | 1 |
| Thy honour and glory To sinners forth show | 200 | 2 |
| Thy humble state I sing | 195 | 4 |
| Thy hungry children feed | 653 | 4 |
| Thy hungry children feed | 1010 | — |
| Thy hungry children feed | 1011 | — |
| Thy image here retrieve | 342 | 2 |
| Thy joy in that happiest day | 78 | 2 |
| Thy joy to do the Father's will | 857 | 1 |
| Thy joyous presence shall remove | 392 | 4 |
| Thy judgments are a mighty deep | 563 | 2 |
| Thy judgment's deep abyss explain | 244 | 3 |
| Thy judgments to the nations show | 444 | 2 |
| Thy justice and thy mercy praise | 670 | 2 |
| Thy justifying grace | 97 | 1 |
| Thy Keeper can surprise | 618 | 3 |
| †Thy killing and thy quickening power | 409 | 3 |
| Thy kind but searching glance can scan | 969 | 6 |
| Thy kind continued aid engage | 916 | 2 |
| Thy kind invitation I gladly embrace | 3 | 4 |
| Thy kingdom come, and hell's o'erpower | 457 | 1 |
| Thy kingdom come, thy perfect will | 366 | 5 |
| Thy kingdom come to every heart | 394 | 4 |
| Thy kingdom come to every heart | 993 | 6 |
| †Thy kingdom come, with power and grace | 251 | 3 |
| Thy kingdom in our souls restore | 524 | 2 |
| Thy kingdom in the isles to prove | 448 | 3 |
| Thy kingdom is not there | 447 | 1 |
| †Thy kingdom, Lord, we long to see | 445 | 2 |
| Thy kingdom now restore | 410 | 2 |
| Thy kingdom of glory to share | 78 | 2 |

| | HYMN | VERSE |
|---|---|---|
| Thy kingdom shall increase | 731 | 5 |
| Thy kingdom shall remain | 731 | 9 |
| Thy kiss forgave me all | 191 | 4 |
| Thy knowledge and dread | 219 | 7 |
| Thy largest promises | 895 | 1 |
| Thy last mysterious agony | 181 | 1 |
| Thy latest foe in death o'ercome | 69 | 4 |
| †Thy lawful servant, Lord, I owe | 614 | 11 |
| Thy laws are pure, thy judgments right | 558 | 5 |
| Thy laws with all my heart obey | 275 | 6 |
| Thy liberal hand provides them meat | 637 | 3 |
| Thy light and easy burden prove | 388 | 5 |
| Thy light and life to me | 609 | 1 |
| †Thy light, and strength, and pardoning grace | 903 | 3 |
| Thy like nor man nor angel knows | 858 | 1 |
| Thy little flock in safety keep | 501 | 1 |
| Thy living temples down | 94 | 3 |
| Thy love alone can comfort give | 437 | 2 |
| Thy love and guardian care | 831 | 15 |
| Thy love attend me all my days | 431 | 6 |
| Thy love can find a thousand ways | 288 | 4 |
| Thy love compassionately sees | 136 | 2 |
| Thy love each believer Shall gladly adore | 199 | 5 |
| Thy love endures the same | 888 | 4 |
| Thy love for a sinner declare | 228 | 2 |
| Thy love for every sinner free | 33 | 5 |
| Thy love immense, unsearchable | 26 | 7 |
| †Thy love is all my plea | 151 | 5 |
| †Thy love I soon expect to find | 384 | 6 |
| Thy love let it my heart o'erpower | 438 | 1 |
| Thy love my plea I make | 772 | 2 |
| Thy love my ravished heart o'erflows | 437 | 6 |
| Thy love on the tree | 160 | 2 |
| Thy love permits, invites, commands | 893 | 1 |
| Thy love shall burst the shades of death | 288 | 5 |
| †Thy love the conquest more than gains | 275 | 8 |
| †Thy love the day designed | 952 | 2 |
| Thy love to Adam's seed | 717 | 1 |
| Thy love unsearchable | 423 | 1 |
| Thy love we praise | 853 | 2 |
| Thy love's ecstatic height | 253 | 3 |
| Thy love's pavilion spread | 465 | 4 |
| Thy loving-kindness and thy truth | 566 | 6 |
| Thy loving self, inspire | 527 | 2 |
| Thy majesty did not disdain | 322 | 1 |
| Thy Maker and thy friend | 407 | 2 |
| Thy meek humility | 109 | 7 |
| Thy members here | 853 | 1 |
| Thy members on thy throne to place | 62 | 6 |
| Thy mercies and my wants to tell | 290 | 5 |
| Thy mercies, heavenly Lord, descend | 636 | 1 |
| Thy mercies how tender, How firm to the end | 611 | 5 |
| Thy mercies never shall remove | 141 | 4 |

| | Hymn | Verse |
|---|---|---|
| Thy mercies reach to all | 245 | 1 |
| Thy mercies to my soul reveal | 155 | 4 |
| Thy mercy doth supply | 602 | 5 |
| Thy mercy I receive | 162 | 5 |
| Thy mercy is for me | 167 | 2 |
| Thy mercy lent an ear | 657 | 3 |
| Thy mercy make known, And sprinkle thy blood | 40 | 7 |
| Thy mercy makes salvation sure | 124 | 3 |
| †Thy mercy never shall remove | 637 | 10 |
| Thy mercy shall proclaim | 543 | 7 |
| Thy mercy spoke it to my heart | 561 | 5 |
| Thy mercy so tender To all the lost race | 5 | 1 |
| †Thy mercy's early light | 635 | 3 |
| Thy mercy's gates are open wide | 797 | 1 |
| †Thy meritorious sufferings past | 702 | 6 |
| *Thy messengers make known | 735 | 1 |
| Thy mighty hand shall set me free | 487 | 9 |
| Thy mighty hand sustains | 989 | 2 |
| Thy mighty name hath been | 482 | 1 |
| †Thy mighty name salvation is | 209 | 2 |
| Thy mighty working let me feel | 351 | 1 |
| Thy mighty working may I feel | 351 | 8 |
| †Thy mind throughout my life be shown | 364 | 4 |
| Thy ministers are living flame | 651 | 4 |
| Thy ministers attend | 734 | 2 |
| Thy miracles repeat | 135 | 3 |
| Thy moon and stars I see | 544 | 2 |
| Thy mortal groan, "My God! my God!" | 157 | 2 |
| Thy most unworthy servant leave | 917 | 1 |
| †Thy mouth, O Lord, hath spoke, hath sworn | 401 | 5 |
| Thy mystery of grace display | 113 | 3 |
| Thy mystic name in me reveal | 144 | 4 |
| Thy name and nature let me prove | 109 | 7 |
| Thy name and temple I profaned | 93 | 2 |
| Thy name be praised on earth, on high | 323 | 2 |
| Thy name confessed and glorified | 473 | 6 |
| Thy name is life, and health, and peace | 485 | 1 |
| Thy name I will in songs record | 545 | 1 |
| †Thy name, Jehovah, be adored | 642 | 6 |
| Thy name let every soul adore | 206 | 4 |
| †Thy name, O God, upon my bed | 437 | 7 |
| Thy name, or place thy house of prayer | 590 | 1 |
| Thy name salvation is | 485 | 1 |
| Thy name, thy all-restoring name | 397 | 1 |
| †Thy name to me, thy nature grant | 403 | 6 |
| Thy name we magnify | 653 | 1 |
| Thy nature and thy name is Love | 141 | Cho. |
| †Thy nature be my law | 340 | 3 |
| †Thy nature, gracious Lord, impart | 343 | 8 |
| Thy nature in my soul proclaim | 283 | 2 |
| Thy nature into every heart | 527 | 2 |
| Thy nature to my soul impart | 369 | 1 |
| Thy needy creatures good | 135 | 2 |

| | Hymn | Verse |
|---|---|---|
| Thy confessors to approve | 62 | 6 |
| Thy conscience as the noon-day clear | 964 | 3 |
| Thy constancy of love | 250 | 5 |
| Thy constant comfort place | 627 | 4 |
| Thy counsel doth excel | 244 | 3 |
| Thy counsel we approve | 387 | 2 |
| Thy countless attributes to show | 240 | 1 |
| Thy courts with grateful fragrance fill | 494 | 4 |
| Thy covenant cannot move | 162 | 5 |
| Thy creature, Lord, again create | 340 | 1 |
| Thy creatures more than thee I loved | 210 | 3 |
| Thy cross and passion on the tree | 33 | 3 |
| Thy cross can abide | 160 | 3 |
| Thy daily stage of duty run | 964 | 1 |
| Thy dainties, and be satisfied | 507 | 4 |
| Thy dearest children are | 818 | 1 |
| †Thy death hath bought the power | 162 | 4 |
| Thy debt is paid, thy soul is free | 36 | 4 |
| Thy deeds, O Lord, are wonder | 587 | 4 |
| Thy Deity of love | 150 | 2 |
| †Thy Deity the saints adore | 770 | 2 |
| Thy delegate and thee | 465 | 5 |
| Thy depth of mercy prove | 184 | 9 |
| Thy drawings from above | 97 | 2 |
| Thy dreadful wrath severe | 43 | 5 |
| Thy dwelling in the sky | 464 | 1 |
| Thy dying in my body bear | 330 | 4 |
| Thy earthly loss is heavenly gain | 857 | 2 |
| Thy earthly temples, are | 591 | 1 |
| Thy easy service prove | 471 | 5 |
| Thy eternal house above | 554 | 6 |
| Thy everlasting arms of love | 227 | 4 |
| Thy everlasting love to man | 377 | 4 |
| Thy everlasting righteousness | 303 | 5 |
| †Thy everlasting truth | 831 | 5 |
| Thy everlasting truth declare | 492 | 5 |
| Thy every act pure blessing is | 831 | 6 |
| †Thy every perfect servant, Lord | 330 | 5 |
| Thy every promise, true | 356 | 1 |
| Thy eyes must all my thoughts survey | 99 | 2 |
| Thy face I am strengthened to see | 70 | 2 |
| Thy face, Lord, will I seek | 558 | 3 |
| Thy fainting pangs, and bloody sweat | 181 | 1 |
| Thy fair, unspotted bride | 531 | 3 |
| Thy faithful followers to cheer | 861 | 4 |
| Thy faithful mercies never end | 576 | 2 |
| Thy faithful mercies own | 335 | 4 |
| Thy faithful promise seal | 342 | 1 |
| †Thy faithful, wise, and mighty love | 288 | 5 |
| Thy faithful witness will I be | 279 | 10 |
| *Thy faithfulness, Lord, Each moment we find | 5 | 1 |
| Thy faith hath made thee whole | 164 | 6 |
| Thy family complete | 452 | 6 |

| | Hymn | Verse |
|---|---|---|
| Thy Father calls for thee | 792 | 1 |
| †Thy fatherly chastisements own | 455 | 4 |
| Thy Father's perfect will | 193 | 6 |
| †Thy favour, and thy nature too | 252 | 2 |
| Thy favourite creature, man | 239 | 7 |
| Thy favourite Jesu's name | 138 | 8 |
| Thy feeble flesh abhorred to bear | 181 | 2 |
| Thy feeble, tempted followers here | 483 | 2 |
| Thy feet, alas, I cannot see | 861 | 2 |
| Thy feet, thy hands, thy side | 35 | 5 |
| †Thy feet were nailed to yonder tree | 35 | 6 |
| Thy fertilizing power | 771 | 4 |
| Thy fiery pillar brightened | 587 | 5 |
| Thy finger on my Bible trace | 770 | 5 |
| Thy flesh for all the world is given | 901 | 4 |
| Thy flowing wounds supply | 798 | 4 |
| Thy foot sinks deep as hell | 382 | 1 |
| Thy footsteps are not known | 587 | 6 |
| Thy footsteps in my closet hear | 770 | 5 |
| Thy former mercies here renew | 864 | 3 |
| Thy free, thine everlasting love | 365 | 6 |
| Thy free, unbounded grace | 983 | 6 |
| Thy full channels gushing o'er | 579 | 2 |
| Thy fulness I require | 416 | 3 |
| Thy gates with praises shine | 942 | 7 |
| Thy gifts abundantly increase | 523 | 2 |
| †Thy gifts, alas, cannot suffice | 415 | 5 |
| Thy gifts I only can receive | 131 | 2 |
| Thy gifts to thee we render back | 587 | 1 |
| †Thy glories blaze all nature round | 226 | 10 |
| Thy glorious arm display | 450 | 4 |
| †Thy glorious face in Christ display | 126 | 6 |
| †Thy glorious name and nature's powers | 248 | 6 |
| Thy glorious name to bless | 652 | — |
| Thy glorious power we sing | 248 | 1 |
| Thy glorious Son reveal | 717 | 3 |
| Thy glory and thy grace | 667 | 3 |
| Thy glory be my aim | 323 | 2 |
| Thy glory be our single aim | 524 | 1 |
| Thy glory be our whole design | 204 | 2 |
| Thy glory be the end | 108 | 7 |
| Thy glory fills both earth and sky | 244 | 1 |
| Thy glory fills both earth and sky | 647 | 2 |
| Thy glory if we now intend | 526 | 2 |
| Thy glory let all flesh behold | 444 | 4 |
| †Thy glory never hence depart | 993 | 6 |
| Thy glory not our own | 204 | 2 |
| Thy glory to display | 97 | 5 |
| Thy glory to the perfect day | 431 | 2 |
| Thy glory was our rear-ward | 276 | 3 |
| Thy glory why didst thou enshrine | 772 | 3 |
| †Thy Godhead brooding o'er the abyss | 750 | 2 |
| Thy Godhead we adore | 239 | 3 |

| | Hymn | Verse |
|---|---|---|
| Thy golden gates appear | 944 | 3 |
| †Thy golden sceptre from above | 133 | 4 |
| †Thy good and holy will | 653 | 3 |
| †Thy goodness and thy truth to me | 250 | 3 |
| Thy goodness and thy truth we praise | 377 | 1 |
| Thy goodness and thy truth we prove | 377 | 1 |
| Thy goodness bade me be | 229 | 1 |
| Thy goodness I'll pursue | 657 | 9 |
| Thy goodness in full glory shines | 563 | 1 |
| Thy goodness is the sight I prize | 283 | 2 |
| Thy goodness is unchangeable | 708 | 2 |
| Thy goodness, Lord, is over all | 576 | 2 |
| Thy goodness, Lord, shall still defend | 602 | 4 |
| Thy goodness thankfully adores | 384 | 5 |
| Thy goodness to proclaim | 204 | 7 |
| Thy goodness to proclaim | 526 | 2 |
| Thy goodness we'll adore | 1002 | 5 |
| Thy goodness we praise | 808 | 1 |
| Thy goodness we proclaim | 482 | 1 |
| Thy goodness we rehearse | 239 | 6 |
| Thy gospel makes the simple wise | 553 | 5 |
| †Thy gospel-minister | 877 | 3 |
| Thy gospel then shall greatly grow | 453 | 1 |
| Thy gospel through the world to spread | 474 | 4 |
| Thy grace and mercy prove | 252 | 4 |
| Thy grace be to our spirits given | 1011 | — |
| Thy grace for every sinner free | 492 | 3 |
| †Thy grace I languish to receive | 119 | 4 |
| Thy grace is always nigh | 175 | 2 |
| Thy grace is ever nigh | 637 | 9 |
| Thy grace is free for all | 164 | 3 |
| Thy grace is free for all | 164 | 4 |
| Thy grace is life for evermore | 559 | 2 |
| Thy grace let every sinner know | 206 | 4 |
| Thy grace restores below | 750 | 5 |
| Thy grace to minister | 872 | 2 |
| Thy grace to wantonness | 307 | 3 |
| Thy grace was my relief | 584 | 4 |
| Thy grace will here be free indeed | 774 | 2 |
| Thy grace with glory crown | 74 | 5 |
| Thy gracious eye surveyed us | 667 | 3 |
| Thy gracious Father's sovereign will | 353 | 4 |
| Thy gracious Father to proclaim | 616 | 10 |
| Thy gracious plenitude reveal | 525 | 3 |
| Thy great confirming grace bestow | 649 | 2 |
| Thy great design fulfil | 788 | 4 |
| Thy great mysterious majesty | 121 | 2 |
| Thy great will delight to prove | 390 | 1 |
| Thy greatness to proclaim | 248 | 5 |
| Thy hallowed courts I trod | 93 | 2 |
| Thy hand hath conducted me through | 231 | 5 |
| †Thy hand, how wide it spreads the sky | 226 | 2 |
| †Thy hand in autumn richly pours | 978 | 3 |

|  | HYMN | VERSE |
|---|---|---|
| †Thy hand, in sight of all my foes | 555 | 4 |
| Thy hand shall save me from my fall | 130 | 4 |
| †Thy hands created me, thy hands | 614 | 12 |
| Thy hands have brought salvation down | 879 | 1 |
| Thy hands stretched out they all may see | 35 | 6 |
| Thy happy name, they weep | 943 | 4 |
| Thy harmonizing name | 204 | 7 |
| Thy head, my Saviour and my Lord | 879 | 1 |
| Thy healing influence give | 108 | 5 |
| Thy healing influence give | 1009 | — |
| Thy health's eternal spring | 567 | 4 |
| †Thy heart, I know, thy tender heart | 144 | 2 |
| Thy heart still melts with tenderness | 189 | 2 |
| Thy heavenly Father's will | 340 | 3 |
| Thy heavenly Father's will | 756 | 3 |
| Thy heavenly succour give | 696 | 1 |
| Thy help in utmost need implore | 770 | 2 |
| Thy help is always nigh | 146 | 2 |
| Thy help is ever near | 546 | 4 |
| Thy holiness is all thy own | 247 | 1 |
| Thy holy arm display | 271 | 1 |
| Thy holy mount to gain | 452 | 5 |
| Thy Holy Spirit breathe | 347 | 1 |
| Thy honour and glory To sinners forth show | 200 | 2 |
| Thy humble state I sing | 195 | 4 |
| Thy hungry children feed | 653 | 4 |
| Thy hungry children feed | 1010 | — |
| Thy hungry children feed | 1011 | — |
| Thy image here retrieve | 342 | 2 |
| Thy joy in that happiest day | 78 | 2 |
| Thy joy to do the Father's will | 857 | 1 |
| Thy joyous presence shall remove | 392 | 4 |
| Thy judgments are a mighty deep | 563 | 2 |
| Thy judgment's deep abyss explain | 244 | 3 |
| Thy judgments to the nations show | 444 | 2 |
| Thy justice and thy mercy praise | 670 | 2 |
| Thy justifying grace | 97 | 1 |
| Thy Keeper can surprise | 618 | 3 |
| †Thy killing and thy quickening power | 409 | 3 |
| Thy kind but searching glance can scan | 969 | 6 |
| Thy kind continued aid engage | 916 | 2 |
| Thy kind invitation I gladly embrace | 3 | 4 |
| Thy kingdom come, and hell's o'erpower | 457 | 1 |
| Thy kingdom come, thy perfect will | 366 | 5 |
| Thy kingdom come to every heart | 394 | 4 |
| Thy kingdom come to every heart | 993 | 6 |
| †Thy kingdom come, with power and grace | 251 | 3 |
| Thy kingdom in our souls restore | 524 | 2 |
| Thy kingdom in the isles to prove | 448 | 3 |
| Thy kingdom is not there | 447 | 1 |
| †Thy kingdom, Lord, we long to see | 445 | 2 |
| Thy kingdom now restore | 410 | 2 |
| Thy kingdom of glory to share | 78 | 2 |

| | Hymn | Verse |
|---|---|---|
| Thy kingdom shall increase | 731 | 5 |
| Thy kingdom shall remain | 731 | 9 |
| Thy kiss forgave me all | 191 | 4 |
| Thy knowledge and dread | 219 | 7 |
| Thy largest promises | 805 | 1 |
| Thy last mysterious agony | 181 | 1 |
| Thy latest foe in death o'ercome | 69 | 4 |
| †Thy lawful servant, Lord, I owe | 614 | 11 |
| Thy laws are pure, thy judgments right | 558 | 5 |
| Thy laws with all my heart obey | 275 | 6 |
| Thy liberal hand provides them meat | 637 | 3 |
| Thy light and easy burden prove | 388 | 5 |
| Thy light and life to me | 609 | 1 |
| †Thy light, and strength, and pardoning grace | 903 | 3 |
| Thy like nor man nor angel knows | 353 | 1 |
| Thy little flock in safety keep | 501 | 1 |
| Thy living temples down | 94 | 3 |
| Thy love alone can comfort give | 437 | 2 |
| Thy love and guardian care | 831 | 15 |
| Thy love attend me all my days | 431 | 6 |
| Thy love can find a thousand ways | 288 | 4 |
| Thy love compassionately sees | 136 | 2 |
| Thy love each believer Shall gladly adore | 199 | 5 |
| Thy love endures the same | 888 | 4 |
| Thy love for a sinner declare | 228 | 2 |
| Thy love for every sinner free | 33 | 5 |
| Thy love immense, unsearchable | 26 | 7 |
| †Thy love is all my plea | 151 | 5 |
| †Thy love I soon expect to find | 384 | 6 |
| Thy love let it my heart o'erpower | 438 | 1 |
| Thy love my plea I make | 772 | 2 |
| Thy love my ravished heart o'erflows | 437 | 6 |
| Thy love on the tree | 160 | 2 |
| Thy love permits, invites, commands | 898 | 1 |
| Thy love shall burst the shades of death | 288 | 5 |
| †Thy love the conquest more than gains | 275 | 8 |
| †Thy love the day designed | 952 | 2 |
| Thy love to Adam's seed | 717 | 1 |
| Thy love unsearchable | 423 | 1 |
| Thy love we praise | 853 | 2 |
| Thy love's ecstatic height | 253 | 3 |
| Thy love's pavilion spread | 465 | 4 |
| Thy loving-kindness and thy truth | 566 | 6 |
| Thy loving self, inspire | 527 | 2 |
| Thy majesty did not disdain | 322 | 1 |
| Thy Maker and thy friend | 407 | 2 |
| Thy meek humility | 109 | 7 |
| Thy members here | 858 | 1 |
| Thy members on thy throne to place | 62 | 6 |
| Thy mercies and my wants to tell | 290 | 5 |
| Thy mercies, heavenly Lord, descend | 636 | 1 |
| Thy mercies how tender, How firm to the end | 611 | 5 |
| Thy mercies never shall remove | 141 | 4 |

| | HYMN | VERSE |
|---|---|---|
| Thy mercies reach to all | 245 | 1 |
| Thy mercies to my soul reveal | 155 | 4 |
| Thy mercy doth supply | 602 | 3 |
| Thy mercy I receive | 162 | 3 |
| Thy mercy is for me | 167 | 2 |
| Thy mercy lent an ear | 657 | 3 |
| Thy mercy make known, And sprinkle thy blood | 40 | 7 |
| Thy mercy makes salvation sure | 124 | 3 |
| †Thy mercy never shall remove | 687 | 10 |
| Thy mercy shall proclaim | 543 | 7 |
| Thy mercy spoke it to my heart | 561 | 5 |
| Thy mercy so tender To all the lost race | 5 | 1 |
| †Thy mercy's early light | 635 | 3 |
| Thy mercy's gates are open wide | 797 | 1 |
| †Thy meritorious sufferings past | 702 | 6 |
| *Thy messengers make known | 735 | 1 |
| Thy mighty hand shall set me free | 437 | 9 |
| Thy mighty hand sustains | 989 | 2 |
| Thy mighty name hath been | 482 | 1 |
| †Thy mighty name salvation is | 209 | 2 |
| Thy mighty working let me feel | 351 | 1 |
| Thy mighty working may I feel | 351 | 8 |
| †Thy mind throughout my life be shown | 364 | 4 |
| Thy ministers are living flame | 651 | 4 |
| Thy ministers attend | 734 | 2 |
| Thy miracles repeat | 135 | 3 |
| Thy moon and stars I see | 544 | 2 |
| Thy mortal groan, "My God! my God!" | 157 | 2 |
| Thy most unworthy servant leave | 917 | 1 |
| †Thy mouth, O Lord, hath spoke, hath sworn | 401 | 5 |
| Thy mystery of grace display | 113 | 3 |
| Thy mystic name in me reveal | 144 | 4 |
| Thy name and nature let me prove | 109 | 7 |
| Thy name and temple I profaned | 93 | 2 |
| Thy name be praised on earth, on high | 323 | 2 |
| Thy name confessed and glorified | 473 | 6 |
| Thy name is life, and health, and peace | 485 | 1 |
| Thy name I will in songs record | 545 | 1 |
| †Thy name, Jehovah, be adored | 642 | 6 |
| Thy name let every soul adore | 206 | 4 |
| †Thy name, O God, upon my bed | 437 | 7 |
| Thy name, or place thy house of prayer | 590 | 1 |
| Thy name salvation is | 485 | 1 |
| Thy name, thy all-restoring name | 397 | 1 |
| †Thy name to me, thy nature grant | 403 | 6 |
| Thy name we magnify | 653 | 1 |
| Thy nature and thy name is Love | 141 | Cho. |
| †Thy nature be my law | 340 | 3 |
| †Thy nature, gracious Lord, impart | 343 | 8 |
| Thy nature in my soul proclaim | 283 | 2 |
| Thy nature into every heart | 527 | 2 |
| Thy nature to my soul impart | 369 | 1 |
| Thy needy creatures good | 135 | 2 |

| | HYMN | VERSE |
|---|---|---|
| Thy needy servants cry | 745 | 1 |
| Thy never-ceasing glories shine | 237 | 3 |
| Thy never-ceasing glories shine | 241 | 4 |
| Thy new, best name of love | 343 | 8 |
| Thy new-made creature crown | 785 | 4 |
| Thy new, unutterable name | 140 | 4 |
| Thy numerous glories show | 226 | 4 |
| †Thy offering still continues new | 708 | 2 |
| Thy offices of mercy bless | 770 | 2 |
| †Thy only glory let them seek | 744 | 6 |
| Thy only glory we declare | 247 | 2 |
| Thy only love resolved to know | 772 | 2 |
| Thy only love to know | 137 | 11 |
| Thy only Son for sinners gave | 39 | 1 |
| Thy only will be done, not mine | 332 | 5 |
| Thy only will we fain would seek | 108 | 6 |
| Thy opening hands to each convey | 636 | 3 |
| Thy orders to obey | 226 | 5 |
| Thy own eternal power reveal | 150 | 2 |
| Thy own fulness to require | 372 | — |
| Thy own holiness impart | 287 | 5 |
| †Thy own peculiar servant claim | 375 | 5 |
| Thy own this moment seize | 296 | 3 |
| Thy own universe to thee | 653 | 7 |
| Thy pardoning grace is rich and free | 795 | 1 |
| Thy pardoning mercy to show | 174 | 4 |
| †Thy parent-hand, thy forming skill | 240 | 3 |
| Thy passion and death on the tree | 228 | 2 |
| Thy passion speaks for me | 151 | 5 |
| Thy path unsullied light | 831 | 6 |
| †Thy patience lifts us up | 983 | 6 |
| Thy peace, and joy, and righteousness | 251 | 3 |
| Thy peace and love my portion be | 196 | 2 |
| Thy peace in my conscience reveal | 911 | 4 |
| Thy peace to my conscience reveal | 165 | 3 |
| Thy peculiar blessing shared | 989 | 2 |
| Thy people, and for ever thine | 511 | 3 |
| †Thy people in thy day of might | 613 | 2 |
| †Thy people, Lord, are sold for nought | 82 | 4 |
| †Thy people saved below | 732 | 2 |
| Thy people still are fed | 664 | 1 |
| Thy people to redeem | 717 | 2 |
| Thy perfections to proclaim | 653 | 1 |
| Thy perfect love on earth shall taste | 590 | 6 |
| Thy perfect strength displayed in me | 836 | 1 |
| Thy pitiful and tender mind | 304 | 4 |
| Thy pity hath been my relief | 165 | 4 |
| Thy pity looked me near | 191 | 3 |
| Thy poor helpless creature hide | 819 | 3 |
| Thy power and constancy | 531 | 3 |
| Thy power and faithful love declare | 561 | 6 |
| Thy power and goodness here display | 993 | 1 |
| Thy power and grace proclaim | 634 | 4 |

# THY POWER — THY PURPOSE

| | Hymn | Verse |
|---|---|---|
| Thy power and love diffused abroad | 473 | 6 |
| Thy power and praise proclaim | 637 | 5 |
| *Thy power and saving truth to show | 439 | 1 |
| †Thy power, and truth, and love divine | 396 | 3 |
| Thy power and will to save | 335 | 3 |
| Thy power and will to save | 874 | 1 |
| Thy power infused doth all sustain | 241 | 3 |
| †Thy power, in human weakness shown | 329 | 2 |
| †Thy power I pant to prove | 27 | 5 |
| Thy power is present now to heal | 781 | 5 |
| Thy power let every tongue proclaim | 206 | 4 |
| Thy power my strength and fortress is | 337 | 5 |
| Thy power: O let us taste thy love | 666 | 2 |
| †Thy power omnipotent assume | 64 | 8 |
| †Thy power through Jesu's life displayed | 750 | 4 |
| Thy power to us make known | 84 | 1 |
| †Thy power unparalleled confessed | 247 | 4 |
| Thy power unto salvation show | 17 | 3 |
| †Thy powerful Spirit shall subdue | 139 | 5 |
| †Thy powerful, wise, and loving mind | 256 | 4 |
| Thy praise shall our glad tongues employ | 977 | 3 |
| Thy praise shall sound from shore to shore | 615 | 2 |
| Thy praise their happy lives employ | 629 | 3 |
| Thy precious blood has paid | 818 | 4 |
| Thy precious death and life—I pray | 33 | 3 |
| Thy precious death hath won for me | 923 | 3 |
| Thy presence is my stay | 555 | 3 |
| Thy presence let me always find | 188 | 5 |
| Thy presence makes my paradise | 415 | 5 |
| Thy presence makes the perfect bliss | 548 | 6 |
| Thy presence through my journey shine | 843 | 3 |
| Thy presence who can fly | 750 | 3 |
| Thy priesthood still remains the same | 708 | 2 |
| †Thy priests be clothed with righteousness | 629 | 3 |
| Thy proffer I embrace | 175 | 4 |
| Thy proffer we receive | 983 | 4 |
| Thy promised aid I claim | 138 | 8 |
| Thy promised presence claim | 485 | 1 |
| Thy promise deeper lies | 460 | 2 |
| †Thy promise, Lord, is ever sure | 600 | 4 |
| Thy promise made to Adam's race | 460 | 1 |
| Thy promises bind thee Compassion to have | 273 | 1 |
| Thy promises, how firm they be | 879 | 3 |
| Thy prophetic character | 676 | 1 |
| Thy providence displayed | 245 | 2 |
| †Thy providence is kind and large | 563 | 3 |
| †Thy Providence my life sustained | 657 | 2 |
| Thy providence to obey | 510 | 1 |
| Thy pure and heavenly nature share | 159 | 3 |
| Thy purifying blood apply | 184 | 1 |
| Thy purity I still abhorred | 93 | 3 |
| Thy purity I want | 109 | 2 |
| Thy purpose firm none can withstand | 244 | 2 |

| | Hymn | Verse |
|---|---|---|
| Thy quickening Spirit give. | 196 | 1 |
| Thy quickening word shall raise me up | 860 | 7 |
| Thy quiet and peaceable reign | 220 | 4 |
| Thy ransomed people lead. | 704 | 1 |
| Thy ransomed people raise. | 948 | 5 |
| †Thy ransomed servant, I | 426 | 2 |
| Thy real worshipper | 88 | 2 |
| Thy regal state I sing | 727 | 1 |
| Thy reign of grace, I sing. | 675 | 8 |
| Thy resurrection's power make known | 861 | 1 |
| Thy resurrection's power to know. | 290 | 4 |
| Thy revealing Spirit give. | 517 | 3 |
| Thy righteousness accounted theirs | 461 | 5 |
| Thy righteousness, brought in | 417 | 2 |
| Thy righteousness wearing, And cleansed by thy | 198 | 3 |
| Thy ruined work restore. | 256 | 5 |
| Thy ruling Providence I see | 289 | 2 |
| Thy sacred energy, and bless | 253 | 3 |
| Thy sacred word is passed. | 282 | 2 |
| Thy sacrifice shall be | 1002 | 6 |
| Thy saints in full prosperity | 612 | 4 |
| Thy saints to thee in hymns impart | 686 | 1 |
| Thy sanctifying grace | 354 | 2 |
| †Thy sanctifying Spirit pour | 891 | 3 |
| Thy saving power display. | 572 | 2 |
| Thy saving strength, O Lord, restore | 574 | 9 |
| Thy saving truth, and live. | 242 | 3 |
| Thy Saviour's sacrifice | 194 | 1 |
| Thy sceptre and thy cross we own. | 891 | 1 |
| Thy sceptre and thy sword. | 675 | 8 |
| Thy sceptre o'er the nations shake. | 445 | 2 |
| Thy sceptre, till to thee shall bend. | 618 | 1 |
| Thy secret thoughts, thy words and ways. | 964 | 3 |
| Thy secret to me Shall soon be made known | 198 | 6 |
| †Thy secret voice invites me still | 344 | 2 |
| Thy selected people spare. | 60 | 1 |
| Thy servant had not died | 184 | 7 |
| Thy servant mightily defend | 916 | 5 |
| Thy servant's life to scan | 635 | 1 |
| Thy servant's sayings to receive | 884 | — |
| Thy shadowing wings around my head | 279 | 5 |
| †Thy side an open fountain is | 85 | 7 |
| Thy sign let them see | 219 | 6 |
| †Thy single arm, almighty Lord | 203 | 4 |
| †Thy sinless mind in me reveal | 368 | 2 |
| Thy sins are forgiven, Accepted thou art. | 40 | 4 |
| †Thy smiling face lights mine | 888 | 5 |
| Thy Son thou hast given The world to redeem | 199 | 4 |
| Thy Son thou hast given to die in our place | 808 | 1 |
| Thy son, thy servant bought with blood | 577 | 2 |
| †Thy soul for sin an offering made. | 830 | 2 |
| Thy sovereign everlasting love | 38 | 5 |
| Thy sovereign goodness we record. | 248 | 1 |

| | Hymn | Verse |
|---|---|---|
| †Thy sovereign grace to all extends. | 216 | 3 |
| Thy sovereign light within my heart | 437 | 1 |
| Thy sovereign Majesty blaspheme | 254 | 3 |
| Thy sovereign power to save | 584 | 5 |
| Thy sovereign will be done | 733 | 2 |
| Thy sovereign will denies | 843 | 1 |
| Thy Spirit and thyself on me | 364 | 1 |
| †Thy Spirit hath the difference made | 81 | 2 |
| Thy Spirit, Lord, supply | 527 | 5 |
| Thy Spirit now demands thy name. | 144 | 3 |
| Thy Spirit on the heart shall trace. | 891 | 5 |
| Thy Spirit sunk beneath its load | 181 | 2 |
| †Thy Spirit's gracious aid impart | 955 | 4 |
| Thy Spirit's plenitude impart | 968 | 2 |
| Thy spotless charity | 504 | 6 |
| Thy spotless sanctity | 340 | 3 |
| Thy sprinkled blood to feel. | 783 | 1 |
| †Thy statutes, Lord, are sure | 601 | 5 |
| Thy steadfast truth declare | 831 | 15 |
| Thy still continued care | 979 | 3 |
| Thy streets with gold are spread | 942 | 7 |
| †Thy strength and thy power I now can proclaim | 200 | 3 |
| Thy strength be in our weakness seen | 475 | 3 |
| Thy strength was in our weakness shown. | 483 | 3 |
| Thy strengthening hands uphold the weak | 637 | 6 |
| Thy strong and bitter cries and tears | 157 | 2 |
| Thy succour afford, Thy righteousness bring | 273 | 1 |
| Thy succours from above | 311 | 1 |
| Thy suffering and my faith are vain | 375 | 2 |
| Thy suffering servants, Lord, address | 636 | 4 |
| Thy suffering, well-beloved Son | 394 | 1 |
| Thy sun thou bidd'st his genial ray | 241 | 3 |
| Thy sway it doth not, cannot own | 391 | 6 |
| Thy sway o'er all the earth maintain | 445 | 1 |
| Thy sweet constraining love | 528 | 4 |
| Thy sweet forgiving love | 97 | 2 |
| Thy sweet refreshing grace. | 292 | 2 |
| Thy sweet return to feel | 188 | 3 |
| Thy tabernacle spread | 998 | 2 |
| Thy table in our heart | 908 | 1 |
| Thy table in our heart | 1024 | — |
| Thy talents to improve take care | 964 | 2 |
| Thy tender care bestowed | 657 | 4 |
| †Thy tender heart is still the same | 343 | 5 |
| Thy tender mercies ever last | 397 | 5 |
| Thy thoughts to us-ward overflow | 566 | 5 |
| Thy thunder shakes our coast | 225 | 6 |
| Thy timely help bring in | 818 | 2 |
| †Thy tokens we with joy confess | 62 | 4 |
| †Thy touch has still its ancient power | 969 | 7 |
| Thy true and only Son adore | 647 | 5 |
| Thy truth and grace the heavens transcend | 576 | 2 |
| Thy truth and power defy | 546 | 2 |

| | Hymn | Verse |
|---|---|---|
| Thy truth I lovingly receive. | 401 | 1 |
| Thy truth shall break through every cloud | 563 | 1 |
| Thy trying power display | 152 | 3 |
| Thy tuneful praises, raised on high | 658 | 2 |
| †Thy undistinguishing regard | 39 | 3 |
| Thy unexhausted grace divine | 874 | 1 |
| Thy universal grace proclaim | 745 | 5 |
| Thy universe is full of thee | 259 | 2 |
| Thy utmost goodness called to prove | 114 | 4 |
| Thy uttermost mercy exert | 165 | 2 |
| Thy various offices make known | 261 | 1 |
| Thy vesture dipped in blood | 901 | 1 |
| Thy vesture keeps its bloody hue | 708 | 2 |
| Thy voice, and know that love is near | 373 | 8 |
| †Thy voice produced the sea and spheres | 651 | 2 |
| Thy voice still let me hear | 305 | 3 |
| Thy waiting servants, Lord, inspire | 733 | 3 |
| Thy wakened wrath doth slowly move | 241 | 2 |
| †Thy walls, sweet city! thine | 942 | 7 |
| Thy warfare's past, thy mourning's o'er | 134 | 5 |
| Thy watchman never sleeps | 618 | 2 |
| †Thy way is in great waters | 587 | 6 |
| *Thy way, not mine, O Lord | 837 | 1 |
| Thy ways unsearchable | 244 | 3 |
| Thy weakest servant keep | 188 | 6 |
| Thy whole economy of grace | 261 | 1 |
| Thy whole immensity of love | 513 | 3 |
| Thy will be done | 841 | Cho. |
| Thy will be done, thy name adored. | 279 | 9 |
| Thy will by all be done | 323 | 2 |
| †Thy will by me on earth be done | 357 | 2 |
| Thy will in all things may I see | 338 | 2 |
| Thy will is my salvation, Lord | 307 | 4 |
| Thy will they all perform | 560 | 3 |
| Thy willing mercy flies apace | 241 | 2 |
| Thy wisdom, equal to thy might | 240 | 3 |
| †Thy wisdom here we learn to adore | 1001 | 5 |
| Thy wisdom in our folly show | 475 | 3 |
| Thy wisdom in their lives be shown | 473 | 6 |
| Thy wisdom, power, and might | 242 | 2 |
| Thy wisdom, truth, and power, and love | 377 | 3 |
| Thy witnesses, we | 219 | 4 |
| †Thy witness with my spirit bear | 351 | 2 |
| Thy wonderful design | 128 | 3 |
| †Thy wonders wrought already | 736 | 3 |
| †Thy wondrous love the Godhead showed | 665 | 3 |
| Thy word and mystery to fulfil | 62 | 6 |
| Thy word may to the utmost prove | 391 | 7 |
| Thy word, or seen the gospel light. | 454 | 5 |
| Thy Word, thy all-creating Word | 203 | 4 |
| Thy word, thy oath, to Abraham's race | 342 | 1 |
| Thy words are more than empty sound | 881 | 1 |
| Thy words of promise sure | 610 | 11 |

| | HYMN | VERSE |
|---|---|---|
| Thy words to hear, thy power to feel | 396 | 1 |
| Thy work, O Lord, is all complete | 429 | 3 |
| Thy work we own | 736 | 1 |
| Thy works are all divine | 572 | 2 |
| Thy works of grace, how bright they shine | 599 | 3 |
| Thy wounds and death uphold me | 923 | 2 |
| Thy wounds upon my heart impress | 373 | 5 |
| Thy wrath withdraw, thy hand remove | 283 | 4 |
| Thy yearning pity for mankind | 300 | 1 |
| Thy years, O God, can never fail | 708 | 2 |
| Thy zeal for God in me | 300 | 1 |
| Thyself hast called me by my name | 140 | 2 |
| Thyself in me reveal | 43 | 6 |
| Thyself in us reveal | 299 | 4 |
| Thyself the blessing give | 435 | 3 |
| Thyself The Lord, The God, approve | 412 | 4 |
| Thyself to sinners join | 153 | 3 |
| Thyself to whom I now apply | 881 | 1 |
| Thyself unseen, unknown | 117 | 3 |
| Tidings of their humbled Lord | 684 | 2 |
| †Till added to that heavenly choir | 377 | 4 |
| Till all appear before his throne | 497 | 1 |
| Till all attain the heavenly goal | 536 | 3 |
| Till all before their God appear | 590 | 3 |
| Till all before thy face appear | 592 | 5 |
| Till all his foes submit | 729 | 4 |
| Till all I have is lost in thine | 361 | 1 |
| Till all in thy whole image rise | 524 | 2 |
| Till all mankind shall learn thy name | 492 | 3 |
| Till all my griefs are past | 778 | 4 |
| Till all my hallowed soul is thine | 374 | 3 |
| Till all my sins are purged away | 282 | 4 |
| Till all of pride and wrath be slain | 511 | 2 |
| Till all our souls are filled below | 901 | 4 |
| Till all our wanderings cease | 664 | 4 |
| Till all shall meet in heaven at length | 592 | 5 |
| Till all receive the starry crown | 510 | 5 |
| Till all that are distressed | 562 | 2 |
| Till all the earth is filled with God | 473 | 6 |
| †Till all the earth, renewed | 719 | 6 |
| Till all the hardness he remove | 312 | 5 |
| Till all the ransomed church of God | 798 | 3 |
| Till all the world thy glory see | 731 | 5 |
| Till all thy foes confess thy sway | 236 | 1 |
| Till, all thy foes thy footstool made | 613 | 1 |
| Till all thy grace is given | 548 | 6 |
| Till all thy nature I partake | 576 | 1 |
| Till all thy perfect mind they gain | 474 | 2 |
| Till all thy utmost goodness prove | 510 | 3 |
| Till all thy will be done | 325 | 3 |
| Till all thy will be done | 775 | 4 |
| Till all transformed I know thy name | 284 | 6 |
| †Till, at thy coming from above | 123 | 2 |

| | HYMN | VERSE |
|---|---|---|
| Till bold to say, My hallowing Lord | 370 | 2 |
| Till by faith again I live | 173 | 5 |
| Till Christ, descending from on high | 108 | 4 |
| Till Christ has all the nations blest | 553 | 4 |
| Till Christ the curse repeal | 108 | 4 |
| Till Christ, the Judge, shall come | 54 | 4 |
| Till Christ the Lord descend from high | 268 | 4 |
| Till coming with thy heavenly train | 525 | 8 |
| Till death expires beneath his feet | 629 | 9 |
| Till death expires beneath thy feet | 275 | 9 |
| Till death thy endless mercies seal | 327 | 4 |
| Till each in heaven appears | 591 | 8 |
| Till each o'ercomes at length | 591 | 3 |
| Till each remotest nation | 747 | 3 |
| Till every heartfelt word be mine | 328 | 1 |
| Till every soul is sanctified | 622 | 3 |
| Till faith filled up in sight shall end | 810 | — |
| Till faith shall make my spirit whole | 356 | 5 |
| Till faith shall make us whole | 303 | 6 |
| Till faith to sight improve | 346 | 4 |
| Till far and wide | 595 | 4 |
| Till flesh and earth return me | 943 | 7 |
| Till for all thy glory meet | 530 | 3 |
| Till from every sin set free | 156 | 2 |
| Till, gathered to the church above | 614 | 14 |
| Till God create my peace | 92 | 5 |
| Till, guided by thy Spirit here | 840 | 2 |
| Till heaven and earth flee from thy face | 196 | 3 |
| "Till he come" himself revealed | 990 | 5 |
| Till he feels the cleansing blood | 349 | 1 |
| Till he his glorious self reveals | 117 | 2 |
| Till he his light impart | 117 | 2 |
| Till he shall bid it rise | 930 | 3 |
| Till his banner unfurled in the air | 491 | 8 |
| Till his sign in the heavens appear | 231 | 2 |
| Till his very voice is heard | 817 | 4 |
| Till hope be lost in sight | 943 | 15 |
| Till hope in full fruition die | 346 | 4 |
| Till I am every whit made whole | 436 | 7 |
| Till I am fixed on thee | 271 | 3 |
| Till I am of thee possessed | 156 | 2 |
| Till I am pure in heart | 368 | 8 |
| Till I am saved indeed | 416 | 4 |
| Till I am wholly lost in thee | 388 | 4 |
| Till I become one spirit with thee | 873 | 7 |
| Till I can all things do | 301 | 1 |
| Till I close my earthly race | 672 | 6 |
| Till I, even I, am crowned above | 649 | 3 |
| Till I fully rest in thee | 156 | 2 |
| Till I my Canaan gain | 68 | 5 |
| Till I my principle rejoin | 368 | 1 |
| Till I my strength renew | 356 | 1 |
| Till I my suit obtain | 342 | 3 |

| | Hymn | Verse |
|---|---|---|
| Till I say, by grace restored | 401 | 3 |
| Till I the blessing find | 805 | 2 |
| Till I thine enemies have made | 275 | 1 |
| Till I thy glory see | 214 | 5 |
| Till I thy love retrieve | 356 | 5 |
| Till I thy mercy know | 151 | 4 |
| Till I thy name, thy nature know | 140 | 3 |
| Till I thy name, thy nature know | 140 | 4 |
| Till I thy perfect glory see | 292 | 5 |
| Till I to thy house remove | 554 | 6 |
| Till in glory we appear | 722 | 3 |
| Till in heaven we take our place | 385 | 3 |
| Till in life's latest hour I bow | 912 | 5 |
| Till in the ocean of thy love | 973 | 6 |
| Till in this earth thy judgments dwell | 157 | 8 |
| Till in us thy full likeness shine | 666 | 6 |
| Till Jesu's blood hath washed thy heart | 439 | 3 |
| †Till Jesus in the clouds appear | 979 | 6 |
| Till joined with thine, and made to share | 702 | 3 |
| Till life itself depart | 684 | 3 |
| Till life's fierce tyranny be past | 114 | 1 |
| Till, like a sea of glory | 747 | 4 |
| Till like burnished gold I shine | 336 | 2 |
| Till, like his, their bodies rise | 817 | 7 |
| Till lodged again in Jesu's breast | 461 | 6 |
| Till loose from flesh and earth I rise | 23 | 9 |
| Till man's first heavenly state again takes place | 681 | 5 |
| Till mercy take our sins away | 121 | 5 |
| Till mercy, with its balmy aid | 370 | 1 |
| Till, moulded from above | 329 | 4 |
| Till my all in all thou art | 185 | 2 |
| Till my appointed time shall come | 177 | 5 |
| Till my Deliverer come | 948 | 2 |
| Till my place above I claim | 175 | 5 |
| Till my triumphant spirit comes | 950 | 2 |
| Till nature shall her Judge survey | 665 | 5 |
| Till o'er our ransom'd nature | 747 | 4 |
| Till o'er the earth its branches bend | 589 | 5 |
| Till, of my Eden re-possessed | 348 | 6 |
| Till on earth by every creature | 743 | 3 |
| Till on the margin of the grave | 916 | 4 |
| Till, on the wings of perfect love | 330 | 6 |
| Till our conquering Lord appear | 238 | 4 |
| Till our earthly course is run | 529 | 4 |
| Till our earthly praise be ended | 990 | 6 |
| Till our souls thou receive | 488 | 7 |
| Till pain and woe are past | 818 | 2 |
| Till perfected in holiness | 990 | 4 |
| Till perfect I am found in thee | 196 | 2 |
| Till perfect we are made in one | 351 | 2 |
| Till saved from sins remains | 387 | 3 |
| Till she may behold his face | 990 | 4 |
| Till sinners adore thee, And own thou art true | 200 | 2 |

| | Hymn | Verse |
|---|---|---|
| Till sought and gathered in by thee | 744 | 1 |
| Till sprinkled with thy blood | 102 | 1 |
| Till steadfastly by faith I stand | 361 | 2 |
| Till summoned to the marriage-feast | 217 | 4 |
| Till suns shall rise and set no more | 585 | 7 |
| Till suns shall rise and set no more | 615 | 2 |
| Till sweetly thou hast breathed thy mild | 873 | 7 |
| †Till that welcome hour I see | 554 | 5 |
| Till the blessing thou bestow | 390 | 3 |
| Till the day of doom to last | 604 | 2 |
| Till the earth is o'erflowed | 219 | 7 |
| Till the full course of time be past | 585 | 3 |
| Till the decisive hour | 811 | 3 |
| Till the Lamb shall take us home | 516 | 3 |
| Till the promise is fulfilled | 479 | 3 |
| Till the sprinkling of thy blood | 292 | 5 |
| Till the storm of life be past | 143 | 1 |
| †Till then I would thy love proclaim | 679 | 6 |
| Till then, thou searchest out in vain | 69 | 4 |
| †Till then, to sorrow born, I sigh | 154 | 2 |
| †Till then with us vouchsafe to stay | 649 | 2 |
| Till they gain their full reward | 325 | 5 |
| Till they reach thy throne at length | 593 | 3 |
| Till they seal their faith with blood | 737 | 9 |
| Till they sink in their own eyes | 508 | 5 |
| Till thou again thy blood apply | 180 | 6 |
| Till thou all thy mind declare | 530 | 4 |
| †Till thou anew my soul create | 313 | 4 |
| Till thou appear | 853 | 1 |
| Till thou art saved from sin | 618 | 5 |
| Till thou bring thy nature in | 185 | 2 |
| Till thou collect them with thine eye | 16 | 7 |
| Till thou com'st, the world's desire | 60 | 2 |
| Till thou create my peace | 343 | 6 |
| Till thou destroy the tyrant foe | 187 | 3 |
| Till thou hast made me whole | 105 | 3 |
| Till thou hast made us free indeed | 503 | 5 |
| Till thou hast won the day | 274 | 2 |
| †Till thou into my soul inspire | 342 | 4 |
| Till thou inward light impart | 963 | 2 |
| Till thou, my God, come down | 153 | 3 |
| Till thou, my only rest, return | 134 | 2 |
| Till thou my patient spirit guide | 301 | 6 |
| Till thou my peace again create | 180 | 5 |
| Till thou my sins destroy | 303 | 4 |
| Till thou my sins subdue | 303 | 4 |
| Till thou my unbelief remove | 130 | 2 |
| Till thou our hidden life reveal | 333 | 7 |
| Till thou our ravished spirits fill | 333 | 7 |
| Till thou our wants relieve | 900 | 4 |
| Till thou repeat my sins forgiven | 180 | 6 |
| Till thou shalt all things new create | 303 | 6 |
| Till thou shalt bid us rise | 389 | 1 |

|  | Hymn | Verse |
|---|---|---|
| Till thou the abiding Spirit breathe | 292 | 4 |
| Till thou the power bestow | 153 | 1 |
| Till thou, the Prince of peace, appear | 134 | 2 |
| Till thou the veil remove | 118 | 2 |
| Till thou thine own desires fulfil | 153 | 3 |
| Till thou this alien heart prepare | 770 | 4 |
| Till thou thy blood apply | 982 | 4 |
| †Till thou thy perfect love impart | 297 | 4 |
| Till thou thy quickening influence give | 773 | 3 |
| Till thou thy quickening Spirit breathe | 26 | 4 |
| Till thou thy secret counsel show | 836 | 3 |
| Till thou thy Spirit give | 784 | 5 |
| Till thou thyself bestow | 297 | 4 |
| Till thou thyself declare | 150 | 1 |
| Till thou, who call'dst a world from nought | 294 | 2 |
| †Till, throughly saved, my new-born soul | 180 | 8 |
| Till through the soul thy power is spread | 157 | 6 |
| Till through the world thy truth has run | 553 | 4 |
| Till thy face in heaven they see | 878 | 7 |
| Till thy favour I retrieve | 173 | 5 |
| Till thy lovely face appears | 173 | 5 |
| Till thy love shall make me whole | 183 | 1 |
| Till thy mercy's beams I see | 963 | 2 |
| Till thy mercy visit me | 620 | 2 |
| Till thy Spirit here abides | 109 | 5 |
| Till time shall be no more | 452 | 2 |
| Till time shall be no more | 464 | 1 |
| Till time shall be no more | 466 | 2 |
| Till time shall be no more | 985 | 5 |
| Till to a perfect man we rise | 489 | 2 |
| Till to the home of gladness | 996 | 8 |
| Till toil, and grief, and pain shall cease | 339 | 6 |
| Till, transformed by faith divine | 368 | 3 |
| Till washed in Jesu's blood | 123 | 1 |
| Till we all, in love renewed | 479 | 3 |
| Till we all to God return | 50 | 5 |
| Till we apply to thee alone | 879 | 2 |
| Till we are in Jesus found | 480 | 3 |
| Till we are of thee possessed | 479 | 3 |
| Till we are raised to sing thy name | 677 | 4 |
| Till we can sin no more | 478 | 3 |
| Till we cast our crowns before thee | 385 | 3 |
| Till we feel the stamp divine | 852 | 1 |
| Till we find salvation nigh | 299 | 2 |
| Till we from sin are fully freed | 299 | 1 |
| Till we in full chorus join | 221 | 4 |
| Till we join the church above | 975 | 5 |
| Till we meet at the feast of the Lamb | 491 | 5 |
| Till we, on the sacred tree | 529 | 4 |
| Till we reach the courts above | 905 | 2 |
| Till we receive the crown | 539 | 3 |
| Till we see our Lord appear | 521 | 4 |
| Till we see the perfect day | 295 | 4 |

| | Hymn | Verse |
|---|---|---|
| Till we see the Saviour-God | 295 | 5 |
| Till we take our seats above | 207 | 2 |
| Till we take our seats above | 588 | 4 |
| Till we the crown obtain | 476 | 3 |
| Till we thy name, thy nature know | 380 | 5 |
| Till we, too, change from grace to grace | 698 | 4 |
| Till, within these walls completed | 990 | 2 |
| Till with joy I remove | 205 | 6 |
| Timbrels soft and cymbals loud | 641 | 3 |
| †Time, like an ever-rolling stream | 41 | 6 |
| †Time to repent thou dost bestow | 982 | 2 |
| Tinged with a blue of heavenly dye | 226 | 2 |
| †Tired with the greatness of my way | 25 | 2 |
| 'Tis all but vanity | 809 | 2 |
| 'Tis all I live to know | 92 | 3 |
| 'Tis all I wish to seek | 214 | 4 |
| 'Tis all my business here below | 37 | 5 |
| 'Tis all their happiness to gaze | 34 | 3 |
| 'Tis all we dare entreat | 696 | 4 |
| 'Tis better far to die | 925 | 1 |
| 'Tis better in thee to be gone | 946 | 3 |
| 'Tis but the voice that Jesus sends | 929 | 1 |
| 'Tis certain, though impossible | 401 | 3 |
| †'Tis done! my God hath died | 27 | 2 |
| †'Tis done, the great transaction's done | 912 | 3 |
| †'Tis done! the precious ransom's paid | 22 | 3 |
| †'Tis done! thou dost this moment save | 417 | 6 |
| †'Tis finished! all the debt is paid | 706 | 2 |
| 'Tis finished! he expires for me | 706 | 6 |
| 'Tis finished! he hath died for me | 127 | 8 |
| *'Tis finished! The Messias dies | 706 | 1 |
| †'Tis fit we should to dust return | 913 | 2 |
| 'Tis fixed; I can do all through thee | 279 | 10 |
| 'Tis for such, thyself declarest | 895 | 1 |
| 'Tis found beneath the mercy-seat | 825 | 1 |
| 'Tis God invites the fallen race | 4 | 1 |
| 'Tis God made man, for man to die | 38 | 7 |
| 'Tis good at thy word to be here | 946 | 3 |
| 'Tis grace salvation brings | 383 | 1 |
| 'Tis heaven to see our Jesu's face | 34 | 3 |
| †'Tis he forgives thy sins | 610 | 3 |
| 'Tis he relieves thy pain | 610 | 3 |
| 'Tis he that heals thy sickness | 610 | 3 |
| 'Tis he! 'tis he | 854 | 1 |
| †'Tis here, in hope my God to find | 781 | 4 |
| †'Tis here thine unknown paths we trace | 1001 | 3 |
| †'Tis his almighty love | 814 | 2 |
| †'Tis his the drooping soul to raise | 107 | 4 |
| 'Tis immortality | 944 | 1 |
| 'Tis I thy sacred flesh have torn | 23 | 3 |
| 'Tis Jesus calls for thee | 792 | 2 |
| 'Tis Jesus, the First and the Last | 660 | — |
| 'Tis just;—but O thy Son hath died | 127 | 7 |

| | Hymn | Verse |
|---|---|---|
| 'Tis just the sentence should take place | 127 | 7 |
| 'Tis life, and health, and peace | 1 | 3 |
| 'Tis life and victory | 34 | 4 |
| 'Tis life everlasting, 'tis heaven below | 205 | 4 |
| †'Tis Love! 'tis Love! thou diedst for me | 141 | 2 |
| 'Tis madness to delay | 792 | 3 |
| 'Tis manna to the hungry soul | 679 | 2 |
| 'Tis mercy all, immense and free | 201 | 3 |
| 'Tis mercy all, let earth adore | 201 | 2 |
| †'Tis mercy all, that thou hast brought | 344 | 3 |
| 'Tis more than angel-tongues can tell | 384 | 8 |
| 'Tis music in his ears | 34 | 4 |
| 'Tis music in the sinner's ears | 1 | 3 |
| †'Tis mystery all! The Immortal dies | 201 | 2 |
| 'Tis nature all, and all delight | 456 | 6 |
| 'Tis not thou, but she must die | 921 | 3 |
| 'Tis seized by violent hands | 277 | 4 |
| †'Tis strung and tuned for endless years | 798 | 7 |
| 'Tis swallowed up in victory | 706 | 5 |
| 'Tis there I would always abide | 228 | 3 |
| †'Tis there, with the lambs of thy flock | 228 | 3 |
| 'Tis the Spirit's rising beam | 791 | 3 |
| †'Tis thine a heart of flesh to give | 131 | 2 |
| 'Tis thine arm alone that saves | 878 | 1 |
| 'Tis thine own work, Almighty God | 617 | 4 |
| 'Tis thine the blood to apply | 85 | 1 |
| 'Tis thine the first good thought to inspire | 770 | 1 |
| 'Tis this alone can cast out sin | 132 | 4 |
| 'Tis this alone can make me clean | 132 | 4 |
| 'Tis thou alone canst make me whole | 132 | 2 |
| 'Tis thou must make it new | 91 | 7 |
| 'Tis through thy light and comes from thee | 210 | 3 |
| †'Tis through thy love alone we gain | 626 | 2 |
| 'Tis thy wounds my healing give | 904 | 2 |
| 'Tis worth living for this | 231 | 11 |
| 'Tis written by his finger | 856 | 4 |
| To Abraham and his seed | 888 | 1 |
| †To accomplish his design | 832 | 6 |
| To Adam's offspring given | 459 | 4 |
| To administer bliss | 231 | 11 |
| To adore the all-atoning Lamb | 34 | 1 |
| To a dry, barren place | 292 | 2 |
| To a forgiving God | 123 | 1 |
| To a poor virgin's womb | 413 | 2 |
| To a reigning church above | 52 | 4 |
| To a taste of the banquet above | 499 | 1 |
| To aggravate my present care | 835 | 2 |
| To aid me in distress | 634 | 2 |
| To aid the common good | 822 | 3 |
| To alarm their fear, excite their hope | 468 | 5 |
| To all believing hearts | 875 | 3 |
| To all by sin and hell oppressed | 545 | 2 |
| To all eternity | 18 | 3 |

| | Hymn | Verse |
|---|---|---|
| To all eternity | 43 | 6 |
| To all eternity | 44 | 1 |
| To all eternity | 58 | 2 |
| To all eternity | 83 | 8 |
| To all eternity | 169 | 5 |
| To all eternity | 256 | 6 |
| To all eternity | 274 | 2 |
| To all eternity | 382 | 5 |
| To all eternity | 423 | 4 |
| To all eternity | 428 | 4 |
| To all eternity | 506 | 3 |
| To all in earth and all in heaven | 721 | 1 |
| To all I shall proclaim | 275 | 8 |
| To all my Saviour's righteous will | 408 | 1 |
| †To all my weak complaints and cries | 657 | 3 |
| To all so freely given | 543 | 5 |
| To all the heights of love I rise | 365 | 2 |
| To all the nations call | 314 | 2 |
| To all their fierce or cool disdain | 439 | 1 |
| To all their paradise restored | 473 | 2 |
| To all thy Church and me | 179 | 2 |
| To all thy inward life restored | 330 | 5 |
| To all thy people known | 403 | 1 |
| To all thy tempted followers give | 297 | 1 |
| To all, to all, thy bowels move | 39 | 5 |
| To all, who hate or bless thy sway | 241 | 3 |
| To all who seek thy love | 781 | 7 |
| To all who speak for thee | 873 | 3 |
| †To an unrighteous judge she came | 827 | 3 |
| To apply, and witness with the blood | 9 | 3 |
| To apprehend his love | 781 | 4 |
| To ask thy pardoning grace | 119 | 1 |
| To attend the whispers of thy grace | 214 | 4 |
| To augment the source of perfect bliss | 291 | 1 |
| †To baffle the wise, And noble, and strong | 212 | 4 |
| To battle all proceed | 266 | 4 |
| To battle all proceed | 277 | 3 |
| To be at last restored | 61 | 4 |
| To be dissolved in love | 415 | 3 |
| To be employed for us | 322 | 1 |
| To be exalted thus | 678 | 2 |
| To be honoured and adored | 233 | 3 |
| To be honoured and adored | 1021 | 2 |
| To be received and reared for heaven | 896 | 2 |
| To be redeemed from sin | 417 | 2 |
| To be so loved by thee | 544 | 2 |
| To be the house of God | 18 | 1 |
| To be thus shy of death | 931 | 5 |
| †To Bethlehem straight the enlightened shepherds ran | 691 | 4 |
| To bid their hearts rejoice | 34 | 7 |
| To blast the blooming work of grace | 458 | 4 |
| To bleed and die for thee | 22 | 1 |

| | HYMN | VERSE |
|---|---|---|
| TO BLESS | | |
| To bless me, thou a curse wast made | 23 | 4 |
| To bless our earth again | 730 | 1 |
| To bless them as they kneel | 996 | 6 |
| To bless the sacred name | 678 | 4 |
| *To bless thy chosen race | 581 | 1 |
| To bow beneath thy feet | 275 | 1 |
| To break, and to bind up my heart | 782 | 2 |
| To break the power of cancelled sin | 456 | 5 |
| To brighten and refine | 414 | 2 |
| To bring fire on earth he came | 115 | 4 |
| To bring fire on earth he came | 218 | 1 |
| To bring our vileness near | 685 | 4 |
| To bring the long-sought Saviour down | 902 | 5 |
| To bring the rebel near to God | 365 | 4 |
| To bring thy sayings to our mind | 754 | 3 |
| To bring us, daily, nearer God | 965 | 6 |
| To bring us rebels back to God | 28 | 3 |
| To build and finish me | 383 | 1 |
| To build our heavenly hopes upon | 617 | 1 |
| To build our hopes, to fix our eyes | 865 | 4 |
| To buy me from the power of sin | 146 | 4 |
| To call and invite you His triumph to prove | 40 | 1 |
| To call in vain on *me* | 697 | 4 |
| To call the Hebrews home | 452 | 5 |
| To call them to his arms | 929 | 1 |
| To Calvary alone I flee | 795 | 4 |
| To Canaan's bounds I urge my way | 800 | 5 |
| To Canaan's bounds thou hast me led | 293 | 3 |
| To carnal minds unknown | 539 | 9 |
| To carry us above | 12 | 2 |
| To cast our arms, our sins, away | 11 | 2 |
| To cast the children's bread | 164 | 4 |
| †To cast their crowns before thee | 996 | 8 |
| To catch the wandering of my will | 808 | 1 |
| To celebrate thy fame | 581 | 3 |
| To celebrate with me | 84 | 1 |
| To certain victory | 314 | 3 |
| To change my human to divine | 330 | 2 |
| To change this old rebellious heart | 416 | 5 |
| To charm the multitude at will | 695 | 2 |
| To chase our darkness by his light | 686 | 2 |
| To cheer it after rain | 804 | 1 |
| To cheer the souls he loves | 637 | 4 |
| To child-like innocence | 528 | 2 |
| To choose and to command | 831 | 12 |
| To Christ alone he dies | 428 | 2 |
| To Christ alone resolved to live | 285 | 6 |
| To Christ, the power of God in man | 401 | 6 |
| To claim my mansion in the skies | 190 | 6 |
| To cleanse from all iniquity | 330 | 2 |
| To cleanse from all unrighteousness | 380 | 2 |
| To cleanse us all, both you and me | 345 | 3 |
| TO CLOTHE | | |
| To clothe them with the robes of praise | 107 | 4 |

| | Hymn | Verse |
|---|---|---|
| To all eternity | 43 | 6 |
| To all eternity | 44 | 1 |
| To all eternity | 58 | 2 |
| To all eternity | 83 | 8 |
| To all eternity | 169 | 5 |
| To all eternity | 256 | 6 |
| To all eternity | 274 | 2 |
| To all eternity | 382 | 5 |
| To all eternity | 423 | 4 |
| To all eternity | 428 | 4 |
| To all eternity | 506 | 3 |
| To all in earth and all in heaven | 721 | 1 |
| To all I shall proclaim | 275 | 8 |
| To all my Saviour's righteous will | 408 | 1 |
| †To all my weak complaints and cries | 657 | 3 |
| To all so freely given | 543 | 5 |
| To all the heights of love I rise | 365 | 2 |
| To all the nations call | 314 | 2 |
| To all their fierce or cool disdain | 439 | 1 |
| To all their paradise restored | 473 | 2 |
| To all thy Church and me | 179 | 2 |
| To all thy inward life restored | 330 | 5 |
| To all thy people known | 403 | 1 |
| To all thy tempted followers give | 297 | 1 |
| To all, to all, thy bowels move | 39 | 5 |
| To all, who hate or bless thy sway | 241 | 3 |
| To all who seek thy love | 781 | 7 |
| To all who speak for thee | 873 | 3 |
| †To an unrighteous judge she came | 827 | 3 |
| To apply, and witness with the blood | 9 | 3 |
| To apprehend his love | 781 | 4 |
| To ask thy pardoning grace | 119 | 1 |
| To attend the whispers of thy grace | 214 | 4 |
| To augment the source of perfect bliss | 291 | 1 |
| †To baffle the wise, And noble, and strong | 212 | 4 |
| To battle all proceed | 266 | 4 |
| To battle all proceed | 277 | 3 |
| To be at last restored | 61 | 4 |
| To be dissolved in love | 415 | 3 |
| To be employed for us | 322 | 1 |
| To be exalted thus | 678 | 2 |
| To be honoured and adored | 233 | 3 |
| To be honoured and adored | 1021 | 2 |
| To be received and reared for heaven | 896 | 2 |
| To be redeemed from sin | 417 | 2 |
| To be so loved by thee | 544 | 2 |
| To be the house of God | 18 | 1 |
| To be thus shy of death | 931 | 5 |
| †To Bethlehem straight the enlightened shepherds ran | 691 | 4 |
| To bid their hearts rejoice | 34 | 7 |
| To blast the blooming work of grace | 458 | 4 |
| To bleed and die for thee | 22 | 1 |

| | Hymn | Verse |
|---|---|---|
| To bless me, thou a curse wast made | 23 | 4 |
| To bless our earth again | 730 | 1 |
| To bless them as they kneel | 996 | 6 |
| To bless the sacred name | 678 | 4 |
| *To bless thy chosen race | 581 | 1 |
| To bow beneath thy feet | 275 | 1 |
| To break, and to bind up my heart | 782 | 2 |
| To break the power of cancelled sin | 456 | 5 |
| To brighten and refine | 414 | 2 |
| To bring fire on earth he came | 115 | 4 |
| To bring fire on earth he came | 218 | 1 |
| To bring our vileness near | 685 | 4 |
| To bring the long-sought Saviour down | 902 | 5 |
| To bring the rebel near to God | 365 | 4 |
| To bring thy sayings to our mind | 754 | 3 |
| To bring us, daily, nearer God | 965 | 6 |
| To bring us rebels back to God | 28 | 3 |
| To build and finish me | 383 | 1 |
| To build our heavenly hopes upon | 617 | 1 |
| To build our hopes, to fix our eyes | 865 | 4 |
| To buy me from the power of sin | 146 | 4 |
| To call and invite you His triumph to prove | 40 | 1 |
| To call in vain on *me* | 697 | 4 |
| To call the Hebrews home | 452 | 5 |
| To call them to his arms | 929 | 1 |
| To Calvary alone I flee | 795 | 4 |
| To Canaan's bounds I urge my way | 800 | 5 |
| To Canaan's bounds thou hast me led | 293 | 3 |
| To carnal minds unknown | 539 | 9 |
| To carry us above | 12 | 2 |
| To cast our arms, our sins, away | 11 | 2 |
| To cast the children's bread | 164 | 4 |
| †To cast their crowns before thee | 996 | 8 |
| To catch the wandering of my will | 308 | 1 |
| To celebrate thy fame | 581 | 3 |
| To celebrate with me | 84 | 1 |
| To certain victory | 314 | 3 |
| To change my human to divine | 830 | 2 |
| To change this old rebellious heart | 416 | 5 |
| To charm the multitude at will | 695 | 2 |
| To chase our darkness by his light | 686 | 2 |
| To cheer it after rain | 804 | 1 |
| To cheer the souls he loves | 637 | 4 |
| To child-like innocence | 528 | 2 |
| To choose and to command | 831 | 12 |
| To Christ alone he dies | 428 | 2 |
| To Christ alone resolved to live | 285 | 6 |
| To Christ, the power of God in man | 401 | 6 |
| To claim my mansion in the skies | 190 | 6 |
| To cleanse from all iniquity | 830 | 2 |
| To cleanse from all unrighteousness | 380 | 2 |
| To cleanse us all, both you and me | 345 | 3 |
| To clothe them with the robes of praise | 107 | 4 |

| | Hymn | Verse |
|---|---|---|
| To come and pluck me thence | 820 | 6 |
| To comfort a mourner appear | 174 | 3 |
| To comfort and to bless | 943 | 14 |
| To comfort, help, defend me | 923 | 1 |
| To comprehend the Eternal Mind | 384 | 6 |
| To conquer and renew | 416 | 5 |
| To conquer death, my final foe | 69 | 2 |
| To conquest and a crown | 675 | 9 |
| To cross this narrow sea | 938 | 4 |
| To crown him Lord of all | 681 | 1 |
| To cry, "Behold the Lamb!" | 37 | 5 |
| To cut the fig-tree down | 981 | 3 |
| †To damp our earthly joys | 55 | 3 |
| To-day as yesterday the same | 95 | 1 |
| †To-day attend his voice | 603 | 4 |
| †To-day, before to-morrow come | 788 | 2 |
| †To-day on weary nations | 958 | 4 |
| To-day, while it is called to-day | 81 | 3 |
| To-day, while it is called to-day | 410 | 2 |
| To-day, while it is called to-day | 782 | 4 |
| *To-day, while it is called to-day | 788 | 1 |
| To-day, while it is called to-day | 982 | 2 |
| To desecrate our hallowed strain | 204 | 3 |
| †To destroy his work of sin | 299 | 4 |
| To die for sins that man had done | 644 | 1 |
| To different climes repair | 585 | 1 |
| To do my Master's will | 318 | 1 |
| To do on earth thy blessed will | 528 | 4 |
| To doubt and fear give thou no heed | 789 | 1 |
| To draw, redeem, and seal, is thine | 131 | 2 |
| To drink of his pleasures unknown | 79 | 1 |
| To drink the pure river of bliss | 78 | 2 |
| To drive thee from my heart | 182 | 3 |
| To dwell in temples made with hands | 992 | 1 |
| To dwell with Christ is better life | 715 | 8 |
| To dwell within that gate of heaven | 590 | 2 |
| To dwell within thy wounds, then pain | 26 | 1 |
| To each kindred, tribe, and tongue | 604 | 2 |
| †To each the covenant blood apply | 532 | 6 |
| †To each the hallowing Spirit give | 893 | 2 |
| To earth and flesh again | 943 | 7 |
| To earthquake, plague, or sword | 61 | 4 |
| To earth's remotest bounds | 738 | 1 |
| To ease, and joy, and rest | 614 | 6 |
| To ease them of their bitter pain | 698 | 1 |
| To Egypt returned, And fled from his face | 481 | 4 |
| To embrace the happy toil | 536 | 2 |
| To end, as to begin, is thine | 773 | 1 |
| To endless ages still the same | 386 | 2 |
| To endless rest Are called away | 991 | 4 |
| To endless years endure | 610 | 11 |
| To endless years the same | 41 | 3 |
| To enforce and make her suit his own | 827 | 7 |

# TO ERECT — TO FRUSTRATE

| | Hymn | Verse |
|---|---|---|
| To erect that final monarchy | 445 | 2 |
| To everlasting bliss | 956 | 4 |
| To everlasting day | 288 | 5 |
| To every asking sinner given | 411 | 2 |
| To every faithful soul appear | 902 | 5 |
| To every heart of man | 251 | 3 |
| To every nation, And people, and tongue | 40 | 7 |
| †To every one whom God shall call | 759 | 2 |
| To every sinful child of man | 438 | 1 |
| To every soul, abound | 250 | 3 |
| To every soul (all praise to thee) | 237 | 1 |
| To every soul thy Son reveal | 441 | 4 |
| To every waiting soul it comes | 630 | 4 |
| To exclude me from thy people's rest | 161 | 4 |
| To expect his return from above | 488 | 1 |
| To extol thy majesty divine | 647 | 3 |
| To fairer worlds on high | 12 | 4 |
| To faith's discerning eye | 862 | 2 |
| To fall and to suffer no more | 165 | 4 |
| To fall asleep is not to die | 715 | 8 |
| To farther conquests go | 535 | 2 |
| To fashion every passive heart | 528 | 1 |
| To Father, and to Son | 958 | 5 |
| To favour now through thee restored | 1005 | 1 |
| To feel my pardon sealed in blood | 290 | 5 |
| To feel the clouds that round me roll | 100 | 2 |
| To feel the curse remove | 703 | 5 |
| To feel the virtue of thy blood | 92 | 3 |
| To feel thy power, to hear thy voice | 344 | 8 |
| To fight our passage through | 510 | 5 |
| To fight the Philistine | 278 | 4 |
| To fill and rule thy heart | 406 | 5 |
| To fill an humble place | 731 | 8 |
| To fill a throne above | 985 | 4 |
| To fill thy worshippers with dread | 994 | 1 |
| To find the Crucified | 468 | 4 |
| To find the God of love | 661 | 1 |
| To find the new Jerusalem | 71 | 4 |
| To find the way to Zion's gate | 592 | 4 |
| To finish and abolish sin | 443 | 2 |
| To finish the transgression | 818 | 4 |
| †To fit his soul for heavenly grace | 467 | 9 |
| To fly the good I would pursue | 849 | 2 |
| To follow after peace, and prize | 442 | 4 |
| To follow his command | 840 | 1 |
| To follow the heavenly Lamb | 371 | 1 |
| To foolish man unknown | 288 | 4 |
| To forfeit it no more | 256 | 5 |
| To form themselves in prayer | 657 | 3 |
| To form thy favourite, man | 256 | 4 |
| To found the fellowship of saints | 527 | 5 |
| To frail earthen vessels And things of no worth | 869 | 1 |
| To frustrate his decree | 832 | 4 |

| | Hymn | Verse |
|---|---|---|
| To full salvation here | 478 | 1 |
| To gain earth's gilded toys, or flee | 279 | 3 |
| To gain my worthless heart | 137 | 5 |
| To gather home his own | 585 | 6 |
| To Gentiles make thy goodness known | 444 | 2 |
| To give away this bride | 996 | 4 |
| To give me up, so long pursued | 178 | 3 |
| To give salvation, and to pardon sin | 967 | 5 |
| To give them songs for sighing | 586 | 2 |
| To give thy word success | 789 | 3 |
| To glorify my God below | 320 | 2 |
| To glorify our God | 1015 | — |
| To glorious happiness | 44 | 6 |
| †To God, at length I cried | 634 | 3 |
| †To God, most worthy to be praised | 997 | 2 |
| †To God the Father, God the Son | 966 | 6 |
| To God the Father's love | 644 | 1 |
| To God the Master of the feast | 1023 | — |
| *To God, the only wise | 814 | 1 |
| †To God the Son belongs | 644 | 2 |
| †To God the Spirit's name | 644 | 3 |
| To God Three in One Eternally be | 869 | 6 |
| To God with faith draw near | 268 | 1 |
| To God, who all creation made | 663 | — |
| To God, who lengthens out our days | 980 | 1 |
| To God your every want | 267 | 4 |
| †To God your spirits dart | 268 | 2 |
| To God's almighty Word | 407 | 6 |
| To govern each devoted heart | 526 | 5 |
| To govern me and mine | 844 | 1 |
| To grasp the God we seek | 947 | 8 |
| To gratitude and worship drawn | 957 | 3 |
| To grow with wheat—yet be a tare | 935 | 3 |
| To guard and feed the chosen race | 704 | 2 |
| To guard his holy law | 650 | 1 |
| To guard my soul from every ill | 632 | 5 |
| To guard the sacred treasure there | 873 | 4 |
| To guard what thou hast given | 469 | 11 |
| To guide me through the gulf of night | 130 | 2 |
| To guide us through the dreary way | 767 | 1 |
| To happiness they tend | 540 | 6 |
| To hardship, grief, and loss | 301 | 2 |
| To hate the sin with all my heart | 270 | 4 |
| To have our home on high | 943 | 2 |
| To heal me, thou hast borne my pain | 23 | 4 |
| To heal their sorrows, Lord, descend | 924 | 3 |
| To heal thy sin-sick people's care | 294 | 4 |
| To hear and keep thy every word | 429 | 1 |
| To hear his trumpet sound | 949 | 5 |
| To hear the Bridegroom's voice | 147 | 4 |
| To hear thy voice and live | 865 | 3 |
| To hear, to heal me, and to save | 559 | 1 |
| To heaven ascend | 800 | 4 |

| | Hymn | Verse |
|---|---|---|
| To help each other on | 527 | 3 |
| To help his weakness on | 487 | 2 |
| †To help our soul's infirmity | 294 | 4 |
| †To help their grovelling unbelief | 107 | 5 |
| To help the poor and needy | 586 | 2 |
| To help the souls redeemed by thee | 89 | 5 |
| To her eternal rest | 137 | 1 |
| To her God his praise restoring | 604 | 1 |
| To hide thee from thy servant's eyes | 973 | 1 |
| To him commend thy cause, his ear | 831 | 4 |
| †To him continually aspire | 420 | 4 |
| To him devote my happy days | 638 | 1 |
| To him, enthroned above all height | 494 | 2 |
| To him I raised my mournful cry | 634 | 1 |
| To him I would not pay | 93 | 4 |
| †To him mine eye of faith I turn | 272 | 3 |
| To him my thanks and praises give | 638 | 1 |
| To him of old allowed | 249 | 1 |
| †To him our request We now have made known | 496 | 2 |
| To him shall bow the knee | 586 | 4 |
| †To him that in thy name believes | 95 | 4 |
| To him that reigns above | 605 | 4 |
| To him they glory give | 941 | 4 |
| †To him thou hourly deign'st to give | 544 | 3 |
| To *him*, to us, the seal | 892 | 1 |
| To him who gave himself for me | 375 | 4 |
| To him who falls alone | 487 | 2 |
| To him who merits all my love | 912 | 2 |
| To him who rules above | 277 | 1 |
| To him with joyful voices give | 208 | 1 |
| To his beloved embrace | 534 | 4 |
| To his command we bow | 949 | 2 |
| To his eternal joy | 954 | 4 |
| To his everlasting home | 720 | 3 |
| To his everlasting rest | 922 | 3 |
| To his glorious likeness wrought | 921 | 1 |
| To his heavenly palace gate | 720 | 1 |
| To his heaven restored | 760 | 1 |
| To his image here restored | 480 | 3 |
| To his people's cry he hearkened | 606 | 3 |
| To his ransomed worshippers | 66 | 3 |
| To his sure truth and tender care | 831 | 1 |
| To his unerring, gracious will | 846 | 3 |
| To his uttermost salvation | 922 | 3 |
| †To hoary hairs be thou *his* God | 985 | 4 |
| To holy convocations | 958 | 4 |
| To Holy Ghost be praises | 958 | 5 |
| To hurry mortals home | 42 | 4 |
| To hymn the mystic Three in One | 647 | 4 |
| To Immanuel's land | 498 | 3 |
| To increase our gracious fears | 55 | 3 |
| To its Judge an answer making | 933 | 4 |
| To Jesus and each other cleaved | 16 | 1 |

| | Hymn | Verse |
|---|---|---|
| To Jesus and his servants dear | 490 | 1 |
| To Jesus draw nigh | 707 | 1 |
| †To Jesu's name give thanks and sing | 539 | 2 |
| †To Jesu's name if all things now | 136 | 4 |
| To Jesu's name submit | 136 | 3 |
| To join and perfect us in love | 459 | 4 |
| To join, redeemed, a glad triumphant throng | 691 | 6 |
| To join the family above | 997 | 4 |
| To join the music of the skies | 658 | 4 |
| To join their loving hands | 996 | 5 |
| To join with softest sympathy | 510 | 2 |
| To joys celestial rise | 949 | 1 |
| To joys that never end | 761 | 6 |
| To judge the human race | 55 | 2 |
| To judge the nations at thy bar | 59 | 4 |
| To judge the world he made | 605 | 7 |
| To keep and cultivate | 842 | 4 |
| To keep me safe from every snare | 310 | 1 |
| To keep us pure in life and heart | 254 | 2 |
| †To keep your armour bright | 267 | 3 |
| To know, and love, and live to thee | 234 | 3 |
| To know, and love, and see | 941 | 3 |
| To know and love thyself, and find | 264 | 2 |
| To know it now resolved I am | 140 | 4 |
| To know thee, who thou art | 122 | 2 |
| To know the wonders thou hast wrought | 26 | 7 |
| To know thou tak'st me for thine own | 285 | 7 |
| To know thy favour sure | 659 | 6 |
| †To know thy nature, and thy name | 251 | 2 |
| To labour in the gospel field | 524 | 3 |
| To laud and magnify | 262 | 2 |
| To lay my soul at Jesu's feet | 388 | 1 |
| To lay this body down | 43 | 1 |
| To leave his Father's breast | 215 | 2 |
| To lie at the foot of the rock | 228 | 3 |
| To life and happiness | 21 | 1 |
| To life eternal lead | 985 | 2 |
| To live and sin no more | 119 | 4 |
| To live more nearly as we pray | 965 | 7 |
| To live with him in heaven | 80 | 6 |
| To lose our melting will in thine | 528 | 3 |
| To lose, when perfected in love | 375 | 1 |
| To love and serve thee is my share | 920 | 1 |
| †To love is all my wish | 27 | 4 |
| To love my God I only live | 155 | 1 |
| †To love my sins,—a saint to appear | 935 | 3 |
| To love's sweet paradise | 389 | 1 |
| †To magnify thy awful name | 204 | 4 |
| †To make an end of sin | 761 | 3 |
| To make an end of sin | 818 | 4 |
| To make his grace to mortals known | 675 | 3 |
| To make me all my vileness feel | 126 | 5 |
| To make my heart and nature clean | 780 | 2 |

| | Hymn | Verse |
|---|---|---|
| To make my ruin sure | 310 | 3 |
| To make our utmost efforts vain | 475 | 2 |
| To make the depths of Godhead known | 377 | 2 |
| †To make them trees of righteousness | 107 | 6 |
| To make this duty our delight | 225 | 1 |
| To make thy chariot way | 226 | 5 |
| To make us anew, Come, Lord, from above | 481 | 5 |
| To make us in thy will complete | 89 | 4 |
| To make us share the life divine | 377 | 2 |
| To manifest his glorious name | 616 | 10 |
| To mark the bounds of good and ill | 467 | 7 |
| To mature the swelling grain | 631 | 4 |
| *To me, almighty Saviour, give | 884 | — |
| To me, and all the fallen race | 878 | 1 |
| To me be all thy treasures given | 134 | 1 |
| To me did freely move | 137 | 3 |
| To me, for Jesu's sake, impart | 364 | 3 |
| To me he soon shall bring it nigh | 803 | 4 |
| To me in willing mercy bowed | 909 | 1 |
| To me, my Saviour, come | 413 | 2 |
| To me reached out I view | 405 | 3 |
| To me shall all be given | 357 | 8 |
| To me the rest of faith impart | 403 | 4 |
| To me the victor's title give | 72 | 4 |
| To me thou oft hast proved | 335 | 2 |
| To me thy compassionate grace | 911 | 3 |
| To me thy succour bring | 852 | 1 |
| To me! 'tis one great wilderness | 117 | 1 |
| To me, to all restore | 252 | 2 |
| To me, to all, thy bowels move | 141 | 2 |
| To me, to me, thy goodness show | 283 | 1 |
| To me, when I am all renewed | 401 | 6 |
| To me, with thy dear name, are given | 209 | 2 |
| To meet a joyful doom | 59 | 4 |
| To meet him in the skies | 976 | 3 |
| To meet its sentence there | 48 | 3 |
| †To meet our desperate want | 892 | 4 |
| To meet our elder Brother there | 497 | 4 |
| To meet the assemblies of thy saints | 592 | 1 |
| To meet the general doom | 54 | 4 |
| To meet the glad with joyful smiles | 842 | 2 |
| To meet thee from above | 384 | 5 |
| To meet thee in the skies | 62 | 3 |
| To meet thy special presence there | 590 | 1 |
| To meet your God prepare | 63 | 2 |
| To minister his pardoning grace | 107 | 2 |
| To mortal man revealed | 642 | 4 |
| To mortal want and labour born | 692 | 1 |
| †To mourn for thy coming is sweet | 946 | 4 |
| To murderer-Moloch through the fire | 467 | 4 |
| To my atoning God | 982 | 3 |
| To my deceitful prayer | 357 | 4 |
| To my diseased, my fainting soul | 785 | 1 |

|  | Hymn | Verse |
|---|---|---|
| To my eternal bliss | 867 | 3 |
| To my eternal rest | 296 | 2 |
| To my conscience signify | 676 | 1 |
| To my offended Father cry | 178 | 1 |
| To my oppressor's scorn | 567 | 3 |
| To my waiting soul reveal | 358 | 2 |
| To none that asked denied | 842 | 5 |
| To obtain the grace I humbly claim | 806 | 1 |
| To offend thy glorious eyes | 204 | 3 |
| To One God in Persons Three | 720 | Dox. |
| To our dying souls appear | 762 | 2 |
| To our eternal rest | 535 | 4 |
| To our Father and King | 491 | 7 |
| To our great father given | 888 | 3 |
| To our high calling's glorious hope | 500 | 2 |
| To our permanent home | 499 | 3 |
| To our Redeemer's name | 771 | 3 |
| To our steadfast mansion there | 67 | 4 |
| To pardon and bless us, And perfect us here | 481 | 1 |
| To patient faith the prize is sure | 333 | 3 |
| To pay thy morning sacrifice | 964 | 1 |
| To perfect health restore my soul | 363 | 4 |
| To perfect health restore my soul | 408 | 8 |
| To perfect heaven restored | 74 | 2 |
| To perfect holiness | 96 | 6 |
| To perfect holiness and love | 363 | 4 |
| To perfect holiness and love | 408 | 8 |
| To perish in my sins at last | 178 | 3 |
| To persevering prayer | 295 | 4 |
| To pity and forgive | 821 | — |
| To pity or redress | 634 | 2 |
| To plead the merits of thy Son | 574 | 10 |
| To please our God alone | 204 | 2 |
| †To please thee thus, at length I see | 91 | 4 |
| To ploughshares men shall beat their swords | 740 | 5 |
| To point him out his lost estate | 467 | 6 |
| To point us out the narrow road | 468 | 1 |
| To pour the balm of Gilead in | 782 | 2 |
| To pour the wealth of ocean | 586 | 4 |
| To praise a Trinity adored | 262 | 1 |
| To praise in songs divine | 685 | 1 |
| To praise the Lamb who died for all | 39 | 2 |
| To praise thy glorious name | 581 | 3 |
| To praise thy name, give thanks, and sing | 599 | 1 |
| To pray and never cease | 301 | 4 |
| †To pray, and wait the hour | 55 | 2 |
| To preach their sins forgiven | 472 | 6 |
| To procure your peace with God | 8 | 1 |
| To prove and do thy perfect will | 429 | 1 |
| To prove his will | 854 | 3 |
| To pruning-hooks their spears | 740 | 5 |
| †To purest joys she all invites | 14 | 5 |
| To purge all fierce and foul desire | 456 | 4 |

| | Hymn | Verse |
|---|---|---|
| To purge my sins, and loose my bands | 269 | 8 |
| To purge the guilt of all our sins | 705 | 3 |
| To purge the guilty offerer's stain | 702 | 2 |
| To push us to the tomb | 42 | 4 |
| To put it on afresh | 930 | 2 |
| To quench my thirst, and make me clean | 391 | 3 |
| To raise the corn, and cheer the vine | 978 | 2 |
| To raise them strong and fair | 584 | 6 |
| To ransom wretched man | 605 | 4 |
| To reach the land I love | 944 | 4 |
| To read his will aright | 549 | 4 |
| †To real holiness restored | 369 | 2 |
| To realms of endless day | 713 | 5 |
| To realms of everlasting rest | 686 | 2 |
| To receive their heavenly King | 720 | 1 |
| To recognise him from above | 673 | 1 |
| To redeem such a rebel as me | 807 | 3 |
| To render me secure | 310 | 3 |
| To rescue all by sin opprest | 107 | 4 |
| To rescue all mankind | 989 | 3 |
| †To rescue me from woe | 137 | 5 |
| To resound thy name in song | 598 | 1 |
| To rest awhile with thee | 863 | 1 |
| To restore thine image lost | 368 | 4 |
| To rid my soul of one dark blot | 796 | 2 |
| To rise, redeemed from earthly care | 919 | 2 |
| To rouse us, O Lord, From slumber of sin | 869 | 5 |
| To rule my family aright | 470 | 2 |
| To rush into thy kingdom, Lord | 265 | 1 |
| To saints on earth forgiven | 979 | 6 |
| To sanctify here, And bear us away | 484 | 3 |
| To sanctify us by his blood | 394 | 3 |
| To sanctify us while we sing | 752 | 2 |
| To save a fallen race | 34 | 6 |
| To save a ruined race | 245 | 3 |
| To save a wretch like me | 83 | 6 |
| To save, and to forgive | 245 | 4 |
| To save me from all guilt and pain | 133 | 6 |
| To save me from low-thoughted care | 344 | 6 |
| To save me in the trying hour | 292 | 3 |
| To save our souls from Satan's wiles | 966 | 3 |
| To save poor souls out of the fire | 433 | 2 |
| To save rebellious worms | 263 | 4 |
| †To save the race forlorn | 450 | 4 |
| †To save us from our lost estate | 665 | 4 |
| †To save what was lost, From heaven he came | 5 | 3 |
| To scatter, tear, and slay | 501 | 2 |
| To seal our everlasting doom | 648 | 4 |
| To see and praise my Lord | 213 | 4 |
| To see an heir of glory born | 867 | 1 |
| To see a prodigal return | 867 | 1 |
| To see each other's face | 510 | 2 |
| To see him again in the air | 77 | 1 |

|  | HYMN | VERSE |
|---|---|---|
| To see his glorious face | 761 | 5 |
| To see our Lord appear | 65 | 6 |
| To see the face divine | 336 | 2 |
| To see the wonders God had wrought for man | 691 | 4 |
| To see thy face above | 979 | 4 |
| To see thy kingdom here | 450 | 2 |
| To see thy salvation, Thou bidd'st me "Stand still" | 200 | 5 |
| To see, without a veil, his face | 65 | 3 |
| To seek and save the lost | 669 | 2 |
| To seek and taste no other bliss | 137 | 11 |
| To seek my wandering soul, and save | 148 | 4 |
| To seek the wandering souls of men | 279 | 7 |
| To seize the crown of perfect love | 265 | 2 |
| To seize the kingdom given | 854 | 3 |
| To sentence their usurping prince | 443 | 2 |
| To serve my God alone | 426 | 2 |
| To serve my God when I awake | 974 | 4 |
| To serve the Lord with filial fear | 320 | 1 |
| To serve the present age | 818 | 1 |
| To serve thy will, and spread thy praise | 409 | 4 |
| To set the captive free | 586 | 1 |
| To set the guilty captives free | 731 | 2 |
| To sever us, in vain | 537 | 4 |
| To share a moment's pain, and seize | 527 | 3 |
| To share thy glory in the skies | 180 | 8 |
| To shine in my dark, drooping heart | 148 | 8 |
| To show thy love by morning light | 599 | 1 |
| To shun thy presence, Lord, or flee | 632 | 1 |
| To sin! a bubble on the wave | 279 | 4 |
| To sing before the mercy seat | 961 | 1 |
| To sing our Maker's praise | 256 | 3 |
| To sing their Saviour's praise | 460 | 2 |
| To sing thy glory or thy grace | 651 | 5 |
| To sing thy goodness there | 258 | 1 |
| To sing thy praise above | 259 | 5 |
| To sing thy praise above | 894 | 1 |
| To sing thy praise in heaven | 242 | 4 |
| To slake our burning thirst | 595 | 6 |
| To slothful flesh and blood | 295 | 3 |
| To snatch them from the gaping grave | 279 | 7 |
| To snatch them from the verge of hell | 433 | 2 |
| To soar to endless day | 920 | 2 |
| To Sodom and Gomorrah prove | 454 | 8 |
| To soothe and sympathize | 842 | 2 |
| To soothe my incurable wound | 777 | 1 |
| To souls for ages dead | 450 | 1 |
| To sound in God the Father's ears | 798 | 7 |
| To sound the depths of love divine | 201 | 2 |
| To sound thy endless praise be mine | 731 | 9 |
| To spare such a rebel as me | 174 | 1 |
| To spend, and to be spent, for them | 433 | 3 |
| To spirits of the blest | 958 | 5 |
| To spread Messiah's praise | 731 | 1 |

| | Hymn | Verse |
|---|---|---|
| To spread the honour of his grace | 107 | 6 |
| To spread the honours of the Lamb | 204 | 4 |
| To spread through all the earth abroad | 1 | 2 |
| To spread thy fame, Redeeming Love | 731 | 8 |
| To spread thy praise our common end | 527 | 3 |
| To stand, or how thine anger bear | 279 | 2 |
| †To steer our dangerous course between | 468 | 2 |
| To stop the mouth of every foe | 319 | 2 |
| To strengthen faith and sweeten care | 864 | 4 |
| To succour and defend | 407 | 2 |
| To suffer and triumph with thee | 228 | 2 |
| To swallow up its careless prey | 82 | 5 |
| To take, and not bestow on thee | 175 | 4 |
| To take away transgression | 586 | 1 |
| To take me to his breast | 947 | 3 |
| To take my sins away | 778 | 1 |
| To take us up to heaven | 853 | 4 |
| To take thy murderers in | 85 | 6 |
| To taste thy love, be all my choice | 344 | 8 |
| To teach and to inspire is thine | 90 | 1 |
| To teach as taught by thee | 468 | 3 |
| To teach, convince, correct, reprove | 89 | 5 |
| To teach his heavenly grace | 675 | 2 |
| To teach our faint desires to rise | 864 | 4 |
| To teach us all thy perfect will | 754 | 2 |
| To tear my soul from earth away | 137 | 7 |
| To that bright celestial place | 941 | 1 |
| To that celestial hill | 833 | 1 |
| To that celestial hill | 497 | 2 |
| To that celestial shore | 52 | 2 |
| To that eternal throne | 550 | 3 |
| To that far country show | 840 | 2 |
| To that immortal state | 12 | 3 |
| †To that Jerusalem above | 947 | 3 |
| To that our labouring souls aspire | 959 | 2 |
| †To the blest fountain of thy blood | 786 | 4 |
| †To the cross, thine altar, bind | 188 | 4 |
| To the dust their hearts were bowed | 606 | 4 |
| To the dying health restore | 109 | 6 |
| To the family above | 509 | 6 |
| To the Father of grace | 231 | 10 |
| To the font baptismal hastening | 895 | 2 |
| To the glory of their King | 663 | — |
| To the great everlasting I AM | 499 | 6 |
| To the great Three in One | 958 | 1 |
| *To the haven of thy breast | 292 | 1 |
| To the heavenly feast | 205 | 5 |
| To the heavenly shore | 499 | 2 |
| To the heaven of heavens in Jesus's love | 205 | 6 |
| *To the hills I lift mine eyes | 618 | 1 |
| To the honour and glory of God | 491 | 3 |
| To the image of my Lord | 855 | 13 |
| To the King of the sky | 499 | 6 |

| | Hymn | Verse |
|---|---|---|
| To the Lamb that was slain. | 491 | 7 |
| To the Lamb that was slain. | 499 | 6 |
| To the land of cloudless sky | 672 | 11 |
| To the Land where rest is given | 995 | 4 |
| To the living fountains lead | 76 | 4 |
| †To the Lord I cried; the cry | 542 | 2 |
| To the Lord our God we give | 748 | 7 |
| To the mansions above | 808 | 7 |
| To the marriage of the Lamb | 520 | 4 |
| †To the never-ceasing cries | 299 | 6 |
| To the new Jerusalem | 572 | 4 |
| To the old Tempter's will | 295 | 2 |
| To the penitent poor | 219 | 3 |
| To the posts of mercy's door | 188 | 4 |
| †To the sheep of Israel's fold | 164 | 2 |
| To the sight of Jesus, go | 922 | 1 |
| To the Spirit, and Son, I return | 231 | 10 |
| †To the supper of the Lord | 714 | 6 |
| To the surviving race | 584 | 3 |
| To the third heaven we go | 58 | 3 |
| To the truths we have embraced | 882 | 7 |
| To thee, against myself, to thee | 59 | 1 |
| To thee and thy co-equal Son | 438 | 2 |
| To thee and thy great name | 801 | 5 |
| To thee, baptized into thy name | 893 | 1 |
| †To thee, benign and saving Power. | 155 | 2 |
| To thee, blest Three in One | 958 | 5 |
| To thee by angel-hosts confest | 444 | 4 |
| †To thee, by whom we live | 983 | 7 |
| To thee for faith I call | 150 | 2 |
| To thee for help we call | 469 | 2 |
| To thee for help we cry | 767 | 1 |
| To thee for help we fly | 501 | 1 |
| †To thee for refuge may I run | 998 | 3 |
| *To thee, great God of love! I bow. | 284 | 1 |
| To thee his hope, his harbour, and his home | 596 | 3 |
| To thee I all resign | 844 | 6 |
| To thee I feebly pray | 167 | 1 |
| To thee I lift mine eye | 175 | 2 |
| †To thee I lift my mournful eye | 146 | 3 |
| To thee I look; my heart prepare | 99 | 1 |
| To thee I look up For certain relief | 273 | 2 |
| To thee I then the whole resign | 92 | 7 |
| To thee in all things rise | 322 | 2 |
| To thee in every wish return | 513 | 4 |
| To thee, in fierce temptation's hour | 237 | 2 |
| To thee in their behalf we cry | 82 | 1 |
| †To thee, inseparably joined | 504 | 5 |
| †To thee let all the nations flow | 749 | 4 |
| To thee, lo! all our souls we bow | 26 | 8 |
| To thee may all our thoughts arise | 494 | 4 |
| †To thee may each united house | 997 | 3 |
| To thee my every breath | 229 | 3 |

| | Hymn | Verse |
|---|---|---|
| †To thee my last distress I bring | 181 | 5 |
| To thee, my Lord, I here restore | 291 | 4 |
| To thee my spirit flies | 587 | 1 |
| To thee my thoughts are kindled | 943 | 6 |
| To thee my weakness show | 311 | 3 |
| To thee, O Jesus, I confess | 397 | 7 |
| To thee O let me live | 229 | 3 |
| To thee, O Lord, I cry | 625 | 1 |
| †To thee, O Lord of life, I prayed | 614 | 4 |
| To thee our cause we bring | 546 | 3 |
| To thee our hearts and hands we give | 26 | 8 |
| To thee our hearts we raise | 654 | 1 |
| To thee our hearts we raise | 1020 | — |
| †To thee our humble hearts aspire | 95 | 2 |
| To thee our longing souls aspire | 666 | 1 |
| To thee our thankful hearts we give | 203 | 6 |
| To thee our will, soul, flesh, we give | 494 | 3 |
| To thee ourselves we give | 654 | 2 |
| To thee presenting, through thy Son | 979 | 3 |
| †To thee shall earth and hell submit | 275 | 9 |
| To thee the creatures lead | 108 | 2 |
| †To thee the glory of thy power | 360 | 10 |
| To thee, the Lord of earth and skies | 431 | 1 |
| To thee, the only ease in pain | 210 | 2 |
| To thee the praise belongs | 742 | 3 |
| To thee the praise designed | 239 | 8 |
| To thee the praise we give | 244 | 2 |
| To thee the ransomed seed shall come | 386 | 4 |
| To thee, the sinner's friend, draw nigh | 395 | 2 |
| To thee the when and how we leave | 380 | 9 |
| To thee their prayer in each distress | 636 | 4 |
| To thee their source; thy love the guide | 108 | 7 |
| †To thee they all pertain; to thee | 992 | 4 |
| To thee, this temple, Lord, we build | 993 | 1 |
| To thee through Jesus we draw near | 394 | 1 |
| To thee thy various works shall raise | 636 | 1 |
| To thee we die, to thee we live | 203 | 6 |
| To thee we lift our voice | 733 | 1 |
| To thee, whate'er is mine | 614 | 11 |
| To thee what shall I say | 93 | 1 |
| To thee, who call'dst us into light | 203 | 6 |
| To thee, who from the eternal throne | 666 | 3 |
| To thee, who wouldst not have me die | 118 | 1 |
| To thee, whose blood can cleanse each spot | 796 | 2 |
| To thee with my whole soul aspire | 351 | 5 |
| To their distant heirs secure | 67 | 1 |
| To their eternal home | 729 | 6 |
| To their first state restored | 452 | 4 |
| To them that mourn their sin | 797 | 1 |
| To these be thy salvation showed | 82 | 7 |
| To these, thy lower courts, it comes | 902 | 4 |
| To thine abode My heart aspires | 591 | 1 |
| To thine arms of mercy fly | 29 | 2 |

| | Hymn | Verse |
|---|---|---|
| To thine eternal throne | 894 | 2 |
| To thine own effectual prayer | 517 | 1 |
| To this house, and all herein | 479 | 2 |
| †To this sure covenant of thy word | 903 | 2 |
| †To this the joyful nations round | 740 | 2 |
| To those that fear his name | 610 | 9 |
| To those who fall how kind thou art | 680 | 3 |
| To those who suffer wrong | 586 | 2 |
| †To those who thee in *him* obey | 465 | 9 |
| To thy benign indulgent care | 241 | 2 |
| †To thy blessed will resigned | 335 | 4 |
| To thy dear Redeemer's breast | 922 | 3 |
| To thy dear wounds I fain would flee | 177 | 1 |
| To thy dread sceptre will I bow | 353 | 4 |
| To thy chosen messenger | 876 | 1 |
| To thy church the pattern give | 509 | 4 |
| To thy cross I look and live | 904 | 2 |
| To thy cross my spirit bind | 350 | 3 |
| To thy glorious life restored | 512 | 3 |
| To thy great praise abound | 981 | 5 |
| To thy great sacrifice | 321 | 3 |
| To thy house, O Lord, in heaven | 995 | 4 |
| To thy human temples come | 399 | 1 |
| To thy name hosannas sing | 737 | 8 |
| To thy perfect love restored | 402 | 2 |
| To thy poor suppliant give | 778 | 3 |
| To thy redeeming grace appeal | 917 | 2 |
| †To thy sure love, thy tender care | 655 | 4 |
| To thy sweet yoke my spirit bow | 186 | 5 |
| †To thy wise and gracious will | 925 | 3 |
| †To time our every smile or frown | 467 | 7 |
| To touch their hearts with filial fear | 468 | 7 |
| To touch, to heal me—in this hour | 779 | 3 |
| To trace thy example, The world to disdain | 484 | 1 |
| To train and bring them up for heaven | 473 | 1 |
| To train our infant up for heaven | 467 | 2 |
| To trample down their sin | 35 | 6 |
| To trample on my mortal foe | 72 | 1 |
| To tread in Christ's long-suffering way | 961 | 4 |
| To tread that path, but this, Thou knowest, Lord | 850 | 4 |
| To tread the thorny road | 844 | 4 |
| To triumph in thy love | 652 | — |
| To triumph in your blest estate | 9 | 4 |
| To undiscerning men | 871 | 1 |
| To urge our God-commanding plea | 294 | 4 |
| *To us a child of royal birth | 689 | 1 |
| To us and ours the promise made | 456 | 1 |
| †To us and to them is published the word | 40 | 6 |
| †To us at thy feet The Comforter give | 10 | 4 |
| To us be graciously the same | 456 | 1 |
| To us, by the commandment slain | 284 | 4 |
| To us he hath, in special love | 673 | 1 |
| To us his Spirit doth impart | 96 | 5 |

| | Hymn | Verse |
|---|---|---|
| To us, in our degenerate age | 89 | 1 |
| To us it is given In Jesus to know | 19 | 3 |
| †To us our gracious God | 623 | 4 |
| To us perform the promise due | 457 | 4 |
| To us that ask impart | 469 | 1 |
| To us the great salvation brought | 203 | 4 |
| To us thy Father's name declare | 505 | 8 |
| To us who for thy coming stay | 294 | 5 |
| To utter all thy praise | 657 | 10 |
| To utter our complaint | 299 | 1 |
| To visit a sorrowful breast | 165 | 1 |
| To walk, and perfectly to obey | 528 | 4 |
| To walk this dangerous road | 42 | 7 |
| To walk with him in white | 54 | 3 |
| To wash his dear disciples' feet | 17 | 6 |
| To wash me in thy cleansing blood | 26 | 1 |
| To wash out all your stains | 625 | 5 |
| To watch, and tremble, and prepare | 44 | 2 |
| †To watch their will, to sense inclined | 468 | 8 |
| To wave its palm before thy throne | 126 | 4 |
| To weep at thy longer delay | 946 | 4 |
| To which thou shalt restore us | 853 | 4 |
| To whom did he his help deny | 32 | 2 |
| To whom I long did bow | 274 | 4 |
| To whom it first was given | 421 | 2 |
| To whom our more than all is due | 286 | 3 |
| To whom our more than all we owe | 492 | 2 |
| To whom should I my troubles show | 152 | 1 |
| To whom we for our children cry | 473 | 1 |
| To work, and speak, and think for thee | 827 | 3 |
| To worship at his shrine | 740 | 7 |
| To worship God aright | 262 | 1 |
| To wrestle till we see thy face | 297 | 3 |
| To write thy law of love within | 380 | 6 |
| To you and all the nations upon earth | 691 | 2 |
| To you far off; he calls you all | 759 | 2 |
| To you is it nothing that Jesus should die | 707 | 1 |
| To Zion above | 760 | 5 |
| To Zion's chosen race | 630 | 8 |
| Together let us die | 501 | 6 |
| †Together let us sweetly live | 501 | 6 |
| Together seek his face | 500 | 1 |
| Together spread the gospel sound | 524 | 3 |
| Together to thy glory live | 527 | 5 |
| Together travel on | 510 | 3 |
| Toil, man, to gain that light | 943 | 15 |
| †Toil on, and in thy toil rejoice | 857 | 6 |
| †Toil on, faint not, keep watch, and pray | 857 | 5 |
| Toil ye shall have; yet all despise | 277 | 5 |
| Tongue cannot express | 807 | 1 |
| Too few we find the happy hours | 222 | 3 |
| Too great, on thee, my Lord, was laid | 23 | 4 |
| "Too late, too late!" will be your cry | 695 | 6 |

| | Hymn | Verse |
|---|---|---|
| Too mean to set our Saviour forth | 675 | 1 |
| Too much I cannot do for thee | 23 | 7 |
| †Too much to thee I cannot give | 23 | 7 |
| Too short to sing thy praise | 222 | 3 |
| Too short to utter all his love | 638 | 6 |
| Too strong for us to turn | 469 | 7 |
| *Too strong I was to conquer sin | 126 | 1 |
| Took all our load of guilt away | 493 | 4 |
| Tophet is moved, and opens wide | 442 | 2 |
| Torn, and forsook of all, I lay | 23 | 5 |
| Tossed about with every wind | 355 | 2 |
| †Touched by the loadstone of thy love | 504 | 4 |
| †Touched with a sympathy within | 725 | 2 |
| Touched with softest sympathy | 518 | 7 |
| †Touch me, and make the leper clean | 184 | 2 |
| Towards thy holy place | 635 | 2 |
| Toward the mark unwearied press | 521 | 2 |
| Trace we the Babe, who hath retrieved our loss | 691 | 5 |
| †Train up thy hardy soldiers, Lord | 474 | 4 |
| Trampled on the Son of God | 168 | 2 |
| Trampling down sin, hell, and death | 58 | 3 |
| Transcripts of the Deity | 7 | 3 |
| Transcripts of thy holiness | 531 | 3 |
| Transformed in all its powers | 96 | 5 |
| Transgression, sin, iniquity | 144 | 6 |
| Transient fears beneath the rod | 768 | 3 |
| Transmitted through thy word, repeat | 89 | 4 |
| Transported far into the deep | 63 | 3 |
| Transported from this vale to live | 59 | 6 |
| Transported with the view, I'm lost | 657 | 1 |
| Travel hand in hand to heaven | 512 | 3 |
| Travelling through this wilderness | 1008 | 1 |
| Treacherous trifling with my God | 768 | 3 |
| Treachery lurked within thy fold | 710 | 3 |
| Tread all the powers of darkness down | 268 | 4 |
| Tread down its strength, o'erturn its sway | 456 | 5 |
| Tread down thy foes, with power control | 132 | 3 |
| Tread in his steps, assisted by his grace | 691 | 5 |
| Tree of Life eternal, rise | 531 | 1 |
| Trees and cattle, creeping things | 639 | 5 |
| Tremble before thy piercing eye | 235 | 3 |
| Tremble, where the proud wave urges | 570 | 2 |
| Trembles, and dreads the swelling tide | 569 | 3 |
| †Trembling at thine altar stand | 910 | 2 |
| Trembling on with steady aim | 766 | 2 |
| Trembling they stand before his throne | 932 | 3 |
| Trembling they strike the golden lyre | 241 | 1 |
| †Trembling we taste; for, ah! no more | 108 | 2 |
| *Tremendous God, with humble fear | 913 | 1 |
| †Triumph and reign in me | 352 | 4 |
| Triumph in his sovereign grace | 571 | 1 |
| Triumph in redeeming grace | 1008 | 1 |
| Triumph in thy saving grace | 890 | 1 |

| TRIUMPH O'ER | | TRY US | |
|---|---|---|---|
| | | HYMN | VERSE |
| Triumph o'er the shades of night | | 963 | 1 |
| Triumphant arise | | 760 | 5 |
| Triumphant here below | | 950 | 1 |
| †Triumphant host! they never cease | | 262 | 2 |
| Triumphant in his sight | | 678 | 3 |
| Triumphant joy for sad despair | | 107 | 5 |
| Triumphant Lord, appear | | 62 | 5 |
| Triumphant o'er his foes | | 731 | 3 |
| Triumphant o'er the world and sin | | 800 | 7 |
| Triumphant through the skies | | 504 | 8 |
| Triumphant with our Head | | 333 | 4 |
| Triumphantly descend | | 761 | 6 |
| Triumphantly sitting In glory with thee | | 484 | 3 |
| Triumphing in Paradise | | 50 | 3 |
| Triumphs in immortal powers | | 61 | 2 |
| Triumphs in thy pardoning grace | | 850 | 5 |
| Trouble, and wash the troubled heart | | 84 | 6 |
| True and faithful | | 748 | 1 |
| †True and faithful as thou art | | 179 | 2 |
| True and faithful is his word | | 142 | 2 |
| True and faithful to thy word | | 50 | 1 |
| *True and faithful Witness, thee | | 418 | 1 |
| *True and faithful Witness, thou | | 449 | 1 |
| †True and faithful Witness, thou | | 506 | 2 |
| True and gracious as thou art | | 29 | 3 |
| True, and merciful, and wise | | 18 | 2 |
| True belief, and true repentance | | 791 | 2 |
| †True believers have seen | | 488 | 5 |
| True followers of the Lamb | | 630 | 2 |
| True followers of the Lamb | | 897 | 3 |
| True in the fiery trial prove | | 878 | 4 |
| †True pleasures abound | | 205 | 3 |
| True Recorder of his passion | | 899 | 1 |
| True riches, and immortal praise | | 14 | 4 |
| †True, 'tis a strait and thorny road | | 802 | 2 |
| †True to his everlasting word | | 638 | 5 |
| True wisdom can impart | | 671 | 2 |
| True witness of mercy divine | | 165 | 5 |
| True witness of my sonship, now | | 374 | 4 |
| True yoke-fellows, by love compelled | | 524 | 3 |
| †Truly our fellowship below | | 490 | 6 |
| Trumpet forth his conquering love | | 571 | 5 |
| Trust him, praise him, evermore | | 628 | 4 |
| Trust in an Almighty Lord | | 278 | 4 |
| Trust in pain and care and strife | | 817 | 6 |
| Trust to be redeemed from sin | | 400 | 6 |
| Trusting by his help to crown it | | 990 | 1 |
| *Trusting in our Lord alone | | 724 | 1 |
| †Trusting in thy word alone | | 915 | 2 |
| †Truthful Spirit, dwell with me | | 769 | 2 |
| Truth in the inward parts | | 91 | 5 |
| Truth, immortal truth, shall reign | | 604 | 4 |
| *Try us, O God, and search the ground | | 503 | 1 |

|  | Hymn | Verse |
|---|---|---|
| Tune my heart to sing thy grace | 866 | 1 |
| Tune your harps, celestial choir | 727 | 2 |
| Tuning their harps, they long to praise | 9 | 4 |
| Turn, and look upon me, Lord | 106 | Cho. |
| Turn, and revive us, Lord, again | 654 | 4 |
| †Turn, he cries, ye sinners, turn | 8 | 2 |
| Turn into flesh my heart | 145 | 1 |
| Turn into flesh my heart of stone | 145 | 1 |
| Turn my darkness into light | 109 | 3 |
| Turn my nature's rapid tide | 158 | 3 |
| Turn my stronger foe aside | 819 | 3 |
| Turn my tempted heart away | 819 | 2 |
| Turn not in silence from my tears | 565 | 7 |
| Turn, O turn a favouring eye | 710 | 2 |
| Turn our darkness into light | 971 | 2 |
| Turn our darkness into light | 971 | 3 |
| Turn our earth to paradise | 756 | 1 |
| †Turn the full stream of nature's tide | 108 | 7 |
| †Turn then, thou good Physician, turn | 779 | 2 |
| Turn thou for us its darkness into light | 962 | 3 |
| Turn to Jesus crucified | 20 | 1 |
| Turned, and stood still with awe | 587 | 5 |
| Turned my glory into shame | 112 | 1 |
| Turned our soul's captivity | 623 | 1 |
| Turning sorrow | 715 | 3 |
| †Turning to my rest again | 809 | 3 |
| Turning water into wine | 995 | 3 |
| Turns from his sin to thee | 162 | 3 |
| †'Twas a wondrous war I trow | 714 | 3 |
| 'Twas greater to redeem | 950 | 2 |
| 'Twas great to speak a world from nought | 950 | 2 |
| †'Twas he who found me on the deathly wild | 794 | 5 |
| 'Twas purchased with a dying groan | 903 | 4 |
| 'Twas thy wisdom appointed it so | 231 | 3 |
| Twelve hours, in which he safely may | 281 | 1 |
| 'Twixt the mount and multitude | 529 | 4 |
| 'Twixt two unbounded seas I stand | 59 | 2 |
| *Two are better far than one | 487 | 1 |
| *Two or three in Jesu's name | 862 | 1 |
| †Two worlds are ours; 'tis only sin | 662 | 3 |
| Type of that everlasting rest | 954 | 2 |
| Unable to rejoice in pain | 331 | 1 |
| Unaccompanied by thee | 963 | 2 |
| Unalienably ours | 67 | 5 |
| Unalterably sure | 250 | 6 |
| †Unappalled by guilty fear | 554 | 4 |
| Unashamed proclaim their king | 737 | 8 |
| Unblamable before thy sight | 364 | 3 |
| Unblamable in grace | 809 | 5 |
| Unblemished and complete | 814 | 3 |
| Unchangeable, all-perfect Lord | 240 | 2 |
| *Unchangeable, almighty Lord | 505 | 1 |

| | Hymn | Verse |
|---|---|---|
| *Unclean, of life and heart unclean | 779 | 1 |
| Unconquerable sin | 139 | 5 |
| †Under his banner thus we sing | 907 | 3 |
| Under my feet at last | 421 | 1 |
| Under one Shepherd make one fold | 505 | 7 |
| †Under the shadow of thy throne | 41 | 2 |
| Under thy mighty hand I stoop | 163 | 6 |
| Under thy protection take | 287 | 2 |
| Under thy protection, we | 1000 | 1 |
| Undevoured we still remain | 238 | 3 |
| Undo the evil done | 892 | 3 |
| Unfaithful Peter's heart | 309 | 4 |
| Unfaithful stewards of thy grace | 176 | 2 |
| Unfathomable depths of love | 1001 | 5 |
| Unfathomable depths thou art | 240 | 1 |
| Unfathomable wonder | 667 | 4 |
| Unfolding every hour | 845 | 3 |
| Unfold the wonders of thy love | 90 | 3 |
| †Ungodly men and their attempts | 540 | 4 |
| Ungrasp the hold of thy right hand | 138 | 6 |
| Unhurt on snares and death I'll tread | 272 | 7 |
| Union to the world unknown | 516 | 3 |
| Unite, and perfect them in one | 17 | 2 |
| Unite and perfect us in one | 505 | 8 |
| Unite my scattered thoughts, and fix | 785 | 3 |
| †Unite the pair so long disjoined | 473 | 5 |
| Unite to praise thy love | 251 | 1 |
| Unite us all in thee | 459 | 3 |
| United in a bond unknown | 527 | 2 |
| United to our Head | 673 | 2 |
| Unites in mystic love and seals | 749 | 1 |
| Universal nature join | 727 | 5 |
| †Universal Saviour, thou | 730 | 3 |
| Unknown to every other nation | 595 | 3 |
| Unless he first divide | 501 | 4 |
| Unless, in answer to our Lord | 435 | 3 |
| Unless my omnipotent God | 911 | 2 |
| †Unless restrained by grace we are | 469 | 3 |
| Unless the fold we first forsake | 501 | 3 |
| Unless the Lord the city keep | 624 | 1 |
| †Unless the power of heavenly grace | 475 | 4 |
| Unless they spring from love | 91 | 4 |
| Unless they spring from love | 822 | 1 |
| Unless thou magnify thy grace | 441 | 3 |
| Unless thou plantest in my heart | 405 | 6 |
| Unless thou purge my every stain | 375 | 2 |
| Unless thou take the veil away | 85 | 2 |
| Unless thou wash my soul from sin | 184 | 2 |
| Unless thyself be given | 415 | 5 |
| Unless thy Spirit lend the key | 90 | 2 |
| Unlimited his bounteous grant | 590 | 5 |
| Unlock the truth, thyself the key | 87 | 2 |
| Unloose our stammering tongues, to tell | 26 | 7 |

| | Hymn | Verse |
|---|---|---|
| Unloose the bands of wickedness | 105 | 2 |
| Unmarked by human eye | 685 | 2 |
| Unmerited and free | 250 | 1 |
| Unmindful of his favours prove | 30 | 3 |
| Unmixed with selfishness and pride | 524 | 1 |
| Unmoved above the storm they lie | 62 | 1 |
| Unmoved by threatening or reward | 301 | 5 |
| †Unnumbered comforts on my soul | 657 | 4 |
| Unnumbered worlds attend | 642 | 1 |
| Unpierced by human thought | 43 | 1 |
| *Unprofitable all and vain | 838 | 1 |
| Unpurged and unforgiven | 150 | 1 |
| Unrenewed and unrestored | 109 | 4 |
| Unsaved, unchanged by hallowing grace | 830 | 1 |
| Unseal the sacred book | 87 | 2 |
| †Unsearchable the love | 685 | 3 |
| Unseen by reason's glimmering ray | 95 | 5 |
| Unspeakable I now receive | 141 | 3 |
| †Unspotted are the ways of God | 551 | 6 |
| †Unspotted from the world and pure | 474 | 2 |
| Unspotted from the world and sin | 364 | 5 |
| Unspotted in so foul a place | 482 | 2 |
| Unspotted purity | 110 | 5 |
| Until he bent down from his throne | 566 | 1 |
| Until that day, When all the blest | 991 | 4 |
| Until the Son of God appear | 690 | 1 |
| Until the Spirit from on high | 153 | 2 |
| Untimely withered and dispersed | 540 | 4 |
| Unto dogs it is not right | 164 | 4 |
| Unto earth's remotest end | 582 | 1 |
| Unto joy or sorrow grown | 987 | 2 |
| Unto salvation wise | 65 | 1 |
| Unto that heavenly bliss | 21 | 5 |
| Unto thee, betrothed in love | 516 | 2 |
| *Unto thee I lift my eyes | 620 | 1 |
| Unto thee, my bleeding Lord | 182 | 5 |
| Unto the perfect day | 446 | 6 |
| Unutterable praise | 423 | 3 |
| Unwatered still, and dry | 115 | 3 |
| Unwavering I believe | 764 | 4 |
| †Unwearied may I this pursue | 373 | 4 |
| Unworthy though I be | 798 | 6 |
| Unworthy to behold thy face | 176 | 2 |
| Upborne by the unyielding wave | 272 | 5 |
| Upheld by mutual prayer | 487 | 2 |
| †Uphold me in the doubtful race | 210 | 5 |
| †Uphold me, Saviour, or I fall | 812 | 7 |
| Uphold thou me, and I shall stand | 944 | 6 |
| †Up into thee, our living Head | 503 | 5 |
| Up-raise me with thy gracious hand | 161 | 6 |
| Up to his care myself I yield | 626 | 3 |
| Up to thee in all things grow | 193 | 5 |
| Up to thee our bodies yield | 427 | 1 |

| | Hymn | Verse |
|---|---|---|
| Up to thee our hearts we raise | 1007 | — |
| Up to thee our souls we raise | 427 | 1 |
| Up to the hill of God, they'll say | 740 | 2 |
| Up to the Lord our flesh shall fly | 929 | 3 |
| Upon his altar lay | 614 | 10 |
| Upon life's feeble strings | 42 | 5 |
| Upon my heart to shine | 252 | 3 |
| Upon our lips be simple truth | 966 | 2 |
| Upon the brink of death | 42 | 6 |
| Upon the chaos dark and rude | 1004 | 3 |
| Upon the fruitful earth | 586 | 3 |
| Upon the Lord relies | 566 | 4 |
| Upon the world's work-wearied breast | 957 | 1 |
| Upon thy love alone | 288 | 4 |
| Upon thy word myself I stay | 134 | 6 |
| *Upright, both in heart and will | 98 | 1 |
| Upright both in life and heart | 368 | 2 |
| Upstarting at the midnight cry | 65 | 1 |
| Upward I send my streaming eye | 154 | 2 |
| Upward still for this we gaze | 852 | 1 |
| Upwards I fly | 848 | 5 |
| Urged by faith's incessant prayer | 449 | 2 |
| †Urge on your rapid course | 277 | 4 |
| Urging them their Lord to embrace | 876 | 3 |
| Us and ours preserve from dangers | 970 | 2 |
| Us and our works canst thou behold | 454 | 1 |
| Us before thy Father's face | 724 | 3 |
| Us fellowship with thee | 1005 | 3 |
| Us from earth to call away | 1008 | 3 |
| †Us from ourselves thou canst secure | 469 | 9 |
| †Us, in the stead of Christ, they pray | 11 | 2 |
| Us, in the stead of God, intreat | 11 | 2 |
| Us into thy hands receive | 989 | 4 |
| †Us into thy protection take | 501 | 3 |
| Us, thine anointed ones receive | 629 | 4 |
| Us thou dost in pity spare | 245 | 1 |
| Us thou mak'st thy tenderest care | 693 | 3 |
| Us, thy lisping creatures, hear | 260 | 2 |
| Us to save from sin and hell | 724 | 2 |
| *Us, who climb thy holy hill | 424 | 1 |
| Use the grace on each bestowed | 518 | 6 |
| Use the rod, and not the sword | 179 | 1 |
| Utterance, Lord, thou dost impart | 876 | 1 |
| Uttered or unexpressed | 823 | 1 |
| Utterly abolish sin | 522 | 3 |
| | | |
| Vain are the cares which rack his mind | 564 | 3 |
| *Vain, delusive world, adieu | 809 | 1 |
| †Vain his ambition, noise, and show | 564 | 3 |
| †Vain in themselves their duties were | 702 | 3 |
| Vain man! thy wisdom folly own | 240 | 4 |
| Vain the hope to purchase thee | 24 | 1 |
| †Vain the stone, the watch, the seal | 716 | 3 |

| | Hymn | Verse |
|---|---|---|
| Vainly I hoped and strove | 91 | 4 |
| Vales, with gleaming harvest white | 579 | 3 |
| †Vanish, then, this world of shadows | 60 | 4 |
| Vapours, lightning, hail, and snow | 639 | 4 |
| Vast as eternity thy love | 608 | 4 |
| †Veiled in flesh the Godhead see | 683 | 3 |
| Veil your eyes, and prostrate fall | 727 | 3 |
| Venture all thy care on him | 921 | 4 |
| Venture on him, venture wholly | 791 | 5 |
| †Vessels, instruments of grace | 529 | 4 |
| Vested with thy authority | 470 | 1 |
| Vexed with the dire remains of sin | 547 | 2 |
| *Victim Divine, thy grace we claim | 902 | 1 |
| Vile, like her, and self-abhorred | 106 | 6 |
| †Vilest of all the sons of men | 365 | 5 |
| Vilest of all thy children, I | 178 | 1 |
| Vilest of the sinful race | 164 | 3 |
| †Vilest of the sinful race | 430 | 2 |
| Vine, abundant fruit providing | 895 | 3 |
| †Vine of heaven! thy blood supplies | 904 | 2 |
| Visit them, and visit me | 479 | 2 |
| †Visit then this soul of mine | 963 | 3 |
| †Visit us, bright morning Star | 449 | 2 |
| Visit us with thy salvation | 385 | 1 |
| Void of true wisdom is my heart | 240 | 1 |
| Vouchsafe me now the victory | 126 | 3 |
| Vouchsafe, O Lord, to rescue me | 566 | 8 |
| Vouchsafe the aid thy grace supplies | 821 | — |
| Vouchsafe the grace we humbly claim | 204 | 1 |
| *Vouchsafe to keep me, Lord, this day | 820 | 1 |
| †Vouchsafe us eyes of faith to see | 122 | 2 |
| Vouchsafe us faith to venture near | 896 | 1 |
| Vouchsafes our intercourse to bless | 489 | 1 |
| †Vying with that happy choir | 221 | 3 |
| Wafted on the wings of love | 718 | 9 |
| Wafting us to realms above | 720 | 8 |
| Waft our happy spirits o'er | 999 | 4 |
| †Waft, waft, ye winds, his story | 747 | 4 |
| Wait for thy unguarded hours | 829 | 2 |
| Wait for your God's appearing | 626 | 4 |
| †Wait on the Lord, with courage wait | 558 | 6 |
| Wait the leisure of thy Lord | 142 | 2 |
| Wait thou his time, so shall this night | 831 | 9 |
| Wait thy passage through the shade | 921 | 5 |
| Wait, till he appear within | 400 | 6 |
| Wait to catch the signal given | 921 | 2 |
| Wait to see the perfect grace | 542 | 3 |
| †Wait we all in patient hope | 54 | 4 |
| Wait we till the Spouse shall come | 516 | 3 |
| Waiting for my last remove | 915 | 1 |
| Waiting for redemption still | 925 | 3 |
| Waiting for the general doom | 51 | 5 |

| | Hymn | Verse |
|---|---|---|
| Waiting for their food on thee | 1012 | — |
| Waiting for us they are | 482 | 3 |
| Waiting, like attentive Mary | 530 | 3 |
| Waiting souls, rejoice, rejoice | 54 | 1 |
| †Waiting to receive thy spirit | 922 | 2 |
| Waits his promise to fulfil | 606 | 6 |
| †Wake, and lift up thyself, my heart | 964 | 4 |
| Wake we in thy similitude | 261 | 4 |
| Waked by the trumpet's sound | 43 | 2 |
| †Waken, O Lord, our drowsy sense | 42 | 7 |
| Walk as children of the light | 400 | 4 |
| Walk as Jesus walked below | 529 | 1 |
| Walk in all the works prepared | 325 | 5 |
| Walk in all thy righteous laws | 166 | 4 |
| Walk in him we have received | 522 | 1 |
| Walk in holiness of life | 521 | 2 |
| Walk in thee, the Truth, the Way | 886 | — |
| Walk in the works by thee prepared | 440 | 2 |
| †Walk with me through the dreadful shade | 919 | 3 |
| Walk with me through the floods and fires | 916 | 6 |
| †Walk with me through the lions' den | 916 | 6 |
| Walking in all his ways they find | 15 | 1 |
| Walking over life's rough sea | 183 | 3 |
| Walks forth with tainted breath | 986 | 2 |
| Walled within the threatening waters | 580 | 2 |
| Wandering from the fold of God | 866 | 2 |
| Want, pain defy, enjoy disgrace | 351 | 6 |
| Warm as these prayers upon *his* head | 896 | 4 |
| Warm their hearts with heavenly zeal | 733 | 3 |
| Warn by thy Spirit's inward call | 306 | 2 |
| Warn me of my approaching end | 913 | 4 |
| *Warned of my dissolution near | 919 | 1 |
| War shall then be learnt no more | 730 | 3 |
| Was cast on Adam's fallen race | 39 | 3 |
| Was closed, that we might live | 106 | 7 |
| Was early ripe to ill | 697 | 5 |
| Was ever grief like thine | 27 | 1 |
| Was ever love, like thine | 22 | 4 |
| Was found in fashion as a man | 137 | 6 |
| Was mightier than death | 167 | 4 |
| Was my joy and my song | 807 | 3 |
| Was nature's God displeased with thee | 223 | 3 |
| Was never love like thine | 701 | 2 |
| Wash all my sins away | 798 | 2 |
| †Wash me, and make me thus thine own | 346 | 3 |
| Wash me, and mine thou art | 346 | 3 |
| Wash me, but not my feet alone | 346 | 3 |
| †Wash out its stains, refine its dross | 339 | 2 |
| Wash us in the atoning blood | 530 | 1 |
| Washed all our sins away | 423 | 1 |
| Washed in the Lamb's all-cleansing blood | 16 | 4 |
| Washed in the sanctifying blood | 254 | 1 |
| Washed their robes by faith below | 76 | 2 |

| | Hymn | Verse |
|---|---|---|
| Washed them in his bleeding side | 735 | 2 |
| Watch, and hold me back from sinning | 819 | 2 |
| Watch and pray | 829 | Cho. |
| †Watch, as if on that alone | 829 | 6 |
| †Watch by the sick, enrich the poor | 973 | 5 |
| Watch his earthly prison | 715 | 4 |
| Watch over them to tear and slay | 458 | 3 |
| *Watched by the world's malignant eye | 819 | 1 |
| Watches every numbered hair | 245 | 2 |
| Watches our every sigh and look | 827 | 6 |
| Watching let us be found | 65 | 6 |
| Watching the glistening raiment glow | 698 | 4 |
| Watching to see him come | 54 | 5 |
| Water at thy word gushed out | 348 | 6 |
| Water from salvation's well | 197 | 4 |
| Watered by thy almighty hand | 734 | 1 |
| †Waters hanging in the air | 639 | 3 |
| Waters in the desert rise | 593 | 2 |
| Way of life, *his* pathway show | 895 | 3 |
| Wayward, and impotent, and blind | 99 | 3 |
| We a better lot shall share | 50 | 4 |
| We are all forgiven For Jesus's sake | 5 | 5 |
| We all delight to prove | 500 | 3 |
| We all hell's host o'erthrow | 315 | 3 |
| We all his steps pursue | 96 | 6 |
| We all his unknown peace receive | 96 | 2 |
| †We all, in perfect love renewed | 492 | 6 |
| †We all partake the joy of one | 500 | 5 |
| †We all shall commend | 808 | 10 |
| We all shall in amity join | 220 | 5 |
| We all shall praise our common Lord | 505 | 4 |
| We all shall soon appear | 55 | 1 |
| We all shall soon from earth remove | 913 | 3 |
| We all shall then in one agree | 505 | 5 |
| †We all shall think and speak the same | 505 | 6 |
| We all thy words behind us cast | 203 | 7 |
| We all with vows and anthems new | 979 | 2 |
| We alone can declare | 495 | 2 |
| We, and all thy creatures, are | 244 | 1 |
| We are banqueting here | 488 | 2 |
| We are bold to outride | 499 | 2 |
| We are freely forgiven through mercy alone | 219 | 4 |
| We are his flock, he doth us feed | 607 | 2 |
| We are his works, and not our own | 603 | 3 |
| We are Jesu's witnesses | 519 | 3 |
| We are marching through Immanuel's ground | 12 | 4 |
| We are met in Jesu's name | 480 | 1 |
| We are met in thy great name | 620 | 2 |
| †We are now his lawful right | 400 | 4 |
| We are travelling to the grave | 42 | 3 |
| We ask for every waiting soul | 977 | 4 |
| We ask for wisdom from on high | 467 | 2 |
| †We ask not, Lord, thy cloven flame | 767 | 2 |

| | Hymn | Verse |
|---|---|---|
| We ask the constant power to pray | 294 | 5 |
| We at his feet may fall | 681 | 8 |
| We, at our judge's instance, live | 11 | 4 |
| We bade the grateful vespers swell | 961 | 1 |
| We banquet on the heavenly bread | 875 | 3 |
| We bear *him* to thy throne | 465 | 3 |
| We bear our heaven about us still | 536 | 2 |
| We bear the character divine | 329 | 4 |
| We behold (the abjects we) | 348 | 3 |
| †We bid life's cares and trifles fly | 955 | 2 |
| We bless the Lamb with cheerful voice | 703 | 5 |
| We bless thy holy name | 945 | 1 |
| We blest and pious grow | 950 | 1 |
| †We boast of our recovered powers | 1001 | 10 |
| We bow before the heavenly voice | 698 | 6 |
| †We bow before thy gracious throne | 83 | 2 |
| We break the hallowed bread | 901 | 1 |
| †We bring them, Lord, in thankful hands | 889 | 3 |
| We but present thee with thine own | 992 | 4 |
| We by faith behold our own | 720 | 5 |
| †We by his Spirit prove | 96 | 4 |
| We by our God were made | 98 | 1 |
| †We call thee Lord, thy faith profess | 454 | 2 |
| We cannot feel a good desire | 294 | 2 |
| We cannot in thy judgment stand | 176 | 1 |
| †We cannot speak one useful word | 435 | 3 |
| We cannot there the fall lament | 482 | 5 |
| †We cannot think a gracious thought | 294 | 2 |
| We cannot want, if thou art here | 533 | 3 |
| †We can, O Jesus, for thy sake | 977 | 3 |
| We can, we now rejoice to tear | 286 | 5 |
| We cheerfully can say | 804 | 2 |
| We choose the better part at last | 977 | 1 |
| We claim thy providential care | 1001 | 8 |
| We clap our hands exulting | 853 | 2 |
| We come before thee at thy gracious word | 850 | 1 |
| We come to train in all thy ways | 468 | 3 |
| We complete in thee are found | 990 | 2 |
| We cumbered long the ground | 981 | 2 |
| We do in Christ believe | 897 | 3 |
| We draw our blessings thence | 591 | 4 |
| We drink of the stream | 488 | 3 |
| We each, as dying Stephen | 853 | 4 |
| We each other's burdens bear | 487 | 2 |
| We each to other fly | 537 | 5 |
| We faithfully depend | 469 | 10 |
| We feast in his sight | 499 | 8 |
| We feed upon thee in our hearts | 507 | 6 |
| We feel the resurrection near | 947 | 7 |
| We extol the slaughtered Lamb | 221 | 3 |
| We eye to eye behold the Man | 525 | 3 |
| We find it nearer while we sing | 71 | 5 |
| We find it now | 276 | 2 |

| | Hymn | Verse |
|---|---|---|
| We find within our hearts, and dare | 96 | 3 |
| We first received the pledge of love | 677 | 2 |
| We for Christ, our Master, stand | 519 | 3 |
| †We, for his sake, count all things loss | 539 | 3 |
| We forfeit all our grace | 806 | 1 |
| We from out our graves may spring | 720 | 9 |
| We gain a pure drop of his love | 79 | 2 |
| We gain in what we seem to give | 896 | 3 |
| We gave up our all | 498 | 2 |
| *We give immortal praise | 644 | 1 |
| We gladly let thee go | 52 | 4 |
| We gladly to the temple go | 860 | 1 |
| We hand in hand go on | 500 | 2 |
| We hand in hand go on | 537 | 3 |
| We haste again to see | 949 | 4 |
| We have access to God | 1005 | 1 |
| We have a house above | 74 | 1 |
| †We have laid up our love | 491 | 2 |
| †We have no abiding city here | 71 | 3 |
| †We have no outward righteousness | 774 | 2 |
| †We have not, Lord, thy gifts improved | 176 | 3 |
| †We have now begun to cry | 299 | 2 |
| We have the treasure to dispense | 874 | 1 |
| We have through fire and water gone | 483 | 2 |
| We hear the rumbling wheels, and pray | 62 | 5 |
| We hear thy voice, and open now | 507 | 1 |
| We his open face shall see | 936 | 7 |
| We his pardoning love have known | 572 | 4 |
| We his quickening Spirit breathe | 519 | 4 |
| We humbly hope with joy to see | 254 | 1 |
| We in his image shine | 21 | 6 |
| We in songs our lives employ | 50 | 5 |
| We in the body mourn | 74 | 4 |
| We in the Godhead own | 256 | 2 |
| We in the kingdom of thy grace | 15 | 3 |
| We in thy passion find | 701 | 1 |
| We in thy sacrifice behold | 702 | 5 |
| We in thy temple stay | 572 | 2 |
| We joyfully adore thee | 853 | 1 |
| We joyfully confess | 652 | — |
| We joyfully submit | 801 | 2 |
| We keep the sacred feast | 907 | 1 |
| We know and feel that thou art here | 969 | 2 |
| *We know, by faith we know | 74 | 1 |
| *We know, by faith we surely know | 673 | 1 |
| †We know it must be done | 452 | 4 |
| We know no help but thee | 696 | 6 |
| We languish to be freed | 818 | 3 |
| †We laugh to scorn his cruel power | 501 | 4 |
| We launch into the foaming deep | 1000 | 1 |
| We lay it not to heart so sore | 856 | 3 |
| We lay the treasure thou hast given | 896 | 2 |
| We let each other go | 533 | 2 |

| | Hymn | Verse |
|---|---|---|
| We lift our hearts and voices | 853 | 1 |
| We lift our hearts to thee | 968 | 2 |
| †We lift our joyful eyes | 723 | 2 |
| We lift up our voice, And call him our Lord | 211 | 1 |
| †We, like Jesse's son, would raise | 989 | 3 |
| We, like them, may live and love | 519 | 2 |
| †We live, and move, and are | 661 | 2 |
| We live, and move, and breathe | 88 | 1 |
| †We live in pleasure, and are dead | 454 | 3 |
| We live our God to please | 96 | 6 |
| We long thy appearing to see | 946 | 3 |
| We long thy praises to repeat | 222 | 4 |
| We look for thee again | 1005 | 3 |
| We look to see restored | 536 | 7 |
| We lose ourselves in heaven above | 973 | 6 |
| We lose the duty in the joy | 957 | 4 |
| We lose the talent we conceal | 806 | 1 |
| We love to hear of thee | 682 | 1 |
| We magnify and love | 259 | 5 |
| We march hand in hand | 498 | 3 |
| †We mark the idolizing throng | 469 | 5 |
| We mark the vengeful day begun | 62 | 2 |
| We may a place provide | 63 | 5 |
| We may face the foe | 715 | 9 |
| We may safely go | 715 | 9 |
| We may, we must draw near | 865 | 1 |
| We meet on earth for thy dear sake | 485 | 2 |
| We meet, the grace to take | 485 | 2 |
| We meet with on earth; for eternity's near | 498 | 3 |
| We met, O Jesus, in thy name | 537 | 2 |
| We more than taste the heavenly powers | 947 | 7 |
| †We mourn not that prophetic skill | 767 | 3 |
| We myriads see | 736 | 2 |
| †We need not now go up to heaven | 902 | 5 |
| †We need not to confess our fault | 797 | 2 |
| †We never will throw off his fear | 532 | 4 |
| †We no miracle require | 995 | 3 |
| We nothing good can do | 435 | 2 |
| We now adore thy name | 617 | 2 |
| We now approach to God | 901 | 1 |
| †We now divinely bold | 723 | 3 |
| We now for succour fly | 986 | 1 |
| We now recall to mind | 900 | 1 |
| We now stand still | 854 | 3 |
| We now thy guardian presence own | 329 | 2 |
| †We now thy promised presence claim | 476 | 2 |
| We now thy promised presence find | 476 | 2 |
| We, O Lord, have found thee true | 348 | 5 |
| We on eagles' wings aspire | 221 | 3 |
| We on his love our spirits stay | 1000 | 2 |
| We on thyself rely | 873 | 1 |
| We only can be saved by grace | 774 | 2 |
| We only hang upon thy word | 380 | 9 |

| | HYMN | VERSE |
|---|---|---|
| WE, ONLY | | |
| We, only, we, can say | 533 | 1 |
| We ought in all his paths to move | 319 | 1 |
| We our dying Lord confess | 519 | 3 |
| We our hearts and voices raise | 260 | 1 |
| †We ourselves are God's own field | 987 | 2 |
| We own him our Jesus, Continually near | 481 | 1 |
| We own the conscious want of grace | 874 | 2 |
| We own thy way is in the sea | 1001 | 4 |
| †We part in body, not in mind | 537 | 3 |
| †We perish if we cease from prayer | 865 | 2 |
| We please the Lord, and work for him | 858 | 2 |
| *We plough the fields, and scatter | 988 | 1 |
| We pray thee now that sinless | 968 | 1 |
| We pray the Spirit of our Head | 539 | 8 |
| We quietly submit | 925 | 3 |
| We raise our hymn to thee | 968 | 3 |
| We raise our songs of triumph higher | 377 | 4 |
| We raise the happiness of heaven | 203 | 5 |
| We reach the rest remaining | 958 | 5 |
| We read thy name in fairer lines | 553 | 1 |
| We read thy patience still | 263 | 2 |
| We remember his word | 491 | 2 |
| †We remember the word | 488 | 6 |
| We rise and come away | 54 | 5 |
| *We rose to-day with anthems sweet | 961 | 1 |
| We search with trembling awe | 88 | 2 |
| We see, adore, and love | 226 | 12 |
| We see, and rush into the snare | 469 | 3 |
| We see by faith to us brought back | 702 | 6 |
| We see it still stretched out to save | 616 | 5 |
| We see the fabric stand | 67 | 4 |
| We see the new city descend | 73 | 2 |
| We see the truth, we judge aright | 469 | 4 |
| We see them all before | 583 | 2 |
| We see them now far off removed | 461 | 2 |
| We seek sometimes, but never strive | 454 | 3 |
| We seek thy perfect way | 510 | 1 |
| We seem agreed to seek thy face | 81 | 1 |
| WE SHALL | | |
| We shall after thee mount up | 723 | 4 |
| We shall all be as our Lord | 400 | 7 |
| We shall all be free indeed | 86 | 3 |
| We shall before his face appear | 333 | 3 |
| We shall from all our sins be free | 345 | Cho. |
| We shall from earth remove | 685 | 5 |
| We shall from Sodom flee | 482 | 2 |
| We shall from the vale remove | 53 | 4 |
| †We shall gain our calling's prize | 400 | 5 |
| We shall in heart be pure | 345 | 6 |
| We shall meet him in the air | 58 | 2 |
| We shall not continue long | 50 | 4 |
| We shall not full direction need | 326 | 2 |
| We shall not in the desert stray | 326 | 2 |
| We shall not then from thee remove | 511 | 3 |

| | Hymn | Verse |
|---|---|---|
| We shall obtain delivering grace | 725 | 5 |
| †We shall our time beneath | 535 | 6 |
| We shall quit the house of clay | 50 | 4 |
| We shall see him again | 488 | 5 |
| We shall see the realms of day | 50 | 4 |
| We shall see the welcome day | 52 | 6 |
| We shall sing to our lyres | 491 | 6 |
| We shall soon be all caught up | 54 | 4 |
| We shall soon be pure within | 623 | 4 |
| We shall soon be taken up | 53 | 4 |
| We shall soon obtain the grace | 400 | 4 |
| We shall suddenly meet | 491 | 6 |
| We shall to the summons bow | 52 | 6 |
| We shall with all our brethren rise | 536 | 4 |
| We shall with them be blest | 535 | 4 |
| We sing the songs of heaven | 614 | 14 |
| We sing thine arm unshortened | 276 | 2 |
| We sink into thy side | 64 | 2 |
| We sit under our Vine | 488 | 1 |
| We sleep our useless lives away | 454 | 2 |
| We soon his face shall see | 497 | 5 |
| We soon in Paradise shall find | 482 | 3 |
| †We soon shall do what we condemn | 469 | 7 |
| We soon shall hear the archangel's voice | 729 | 6 |
| We soon shall recover our home | 73 | 1 |
| We soon with open face shall see | 333 | 5 |
| We spend our wretched strength for nought | 526 | 1 |
| We stand to bless thee ere our worship cease | 962 | 1 |
| We still are one in heart | 534 | 1 |
| We still are preparing To meet our reward | 484 | 2 |
| We still shall adore | 808 | 11 |
| We still to conquer go | 315 | 3 |
| We sweetly then pursue | 804 | 2 |
| We take the pardon of our God | 656 | 3 |
| We taste our glorious liberty | 419 | 1 |
| We thankfully embrace | 387 | 2 |
| We thank thee for the past | 875 | 2 |
| We thank thee for the past | 1016 | 1 |
| †We thank thee then, O Father | 988 | 3 |
| We then pursue our sole design | 528 | 3 |
| We then through faith shall understand | 121 | 2 |
| †We, the sons of men, rejoice | 684 | 4 |
| We the Spirit receive | 488 | 3 |
| We there shall enjoy | 808 | 8 |
| We thine altars will adorn | 580 | 3 |
| We thither repair | 498 | 3 |
| We, through the Holy Ghost | 21 | 3 |
| We through thy gracious Spirit feel | 419 | 3 |
| We through thy Spirit and thy Son | 865 | 5 |
| We thus our right maintain | 897 | 4 |
| We thy confessors scorn to shun | 891 | 2 |
| We thy kindest word obey | 29 | 2 |
| We to Jesus look up | 491 | 8 |

| | Hymn | Verse |
|---|---|---|
| We to our country come | 497 | 2 |
| We to our Father's house repair | 497 | 4 |
| We too will his grace implore | 606 | 5 |
| †We too with him are dead | 898 | 4 |
| We travel to the mount of God | 71 | 6 |
| †We tremble at the danger near | 467 | 3 |
| We triumph and sing Of Jesus's name | 211 | 2 |
| We triumph in thy favour | 276 | 4 |
| We trust our whole salvation here | 617 | 2 |
| We trust thee, though thy face be hid | 546 | 1 |
| We turn, who oft have strayed | 986 | 4 |
| We urge our way with strength renewed | 71 | 6 |
| We urge the restless strife | 74 | 3 |
| We view our promised land | 958 | 3 |
| We wait, according to thy word | 486 | 2 |
| We wait for all the power of love | 448 | 3 |
| We wait the Pentecostal powers | 759 | 4 |
| We wait thy Spirit's latest call | 448 | 1 |
| We wait to catch the spreading flame | 490 | 4 |
| We walk upon our subject seas | 1001 | 9 |
| †We weep for those that weep below | 441 | 2 |
| We, we have seen a gospel day | 493 | 1 |
| †We, while the stars from heaven shall fall | 57 | 4 |
| †We who in Christ believe | 96 | 2 |
| We who Jesus have put on | 518 | 9 |
| We who prayed for their success | 735 | 1 |
| We whom thy love delights to keep | 1001 | 2 |
| We will covet nothing less | 399 | 2 |
| We will no more our God forsake | 532 | 3 |
| †We will not close our wakeful eyes | 977 | 2 |
| We will not let our eyelids sleep | 977 | 2 |
| We wist not what to think or say | 698 | 5 |
| We with Christ our Lord may dwell | 720 | 8 |
| We with him are crucified | 519 | 4 |
| We worship evermore | 259 | 3 |
| We worship evermore | 673 | 3 |
| We worship thee | 800 | 10 |
| We worship thee, the common Lord | 647 | 1 |
| We worship toward that holy place | 121 | 3 |
| We worshipped Thor and Woden still | 454 | 7 |
| We would adore our Maker too | 316 | 3 |
| We would employ in works divine | 955 | 1 |
| †We would in every step look up | 468 | 5 |
| †We would persuade their hearts to obey | 468 | 6 |
| We would thy law receive | 886 | — |
| †We wrestle for the ruined race | 441 | 3 |
| We wretched sinners lay | 699 | 1 |
| We yield to be set free | 387 | 2 |
| †We'll crowd thy gates with thankful songs | 608 | 3 |
| We'll mount aloft to thine abode | 802 | 5 |
| We'll praise him for all that is past | 660 | — |
| We'll praise thee for thy mercies past | 1002 | 5 |
| We'll sing our Jesu's lovely name | 682 | 3 |

| | Hymn | Verse |
|---|---|---|
| We'll think upon his wondrous grace | 573 | 4 |
| We'll to his house repair | 573 | 4 |
| Weak and helpless as I am | 142 | 4 |
| Weak and wounded, sick and sore | 791 | 1 |
| †Weak is the effort of my heart | 679 | 5 |
| Weakness itself thou know'st I am | 126 | 3 |
| †Wealth, honour, pleasure, and what else | 285 | 6 |
| †Wealth, labour, talents, freely give | 746 | 2 |
| Wealth, pleasure, fame, for thee alone | 494 | 3 |
| Weaned from every creature good | 628 | 3 |
| †Weaned from his mother's breast | 627 | 3 |
| Wean my soul, and keep it low | 302 | 1 |
| Wearied we lie down to rest | 970 | 1 |
| Wear it ever night and day | 829 | 3 |
| Weary and faint through long delay | 379 | 1 |
| †Weary and sick of sin I am | 177 | 3 |
| Weary hearts and troubled spirits | 990 | 3 |
| Weary, I come to thee for rest | 395 | 3 |
| *Weary of earth and laden with my sin | 794 | 1 |
| Weary of earth, myself, and sin | 132 | 1 |
| †Weary of life, through inbred sin | 230 | 3 |
| Weary of mine own righteousness | 25 | 2 |
| †Weary of passions unsubdued | 25 | 3 |
| Weary of sin, from sin would cease | 25 | 2 |
| Weary of vows in vain renewed | 25 | 3 |
| *Weary of wandering from my God | 186 | 1 |
| Weary, O Lord, thou know'st I am | 388 | 2 |
| Weary, parched with thirst, and faint | 292 | 4 |
| *Weary souls, that wander wide | 20 | 1 |
| Weep, believe, and sin no more | 168 | 6 |
| †Welcome as the water-spring | 292 | 2 |
| †Welcome from earth: lo, the right hand | 490 | 2 |
| Welcome news of saving grace | 873 | 1 |
| *Welcome, sweet day of rest | 956 | 1 |
| Welcome to this reviving breast | 956 | 1 |
| Well and faithfully done | 47 | 6 |
| Well may I fill the allotted space | 440 | 2 |
| Well may I tremble at thy word | 93 | 1 |
| Well may this glowing heart rejoice | 912 | 1 |
| Well may thy praise our lips employ | 978 | 1 |
| Well pleased in thee, our God looked down | 902 | 3 |
| Well pleased with me, when mine thou art | 321 | 4 |
| Well-pleasing in thy sight | 367 | 3 |
| Well supply thy sons and daughters | 594 | 2 |
| †Well thou know'st I cannot rest | 156 | 2 |
| Well thou know'st my desperate case | 151 | 2 |
| Wept like a weaned child | 697 | 3 |
| Wept o'er my soul thy pitying eye | 206 | 2 |
| Were hidden from thine eye | 546 | 2 |
| Were I built upon the rock | 271 | 2 |
| Were precious in his sight | 586 | 2 |
| †Were the whole realm of nature mine | 700 | 4 |
| What a blessing to know that my Jesus is mine | 205 | 1 |

| | Hymn | Verse |
|---|---|---|
| What a comfort divine | 205 | 1 |
| What a concert of praise | 499 | 4 |
| What a countless company | 75 | 1 |
| What a heaven in Jesus's name | 807 | 2 |
| What a heaven of bliss | 231 | 6 |
| What a joy it received | 807 | 2 |
| †What a mercy is this | 231 | 6 |
| †What a rapturous song | 499 | 5 |
| What after death for me remains | 44 | 1 |
| †What ailed thee, O thou trembling sea | 223 | 3 |
| \*What am I, O thou glorious God | 206 | 1 |
| What angel-tongue can tell | 216 | 6 |
| †What are our works but sin and death | 26 | 4 |
| \*What are these arrayed in white | 76 | 1 |
| What best for each will prove | 831 | 5 |
| What blessed light breaks on my soul | 697 | 9 |
| What bliss beyond compare | 943 | 8 |
| What, but one drop! one transient sight | 284 | 3 |
| What but thy grace can foil the tempter's power | 972 | 3 |
| †What but thy manifested grace | 124 | 3 |
| What but thyself canst thou desire | 38 | 5 |
| What can his love withstand | 267 | 2 |
| What can my hopes withstand | 275 | 2 |
| What can my weakness do | 91 | 7 |
| What can our foundation shock | 67 | 2 |
| What can shake thy sure repose | 594 | 1 |
| What can the Rock of ages move | 227 | 4 |
| What can withstand his will | 384 | 3 |
| What Christ hath for his saints prepared | 69 | 8 |
| What condescending ways | 675 | 2 |
| What conflicts have we passed | 478 | 2 |
| †What could my Redeemer move | 215 | 2 |
| \*What could your Redeemer do | 8 | 1 |
| What cries to heaven's gates ascending | 595 | 6 |
| What desolations he hath made | 569 | 7 |
| †What did thy only Son endure | 784 | 2 |
| †What doth then my hopes prevent | 910 | 6 |
| What dying worms we be | 42 | 1 |
| What endless glory shines | 880 | 1 |
| What every member bears | 725 | 3 |
| What every member wants | 487 | 4 |
| What flesh and blood can ne'er reveal | 148 | 2 |
| What forms of love he bears for thee | 675 | 2 |
| What God by them hath done | 735 | 1 |
| †What hast thou done for me | 151 | 6 |
| What hast thou suffered on the tree | 330 | 1 |
| What hath he at last | 793 | 5 |
| What hath your Saviour done for you | 746 | 2 |
| †What have I then wherein to trust | 127 | 6 |
| What heights of rapture shall we know | 500 | 6 |
| What his guerdon here | 793 | 4 |
| What hope of a second release | 174 | 1 |
| What horror turned the river back | 223 | 3 |

| | Hymn | Verse |
|---|---|---|
| †What if a sternly righteous doom | 799 | 2 |
| What if thy form we cannot see | 969 | 2 |
| What in him seemeth righteous | 626 | 2 |
| †What is a worthless worm to thee | 773 | 2 |
| What is in man thy grace to move | 773 | 2 |
| †What is it keeps me back | 152 | 2 |
| *What is our calling's glorious hope | 406 | 1 |
| †What is the creature's skill or force | 225 | 5 |
| What is the length, and breadth, and height | 136 | 10 |
| What is the length, and breadth, and height | 370 | 4 |
| †What is there here to court my stay | 947 | 4 |
| What I've committed to his hands | 811 | 3 |
| What keeps me out of thee | 152 | 3 |
| What lives and moves, lives by thy word | 240 | 2 |
| †What means my trembling heart | 931 | 5 |
| What means that strange expiring cry | 33 | 1 |
| *What means this eager, anxious throng | 695 | 1 |
| What means this strange commotion, pray | 695 | 1 |
| What meant the suffering Son of man | 128 | 3 |
| †What mighty troubles hast thou shown | 483 | 2 |
| What mortal eloquence can raise | 612 | 2 |
| What most I prize—it ne'er was mine | 841 | 3 |
| *What! never speak one evil word | 363 | 1 |
| What now is my hope and desire | 371 | 1 |
| *What now is my object and aim | 371 | 1 |
| What numbers fall by thee and rise | 670 | 1 |
| What once for all the world was done | 595 | 4 |
| What only conquest can explain | 69 | 4 |
| What our dim eye could never see | 240 | 4 |
| What our God for us hath done | 580 | 4 |
| What pain, what labour, to secure | 784 | 2 |
| †What peaceful hours I then enjoyed | 787 | 3 |
| What people is like thee | 407 | 6 |
| What pleasure to our ears | 742 | 1 |
| What power shall be the sinner's stay | 934 | 1 |
| †What profit in my blood is found | 559 | 4 |
| What radiancy of glory | 943 | 8 |
| †What seek I now, O Lord | 565 | 4 |
| What shall I bring to gain thy grace | 127 | 1 |
| †What shall I do my God to love | 216 | 2 |
| *What shall I do my God to love | 378 | 1 |
| †What shall I do my suit to gain | 145 | 4 |
| †What shall I do to keep | 172 | 3 |
| What shall I do to make it known | 34 | 6 |
| †What shall I, frail man, be pleading | 933 | 7 |
| *What shall I render to my God | 614 | 8 |
| †What shall I say thy grace to move | 132 | 6 |
| What shall thy work withstand | 831 | 7 |
| *What shall we offer our good Lord | 492 | 1 |
| What social joys are there | 943 | 8 |
| What the agony to part | 914 | 6 |
| What the depth of love like thine | 27 | 5 |
| What the length, and breadth, and height | 27 | 5 |

| | Hymn | Verse |
|---|---|---|
| What the length, and breadth, and height | 413 | 8 |
| †What then is he whose scorn I dread | 279 | 4 |
| What then to me thine eyes could turn | 38 | 6 |
| What thickest darkness veils, to thee | 240 | 4 |
| What thine own Spirit doth inspire | 558 | 1 |
| What thou for all mankind hast done | 34 | 6 |
| What thou for me hast done | 150 | 5 |
| What thou hast bought so dear | 35 | 3 |
| What thou more willing art to give | 782 | 1 |
| †What though a thousand hosts engage | 269 | 2 |
| †What though I cannot break my chain | 138 | 4 |
| †What though in solemn silence all | 552 | 5 |
| What though my flesh and heart decay | 210 | 7 |
| †What though my shrinking flesh complain | 140 | 5 |
| What though no real voice or sound | 552 | 5 |
| †What though the gates of hell withstood | 617 | 4 |
| †What though the spicy breezes | 747 | 2 |
| †What though thou rulest not | 831 | 11 |
| What thy estimate may be | 24 | 2 |
| What thy mysterious name shall be | 69 | 4 |
| What tongue can tell the almighty grace | 298 | 1 |
| †What troubles have we seen | 478 | 2 |
| What voices from the tomb are heard | 559 | 4 |
| What we have done, and what we are | 797 | 2 |
| What we have felt and seen | 96 | 1 |
| What will become of me | 43 | 2 |
| What will thy glory be | 920 | 4 |
| †What without thy aid is wrought | 753 | 6 |
| †Whate'er beneath thy searching eyes | 961 | 3 |
| †Whate'er events betide | 560 | 3 |
| Whate'er has risen from heart sincere | 961 | 2 |
| †Whate'er I fondly counted mine | 291 | 4 |
| †Whate'er I have of evil done | 917 | 3 |
| Whate'er I have, or can, or am | 375 | 1 |
| Whate'er I have was freely given | 332 | 4 |
| Whate'er I have, whate'er I am | 229 | 3 |
| Whate'er I have, whate'er I am | 772 | 6 |
| †Whate'er I say or do | 323 | 2 |
| Whate'er in earth, or sea, or sky | 240 | 3 |
| †Whate'er in me seems wise, or good | 217 | 3 |
| Whate'er is done | 736 | 1 |
| Whate'er is pleasing in thy sight | 438 | 2 |
| †Whate'er my sinful flesh requires | 332 | 2 |
| †Whate'er obstructs thy pardoning love | 97 | 5 |
| Whate'er obstructs thy work of grace | 528 | 2 |
| †Whate'er offends thy glorious eyes | 502 | 4 |
| Whate'er of sin in us is found | 503 | 1 |
| †Whate'er our pardoning Lord | 96 | 6 |
| Whate'er our souls can need | 905 | 2 |
| Whate'er that idol be | 787 | 5 |
| †Whate'er the ancient prophets spoke | 90 | 2 |
| †Whate'er the Father views as thine | 321 | 3 |
| †Whate'er thou dost on one bestow | 524 | 2 |

| | Hymn | Verse |
|---|---|---|
| Whate'er thou hast, whate'er thou art | 806 | 2 |
| Whate'er thou wilt, be done | 842 | 4 |
| †Whate'er thou wilt, in earth below | 239 | 5 |
| Whate'er thy bounteous grace hath given | 824 | 5 |
| Whate'er thy children want, thou giv'st | 831 | 7 |
| Whate'er thy every creature needs | 99 | 1 |
| Whate'er thy will decrees is done | 240 | 3 |
| Whate'er we do, where'er we be | 42 | 3 |
| Whate'er we have or are | 979 | 3 |
| Whate'er we hope, by faith we have | 95 | 3 |
| †Whatever ills the world befall | 62 | 5 |
| Whatever is, is best | 533 | 1 |
| Whatever part he please | 844 | 3 |
| Wheat and tares together sown | 987 | 2 |
| †When affliction clouds my sky | 672 | 3 |
| †When all are sweetly joined | 630 | 2 |
| When all my warfare's past | 421 | 1 |
| When all our toils are o'er | 536 | 4 |
| When all shall be brought home | 537 | 12 |
| When all the weary wheels stand still | 961 | 5 |
| When all things else decay | 682 | 3 |
| When all thy church shall chant above | 648 | 6 |
| When all thy foes thou shalt destroy | 602 | 1 |
| *When all thy mercies, O my God | 657 | 1 |
| When all who on their God believe | 254 | 3 |
| When an heir of salvation was born | 231 | 1 |
| †When anxious cares would break my rest | 658 | 2 |
| When as a flood the foe comes in | 230 | 3 |
| When a thousand feel the blow | 597 | 2 |
| When brethren all in one agree | 630 | 1 |
| When brethren cordially agree | 489 | 1 |
| When brought into bondage again | 174 | 1 |
| †When by our bed the loved ones weep | 961 | 6 |
| †When by the dreadful tempest borne | 1002 | 3 |
| When caught in the rapturous flame | 946 | 2 |
| When children's voices raise that song | 993 | 4 |
| When Christ himself imparts | 875 | 3 |
| When comforts are declining | 804 | 1 |
| When darkling in the depths of night | 698 | 6 |
| †When darkness intercepts the skies | 272 | 6 |
| When dazzled with excess of light | 698 | 6 |
| †When death o'er nature shall prevail | 658 | 3 |
| When death shall all be done away | 534 | 6 |
| When death was full in view | 697 | 6 |
| When dust he turns to dust again | 422 | 1 |
| When earth and heaven are fled away | 240 | 2 |
| When earth and hell oppress us | 276 | 1 |
| When earth and hell their forces join | 475 | 1 |
| When earth's foundations melt away | 189 | 6 |
| When every star its course hath run | 694 | 2 |
| When faith in sight shall end | 212 | 4 |
| When father, mother, kindred fail | 558 | 4 |
| When fears distract my mind | 602 | 4 |

| | Hymn | Verse |
|---|---|---|
| When first I saw the Lord | 787 | 2 |
| When from flesh the spirit freed | 51 | 3 |
| When from heaven the Judge descendeth | 933 | 2 |
| When from on high his thunder roars | 569 | 8 |
| †When from the dust of death I rise | 190 | 6 |
| When from the flesh they fly | 941 | 1 |
| When fully he the work hath wrought | 831 | 13 |
| When 'gainst it first I turned my face | 126 | 1 |
| *When gathering clouds around I view | 849 | 1 |
| †When glorious in the nightly sky | 544 | 2 |
| When God doth all his wrath reveal | 63 | 1 |
| When God himself imparts | 262 | 2 |
| †When God is mine, and I am his | 384 | 7 |
| When God is on my side | 575 | 1 |
| When God the nations shall survey | 994 | 5 |
| When grace has well refined my heart | 599 | 5 |
| When grace in glory ends | 258 | 3 |
| *When, gracious Lord, when shall it be | 163 | 1 |
| When grief my wounded soul assails | 338 | 3 |
| When hanging on the accursed tree | 703 | 4 |
| When heated in the chase | 567 | 1 |
| When heaven and earth are fled | 253 | 4 |
| When heaven and earth are fled and gone | 63 | 4 |
| When heaven and earth are fled away | 189 | 1 |
| When heaven and earth shall pass away | 932 | 4 |
| When heaven and earth shall pass away | 934 | 1 |
| When he bled on the cross | 707 | 7 |
| †When he first the work begun | 218 | 2 |
| When he had purged our stains | 729 | 2 |
| When he went to prepare us a place | 488 | 6 |
| When high the storms of passion rise | 272 | 6 |
| When I am pure in heart | 175 | 5 |
| When I am weak, then I am strong | 140 | 5 |
| †When I, beset with pain and grief | 551 | 2 |
| †When I feel it fixed within | 355 | 9 |
| When I forsake his ways | 555 | 2 |
| When I have lived to thee alone | 440 | 2 |
| When I have my Saviour, My sin shall depart | 273 | 8 |
| When I in Christ am formed again | 401 | 6 |
| †When I lie buried deep in dust | 584 | 6 |
| †When I my Saviour love | 877 | 2 |
| When I rise to worlds unknown | 709 | 3 |
| When I shall quit my place | 584 | 3 |
| *When I survey the wondrous cross | 700 | 1 |
| When I thy joys shall see | 939 | 6 |
| When I to folly turned again | 365 | 5 |
| †When I touch the blessed shore | 672 | 10 |
| †When I tread the verge of Jordan | 839 | 3 |
| †When I walk through the shades of death | 555 | 3 |
| When in distress to him I called | 562 | 3 |
| †When in his strength I struggle | 943 | 13 |
| When in my sin I totter | 943 | 13 |
| †When in the slippery paths of youth | 657 | 5 |

# WHEN IN — WHEN SHALL

| | Hymn | Verse |
|---|---|---|
| When in thy hands I lay | 274 | 2 |
| When in thy presence we appear | 896 | 1 |
| When, invoked by priest and seer | 606 | 3 |
| *When Israel out of Egypt came | 223 | 1 |
| When it hath found repose in thee | 344 | 4 |
| When Jesus doth his blood apply | 422 | 2 |
| When Jesus enters in | 216 | 7 |
| When Jesus doth the heavens bow | 65 | 6 |
| †When Jesus makes my heart his home | 406 | 5 |
| †When justice bared the sword | 981 | 3 |
| †When, like a tent to dwell in | 667 | 2 |
| When love will do the deed | 468 | 6 |
| When man to judgment wakes from clay | 934 | 3 |
| When men and devils join | 311 | 2 |
| When my eyes shall close in death | 709 | 3 |
| When my heart it believed | 807 | 2 |
| *When, my Saviour, shall I be | 381 | 1 |
| When my sorrows most increase | 336 | 1 |
| When my strength and spirit fail | 101 | 5 |
| When nature is destroyed | 64 | 5 |
| When nature shall expire | 642 | 5 |
| †When new triumphs of thy name | 672 | 4 |
| When none but God is near | 823 | 2 |
| When none thy Godhead shall deny | 254 | 3 |
| When old things shall be passed away | 367 | 2 |
| †When, O my God, shall I | 27 | 3 |
| When onward to thine altar | 996 | 7 |
| When other helpers fail, and comforts flee | 972 | 1 |
| When our bitter tears o'erflow | 711 | 1 |
| When our eyes shall see thee near | 852 | 3 |
| *When our heads are bowed with woe | 711 | 1 |
| When our Jesus's grace | 499 | 4 |
| When our Redeemer shall come down | 954 | 3 |
| *When our redeeming Lord | 623 | 1 |
| When our voice in prayer was strong | 580 | 4 |
| †When pain o'er my weak flesh prevails | 338 | 3 |
| †When, passing through the watery deep | 272 | 2 |
| When perfected in grace | 436 | 8 |
| When perfected in love | 482 | 2 |
| When perfect love shall cast out fear | 547 | 6 |
| *When quiet in my house I sit | 328 | 1 |
| When, raised by the life-giving word | 73 | 2 |
| When, repentant, to the skies | 710 | 1 |
| †When rising floods my soul o'erflow | 339 | 4 |
| When, robed in majesty and power | 55 | 2 |
| When, robed with majesty and power | 483 | 5 |
| When rolling years shall cease to move | 608 | 4 |
| When round his throne we meet | 500 | 6 |
| When saints and angels join | 537 | 9 |
| When shall I call thee mine | 731 | 6 |
| When shall I find my willing heart | 147 | 1 |
| †When shall I hear the inward voice | 376 | 2 |
| †When shall I see the welcome hour | 361 | 3 |

| | Hymn | Verse |
|---|---|---|
| †When shall mine eyes behold the Lamb | 388 | 2 |
| When shall my labours have an end | 939 | 1 |
| When shall my soul return again | 137 | 1 |
| When shall my soul triumphant prove | 290 | 6 |
| †When shall these eyes thy heaven-built walls | 939 | 2 |
| *When shall thy love constrain | 137 | 1 |
| †When shall thy Spirit reign | 653 | 2 |
| When short-lived worlds are lost, shall shine | 240 | 2 |
| †When shrivelling like a parched scroll | 934 | 2 |
| When sin is all destroyed | 436 | 10 |
| When sin shall all be purged away | 365 | 9 |
| When sinks my heart in waves of woe | 339 | 4 |
| When sinks the sun behind the hill | 961 | 5 |
| †When sorrow bows the spirit down | 637 | 7 |
| †When sorrowing o'er some stone I bend | 849 | 4 |
| When stars and sun no more shall shine | 731 | 9 |
| When storms of sharp distress invade | 569 | 1 |
| †When stronger souls their faith forsook | 483 | 3 |
| When success attends their mission | 878 | 7 |
| When that righteous doom shall be | 604 | 3 |
| When the archangel's trump shall blow | 51 | 5 |
| When the evening stars arise | 598 | 1 |
| When the favour divine | 807 | 2 |
| When the glorified throng | 499 | 5 |
| †When the heart is sad within | 711 | 2 |
| †When the Judge his seat attaineth | 933 | 6 |
| When the Judge, to earth descending | 604 | 4 |
| When the just are mercy needing | 933 | 7 |
| When the morning paints the skies | 598 | 1 |
| †When the morn shall bid us rise | 975 | 4 |
| †When the soft dews of kindly sleep | 973 | 2 |
| When the spirit shrinks with fear | 711 | 2 |
| When the waves in wild commotion | 878 | 3 |
| When thee we behold in the cloud | 946 | 4 |
| When thee with all my heart I love | 357 | 7 |
| When they awake | 595 | 5 |
| †When they once are entered there | 941 | 2 |
| †When they reach the land of strangers | 878 | 4 |
| When they sought his face once more | 606 | 5 |
| †When they think of home, now dearer | 878 | 5 |
| When this poor lisping, stammering tongue | 798 | 5 |
| †When thou arisest, Lord | 831 | 7 |
| When thou art seen in us below | 505 | 9 |
| When thou com'st on earth to abide | 885 | 2 |
| †When thou didst our Isaac give | 914 | 2 |
| When thou dost know before we speak | 797 | 8 |
| †When thou hadst all thy foes o'ercome | 72 | 5 |
| †When thou hadst rendered up thy breath | 648 | 3 |
| When thou hast bid me live | 778 | 3 |
| *When thou hast disposed a heart | 876 | 1 |
| †When thou in our flesh didst appear | 220 | 2 |
| When thou record'st my sins no more | 778 | 3 |
| When thou return'st to set them free | 612 | 3 |

| | Hymn | Verse |
|---|---|---|
| When thou the gift hast given | 292 | 5 |
| †When thou the work of faith hast wrought | 857 | 5 |
| †When thou the work of faith hast wrought | 401 | 4 |
| When thou wilt the blessing give | 925 | 3 |
| When thou wilt to work proceed | 244 | 2 |
| When thou with clouds shalt come | 59 | 4 |
| When thus I heard thee speak | 558 | 3 |
| When thy quickening power we prove | 850 | 7 |
| When time and death shall be no more | 638 | 6 |
| When time and death shall be no more | 649 | 1 |
| †When time is no more | 808 | 11 |
| When time shall cease to be | 665 | 6 |
| †When 'tis deeply rooted here | 355 | 8 |
| When to me my Lord shall come | 383 | 2 |
| †When to the right or left I stray | 312 | 4 |
| When to the right or left I turn | 305 | 3 |
| †When to the right or left we stray | 503 | 2 |
| †When tongues shall cease, and power decay | 767 | 5 |
| When truth's opposers rise | 733 | 2 |
| When war's and tumult's waves run high | 62 | 1 |
| When we all our work have done | 925 | 2 |
| †When we appear in yonder cloud | 682 | 4 |
| When we can to thee draw near | 882 | 1 |
| When we have our grief filled up | 925 | 2 |
| When we in thy house appear | 975 | 4 |
| When we made our supplication | 580 | 4 |
| When we mourn the lost, the dear | 711 | 1 |
| When we our whole hearts resign | 179 | 3 |
| When we reach yon blissful station | 1007 | — |
| †When we would have spurned His mercy and grace | 481 | 4 |
| When will it reach to all mankind | 444 | 1 |
| When wilt thou all my load remove | 177 | 3 |
| When wilt thou banish my complaints | 765 | 2 |
| When wilt thou come into my heart | 379 | 1 |
| †When wilt thou my whole heart subdue | 351 | 3 |
| When wilt thou rid me of my shame | 177 | 3 |
| When wise ones reject His offers of grace | 212 | 3 |
| When, with all his bright train | 488 | 5 |
| When, with angel-hosts surrounded | 936 | 3 |
| When with foes we stood at bay | 621 | 1 |
| When with ravished eyes I see | 18 | 3 |
| *When, with wasting sickness worn | 672 | 7 |
| †When worn with sickness, oft hast thou | 657 | 7 |
| †When, wrestling in the strength of prayer | 181 | 2 |
| When youth its pride of beauty shows | 46 | 3 |
| Whence all our hope and comfort springs | 563 | 4 |
| Whence all the streams of mercy flow | 364 | 3 |
| Whence it may ne'er remove | 340 | 2 |
| Whence the healing stream shall flow | 839 | 2 |
| Whence to me this waste of love | 168 | 2 |
| Whene'er I hear the Bridegroom's voice | 974 | 7 |
| ✦Whene'er in error's paths we rove | 89 | 3 |
| †Whene'er my careless hands hang down | 309 | 3 |

| | Hymn | Verse |
|---|---|---|
| Whene'er the wicked man | 162 | 3 |
| Whene'er thou dost my soul require | 919 | 2 |
| †Whenever on the Lord I cry | 575 | 3 |
| Where Afric's sunny fountains | 747 | 1 |
| Where all are wont to meet | 619 | 3 |
| Where all is assurance and peace | 49 | 2 |
| Where all is calm, and joy, and peace | 339 | 6 |
| Where all is love and harmony | 505 | 7 |
| Where all may freely go | 35 | 7 |
| Where all may see their sins forgiven | 111 | 7 |
| Where all my fathers once, like me | 565 | 8 |
| Where all our labours end | 535 | 3 |
| Where all our thoughts are drowned | 250 | 3 |
| Where all our toils are o'er | 535 | 3 |
| Where all that find acceptance stand | 283 | 3 |
| Where all the righteous go | 771 | 2 |
| Where all things are forgot | 43 | 1 |
| Where all, who their Shepherd obey | 228 | 1 |
| †Where am I now, or what my hope | 91 | 7 |
| Where are thy old mercies? where | 151 | 3 |
| Where can a creature hide | 632 | 4 |
| Where danger fiercely rides | 1003 | 1 |
| Where days and years revolve no more | 978 | 6 |
| Where every humble, contrite heart | 907 | 1 |
| Where faith in sight is swallowed up | 297 | 6 |
| Where faith is sweetly lost in sight | 59 | 6 |
| Where fear, and sin, and grief expire | 403 | 2 |
| Where God delights to hear | 591 | 2 |
| Where gospel-light is glowing | 958 | 4 |
| Where he appoints we go | 534 | 2 |
| †Where he displays his healing power | 585 | 11 |
| Where he sits enthroned in glory | 720 | 8 |
| Where in ocean's heart they lie | 570 | 1 |
| Where is death's sting? where, grave, thy victory | 972 | 4 |
| Where is his blest abode | 595 | 4 |
| Where is that soul-refreshing view | 787 | 2 |
| †Where is the blessedness bestowed | 134 | 3 |
| †Where is the blessedness I knew | 787 | 2 |
| Where is the earnest of my heaven | 376 | 4 |
| Where is the Son of God | 595 | 4 |
| †Where is the way? Ah, show me where | 288 | 2 |
| Where Jesus hath fixed his abode | 70 | 1 |
| Where Jesus is pleased to reveal | 946 | 2 |
| Where Jesus reigns alone | 343 | 2 |
| Where Jesus's beauties display | 73 | 4 |
| Where Jesus's Spirit o'erflows | 220 | 5 |
| Where knowledge grows without decay | 789 | 4 |
| Where many mightier have been slain | 469 | 2 |
| Where men each other tear | 447 | 1 |
| Where men like fiends each other tear | 442 | 1 |
| Where men profanely talk | 540 | 1 |
| Where my Redeemer died | 982 | 3 |
| †Where no fruit appears to cheer them | 878 | 6 |

| | Hymn | Verse |
|---|---|---|
| Where, O death, is now thy sting | 716 | 4 |
| Where only Christ is heard to speak | 343 | 2 |
| †Where our banner leads us | 715 | 9 |
| Where our Chief precedes us | 715 | 9 |
| Where praying saints were met | 733 | 3 |
| †Where pure, essential joy is found | 386 | 6 |
| Where reason fails, with all her powers | 644 | 4 |
| Where rest the souls that dwell with thee | 698 | 2 |
| Where saints and angels meet | 535 | 4 |
| Where saints immortal reign | 938 | 1 |
| Where saints in an ecstasy gaze | 228 | 2 |
| Where shadowy joy or solid woe | 154 | 1 |
| Where shall I find my destined place | 44 | 4 |
| Where shall I myself conceal | 633 | 1 |
| *Where shall my wondering soul begin | 30 | 1 |
| Where shall the man of sin appear | 625 | 2 |
| *Where shall true believers go | 941 | 1 |
| Where should the dying members rest | 929 | 2 |
| Where sin can never come | 172 | 2 |
| Where sorrow and death are no more | 946 | 1 |
| Where stand revealed to mortal gaze | 698 | 2 |
| Where stars revolve their little rounds | 316 | 1 |
| Where tares and wheat together grow | 935 | 3 |
| Where tears are ever banished | 943 | 5 |
| *Where the ancient dragon lay | 349 | 1 |
| Where the angels praise their King | 192 | 1 |
| Where the cherubim adore him | 606 | 1 |
| Where the Eternal fixed his tent | 570 | 3 |
| †Where the indubitable seal | 876 | 5 |
| Where the ruined world hath mourned | 730 | 2 |
| Where the Son of man in glory | 720 | 6 |
| Where the weary are at rest | 50 | 2 |
| Where their Head hath gone before | 51 | 2 |
| Where then are all his vain desires | 638 | 3 |
| †Where they all thy laws have spurned | 730 | 2 |
| Where they thy name profane | 730 | 2 |
| Where thou art guide no ill can come | 751 | 2 |
| Where thou dost in glory reign | 762 | 1 |
| Where thou, my Lord, hast been | 956 | 3 |
| Where thy bride, thy church redeemed | 990 | 4 |
| Where thy people | 878 | 5 |
| Where two or three are met below | 630 | 7 |
| Where unaided man must fail | 769 | 4 |
| †Where unity is found | 630 | 4 |
| †Where unity takes place | 630 | 3 |
| Where vengeance and compassion join | 263 | 4 |
| Where war is learned, they must confess | 447 | 1 |
| Where weary pilgrims rest | 731 | 6 |
| Where we our maker see | 701 | 2 |
| Where we thy children kneel | 892 | 1 |
| Where'er in lands unknown | 452 | 5 |
| Where'er peace dwells, or truth hath trod | 770 | 7 |
| Where'er they seek thee thou art found | 864 | 1 |

| | Hymn | Verse |
|---|---|---|
| Where'er thou bidd'st me roam | 840 | 2 |
| Where'er thou choosest to record | 590 | 1 |
| Where'er thou go'st to follow thee | 332 | 1 |
| Where'er thy healing beams arise | 378 | 3 |
| Wherefore hast thou for sinners died | 774 | 7 |
| †Wherefore in never-ceasing prayer | 282 | 5 |
| †Wherefore, let every creature give | 239 | 8 |
| Wherefore let us all rejoice | 714 | 1 |
| †Wherefore my heart doth now rejoice | 548 | 5 |
| †Wherefore my hope is in the Lord | 626 | 3 |
| †Wherefore of thy love We sing and rejoice | 199 | 5 |
| Wherefore to beg and to entreat | 797 | 2 |
| †Wherefore to him my feet shall run | 246 | 2 |
| †Wherefore to thee I all resign | 332 | 5 |
| †Wherefore to thee my heart I give | 234 | 4 |
| †Wherefore we now for mercy pray | 648 | 5 |
| Wherefore we sing, both heart and voice awaking | 663 | — |
| Wherein all hath been recorded | 933 | 5 |
| Wherein thou causest me to trust | 780 | 1 |
| Wherein thou may'st be sought | 863 | 2 |
| Whereon the Saviour of mankind was born | 691 | 1 |
| Where's thy victory, boasting grave | 716 | 4 |
| †Wherever in the world I am | 842 | 4 |
| *Wherewith, O God, shall I draw near | 127 | 1 |
| Whether I die or live | 920 | 1 |
| Which all contains in one | 870 | 3 |
| Which all mankind with me may feel | 365 | 6 |
| Which all that feel shall surely know | 304 | 1 |
| Which all thy great salvation brings | 880 | 7 |
| Which always shall endure | 693 | 4 |
| Which angel-choirs, and saints in light | 259 | 4 |
| Which angels would search out in vain | 413 | 3 |
| Which arms us for the war | 277 | 6 |
| Which at the mercy-seat of God | 190 | 4 |
| Which bids bewildered souls rejoice | 698 | 6 |
| Which bought for me the sacred peace | 363 | 8 |
| Which bows before the Lord | 104 | 1 |
| Which bows thee down to me, who less | 88 | 3 |
| Which brings thy grace on sinners down | 394 | 2 |
| Which brings us here to meet again | 482 | 1 |
| Which bruises now my sinful soul | 181 | 4 |
| Which calms the waves of strife | 822 | 2 |
| Which can no more remove | 251 | 5 |
| Which can the test abide | 805 | 1 |
| Which cannot ask in vain | 842 | 3 |
| Which cannot be o'erthrown | 67 | 3 |
| Which covers what was once a friend | 849 | 4 |
| Which crowns our families with peace | 997 | 1 |
| Which dark to human eyes appear | 1001 | 3 |
| Which doth the mountain move | 342 | 6 |
| Which dwells in thee alone | 258 | 2 |
| Which echo through the heavenly plains | 658 | 5 |
| Which evermore makes all things new | 965 | 1 |

| | Hymn | Verse |
|---|---|---|
| Which first did for our sins atone | 438 | 1 |
| Which first was fixed on God alone | 98 | 1 |
| Which for thee we ever feel | 530 | 2 |
| Which from repentance flow | 104 | 1 |
| Which gave thy Son to die | 221 | 4 |
| Which God delights to bless | 424 | 2 |
| Which God in Christ imparts | 539 | 8 |
| Which God in Zion lays | 617 | 1 |
| Which grieves at having grieved its Lord | 341 | 3 |
| Which guards these sacred courts in peace | 994 | 1 |
| Which gushed from Immanuel's side | 371 | 2 |
| Which hath joined us in Jesus's name | 491 | 5 |
| Which hath my refuge been | 813 | — |
| Which heavenly truth imparts | 662 | 1 |
| Which here by faith we know | 88 | 4 |
| Which here has sought and found salvation | 595 | 6 |
| Which here speaks peace | 595 | 3 |
| Which here we come to prove | 485 | 1 |
| Which holds, and will not let thee go | 342 | 3 |
| Which hosts of angels chanted from above | 691 | 1 |
| Which human hope transcends | 258 | 3 |
| Which I felt in the life-giving blood | 807 | 4 |
| Which I have feared to see | 152 | 3 |
| Which in our hearts thy laws may write | 456 | 6 |
| Which Jesus did bequeath | 903 | 4 |
| Which kings and prophets waited for | 741 | 3 |
| Which knows our days | 853 | 2 |
| Which lifts poor dying worms to heaven | 206 | 3 |
| Which, like thee, no beginning knew | 240 | 2 |
| Which longs to build thy house again | 433 | 1 |
| Which love cannot untie | 288 | 3 |
| Which made us thine | 853 | 2 |
| Which makes the wounded whole | 308 | 3 |
| Which may to heaven ascend | 119 | 7 |
| Which more and more thy praise may show | 424 | 2 |
| Which moves with busy haste along | 695 | 1 |
| Which nature dreads, alas! to know | 775 | 3 |
| Which neither life nor death can part | 343 | 3 |
| Which never can be broke | 504 | 2 |
| Which never is followed by night | 73 | 4 |
| Which nought on earth may break | 996 | 3 |
| Which now I embrace | 707 | 6 |
| Which now our spirits feel | 693 | 2 |
| Which now, through Christ, I offer thee | 245 | 4 |
| Which now to thee we give | 83 | 1 |
| Which now we for our Israel plead | 298 | 3 |
| Which now we prove | 276 | 4 |
| Which offers life to all | 270 | 2 |
| Which of the glories brightest shone | 263 | 5 |
| Which of you dares meet his day | 54 | 5 |
| Which only faithful souls can hear | 376 | 2 |
| Which only Jesus can bestow | 816 | 1 |
| Which pants to have no other will | 285 | 2 |

| | Hymn | Verse |
|---|---|---|
| Which pardon and salvation brings. | 693 | 4 |
| Which peace and joy imparts | 822 | 1 |
| Which pride would not permit to last | 365 | 3 |
| Which purges every stain | 356 | 4 |
| Which purges me from every stain | 364 | 5 |
| Which reigns in faithful hearts | 872 | 1 |
| Which saves from sin, the world, and hell. | 472 | 5 |
| Which saves us from wrath, And brings us to God | 3 | 6 |
| Which saves us to the uttermost | 478 | 3 |
| Which seals my pardon on my heart | 780 | 1 |
| Which seals thee ours for ever | 1026 | — |
| Which shall for ever save | 387 | 3 |
| Which shall from age to age endure | 391 | 1 |
| Which shall in glory end | 119 | 7 |
| Which shall my sins consume | 367 | 2 |
| Which shall no change or period see | 600 | 2 |
| Which shall our flesh restore | 534 | 6 |
| Which spake us justified | 1005 | 2 |
| Which suits a sinner best | 249 | 5 |
| Which swells the formal song | 204 | 6 |
| Which take their everlasting flight. | 422 | 1 |
| Which takes our sins away | 532 | 6 |
| Which the words of life contain | 882 | 2 |
| Which thou hast already given | 243 | 2 |
| Which thou hast already given | 1018 | — |
| Which thou hast ever used below | 475 | 1 |
| Which thou hast freely given | 485 | 2 |
| Which thou hast set before us | 853 | 4 |
| Which thou, my Lord, hast borne before | 166 | 4 |
| Which thou to me hast given | 281 | 4 |
| Which thou wilt guide aright | 436 | 1 |
| Which thou wouldst fain remove | 152 | 4 |
| Which throbbed and bled for you | 713 | 2 |
| Which thy great Spirit imparts | 872 | 1 |
| Which unknown heirs divide | 565 | 3 |
| Which waits us in the skies. | 535 | 2 |
| Which warble from immortal tongues | 959 | 3 |
| Which was in Christ your Head | 277 | 3 |
| Which whosoe'er receives | 85 | 4 |
| Which will not let my Saviour take | 152 | 2 |
| Which wraps us in its awful shroud | 698 | 5 |
| Which wrestles and receives in prayer | 805 | 1 |
| While all I am declares thy grace | 159 | 3 |
| †While all my old companions dear | 80 | 2 |
| While all our souls fly up to thee | 513 | 4 |
| While all our souls with restless strife | 513 | 3 |
| While all the armies of the sky | 742 | 2 |
| While all the long day I publish thy grace | 200 | 2 |
| While all with one accord | 731 | 7 |
| While angels beckon me away | 947 | 4 |
| While angels delight To hymn thee above | 611 | 6 |
| While angels in their songs rejoice | 823 | 4 |
| While as a penitent I stand. | 703 | 3 |

| | Hymn | Verse |
|---|---|---|
| While at thy cross I lie | 410 | 3 |
| While by our Shepherd's side | 501 | 4 |
| While Christ to me it brings | 192 | 3 |
| *While dead in trespasses I lie | 136 | 1 |
| While distant lands their tribute pay | 581 | 2 |
| While earth repeats the joyful song | 253 | 1 |
| While eternal ages roll | 197 | 6 |
| While eternal ages roll | 737 | 1 |
| While eternal ages roll | 941 | 4 |
| While even our enemies exclaim | 822 | 4 |
| While every nation, every shore | 569 | 3 |
| †While, feebly gasping at thy feet | 881 | 2 |
| †While, full of anguish and disease | 136 | 2 |
| While gathered in by thee | 460 | 3 |
| While God prolongs the kind reprieve | 44 | 2 |
| While guarded by his mighty hand. | 868 | 3 |
| †While, hanging on thy faithful word | 916 | 4 |
| While hanging on thy love | 813 | — |
| While held in life's uneven way | 71 | 1 |
| †While he lifts his hands in blessing | 720 | 3 |
| While here o'er earth we rove | 214 | 1 |
| While here on earth we stay | 947 | 7 |
| While his foes from him receive | 758 | 2 |
| While his streaming grace ye feel | 197 | 4 |
| †While I am a pilgrim here | 824 | 6 |
| While I at thy altar bow | 910 | 7 |
| †While I draw this fleeting breath | 709 | 3 |
| While I have breath to pray or praise | 577 | 5 |
| †While in affliction's furnace. | 853 | 2 |
| While in the flesh, my hope and love | 947 | 3 |
| †While in the heavenly work we join | 204 | 2 |
| While in the narrow path I stand | 471 | 2 |
| While in the silent womb I lay | 657 | 2 |
| While in this desert land I live | 437 | 2 |
| †While in this region here below | 285 | 3 |
| While in this world we stay | 682 | 3 |
| While in thy temple we appear | 978 | 1 |
| †While in thy word we search for thee | 88 | 2 |
| While Jesu's blood, through earth and skies | 189 | 3 |
| While Jesus can restore | 274 | 3 |
| While Jordan rolled between | 938 | 3 |
| While justice hears thy praying faith | 298 | 2 |
| While life, and thought, and being last | 224 | 1 |
| While life, and thought, and being last | 224 | 4 |
| While, listening to the wretch's cry | 364 | 4 |
| *While lone upon the furious waves | 1003 | 1 |
| While love, almighty love, is near | 326 | 2 |
| While lovely tempers, fruits of grace | 457 | 3 |
| While low at Jesu's cross I bow | 726 | 2 |
| While, marked with blessings, every hour. | 155 | 2 |
| †While now thine oracles we read | 89 | 2 |
| While o'er the happy plains they range | 482 | 4 |
| While on earth in heaven to be | 817 | 1 |

| | Hymn | Verse |
|---|---|---|
| While on in Jesu's steps we go | 979 | 4 |
| While, on the bosom of my Lord | 328 | 3 |
| While on the wings of faith and prayer | 537 | 5 |
| While, purified by grace | 361 | 10 |
| While realms beneath its shadow rest | 589 | 6 |
| While Satan cries, " Be still " | 295 | 2 |
| †While still to thee for help I call | 282 | 4 |
| While stronger and stronger In Jesus's power | 200 | 7 |
| While such as trust their native strength | 802 | 4 |
| While the dew on all around | 115 | 3 |
| While the glorious Judge draws nigh | 936 | 4 |
| While the long cloud of witnesses | 940 | 5 |
| While the nearer waters roll | 143 | 1 |
| While the red lightnings wave along | 226 | 6 |
| While the Spirit of love and prayer | 862 | 2 |
| While the tempest still is high | 143 | 1 |
| †While the wicked are confounded | 933 | 16 |
| While thee, all-infinite, I set | 240 | 1 |
| While thee my Advocate I have | 275 | 2 |
| While thee we testify | 873 | 1 |
| While their eager eyes behold him | 720 | 3 |
| While they traverse sea and land | 878 | 2 |
| †While thou art intimately nigh | 227 | 5 |
| While thou art near | 853 | 3 |
| While thou bow'dst the heavens beneath | 737 | 2 |
| †While thou didst on earth appear | 529 | 2 |
| While thou our long-lost paradise | 447 | 3 |
| While thou visitest the nations | 60 | 1 |
| While through the mighty waves we pass | 1001 | 3 |
| While thus thy precious death we show | 902 | 1 |
| While to love and good works we each other provoke | 495 | 2 |
| While to that sacred shrine I move | 912 | 2 |
| While to thee alone we live | 427 | 1 |
| While twice ten thousand thunders roar | 57 | 1 |
| While unborn churches by their care | 868 | 4 |
| While upright both in life and heart | 319 | 2 |
| While we are adoring, He always is near | 859 | 2 |
| While we die to thee alone | 427 | 1 |
| While we Jesu's praise repeat | 538 | 4 |
| While we may acceptance find | 463 | 1 |
| †While we pray for pardoning grace | 975 | 3 |
| While we so near thy presence dwell | 569 | 11 |
| While we survey the awful scene | 57 | 5 |
| While we vital breath enjoy | 737 | 1 |
| †While we walk with God in light | 522 | 2 |
| While with the Father and the Son | 823 | 6 |
| While worshipping thine altar near | 909 | 1 |
| While ye surround his throne | 12 | 1 |
| While yet I am calling, Thy succour I feel | 273 | 3 |
| While yet my hands are here employed | 325 | 4 |
| †While yet the life-proclaiming word | 799 | 5 |
| While yet thou dwelledst not in me | 770 | 3 |

| | Hymn | Verse |
|---|---|---|
| While yet we in the flesh remain | 423 | 2 |
| While young and old, in many a band | 619 | 2 |
| †Whilst all the stars that round her burn | 552 | 4 |
| Whilst thou art calling, O call me | 790 | 5 |
| †Whispering thy love into my heart | 913 | 4 |
| Whisper within, thou Love divine | 184 | 3 |
| Whiter than Hermon's whitest snow | 698 | 4 |
| Whither, ah! whither would ye go | 4 | 6 |
| †Whither, O whither should I fly | 289 | 5 |
| *Whither shall a creature run | 633 | 1 |
| Whither shall my vileness run | 185 | 1 |
| Whither should a sinner go | 809 | 4 |
| Whither should a sinner fly | 116 | 1 |
| Who all mankind oppressed | 583 | 1 |
| Who all night long unwearied sing | 964 | 4 |
| Who all your toil foreknew | 277 | 5 |
| Who always ready art | 783 | 2 |
| Who always see thee on thy throne | 357 | 2 |
| Who ask, shall all receive thy love | 380 | 3 |
| †Who ask thine aid with heart sincere | 636 | 4 |
| Who bad'st its angry tumult cease | 1004 | 3 |
| Who bears the general sin away | 129 | 6 |
| Who bidd'st the mighty ocean deep | 1004 | 1 |
| Who bids us confidently claim | 827 | 3 |
| Who blest us in his will | 903 | 5 |
| Who, blindly fond, their children rear | 467 | 3 |
| Who bought me with his blood | 669 | 1 |
| Who bought me with his blood | 809 | 1 |
| Who bought my soul with blood divine | 927 | 1 |
| Who bought the sight for me | 947 | 8 |
| Who bought us with a price | 428 | 2 |
| Who bought us with his blood | 644 | 2 |
| Who bow to Christ's commands | 314 | 1 |
| Who braved a tyrant's ire | 359 | 1 |
| Who bring salvation in their tongues | 741 | 1 |
| Who build, O Lord, on thee | 67 | 2 |
| Who build on that alone | 989 | 1 |
| Who can answer to his word | 54 | 5 |
| Who can approach consuming flame | 651 | 6 |
| †Who can before my Captain stand | 293 | 9 |
| †Who can behold the blazing light | 651 | 6 |
| Who can break a threefold cord | 487 | 3 |
| *Who can describe the joys that rise | 867 | 1 |
| Who can explore his strange design | 201 | 2 |
| Who can faint, while such a river | 594 | 2 |
| †Who can his mighty deeds express | 612 | 2 |
| †Who can now lament the lot | 51 | 3 |
| Who can resist thy will | 303 | 6 |
| †Who can resolve the doubt | 43 | 4 |
| †Who can sound the depths unknown | 245 | 3 |
| Who can sound the mystery | 244 | 3 |
| †Who can tell the happiness | 58 | 3 |
| Who can the sons of Anak meet | 293 | 6 |

| | Hymn | Verse |
|---|---|---|
| Who can to him for succour flee | 638 | 4 |
| *Who can worthily commend | 423 | 1 |
| Who cannot doubt thy gracious will | 668 | 2 |
| Who cannot do what is unjust | 844 | 2 |
| Who cast on him their griefs and cares | 595 | 2 |
| Who chant thy praise above | 221 | 3 |
| Who choosest for thine The weak and the poor | 869 | 1 |
| Who conquers sin for you | 278 | 6 |
| Who conquer through their Saviour's might | 69 | 3 |
| Who, conscious of their pardon sealed | 493 | 2 |
| Who could thy sacred body wound. | 23 | 2 |
| Who daily, Lord, ascend with thee | 419 | 1 |
| Who dare expect salvation here | 111 | 2 |
| Who dare not lift mine eyes to thee | 779 | 2 |
| Who did for every sinner die | 85 | 1 |
| Who did for us his life resign | 254 | 1 |
| Who did his peace to all bequeath | 733 | 6 |
| Who did our lower world redeem | 721 | 3 |
| Who did the world redeem | 125 | 1 |
| Who didst for all fulfil | 340 | 3 |
| Who didst from heaven come | 883 | 2 |
| Who didst my every pain endure | 816 | 1 |
| Who didst thy ancient saints inspire | 255 | 1 |
| Who didst thyself our ransom pay. | 423 | 1 |
| Who died, and lives, to die no more | 277 | 2 |
| Who died for me, even me, to atone | 190 | 3 |
| Who died the whole world to redeem | 231 | 12 |
| Who died to save the world he made | 953 | 1 |
| Who diedst thyself, my soul to save | 43 | 5 |
| Who dost free salvation send us | 933 | 8 |
| Who dost thy right maintain | 248 | 3 |
| Who dost thy sevenfold gifts impart | 751 | 1 |
| Who doth my Advocate appear | 982 | 1 |
| Who dwelt among the dead | 713 | 4 |
| Who dying bought us with his blood | 438 | 1 |
| Who fain would prove thine utmost will | 527 | 1 |
| Who feel thee, Saviour, in their heart | 590 | 2 |
| Who felt on earth severer woe | 849 | 3 |
| Who finds in Jesu's wounds his rest | 561 | 1 |
| Who fit for glory are | 65 | 2 |
| Who follow after righteousness | 111 | 1 |
| Who follows not the proud, nor those | 566 | 4 |
| Who for full redemption groan | 937 | 3 |
| Who for full redemption weep | 623 | 5 |
| Who for lost man's redemption died | 752 | 5 |
| Who for me be interceding | 933 | 7 |
| Who for me, for me, hast died | 193 | 1 |
| Who for me vouchsafed to die | 554 | 3 |
| Who for my sake his soul in death outpoured | 851 | 3 |
| Who for our offence was slain | 714 | 1 |
| †Who for thy coming wait | 623 | 5 |
| Who formed me man, forbids my fear | 272 | 1 |
| Who from his altar call | 681 | 3 |

| | Hymn | Verse |
|---|---|---|
| Who from the Father's bosom came | 190 | 8 |
| Who gasp for help from thee | 112 | 2 |
| Who gasp to admit Thy Spirit, and live | 10 | 4 |
| Who gave his life, that I might live | 125 | 1 |
| Who gave us our triumphal song | 493 | 3 |
| Who gav'st my soul to be | 249 | 8 |
| Who gives the lilies clothing | 804 | 3 |
| Who hast entrusted to our care | 467 | 1 |
| Who hast led them safe through all | 593 | 3 |
| Who hast on me bestowed | 18 | 1 |
| Who hast the earnest given | 74 | 5 |
| Who hast through life delivered me | 894 | 1 |
| Who hath an everlasting right | 844 | 1 |
| Who hath for us a table spread | 1023 | — |
| Who hath my sins forgiven | 614 | 14 |
| Who hath my sins forgiven | 669 | 2 |
| *Who hath slighted or contemned | 883 | 1 |
| †Who hath these little ones despised | 891 | 4 |
| Who have not yet my Saviour known | 483 | 8 |
| Who heard the angelic herald's voice: "Behold" | 691 | 2 |
| Who hears our solemn vow | 532 | 4 |
| Who heaven and earth commands | 881 | 1 |
| Who here thy last appearing love | 254 | 8 |
| Who his loved Israel keeps | 595 | 1 |
| Who his quiet shall molest | 18 | 1 |
| Who his salvation make | 602 | 2 |
| Who hold it with our Head | 897 | 4 |
| Who honoured thy name | 231 | 3 |
| Who humbly comes to thee | 167 | 2 |
| Who humbly for thy mercy groan | 170 | 2 |
| Who hungry still on thee attend | 875 | 1 |
| †Who, I ask in amaze | 231 | 9 |
| †Who in heart on thee believes | 350 | 5 |
| Who in his truth confide | 562 | 5 |
| Who in Jesus agree | 488 | 1 |
| Who in Jesus believe | 488 | 3 |
| †Who in Jesus confide | 499 | 2 |
| Who in our unity delights | 489 | 1 |
| Who in thee begin to live | 850 | 1 |
| *Who in the Lord confide | 622 | 1 |
| Who in the strength of Jesus trusts | 266 | 1 |
| Who in thy glorious image shine | 511 | 3 |
| Who in thy guardian mercy rest | 649 | 3 |
| Who in thy name are joined | 486 | 2 |
| Who is a pardoning God like thee | 656 | Cho |
| Who is so great a King as mine | 293 | 9 |
| *Who is this gigantic foe | 278 | 1 |
| †Who is this Jesus? why should he | 695 | 2 |
| †Who is this King of Glory? Who | 557 | 9 |
| †Who is this King of Glory? Who | 557 | 11 |
| †Who is this that comes in glory | 720 | 2 |
| *Who Jesus our example know | 860 | 1 |
| †Who Jesu's sufferings share | 345 | 5 |

| | Hymn | Verse |
|---|---|---|
| Who joins us by his grace | 500 | 1 |
| Who, joyful, in harmonious lays | 950 | 1 |
| Who keeps his saints in perfect peace | 833 | 2 |
| Who kindly lengthens out our days | 979 | 1 |
| Who know his power, his grace who prove | 494 | 1 |
| Who knows his sins forgiven | 947 | 1 |
| Who knows the joys of unity | 630 | 1 |
| Who knows, The Saviour died for me | 14 | 2 |
| Who launched this floating ball | 681 | 2 |
| Who leads them captive at his will | 461 | 3 |
| Who lengthens out our trial here | 981 | 1 |
| Who life and strength from thence derive | 26 | 3 |
| Who light thy dwelling-place hast made | 974 | 8 |
| Who like thyself my guide and stay can be | 972 | 3 |
| Who lived to yield our ills relief | 692 | 2 |
| Who live in pomp, and wealth, and ease | 94 | 2 |
| †Who live, O God, in thee | 661 | 3 |
| Who live to serve our God alone | 222 | 2 |
| Who load us with reproach and shame | 319 | 1 |
| Who long thy appearing to know | 220 | 4 |
| Who, Lord of heaven, yet deigns to come | 997 | 2 |
| Who love the way To Zion's hill | 591 | 2 |
| Who made intercession, "My Father forgive" | 707 | 4 |
| Who made me, and who saved | 943 | 12 |
| Who make to thee their timely prayer | 561 | 6 |
| Who may be saved—shall I | 80 | 1 |
| Who may the test abide | 625 | 2 |
| Who, meanly in Bethlehem born | 220 | 1 |
| Who meet on that eternal shore | 535 | 3 |
| Who mercy through their fall obtain | 451 | 1 |
| Who mildly comes to meet my soul | 779 | 3 |
| Who mocked our scanty grace | 531 | 2 |
| Who must be righteous still | 844 | 2 |
| Who my anguish can reveal | 112 | 1 |
| Who my cause hath undertook | 243 | 3 |
| Who myself can nothing do | 819 | 4 |
| Who nailed thy body to the tree | 157 | 3 |
| Who ne'er began to be | 731 | 9 |
| Who never canst thyself forget | 181 | 1 |
| Who never knew our God | 12 | 1 |
| †Who now against each other rise | 442 | 4 |
| Who now by faith approach to thee | 284 | 5 |
| Who now go on their way and weep | 120 | 2 |
| Who now in bodies live | 535 | 5 |
| Who now is reviving His work in our days | 40 | 6 |
| †Who of other help despair | 693 | 3 |
| †Who of twain hath made us one | 487 | 3 |
| †Who on earth can conceive | 499 | 4 |
| Who on his love rely | 572 | 4 |
| Who on his succour trust | 562 | 4 |
| Who on Jesus rely | 707 | 5 |
| Who on the Anointed fix their trust | 541 | 5 |
| Who on thee alone depend | 508 | 1 |

| | Hymn | Verse |
|---|---|---|
| Who on thy love depend | 310 | 4 |
| Who, once in mortal weakness shrined | 989 | 3 |
| Who once received on Horeb's height | 698 | 2 |
| Who only canst my plague remove | 779 | 2 |
| Who our dying souls reviveth | 580 | 3 |
| †Who, passing through the mournful vale | 590 | 3 |
| †Who points the clouds their course | 831 | 2 |
| Who praise thee with a stammering tongue | 494 | 2 |
| Who press to enter in | 828 | 3 |
| Who, prompted by thy foe | 447 | 1 |
| Who quits his throne on earth to live | 689 | 4 |
| Who reap the pleasures there | 948 | 5 |
| Who reigns enthroned above | 800 | 1 |
| Who reigns enthroned on high | 981 | 1 |
| Who round us hath shed His marvellous light | 869 | 6 |
| Who, safe beneath their guardian Rock | 62 | 1 |
| Who sailed with the Saviour beneath | 49 | 3 |
| Who scatters abroad | 219 | 1 |
| †Who seed immortal bears | 623 | 6 |
| Who seek redemption in thy blood | 505 | 2 |
| Who seek thy praise to show | 989 | 1 |
| Who sees what is best For each of his own | 496 | 2 |
| Who, sent by thee, proclaim | 872 | 1 |
| Who serve the Lord most high | 840 | 1 |
| Who shall a helpless worm redeem | 918 | — |
| Who shall ascend on high | 192 | 1 |
| Who shall ascend the heavenly place | 557 | 3 |
| Who shall at last set Israel free | 626 | 5 |
| Who shall contend with God? or who | 337 | 6 |
| Who shall dare with thee to vie | 737 | 6 |
| Who shall sustain my sinking years | 584 | 2 |
| Who shall violate his rest | 13 | 1 |
| Who sink into perfection's height | 69 | 3 |
| Who sits upon the throne | 232 | 3 |
| Who sittest on thy righteous throne | 733 | 2 |
| †Who sow in tears, in joy shall reap | 120 | 2 |
| Who sows in tears in joy shall reap | 545 | 3 |
| Who spares us yet another year | 980 | 1 |
| Who speaks our sins forgiven | 705 | 4 |
| Who spreads his clouds along the sky | 225 | 3 |
| Who stand on Zion's hill | 741 | 1 |
| Who steadfastly believes in thee | 590 | 6 |
| Who still conceal'st thyself from me | 130 | 1 |
| Who still in strength excel | 315 | 1 |
| Who still is hovering round | 966 | 3 |
| Who still your bodies feel | 333 | 1 |
| †Who stoops to clothe a fading flower | 833 | 3 |
| †Who suffer with our Master here | 333 | 3 |
| Who thankfully own | 219 | 4 |
| Who thankless spurn thy easy reign | 241 | 3 |
| †Who the calm can understand | 1000 | 2 |
| Who the heavenly realm has won | 720 | Dox. |
| Who the Saviour obey | 807 | 1 |

| | Hymn | Verse |
|---|---|---|
| Who the victory gave | 219 | 1 |
| Who the worth of love can tell | 434 | 5 |
| Who their God can never know | 7 | 1 |
| Who their heaven in Christ have found | 115 | 2 |
| Who then can that vast love express | 38 | 3 |
| †Who then shall live, and face the throne | 63 | 4 |
| Who therefore hath bestowed | 981 | 4 |
| Who think and speak the same | 539 | 5 |
| Who this mighty champion is | 278 | 2 |
| Who through God's grace | 595 | 1 |
| Who through this weary pilgrimage | 664 | 1 |
| †Who thus our faith employ | 898 | 3 |
| Who thy mystic body are | 518 | 1 |
| Who thy wonders can express | 598 | 2 |
| Who to death upon the tree | 714 | 4 |
| Who to God their spirits give | 925 | 1 |
| Who to Messiah fly | 731 | 4 |
| Who, to ransom wretched thee | 24 | 2 |
| Who to the deep shall stoop | 192 | 2 |
| Who to thy glory live | 734 | 1 |
| Who to thy tribes, on Sinai's height | 690 | 5 |
| Who trembled, wept, and bled for me | 181 | 6 |
| Who truly turn to thee | 242 | 4 |
| †Who trusting in their Lord depart | 926 | 2 |
| Who trust in him alone | 801 | 1 |
| Who trust the blood of God to cleanse | 254 | 2 |
| Who tuned his golden lute | 948 | 6 |
| Who, turning to that heavenly shrine | 121 | 4 |
| Who turns our darkness into light | 976 | 2 |
| Who turns our hell to heaven | 976 | 2 |
| Who use religion as a screen | 858 | 1 |
| Who wait for us above | 482 | 2 |
| Who walkedst on the foaming deep | 1004 | 2 |
| Who walk with him in white | 535 | 1 |
| Who was, and is for evermore | 255 | 3 |
| Who was and is the same | 800 | 10 |
| Who wert, and art, and evermore shalt be | 646 | 2 |
| Who, when this precious faith he gave | 810 | — |
| Who, when we saw thee slighted | 667 | 4 |
| †Who, who, my Saviour, this hath done | 23 | 2 |
| †Who, who shall in thy presence stand | 138 | 6 |
| Who, who shall violate my rest | 227 | 5 |
| Who with clamour pursued thee to Calvary's top | 160 | 1 |
| Who would not give his heart to thee | 38 | 1 |
| Who would not give his heart to thee | 38 | 8 |
| Who would not his whole soul and mind | 38 | 1 |
| Who would not his whole soul and mind | 38 | 8 |
| Who would not love thee with his might | 38 | 1 |
| Who would not love thee with his might | 38 | 8 |
| Who would not own thy sway | 347 | 4 |
| Who would on thee alone rely | 71 | 1 |
| Who wrote from thee the sacred page | 89 | 1 |
| Whoe'er by grace is saved from sin | 557 | 4 |

| | Hymn | Verse |
|---|---|---|
| Whoe'er to Jesus bow | 539 | 6 |
| †Whoe'er to thee themselves approve | 127 | 4 |
| †Whoever receives The life-giving word | 3 | 3 |
| Wholesome grain and pure may be | 987 | 2 |
| Wholly to thyself devoted | 530 | 3 |
| Whom all the heavens cannot contain | 648 | 2 |
| Whom angels dimly see | 128 | 1 |
| Whom angels dimly see | 128 | 8 |
| Whom angels dimly see | 642 | 2 |
| Whom believingly we claim | 755 | 1 |
| Whom David Lord did call | 681 | 5 |
| Whom God himself hath bidden | 856 | 2 |
| Whom have I in heaven but thee | 434 | 4 |
| †Whom have I on earth below | 434 | 4 |
| Whom heaven and earth their Maker own | 157 | 5 |
| Whom heaven cannot contain | 684 | 3 |
| Whom he would again create | 7 | 3 |
| Whom I devote to thee | 893 | 2 |
| †Whom I to thy grace commend | 915 | 3 |
| Whom I would gladly die to know | 113 | 1 |
| Whom in his days of flesh pass by | 32 | 2 |
| Whom in life and death ye loved | 737 | 7 |
| *Whom Jesu's blood doth sanctify | 801 | 1 |
| †Whom man forsakes thou wilt not leave | 163 | 4 |
| Whom man refused and doomed to die | 616 | 7 |
| Whom none but thy essential Word | 642 | 6 |
| Whom none can comprehend | 642 | 1 |
| †Whom now we seek, O may we meet | 486 | 5 |
| Whom one all-perfect God we own | 261 | 1 |
| Whom One in Three we know | 259 | 1 |
| Whom only I languish to love | 77 | 2 |
| Whom still I hold, but cannot see | 140 | 1 |
| Whom still we love with grief and pain | 461 | 2 |
| Whom the heavens cannot contain | 195 | 2 |
| Whom the heavens cannot contain | 758 | 3 |
| Whom the world cannot receive | 517 | 3 |
| Whom thickest darkness compassed round | 353 | 1 |
| Whom thou didst by thy Spirit join | 489 | 2 |
| Whom thou hast out of Egypt freed | 298 | 3 |
| Whom thou hast saved, persist to save | 806 | 2 |
| Whom we ask in Jesu's name | 755 | 1 |
| Whom we first received from thee | 890 | 1 |
| Whom winds and seas obey | 831 | 2 |
| Whom winds and seas obey | 1000 | 2 |
| Whose all-sufficient grace | 800 | 8 |
| Whose anger is so slow to rise | 610 | 6 |
| Whose arm doth bind the restless wave | 1004 | 1 |
| Whose arms are still your sure defence | 561 | 11 |
| Whose blood for us was shed | 704 | 1 |
| Whose blood proclaims our sins forgiven | 298 | 5 |
| Whose boundless mercy hath for me | 190 | 8 |
| Whose bowels of compassion move | 378 | 1 |
| Whose bowels of compassion move | 438 | 1 |

| | Hymn | Verse |
|---|---|---|
| Whose chariots of wrath Deep thunder-clouds form | 611 | 2 |
| Whose countless seed shall soon arise | 883 | 3 |
| Whose depth unfathomed, no man knows | 344 | 1 |
| Whose everlasting birth | 883 | 3 |
| Whose every sin was counted thine | 378 | 2 |
| Whose eyelids never sleep | 305 | 5 |
| Whose eyes my inmost substance see | 324 | 3 |
| Whose favours are divine | 610 | 1 |
| Whose forming hand on every part | 241 | 1 |
| Whose founder is the living God | 71 | 3 |
| Whose garments rolled in blood appear | 38 | 7 |
| Whose glorious mercies never end | 648 | 1 |
| Whose glory fills the sky | 262 | 2 |
| Whose glory to this earth extends | 262 | 2 |
| Whose Godhead with the manhood joined | 860 | 2 |
| Whose goodness crowns the circling year | 978 | 1 |
| Whose goodness, providently nigh | 99 | 1 |
| Whose goodness shall send Us bread from the sky | 1013 | 2 |
| Whose grace to all did freely move | 39 | 1 |
| Whose hand doth earth and heaven sustain | 1001 | 1 |
| Whose hope is in the Lord his God | 638 | 4 |
| Whose hope, still hovering round thy word | 574 | 5 |
| Whose hours divided are | 222 | 1 |
| Whose joys eternal flow | 671 | 4 |
| Whose lamps are burning bright | 54 | 3 |
| Whose love hath gently led me on | 97 | 1 |
| Whose love is as great as his power | 660 | — |
| Whose love is ever new | 701 | 1 |
| Whose mercies are so great | 610 | 6 |
| Whose mercies never end | 539 | 2 |
| Whose mercies over all rejoice | 235 | 1 |
| Whose mercy firm through ages past | 612 | 1 |
| Whose mercy is divinely free | 378 | 1 |
| Whose mercy shall unshaken stay | 189 | 1 |
| Whose new-creating power | 644 | 3 |
| Whose nod restores the universe | 536 | 6 |
| Whose only name, to sinners given | 448 | 1 |
| Whose power does heaven and earth command | 752 | 3 |
| Whose power inverted nature owns | 223 | 4 |
| Whose power the wind, the sea, controls | 1001 | 1 |
| Whose power through endless ages lives | 636 | 2 |
| Whose presence fills both earth and heaven | 255 | 2 |
| Whose robe is the light, Whose canopy space | 611 | 2 |
| Whose souls, condemned and dying | 586 | 2 |
| Whose Spirit breathes the active flame | 95 | 1 |
| Whose spirit is by grace restored | 561 | 2 |
| Whose Spirit leads believing souls | 1001 | 1 |
| Whose Spirit shall guide us safe home | 660 | — |
| Whose spirit trusts Alone in thee | 591 | 5 |
| Whose strength and confidence thou art | 590 | 2 |
| Whose threatening looks dry up the sea | 138 | 5 |
| Whose throne all nature's wreck survives | 636 | 2 |
| Whose virtue every heart may feel | 472 | 5 |

| | Hymn | Verse |
|---|---|---|
| Whose wickedness is all forgiven | 561 | 1 |
| Whose wisdom, love, and truth, and power | 832 | 5 |
| Whose word, when heaven and earth shall pass | 391 | 1 |
| Whose works are all divine | 844 | 1 |
| Whose wrath or hate makes me afraid | 279 | 4 |
| Why am I thus?—O tell me why | 146 | 3 |
| Why breaks not out the fire within | 290 | 6 |
| Why cannot I this moment give | 775 | 2 |
| Why didst thou groan thy mortal groan | 330 | 1 |
| †Why do not I the call obey | 775 | 2 |
| *Why do we mourn departing friends | 929 | 1 |
| Why hangs he then on yonder tree | 33 | 1 |
| †Why hast thou cast our lot | 510 | 2 |
| Why is the grace so long delayed | 444 | 1 |
| *Why not now, my God, my God! | 149 | 1 |
| Why rage they with vain menacing | 541 | 1 |
| †Why restless, why cast down, my soul | 567 | 4 |
| †Why seek ye that which is not bread | 4 | 5 |
| †Why should I ask the future load | 835 | 2 |
| †Why should I shrink at pain and woe | 939 | 4 |
| *Why should I till to-morrow stay | 782 | 1 |
| *Why should the children of a king | 765 | 1 |
| †Why should the foe thy purchase seize | 82 | 6 |
| †Why should the men of pride and sin | 546 | 2 |
| Why should *they* die, when *thou* hast died | 82 | 5 |
| †Why should we doubt his equal love | 846 | 3 |
| Why, sinners, will ye perish, why | 31 | 4 |
| Why, sinner, wilt thou perish, why | 773 | 2 |
| †Why then, thou universal Love | 39 | 5 |
| Why unfulfilled the saving plan | 444 | 1 |
| Why will ye folly love | 21 | 1 |
| Why will you for ever die | 6 | 4 |
| Why will you for ever die | 7 | Cho. |
| Why will you resolve to die | 8 | Cho. |
| Why will you, ye Christians, why | 7 | 4 |
| Why will you your Lord deny | 8 | 1 |
| †Why wilt thou not for all my life | 820 | 4 |
| Why, ye long-sought sinners, why | 6 | 3 |
| Why, ye ransomed sinners, why | 6 | 2 |
| Why, ye thankless creatures, why | 6 | 1 |
| Wide as infinity | 216 | 4 |
| †Wide as the world is thy command | 608 | 4 |
| †Wide earth's remotest bound | 737 | 10 |
| Wide unfold the radiant scene | 718 | 2 |
| Wider, and yet wider still | 372 | — |
| Widest extremes to join | 685 | 4 |
| †Wild as the untaught Indian's brood | 82 | 3 |
| Wild human bears on slaughter bent | 810 | 2 |
| Wild war chariots | 570 | 5 |
| Will angel-bands convey | 43 | 3 |
| Will clothe his people too | 804 | 3 |
| Will every needful blessing give | 833 | 3 |
| Will furnish all we ought to ask | 965 | 6 |

| | HYMN | VERSE |
|---|---|---|
| †Will gifts delight the Lord most high | 127 | 2 |
| Will give his children bread | 804 | 3 |
| †Will he forsake his throne above | 128 | 2 |
| Will he not his help afford | 618 | 1 |
| Will he say me nay | 793 | 6 |
| Will join the glorious band | 939 | 5 |
| Will mercy itself be so kind | 174 | 1 |
| Will multiplied oblations please | 127 | 2 |
| Will not murmur or complain | 914 | 3 |
| Will not now his servant leave | 335 | 1 |
| Will outward good provide | 834 | 2 |
| Will say concerning me | 182 | 1 |
| Will still in every future hour | 813 | — |
| Will still my sure refreshment prove | 279 | 5 |
| Will the house of Israel die | 7 | 4 |
| Will the Unsearchable be found | 128 | 1 |
| †Will they not charge my fall on thee | 547 | 5 |
| Will they not dare my God to blame | 547 | 5 |
| Will ye cross his love, and die | 6 | 1 |
| Will you grieve your God, and die | 6 | 3 |
| Will you let him die in vain | 6 | 2 |
| Will you not his grace receive | 6 | 3 |
| Will you not his OATH believe | 8 | 4 |
| Will you not his word receive | 8 | 4 |
| Will you slight his grace, and die | 6 | 2 |
| Will you still in sin remain | 6 | 4 |
| Will you still refuse to live | 6 | 8 |
| Willing, able, all to save | 142 | 8 |
| Willing thee alone to know | 302 | 1 |
| Willing thou art and ready still | 146 | 2 |
| †Willing thou that all should know | 242 | 3 |
| Willing to retain her guest | 921 | 3 |
| Willing we should all repent | 463 | 2 |
| Wilt all thy creatures bless | 730 | 3 |
| Wilt freely my backslidings heal | 180 | 4 |
| Wilt from the dreadful day remove | 104 | 2 |
| Wilt keep me still in perfect peace | 227 | 6 |
| Wilt keep us every moment here | 812 | — |
| Wilt keep us faithful to the end | 524 | 3 |
| †Wilt keep us tenderly discreet | 469 | 11 |
| Wilt not give the sinner o'er | 182 | 3 |
| †Wilt thou cast a sinner out | 167 | 2 |
| Wilt thou for ever hide thy face | 547 | 1 |
| †Wilt thou forsake my hoary hairs | 584 | 2 |
| Wilt thou not bid the outcasts look | 451 | 2 |
| Wilt thou not in the midst appear | 861 | 1 |
| Wilt thou not the light afford | 854 | 2 |
| †Wilt thou not the promise seal | 755 | 3 |
| Wilt thou not the wrong forget | 168 | 5 |
| †Wilt thou not yet to me reveal | 140 | 4 |
| †Wilt thou suffer me to go | 854 | 2 |
| Wilt welcome, pardon, cleanse, relieve | 796 | 5 |
| Winding or straight, it leads | 837 | 1 |

| | Hymn | Verse |
|---|---|---|
| Winds may rise, and seas may roar | 1000 | 2 |
| Wine of the soul, in mercy shed | 906 | 1 |
| Wiped for ever from his eyes | 52 | 3 |
| Wipe the tears from every face | 76 | 4 |
| Wipe the tears from every face | 349 | 4 |
| Wisdom, and Christ, and heaven are one | 14 | 6 |
| Wisdom, and might, and love are thine | 235 | 2 |
| *Wisdom ascribe, and might, and praise | 980 | 1 |
| †Wisdom divine! Who tells the price | 14 | 3 |
| Wisdom in a mystery | 358 | 3 |
| †Wisdom is due to thee | 727 | 6 |
| Wisdom, pure religious fear | 454 | 2 |
| Wisdom to silver we prefer | 14 | 3 |
| Wise and merciful and just | 914 | 8 |
| Wise are the wonders of thy hands | 563 | 2 |
| Wise to fathom things divine | 27 | 5 |
| With a glad heart and free | 426 | 1 |
| With a high hand and outstretched arm | 916 | 1 |
| With a triumphant noise | 719 | 1 |
| With Alleluia evermore | 663 | — |
| With all-engaging charms | 889 | 1 |
| With all flesh is now begun | 60 | 2 |
| With all his plenitude of grace | 689 | 2 |
| With all his recent prints of love | 721 | 5 |
| With all his saints ascend | 65 | 3 |
| With all his saints in light | 54 | 4 |
| With all his strength endued | 266 | 2 |
| With all his strength, to thee unite | 38 | 1 |
| With all his strength, to thee unite | 38 | 8 |
| With all its glittering snares, adieu | 285 | 3 |
| With all its powers | 855 | 1 |
| With all mankind and me | 162 | 2 |
| With all my heart, and all my might | 470 | 2 |
| With all my idols part | 102 | 1 |
| With all my loving heart | 243 | 3 |
| With all my nature's weight oppressed | 25 | 4 |
| With all my sins to part | 414 | 1 |
| With all my soul submit | 275 | 6 |
| With all of creature-good | 809 | 1 |
| With all our ransomed powers | 411 | 1 |
| With all pollutions stained | 93 | 2 |
| †With all-sufficient grace supply | 472 | 5 |
| With all that favoured throng | 682 | 4 |
| With all that God can give | 418 | 2 |
| With all the blue ethereal sky | 552 | 1 |
| With all the dead awake | 65 | 1 |
| With all the fruits of Paradise | 800 | 8 |
| With all the hosts of God | 719 | 6 |
| With all the life of God | 901 | 4 |
| With all the powers of love | 775 | 3 |
| With all the powers of prayer | 268 | 1 |
| With all the ransomed throng I dwell | 795 | 5 |
| With all the sanctified | 503 | 6 |

| | Hymn | Verse |
|---|---|---|
| With all their cares and fears | 41 | 5 |
| With all thou hast, and art | 323 | 3 |
| With all thy Father's dazzling train | 55 | 2 |
| With all thy fulness fill | 510 | 6 |
| With all thy fulness fill | 654 | 4 |
| With all thy glorious grace | 55 | 2 |
| With all thy great salvation bless | 297 | 5 |
| With all thy quickening powers | 763 | 1 |
| With all thy quickening powers | 763 | 4 |
| With all thy saints below | 27 | 6 |
| With all thy saints shall prove | 136 | 10 |
| With all thy servants there | 941 | 4 |
| With all thy weight of love | 137 | 10 |
| With all thy wounds appear | 35 | 3 |
| †With all who chant thy name on high | 222 | 4 |
| With all who finally o'ercome | 72 | 2 |
| †With all who for redemption groan | 121 | 5 |
| With angels above We lift up our voice | 199 | 5 |
| With angels round the throne | 678 | 1 |
| With an immortal pen | 659 | 3 |
| With anxious thoughts distrest | 614 | 6 |
| With ardent pangs of strong desire | 959 | 2 |
| With awe even we thy children prove | 666 | 2 |
| With azure canopy o'erspread | 862 | 1 |
| With Babylon must cope | 943 | 3 |
| With balm of bleeding love | 693 | 3 |
| With beams of sacred bliss | 213 | 3 |
| With beatitude unknown | 633 | 2 |
| With blessings from above | 704 | 4 |
| With blessings from thy boundless store | 973 | 5 |
| With blest anticipation | 853 | 1 |
| With bliss ineffable, divine | 258 | 3 |
| With blood of millions slain | 730 | 2 |
| With boldness at thy throne | 775 | 4 |
| With boldness to the throne of grace | 365 | 1 |
| With boundless charity divine | 433 | 5 |
| With boundless stores of grace | 679 | 3 |
| *With broken heart and contrite sigh | 795 | 1 |
| With calm and tempered zeal | 270 | 2 |
| With calmest pity I submit | 439 | 1 |
| †With calmly-reverential joy | 204 | 8 |
| With choicest tokens of thy grace | 994 | 2 |
| With Christ may I be crucified | 351 | 5 |
| With Christ's own bride they rise | 996 | 8 |
| With claims and blessings all its own | 951 | 2 |
| With clearer light thy witness bear | 374 | 5 |
| With comfortable words and kind | 397 | 2 |
| With condescending dignity | 470 | 8 |
| With confidence divine | 94 | 5 |
| With confidence I now draw nigh | 202 | 5 |
| With confidence we seek thy face | 504 | 1 |
| With confidence we tell | 96 | 1 |
| With contrite anguish sore | 696 | 2 |

| | Hymn | Verse |
|---|---|---|
| †With contrite hearts to thee, our King | 986 | 4 |
| With cords of love our spirit bind | 616 | 11 |
| With creatures such as we | 667 | 4 |
| With cries, entreaties, tears, to save | 279 | 7 |
| With crowns of joy upon our head | 497 | 3 |
| With crowns of joy upon our heads | 976 | 3 |
| †With daily toil oppressed | 838 | 2 |
| With daily triumph we proclaim | 649 | 1 |
| With deep and conscious guilt oppressed | 795 | 2 |
| With downcast eye the angelic choir | 241 | 1 |
| With drops of creature happiness | 291 | 1 |
| With duteous reverence at thy feet | 353 | 4 |
| With each new return of day | 604 | 1 |
| With each other, and with thee | 995 | 1 |
| With each other in the Lord | 1006 | — |
| With eagles' eyes on thee to gaze | 284 | 2 |
| †With earnest desire | 488 | 7 |
| With earnest prayer and strong desire | 89 | 2 |
| †With ease our souls through death shall glide | 504 | 8 |
| With echoing joys resound | 727 | 4 |
| With ever-growing praise | 844 | 5 |
| With everlasting gladness crowned | 386 | 6 |
| With every blessing blest | 404 | 3 |
| With every fleeting breath | 679 | 6 |
| With every morning sacrifice | 585 | 8 |
| With every useless load | 775 | 2 |
| With eyes of flesh refined, restored | 927 | 3 |
| †With fainting heart, and lifted hands | 577 | 3 |
| With faith into our hearts receive | 689 | 4 |
| †With faith I plunge me in this sea | 189 | 4 |
| With faith, with hope, with love | 767 | 5 |
| With faith's strong arm on thee lay hold | 144 | 1 |
| †With favour look upon *his* face | 465 | 4 |
| With fervency of spirit stands | 858 | 2 |
| With fervour in our own | 767 | 2 |
| With fiends, or angels spend | 44 | 4 |
| With filial awe revere thy rod | 455 | 4 |
| With filial fear thy goodness see | 625 | 3 |
| With floods of wickedness o'erflowed | 442 | 1 |
| †With force of arms we nothing can | 856 | 2 |
| †With fraudless, even, humble mind | 338 | 2 |
| With full salvation bless | 417 | 6 |
| †With garments of salvation deck | 629 | 7 |
| With gifts his hands are filled | 591 | 4 |
| With glad exultation Your triumph proclaim | 19 | 1 |
| With glorious beams of endless bliss | 121 | 1 |
| *With glorious clouds encompassed round | 128 | 1 |
| With glory and light from above | 70 | 1 |
| *With glory clad, with strength arrayed | 600 | 1 |
| With God and man for ever one | 525 | 2 |
| With God essentially the same | 668 | 1 |
| With God eternally shut in | 65 | 5 |
| With God interceding For sinners beneath | 5 | 4 |

# WITH GOD — WITH JOY

| | Hymn | Verse |
|---|---|---|
| With God Messiah ever reign | 731 | 6 |
| †With grace abundantly endued | 16 | 3 |
| With grateful love to thee | 842 | 6 |
| With grief and pain extreme | 950 | 2 |
| With grief who seeks with joy shall find | 545 | 3 |
| With groans unspeakable | 144 | 3 |
| With groves of living joys | 800 | 8 |
| With harp and psaltery | 641 | 3 |
| With healing in his wings | 804 | 1 |
| With healing in thy wing | 785 | 1 |
| With health renewed my face | 657 | 7 |
| With heart and voice | 276 | 2 |
| With heaven's host lift up your voice | 684 | 4 |
| With heedless footsteps there | 697 | 2 |
| With heedless steps I ran | 657 | 5 |
| With him enthroned above all height | 668 | 1 |
| †With him I on Zion shall stand | 70 | 2 |
| With him of every good possest | 912 | 4 |
| With him on Zion's hill | 537 | 8 |
| †With him we are gone up on high | 1001 | 9 |
| With him we reign above the sky | 1001 | 9 |
| †With him we walk in white | 21 | 6 |
| With him whose last, best word is love | 698 | 3 |
| With his blood, within the veil | 720 | 4 |
| With his mercy's full blaze | 499 | 7 |
| With his people to stay | 760 | 2 |
| With his true saints alone | 991 | 1 |
| With holy beauties shine | 740 | 7 |
| With holy fear and humble love | 819 | 1 |
| With holy hope inflame | 785 | 2 |
| With holy joy, or guilty dread | 55 | 1 |
| With humble awe I come behind | 781 | 4 |
| With humble awe thy rod we hear | 176 | 1 |
| With humble confidence look up | 301 | 1 |
| With humble confidence to find | 836 | 1 |
| †With humble faith his death I plead | 917 | 4 |
| With humble supplication | 587 | 1 |
| With humble zeal to do thy will | 281 | 5 |
| With hymns of praise to usher in | 983 | 2 |
| With inextinguishable blaze | 327 | 2 |
| With Israel's myriads sealed | 452 | 6 |
| With Jesus ineffably one | 73 | 4 |
| With Jesus in his heart | 407 | 4 |
| With Jesus in my view | 281 | 1 |
| With Jesus in my view | 800 | 5 |
| With Jesus in the ship | 1000 | 1 |
| With Jesu's priests and kings | 404 | 1 |
| With joy and pious mirth | 581 | 4 |
| With joy I drop my mouldering clay | 927 | 4 |
| †With joy like his shall every saint | 713 | 5 |
| With joy or sorrow fill | 837 | 3 |
| With joy our grateful hearts receive | 655 | 3 |
| With joy shall I lift up my head | 190 | 1 |

| | Hymn | Verse |
|---|---|---|
| With joy the appointed race | 536 | 3 |
| †With joy the Father doth approve | 867 | 2 |
| With joy their Lord surrounding | 932 | 2 |
| With joy they doubtless shall return | 120 | 2 |
| With joy unspeakable adore | 377 | 3 |
| With joy upon our heads arise | 71 | 6 |
| With joy upon our heads return | 977 | 5 |
| *With joy we meditate the grace | 725 | 1 |
| †With joy we now approve | 735 | 2 |
| With joy we render thee | 428 | 4 |
| With joy we seek the things above | 419 | 2 |
| †With joy we shall behold | 535 | 5 |
| With joy we welcome from the sky | 689 | 4 |
| With joyful fear O serve the Lord | 541 | 4 |
| With joyful haste he sped | 699 | 3 |
| With joys divinely great | 814 | 3 |
| †With labour faint thou wilt not fail | 157 | 8 |
| With lamb-like patience arm my breast | 338 | 8 |
| With life and liberty | 872 | 2 |
| With life everlasting o'erflowed | 78 | 2 |
| With life I shall not part | 931 | 5 |
| With long despair our spirit breaks | 879 | 2 |
| †With longing eyes the creatures wait | 637 | 3 |
| With longing sick, with groaning faint | 155 | 6 |
| With loudest hallelujahs met | 721 | 4 |
| With love embrace and cover me | 240 | 1 |
| With loving gratitude | 320 | 1 |
| With lowliness and purity | 431 | 5 |
| †With lowly reverential fear | 781 | 7 |
| With lowly shame I own | 270 | 3 |
| With lustre brighter far shall shine | 46 | 5 |
| With majesty divine | 730 | 2 |
| With man this is impossible | 830 | 1 |
| With many a conflict, many a doubt | 796 | 3 |
| With many a gloomy care oppressed | 602 | 3 |
| With Mary at the Master's feet | 147 | 4 |
| With meekness hear the gospel-word | 953 | 3 |
| With meekness to reprove | 270 | 4 |
| With me exalt his name | 562 | 3 |
| †With me if of old thou hast strove | 165 | 2 |
| †With me, I know, I feel, thou art | 405 | 6 |
| With me in the fire remain | 336 | 2 |
| †With me O continue, Lord | 156 | 3 |
| †With me, your chief, ye then shall know | 1 | 10 |
| With mercy crowned | 800 | 6 |
| With mercy, grace, and love | 566 | 5 |
| †With mercy's mildest grace | 731 | 4 |
| With mercy's outstretched arms embrace | 258 | 1 |
| With mildest zeal proceed | 468 | 6 |
| With milk and honey blest | 943 | 8 |
| †With mine enemies surrounded | 819 | 3 |
| †With my burden I begin | 824 | 3 |
| With my distempered soul | 166 | 3 |

| | Hymn | Verse |
|---|---|---|
| With my lamp burning in my hand | 974 | 7 |
| With my pastoral crook | 231 | 8 |
| With my Redeemer's presence blessed | 124 | 1 |
| With my Saviour in my heart | 287 | 5 |
| †With my sling and stone I go | 278 | 4 |
| With nature's stern decree | 44 | 1 |
| With never-ceasing prayer | 310 | 4 |
| With no kind shepherd near to guide | 744 | 2 |
| With offerings of devotion | 586 | 4 |
| With one accord our parting hymn of praise | 962 | 1 |
| With only sin and misery | 163 | 5 |
| With open hearts and hands we stand | 490 | 2 |
| With opening light, and evening shade | 978 | 4 |
| With our great Forerunner we | 723 | 5 |
| With our Head to ascend | 488 | 8 |
| With our youth renewed like eagles | 720 | 9 |
| With peace, and joy, and heaven, and God | 237 | 2 |
| With peace and plenty blest | 800 | 6 |
| With pearls are garnished | 942 | 7 |
| With perfect charity | 270 | 2 |
| With pitying eyes behold me fall | 135 | 3 |
| †With pitying eyes, the Prince of peace | 699 | 2 |
| With pity we look down | 21 | 6 |
| With pleasing force on earth detain | 108 | 3 |
| With plenitude of grace | 258 | 2 |
| With plenteous food and gladness fills | 241 | 3 |
| †With power he vindicates the just | 585 | 3 |
| With power to speak thy gracious word | 190 | 9 |
| With praises of redeeming love | 926 | 4 |
| With present pardon blest | 123 | 4 |
| †With publicans and harlots, I | 395 | 2 |
| With pure and radiant beams | 958 | 4 |
| With pure delight and inward bliss | 285 | 7 |
| With pure seraphic joy | 729 | 5 |
| With purest love thy servant fill | 982 | 4 |
| With purest lustre shine | 526 | 6 |
| With rage that never ends | 315 | 1 |
| With rapture ascribe our salvation to thee | 219 | 4 |
| With rapturous amaze | 262 | 4 |
| With resolute wisdom us endue | 467 | 6 |
| With reverence and with fear | 865 | 1 |
| With ripe, millennial love | 449 | 2 |
| With sacred horror fly | 103 | 2 |
| With sacred jealousy | 204 | 5 |
| With salvation's walls surrounded | 594 | 1 |
| With self-abasing shame | 243 | 5 |
| With self-distrusting care | 311 | 3 |
| With serious industry and fear | 59 | 5 |
| With shame confess our nature's stream | 469 | 7 |
| With shawms and trumpets praise | 605 | 5 |
| With shouting each other they greet | 49 | 3 |
| With shouts, and garments rolled in blood | 493 | 5 |
| With shouts proclaiming Jesu's love | 616 | 4 |

| | Hymn | Verse |
|---|---|---|
| †With simple faith on thee I call | 131 | 3 |
| With sin, and dim with error's night | 133 | 1 |
| With singing I repair | 947 | 3 |
| †With singing we praise | 491 | 3 |
| With sins, and doubts, and fears | 940 | 2 |
| With smiles of acceptance, our labour of love | 495 | 1 |
| With smiles, the flaming void | 61 | 3 |
| With softening pity look | 102 | 2 |
| †With solemn faith we offer up | 394 | 2 |
| With solemn prayer approach the throne | 953 | 3 |
| With songs let us follow his flight | 49 | 1 |
| With songs of praise | 276 | 4 |
| With songs of praise return | 497 | 3 |
| With songs that rival those above | 616 | 4 |
| With songs to Zion we return | 71 | 5 |
| With sore perplexity distrest | 836 | 2 |
| With soul athirst, like weary lands | 635 | 2 |
| With soul-refreshing streams | 958 | 4 |
| With sounding wings they sweep the air | 226 | 5 |
| With speechless wonder at thy feet | 369 | 3 |
| With spotless love, and lowly fear | 337 | 2 |
| With steadfast eye mark every step | 338 | 4 |
| With steadfast patience arm my breast | 337 | 2 |
| †With steady course the shining sun | 788 | 2 |
| With streams of sacred bliss | 800 | 8 |
| With strength of youth their King obey | 613 | 2 |
| With strictest justice give | 242 | 3 |
| With strong, commanding evidence | 95 | 5 |
| With strong desire my spirit faints | 592 | 1 |
| With such an abject worm as me | 113 | 3 |
| With such light, and love, and power | 882 | 6 |
| With sufficient strength defend | 653 | 6 |
| With sweetness fills my breast | 680 | 1 |
| With tears and bitter cry | 797 | 1 |
| With tears we come to thee | 797 | 2 |
| With terror and delight | 226 | 10 |
| With terror clothed, hell's kingdom shake | 386 | 1 |
| With thankful hearts to thee we sing | 666 | 1 |
| With thankfulness acknowledge | 736 | 1 |
| With thanks for thy continued gift | 483 | 1 |
| With thanks his dying love record | 953 | 3 |
| †With thanks I rejoice | 231 | 3 |
| †With thanks we approve | 491 | 5 |
| With that beatific sight | 941 | 3 |
| With that enraptured host to appear | 948 | 7 |
| With that last glorious shower | 409 | 6 |
| With that pure love of thine | 414 | 2 |
| With the abundance of thy grace | 751 | 2 |
| With the dawn of endless day | 60 | 4 |
| With the Father above | 160 | 5 |
| With the Father, in the Son | 817 | 8 |
| With the gospel-blessing blest | 542 | 3 |
| With the great archangel's voice | 58 | 1 |

|  | Hymn | Verse |
|---|---|---|
| With the heavenly choirs | 491 | 6 |
| With the Holy Spirit's favour | 1006 | — |
| With the indwelling Spirit give | 354 | 3 |
| With the lamp of truth precede us | 882 | 4 |
| With the Lord in Paradise | 817 | 7 |
| With the man of peace abide | 479 | 1 |
| With the plague-spot in my flesh | 768 | 8 |
| With the plummet in his hands | 383 | 1 |
| With the prophet we soar | 499 | 2 |
| With the saving truths impress us | 882 | 2 |
| With the shadow of thy wing | 143 | 2 |
| With the sheep at thy right hand | 13 | 4 |
| With the sight of his face | 499 | 7 |
| With the Spirit remove | 760 | 5 |
| With the streams of peace o'erflowed | 418 | 2 |
| With the thought of all its sin | 711 | 2 |
| With the top-stone in its day | 990 | 1 |
| With the tree of life sustain | 76 | 4 |
| With the trump of jubilee | 720 | 2 |
| With the virtue of his blood | 724 | 1 |
| With the wings of his protection | 597 | 3 |
| With the word a power convey | 299 | 1 |
| With thee all night I mean to stay | 140 | 1 |
| With thee and with the Father is | 490 | 6 |
| With thee, and with thy faithful three | 698 | 3 |
| With thee began, with thee shall end the day | 962 | 2 |
| †With thee conversing we forget | 214 | 2 |
| With thee for evermore | 549 | 7 |
| With thee importunately plead | 299 | 2 |
| With thee in strength divine | 436 | 6 |
| With thee, into the souls of men | 448 | 4 |
| With thee, the great I AM | 360 | 6 |
| With them the joyful tidings first begun | 691 | 1 |
| †With them we lift our voice | 735 | 4 |
| With this true and living bread | 904 | 1 |
| With those that went before | 949 | 4 |
| With those to glory gone | 949 | 1 |
| With thought and love of thy great name | 974 | 9 |
| With thy daily wrongs unwept | 768 | 7 |
| With thy dead men arise | 362 | 6 |
| †With thy favoured sheep O place me | 933 | 15 |
| With thy fulness fill me, Lord | 109 | 7 |
| With thy gifts of priceless worth | 753 | 2 |
| †With thy gifts the year is crowned | 579 | 3 |
| With thy heavenly presence blest | 260 | 3 |
| With thy high praise resounds | 737 | 8 |
| With thy loved name, rocks, hills, and seas | 226 | 1 |
| With thy name thy praise is known | 572 | 2 |
| With thy people enrolled | 231 | 6 |
| With thy people to live and to die | 231 | 6 |
| With thy sincere disciples meet | 861 | 2 |
| With thy Spirit's two-edged sword | 299 | 7 |
| With thy streaming glory flames | 737 | 10 |

| | Hymn | Verse |
|---|---|---|
| With thy sweet Spirit for its guest. | 841 | 5 |
| With timely care depart | 187 | 3 |
| With timely fruit doth bend | 540 | 3 |
| With trembling awe, in midnight shade | 437 | 7 |
| With trembling joy embrace his Word | 541 | 4 |
| With triumph or regret | 43 | 3 |
| With triumph we proclaim | 259 | 2 |
| With true adoration Shall lisp to thy praise | 611 | 6 |
| With true sincerity of woe | 102 | 2 |
| With unavailing pain | 91 | 1 |
| With unbeclouded eyes | 938 | 5 |
| With us evermore be found | 1008 | 2 |
| With us he vouchsafes to dwell | 755 | 2 |
| With us, in us, here below | 299 | 4 |
| With us, in us, live and dwell | 506 | 3 |
| †With us no melancholy void | 222 | 2 |
| With us shall abide | 760 | 3 |
| With us shall aspire | 808 | 9 |
| †With us thou art assembled here | 486 | 3 |
| With us while unseen he stays | 755 | 2 |
| With utmost care the time improve | 953 | 4 |
| With vigour arise | 498 | 1 |
| With violence, wrong, and cruelty | 442 | 1 |
| With violent faith and patience | 854 | 3 |
| With warm desires To see my God | 591 | 1 |
| With wealth, prosperity, and peace | 985 | 5 |
| †With what different exclamation | 936 | 5 |
| With what glad accents shall I rise | 658 | 4 |
| With what rapture | 66 | 3 |
| With which he doth embrace | 595 | 2 |
| With which my soul and flesh are filled | 331 | 3 |
| With which our souls are fed | 907 | 2 |
| †With whom dost thou delight to dwell | 655 | 2 |
| With whom I once did live | 80 | 2 |
| With whom thou always art | 871 | 2 |
| With wisdom from on high | 747 | 3 |
| With wishful looks we stand | 949 | 3 |
| With you we now appear | 539 | 7 |
| Withered my nature's strength; from thee | 141 | 5 |
| Withhold the hurtful food | 468 | 8 |
| Within my broken heart | 153 | 2 |
| Within the overshadowing cloud | 698 | 5 |
| Within the paths of righteousness | 556 | 2 |
| Within the temple door | 619 | 2 |
| Within the temple of thy grace | 592 | 3 |
| Within the veil, and see | 940 | 1 |
| Within the veil is cast | 723 | 4 |
| Within the verge of sin | 818 | 2 |
| †Within these walls may peace | 619 | 5 |
| Within those courts are found | 942 | 12 |
| Within thy circling arms I lie | 632 | 4 |
| Within us, and around | 662 | 2 |
| Without a hope to cheer the tomb | 857 | 4 |
| Without any alloy | 498 | 3 |

| | Hymn | Verse |
|---|---|---|
| Without committing sin | 820 | 1 |
| Without committing sin shall live | 282 | 2 |
| Without money | 791 | 2 |
| Without one cheerful beam of hope | 699 | 1 |
| Without our aid he did us make | 607 | 2 |
| Without reserve, or cloaking art | 561 | 5 |
| Without superior love | 469 | 4 |
| Without thee, wretched, poor, and blind | 770 | 2 |
| Without the inward witness live | 97 | 3 |
| Without the Spirit of thy Son | 435 | 2 |
| Without this blessed bond of peace | 822 | 2 |
| Without,—'tis misery all, and woe | 290 | 8 |
| Witnesser of Jesu's merit | 790 | 4 |
| †Witnesses of the all-cleansing blood | 524 | 3 |
| †Witnesses that Christ hath died | 519 | 4 |
| Witnessing to all mankind | 355 | 13 |
| Witness of thy power to save | 173 | 3 |
| Witness of thy saving will | 877 | 3 |
| Witness that streaming blood | 146 | 3 |
| Witness to all thy pardoning love | 439 | 3 |
| Witness to the solemn vow | 910 | 7 |
| *Woe is me! what tongue can tell | 112 | 1 |
| †Woe to him whose spirits droop | 487 | 2 |
| *Woe to the men on earth who dwell | 63 | 1 |
| Woe to the traveller who strayed | 697 | 2 |
| †Woke to holy labours fresh | 768 | 8 |
| Woman's seed, appear within | 271 | 1 |
| Wonder and joy shall tune my heart | 263 | 7 |
| Wonder asked, "And can it be" | 623 | 1 |
| †Wonderful in saving power | 571 | 7 |
| Wonderful thy truth is found | 579 | 1 |
| Wonderful thy works we own | 244 | 3 |
| Wondering gazed the angelic train | 737 | 2 |
| Wonders he for us hath done | 623 | 3 |
| Wonders his right hand hath wrought | 605 | 1 |
| †Wondrous sound the trumpet flingeth | 933 | 3 |
| Wondrous things the Lord hath done | 197 | 5 |
| Wooed you to embrace his love | 6 | 3 |
| Words that endless bliss impart | 885 | 1 |
| Words that made the Saviour mine | 191 | 4 |
| Words which did from thee proceed | 885 | 1 |
| Work in me both to will and do | 472 | 4 |
| Work in me to will and do | 158 | 3 |
| Work in my heart the saving grace | 118 | 1 |
| Work shall be prayer, if all be wrought | 863 | 3 |
| Works of faith and charity | 529 | 2 |
| Works of love on man bestowed | 529 | 2 |
| Works of purest love are thine | 693 | 1 |
| †Worldly cares at worship-time | 768 | 5 |
| †Worldly good I do not want | 167 | 3 |
| Worlds his mighty voice obeyed | 640 | 1 |
| World without end we worship thee | 255 | 1 |
| *Worship, and thanks, and blessing | 276 | 1 |
| Worship at his holy hill | 606 | 6 |

| | Hymn | Verse |
|---|---|---|
| †Worship, honour, power, and blessing | 722 | 4 |
| †Worshipping in spirit now | 817 | 3 |
| Worth can ne'er create in me | 24 | 1 |
| †Worthless are my prayers and sighing | 933 | 14 |
| Worthy him who fills the skies | 516 | 1 |
| Worthy, in your Saviour's worth | 54 | 3 |
| Worthy is the work of him | 218 | 3 |
| †Worthy, O Lord, art thou | 727 | 5 |
| " Worthy the Lamb ! " our hearts reply | 678 | 2 |
| †" Worthy the Lamb that died," they cry | 678 | 2 |
| Worthy thou of all our love | 727 | 6 |
| Worthy thou of endless praise | 53 | 2 |
| Worthy thou, our heavenly Lord | 233 | 3 |
| †Worthy thou, our heavenly Lord | 1021 | 2 |
| Worthy to be feared, adored | 244 | 1 |
| Would all mankind embrace | 57 | 4 |
| †Would aught on earth my wishes share | 291 | 3 |
| Would bear me conqueror through | 213 | 5 |
| Would blush to put that name on them | 891 | 4 |
| Would fain, like Peter, weep | 106 | 1 |
| Would for Christ my Saviour speak | 769 | 1 |
| Would he ask, obtest, and cry | 8 | 2 |
| Would he not testify of thee | 97 | 4 |
| Would he you to life invite | 8 | 2 |
| Would I not die this hour | 362 | 5 |
| Would in all thy footsteps go | 529 | 1 |
| *Would Jesus have the sinner die | 33 | 1 |
| Would light on some sweet promise there | 574 | 5 |
| Would nail my passions to the cross | 982 | 3 |
| Would not hearken to his calls | 168 | 1 |
| Would thy life in mine reveal | 769 | 1 |
| †Wouldst thou the body's health restore | 397 | 6 |
| Wound, and pour in, my wounds to heal | 105 | 2 |
| †Wounded by the grief of one | 518 | 8 |
| Wrestle, and fight, and pray | 268 | 4 |
| Wrestle with Christ in mighty prayer | 380 | 5 |
| Wrestling, I will not let thee go | 140 | 3 |
| Wrestling, I will not let thee go | 140 | 4 |
| Wrestling, I will not let thee go | 155 | 5 |
| †Wrestling on in mighty prayer | 530 | 4 |
| *Wretched, helpless, and distrest | 109 | 1 |
| Wretched I, and poor, and blind | 116 | 1 |
| Wretched sinners to receive | 182 | 4 |
| Write forgiveness on my heart | 173 | 1 |
| Write forgiveness on our heart | 29 | 3 |
| Write forgiveness on our heart | 900 | 4 |
| Write it in the book of heaven | 895 | 4 |
| Write kindness on our inward parts | 442 | 3 |
| Write the name we now have given | 895 | 4 |
| Write the new precept in our hearts | 511 | 3 |
| Write thy law of love within | 522 | 3 |
| Write thy new name upon my heart | 343 | 8 |
| Write thy salvation on my heart | 789 | 3 |
| †Write upon me the name divine | 72 | 3 |

| | Hymn | Verse |
|---|---|---|
| Yea, a crown, in very surety | 793 | 3 |
| Yea, all I need, in thee to find | 796 | 4 |
| †Yea, Amen! let all adore thee | 66 | 4 |
| Yea, and before we rise | 12 | 3 |
| Yea, by his blessing do my reins | 549 | 4 |
| Yea, even our crimes, though numberless | 655 | 5 |
| Yea, he himself becomes my guard | 227 | 3 |
| †Yea, let men rage, since thou wilt spread | 279 | 5 |
| Yea, let the world, O Lord, combine | 581 | 3 |
| †Yea, let thy Spirit in every place | 457 | 3 |
| Yea, life itself, that they may live | 746 | 2 |
| Yea, the far-resounding ocean | 604 | 3 |
| †Yea, though I walk in death's dark vale | 556 | 3 |
| †Yea, thou wilt answer for me, righteous Lord | 794 | 7 |
| Yea, 'tis as the Scripture saith | 714 | 3 |
| Ye all are bought with Jesu's blood | 28 | 3 |
| Ye all may come to Christ and live | 2 | 6 |
| Ye all may find favour, Who come at his call | 5 | 2 |
| †Ye all may freely take | 86 | 2 |
| Ye all may hide you in my breast | 31 | 3 |
| Ye all may live, for Christ hath died | 2 | 5 |
| Ye all may now be justified | 2 | 5 |
| Ye all may receive | 707 | 4 |
| †Ye all shall find, whom in his word | 380 | 2 |
| Ye blind, behold your Saviour come | 1 | 6 |
| Ye blood-besprinkled bands | 277 | 4 |
| Ye clouds that onward sweep | 663 | — |
| Ye count our life beneath | 21 | 2 |
| Ye creatures of a day | 983 | 1 |
| Ye days of cloudless beauty | 663 | — |
| Ye dead, the Judge is come | 55 | 3 |
| †Ye different sects, who all declare | 16 | 5 |
| Ye everlasting doors give way | 557 | 7 |
| Ye everlasting doors give way | 557 | 10 |
| †Ye faithful souls confide in God | 625 | 5 |
| †Ye faithful souls rejoice in him | 561 | 11 |
| *Ye faithful souls, who Jesus know | 420 | 1 |
| †Ye fearful saints, fresh courage take | 845 | 2 |
| Ye floods and ocean billows | 663 | — |
| Ye followers of the Lamb | 539 | 1 |
| †Ye Gentile sinners, ne'er forget | 681 | 6 |
| Ye groves that wave in spring | 663 | — |
| Ye happy saints receive | 418 | 2 |
| Ye heavenly choirs proclaim | 253 | 2 |
| Ye heavens, from above | 86 | 6 |
| Ye hills, that leaped as frighted lambs | 223 | 3 |
| Ye hosts that to his courts belong | 241 | 4 |
| *Ye humble souls that seek the Lord | 713 | 1 |
| Ye labouring, burdened, sin-sick souls | 4 | 3 |
| Ye lightnings wildly bright | 663 | — |
| Ye lovers of the Lamb | 539 | 5 |
| Ye may now be happy too | 20 | 3 |
| Ye may o'ercome through Christ alone | 266 | 2 |
| Ye mountains huge, that skipped like rams | 223 | 2 |

| | Hymn | Verse |
|---|---|---|
| Ye mournful souls, be glad | 738 | 2 |
| Ye nations, bow with sacred joy | 608 | 1 |
| Ye need not one be left behind | 2 | 1 |
| *Ye neighbours and friends Of Jesus draw near | 40 | 1 |
| Ye nothing seek or want beside | 420 | 5 |
| Ye of fearful hearts, be strong | 348 | 4 |
| Ye of the Spirit born indeed | 626 | 4 |
| Ye poor, and maimed, and halt, and blind | 2 | 3 |
| Ye pure in heart, obtain the grace | 65 | 3 |
| Ye ransomed from the fall | 681 | 4 |
| *Ye ransomed sinners, hear | 345 | 1 |
| Ye restless wanderers after rest | 2 | 3 |
| Ye saints, ascend the skies | 929 | 4 |
| †Ye seed of Israel's chosen race | 681 | 4 |
| †Ye seraphs nearest to the throne | 262 | 4 |
| *Ye servants of God, Your Master proclaim | 859 | 1 |
| Ye shall not be forgotten long | 380 | 4 |
| *Ye simple souls that stray | 21 | 1 |
| †Ye slaves of sin and hell | 738 | 4 |
| Ye sons of men, for God is man | 494 | 5 |
| Ye sons of men, rejoice | 277 | 1 |
| Ye soon shall meet him in the skies | 420 | 6 |
| Ye soon shall see his smiling face | 120 | 1 |
| Ye soon the wreath shall wear | 345 | 5 |
| Ye spend your little all in vain | 4 | 5 |
| Ye storms and winter snow | 663 | — |
| Ye tempted, there's a refuge nigh | 695 | 5 |
| †Ye that have here received | 65 | 4 |
| †Ye that tremble at his frown | 348 | 4 |
| *Ye thirsty for God, To Jesus give ear | 10 | 1 |
| Ye thunders, echoing loud and deep | 663 | — |
| Ye toil with unavailing strife | 4 | 6 |
| Ye tracts of earth and continents, reply Alleluia | 663 | — |
| †Ye vagrant souls, on you I call | 2 | 5 |
| *Ye virgin souls, arise | 65 | 1 |
| Ye wanderers from a father's face | 695 | 5 |
| Ye weary spirits, rest | 738 | 2 |
| †Ye who faint beneath the load | 54 | 2 |
| †Ye who have sold for nought | 738 | 5 |
| †Ye whose loins are girt, stand forth | 54 | 3 |
| Ye winds on pinions light | 663 | — |
| *Ye worms of earth, arise | 983 | 1 |
| Yes, broke out our joyful tongue | 623 | 2 |
| *Yes, from this instant now, I will | 178 | 1 |
| Yes, gracious Lord, thy word is passed | 451 | 2 |
| Yes, I have touched thy clothes, and own | 781 | 6 |
| Yes, I yield, I yield at last | 182 | 5 |
| †Yes, Lord, I shall see The bliss of thine own | 198 | 6 |
| †Yes, Lord, we must believe thee kind | 380 | 3 |
| Yes, our bounding heart replied | 623 | 2 |
| Yes; self-sufficient as thou art | 38 | 5 |
| †Yes, the Christian's course is run | 50 | 3 |
| †Yes, the prize shall now be given | 936 | 7 |
| Yes, thou must the grace bestow | 755 | 3 |

|  | HYMN | VERSE |
|---|---|---|
| Yet a lowly heart, that leans on thee | 842 | 7 |
| Yet am I unredeemed at last | 776 | 1 |
| Yet blessed when most sad | 602 | 1 |
| Yet cannot come to thee | 25 | 4 |
| Yet choose not, Lord, this house alone | 993 | 6 |
| †Yet could I hear him once again | 697 | 7 |
| †Yet do not drive us from thy face | 176 | 4 |
| Yet doth he us in mercy spare | 981 | 2 |
| Yet earth partakes thy gracious sway | 240 | 4 |
| †Yet, for thy own mercy's sake | 173 | 3 |
| Yet free as air thy bounty streams | 38 | 2 |
| Yet from the world they break not free | 969 | 4 |
| †Yet, glorified by grace alone | 926 | 4 |
| †Yet God is above Men, devils, and sin | 273 | 6 |
| Yet, God the same abiding | 804 | 4 |
| Yet, good Lord, in grace complying | 933 | 14 |
| Yet have not sought a friend in thee | 969 | 4 |
| Yet heaven, and earth, and hell | 831 | 11 |
| Yet hindrances strew all the way | 344 | 2 |
| Yet hope to feel thy comfort near | 767 | 4 |
| †Yet, if so thy will ordain | 925 | 2 |
| Yet in my dreams I'd be | 848 | 2 |
| †Yet, in thy Son, divinely great | 1001 | 8 |
| Yet is our sure trust in thee | 400 | 7 |
| Yet is their profit small | 856 | 4 |
| Yet let me hear thy call | 139 | 6 |
| †Yet let me not my place forsake | 470 | 6 |
| Yet let me now consent to know | 152 | 3 |
| Yet let my full heart what it can bestow | 794 | 8 |
| †Yet, Lord, well might I fear | 93 | 2 |
| Yet must I own it from my heart | 130 | 3 |
| Yet must this building rise | 617 | 4 |
| Yet my Lord I cannot blame | 115 | 3 |
| Yet, nearer to thy sacred throne | 241 | 2 |
| Yet nightly pitch my moving tent | 944 | 2 |
| †Yet not many wise His summons obey | 212 | 2 |
| Yet O! by faith I see | 947 | 1 |
| Yet, O disdain to fear | 277 | 5 |
| †Yet O! the chief of sinners spare | 161 | 4 |
| †Yet, O the riches of thy grace | 180 | 4 |
| Yet once again I pray | 110 | 1 |
| Yet once again I seek thy face | 186 | 2 |
| Yet on mine ears the gracious tidings fall | 794 | 3 |
| Yet on this rock the church shall rest | 617 | 3 |
| †Yet onward I haste | 205 | 5 |
| Yet patient vigil keep | 838 | 2 |
| †Yet save a trembling sinner, Lord | 574 | 5 |
| Yet shall it be, I know it shall | 401 | 2 |
| Yet still by sovereign grace I live | 365 | 8 |
| Yet still I cannot come to thee | 388 | 2 |
| †Yet still the Lord, the Saviour reigns | 64 | 5 |
| †Yet still we wait the end | 460 | 2 |
| Yet the dogs the crumbs may eat | 164 | 4 |
| Yet the Gentiles now behold | 164 | 2 |

| | Hymn | Verse |
|---|---|---|
| Yet the place of old prepared | 989 | 2 |
| Yet thee, my Lord, have I not known | 113 | 2 |
| Yet there are hands stretched out to draw me near | 794 | 2 |
| Yet there our Lord we cannot see | 90 | 2 |
| †Yet these are not the only walls | 863 | 2 |
| †Yet these, new rising from the tomb | 46 | 5 |
| †Yet thou know'st what pangs of love | 914 | 6 |
| Yet, through the garment of his word | 779 | 1 |
| Yet thy prey thou couldst not keep | 274 | 1 |
| †Yet thy wrath I cannot fear | 215 | 4 |
| †Yet we know our Mediator | 748 | 4 |
| Yet we will the cross sustain | 295 | 3 |
| Yet, when melted in the flame | 115 | 5 |
| †Yet, when the fullest joy is given | 504 | 9 |
| †Yet when the work is done | 674 | 2 |
| †Yet, while at length who scorned thy might | 241 | 4 |
| Yet, while I seek but find thee not | 344 | 3 |
| Yet will I fear no ill | 556 | 3 |
| †Yet will I in my God confide | 779 | 3 |
| Yet will I in my Saviour trust | 803 | 3 |
| Yet will I, Lord, the work complete | 281 | 4 |
| Yet will I thee my Father own | 178 | 1 |
| Yet will I thee my Saviour call | 130 | 4 |
| Yet will I triumph in the Lord | 803 | 2 |
| †Yet with truer nobler beauty | 990 | 4 |
| †Yet would I not regard thy stroke | 180 | 2 |
| Yield thee up, and ask no more | 24 | 2 |
| Yield to be saved from sin | 208 | 3 |
| Yield to his love's resistless power | 2 | 7 |
| *Yield to me now, for I am weak | 141 | 1 |
| Yield we now our bodies up | 61 | 4 |
| You, accustomed to obey | 639 | 6 |
| You for higher ends were born | 7 | 1 |
| You, for whom himself was sold | 7 | 3 |
| You, his chosen people, you | 7 | 4 |
| You, his saints, resound his praise | 639 | 9 |
| You, his sons, his chosen race | 639 | 9 |
| You may all to God return | 7 | 1 |
| You, of reason's powers possest | 7 | 2 |
| †You on our minds we ever bear | 539 | 6 |
| †You, on whom he favours showers | 7 | 2 |
| You, on whom he still doth wait | 7 | 3 |
| You, possest of nobler powers | 7 | 2 |
| †You, who awful sceptres sway | 639 | 6 |
| You, who bow with age's weight | 639 | 7 |
| You, who call the Saviour Lord | 7 | 4 |
| *You, who dwell above the skies | 639 | 1 |
| †You, who own his record true | 7 | 4 |
| You, who read his written word | 7 | 4 |
| You, who see the gospel-light | 7 | 4 |
| You, who were but born of late | 639 | 7 |
| You, whom he in life doth hold | 7 | 3 |
| †You, whom he ordained to be | 7 | 3 |
| You, whom highest heaven embowers | 639 | 1 |

|  | Hymn | Verse |
|---|---|---|
| You will never come at all | 791 | 4 |
| You, with finer sense endued | 7 | 2 |
| You, with will and memory blest | 7 | 2 |
| *Young men and maidens, raise | 232 | 1 |
| Your arms and hearts prepare | 314 | 1 |
| Your basest crime he bore | 36 | 2 |
| Your bitter prayer for pardon spurn | 695 | 6 |
| Your Captain gives the word | 267 | 4 |
| Your Captain's footsteps see | 314 | 3 |
| Your creature-love is crucified | 420 | 5 |
| Your debt he hath paid, and your work he hath done | 707 | 4 |
| Your downcast eyes and hands lift up | 380 | 4 |
| Your everlasting Friend | 65 | 3 |
| Your faces Zion-ward | 497 | 1 |
| †Your faith by holy tempers prove | 420 | 2 |
| Your God, in Jesus reconciled | 721 | 1 |
| Your God, ye fallen race | 1 | 7 |
| Your guides and brethren bear | 268 | 3 |
| Your Head to glorify | 65 | 3 |
| Your hearts and voices in his praise | 225 | 1 |
| Your heritage above | 738 | 5 |
| Your liberty receive | 738 | 4 |
| Your loosened tongues employ | 1 | 6 |
| Your Lord and King adore | 729 | 1 |
| Your Lord is mighty to redeem | 561 | 11 |
| Your prison-doors stand open wide | 107 | 3 |
| Your proffered liberty | 983 | 3 |
| Your ransom and peace | 707 | 1 |
| †Your real life, with Christ concealed | 420 | 6 |
| Your routed foe pursue | 278 | 6 |
| Your Saviour on the cross hath bled | 721 | 1 |
| Your secret, sworn, eternal foes | 815 | 1 |
| Your sins on the Lamb, and he bore them away | 707 | 2 |
| Your souls in words declare | 268 | 2 |
| Your stronger proofs divinely give | 16 | 5 |
| Your surety he is | 707 | 1 |
| Your tuneful voices high | 232 | 1 |
| †Your willing ear and heart incline | 4 | 9 |
| †Youths and virgins flourishing | 639 | 7 |
| Zion, behold thy Saviour King | 741 | 2 |
| Zion, city of our God | 594 | 1 |
| ‡Zion enjoys her monarch's love | 569 | 5 |
| †Zion, God saith, my rest shall be | 629 | 5 |
| Zion, in all thy palaces | 619 | 5 |
| †Zion, shout thy Lord and King | 197 | 6 |
| Zion, tell the world his fame | 606 | 2 |
| ‡Zion's gates Jehovah loveth | 595 | 2 |
| †Zion's God is all our own | 572 | 4 |
| Zion's joy, flow clear and still | 570 | 2 |

M'CORQUODALE AND CO., PRINTERS, LEEDS.

www.ingramcontent.com/pod-product-compliance
Lightning Source LLC
Chambersburg PA
CBHW031943290426
44108CB00011B/658